WORKING OUT OF CRIME

PIONEERS IN CONTEMPORARY CRIMINOLOGY

Series Editor: David Nelken

The titles in this series bring together the best published and unpublished work by the leading authorities in contemporary criminological theory. By drawing together articles from a wide range of journals, conference proceedings and books, each title makes readily available the authors' most important writings on specific themes. Each volume in this series includes a lengthy introduction, written by the editor and a significant piece of scholarship in its own right, which outlines the context of the work and comments on its significance and potential. The collected essays complement each other to give a retrospective view of the authors' achievements and a picture of the development of criminology as a whole.

Titles in the series

A Criminological Imagination
Pat Carlen

Working Out of Crime
David Downes

Building Modern Criminology: Forays and Skirmishes
David F. Greenberg

Breaking Criminological Convention: Selected Essays of Richard Ericson
Kevin D. Haggerty, Aaron Doyle and Janet Chan

Policing, Popular Culture and Political Economy
Robert Reiner

Victims, Policy-making and Criminological Theory
Paul Rock

Essays on Transnational Crime and Policing
James Sheptycki

Thinking about Punishment
Michael Tonry

Working Out of Crime

DAVID DOWNES
London School of Economics, UK

PIONEERS IN CONTEMPORARY CRIMINOLOGY SERIES

ASHGATE

Published by
Ashgate Publishing Limited
Wey Court East
Union Road
Farnham
Surrey GU9 7PT
England

Ashgate Publishing Company
Suite 420
101 Cherry Street
Burlington, VT 05401-4405
USA

Ashgate website: http://www.ashgate.com

ISBN 978-0-7546-2893-4

British Library Cataloguing in Publication Data
Working out of crime. – (Pioneers in contemporary criminology)
1. Crime. 2. Criminology. 3. Criminal justice, Administration of.
I. Series II. Downes, David M.
364-dc23

Library of Congress Control Number: 2011945741

MIX
Paper from responsible sources
FSC® C018575

Printed and bound in Great Britain by the MPG Books Group, UK

Contents

Acknowledgements

We are most grateful that permission has been granted to reprint the articles and excerpts above by the publishers concerned. In Chapter 5 above, the publisher is now Taylor and Francis; in Chapter 10, John Wiley. In the case of the Scottish Academic Press, despite our best efforts, we have been unable to contact the publisher. My thanks also that permission to reprint the chapters comprising Chapter 4 has been given by my co-authors, Professors Miriam David and Bleddyn Davies, and Mr Peter Stone; and for Chapter 12 by Professor Rod Morgan. I would also like to thank Paul Rock, Alice Sampson and Betsy Stanko for helpful comments.

Introduction

The rather cumbersome title *Working Out of Crime* is an attempt to convey a constant thread throughout my working life, which has been primarily to do with the study of crime, criminal justice and penal policy, and teaching students about those fields. It covers several aspects: a career spent trying to make sense of crime, deviance and control; the implications of crime and punishment for an understanding of the wider society and social trends; and the potential of work for people to lift themselves out of crime, and how they might best be helped in the process. Without being able to nail the links conclusively, in my view the balance of evidence substantially favours decent employment as the best antidote to crime. This view has been greatly strengthened by life-course studies of crime and desistance (see esp. Sampson and Laub, 1993; Laub and Sampson, 2003).

The first two pieces reprinted here are to do with young people and the limitations of their education and work as generating an over-emphasis on leisure as *the* source of fulfilment in their lives. The short piece on experimental youth work (here Chapter 1) was published in *Anarchy*, a journal of anarchist ideas edited throughout the 1960s by Colin Ward, the most persuasive advocate of anarchist ideas in Britain. His work has been deftly analysed by Stuart White (2007) as 'respectable' anarchism, a way of bringing into view the 'seed beneath the snow' of mutual aid and co-operative impulses that are at work in everyday life, though we rarely realize their importance at any conscious level. While never fully subscribing to even so sympathetic a version of anarchist philosophy – to me it remained unable to grapple with the fundamental problem of power, the emergence of the *fuhrer* in various forms – I was always attracted to its sheer rightness in most circumstances. One only has to think of the flooding of New Orleans by Hurricane Katrina to grasp the anarchist point. In the crunch, government assistance failed almost completely, yet people were strikingly ready to help each other out; but the authorities, the police and military, forestalled such efforts and misused their power quite appallingly, as chronicled in Dave Eggers's *Zeitoun* (2009). Such is not necessarily the case, as when – for example, in the London Blitz of 1940 or the aftermath of 9/11 – governments and people work co-operatively together. But the anarchist wisdom still prevails there too.

The second piece (Chapter 2) is a 1965 Fabian pamphlet on Further Education co-authored with the late Fred Flower, then Principal of Kingsway College, one of the most successful FE colleges in the country for its imaginative provision for part-time students on day release from their jobs. The time was right for a big expansion in further education as a complement to the comprehensive reorganisation of secondary schools and as a crucial adaptation to what was clearly a looming transformation in the technological basis of the economy. A far more comprehensive framework was needed for training and retraining in the rapidly changing industrial division of labour. In the event, the scale and character of further education has remained impoverished compared with the endless expansion of higher education, leaving the UK far less well equipped than comparable European countries to cope with deindustrialisation in the context of globalisation.

That analysis grew out of my research on delinquency in East London. I had signed on at the London School of Economics to do post-graduate research in criminology in 1959. Criminology in Britain was then largely in embryo compared with the USA. Barbara Wootton had just published a devastating critique of the field in her *Social Science and Social Pathology*, but her strictures against the then current social factor and psychological approaches did not really engage with the sociological approaches being developed in the USA. Her book came too early to encompass the work of Cloward and Ohlin (1960), though she did allude to Albert Cohen's subcultural theory (1955) and Robert Merton's anomie theory (1938), both of which she over-simplified. Her dismissal of subcultural theory as a 'way of life' (culture) explaining a 'way of life' (delinquent gangs) was far too brisk. In reality, the American theories were streets ahead in facing the task of addressing the paradox of rising rates of crime and delinquency in the context of growing prosperity.

Taking these theories seriously led on to the aim of testing their significance in the British context. The then dominant model of social research would have entailed conducting a social survey of a random sample of young people involved in delinquency with a control group to test the significance of key variables: status frustration, alienation and anomie. This daunting prospect seemed far too schematic. Fortunately, Terence Morris, my co-supervisor (with Eryl Hall Williams) at the LSE was a strong, indeed passionate advocate of the methods of the 'Chicago School'. The hallmark of the Chicagoans was to combine a commitment to quantitative measures of the social sources and character of delinquency with the need to 'go out and observe', in Robert Park's celebrated phrase, though quite how to do so was not that obvious. My main aim was to see how far, if at all, young offenders in British cities pursued a 'way of life' comparable to that documented and theorized in the USA. In particular, I looked for resemblances in terms of gang behaviour and expressive forms of delinquency which might flow from subcultural, or even contracultural beliefs and values. London's East End seemed an obvious place to start, and I recall nervously treading the streets as if about to be pounced on as a nosey intruder. In the event, it proved none too difficult to strike up conversations in cafes, pubs and youth clubs touching on my interest in the area which, if asked, boiled down to writing a book about teenagers in London. In one caff, I struck up enough rapport with one group of boys to sustain their company, on and off, for several months, and that experience formed the core of the observations in the chapter reprinted here as Chapter 3.

What came out of that for me was a convincing set of reasons for distinguishing patterns of delinquency in Britain from those in the USA. In that vanished world of fifty years ago, working-class community was cohesive enough to hold anomie at bay (for a distillation of the sweeping changes since that era, see Hobbs, 2005). Though crime and delinquency were very much a fact of life in the East End, especially as the Krays were on the verge of becoming headline news throughout most of the decade, they were not fuelled by status frustration, alienation or intense anomie. Youthful offending was typically what David Matza (1964) was to call 'intermittent and mundane' fringe delinquency, even in the USA. The more virulent and violent forms of youth gang delinquency theorized by Cohen (1955) and Cloward and Ohlin (1960), and romanticized in *West Side* Story, were hardly evident in Britain, other than in Glasgow's gang culture (Patrick, 1973). This did not mean, however, *pace* Matza, that the subcultural theorists were in error. The Britain of 1960 was a country of full employment, solidary working class communities, politically versed in trade unionism and Labour politics, and still socialized into a 'Them and Us' culture which held to a non-revolutionary but strongly conflictual identity. My anglicization of anomie theory (the phrase is Paul Rock's) is not its refutation but an affirmation of variance. Should things change structurally, as they have, with a 'Them and Us' culture being eroded by a 'winner-loser culture', in Oliver James's phrase (1995), in many ways emulating that in the USA, then crime and delinquency would change too – and, arguably, they have. Though the terrain is much contested, levels of violence and intimidation are both higher and occur in youth groups which approximate far more to gang formations than half a century ago. We are still, however, a long way from being a USA in miniature, and lethal violence remains strikingly lower in Britain than in America, despite the latter's capitulation to the false logic of mass imprisonment.

Having avoided the straitjacket of heavy-duty quantitative research on my first project, I was to walk into that trap in my second. In 1964, I undertook with a colleague, Bleddyn Davies, to embark on a study of gambling, funded by the newly formed Churches' Council on Gambling (see Chapter 4). It seemed like a good idea at the time. In Britain, next to nothing had been published on the subject, other than media rants about the country becoming a 'nation of gamblers' following the legalisation of off-course betting and casino gaming in 1961. Even in the USA no more than a handful of worthwhile studies had been conducted on the subject. However, in the event, the project was to take over a decade from start to publication of the results in 1976. There was for me a big opportunity cost of other projects abandoned or still-born, not least a book on further education and industrial training commissioned by Penguin Education. Much of this had to do with sheer inexperience in the operation of large-scale projects. Now constrained by work and family commitments, we decided against an ethnographic component to the study, plumping instead for three area surveys covering people's involvement in the major commercial forms of gambling. Gathering data also on respondents' work, income, leisure, religion, family commitments and assorted beliefs generated a mountain of data which, with the computer technology of the day, we had difficulty in processing. Endless meetings were spent listening to Peter Stone, our Research Officer, detailing technical problems of computer breakdown which, a few years later, had been ironed out. But Peter bequeathed a working database; Bleddyn wrote the methodology chapter; and Miriam David later did vital editing of a sprawling typescript. But without two years of a Nuffield College Fellowship, the eventual analysis would, in all likelihood, never have appeared. What did it achieve? First, it provided a baseline of sorts against which to assess future trends. Secondly, where possible, it established little change in the prevalence of gambling over the previous few decades: legalisation had not opened the floodgates. Thirdly, it showed the significance of parental gambling on the next generation – no great surprise, as much the same applies to most forms of conduct. And fourthly, it gave context, both historically and empirically, to the relative success with which Britain had fashioned a genuine 'third way' in the regulation of gambling, in parallel with similar pragmatism in relation to 'hard' drugs (until the mid-1970s) and the broadcast media. In all such fields a compromise was struck between the extremes of *laisser faire*, in which the market ruled without state competition, on the one hand; and Prohibition, as in most of the pre-1960s field of gambling in Britain, and even more extensively in the USA, where its illegal status, as with alcohol in the 1920s, fuelled an immense growth in organized crime. In Britain, the compromise was *unstimulated demand*: to allow all forms of gambling but to constrain their stimulation by advertising, and on-site food, drink and entertainment. The Rothschild Royal Commission on Gambling (1978) reaffirmed the wisdom of this model, which was not seriously challenged until the advent of on-line gambling and the National Lottery blew many of these key constraints out of the water. 'It could be *you*', was the launch advertisement for the latter – a huge finger pointing at the lucky winner, the myriad losers left out of the frame.

'Praxis Makes Perfect' (here Chapter 6) was published in 1979 as one of several ripostes to *The New Criminology* (Taylor, Walton and Young 1973) which had exploded onto the scene six years earlier. The story went back to the formation of the National Deviancy Symposium (later Conference – NDC) in 1968 by Stan Cohen, Laurie Taylor, Paul Rock, W.G. 'Kit' Carson and myself during a British Society of Criminology conference convened at the Institute of Criminology at Cambridge. We felt the need for a more informal and direct way of discussing issues of crime, deviance and control than more formal conferences allowed. At the same time, we thought the dominant model of criminological research in Britain too restrictive, with its heavy emphasis on tight medico-legal definition of the field to be researched by orthodox empirical methods. 'Deviance' was a break from 'crime', affording far more scope for the study of neglected and emergent forms of expressive and creative transgression, from drug use to student protest. American work along interactionist lines offered a more engaged role for political and policy inferences to be drawn from academic research. An earlier paper, 'Promise and performance in British criminology' (1978; here Chapter 5) analysed the turbulent character of the field at this point, when paradigmatic revolution eclipsed 'normal science'.

The opposition to what had been dismissed in a somewhat overdrawn depiction of sterile positivism (see esp. Matza, 1964) united intellectual radicals, primarily interested in methodology and epistemology, and radical intellectuals, focussed on bringing crime and its control onto a revolutionary agenda. For a few years, it all went with a swing. The wealth of lectures and debates, covering a range of topics from sexual deviance to the social history of crime and dissent, produced two edited volumes, *Images of Deviance* (Cohen, 1971) and *The Politics of Deviance* (Taylor and Taylor, 1973). But the 'New Criminology' was a clear break with the scepticism that had been the hallmark of the NDC. The neo-Marxist approach brooked no alternative, though the history of the subject was scoured for useful insights. Social Democratic reformism was to be rejected, with 'Fabian criminology' singled out as a particular *bête noire* .though a few years later 'Left Realism' somewhat redressed the balance (Lea and Young, 1984).

Deviant Interpretations (Downes and Rock, 1979) was an attempt to articulate just what made former adherents to the same cause so uneasy about the New Crim. In my own case, it was their failure to acknowledge the bloody precedents of past revolutions as even faintly relevant to what was meant to be the birth of history. Moreover, 'praxis' was a celebration of the necessity for a *carte blanche* view of revolutionary change. As the future is unknowable, it would be wrong to restrict post-revolutionary developments by adherence to pre-revolutionary blueprints. But Social Democrats don't insist on a blueprint, only a debatable set of proposals about what a better society would look like. Evan Durbin, a likely future leader of the Labour Party but for a tragically early death, had made the point extremely well in his *The Politics of Democratic Socialism* (1940): the non-revolutionary Left agreed with most of Marx and Engels' diagnosis of what was wrong with capitalism. What they did not share was the Marxist prognosis of what was to be done. As David Matza once put it in conversation, with Brooklynesque irony, about this gap in revolutionary thought : 'I mean, I know we won't need political parties, but can we have them anyway?' The problem with praxis is that it makes a virtue of *not* attempting to delineate what a 'truly' socialist society would look like.

The 1970s saw a parallel, and far more consequential, development politically. Labour had lost the 1970 election despite a creditable record of six years in government, which encompassed – largely via Private Members' Bills – such notable reforms as the abolition of capital punishment, homosexual and abortion law reform, the ending of theatre censorship and the pragmatic consolidation of liberal frameworks for the regulation of drugs and gambling. There were steady gains in prosperity. So what went wrong? In all probability, Labour would have won that election if the concordat proposed by Barbara Castle between government and trade unions, including a 'cooling-off' period before strike action, had been accepted and not rejected outright by the Labour movement and the TUC. People were becoming increasingly disaffected by the worsening record of strike action, much of it 'wildcat' strikes which brooked little opportunity for mediation or conflict resolution by conciliation. Underlying factors were the loss of jobs due to automation and the continuing class-ridden nature of British society. But the pursuit of 'free collective bargaining' at all costs to the industrial base, full employment and inflation was in sharp contrast to the constraints against strike action accepted by several Continental labour movements, as in Germany and Scandinavia.

Matters were made worse in the 1970s as the Labour Left drew exactly the wrong conclusions from the election defeat in 1970, which they saw as due to the Labour programme being insufficiently left-wing. When the Tory government under Edward Heath fell in 1974, thanks to their inability to deal with growing industrial conflict – especially the confrontation with the miners in 1973 and the ensuing three-day week – Labour were returned twice in the same year; first with a narrow, next with a workable majority. Labour was re-elected, the Tories having failed that test, in the hope that they could now establish effective relations with the unions. But in 1975 the trade unions dealt the Labour government, and themselves in the long run, a devastating blow. As Will Hutton tells it:

> I was working in the City in the mid-1970s, and could scarcely believe British trade unionists protesting against the Bullock Committee's proposals to create statutory obligation for trade unions to be represented on company boards. Couldn't they see that the City believed the proposal the work of the devil? But the City could relax. Trade unions thought to sit on boards would represent collaboration, castrate them in their fight against capitalism and undermine free collective bargaining. Their resistance was an act of supreme folly that would contribute to the decline and fall of meaningful trade unionism while the stock market jumped in unexpected delight at their mulish opposition – but it is rare even today to find a leading trade unionist who will recognize the craziness of that decision. (Hutton, 2010)

That refusal left industrial conflict as the main weapon in the union armoury. Three years later, the 'Winter of Discontent' pitched union strength against a Labour government struggling to survive on a minority vote. The 1979 election brought in the Conservative Party under Margaret Thatcher, a Prime Minister committed to breaking with the Social Democratic consensus that had held sway since 1945. The rise of neo-liberalism ever since, even under a 'New Labour' government, changed the political economy, including that of crime and its control by the politicisation of the law and order issue, though it was not until the 1990s that the full logic of that position was actualized (Farrell and Hay, 2010).

My engagement with the study of criminal justice and penal policy had been pretty well non-existent until the late 1970s. I optimistically assumed that prison was so obviously a repressive and counter-productive instrument of control that its use would recede gradually to the point where only the lethally violent would be held in custody for any length of time. The steady rise of the prison population showed that view to be increasingly naive. While the establishment of the therapeutic prison at Grendon (Genders and Player, 1995) showed another way forward, it was to remain an anomaly in the system that seemed in the 1970s to be in dire straits (see esp. Cohen and Taylor, 1972; Fitzgerald, 1978). But it was as late as 1977 that a conversation with David Donnison prompted me to visit the Barlinnie Special Unit, about which he had written in strongly positive terms in *New Society*. The Unit was an experimental regime, within a large metropolitan jail in Glasgow, which allowed prisoners an unusual degree of self-government. It had been set up in 1973 as a radical alternative to the punitive 'cages' at Peterhead for the close confinement of violent and disruptive prisoners. In England, facing similar problems, no attempt was seemingly made, either then or later, to learn from this Scottish experiment, much as the welfare-based Scottish system of juvenile justice was also ignored. Instead, the Home Office in 1974 set up a far more constraining Control Unit at Wakefield Prison which proved abortive, closing within a year following the exposé of its impact on at least one prisoner. By contrast, the Barlinnie Special Unit worked on democratic lines to reduce violence among Scotland's most notorious prisoners. Through Kay Carmichael, the psychiatric social worker who was a leading light in its establishment, I met Jimmy Boyle, a Glasgow gang leader who had discovered his prowess as a sculptor in the Unit, and Ken Murray, the prison officer who led the staff to man and support the Unit.[1] Both gave strongly convincing accounts of its importance in extending to prisoners a new freedom – to run their own lives within jail to the maximum extent possible consonant with security. Though I never wrote at length about the Unit, later studied and vindicated by David Cooke (1989), and though the Unit was to be closed abruptly in 1995, this brief glimpse of potential alternatives to repressive regimes for even the allegedly most violent prisoners, remains an inspiration, and led me to change tack in the focus of my research.

A further stimulus to studying criminal justice policy, as distinct from the causes and character of crime and deviance, was the formation of the Labour Campaign for Criminal Justice (LCCJ) in 1978 by Alex Lyon MP. The idea was born of developments in the 1970s which implied a series of setbacks to liberal reform, following the striking successes of the 1960s, were becoming institutionalized. The crime rate and the prison population with it were rising steadily. The high hopes for juvenile justice reform were being dashed by increasing numbers of young offenders in custody and the abandonment of many of the welfare provisions of the 1969 Act. Terrorist outrages led to trials whose verdicts, as in the cases of the Guildford Four and Birmingham Six, were at the time widely felt to be 'unsafe' – and much later found to be so. The LCCJ throughout the 1980s and early '90s provided a forum for interested supporters of the Labour Party to meet regularly to discuss and mount campaigns against what were felt to be injustices, the excessive use of imprisonment, undemocratic policing and insufficient investment in crime prevention and community penalties. LCCJ members were a mix of Labour MPs such as Alex Lyon, Alf Dubs, Clive Soley and Barry

[1] Murray was evidently forced to resign from the Unit under protest. See the debate on the Unit in the House of Commons, 12 February 1980: Hansard, vol. 978, cc. 1493–502.

Sheerman, practitioners from the criminal justice professions, lawyers, probation, social work and even the occasional Prison Governor, academics, reform group agencies – Vivien Stern was a driving force throughout – and civil libertarians – before becoming an MP, Harriet Harman, later Deputy Leader of the Labour Party, was its first secretary. My 1983 Fabian/LCCJ pamphlet, reprinted here as Chapter 8, argued the case for Labour to seize back the initiative on law and order to which, on the evidence, they could claim more success than the Conservatives. The LCCJ arguably helped reinforce the Labour Opposition to press for alternatives to prison and for new constraints on the abuses of power. That in its turn enabled the Tory Government to accept the policies of successive Home Secretaries, Douglas Hurd in particular, to look for principled ways of reducing the prison population and bolstering community penalties. A striking success in the juvenile justice field, following increased government funding, was the practitioner-led development of Intermediate Treatment that proved successful at local level and began to spread both nationally and in schemes for adult offenders. The pay-off was a marked reduction in the prison population – from 50,000 in 1988 to 42,000 in 1992; a development that would have been inconceivable if the Labour Opposition had been lambasting the Government for being 'soft on crime'.

All that was to change after Labour lost its fourth successive General Election in 1992. Shortly after that defeat, all the more traumatizing due to high Labour hopes of victory following the lengthy recession, I met one of the LCCJ's most active members in Whitehall. Now a leading member of the team working for the new Shadow Home Secretary, Tony Blair, I asked what was likely to be our next step. To the best of my recollection, the reply was 'Well, we have to get rid of the '91 Act.' I was stunned: 'But we spent years campaigning for it.' 'Yes, but it's got to go.' Even revision of the key 'just deserts' clause, which had been crucial for reducing the imprisonment of the petty, persistent offender by focussing more on the current offence, far less on previous convictions, was ruled out. So that was that. When Kenneth Clarke (Home Secretary 1992–93), proposed its repeal, Labour did not oppose it. Phase 2 of the new era of political rivalry over effectiveness on law and order – which led to the so-called 'arms race' of prison-building and sentencing – was ushered in. Following Blair's 'tough on crime, tough on the causes of crime' speech in May 1993, Labour's opinion poll rating as the most trusted party on law and order shot ahead of the Tories, for the first time. In clear retaliation, Michael Howard, the new Home Secretary by October 1993, made his 'Prison Works' speech to the Tory Party Conference. The prison population resumed its growth: byAutumn 2011 it stood at 87,200, over double its size in the early 1990s.

Another experience of involvement in debate about penal policy stemmed in 1981 from an initiative sparked by David Faulkner (Director of Operational Policy in the Prison Department of the Home Office, 1980–82[2]), who had been given the brief to explore ways of bringing greater coherence to penal policy, not least in stemming the seemingly incessant rise in the prison population. Not only would this be less costly in financial, but also in human terms, as more humane regimes could be introduced more effectively. A small discussion group of civil servants, practitioners and academic criminologists was convened to meet every so often at the offices of the National Association for the Care and Resettlement of Offenders (NACRO), under the aegis of Vivien Stern. The Home Office team, led by Faulkner, included *inter alia*

[2] Faulkner was then promoted to Deputy Under-Secretary of State, Criminal, Research and Statistics Department (1982–90).

Bill Bohan, Philippa Drew and Mary Tuck; the practitioners included Cedric Fullwood (head of Manchester Probation) and Bryan Gibson (a Clerk of the Courts and Editor of the *Justice of the Peace*); the academics were chiefly Rod Morgan, Roy King, Andrew Rutherford and myself. A key influence as the decade wore on was Andrew Ashworth who – with Andrew von Hirsch – was a major influence arguing for 'just deserts', the key principle behind the 1991 Criminal Justice Act's attempt to legislate for dealing non-custodially with offenders jailed for their persistence rather than the seriousness of their crimes. Few Bills have been more assiduously canvassed than the 1991 Act, with two important conferences, at Leeds Castle and Ditchley, being path-making steps on the way, the latter unprecedentedly involving senior civil servants, leading members of the judiciary and key practitioners, all taking part in debates on what was at stake. Despite these foundations, the Act foundered in operation due to the antagonism of a critical mass of the judiciary, the tabloids and Conservative MPs.

My contribution to these debates and forums chiefly stemmed from the comparative research I was conducting on Dutch penal policy and that of England and Wales (see Chapter 9). John Croft, the Head of the Home Office Research Unit, had sent a circular round the universities inviting bids for research funding. I put in a bid prompted by the need to challenge the view, put about to explain the rising prison population, that, if the crime rate rose, so must prison numbers. Just across the Channel, the Netherlands' experience seemed to refute that line. Hence I proposed to study the causes, character and consequences of that contrast with the English experience, a choice which dominated my research work for the next ten years.

Cross-national studies of crime and punishment were then surprisingly few and far between. But if the relations between crime rates and penal policy was to be understood, exploring the links comparatively, looking at more than one country's experience, seemed crucial. Four findings emerged that made it worthwhile. First, the disparity between the two countries was real. The 4:1 ratio between the then English and Dutch prison population rates was not simply due to confounding variables, such as the Dutch crime rate being four times lower. It was indeed lower, but not by that much. Nor did the Dutch do other, institutionally equivalent things to offenders, such as hiving them off into mental institutions, on a large enough scale to account for the gap. Secondly, the much lower prison numbers in the Netherlands enabled their regimes to be far more humane than the English, a difference which has proved durable to the present day (Kruttschnitt and Dirkzwager, 2011). Nor, thirdly, did greater Dutch leniency spell a crime rate spiralling out of control. That it rose faster than that in England in the late 1970s and early '80s was due to a 'depillarization' effect well analysed by the Dutch Committee Report *Society and Crime* (1985). The 'recarceration' following that boom, even after it levelled out, led Rene van Swaaningen and myself (Downes and van Swaaningen, 2007) to warn of the dangers of a 'dystopian' trend, though recent years have seen a fall back in the prison population, despite the fears of civil strife engendered by the murders of Pim Fortuyn and Theo van Gogh.

The 'working out of crime' theme recurred with a Home Office project on revictimization and violence which was masterminded in 1990–91 by Ken Pease, Gloria Laycock and Alice Sampson. Pease had made a real breakthrough in his study of revictimization and property crime, establishing that substantially higher rates of burglary occurred within a short time after the initial break-in. This led to a seemingly successful crime prevention strategy of 'cocooning' victims, by the rapid upgrading of domestic security and by alerting neighbours to the offence. This later project was an attempt to establish whether or not the same dynamic applied to victims of 'public violence' (as distinct from domestic violence). Five projects were set up, of which mine (see Chapter 10) was to focus on two high-crime estates, one in East London, the other in Liverpool. Two stages were involved in a project lasting three months: first, an ethnographic study of violent crime on the London estate (that in Liverpool was curtailed); and, secondly, a study (reprinted here) of several employment-related crime prevention schemes for ex-offenders. The two main results were, first, that several projects around the country were working with some success to steer offenders away from crime. Though none focussed on violent offenders, they were included. The projects that worked best gave real emphasis to gauging trainees' job preferences and potential, and instilling the confidence they needed to enter the world of work. A key finding was that all too often successful schemes' funding lasted for three years or less, leaving it to other agencies or the local authority to keep them going (Downes, 1993). The second finding was that the main victims of public violence on the London estate were Bengali immigrants subject to resentment by indigenous groups who felt discriminated against by comparison with the newcomers in terms of public housing. There was little evidence for such positive discrimination but it animated high rates of low-level vandalism and harassment which made their lives a misery. The police method of recording each offence separately led to the error of failing to discern the pattern, each offence being dismissed as of little account, when the offences in aggregate were a clear case of mounting revictimisation. Though these studies were not published as a whole independently[3], they fed into the work of and later publications by the team (see, for example, Stanko 2008); and into the case for a New Deal for youth training and employment later brought in, with mixed results, by New Labour after 1997 (Downes, 1994; here Chapter 11).

The work theme recurred in relation to analysis of the rise of mass imprisonment in the USA. In 1997, I wrote a brief article for the *Guardian*[4] on how the extent of imprisonment in the USA masked the true rate of unemployment there, a figure that was then deployed in cross-national comparisons to assert that the neo-liberal economic policies of the USA were far more effective in generating jobs than the Social Democratic societies of Western Europe. Quite independently of my work, Bruce Western was making a more extensively grounded analysis along the same lines (Western and Beckett, 1997). With Katherine Beckett, he went on to establish the increasingly inverse relationship between welfare and imprisonment across US states (Beckett and Western, 2001). Both their analysis, and a second cross-national trend comparison which I conducted with Kirstine Hansen (2006) signified that commitment to welfare was increasingly important as a barrier to the 'punitive turn'.[5] At a conference organized by David Garland in New York University in 2000, these themes were debated and discussed, though no one made the link between the scale of imprisonment in the USA and its electoral implications. It has since been established (Manza and Uggen, 2006) that the disenfranchisement of prisoners not only whilst in jail but, in several key states, for life after their release held momentous consequences for elections at both state and national level, not least the knife-edge election of George W. Bush to the presidency in 2000. Penal politics in the USA has thereby shaped world politics to a remarkable and woefully damaging extent.

[3] The study of employment projects, *Employment Schemes for Offenders* (1993), was published by the Home Office 'for distribution to Probation Services'.

[4] 'Prison does wonders for the jobless figures', 25 November 1997.

[5] Our interpretation of the effect is overstated in this case (2006, p. 153), though it remains noteworthy. For clarification, see Downes in Snacken and Dumortier (2012), pp. 27 and 33, note 18.

Why did the American mass incarceration happen as and when it did, from the mid-1970s onwards? Highly sophisticated theories abound: Simon's 'governing through crime' (2007), Whitman's 'harsh justice' (2006) and Garland's 'culture of control' (2001) go far to explaining why and how, albeit not when, so marked a phenomenon could happen. Loic Wacquant's (2001) theory of the prison as ghetto in the neo-liberal era of crisis links the politics of race, class and political economy to powerful effect. But many such critical conflicts were occurring in societies where prison populations were little changed (Tonry, 1999). My argument (reprinted here as Chapter 13) is that the *macho* penal economy is a logical outgrowth of American exceptionalism, the belief that the USA is a perfect society in embryo, indeed in many ways a *prefect* society, on a 'sacred errand' to save the world, declension from which is the American nightmare, justifying the harshest retribution. Such extremes were long held in check by the belief in rehabilitation and social reform. It was only with the dawn of 'Nothing Works' pessimism coinciding with the end of the New Deal era that such constraints were abandoned. Though social reform and resistance to mass imprisonment are resilient and even growing movements, the 'Prison Works' credo of sheer incapacitation, once embarked upon, is remarkably difficult to discredit.

One society that shows signs of having done so is the Netherlands, where the prison population, having risen so sharply for two decades, receded to below the European average for the past few years. Much of my primary research activity for the last few decades concerned Dutch penal policy. It has been a most rewarding experience to enjoy the warm, if often astringent, co-operation of Dutch criminologists, lawyers and penal administrators. Not having learnt the language, I ran a grave risk of criminological tourism. Insofar as I avoided it, it was thanks both to Dutch fluency in English, not least of the Dutch prisoners I interviewed, and the ease of exchanging ideas with especially Pia Mitchell (who assisted greatly in my first year of research), Nico Keijzer, Jos Verhaegen, Jan van Dijk and Maurice Punch. The recarceration trend from the mid-1980s was a particular challenge, and it was a distinct pleasure to explore the issues involved with Rene van Swaaningen (2007), as part of a project on crime and criminal justice in the Netherlands for the monumental 'Crime and Justice' series edited by Michael Tonry. Reprinted here is a chapter from the following volume, which takes a broader cross-national perspective (see Chapter 15). The title links with the work of Stanley Cohen, a great sociologist of crime, deviance and control, who in his *States of Denial* (2001) brought criminological insights to bear on the most pressing issues of human rights.

The politics of law and order is a theme on which I have written for some two decades with Rod Morgan, a tireless upholder of the rule of law and human rights. In five editions of the *Oxford Handbook of Criminology* (1994, 1997, 2002, 2007, and 2012) we have traced the changing character of the politics of crime control from the hesitancy of pre-Blair 'Old Labour' in engaging the Tories on that ground to the post-Blair embrace of a 'governing through crime' 'arms race' rivalry. The chapter reprinted here from the 1997 edition (as Chapter 12) analyses the distancing of New Labour from what were seen as the electoral liabilities of key Old Labour 'hostages to fortune'. Criminal justice was no longer a non-partisan backwater but in many ways a catalyst of real changes in political economy, strengthening the trend to the neo-liberal 'false dawn' (Gray, 1998) which has proved so destructive of what Durkheim (1893) called the 'non-contractual elements in contract': trust, co-operation, and mutual aid. Without these taken-for-granted products of *social* institutions – families, friendships, schools, communities – any 'advanced' economic exchanges would be impossible. As Blair himself has acknowledged, the short-term electoral pay-off of his 'tough on crime, tough on the causes of crime' rebranding of New Labour has been damaging in the longer term. Included here (as Chapter 14) is a related article on that theme in 1998, just after the election of New Labour, spelling out the likely ill effects of the short-term 'tough on crime' agenda overwhelming the longer-term focus on its causes.

I have not included here any extracts from successive editions of *Understanding Deviance* (1982, 1988, 1995, 2003, 2007 and 2011), the textbook which Paul Rock and I worked on for three decades and six editions. That is not to say that I disregard it but, as it is still in print, it seems unwarranted. I have taught the sociology of deviance and control for over forty years with Paul, a most stimulating alliance. The textbook grew from our attempt in teaching to cover the field of crime, deviance and control in a disinterested way that gave theorists their 'best shot' and critics their most telling points. Important as it is to remain dispassionate, there remains plenty of support for the anomie-based theories of crime to sustain the view that meaningful work, as distinct from forced, exploited and exploiting labour, is the best antidote to crime. Via restorative justice, it could be the best antidote to punishment (Downes, 2011). It is also the key to a socially just and only moderately crime-ridden society which is, I think, the best we can hope for. As Robert Reiner, an unfailingly inspiring colleague, put it, paraphrasing Rosa Luxemburg: 'Social Democracy is the only alternative to barbarism' (2005).

I am now revisiting many of these themes, in the course of research – with Tim Newburn and Paul Rock – for the official history of criminal justice policy in England and Wales from the 1960s to 1997.

References

Beckett, K. and Western, B. (2001) 'Governing Social Marginality', in D. Garland (ed.), *Mass Imprisonment: Social Causes and Consequences*, London: Sage, pp. 35–51.

Cloward, R.A. and Ohlin, L.E. (1960), *Delinquency and Opportunity: A Theory of Delinquent Gangs*, New York: The Free Press.

Cohen, A.K. (1955) *Delinquent Boys: The Culture of the Gang*, Glencoe: The Free Press.

Cohen, S. (ed.) (1971), *Images of Deviance*, Harmondsworth: Penguin.

Cohen, S. (2001), *States of Denial: Knowing about Atrocities and Suffering*, Cambridge: Polity Press.

Cooke, D. J. (1989) 'Containing Violent Prisoners: An Analysis of the Barlinnie Special Unit', *British Journal of Criminology*, **29**, pp. 129–43.

Downes, D. (1993), *Employment Opportunities for Offenders*, London: Home Office.

Downes, D. (2011), 'Comparative Criminology, Globalization and the 'Punitive Turn', in D. Nelken (ed.), *Comparative Criminal Justice and Globalization*, Farnham: Ashgate, pp. 27–48.

Downes, D. and Rock, P. (1982), *Understanding Deviance: A Guide to the Sociology of Crime and Rule-Breaking*, Oxford: Oxford University Press; successive editions 1988, 1998, 2003, 2007, 2011.

Downes, D. and Hansen K. (2006), 'Welfare and Imprisonment in Comparative Perspective', in S. Armstrong and L. McAra (eds), *Perspectives on Punishment*, Oxford: Oxford University Press, pp. 133–54.

Downes, D. and Van Swaaningen, R. (2007), 'The Road to Dystopia?: Changes in the Penal Climate of the Netherlands', in M. Tonry and C. Bijleveld (eds), *Crime and Justice in the Netherlands*, Chicago: Chicago University Press, pp. 31–71.

Durbin, E. (1940) *The Politics of Democratic Socialism*, London: Routledge.

Durkheim, E. (1933 [1893]) *The Division of Labor in Society,* New York: Macmillan.
Eggers, D. (2009), *Zeitoun*, San Francisco: McSweeney's.
Farrell, S. and Hay, C. (2010), 'Not So Tough on Crime? Why Weren't the Thatcher Governments More Radical in Reforming the Criminal Justice System?', *British Journal of Criminology*, **50**, pp. 550–69.
Garland, D. (2001), *The Culture of Control*, Oxford: Oxford University Press.
Genders, E. and Player, E. (1995), *Grendon: A Study of a Therapeutic Prison*, Oxford: Oxford University Press.
Gray, J. (1998), *False Dawn: The Delusions of Global Capitalism*, Cambridge: Granta.
Hobbs, D. (2005), 'East Ending: Dissociation, De-industrialization, and David Downes', in T. Newburn and P. Rock (eds), *The Politics of Crime Control: Essays in Honour of David Downes*, Oxford: Oxford University Press, pp. 117–46.
Hutton, W. (2010), 'We Had It All – Sex, Freedom, Money. Did We Throw It All Away?', *The Observer, New Review*, 22 August, p. 13.
James, O. (1995), *Juvenile Violence in a Winner-Loser Culture*, London: Free Association Books.
Kruttschnitt, C. and Dirkzwager, A. (2011), 'Are there still Contrasts in Tolerance? Imprisonment in the Netherlands and England 20 years later', *Punishment and Society*, **13**, pp. 283–306.
Laub, J.H. and Sampson, R.J. (2003), *Shared Beginnings, Divergent Lives: Delinquent Boys to Age 70*, Cambridge, MA: Harvard University Press.
Lea, J. and Young, J. (1984), *What Is To Be Done About Law and Order?* Harmondsworth: Penguin.
Manza, J. and Uggen, C. (2006), *Locked Out: Felon Disenfranchisement and American Democracy*, New York: Oxford University Press.
Matza, D. (1964), *Delinquency and Drift*, New York: Wiley.
Merton, R. (1938), 'Social Structure and Anomie', *American Sociological Review*, **3**, pp. 672–82.
Netherlands, Ministry of Justice (1985), *Society and Crime: A policy plan for The Netherlands*, (English version), Schiedam: Van Rossum.
Patrick, J. (1973), *A Glasgow Gang Observed*, London: Eyre Methuen.
Reiner, R. (2005), 'Beyond Risk: A Lament for Social Democratic Criminology', in T. Newburn and P. Rock (eds), *The Politics of Crime Control: Essays in Honour of David Downes*, Oxford: Oxford University Press, pp. 7–50.
Royal Commission on Gambling (1978), (Rothschild Report), London: HMSO (Cmnd. 7200).
Sampson, R.J. and Laub, J.H. (1993), *Crime in the Making: Pathways and Turning Points through Life*, Cambridge, MA: Harvard University Press.
Simon, J. (2007), *Governing Through Crime*, New York: Oxford University Press.
Snacken, S. and Dumortier, E. (2012), *Resisting Punitiveness in Europe*, London: Routledge.
Stanko, B. (2008), 'Strategic Intelligence: Methodologies for understanding What Other Services Already 'Know' to Reduce Harm', in C. Harfield, A. MacVeen, J. Grieve and D. Phillips (eds), Oxford: Oxford University Press, pp. 227–37.
Taylor, I. and Taylor, L. (eds) (1973), *The Politics of Deviance*, Harmondsworth: Penguin.
Taylor, I., Walton, P. and Young, J. (1973), *The New Criminology*, London: Routledge.
Tonry, M. (1999), 'Why are US incarceration rates so high?', *Crime and Delinquency*, **45**, pp. 419–37.
Wacquant, L. (2001), 'Deadly Symbiosis: When Ghetto and Prison Meet and Mesh', in D. Garland (ed.), *Mass Imprisonment: Social Causes and Consequences*, London: Sage, pp. 82–120.
Western, B. and Beckett, K. (1997), 'The Penal System as Labor Market Institution: Jobs and Jail, 1980–1995', *Overcrowded Times*, **8**, pp. 1, 9–13.
White, S. (2007), 'Making Anarchism Respectable? The Social Philosophy of Colin Ward', *Journal of Political Ideologies*, **12**, pp. 11–28.
Whitman, J. (2005), *Harsh Justice*, New York: Oxford University Press.
Wootton, B. (1959), *Social Science and Social Pathology*, London: Allen and Unwin.

Published Writings

Books

The Delinquent Solution: A Study in Subcultural Theory (Routledge and Kegan Paul), 1966.
Gambling, Work and Leisure: A Study Across Three Areas (Routledge and Kegan Paul), 1976; with B.P. Davies, M.E. David and P. Stone.
Understanding Deviance (Oxford University Press), 1982; 2nd edn 1988; 3rd edn 1998; 4th edn 2003; 5th edn 2007; Canadian edn 2009; 6th edn 2011; with Paul Rock.
Contrasts in Tolerance: Post-war Penal Policy in the Netherlands and England and Wales (Oxford University Press), 1988.

Edited Books

Deviant Interpretations: Problems in Criminological Theory (Martin Robertson) 1979; with Paul Rock.
Crime and the City: Essays in Memory of John Barron Mays (Macmillan) 1989.
Unravelling Criminal Justice: Eleven British Studies (Macmillan) 1992.
Crime, Social Control and Human Rights: From Moral Panics to States of Denial – Essays in Honour of Stanley Cohen (Willan) 2007; with P. Rock, C. Chinkin and C. Gearty.
The Eternal Recurrence of Crime and Control: Essays in Honour of Paul Rock (Oxford University Press) 2010; with D. Hobbs and T. Newburn.

Articles and Chapters

'The Teen Canteen: In at the End', *Anarchy: A Journal of Anarchist Ideas,* May 1963, **27**, pp. 131–4.
'Perks *v.* the Criminal Statistics', *Criminal Law Review*, January 1965, pp. 12–18.
'The Gang Myth', *The Listener*, 14 April 1966, pp. 534–7.
'Delinquency, Work, and Leisure', *The Listener*, 26 May 1966, pp. 755–7.
'Drug Takers and the Community', in T. Weston (ed.), *Behind the Drug Scene* (British Medical Association) n. D. (1968), pp. 21–6.
'Social Reaction to Deviance and Its Effects on Crime and Criminal Careers', *British Journal of Sociology*, **22**, 1971, pp. 351–64; with Paul Rock.
'Interpreting Delinquency', in G. Croton (ed.), *Signs of Trouble* (British Broadcasting Association), 1976, pp. 41–55.
'Promise and Performance in British Criminology', *British Journal of Sociology*, **29**, December 1978, pp. 483–502.
'From Raffles to Heart-Stoppers: The Social Control of Gambling', *British Journal of Law and Society*, **6**, 1979, pp. 235–43.
'Praxis makes Perfect: A Critique of Critical Criminology', in D. Downes and P. Rock (eds), *Deviant Interpretations: Problems of Criminological Theory* (Martin Robertson), 1979, pp. 1–16.
'Abolition: Possibilities and Pitfalls', in A.E. Bottoms and R.H. Preston (eds), *The Coming Penal Crisis* (Scottish Academic Press), 1980, pp. 71–83.

'The Origins and Consequences of Dutch Penal Policy since 1945: A Preliminary Analysis' *British Journal of Criminology*, **22**, October 1982, pp. 325–62.

'Back to Basics: Reflections on Barbara Wootton's 'Twelve Criminological Hypotheses'", in P. Bean and D. Whynes (eds), *Barbara Wootton: Social Science and Public Policy* (Tavistock), 1986, pp. 195–215.

'Only Disconnect: Law and Order, Social Policy and the Community', in M. Bulmer, J. Lewis and D. Piachaud (eds), *The Goals of Social Policy* (Unwin Hyman), 1989, pp. 234–44.

(with Rod Morgan) '"Hostages to Fortune"?: The Politics of Law and Order in Post-war Britain', in M. Maguire, R. Morgan and R. Reiner (eds), *The Oxford Handbook of Criminology*, Oxford University Press, 1994; 'Dumping the "Hostages to Fortune"?: The Politics of Law and Order in Post-war Britain', 2nd edn, 1997, pp. 87–134; 'The Skeletons in the Cupboard. The Politics of Law and Order at the Turn of the Millennium', 3rd edn, 2002, pp. 286–321; 'No Turning Back: The Politics of Law and Order into the Millennium', 4th edn, 2007, pp. 201–40.

'Broken Windows of Opportunity: Crime, Inequality and Employment', in H. Jones and J. Lansley (eds), *Social Policy and the City* (Avebury), 1995, pp. 135–48.

'Why Inequality Is Still a Factor', *Times Literary Supplement*, 1 September 1995, pp. 11–12. Reprinted as 'Crime and Inequality: Current Issues in Research and Public Debate', in J. Vagg and T. Newburn (eds), *The British Criminology Conferences: Selected Proceedings. Papers from the British Criminology Conference, Loughborough University, 18–21 July, 1995.* British Society of Criminology. www.britsoccrim.org/volume1/001.pdf

'What the Next Government Should Do About Crime', *Howard Journal of Criminal Justice*, **36**, February 1997, pp. 1–13.

'Toughing It Out: New Labour and Crime Control', *Policy Studies* 19, 1998, pp. 191–208.

'The Buckling of the Shields: Dutch Penal Policy 1985–1995', in R. Weiss and N. South (eds), *Comparing Prison Systems* (Gordon and Breach), 1998, pp. 143–74.

'Back to the Future: The Predictive Value of Social Theories of Delinquency', in S. Holdaway and P. Rock (eds), *Thinking about Criminology* (UCL Press), 1998, pp. 99–119.

'The *Macho* Penal Economy: Mass Incarceration in the United States – A European Perspective', in D. Garland (ed.), *Mass Imprisonment: Social Causes and Consequences* (Sage), 2001, pp. 51–69; also *Punishment and Society*, 2001, **3**, pp. 61–80.

'Welfare and Punishment in Comparative Perspective', in S. Armstrong and L. McAra (eds), *Perspectives on Punishment: The Contours of Control* (Oxford University Press), 2006, pp. 133–54; with Kirstine Hansen.

'The Road to Dystopia? Changes in the Penal Climate of the Netherlands', in M. Tonry and C. Bijleveld (eds), *Crime and Justice in the Netherlands* (Chicago University Press), 2007, pp. 31–71; with Rene van Swaaningen.

'Visions of Penal Control in the Netherlands', in M. Tonry (ed.), *Crime, Punishment, and Politics in Comparative Perspective* (Chicago University Press), 2007, pp. 93–125.

'Comments on Mathiesen's "Ten Reasons"', in M. McCarthy (ed.), *Incarceration and Human Rights: The Oxford Amnesty Lectures 2007* (Manchester University Press), 2010, pp. 119–26.

'Against Penal Inflation: Comment on Nicola Lacey's *The Prisoners' Dilemma, Punishment and Society*, 2011, January, Vol.13:114–20.

'What Went Right? New Labour and Crime Control', *Howard Journal of Criminal Justice*, **49**, September 2010, pp. 394–397.

'Comparative Criminology, Globalization and the "Punitive Turn"', in D. Nelken (ed.), *Comparative Criminal Justice and Globalization* (Ashgate), 2011, pp. 27–47.

'Overtaking on the Left? The Politics of Law and Order in the 'Big Society', in M. Maguire, R. Morgan and R. Reiner (eds), *The Oxford Handbook of Criminology*, 5th edn (Oxford University Press); with Rod Morgan, 2012, pp. 182–205.

'Waiting for Ingleby: The Minimum Age of Criminal Responsibility – A Red-line Issue?', in J. Peay and T. Newburn (eds), *Policing: Politics, Culture and Control: Essays in Honour of Robert Reiner* (Oxford: Hart); with Rod Morgan, 2012, pp. 245–64.

'Political Economy, Welfare and Punishment in Comparative Perspective', in S. Snacken and E. Dumortier (eds), *Resisting Punitiveness in Europe*, London: Routledge, 2012, pp. 23–34.

Miscellaneous

Educating for Uncertainty (Fabian Society), 1965; with Fred Flower.

Law and Order: Theft of an Issue (Fabian Society/ Labour Campaign for Criminal Justice), 1983.

Democratic Policing: Towards a Labour Party Policy on Police Accountability (Labour Campaign for Criminal Justice), 1986; with Tony Ward.

Employment Opportunities for Offenders (Home Office), 1993.

'Mitigating the social effects of unemployment' Evidence additional to the contents of *Employment Opportunities for Offenders* (1993) to the Employment Committee, House of Commons, 1994.

Editor: *Ten Years On: Success or Statistics? New Labour and Crime Control* (Centre for Crime and Justice Studies), Criminal Justice Matters no. 67, Spring 2007.

[1]
The Teen Canteen: In at the End

THE TEEN CANTEEN CLOSED DOWN OFFICIALLY IN DECEMBER, 1962. It had run for seven years, and had been successful for perhaps as many as three out of those seven. I became a "voluntary helper" and—later—a committee member at perhaps its lowest ebb, in mid-1960, when it re-opened only two nights a week and was little more than a built-in street-corner. It remained in this state until mid-1961, when a full-time, fully-paid manageress was appointed (Barbara Ward). With her, the Canteen opened five nights in the week, soon attracted about 50-60 customers—about 30 a night—mostly the 'unclubbables', the 'layabouts',

---

DAVID DOWNES has been doing post-graduate research on juvenile delinqeency in East London for the past three years.

the 'yobs', whatever name we call them to single them out for worry, condescension and little else. Within a few months, a football team was organised (by them), the drab cellar was re-decorated, the semblance of a committee was arranged by the regulars. Whether or or not these are criteria of "success" for an "experimental" youth project (*i.e.* a project which attempts to seduce non-Youth Club users from the street-corner), at least things were happening where before there had merely been a social vacuum. At this point the Canteen ran out of money, ran through every possible money-raising scheme[1] and—within a few months—had to admit financial defeat. We were spared one of the problems of our "success": how to retain a self-established in-group without excluding all comers. That we reached this stage at all was something.

What did the Canteen achieve? It kept them off the streets, marvellous. But if there had never been more to it than a negative coralling, an instant delinquency prevention programme, we would not only have failed: we would have been ridiculous. In that respect, the Canteen could never have been more than a holding operation only. More importantly, the Canteen served as a link between "do-gooders" who realised that established youth work was preaching to the converted (however useful that might be) and those adolescents who remained staunchly unconverted, who rejected and resented the cosy paternalism of the Clubs and preferred the uncertain freedom of the streets and the caffs. In this connection, the Canteen tapped—probably by accident—a source of frustration which is especially severe for the working-class adolescent in a dead-end, semi-skilled job, or in no job at all. What is often overlooked about these teenagers is the sheer *importance* they attach to their leisure hours. It is not for them simply a question of "killing time". It is that they increasingly look in their leisure for the purpose and excitement so conspicuously absent from their work. We too easily assume that the only aspirations an adolescent can have are occupational. It is a specifically middle-class assumption that, if a boy lacks 'ambition' in this narrow sense, all we can do is keep him occupied, fill in his time, give him ping-pong, go-kart racing and 'activities'. This is both naive and an insult to his intelligence.

The job aspirations of most working-class teenagers are notoriously —and realistically—limited in range. A few areas have specialities, such as docker and market-porter, but the norm is labourer, van-boy, factory operative. The scope is small for the non-apprentice, and their aspirations reflect this low-ceilinged market-place. They are not *inherently* disillusioned about jobs, any more than they are about education; it is just that the jobs to which they have access are all the same —tedious. Money is, therefore—and quite rightly—their only occupational criterion[2]. Hence the excessive importance of off-work hours, and here it is not only excitement they are looking for. Much more crucially for their self-respect, they seek in leisure the freedom and dignity denied to them in work.

It is precisely on these two fronts that their self-respect is undermined nightly. If he rejects the Youth Club, he is "on the town". One of the best features of Fyvel's book[3] was his evocation of just how little the "town" has to offer: the drab caffs and the sterile Wimpy's are all the working-class 'corner boy' has to hand for rendezvous and conversation; the cinema, Bingo and the occasional dance all he has for entertainment. The more decorous cafés, where open, either charge too much or frown on the milling, drifting chatter of the 'Teds' and their girls. "The Boys" was a film which caustically showed the possible results of this 'closed doors' policy. The Youth Service caters for these adolescents as if they were students or serious grammar-school boys, who sit quietly over espressos talking about the latest Truffaut film, when the least that they want is a place where they feel at home, can relax, which doesn't cost too much but is anti-drab, where they can loll about, drift from table to table, dance if they feel like it, horseplay a little, and so on. This is the necessary basis for the positive things of which they are capable as and when they sense that the 'tone' of a place is right. The triumph of Ray Gosling's Youth Ventures experiment —despite its tragic closure—was his instinctive flair for creating a set-up where—for once—the town 'rowdies' were trusted, not only to refrain from tearing the place apart, but to 'run' it. The Canteen did not go this far: in time it might have done, but its structure was neither big enough nor smart enough to really capture the teenagers' imagination. We lacked the money and the personnel to supply those specialised services—on a semi-commercial basis—which Gosling rightly saw as priorities.[4] But the Canteen *did*—for a spell of a few months at the end of 1961—become a place where the customers' sense of freedom and dignity was not affronted. Under Miss Ward's managership, it not only lacked the outdated Baden-Powellism of the average youth club, it briefly possessed an aura of teenage ownership, and we saw the glimmerings of the potentialities we ignore at great cost. At great cost, not simply because economically "the country" cannot afford a waste of talent and energy on the immense scale of the present. It can't, but we'll realise that too late. It is simply that, by ignoring this vitality and allowing it too often to warp into 'fringe' and chronic delinquency, *we* are the poorer as human beings.

The only consolation for "the boys" is that sooner or later, directly or indirectly, society pays the price. But delinquency is muddled social, never political, protest. The delinquent makes a blind swing at the wrong target, or pursues some futile 'exploit'. As yet, we are fundamentally indifferent to the delinquent potential of a class of adolescents who are—in crude socio-economic terms—expendable. Until recently, the American attitude towards a much larger problem suggested the same acceptance of delinquency as the other side of the coin to free-wheeling, if irresponsible and unequal, affluence. The problem became finally unmanageable, and following a decade of juvenile street warfare culminating in the Michael Farmer killing, existing agencies were given massive governmental and foundation aid to further research and preventive work. 'Mobilisation for Youth' is currently pouring 12 million dollars into one section of the lower East Side in an attempt to create legitimate job-opportunities where previously none or few existed. The situation here is radically different, but the government might have considered pouring a few hundred pounds into the Elephant and Castle, where by all accounts the Teddy Boy movement started. The 1960's will have its equivalent, with a different trigger-point but the same essential causes. The financial failure of the Canteen—which mirrors that of most experimental projects—is just a symptom of the structure of social priorities which underlies much delinquency. But in the case of the Teddy Boy movement, we are not only not wise after the event: we are not even sure what the event was. It is 16 years since the Barge Boys club, 12 since Spencer publicised the danger of the 'unclubbables', 3 since Albemarle, 2 since Leicester. When the Canteen idea began in 1955, it was hoped it would "catch on" all over the country. That it hasn't is only a reflection of our larger failure to *want* to understand the needs of "the boys".

NOTES:

1 LCC administrators well-meaning but far too limited funds. Case for responsibility of universities for fund-giving resources for "experiments".

2 cf. Arthur Seaton's pride in "grafting" for his wages, *i.e.* work hard, not bribery. But if you're, for instance, a van-boy, it's *impossible* to graft. This is incidentally the whole point of Paul Goodman's *Growing Up Absurd*".

3 *The Insecure Offenders*. 1961.

4 tSee *Lady Albemarle's Boys,* (Young Fabian Pamphlet, No. 1).

[2]
Educating for Uncertainty
(*with Fred Flower*)

Since the turn of the century numerous schemes have been proposed, both by individual educationalists and government commissions, for the extension of part time education to all young workers in the period of two or three years after they have left full time education. That these schemes have uniformly been abandoned is principally due to the superior claims on scarce resources of primary and secondary education. Social scientists, themselves in scarce supply, have similarly concentrated on the full time educational structure, at primary, secondary and university level.

There is every reason to think that this period of neglect is coming to an end. Firstly, the primacy of part time education for the manual worker is becoming established *de facto* by the rapidity of technological change. Secondly, the struggle to establish the comprehensive principle has been won intellectually, if not administratively, in secondary education: the next stage must be its extension to the further education system. Thirdly, the inter-dependence of the various sub-systems of education is much more clearly recognised than before, so that changes in one sub-system are now *expected* to affect the total structure. The danger is that resources are not made available to meet the needs that result from change, even though its effects are anticipated in theory. This danger is particularly clear in the likely impact of the Newsom Report on the field of further education.

two assumptions

This pamphlet stems from two assumptions: the first is that the Newsom Committee were correct in stating that "when the school leaving age is raised to 16 for all, there will be a fundamental change in the whole educational situation, and the schools must be equipped, staffed and reorientated in their working to meet it. If they do their job well, the colleges of further education will have to meet rapidly increasing demands for courses by older school leavers" (*Half Our Future,* p8, para 23, HMSO 1963). The second assumption is that the Crowther Committee were correct in recommending that the introduction of county colleges, or compulsory part time education for all until the age of 18, should be planned in three stages. But Crowther then went on to say that "the first stage, which would take place while the Ministry and the local education authorities were heavily engaged with preparations for raising the school leaving age, would be concerned with the development of the voluntary system (of further education), with the assistance of strong encouragement from the Government " The second stage would be the introduction of compulsion in a few carefully selected areas. This should follow hard on the raising of the school leaving age. "This experimental stage would feasibly take about five years . . . The third stage in the introduction of further education for all would be the progressive extension of compulsion to the whole country . . ." in a "phased programme spreading in successive years from region to region" for which "three or four years might be needed" (*15-18,* vol 1, pp188-189, paras 242-294, HMSO 1959). On the basis of Crowther, therefore, we cannot expect a compulsory, part time, paid system of further education for all until the 1980s, while the needs of Newsom demand that it should arrive by the mid-1970s.

The Newsom assumption means that further education is integral, not merely incidental, to the chances of Newsom's proposals succeeding. But the Newsom Committee were prevented, by their terms of reference, from making proposals for the further education system as radical as those made by their Report for the secondary modern system. Hence, the Crowther proposals for further education assume tremendous significance, all the more so because, while Crowther was right in his "three stages" proposal, he was wrong, from the Newsom point of view, in his timing. Insofar as the Newsom proposals work, boys and girls in secondary modern and comprehensive schools who have previously been either apathetic towards or hostile to the idea of school, are going to be stimulated and interested by a different kind of educa-

2

tion which relates much more closely to their work, and to their personal and social development, than the present, narrowly "subject tied" approach. The extra year is the basis for this re-orientation.

Yet, if this education stops at 16, it is probable that more harm will be done than if the system remains as it is. False hopes will have been generated, only for the quick return of cynicism on entry to the labour market, if educational links are not maintained. Unfortunately, this is essentially what Crowther's timing will involve for the first and most crucial decade of the Newsom re-organisation. On the basis of Crowther's timing, the regional experimental stage would begin with the exit from the schools of the first age group to leave at 16, in 1971. Lasting five years or so, this stage would take us to 1976, when phased extensions of further education by compulsion spread regionally to cover the whole country, this stage lasting three or four years at least, and taking us to 1980. Allowing for the usual time lags, we cannot, on the basis of Crowther, expect a national part time further educational system for all up to 18 until well into the 1980s.

This does not simply mean that we are abandoning virtually half a generation to the present inadequacies of the post-secondary modern school system: it means the strong probability that the "head of steam" generated by Newsom will fizzle out, since the demand for further education which it stimulates will not be met.

underlying assumptions

By "Newsom child" we mean the "Jones" and the "Robinsons", the two middle and the lower quarters of the secondary modern age group as assessed by reading ability, and not the "Browns", the top quarter in ability as assessed by reading tests, who are really grammar school boys *manqués,* who go on much more frequently than the rest to white collar and skilled manual jobs, day release and apprenticeships, and who are more likely to be middle class in origin.

The theoretical essence of the Newsom Report is to be found in the work of one of its witnesses, Basil Bernstein, of the Institute of Education. Bernstein's work ("Social Class and Linguistic Development: A Theory of Social Learning" (ed. Floud, Halsey and Anderson), *Education, Economy and Society,* 1961), centres, in brief, on the "linguistic deprivation" of the lower working class child of average or below average ability, whose parents typically have had no education themselves beyond the old elementary stage and neither of whom is of middle class origin.

Bernstein contends that this sort of child is socialised into communicating solely by "restricted" language, the vivid and direct, but limited, language of everyday working class speech. The middle class child, by contrast, is taught to respond not only to this "restricted" language, but is also socialised into the use of "elaborated" language, the vehicle used for concept formation. We are not concerned here with accent, pronunciation, or with class linked quirks of address; but simply with the extent to which the two codes "carry" differing potential for the elaboration of the child's linguistic and intellectual apparatus in the future. "Social class factors have been shown to affect not only the level of educational attainment, but also the very structure of ability itself," according to Basil Bernstein ("Research for the 'Sixties", *Twentieth Century,* Autumn 1963, p92).

The logic of this approach of Bernstein's is that the middle class child is extended linguistically far more than the working class child, in range, diversification and complexity of symbols and thought. This lays the essential groundwork for the smooth entry of the middle class child to the school, and the more tentative and less sure footed entry of his working class counterpart. Subcultural differences are progressively widened by differential parental encouragement, streaming, availability of books, and so on, so that by the age of seven or eight it is axiomatic that each middle class child will be performing academically better than any working class child of equivalent ability at entry. (see J. W. B. Douglas, *The Home and the School,* 1964, and B. Jackson, *Streaming: An Education System in Miniature,* 1964.) While the *weightings* to be adduced to each of these variables are not yet agreed upon, their operation works *cumulatively* in the same direction and towards the same product: the severity of the handicaps under which the working class child competes with his middle class counterpart for restricted educational opportunities.

There is an obvious danger that Bernstein's work, unlike that of Douglas, Jackson, Floud, Halsey and others, will be misunderstood as locating the source of educational "failure" purely in "faulty" or "inadequate" socialisation, rather than in conditions stemming from far less subtle social and economic inequalities.

Access to an "ellaborated" code only frames the conditions under which conceptual thinking becomes possible. Possession of an "elaborated" code does not guarantee higher intelligent or creative *thinking*: thought is not indentical with language, and from the quicker retort of lower working class boys to physical aggression might be inferred the frustration of thinking imprisoned within a restrictive code. There is no necessary corelation between speed or depth of insight and sense or fluency of expression: and too often in education inability to think is inferred from a failure to communicate. An "elaborated" code in language cannot prevent the stereotypy and rigidity of thought deployed at the typical Tory Women's Conference. Nor should concern about "linguistic deprivation" deflect attention from the brute *economic* inequalities and differences in parental privilege, attitude and ambition referred to above.

By the age of 11, the typical "Newsom child" is formed, not only in his vocabulary and linguistic ability, but in his dissociation from academic education. It is at this point that he is "selected" for the secondary modern or the diluted comprehensive school.

extending awareness

The appointment of the Newsom Committee in itself indicated recognition of the secondary modern system's failure to undo the damage inflicted on the "Newsom child" by throwing him into an educational structure based on criteria he was ill prepared to meet. Their job was to propose the appropriate education to enable these children to overcome the cultural "gulf" which increased with age between them and the system of formal education.

Briefly they proposed a set of ideas basically designed to extend the Newsom child's awareness of *choice,* and by implication to extend his range of choices both educationally and occupationally. Their chief notion was that the *content* of the traditional disciplines should be re-examined and taught through and in terms of the culture with which the working class child has most direct and intense experience, and that this content should be expanded to cover issues and themes relevant to the child's own personal and social development. This is not to say that the working class child is to be *hardened* in his own culture: simply that it must be the basis for engaging his energies and attention in the first place. Nor is it to say that the working class child is to be "bourgeoisified" and taught to share middle class values and attitudes: simply that the school should aim at imparting the middle class child's linguistic and intellectual range and awareness. New thinking on the teaching of English and Social Studies combined is abundantly provided. Typical of the new approach are *Reflections,* a textbook for teaching English to 14 to 18 year olds, by Simon Clements, John Dixon and Leslie Stratton, and the ideas contained in *The Popular Arts* by Stuart Hall and Paddy Whannel. In the field of political and "constitutional" history, Philip Abrams has recently attacked the smug circularity and arid parochialism of the major text-books in use at all

4

levels. Sterility in this field is particularly disturbing, and underlies the ease with which even the best intentioned "liberal studies" course degenerates into mere "civics" (P. Abrams, "Notes on the Uses of Ignorance", *Twentieth Century*, Autumn, 1963, pp66-77).Not surprisingly, the young voter typically inclines to political quietism (P. Abrams and A. N. Little, "The Young Voter in British Politics", *British Journal of Sociology*, June, 1965). A new awareness can only be achieved via a re-organisation of the syllabus which makes for flexibility and sensitivity to local as well as national concerns, and which is possible only on the basis of compulsory full time education for all to 16. The CSE examination, which started this year, could—if imaginatively used—be the vehicle by which the Newsom proposals begin to work.

other attempts

The task of the Newsom Committee was essentially to solve a theoretical problem, the cultural gulf between the school and the child of average and below average ability, and an organisation problem, how to build this "solution" into the curriculum within restricted terms of reference.

The task of the Crowther committee, on the other hand, was to *set* the terms of reference for the English educational system for the next two decades, by exhaustive research and the sifting of priorities at the 15-18 stage. As the first major enquiry into the education system since the 1944 Education Act, the main impact of the Crowther Report's findings focussed on how effectively the reconstituted system was working. Here the Report was generally, if guardedly, optimistic: it concentrated on assessing the under use of the potential of the *status quo*, rather than on criticising its basic structure. But inevitably the Report was also charged with deciding how best the unimplemented sections of the 1944 Act could be put into operation. The 1944 Act, and the debates which surrounded it, called for the raising of the leaving age to 16, and the introduction of part time compulsory further education for all, as soon as possible after the raising of the leaving age to 15 in 1945. In 1945 it was assumed that these sections would be operative by the early 1950s.

The idea of releasing young people in industry for one day per week to attend technical college classes dates from long before the 1944 Education Act. The Fisher Education Act of 1918 required authorities to establish "continuation schools" for young people between the school leaving age of 14 and the age of 16, and enforce their attendance for 320 hours per annum. P. I. Kitchen in *From Learning to Earning,* describes the disappointing story of the failure of these schools. Rugby has been the only authority to carry out, continuously since 1919, the intention of this Act. Similarly the 1944 Education Act made provision for continued education in "county colleges" on a part time *or* full time basis, to the age of 17 and, subsequently 18: again, this section of the Act remained unimplemented. Very few county colleges, as such, have been established, and nowhere, save Rugby, is release compulsory.

The onus on the Crowther committee was to analyse the reasons for this stagnation, and press for politically and financially acceptable ways of introducing this long neglected reform. However, despite Crowther's support for the implementation of the ideal as soon after the raising of the school leaving age to 16 as possible, and despite the Report's criticisms of the system which, 40 years after the Fisher Act, still left 70 per cent of young male employees without any further education after leaving school, the prospect of any legislation in the foreseeable future to enforce these recommendations is strikingly absent from the political scene.

2. where Crowther went wrong

To some extent, the seeds of this abandonment were present in the Crowther line of argument. Firstly, Crowther's timing of the introduction of compulsory further education was illogical. Secondly, it gave the county college concept a "liberal studies" non-vocational gloss which was at odds both with the intention of the 1944 Act and with the subsequent Newsom proposals. If the term "liberal studies" is used here pejoratively, this is not to denigrate the field, whose promise we are in essence recommending, but to reflect the emptiness with which the term is currently used and associated. What minor experiments currently exist for further education with semi-skilled and unskilled young workers are termed "*non-vocational* day release", a concept quite contradictory to the intention of Newsom, but inherent in the separate development of technical further education in the 1950s, welcomed by Crowther. This suggests a watered down academic education for those who need it least, and have rejected it since the age of five.

Crowther's timing was the real basis for the neglect now threatening his recommendation for further education. He gave four main reasons for making experiments with compulsory further education follow, rather than precede, the raising of the school leaving age.

As 15 year olds would soon be staying on full time, Crowther thought that to provide for them temporarily in part time further education would be "wasteful". This point has already been partly undermined by the implementation of another Crowther recommendation, the abolition of the Christmas leaving date. This means that, in effect, most leave at 15½: the "gap" between leaving and part time further education is therefore reduced to a matter of a few months for most, and cannot be described as harmful. In other words, if compulsory part time further education was brought in for 16-18 year olds before the raising of the leaving age, it would not necessarily have to provide for 15 year olds.

Secondly, Crowther hoped that raising the leaving age to 16 would automatically mean just as many staying on to 17-18 as had previously stayed on to 16. Therefore, further education would only have to cater for 1½, as distinct from 2½, age groups. Apart from the fact that this assumption seems over optimistic, since staying on tendencies cannot be extrapolated so readily from one age group to the next, the idea of restricting further education to 1½ age groups runs counter to the intention of the county college ideal.

Thirdly, Crowther thought that staff engaged to deal with 15 year olds might have difficulty switching to 17 year olds when the leaving age is raised. This assumption is very dubious; teachers are not that inflexible, and 15 year olds will have to be catered for anyway if Newsom's proposals for spells in further education during the fifth year at school, are widely implemented.

Last, it was thought that full time education for the 16th year was infinitely preferable to part time education for that year. This assumption is valid, but should not be used as an argument against the need to experiment regionally with compulsory further education *before* the raising of the school leaving age. At least three of the arguments used by Crowther for postponing even a regional experiment with compulsory further education for all until after raising of the leaving age are value judgments loosely based on the magical qualities of a fifth year unrelated to a re-organised further education system. Yet, Crowther goes to great pains to stress that *both* are needed, and Newsom makes it adamantly certain that further education for all must rapidly following raising the leaving age to 16.

county colleges

Apart from the negative implications of the Crowther case for postponing the introduction of further education for all, the report further weakened that case by accepting the tripartism of secondary education at further education level. This represented a retreat to the idea of essentially non-vocational further education

6

for those outside the technical college, a notion contrary to the intentions of the framers of the 1944 Act. The Report defined the county college as: "a term sometimes used to cover any institution which might be attended by young people receiving part time compulsory education, and sometimes to refer only to an institution designed to provide for those whose education at this stage *will not be mainly vocational*. Except where otherwise stated, we use the term in the more restricted sense" (p507). Crowther points out the "confusion in usage about the term county college. There is no doubt that the Act of 1944 provides for attendance at county colleges *by all who are not receiving full time education*. . . . There might thus be a widely different curriculum for apprentices and for routine process workers, though both would be attending county colleges. In much common speech, however, the term "county college" has been used as if it excluded most of what now goes on in technical colleges, that is, *as if it applied* only to institutions designed to cater for the great number of young workers who neither need, *nor could benefit from*, a strictly technical education. . . . In what follows, the term . . . is to be understood in this more restricted sense" (*15-18*, pp163-4, para 251).

The implication of this crucial passage is quite simply that Crowther endorsed and accepted the tripartite system at the 15-18 stage. By doing so, and by scaling down the "county college" concept to essentially non-vocational, if occasionally "practical", education. Crowther effectively placed the issue of further education for all at the bottom of the heap of educational priorities. The build up of technical colleges throughout the 1950s, the White Paper on "technical education" in 1956, which set out a five year plan of development for technical education, and pressed home the need for colleges of advanced technology first recommended by the 1945 Percy Report, had both legitimised and institutionalised the trend for technical education, as well as "academic" education, to be separated from the rest. (See M. Argles, *South Kensington to Robbins: An Account of English Scientific and Technical Education since* 1851, pp104-108, Longmans, 1964).

Crowther failed to swim against the tide, and even strengthened it by insisting that the county college ideal, which the report had shredded of any real relevance, was viable only in spanking new buildings with teachers called "tutors". Words like "leadership" and "pastoral care" were invoked to convey the relationship desired between teacher and pupil. Nor could the linking of the county college concept with the Duke of Edinburgh's award scheme and the Youth Service have been conducive to confidence in the idea of further education for all by hard-headed employers who had to foot part of the bill (*15-18*, paras 298-301). The concept was now linked in social thinking with the woolliest kind of "liberal studies" education. Not surprisingly, it has proved infinitely shelvable.

recent developments

Developments *since* the Crowther Report strengthen the view that there is very little prospect of any radical improvement in the voluntary further education system in the foreseeable future. What has happened since Crowther is that education is becoming more stratified, not less, and these trends show up exceptionally clearly in the further education field. We are moving towards a meritocratic system catering for four broad, but clearly distinct strata, with tremendous inequality in the investment of resources at each level.

At the top we have the expanded elite, catered for by the Robbins Report, and in turn meant to cater for our needs for administrators and technologists. The next stratum is the apprenticeship layer, at present covering the bulk of skilled workers, and now extended upwards to take in technician grades. These two strata practically accommodate all boys of middle-class origin and above, if we include black coated workers with apprentices. The third layer is largely prospective, designed to make up for the inadequate numbers in the second layer and overlapping considerably with it. The third layer takes in those skilled workers and top level semi-skilled who are not accommodated by the creaking apprenticeship system, and who are to be catered for by the Industrial Training Act 1964 and the Henniker-Heaton Report proposals for doubling numbers in day release over the next five years. This layer has yet to emerge, but will do so in response to our need for more skilled labour. The fourth layer constituting over 40 per cent of the 15-17 age group, is simply the rest, perhaps a third of whom will, in a decade, constitute an unemployable rump, unless rapid and radical changes are made to their prospects and education at both secondary and further levels.

the Industrial Training Act

The danger is not only that we treat this fourth layer as expendable from the further education and training point of view, but also that we imagine that the provision for the second and third layers is adequate. The deficiencies of our apprenticeship system are indicated below, but they set the tone for the whole further education system. It was in response to these deficiencies, which underlay our chronic shortage of skilled manpower, and helped to perpetuate under employment, demarcation and restrictive practices in industry, that the Industrial Training Act and the Henniker-Heaton Committee were conceived. But the Industrial Training Act is aimed at the limited training and re-training ends demanded by the current estimate that by 1970, $1\frac{1}{2}$ million *less* unskilled, and $1\frac{1}{2}$ million *more* skilled workers will be needed; even if successful beyond current expectations, the Act will only give a narrow practical education for a limited number of skills; and the Henniker-Heaton Report simply recommended an increase in numbers to be granted day release which was inevitable anyway.

It is clear from the publication of the Levy and Grant proposals of the first Industrial Training Boards, 1965/66, that the worst fears of some educationalists about industrial training will not be realised. Further education seems to be a definite requirement in all schemes of training on which grant is to be paid. But it is also quite clear that industrial training is not, nor can it be, any substitute for compulsory day release or its equivalent for all young people not in full time education between 15 and 18, as envisaged by the 1944 Act.

The further education to be included in industrial training schemes will take the form of packaged courses, all with a strongly vocational flavour, even in those areas of work where there can be little purely vocational skill to be acquired. Again, while some benefit may come immediately, or fairly soon. to the "brighter" Newsom children, the middle and lower ranges, the Jones and Robinsons of the report, may not be affected by operative training programmes for a long time to come. They will be the last in the queue, though eventually they may be covered. The very fact that their needs are primarily educational in the broadest sense, that is, they need to be stimulated into further intellectual growth, means that a scheme of education organised by industries is singularly inappropriate. Young workers at this level have far more in common, culturally and in their social needs, than they have with others in the same industry; and an attempt to produce an educational scheme based on the needs of their industry may in fact reinforce the very lack of flexibility which it is one of the aims of industrial training to overcome.

The more formal the education and training these students receive, the more it seems associated with what they did at school, the less there is of personal choice and the meeting of personal needs and preferences, the greater the tendency for these students to drop out of education and training altogether. These are points which may not always be apparent to the outside observer, particularly one who is concerned with the problems of industry, productivity and manpower. Industrial training may therefore be

8

either a step towards a genuine expansion of further education and of educational opportunity for Newsom children out at work; it may equally well become an obstacle to the development of the kind of education they so desperately need. It is for this reason that, however successful the Industrial Training Act may prove in practice, it is really necessary to have an alternative scheme in actual existence to demonstrate the difference between the complete response of the 1944 conception and the partial response of the Industrial Training Act to the needs of the young people themselves.

The need for more skilled manpower has been used as a pretext to bypass Crowther and Newsom. In effect, we have now legislated in the compulsory fifth year for those who would not have stayed on voluntarily, only to leave the situation *after* that fifth year completely unchanged for the same population. The further education recommendations of Crowther have been shelved, if not deliberately abandoned, and without them the promise of the Newsom proposals is seriously threatened.

3. the case for rapid change

The principal inadequacy of the present system of voluntary further education, whereby those whose employers do not encourage them to take advantage of day release facilities are dependent upon evening only education, is that far too few of the population "at risk" benefit from it. This applies particularly to "Newsom children"—by our definition. An unpublished study carried out in 1964 by Peter Willmott in Bethnal Green gives a representative picture. Of 148 boys aged 15-20, who had been to secondary moderns, including a few who had been to comprehensives, 55 per cent had had no education since leaving school at 15. 26 per cent had experienced or were undergoing some form of day release, and an additional 19 per cent some form of evening only education. The Henniker-Heaton Report (*Day Release,* appx A, table 1(a), p36, HMSO 1964) on day release similarly showed that 28 per cent of boys aged 15-17, and not in full time education, were granted day release. Even these rational figures are, misleading, for they take no account of courses discontinued, failure rates and non-attendance. The wastage in evening only education is especially severe, amounting to almost 50 per cent by the end of a course (*15-18,* p168, para 258). Obviously these figures show that the present system is coming nowhere near voluntary implementation of the section of the 1944 Education Act which calls for part time education for all till the age of 18. Yet the merits of expanding the voluntary system are constantly invoked as an alternative to a framework of compulsion.

lack of provision

The system is even unsatisfactory for that minority who achieve day release. The bulk of the students work part time for the qualifications of GCE, the National Certificates (ONC and HNC) and City and Guilds. The National Certificates are gradually outstripping the rest as the system gears itself to catering increasingly for the "abler" students, since the "Higher National" is virtually synonymous with professional status for engineers, who form the majority of entrants.

The failure rates in both ONC and HNC examinations are notoriously high: about 12-13 per cent of those embarking on ONC finally achieve HNC standard four or five years later (depending on whether they were exempt from the first stage of ONC by virtue of possessing enough GCE "O" levels) (Ethel Venables, "The Reserve of Ability in Part Time Technical College Courses," *Universities Quarterly,* vol 17, pp60-75). The failure rate for ONC alone is 75 per cent, though this is reduced to about 55 per cent if those failing at the initial stage are excluded.

Figures of this magnitude indicate wastage of both ability and resources on an immense scale. This wastage will grow as the system becomes increasingly geared to strictly vocational competence and the criteria appropriate to professional status. In 1960-61, of about 86,000 part time day students on ONC courses in England and Wales, roughly 75 per cent were in electrical and mechanical engineering, while the obvious goal was associate membership of the Institution of Mechanical Engineers (AMIMechE).

It is doubtful, however, that this is either the best way to pursue the professionalisation of engineering, for which the "sandwich" course and a Dip. Tech. is more apprpriate, or the best use of existing resources in further education, which should be evenly aimed at catering for students of all levels of ability and aspiration. As it is, those who have most need of the part time route are "selected out" as rigorously as they were from the full time route.

The present system of further education is neither intended for, nor used by, the "Newsom child". He is left to fend for himself in the labour market and, in the largely responsibility free period between leaving school and marriage, he invariably relishes his "freedom" from "school" and any adequate system of vocational guidance. However, earlier marriage and its inroads on means and mobility, brings boys in "dead-end" jobs face to face with the finality of their educational shortcomings at an increasingly early age.

10

As Alan Little and John Westergaard have pointed out ("The Trend of Class Differentials in Educational Opportunity in England and Wales," *British Journal of Sociology,* vol 15, pp301-316), the 1944 Education Act has made for increased opportunities for social mobility, but *only through education*: "career mobility", or mobility *via* routes other than the school system, have contracted proportionately.

Those who do not make it at school do not make it at all: mobility, the opportunity to attain even skilled manual status, is a process which is increasingly peculiar to the adolescent and pre-adolescent stages of the life cycle. Since the war, boys in "dead end" jobs at least had the capacity of temporary high wages and an abundance of opportunities within the same stratum, throughout the life cycle; but even this certitude will likely disappear by the mid-1970s, with a shrinking opportunity structure at the "bottom of the heap" and the closure of access to upward mobility for those without qualifications or the intellectual and practical means of acquiring new skills. Once in the labour market, the only potential avenue to skilled employment for the majority of "Newsom children" would be a vastly expanded system of part time further education.

no short term economic incentives

The case for compulsion as the necessary framework for an adequate system of further education remains the lack of any clear cut, short term economic incentive for either employers to allow, or young, non-skilled workers to demand, part time further education on a voluntary basis. The case for compulsion in further education is essentially that for compulsion up to age 16 in full-time education. Moreover, the two stages are interdependent: the one cannot succeed without the other.

The real trouble, however, is that the present system relies not so much upon the employer's *consent to* young workers participating in further education: it depends upon his *active encouragement* of them to pursue it. This is not only a wrong headed assumption to make about the majority of employers: it is a wrong headed role to impose upon them in the first place. Only employers with joint consultation agreements to keep, or with the need to maximise technical ability of a fairly high order, will take advantage of day release facilities.

day release and the small firm

At present, small and medium sized firms are the most inefficient in their training and granting of day release. Hence the provision in the Industrial Training Act for a levy to be imposed on firms evading their training obligations: the large firms resent the disproportionate burden they carry in training skilled manpower, and the "poaching" of that manpower once the costs have been met. The focus here is strictly on vocational skills rather than all round further education. Even so, a recent study in Leicester (E. T. Keil, D. S. Riddell and C. B. Tipton, "The Entry of School Leavers into Employment," *British Journal of Industrial Relations,* vol 1, pp408-411) found that 70 per cent of young male entrants to industry took their first jobs in firms of less than 250 employees. By contrast, only 45 per cent of the total male labour force is employed by firms of this size. In other words, the firms that give the worst training, even within narrowly defined limits, attract a disproportionate supply of young entrants.

It is not only that the smaller and middle sized firms attract a disproportionate number of young male entrants to industry, whether they are apprenticed or not, and that they have far less access than those entering large firms, of 1,000 persons or more, to both adequate in-training and day release as a result: it is also that the smaller the firm, the greater the likelihood of "drop out" for even that minority who *do* attend college (C. L. Ashton, "Enrolment and Examination Success of Day Release Students by Size of Firm", *British Journal of Industrial relations,* vol 3, pp90-94). If these firms give the most inefficient training in a strictly technical sense, their record in meeting requirements for a voluntary system of "liberalised" further education would be even worse.

This situation is not unique to Leicester. A recent study in Willesden, London, (Joan Maizels, "The Entry of School Leavers into Employment", *British Journal of Industrial Relations,* vol 3, pp 77-89) showed that 62 per cent of boys' first placements were in firms of less than 100 employees, as against 54 per cent in Leicester. In Willesden, only 25 per cent of all males aged 15 and over are employed in firms of this size, compared with 54 per cent of all boys under age 18, and 74 per cent of secondary modern boys in their first placements. Even where the boys gained apprenticeships, it appeared from an analysis of placements by the local Youth Employment Bureau that one in three secondary modern appentices were placed with firms of *ten* persons or less, while less than one fifth of apprentices from selective schools, grammar and technical, were placed with firms of less than 100 persons, and over one half of the latter were placed with firms of 1,000 or more persons. "Presumably this asymmetry reflects the discrimination of the larger firm in favour of applicants for apprenticeships who have secured some "O" level passes in GEC.

This implies, because of difficulties associated with training facilities in the small firm, that boys who have already obtained selective education, are more likely to receive favourable training opportunities, including that of day release, which the large firm can usually provide" (p83). It also implies that, although many of the vast majority of secondary modern boys who enter industry via the smaller firm eventually move to the large firm, thus "leaving their former jobs to the fresh generation of school leavers" (p86), they do so in general *only after they have outgrown* the age at which the training opportunities of the large firm would have been available to them.

Nationally, as locally, the short term economic incentives to press for further education for all are lacking. The picture is one of stretched labour resources, particularly of skilled manpower. Hence the "hoarding" or skilled labour, and the enactment of the Industrial Training Act. This is the current picture: but it has been projected to 1973 at least by the first report of the manpower research unit of the Ministry of Labour (*The Pattern of the Future",* HMSO, 1964). With the fall in numbers of new entrants to industry due with the "valley" in the size of adolescent age groups in the late 1960s, and with the raising of the school leaving age in 1971, the unit states that "up to 1973, the likely picture is . . . one of stretched manpower resources" (p35). They envisage the employment of an additional one million married women by 1973, although this is partly a response to the expected drop, of half a million, in the numbers of single, widowed and divorced women available by 1973.

manpower utilisation

In short, full employment and scarcity of manpower will be as prevalent a decade hence as now. Unfortunately, the unit reported strictly on the basis of past and present trends, with little regard for the commonplace findings of industrial sociology: that full employment is bought at the expense of endemic under employment, that the latter is already pricing us out of world markets, and that another decade of the same practice will bring us problems much more severe than a shortage of cheap labour. Ironically, the Report also notes that "the falling off in the number of young people entering the labour market . . . will call for adjustments, while at the same time making for a *less adaptable and flexible* labour force" (p35). It may be that this is where the logic of our current economic situation is taking us: but it remains a prescription for stagnation and eventual decline. As the Report also calls for the "efficient manpower utilisation . . . (which becomes) even more essential . . . with a labour force which will be smaller in relation to total population" (p35), it must reject the equation of full employment with the under employment, inflexi-

12

bility and immobility of labour to which we are currently training new entrants to industry.

long term economic incentives

If the argument above is valid, then one conclusion is plain: that the factors underlying opposition to further education for all, such as stretched labour resources and pursuit of short term at the expense of long term goals are identical with the factors underlying our relatively poor economic performance as compared with countries at a comparable stage of economic development. This makes us hopeful that the decision to implement the 1944 proposals for further education *to the full* would contribute towards an undermining of those forces most resistant to necessary changes in our social and economic structure. These fall under five main headings: a flexible and adaptable labour force; a mobile labour force; as little under employment and "synthetic" overtime as possible; more voluntary staying on in full time education; and an improvement in the technical and general education offered by local technical colleges.

The case for radical improvements on all five criteria must be synonymous with that for part time further education for all within a framework of compulsion on both employer and student. The terms "flexibility" and "adaptability" have been used by both Crowther and Newsom, and have been assimilated into the "conventional wisdom" long before they have emerged in reality. As concepts, they rest on the assumption that the constellation of technological changes referred to as "automation" will involve, for the majority, an increasing frequency of "bridging" between occupational roles throughout the life cycle (J. H. Smith and L. Broom, " 'Bridging' Occupations", *British Journal of Sociology*, vol 14, pp321-334).

However, the very occupational roles most vulnerable to "de-skilling" and redundancy for their occupants are also those with least potential for "bridging", as their job content is not transferable to other roles. As recent American experience has shown, the blow will fall most heavily on those already at the "bottom of the heap". Feasibly, we need a further education system capable not only of socialising new entrants to industry to an awareness of this likelihood, and geared to providing them with a diversity of skills, but also one which functions as a "bridge" for those adults who in the future find themselves stripped of their "one skill" income producing role.

The same arguments apply to any call for an increasingly mobile labour force, "mobile" at least in the occupational sense. A corollary of immobility is under employment: while this is too complex a problem to be discussed in any detail here, it can at least be noted that the "cheap labour" represented by non-skilled and female, as well as apprenticed, manpower is one of the principal supports perpetuating the under employment of adult workers in industry. As long as the flow of entrants into industry from the schools is unchecked, while the adolescents concerned are untrained and only semi-educated, their exploitation as "cheap labour" to cover up for under employment and low productivity will continue. The uses to which 15 year olds were put in industry served as one of the main arguments for raising the school leaving age to 16: it still stands as such for part time compulsory further education to 18 and beyond.

"dead end" jobs

At present, although "cheap" in comparison with adult male workers, non-skilled adolescents in "dead end" jobs receive relatively higher wages than ever before: this is the incentive for the adolescent who has suffered at the hands of the school system as an academic "failure" to leave and enter the labour market. Yet more full time education is obviously desirable: the more complex needed and marketable skills become, the longer the period of full time education needed to acquire them; and the critical awareness of our society that is to characterise secondary education if Newsom succeeds will take longer to convey. Crowther hoped for a natural increase in "staying on" voluntarily: yet the main improvements to date are slight, except for that produced by the elimination of the Christmas leaving date. However, if part time further education was a necessity for all, and education was not so much brought to a halt as "tapered off" by leaving as early as possible, the impetus to stay on full time would be much more concrete. The way to encourage more full time staying on is not to leave the post school leaving situation open, but to enforce part time further education.

Hence the long term economic incentives for further education for all are considerable. Pressures would be generated on employers and unions alike to cut down on restrictive practices, the most marked of which are systematic overtime and institutionalised under employment due to demarcation and anti-dilution agreements. With a system geared to maximising labour mobility and adaptability, the fears which underlie these practices would begin to be eroded. There is no doubt that the Industrial Training Act aims at similar ends: but the population at which its provisions are aimed is much more diverse than that for which further education would cater.

local technical colleges

An additional point is that compulsory further education for all would mean a shake up for the present further education system: it would be a spur to "broadening out" the present narrow focus on either purely technical or purely "non-vocational" education. As one study has shown, too many local technical colleges are as out of touch with current and prospective manpower needs and industrial requirements as the small and medium sized firms from which they draw too few students (P. F. R. Venables and W. J. Williams, *The Smaller Firm and Technical Education,* 1962).

Unlike the Colleges of Advanced Technology and the Regional Colleges, the evolution of the local technical colleges is very similar to that of the small firm. Their staffs, and the degree of interchange between those staffs and local industry, are inadequate to meet even local needs. It is doubtful whether these problems can be solved without the drastic overhaul implicit in the complete transforation of the local technical colleges into colleges of further education for all.

In short, the under employment position in industry, and the misuse of resources in many technical colleges, means not only that there is a great deal of slack to be taken up via an expanded system of further education, but that long term economic benefits should accrue if it *was* taken up in this direction.

apprenticeship

As at present organised in this country, apprenticeship functions mainly as a buttress for the protection of the skilled worker against the semi-skilled and unskilled: it serves as a means of regulating entry into skilled trades, and this function vitiates its effectiveness as a vehicle for industrial training. It reduces choice, by insisting on 16 as the maximum age of entry for school leavers; it promotes early leaving, by the same token; it embodies no general standard of attainment, mere time serving is enough; and it perpetuates training for "one skill" jobs. Moreover, the insistence in general on the five year term is at odds both with industrial realities *and* the existing practice of most European countries.

In brief, it functions principally as a surrogate for civilised industrial relations and control: and this role militates against its use as an educational and training avenue. Further education for all would be a vehicle for at least modifying the worst features of apprenticeship, since to eliminate it would be unlikely until more enlightened labour relations and income security conditions prevail. A full scale part time compulsory further education system would by-

14

pass the need for apprenticeships, and modify its worst side effects.

no provision for girls

Although the Crowther Report drew attention to the startling disparity between the provision of day release and other forms of further education for girls and the provision for boys, there has been very little progress since 1959 in extending facilities for girls. An ambitious project, sponsored by the YWCA in 1961-62 in collaboration with the LCC, that was based on the assumption that a major factor in the lack of girls' further education was the shortage of suitable accommodation, met with very little success.

On the other hand, it established beyond reasonable doubt that the main obstacle to the expansion of further education for girls was the attitude of employers, especially their objection to the devotion of working time to general education. The provision for girls in part time further education is nothing short of a public scandal; only 8 per cent of girls "at risk" receive day release at present (*Day Release*, appx A, p36), and their needs are almost totally ignored by the present voluntary further education system.

Any scheme of compulsory part time further education must include girls, who are even more likely than boys to be used as "cheap labour" for the purposes analysed above. There are also a number of special problems attaching to the further education of girls. Early school leaving is much more marked amongst girls than amongst boys, and even amongst girls who stay until 16, substantially more who would be intellectually capable of taking a sixth form course choose to leave rather than continue in a school atmosphere. This urge to leave school and to go out to work is often closely related to the fact that a girl in her late teens sees her prime role in life as a wife and mother, and at that stage is less interested in the possibilities of a long term career, even though she may be as intellectually capable of following one as a boy.

At present, many girls are used well below their intellectual capacity in routine jobs in offices and other work, filling in time until they get married. They may subsequently return to employment after a period of child bearing, but with only limited skills and experience to offer. If we are to help not only the Newsom girl, but even some of the girls above the Newsom range, to make their full contribution to the economy and to attain a larger measure of personal development as mature women, they need a further education which, while it may contain certain elements, such as the commercial skills, shorthand and typewriting for example, must also contain a personal element which for many may be related to the home, while for others it may be an academic subject, a science or a social study, or an aesthetic or cultural pursuit. Even more than in the case of the boys, it is essential that this element of personal choice should be present in the girls' curriculum.

It cannot be stressed too strongly that when studies or activities relating to the home are included in a girls' curriculum, at this stage they must be seen as a vehicle of real expanse of education. Housecraft must not become a disguised form of industrial training, but a real and living experience that can be used to promote further literacy, discrimination and development of mature judgment. It is also essential to ensure that while a girl may be able to choose as the personal part of her education something relating to her home and her future role as wife and mother, it must not be restricted to this range; where it is possible for her to undertake further personal academic pursuits, she should be encouraged to do so.

What we are concerned with here is the preliminary training upon which further training and education may be given when, as a mature woman, whose children are at school, she returns to work. The pamphlet, *Youth's Opportunity*, published in 1947, suggested that not more than five eighths of a young person's day should be entirely taken up with material deriving from his job. Certainly for girls it is most important that there should be this balance of time devoted to personal education. Yet under the Industrial Training Act, where office staff of the lowest grades are to be brought into schemes of training and education, they will be encouraged to take the Certificate of Office Studies which, in its present form, is a most unsatisfactory means of meeting the professional and personal needs of girl clerical workers. Four subjects have to be taken, three are compulsory: English, Office Practice and Calculation (or Accounts), and one other subject, from a list that includes, amongst others, Law, Social Studies and Accounts. For this certificate to become an appropriate vehicle for the genuine education and training of the Newsom girl, the compulsory subjects would need to be limited to two, English and Office Practice, the list of options extended to include some purely personal options, and the syllabuses of all the subjects to be looked at really carefully with the individual students rather than the subjects in mind.

Finally, the first priority of the Industrial Training Act remains that of improving and extending the training offered to potentially skilled workers in the staple productive industries. Its scope is huge even by this definition: it is to cover workers at all levels, of all ages and of both sexes. But it would be foolish to pretend that, even by the early 1970s, equal attention and investment will be allocated to the skilled apprentice in engineering and the non-skilled female shop assistant or factory operative. The Act was aimed particularly at the young, male, potentially skilled worker in firms not pulling their weight in the industrial training field; and if it achieves a levelling-up in this sector in the next decade, it will have achieved a great deal. But those adolescents, and particularly the girls, with whom we are most concerned, are not likely to be covered by that date: they will be last in the queue, non-skilled and often outside the productive sector in routine distributive or "service" jobs. And even when they are covered, it may well be inappropriately, as we suggest above: their range will be extended along one narrow dimension only. On both counts, that of priority and that of content, the Industrial Training Act seems unlikely to be the answer for the Newsom girl in the foreseeable future.

The question of provision for girls, therefore, raises in most acute form the deficiencies of an "industrial training" solution to the problems at issue. We believe that the resources at the disposal of the Industrial Training Boards could best be used in re-training *adult* workers faced with "de-skilling" and redundancy prospects: for *adolescent* workers, the problems should be faced in the context of a radically re-organised system of further education based on compulsory day release, though the emphasis on levying firms to provide concurrent on the job training of an acceptable standard should still be as vigorously pursued as now.

no middle class support

It has been argued above that children of middle class origin are, broadly speaking, already effectively catered for by existing arrangements, from which they have benefited proportionately much more than the children of semi-skilled and unskilled manual origins. Hence, the biggest barrier to any scheme for further education for all it not necessarily shortage of resources, but the structural implications of the fact that the middle classes have nothing to gain from the extension of part time education to the whole age group.

It is likely that the extensions of voluntary technical and further education over the last decade have taken place largely at the behest of those sections of the middle and skilled manual working classes whose needs were not met by the narrow intake into selective grammar and higher forms of education. This makes any extrapolation of the expansion of the last decade in the voluntary system into the future extremely hazardous. It also means that there is little hope of active support from the most vocal and articulate sections of society for improvements in the education of the Newsom child.

another route to higher education

As education comes to monopolise the *capacity* for social mobility in our society, so the doors to "higher" education become increasingly closed to those outside the formal education system, even though the volume of mobility experienced by those within it might increase. Unless we can devise alternative routes to higher education, the differentials in access to it will increase between those "staying on" and those leaving "early" who subsequently seek re-entry. As our present system of further education is merely echoing this stratification, it serves at present not as an alternative route to higher education for those *outside* the selective system, but as an alternative form of higher education, for those within it.

The extension of further education *to all* would open up just such an alternative route as is becoming increasingly desirable for Newsom children who *have* the ability, but realise it far too late. A corollary is obviously that we expand the *base* of those entering higher education though not necessarily the apex of those who continue in it.

As a recent study has shown (M. Cooper, "Why Some Prefer CAT's," *New Society*, 4 February, 1965), entrants into colleges of technology are marginally more likely to be skilled manual in origin than middle class: the cultural factors which working class adolescents *and* their parents share involve a "dissociation" from university education as more appropriate to "them": as we cannot expect these factors to disappear in the short term, we must counter the élitism of older universities by evolving institutional routes to forms of higher education more conducive to attracting working class entrants. The "city college" is one such concept. Moreover, the work of Ethel Venables (op. cit.) has shown the pool of ability among the abler boys in local technical schools as measured by non-verbal intelligence tests. There is no reason to suppose that similar potential is absent from those not currently being educated beyond the age of 15.

vocational guidance

At present the Youth Employment Service contacts the school leaver for his first job, after which the young worker resorts to it with dwindling frequency for each successive change of job (M. P. Carter, *Home, School and Work,* 1962). Except for boys in that minority of schools employing a careers adviser on a full time basis, this is the sole extent of vocational guidance offered to the adolescent, who feels that the Youth Employment Service has little to offer beyond routine placements. Psychological testing, systematic contact and recording for each school leaver finds no place in the current Youth Employment Service structure.

Joan Maizels found an imbalance in the investment of resources, in at least one bureau, between first and subsequent placements, and in secondary modern applicants over those from selective schools, and concluded that "the aims of the service are frustrated by the type of employment registered if, as in the case of Willesden, it more frequently represents (particularly for boys) the unskilled or semi-skilled manual work in the very small firm (op cit, p89). However, if the local office of the Youth Employment Service was built into the local county college, continuity of both access and contact would be ensured. More sensitive and individualised advice could be given. Moreover, this kind of vocational guidance, though expensive to administer, would both enhance the mobility of young workers and resurrect the Youth Employment Service as an agency of relevance for the young worker.

At present, since large firms are investing disproportionately in granting their best adolescents day release, they would stand to *lose* promising manpower rather than the reverse: their opposition to such a scheme operating within the present system of further education would be inevitable. But with all firms sending all their young workers to county colleges for a minimum of one day in five, large firms would stand to gain, as well as lose, promising manpower. Within the context of further education for all, there would be no obstacles to re-integrating the Youth Employment Service into the young worker's frame of reference.

delinquency

Delinquency, as measured by court appearances, is assumed to be more prevalent among Newsom children, by our definition, than among any other section of the population "at risk": this assumption has recently been confirmed in a paper by the National Survey of Health and Development. At present, however, delinquency in this country is mundane rather than extremist, its genesis lying in a process of drift and "dissociation" rather than in oppositional and contracultural values. David Matza recently argued that delinquency of this type is generated by "status anxiety" (the relative lack of access to legitimate achievement or "exploit" in an "achieving" society); "preparation" (socialisation in a milieu supportive of, though only rarely committed to, law breaking); and "desperation" (the perception of a lack of self-control over one's own "life chances") (*Delinquency and Drift,* 1964). Insofar as this analysis holds true, the propensity to delinquency will increase as disparities in "life chances" grow, or become more visible.

Over the next decade, and despite the movement towards comprehensive secondary education, these trends appear exceptionally likely to crystallise around the transition from school to occupational and income producing roles. In this situation, a radically re-organised system of comprehensive further education for all becomes a structural pre-requisite in delinquency prevention, not in order to forestall "maladjustment", but in order to reduce differentials in both educational and occupational opportunities at the most crucial transitional stage of the "life cycle".

4. the need for an experiment

The basic fallacy of Crowther was to assume that, because the joint aims of raising the leaving age to 16 and introducing compulsory further education for all were not possible simultaneously, then plans for the introduction of each should be drawn up separately, and the case for each should be made on differing bases. We have tried to show that the logic of Newsom demands a joint plan, and joint arguments, for both stages. If they cannot be implemented simultaneously, they at least need to be implemented as simultaneously *as possible,* and to wait a decade or more would be disastrous.

The need is for a full scale regional experiment in part time compulsory education for all to begin before, not after, the raising of the leaving age to 16 in 1971. If this assumption is made, certain preferences follow: the region chosen must contain all the problems about which decisions have to be made, such as whether further education is based on work or home residence, and what happens when a teenager changes jobs; the region chosen must be a focal point, not a backwater; it would best be in the south, since the north is still too handicapped at the secondary level to undertake a full blown regional experiment. On all criteria, London is the appropriate choice: it contains numerous "problem" areas, such as Notting Hill, Highbury, and parts of the East End; it has the commuting problem; it also has the finest base for pioneering technical and further education for all. It was one of the areas to attempt to do so in 1918. The timing must be at the end of the 1960s to benefit from the "valley" in age group size, before the vast increase in numbers in the 1970s. Greater allocation of resources is the obvious priority, but if these were granted, the experiment is workable. It may be desirable for *two* or *three* experimental regions to be chosen: London, and regions in the North (for example, Newcastle) and the West Country (for example, Bristol).

The mechanisms devised for approaching LEAS and the regions about such a scheme must be flexible, must maximise their advantages, and be politically acceptable. A working party should be set up at once to draft such plans in detail: but the ignoring of the Rugby experiment since 1919 is a warning to those who advocate piecemeal LEA experiment. This leads on to the fundamental requirement that Newsom children should not be "siphoned off" for further education to institutionally separate county colleges. An institutional form must be evolved to accommodate further education for all.

The local technical colleges could well be the basis for this, but must not be maintained as separate, selective establishments. The general pattern of day release on a one day per week basis must not be rigidly adhered to. The current trend to extend block release and sandwich courses for technicians and top level skilled workers must be extended as far as possible to non-skilled grades. But it may well be that day release is the best pattern for workers who are at present rated as non-skilled, though preferably on a two day rather than a one day basis, since they may be hostile to prolonged, continuous periods in further education. Also, further education should not stop at 18, but be extendable to 19 or even 20.

student attitude

The Fisher experiment in compulsory day release in the early 1920s failed for two reasons. First, there was sustained opposition from both employers and from students and their parents, and secondly there was gross inadequacy of resources; neither buildings nor equipment nor teachers were available in sufficient quantity. This last factor led to the opening of schemes for compulsory day release at different dates in adjoining local education authorities, and the discrepancy that existed from one area to another was a further cause of great dissatisfaction.

The opposition of the employers would not have been sufficient to kill the scheme had it not been actively reinforced by reluctance on the part of students to attend and the unwillingness of parents to support the idea of continued education. This experiment was, of course, terminated by the Government economies embodied in the notorious "Geddes Axe". Many people still fear an unholy alliance of employer, parent and young person will kill any attempt to implement the "county college" provision of the 1944 Act. It is quite true that attitudes towards education shade off through the population from enthusiasm at the upper levels through indifference in the middle ranges to mistrust and open hostility at the bottom.

For most of the children in the Newsom group school and education has not been an experience of absorbing interest and excitement unless they have been exceptionally fortunate in their teachers. If what they encounter in further education is merely a repetition of an unsatisfactory experience at school then their attitude is likely to be one of suspicion and eventual hostility. If they meet a new curriculum that relates directly to their life as they see it, that seems both to encourage and make possible their personal aspirations, and, above all, treats them like responsible adults, they may respond very differently.

Yet the position today is quite different, in that while employers might still be reluctant to release students who were not going to train for skills that could be immediately employed within the firm, the prospective students themselves and their parents are much more alive to the value of continued education. Students, too, are older. The Fisher scheme was concerned with day continuation from 14 to 15, and the general level of sophistication of young people in the 1920s was much lower than the present time. The further education to be provided in county colleges was to be for students of 15, 16 after the raising of the school leaving age, until 18, and today's young people, thanks to the continuing period of relatively full employment, are much more independent.

There is at present in many technical colleges a firm belief in the unwillingness of students to attend college unless there is a clear vocational carrot. Many teachers are convinced that students will reject education that is not clearly vocational in character, and they doubt the success of both courses in general education and the general studies portions of existing technical courses. Studies that have been made of students' reaction to day release seem to confirm the prevalent view. These studies invariably ignore the actual provision of general education and of general studies, and its unsatisfactory character in many colleges and the effect of bad courses on students. Student reluctance to participate in any kind of course is not an absolute quality but depends upon what is provided and how it is provided. We know that the characteristic attitude of Newsom children is that they wish to leave school as quickly as possible, but it was the hope of the authors of the Newsom Report that if the principles underlying the curriculum that they suggested were adopted, then this eagerness to leave school might be overcome.

If similar principles can be introduced into the provision of further education courses then the alleged reluctance of students to enter further education willingly may well vanish. Experience in a number of further education colleges confirms this point of view, and the best teaching in further education at the present time, whether on the technical portions of courses or on those sections devoted to general studies, would appear to embody the characteristics that *Half our Future* says should mark the new style of secondary education, that is that it should be vocational, practical, realistic and should offer the student the possibility of choice.

choice of course

It is necessary to comment upon the word "vocational" in this sense. In practice a vocational course usually means a course sanctioned by an employer or a trade or professional organisation, such as a National Certificate course or a City and Guilds course, or one of the courses

20

sponsored by the retail trades. Other work not falling within the scope of these courses or their attendant examinations is lumped together as general education. Much of what is studied in these "vocational" courses bears little relation to the jobs which are actually being undertaken by the students, or, in some cases, ever likely to be undertaken by the students. Many of the items which might appear in the general studies portions of, for example, a general engineering course, such as a discussion of systems of authority with relation to the role of foremen and supervisors or a consideration of problems arising from conditions of work or from the human relationships at a place of work, may have far more relevance to a young person's immediate life and future prospects than the mathematics and engineering science and workshop processes of the rest of the course. "Vocational" used in this sense may well be applied to any portion of a course in which a student perceives a relevance between what he is studying and any adult role he envisages himself playing in the future.

There can be no real hard and fast line drawn between the kinds of courses at present being provided in local technical colleges and the kinds of course which may be devised to meet the operatives who will be coming into the colleges under the terms of the Industrial Training Act, and, eventually, all the young people to whom the 1944 Act promises "day release". The elements may not always be as specific in a vocational sense as the present very tightly drawn courses are, but apart from the basic subjects of education ensuring literacy and numeracy, there must be provision for the mechanical skills that will lay the basis of possible further adaptation and development of the students at a later stage.

In at least one college there has been an attempt to give expression to these principles. The timetable has been so arranged that it is possible for students to choose between what is offered in all the departments, and to make up a timetable consisting of elements drawn from subjects with an academic content, subjects of a more personal character, and subjects which have a direct bearing on the student's work; for example, a typist may take a purely "vocational" course of shorthand, typewriting, office practice and English, but if the only commercial skill she was interested in and that her employer required was typewriting, she might have a programme consisting of typewriting, dressmaking, film study and chemistry ("O" level). These are actual examples of timetables being followed in the College. By offering subjects and activities at different levels, it is possible to make a tailormade timetable for a majority of students. If thought were given to the existing interests and possible lines of development of the Newsom children, who are at present excluded from day release, it should be possible to devise courses within a timetable of this pattern. Students could then choose a combination of subjects and activities that would seem to them relevant to their life and pertinent to their interests.

In this particular college the timetable consists of three sessions of two hours and one session of an hour. All follow the same pattern and therefore the possibilities of combinations of subjects and activities drawn from different departments is enormous. Where necessary two periods of two hours can be allocated to a given field of study and three hours are still disposable for other choices.

not too bitty

Some critics condemn the day release pattern because they say it is too bitty. The rival attractions of full time and block courses seem so much greater to the casual view that some teachers may hesitate to recommend any extension of the existing provision of day release courses. This is unfortunate because from the student's point of view day release is not always so bitty as it might seem. A regular attendance at an intelligently run institution throughout the year will be keeping him in touch with an educational atmosphere that will seem, not something special and extra, like going off to attend a block course, but an essential part of the pattern and fabric of his ordinary life.

Education alongside work can be especially effective for the type of young person we have in mind, especially if there is close collaboration between the firm and the educational institution and the Youth Employment Officer. Teachers who have not experienced teaching in an institution that is mainly concerned with day release students may believe that it is not possible to establish a satisfactory relationship with different groups each day of the week. To some extent this is illusory. A teacher who teaches for 20 or 22 "contact" hours during the week on a programme of the kind outlined above would meet 10 or 11 different groups in a week. Some full time specialist teachers in secondary schools do this already, in much shorter teaching periods. Full time teaching under such conditions can be very much more bitty than teaching day release classes.

local colleges for all

A further thought arises which deserves the most serious consideration, especially at this moment when schemes for the reorganisation of secondary education are being laid down that will set a pattern for the next half century. Even if selection for type of school is abolished at 11, a comprehensive system cannot be truly comprehensive if at the age of 16 one group of pupils leaves school to follow part time, or even full time, education in another institution, while the selected minority continue in the highly privileged atmosphere of a sixth form. The very existence of a sixth form within a school already introduces a measure of differentiation well below the level of the sixth form between those who are going to stay and those who are going to leave. This differentiation will be reflected not merely in a difference of curriculum but in the reciprocal attitudes of staff and pupils.

If all the young people leave school at 16 and proceed to a local college, some of them to undertake full time courses and some part time education side by side until 18 or 19, several advantages would ensue. Many young people, especially girls, leave education at 16 because they have outgrown the atmosphere of school and the teacher pupil relationship characteristic of it. It is difficult to modify this relationship within an institution that contains children of 11 and 12 years old as well as young people of 16 to 18. The establishment of an appropriate relationship is much easier within a college designed specifically for young adults. This is the familiar argument for the junior college. It is immeasurably strengthened if we include within the college not only the traditional sixth form courses, but elements to be found within the local colleges such as pre-apprenticeship courses, pre-nursing courses, secretarial courses, full time and block courses, and all the day release courses, both those already in existence and those eventually to come.

As has already been found in many further education colleges, students on GCE courses profit considerably from the contacts they establish through education, alongside young people already at work. Transfer from one course to another would be facilitated. A student, finding himself on an academic course which did not satisfy him, could transfer to the alternative technical or commercial route within the same institution. The transfer would be easier than at present and would not involve a loss of status or a sense of failure. The process would also operate in reverse. Early leavers who later regret their departure from full time education, and who at present often find it difficult to return, could move easily back into the type of full time education best adapted to their developing interests.

The abolition of sixth forms would entail the disappearance of the "experience of leadership" which a minority of sixth formers enjoy, and on which head teachers, especially those in grammar schools, place such store. Experience of leadership within what tends to be an authoritarian hierachy, however liberal its tyranny, may still not be as valuable as

22

the genuine democratic experience a good local college could provide.

Finally, a careful examination of this proposal might reveal unexpected but substantial economies that could be made, both of plant and of teaching power. The teacher student ratio in further education is very favourable when compared with the ratio in primary schools, but many sixth form ratios, because of the points system by which the establishment is calculated, may be even more favourable in fact than in theory. A scheme of local colleges, which would use in some cases new buildings and in others former grammar school buildings made available by the development of comprehensive schools and the elimination of sixth forms, would permit slightly larger and more economic teaching groups than often obtain at present, while still keeping classes down to reasonable levels of, for example, not more than 20-24 pupils.

incentives and sanctions

If the problem of students' attitudes could be regarded as being solved, the problem of resources in short supply is still very much with us. Unless a target date is fixed, however, when a scheme for compulsory day release is to be adopted, resources will never become available. The Industrial Training Act can either become a milestone on the way towards a compulsory scheme, or it can prove a major deterrent to its establishment. While no doubt industrial training may provide incentives for learning for most of the young people involved, the fact that those most difficult to motivate will be excluded from its operation may lead to the neglect of the problem of incentives, so that even industrial training may not achieve all it could do. Its value as a stage on the journey to compulsory day release for all may be minimised unless there is a experiment in compulsion that can act as a control.

How can a student be compelled to attend? Compulsory attendance cannot be enforced as attendance at school is enforced at present by laying the onus on the parent to ensure attendance. Today's young people are often quite independent of their parents and not only would they regard any such provision as abhorrent, but their parents might be quite incapable of enforcing their attendance against their will.

The most effective way of ensuring attendance would be to regard attendance at an institution of further education as an integral part of employment until the young person had attained the age of 18 and to lay the onus to ensure attendance on the employer. Absence from college would be notified to the employer as is done for the students at present attending under the voluntary scheme. Absence from the college would amount to absence from work and would carry with it the loss of a day's pay, and this would be the simplest and the most effective sanction that could be easily devised.

where to experiment

We need to show what can be done with a completely non-selected group of students attending a local college. We need to experiment on a large scale with teaching techniques, programmes and syllabuses that may have been found useful in other colleges, and therefore we need to select an area in which an experiment in compulsion can be tried which is big enough to provide a viable experiment, and which is sufficiently self-contained to minimise the friction that might occur on the margin between the area of compulsion and the area of voluntary further education.

An obvious area for first consideration is the Greater London Council. The GLC is a unity in a sense that its constituent boroughs are not. The problem of accommodition, while it is a very difficult one, would not be insuperable if we do not think in terms of wishing all students in new buildings. There would need to be some new building, but not all of this need be at the local college level. New secondary schools would release, as they are doing at present, older buildings which, though far from ideal, could be adapted as further education colleges for the time being, and if all the boroughs were to establish, or even to begin to establish, the local colleges which they should be building, many of the students who at present travel in to the ILEA area to receive their further education would be able to follow home based courses.

teacher shortages

The problem of teachers is a much more difficult one. If the GLC were selected as an area in which to try a compulsory experiment, a large percentage of the total age group would be covered. This fact, which makes the proposal so attractive, might also be the reason for not accepting the GLC as a trial area, because it might involve the commitment of too large a volume of resources.

An alternative suggestion would be that two much smaller areas, but of differing character with different problems, might be selected; for example, the north east region or some portion of it, and the south west region or some detachable portion of it, such as Bristol. The same problems of accommodation and teacher supply would present themselves as in the GLC, but perhaps not to the same degree of severity. The investment of resources in educational facilities in the north east region, which is a development area, would probably be met by some new building, by taking over the margins of secondary accommodation as they fall vacant, and by an imaginative use of unorthodox accommodation following up the lead, for example, of the YWCA who, some years ago, proposed that their hostel accommodation might be used for the promotion of day release schemes for girls. Unfortunately, this scheme did not receive the success it deserved because of the reluctance of employers to release girls for anything but the narrowest vocational courses (F. D. Flower, "Failure of an Experiment", *Education,* February, 1965).

In all areas, the main problem would be the shortage of teachers. Teacher shortage is a growing problem for education as a whole, and can only be solved first by an expansion of supply through an extended secondary education and an expanded programme of higher education. It might be mitigated by the introduction of teaching machines on a large scale, not in order that machines should replace teachers, but that they might so organise their work that larger classes could be divided between tutorial work with a teacher and more formal routine work on a machine. Improvements in the remunerative and professional status of the teacher would naturally also assist in recruitment.

The short term problem of a substantial increase in further education teachers in the areas selected for compulsion could be met by a planned expansion of places in the technical teacher training colleges for teachers, especially earmarked for these areas. A scheme of unorthodox recruitment is needed that would accept suitable applicants into the profession and provide courses of in-service training based on the senior technical colleges, and involve a careful reconsideration of the academic standards which are regarded as a minimum for entry into further education. It should not be impossible, if these steps are adopted, to provide the number of teachers required to man the scheme in the selected areas proposed.

These proposals would call for not more than 3,000 full time teachers for the scheme in the GLC area or for 300-500 teachers in each of the other two areas. Present practice would seem to be that colleges are expected to cover at least 25-30 per cent of their work by part time staff, and it would be possible to increase the amount of work covered by part time teachers to well beyond that percentage. In coming decades, we shall inevitably employ increasing numbers of part time teachers. Whether or not their excessive use in schools would lead to adverse consequences, there is no doubt that they have a positive role to play in further education, where in any case it is easier to find a satisfactory niche for them than in schools.

24

The presence of university institutions in all three of the areas proposed for the experiment suggests a limited source of supply for part time teachers among post graduate students. The increased provision of practical activities of all kinds would suggest other sources of part time teachers of a quite different kind. It must be emphasised, however, that the core of any scheme of this kind, if it is to be successful, must be a team of experienced and dedicated teachers who must be assembled in good time in the institutions which will form the kernel of any experiment in compulsory day release.

CONCLUSION

We have argued that the success of Newsom's proposals rests to an as yet unrecognised extent on early implementation of the Crowther proposals for compulsory, part time further education for all until the age of at least 18. A regional experiment should, therefore, be started up *before* the raising of the leaving age to 16. Preferably, this would be scheduled for 1968-9, and would cover the Greater London area and/or two other regions such as those centred on Bristol and Newcastle. Even if this were accomplished, further education for all on a national scale would still lie in the late 1970s. Unless this possibility is re-opened, however, prospects for the Newsom child are gloomy, since his fate will be left to the free play of the labour market in an increasingly uncertain economic future, and no protection will be afforded him by the combined operation of an enlightened further education system and a reoriented secondary education.

[3]
Delinquent Subcultures in Stepney and Poplar: Informal Observation

PRIOR to work on the statistical survey of crime and delinquency in Stepney and Poplar, field-work was carried out in the two boroughs on the basis of 'informal observation'. This approach was thought to be the most feasible means of penetrating street-corner society in the neighbourhoods, outside institutions such as the school and the youth-club. 'Informal observation' is simply meant to convey the approach of 'hanging around', talking and sometimes going around with male adolescents and adults who seemed to be connected with delinquency and crime, although the original emphasis was on contact with delinquent male cliques or gangs. This approach differs fundamentally from that of 'participant observation'. The participant observer seeks direct involvement in the group(s) observed. The classic instance in the field of crime and delinquency is the work of W. F. Whyte with young adults in an Italian-American slum district of Boston. But for this method to work as a basis for research, as distinct from action-research and welfare work, there must be some degree of certainty that the observer is participating without unduly influencing or changing the life of the group(s). Whyte went to great pains to avoid changing the behaviour patterns of the 'Corner boys', but he was a young adult playing a role within a young adult—not an adolescent—group which was almost wholly non-delinquent. An equivalent approach with a delinquent adolescent group would entail not only the probable expectation that the observer participated in delinquent exploits, but also the near-certainty that the behaviour patterns of the group would undergo drastic change. It is one thing for an adult to become sufficiently friendly with such a group to be tolerated in their milieu; it is an entirely different matter for an adult to 'join' the group without some recasting of the group's attitudes and values, and some modification of their way of life. Thus, unless some intervention for delinquency prevention purposes is intended, it is essential for the observer to avoid playing any role *within* the group, the central notion of 'participant observation'.

Likewise, 'residential participation' fails to describe the approach made in the present research. This term connotes the complete sharing by the observer of the environment, if not the behaviour, of the group(s) observed. In this case, while residence within the boroughs was taken up for several months, this was not synonymous with sharing the environment of the boys or adults in question. 'Informal observation' implies also that no attempt was made to gain information by the use of interviews, whether structured or unstructured, questionnaires or any kind of projective technique. At a later stage, unstructured interviews were attempted, but the approach proved abortive for the purposes in mind. The results of this type of observation are impressionistic and are akin to reportage. The role adopted—that of a writer working on a book about teenagers in London—was not unfamiliar to the adolescents involved. No role is without disadvantages, but that of writer appeared to have less than those of youth worker, student etc. The attempted interviews illustrate the difficulties involved. With a view to more extensive interviewing, a 'pilot' sample of 10 names was chosen at random from the electoral registers of Stepney and Poplar. All were 21 year-old males: of these, four were successfully interviewed; two refused; two more consistently not available; one was on 'holiday'; and one had moved elsewhere. The interviewees were approached at home, and on the basis of a survey for London University on how far young people were satisfied with the jobs they were doing. In this respect at least, the refusals were of interest. Those who agreed to be interviewed were a university student, a technician and a skilled craftsman; the other interview gained was with a youth undergoing occupational therapy who had little idea what the interview was about. The direct refusals came from individuals who were in unskilled work, and who reacted against the mention of 'London University'. As there was no reason to assume that more extensive interviewing would reveal a different pattern of acceptance and refusal, the idea was dropped. If contacts refused to talk freely about employment, there was even less chance that they would—on the basis of a doorstep introduction—be drawn into comments on delinquency, their views on the law, the police, etc. Unless large-scale infiltration into the lives of *families*—as opposed to one adolescent—is envisaged, as with the Gluecks' research, and that of the Cambridge Institute in Camberwell—it appears that adolescents can be contacted individually only on their own terms in their own milieux on an informal basis. The only exception to this applies where the population is 'captive'; i.e. in prison, school, or youth-club, but forces of selection operate in these instances which defeat the purpose of sampling the population at large. But there is a more compelling reason why interviews with an East End young adult sample in the home would have been essentially unscientific, even if the response rate had been 100 per cent. Even in the four interviews completed, there were marked differences in the interview situation. Two were interviewed alone, one with both parents present, and one with his wife present. The interview situation is obviously determined by factors such as family size, housing, household leisure interests, marital status, etc. Data gained in such diverse interview situations will be of interest, but cannot be quantified in any meaningful way, particularly when the focus is on attitudes, not simply factual information. As the object of interviewing was to compare impressionistic with systematically-gathered evidence, and the only way to locate a random sample was by home contact, the interview situation—as much as the refusal rate—led to the abandoning of this approach. Significant here is the success of the Institute of Community Studies in interviewing Bethnal Green adults on family and kinship, with a refusal rate of only 5·5 per cent.[1] Three factors were probably crucial in securing this high response rate: (a) the enquiry was family-, not problem-centred; (b) family heads, and not adolescents, were approached; (c) the Institute was situated locally. However, a later enquiry on behalf of the Institute by Ralph Samuel, into adolescents' attitudes

[1] P. Willmott and M. Young, *Family and Kinship in East London* (1957), p. 168.

towards employment, met with a refusal rate of only 4 per cent. If this had been the case in Stepney and Poplar, a programme of interviewing would have been desirable. In the event, however, all the data available were extracted on the basis of 'informal observation'.

Field-work was carried out over a period of six to seven months in Stepney and Poplar. Owing to the way field-work developed, the data do not make for easy comparability between the two boroughs. In Stepney, fleeting contacts were made with adolescent individuals and groups mainly in youth clubs, and with coloured adults in pubs. In Poplar, work centred almost entirely around one 'street-corner group' with whom acquaintance was maintained over the period of several months, and contacts were restricted to the single 'caff' where the group hung out. Fyvel's work has by now familiarised the typically drab caff which all too often is the only resort for teenagers outside the pub, the cinema, the youth club and home. This particular caff conformed to the pattern. Between 8 and 11 p.m., it usually contained about 30 teenagers, mostly male, and the contacted group of 5–6 supplied much of the following information, though where appropriate, data from other sources are presented. At no time throughout the research did observation suggest that this group was especially unrepresentative of adolescent groupings in the two boroughs. This chapter is concerned with relating observed behaviour to concepts central to subcultural theorisation on delinquency.

(a) 'Gang' or Group?

Delinquent groups in the East End lacked both the structured cohesion of the New York gangs described by Cloward and Ohlin, and the fissile impermanence of Yablonsky's 'near-group'. If the definition of delinquent gang is that of a group whose central tenet is the requirement to commit delinquent acts—i.e. 'delinquent subcultures' as defined by Cloward and Ohlin—then observation and information combined point to the absence of delinquent gangs in the East End, except as a thoroughly atypical collectivity. The possible exceptions that were heard of were—by repute—conflict-oriented and 'near-group' in structure, and neither criminal- nor retreatist-oriented gangs were mentioned by respondents even in the legendary sense. The groups responsible for the bulk of delinquency were simply small cliques whose members committed illegal acts sometimes collectively, sometimes in pairs, sometimes individually, in some cases regularly, in others only rarely. Delinquency was no more the central requirement for membership than the experience of sexual intercourse, though the group and the peer group gave collective support to the commission of delinquent acts, much as they would to sexual prowess. Average group size was 4–5, with a few individuals on the periphery. While these street-corner groups persisted over time, and invariably possessed a dominant personality, all the other features commonly attributed to the delinquent 'gang' were absent: i.e. leadership, role allocation, hierarchical structure, consensus on membership, uniform, and name. Girls were attached to the groups only in so far as they were acquainted with individual members, but rarely took part in any delinquent activity. The norm, then, is the fluid, street-corner clique, averse to any form of structure and organisation, but with persistence over time.

Undoubtedly, exceptions to this general pattern existed, but the exceptions also conformed to a distinct type, and it is doubtful if this type conformed to the Cloward-Ohlin criteria. In general, these exceptions were heard of in connection with street forays, and descriptions of the action suggested close parallels to Yablonsky's delineation of the delinquent 'near-group'. The evidence suggests that short-lived mobilisation of groups numbering up to 20–30 is feasible in any urban working-class area for reprisal against a single target, but that such 'near-group' formations can be easily dispersed by police action, and disintegrate even if unscathed once the single act of reprisal is over. For example, a teacher at one of the East End's rougher secondary schools mentioned an incident in which the 'S—— Street boys' converged on the school one afternoon to 'get' an individual Cypriot boy who allegedly had beaten up one of their number. Two squad cars dispersed them before they even reached the school, but in fact nobody had ever heard of the 'S—— Street boys' before or since this incident. They were simply a heterogeneous group of boys living on or around S—— Street, mobilised for the temporary purpose of reprisal by a few friends of the boy who was beaten up. This is not to say that these groups, with their show of violence—they carried bike-chains, etc.—are not dangerous: the legends generated by such occasional acts of mobilisation for conflict purposes are indeed a pure example of the Durkheimian logic that crime serves as normative reinforcement for conventional society. Another example was given by one of the Poplar boys:

> 'The other night . . . I got off the bus down here, and outside the post office there were fifty of 'em having a fight. . . . Honestly, they've got gangs of 25 round here. They walk along in a big gang, they come up against another gang in the street, they have a punch-up.' The boys in the café weren't a gang, 'not really' though 'Ray, he's got a black jacket with a skull painted on the back'. Tony knew nothing about these gangs except 'they get the leader's name. Like Johnson's boys. That's Barry Johnson. They're fairly young, he's only 18.'

From observation, however, in no part of the East End did gangs even obtrude, let alone dominate an area, despite stories such as the following:

> 'I can't see no sense in a big gang going round beating up a couple of fellers. I been beaten up myself. It happened to me and Bill. In Plaistow. We was just walking along, three of us, and three fellers come up towards us, looking for trouble, so we thought well alright, there's three of them, three of us, then twelve more comes round the bleeding corner and kicks us to death. The trouble is, get any one of them on their own and they're bleeding cowards, but put 'em in a gang with all the boys behind 'em, then it's different. I was walking down the main road last Saturday, and there's a kid lying there with his face all smashed in. The boys had come over from the Castle. There's a few of 'em round here. . . . They've got leaders, but take the leaders away and you won't find the gangs no more. . . . Over in Plaistow there were two gangs and two leaders. Now one's in Ireland, the other's in the nick. You go over to Plaistow you won't find the gangs no more.'

Paradoxically, it appears that the Teddy Boy movement brought the gang as a unit into very low repute, especially among working-class people. The view was frequently expressed that 'They're the lowest of the low', 'They're the real morons', etc., so that to move in a large crowd became, for a time at least, an index of cowardice rather than toughness.

The most general attitude towards gangs in the East End was

that they were a thing of the past, even though 'There's a rough lot in every district' and 'There've always been Teds. There always will be. It doesn't make any difference what clothes they wear.' The most that happened was the occasional dance-hall fight, 'no *West Side Story* stuff', just 'the Canning Town boys' coming over to a Stepney dance, 'we expected them to come'. There would be fights in defence of some vaguely defined 'territory', but nothing serious. In the 1950's, each gang had a leader—'all gangs have'—but the names were either vague references to area—the Canning Town boys, the Whitechapel boys, the Roman Road boys—or simply the name of the 'leader'. But even this was dying out. The most usual attitude was that whatever 'gang' problem had ever existed in the East End had both disappeared and shifted to areas like St. Pancras. 'The East End isn't a trouble spot any more. 'It's more Paddington and King's Cross now'; this is the view of most youth workers in the East End. Adolescents themselves thought much the same, that 'Kids aren't in gangs round here' or 'It's like a police sergeant once said: "Go round in twos and you're alright, go round in threes and you're a gang". There's one or two gangs round here, but . . . they don't bust places up, or anything like that', or 'About once a month you'll get a real fight between two of the boys here, but nothing like gangs fighting'. These beliefs were reiterated many times by both adolescents and adults. Chain-swinging, knife-carrying Teds were apparently eliminated in the boroughs of Stepney and Poplar almost before they began, the local community and the police combined taking immediate action against the threat of the institutionalisation of violence in gang form. The feeling against gangs is deep enough for most adolescents themselves to react against the idea of going around in a gang, even though the rare 'punch-up' between groups which resemble mobs rather than gangs takes place; 'You just get into trouble that way'. Preventive work by the police took the form of 'beheading' a gang. 'If they always go round together, the police'll bust them up', and this policy was remarkably effective, if only because other factors in the East End situation worked against the emergence of structured gangs. However, gangs of a conflict-oriented and near-group variety are reported to exist in areas more highly urbanised than the East End, such as Paddington and St. Pancras, which are dominated by the main-line termini and characterised by appalling housing, extreme poverty, immigrant Irish and coloured populations on a large scale, property racketeering, and a prostitution-gambling-drinking club network which appears much more organised than the same elements in west Stepney. But even there incidents are infrequent, though the reports which filter through to other parts of London about gang-activity serve to preserve the delinquent gang myth.

The non-existence in Stepney and Poplar of both gangs and groups based on the pursuit of delinquent activity *per se* is not, however, necessarily a proof of the non-existence of delinquent subcultures. The bulk of delinquency is committed by groups: but the delinquency is one aspect of the group's way of life, not the controlling factor in its formation. The issue now at stake is not what gangs there are, but why none—or very few—exist. What relevance have the Cohen and Cloward-Ohlin concepts to this type of delinquency situation?

(b) Non-utilitarian

The assertion that the bulk of working-class male group delinquency was non-utilitarian is central to Cohen's concept of the parent male subculture, and was consistently borne out by the observation with the Poplar group, even though they were aged 16–17, and would theoretically have been expected to conform to some more distinctive adaptation, such as semi-professional theft or conflict-oriented delinquency. There were obviously exceptions to the pattern, but little of the group's delinquent activities appeared to be consciously and deliberately motivated by the desire for gain, or by any other rational utilitarian purposes. This tendency is more pronounced with younger boys, once it is disentangled from the petty theft endemic to traditionally 'rough' working-class neighbourhoods. For example, a tremendous amount of vandalism takes place in certain East End primary and secondary schools. But it would be naïve to assume, in very poor areas, that all delinquency is non-utilitarian. Poverty —i.e. the lack of many stealable things—is still a real force for crime, and in most parts of Stepney and Poplar it would be abnormal for a boy to refrain from stealing throughout childhood and adolescence—unless he belonged to the fast-disappearing respectable Jewish population. Groups of children stealing from the docks and the big stores may be a commonplace in both working-class areas, but crime as a part of everyday life for children stops at peccadilloes. Essentially non-utilitarian delinquency is a separate tendency.

The delinquent mode for the Poplar boys was usually non-utilitarian:

> 'Pete told me Bill and the boys were out "joy-riding" and the police would probably be in after them tonight.' He dangled a car-key and said it was a Ford Consul, brand-new model. 'The bloke just left it lying around (at work). Well, that's just asking for it, ain't it?' They had been joy-riding 'only just lately. They just got the craze. We do it for enjoyment, you know. There's nothing else to do around here. Anything round here you can get enjoyment from you're breaking the law.' They had this particular craze for only three days, then stopped: 'Best to give up while you're lucky.' Pete had received two years probation at the age of 14 for breaking-and-entering. He had broken into four or five shops a week 'for months' before being caught. They did it 'just for laughs. That's all we do it for. We take a few things, but nothing much.' The next development had been stealing bikes: 'We must have stolen hundreds of the things. People just leave 'em lying about. I did it with Lennie and the boys. When I'd ridden 'em round for a bit, I dumped 'em in the canal or sold 'em at the Lane. Just walk up and down the Lane with a bike and somebody'll give you a couple of quid for it.'

Also, rowdyism—though not vandalism—was a feature of their behaviour in the street and in the cinema, though not so much in the café, due to the threat of a ban by the proprietor. A trip to the cinema was typically 'just for laughs': it had nothing to do with the film. Inside, often by the back exit, activity took the form of races round the aisles, frequent door-banging trips to the lavatory, shouting up 'birds', cat-calls, etc. but nothing serious, no seat-slashing or violence. Later, however, they became more money-minded:

> 'We had three look-outs. We were after one of those cig. machines. They hold ten quid those things. . . . We get the whole thing off the wall and take it away. I'm going for the money now. I'm ten quid in debt. We're off doing things just for a laugh now. Last laugh I had, it cost me twelve weeks' (i.e. two hours a week in an attendance centre). Pete also left his job—his eighth—for a scrap-

> firm as '. . . It's no good now. They stopped all the fiddling. I used to fiddle six or eight quid a week out of that, but the other silly buggers had to go and get caught. One of 'em's due for a stretch. I just got warned.'

'Fiddling' is the adult practice of enlarging income tax-free by theft from one's work-place, the childhood version being theft from stores and school, the justification being that 'Everybody does it'. It is associated with the docks in particular, but is not regarded as a crime, simply as an occupational risk. Non-utilitarian offences are generally reserved for out-of-work hours. Exceptions were reported, but the pattern of delinquency for the Poplar group seemed to be one of pointless break-ins, joy-rides, rowdyism and larcenies for small returns. They rarely capitalised on their law-breaking abilities. For example, although adept at borrowing cars, they apparently made no attempt to sell them, even though they knew of sources for purchase. But the rate of theft of car accessories in conjunction with take-and-drive points to a limited form of utilitarian delinquency.

There is a point which springs from Cohen's treatment of this concept. He states that the objects stolen may often be valued by the delinquent, but the treatment of the object is in no rational proportion to the risks run in its illegal acquisition, i.e. it is the act of theft, not the object stolen, which is the principal motivating force. It may be objected to this that the delinquent steals for imagined utilitarian ends, but possession of the object stolen reveals the illusory nature of the original impulse; e.g. he steals a car because pressurised by commercial-ideological forces into thinking he needs one, but soon realises the falsity of the need and discards it. While this would account for a single car-borrowing, it would not account for a car-borrowing career, for disenchantment with the object stolen would be final, and the delinquent would cease to pursue car-borrowing.

(*c*) *Malice*

A tendency, but not a marked one, and refuted more often than confirmed. With the Poplar boys, it was possible to infer the element of active spite from certain activities—the cinema rowdyism, the discarding of bikes in the canal—but they did not display the 'gratuitous hostility towards non-gang peers as well as adults' which Cohen postulated as one hallmark of the delinquent subculture. Only one incident of active malice was observed, which involved the teasing of a girl in the café by throwing around and damaging a newly-bought under-skirt, but the incident was exceptional and sexually-derived, not the rule. On the other hand, many incidents of vandalism in school were reported, and it is axiomatic that in a middle-class institutional atmosphere, the element of active malice emerges much more clearly. (Cf. the 'irresponsibility' of 'Black' school, as analysed by Webb.) In joy-rides, however, the Poplar boys never took girls along, because 'It'd be wrong to risk anybody except yourselves'. They denied any connection with an episode of vandalism in Poplar, both on their own behalf and for the rest of the boys in the caff: 'What would they get out of it?' They thought that if adolescents had done it, it was 'out of boredom. They get nothing to do round here, and once they get into a gang, they'll do anything.' The attitude towards seat-ripping in provincial cinemas—following an account in the Press—was that it was 'stupid, there's no sense in that kind of thing, is there?' Moreover, youth clubs relied in general on self-discipline by adolescents who frequently had delinquent records: 'If there's a riot, there's nothing we could do about it.' This reliance has considerable point: if the element of malice was so marked in the delinquent subculture, few youth-clubs would be left standing. Possibly the most archetypal piece of 'malice' witnessed in Poplar was that of a group of school-boys throwing stones and systematically breaking glass in a deserted tenement block. No harm was done—the block was due for demolition—and the impulse worked itself out in twenty minutes.

(*d*) *Negativism*

To establish the reality of the element of negativism in delinquent subcultural behaviour, the concept of 'inverse polarity' must be strongly exemplified as a determinant of the delinquent's value-system, i.e. that the delinquent turns the rules of conventional society upside-down, as distinct from simple engagement in rule- and law-breaking. No such evidence can be offered in the case of the Poplar boys; the only episode indicative of negativism is that of cinema rowdyism, where the behaviour of the boys in the cinema exactly opposes that thought desirable by a conventional cinema audience. It should be noted here that on a subsequent visit, barely any rowdyism occurred. The trouble with the concepts of non-utilitarianism, malice and negativism is that they hang together simply as negatives, i.e. the presence of one such element in a delinquent act implies the other two from the view-point of a middle-class observer. Yet the vast majority of the delinquent acts committed by the Poplar group were surreptitious: there was no overt 'flouting' of the rules, no display of prowess to the world at large, only to the peer group. There was no assertion resembling that of Arthur Seaton's 'Rules are there to be broken by blokes like me.'[2] Again, there is the strong probability that these elements are much more noticeable among secondary modern school-boys in the poorer working-class areas (cf. Webb's disclaimer on this point). But no such value-system was encountered with post-school-leaving adolescents, despite their immersion in a social climate conducive towards delinquency.

(e) Versatility

This characteristic was fully borne out. In a short acquaintance, the Poplar group engaged in take-and-drive-away, larceny from slot-machines, rowdyism and some violence. In the past, they had committed break-ins, a variety of simple larcenies, larceny of bicycles and trespass. (Receiving almost goes without saying.) But the avoidance of vandalism, and the periodicity of indulgence in delinquency of all kinds, means that the behaviour of the Poplar group cannot be equated with the 'generalised, diversified, protean "orneriness"' which Cohen attributed to the delinquent gang proper.

(f) Short-Run Hedonism

This strain was very marked in the life of the Poplar group and, as far as could be seen, of all other similar groups encountered. As Cohen asserts, it is a characteristic of working-class life in general, but 'in the delinquent gang it reaches its finest flower'. The Poplar boys spent most evenings—and earnings—hanging around in the caff, with the occasional visit to the cinema, skating or swimming, 'outside' to pick up girls or commit an offence, and—even more rarely—a trip to the West End. They rarely planned for more than the evening ahead, and bouts of

[2] A. Sillitoe, *Saturday Night and Sunday Morning* (1959).

activity came spontaneously. With jobs and school, they had displayed the same inability to think ahead that they revealed with leisure. Throughout the period involved, they planned months ahead for one event only, Bill's eighteenth birthday party. They would 'chuck in' their jobs without any alternative to hand, 'it's like being on holiday', but soon be compelled to take one only fractionally different. Pete, asked what he would do if the boys didn't come in, replied that he had nothing to do: 'There's nothing to do around here, see? Nothing at all.' They did not 'work at' delinquency, least of all in a planning sense: most of the 'enjoyment' stems from improvised illegality. They soon lost interest in any form of regulated activity, even a game of darts or snooker. Cohen's point that only a small fraction of the delinquent gang's time is spent looking for 'fun' via delinquency is carried by definition. 'Hanging around' creates its own tensions only gradually. A corollary is the difficulty of 'hanging around' with them for any period of time. The role of 'writer' eventually caused suspicion owing to lack of an immediate end-product.

(g) Group Autonomy

As all authoritarian settings were avoided, the kind of situation in which the Poplar group's autonomy would have been tested never arose. This avoidance in itself indicated the group's desire for an autonomous existence. Individual members were subject to parental regulation and a modicum of discipline restricting behaviour in the caff. For example, Pete and Lennie had to be in by 11 p.m. and paid £2 10*s*. a week rent to their parents. They obeyed the café owner in several instances regarding misuse of property in the caff. Stan, a 19-year-old on the fringe of the group, was barred from the caff for swearing at the owner. But in no case was the *group* reprimanded, and in no case did the group have to face any threat, whether verbal or physical.

Summary: No group is in stasis. In the period of time—relatively short—in which the Poplar group were contacted, their delinquent behaviour appeared to lack two elements crucial to Cohen's construct of the delinquent subculture, i.e. malice and negativism. The absence of these elements signifies the 'corner boy' rather than the 'delinquent boy' adaptation, although their involvement in delinquency was far greater than Cohen postulated for the typical corner-group, whose delinquent activities implicitly stop at truancy and do not involve property or personal aggression.[3] However, this is not to deny that the group had been subcultural delinquents at an earlier age and while still at school, the forcing-house for the delinquent subculture. According to Cohen, the parent male subculture tapers off at about age 15–16. In this way, the Poplar group can be viewed as en route from subcultural delinquency to young adult 'corner boy' conformity. The question of interpretation must remain open.

(b) Criminal

The three categories of the Cloward-Ohlin typology are discussed here not as delinquent subcultures, but as patterns of behaviour generalised throughout the social and geographical areas studied. The ultimate criterion for the existence of a criminal opportunity structure in an area must be that such a structure has a separable existence as an institution within the area. By this criterion, Stepney can hardly be considered a 'criminal' area, and Poplar even less so. While there are in the East End several well-known (to the police) criminal cliques, and families of a 'professional' nature, i.e. solely engaged in the utilitarian pursuit of break-ins, robbery, and drug-trafficking, these groups are largely independent of each other, and are not organised in such a way as to constitute a visible, coherently patterned criminal opportunity structure on a quasi-bureaucratic basis, as are the big American syndicates. The set-up of adult crime in the East End seems to be that of small autonomous groups, some with their own 'guv'nor', some recruited on a completely *ad hoc* basis. Allerton[4]—in one of the few 'life-histories' of an East End professional criminal available—describes his recruitment for a specific 'job' into just such an *ad hoc* clique. This adult set-up is naturally reflected in the structure and aims of adolescent delinquents, among whom there are very few groups dedicated to deliberate and positive criminality, and these are almost certainly composed of boys with much Approved School and Borstal history. Small pockets of organised crime undoubtedly exist in Stepney, and it has traditionally acted as a

[3] Cohen, op. cit., pp. 129–130.

[4] R. Allerton and T. Parker, *The Courage of his Convictions* (1962), pp. 78–80.

magnet for ex-cons and receivers, as well as for the social 'inadequates' who fill the hostels and whose last resort is the bomb-site. Traditional Stepney crime comprises 'screwing', the used-car racket, H.P. rackets, dog-doping, and—more recently—drug-trafficking, as well as prostitution and illegal gambling and small-time 'protection' exercised against cafés and betting-shops. In a continuum of adult crime in west Stepney in particular, the most organised activities—'screwing', robbery, doping, drug-traffic—would have least personnel involved; more numerous would be those engaged in prostitution, immoral earnings, illegal gambling, drug-use and proneness to violence; mid-way would be larger numbers purposefully engaged in crime as a supplement to their jobs; and finally even more would take the opportunities inherent in their jobs to 'fiddle' extras in a fairly systematic way. The last category, which includes such activities as dockers 'whipping' goods, cannot be considered a criminal 'career', but is rather what Sykes and Matza might term a 'subterranean' aspect of conventional job-routine. 'Fiddled' goods are generally consumed personally or by immediate family, or are sold cheaply on a kind of informal community network, in which those who will buy suspected stolen goods, and those who would disapprove, or who might even 'inform', are known in advance. Where goods whose origin is fairly anonymous are concerned, such as nylons or canned soup, the risk is sometimes taken of hawking them round local pubs. There is little interaction between this kind of amateur crime—where recourse is rarely had to established 'fences'—and the first two categories mentioned. This is not to say that the promising dock 'whipper' or car-borrower never progresses to more ambitious and better-organised crime: but in the cases where this happens, the process is largely one of self-recruitment to a way of life, rather than attraction into a stable hierarchy which provides an alternative route to upward mobility. The latter feasibly occurs more frequently in those activities which are essentially crime-promoting but technically legal, such as property-racketeering and certain forms of bookmaking, and gambling.

The absence of a conspicuously successful adult criminal élite is reflected in the lack of any perceptible aspiring towards professional crime among adolescent delinquents; it is also reflected in the areas of adolescent congregation—which are restricted to stable working-class or wholly teenage locales—and their avoidance of specifically 'criminal' milieux. The self-image of the Poplar boys, for example, was that of the 'hooligan', not the criminal. This is not to say that they had no contact with individual adult criminals—a relative of the café owner was 'inside' for dealing in stolen cars—or that none of them had ever envisaged a full-scale 'job':

> I asked Pete what he'd be doing in ten years time. 'Swinging by the fucking neck', he said. I asked what for. 'Well, if I ever run out of money again, I'm going to go out and do a job for some.' He told me that last weekend a kid had offered to go in with him on a job they'd get £200 each from, 'but why should I?' said Pete. 'If I got caught I could get five or ten years for that. Five years for two hundred quid, it's not worth it. Anyway, the next job I do I'm going to do by myself. I've been to court four times but I've never been caught yet, have I? I've always been split on. Every single time one of my mates has given me away. . . . But there's one job I'm gonna do, as soon as I break up with my girl. I'll get a couple of thousand quid out of it'—The pub radio gave out a bulletin on a mail-van raid when the bandits got away with £4,000—'Good luck to 'em, mate', said Pete vehemently. 'Behind every robbery like that, there's a brain. They do the job and he pays them off. The bloke who gives the inside information gets £500. They don't have to worry about getting rid of the stuff. The brain does that. I read it in the papers.'

This story shows—for one boy at least—intense sympathy for, if not identification with, the adult professional criminal. It also testifies to the efficiency of the various media as vehicles for the dissemination of criminal techniques. This example of aspiration towards the 'big score' was atypical, and probably paranoid. But it serves as a reminder that the tendency for offences to be non-utilitarian declines with age and growth of the appreciation of risk.

A factor which feasibly serves to deflect adolescents from certain offences in the East End, such as prostitution, poncing, drug-use and illegal gambling, is the association of these offences with the 'blacks', although long-established working-class families in the area are traditionally antipathetic towards prostitution. Prostitution is the notorious 'Stepney problem', a term which was actually used in one survey to differentiate the Stepney prostitute from the West-End type: '"Stepney problem" is a special connotation used to describe those girls who were mainly the failures of Approved Schools and Borstals, and went to live in the coloured quarter of Stepney; mentally, physically, and morally they were in a lower grade than the ordinary prostitute.'[5] It is no longer so true that the Stepney prostitute is a pathetic and feeble-minded amateur, absconded from an institution or newly arrived by lorry from the North, sharing a bed often for nothing as the only means of finding one. Since the early and mid-1950's, the girls have been more organised, and a pattern established. There seems to be a distinction between the Cable Street and Spitalfields areas *vis-à-vis* prostitution, the former being centred on the caffs, the latter being much less public and tightly controlled by ethnic cliques, centred in all-night caffs and drinking-clubs. The clubs in Spitalfields are near the City, and cater for businessmen during the day, locals and 'tourists' at night. Many caffs rely on respectable trade during the day, and open at night simply as rendezvous for the girls, ponces and clients. Clubs which are closed simply re-open under a different name and management, on the by now well-established pattern. The Maltese reportedly run the girls in Spitalfields, and have been held to sell them to other cliques, such as Pakistanis, for sums around £10. Few girls are from Stepney or Poplar, and no attempt is made to recruit locally: the influx from the Northern conurbations is consistent. The occasional caff is 'queer' or lesbian, but these circles shift within short periods of time. Underlying the prostitution situation, and in partial explanation of community attitudes towards the 'slags' and the 'blacks' are two main factors. First, the shrinkage of the native resident Cockney and Jewish population of Stepney from about 200,000 in 1939 to just over 90,000 in 1961, due to massive re-housing schemes and migration to the suburbs, both during the war and after, so that while the influx of coloured immigrants is well under 10,000 in number, they stand out disproportionately in the young male population. Second, the housing situation has left west Stepney in particular with tracts of slum, condemned property, some of which is not scheduled to be pulled down until 2005. But the property crucial to prostitution and property racketeering is especially that in re-development areas, with

[5] C. H. Rolph (Ed.), *Women of the Street* (1955), p. 245.

only a decade at most to stand. Whole areas have been bought up cheaply by agents and let off at exorbitant rents, or leased at high rates of interest, to landlords—often coloured—who connive at maximum short-term profits either from the girls and their ponces or sub-letting at exorbitant rents. Since the mid-1950's, therefore, prostitution has spread from the coloured enclave of Cable Street to Cavell Street, Spitalfields and, more recently, to Mile End, a pattern pre-determined by the ownership of crumbling property. Illegal gambling and drug-use has spread correlatively. Local white residents are bitter, but are now resigned to the spread of prostitution and the lack of official action apart from the occasional police raid. Neighbourhood organisation to tackle the problem came to an end with the break-up by the police of the 'Vigilantes' in 1957–58, an attempt by the community to administer the 'rough and ready' justice of the streets to what—in some areas—was beginning to threaten families and children. The fear was that 'children would come to regard prostitution as a possible way of life' but the impetus was given added violence by the identification of prostitution with 'the blacks', whose reliance on the girls was—to a large extent—forced by the absence of their own women, and the stigma attached by the stable working-class community to a girl who went with a coloured man. The only resort for unmarried negroes were those white women the local community itself rejected. White adolescents come to share the blanket aversion of their parents for 'the blacks and their women. . . . I bet you five quid you can't walk with me down Cavell Street and point to three houses that aren't brothels. It's the blacks. Send the cunts back from where they came from. . . . They import girls, most of 'em Irish. There hasn't been a pross nicked in two years.'

(i) Conflict

Both the 'conflict' subculture of Cloward and Ohlin, and the 'conflict-oriented' adaptation of Cohen and Short, are based on the institutionalisation of violence in the street warfare ('rumbles') of juvenile delinquent fighting gangs in New York, Chicago and other metropolitan centres. In both Stepney and Poplar, no inter-gang, and barely any inter-group, fighting was reported or observed, though there was a generally disseminated proclivity towards limited forms of toughness and aggression. A 'punch-up'

Informal Observation

that was witnessed in the Aldgate Wimpy appeared typical of the form taken by most adolescent aggression in the East End, though 'punch-ups' are supposed to be pre-arranged. This particular scuffle took place on a Friday evening about 10.30, began with one male teenager insulting another, blows were exchanged and—as the place was tightly packed with male teenagers and their girls—the fight snowballed so that those who were in the fight and those who were trying to watch became indistinguishable. A young P.C. came into the Wimpy, forced his way through the struggle, had his helmet knocked off but separated the two central protagonists, and ordered them outside. They apparently got away without being charged. This type of scuffle was frequent in this café, there were fights in or around or at the back of the building, usually at weekends following Friday pay-day. But:

> 'They're nothing much. . . . Nothing gets broken, except perhaps somebody's nose. There's no knives or anything more than a bottle, but hardly even that.'

The general view was that 'old-style' battles, between marauding mobs (as distinct from structured gangs) from nearby areas such as Hoxton and local mobs, were very much a thing of the past, of the 40's and early 50's.[6] The 'Teds' never really 'caught on' in Stepney and Poplar, snuffed out by an essentially conservative working-class community which frowned on any real violence as a threat to family life and children. But even at its height, 'old-style' delinquency lacked the gang-structure, the concept of 'turf' and the idealisation of 'heart' which are held to be characteristic of the American street-gang warfare situation.

The Poplar boys were never seen to display even that degree of aggression that took place ritually in Stepney. Lacking in these boys was another characteristic of the American situation, the willingness to 'talk delinquency'. Axiomatic, however, was the absence of any 'real' aggression:

[6] This is not to deny that, more recently, in Islington and Shoreditch, for example, youth workers and police have been worried by the increase in 'tooling up' with guns instead of knives, etc. The case for 'detached work' in such areas, and in Soho—a focal point for buying and selling weapons—is particularly strong. The 'detached worker' would serve as much to give an unbiassed picture of what was happening in an area, as for any possible 'preventive' role. At present, it only needs one 'near-group' mobilised by a seriously disturbed youngster with a gun to spark off claims that 'gang warfare' has broken out.

Delinquent Subcultures in Stepney and Poplar

> . . . I asked him if a big bunch had ever tried to take this particular café over, since it was the only one of its kind nearby. . . . Lennie said no, there was none of that kind of thing. 'It's only common sense. If a bunch came in now, there's not many of us here at the moment, they could clear us out. But we'd find out where they came from and we'd get all the boys from here, and all the boys from Bow, and we'd go and beat them up tomorrow night. No, there's never been anything like that. Stands to reason. If a negro boy comes in, he's going to feel scared because we're all whites, but we don't take any notice. The other night four negro boys came in but nobody took any notice. If seven or eight of 'em come in, then we might tell 'em to clear out, but they'd never do that. No, about once a month you'll get a real fight between two of the boys here, but nothing like gangs fighting.'

In other words, conflict for 'neighbourhood hegemony' just doesn't apply in Poplar, or Stepney, or—with few exceptions—throughout London. Fights occur, but for more straightforward reasons:

> 'Bill's birthday party. . . . That ended up in a fight. These two boys turned up in a van and started messing about with Bill's girl, so we threw 'em out. They came back and there's five more of 'em in the back of the van with fucking great hooks from the docks. We beat 'em off throwing bottles at 'em. One of 'em gets his hook in Ray's jersey. Ray just says, "here, get your hook out of my jersey". The bloke takes it out and Ray just hits him in the face with this bottle. . . . Nobody got hurt bad.'

In general, however, the attitude was one of avoiding violence. Pete refused to use a snooker room because 'the yobs' who hung around the place used violence on newcomers:

> '. . . They come from round Barking. If you go in there, they just beat you up. . . . That's their enjoyment, like ours is hanging around here and stealing cars. . . . They'd never let me in that gang down there, and I wouldn't want to, anyway. *They're too tough.* They don't even let you get to know them. You speak to them and they just walk past you in the street, then two or three of them'll split off and get you. . . .'

But this kind of vicious hostility was the exception, and clearly regarded as such by the boys themselves. Their own aggression, mostly verbal, followed the lines indicated by Miller in his analysis of aggression in a boys' street-corner group, i.e. narrow in content, target and range of expression, and playing itself out within the confines of the group.

The nearest approximation to conflict-orientated adolescent delinquency was the occasional short-term mobilisation for street forays.[7] The difference was well summarised by the director of a well-organised Stepney youth club who had been to New York:

> '. . . I went out to several locations. We have gangs here, there's no denying that, but they're nothing like the ones in New York. They have names, there, like the Comanches. . . . Here, the boys use bike-chains or knives and—occasionally—a kid gets killed by accident. But there they use guns and plan murder in advance, they premeditate that such and such a boy should be liquidated. . . . I give the street-workers there all credit, but they came too late. Here a boy leaves school and is working hard straightaway. There they stay at school until 16 or 17, they're bored, uninterested and don't get into a job when they leave school the way a boy does over here. . . . You can read the statistics any way you like. A twenty per cent rise in juvenile crime could mean just that the kids don't get away with it. When I was a kid, I stole, but I could run faster than any copper. Now the police have cars. . . . It's important to get this in perspective. Thirty years ago, you honestly couldn't walk through Stepney without fear of being molested. . . . Well, I've been here ten to fifteen years and I've never been beaten up yet, even in the worst districts. There's a lot of exaggeration. There's less *real* delinquency than ever before.'

(j) Retreatist

While no evidence at all was found to suggest the existence of an adolescent retreatist subculture, characterised in its ideal-typical form, according to the Cloward-Ohlin criteria, by the consumption of alcohol, drugs, jazz and sex, two subgroups in the populations studied possessed affinities with Merton's category of retreatism, which does not postulate specifically delinquent or criminal behaviour, and which does not entail contracultural self-images of the subgroup as an élite. These two subgroups were the young coloured males who lived or hung around Cable Street and its environs—some of whom were involved in prostitution, gambling, hemp- or marihuana-smoking,

[7] See pp. 198–202.

heavy drinking and violence—and the young adult white 'yobs' or layabouts who shared this milieu, but who are characteristic of any inner urban working-class area, and are not confined to any specific 'quarter'.

(*i*) *The 'blacks'*: Banton, writing on the basis of research in Stepney's coloured quarter of Cable Street between 1950–52,[8] described and analysed the situation of what was then a racial and cultural enclave in terms which still apply to the tensions between white and coloured in west Stepney today, despite the many intervening changes. The biggest change has been the spread of immigrant residence from the immediate Cable Street area to Spitalfields, areas north of the Commercial Road and parts of Mile End and Bow. The Cable Street sector, however, still accommodates those coloured immigrants who are (a) in transit, and (b) lacking in the skills needed for mobility and the ability to cope with life in a complex, technological society. Many of the pressures on this partly residual, partly transitional population are shared by all immigrants to Britain, whether white or coloured. Stepney has been an immigrant area for centuries, and 'antagonism towards immigrants is the rule, not the exception'.[9] Between 1881 and 1901, the number of aliens in the two wards of Whitechapel and St. George's in West Stepney increased by 37 per cent mostly following the immigration of Jews after the pogroms in Russia and Eastern Europe. In 1900, it was estimated that there were 100,000 Jews in East London, nearly all of whom lived in Stepney, and slightly over half being aliens. Prior to this, by about 1880, the last remnants of middle-class respectability had left Stepney with the exodus of the old sea-captains and their families from Wellclose Square, and the merchants from the old Huguenot district around Spitalfields. Stepney was now uniformly working-class, its characteristic industries were becoming established—tailoring in particular—back-yard workshops and 'sweated' garment trades sprang up and increased the shortage of space. Housing conditions attracted philanthropists, and huge blocks of 'model' dwellings went up, such as the Brady Dwellings, barrack-like rewards for the thrifty poor. These charitable activities, although largely beneficial, combined with the construction of the huge Rowton House in 1892

[8] M. Banton, *The Coloured Quarter* (1955).

[9] Banton, op. cit., p. 18.

and the massive Jewish influx to establish Stepney as the home of 'the strangers, the shiftless and the derelict' and it is from this period that Stepney's notoriety for crime and poverty springs, the Press-fostered perpetuation of this reputation being responsible for much harm.[10] Obviously, housing and employment are the most urgent problems for all immigrants to Stepney in particular, or the country as a whole. But the Negro—i.e. West African and West Indian—Cable Street population are unrepresentative of both their own immigrant population as a whole and of all immigrants in general, in that they lack the skills to overcome the handicaps attached to finding employment and housing. The situation is vitiated even further in west Stepney by the critical shortage of housing, and the enormous amount of pre-twentieth century slum property which is both privately owned and almost invariably expensive to rent. Virtually barred from council flats, the 'blacks' inevitable resort is to this deteriorating property. Local white residents link the onset of deterioration with the arrival of the 'blacks' and blame the newcomers for the deterioration, whereas 'they are its result, not its cause'.[11] Also, conventional British attitudes towards coloured people are such that few white women will associate with them; those who do are mostly women who have failed—or been refused the chance—to find a satisfying role in conventional society, and their frequent instability underlies the unhappiness of many mixed marriages. This prohibition by the working-class community of female contact with young coloured males led—in the absence of an equal number of coloured females—to an inevitable market for prostitution. Deprived in the areas of jobs, sex, housing and leisure, this sector of the coloured population—which arrived in this country with high expectations as to earnings and miscegenation—have adopted a retreatist way of life sufficiently desperate to create a sub-group situation of anomie.

The situation is worse for West Africans, West Indians, Maltese and Cypriots than for the other, and quite distinct, coloured groups, such as the Pakistanis, Indians and Arabs. The two groups entertain different aspirations and expectations

[10] For a vivid evocation of 'working-class culture' at this period and its squalor and suffering, see Jack London's *The People of the Abyss* and also *Child of the Jago* by Arthur Morison.

[11] Banton, op. cit., p. 71.

towards life and work in Britain, the first group typically immigrating with settlement in mind, the second with more limited economic ambitions: the one is an immigrant group, the other migrant workers.

> The Pakistanis and Sikhs are examples of non-assimilating or *accommodating* as opposed to *adapting* groups. Many of them are migrant workers who will return to their homeland when they have saved enough money, but those who remain will seek to preserve a group life of their own. . . . The West African and West Indian immigrants begin with an entirely different outlook. One of the factors encouraging them to leave the colonies was their idealisation of Britain and their acceptance of our culture—in many aspects—as superior to their own. The Negro immigrants see no reason for separate practices. They favour amalgamation of ethnic stocks. A person's membership of the immigrant grouping does not in any way hinder him in his relations with non-immigrants.[12]

As Banton asserts, the clear-cut objectives of the accommodating groups have generated a disciplined approach to jobs and housing, via a network of contacts based on café-society: 'cohesion will always be weaker in an adapting group, for the major interests of the members lie outside the group'.[13] This fragmentation makes for a greater vulnerability to adverse social pressures. Lacking the insulation provided by this kind of group-life, and disillusioned with the central impulse underlying immigration—the tragic misconception, in some cases, that Britain was an El Dorado—the less skilled among the young adult Negro males are faced not simply with value-conflict, but with disenchantment with the conventional value-systems of both their own and the host society.

Banton estimated[14] that well over two-thirds (c. 70%) of West Indian and West African males in Stepney were employed in unskilled or semi-skilled work, while the number employed was unknown. Yet: 'No coloured man go home unless he rich. Too much shame. Everyone laugh at him.'[15] For few sectors of

[12] Banton, op. cit., pp. 74–75.

[13] Ibid., p. 233.

[14] Banton, op. cit., p. 132.

[15] J. Lawrie, *The Marriage of Gor* (1960), p. 137; a humane account of ten years' 'respectable' co-habitation in appalling conditions on Cavell Street between a Gambian and an English woman and their family.

Informal Observation

the population is the ends-means disparity more cruelly marked than for the young adult male sector of the Cable Street coloured population: the impregnation of their milieux with prostitution, gambling, hemp-smoking, heavy drinking and violence—the latter a non-correlate for retreatism by Cloward-Ohlin criteria—is a functional outgrowth of their socio-cultural situation. Prostitution flourishes due to the 'blacks' sexual deprivation consequent upon discrimination and socio-cultural apartheid; illegal gambling represents the residue of El Dorado attitudes, subsequent disillusion, and an inability to treat money as sacred; the hemp-smoking minority are strengthened in the habit by the disappointments of immigration; heavy drinking is in part the result of the function of the pub as the blacks' sole means of rendezvous and congregation (much as it used to be for the manual working-classes before World War 2), except for coloured-owned caffs and clubs. Interaction between white and coloured is permissible on a commercial basis. Because of the strength of the resultant makeshift relational system, and because of the placing of blame for failure on external sources,[16] violence is very near the surface—a tendency reinforced by the presence in the area of the female 'misfits' on whom the 'blacks' place such reliance as sexual resource, and white petty criminals who see the 'blacks' as ready-made 'suckers'. A constant factor throughout in this sub-area is the stagnant housing deterioration situation, which attracts the coloured immigrant 'residue' and repels the socially mobile and technically skilled members of the coloured population.

Examples of mutual sponging, room-sharing, disputes over gambling and women leading to unreported petty violence are too numerous to mention. But the volatile situation in which the 'blacks' live also furnishes examples of political extremism and deep-rooted feelings of persecution, springing from treatment in the Press, by the police, by social agencies and labour exchanges, employers, and the white community in general, factors which do not apply in areas attracting the more stable and skilled section of coloured immigrants such as Brixton, where gradual and uneventful assimilation is taking place despite suspicion and initial discriminatory practices by the local white residents:

[16] See J. F. Short, Jr. and A. F. Henry, *Suicide and Homicide* (1955).

Delinquent Subcultures in Stepney and Poplar

> Sam worked in a gas-works as a labourer, had done so for a year, had been in England since 1946, and stayed in Stepney because 'my people are here'—he was Nigerian. He was married and had four kids. We talked in the pub, which accommodated 20–25 Negroes (Arabs, Pakistanis, etc., avoided it), one Negress and several middle-aged-seeming white women, 'slags' to the whites. He was extravagantly dressed, wearing a Cossack hat—'From Moscow. I'm a Communist'—and drank strong bottled ale. He refused a cigarette, and asked me what I did. I said I was a writer. 'Man, I don't like publicity,' he yelled. 'Stupid' journalists gave coloured people 'bad publicity'. 'They all work for government and, you know, if a journalist write good things about coloured man, West African or West Indian, the editor, he censor it.' Sam wore a Nigerian Independence badge, and alternated between saying 'the only hope for the world is that all peoples live in peace and understanding' and 'I hate the English. Why don't they go away, go away from Africa and leave us alone, 'cos I tell you, man, five years ago, even five, Africa was asleep, but now she's waking up, she's *awake*.' He shouted that 'English socialists' were 'hypocrites', the rest were 'capitalists' and he'd 'machine-gun them down' if he got power. He identified himself with the working-classes, but 'the English working-class is the stupidest in the world. They are really ignorant, some of them.' His friend tried to calm him down, and asked me: 'Did you get him on to politics?' The rest kept well away. 'Some men have hundred of thousand of pounds they don't know what to do with except drink champagne, and outside in street'—he jabbed at the window—'poor boy hasn't got a penny, nothing to eat. If I in power, I take all money away from rich, give to poor boys.' He eventually calmed himself down by smoking a reefer in the lavatory, but secretly, he knew it was against the law. The 'cat' would have flaunted his marihuana.

Likewise, the Chicago 'cat' and the New York 'retreatist' would have avoided violence, politics and jobs, would have cultivated an elitist philosophy absent in Cable Street, and would have displayed their knowledge of jazz, hustling and drug-lore. But the affinities with retreatism would increase but for the chink in the armour of white discrimination supplied by the pub-owners—who cannot maintain an impersonal commercial relationship as white café-owners and shop-keepers typically do—and the 'blacks' women', who mix despite sanctions from both white and coloured:

Informal Observation

'Some people spit at us in the street, black people, his own people. One came in here the other day and shouted 'nigger' at him. His own people. And we hate that word anyway, we hate 'blacks' as well, even though they call themselves that.'

(*ii*) *The 'double failures'*: Sharing the milieux of the 'blacks' in west Stepney, and 'the boys' in Poplar and the rest of Stepney the young adult, frequently ex-institutional 'yobs' are typically out-of-work or in jobs which can barely be described as occupations, such as serving in and sweeping up caffs on a casual basis. They live on the dole, by sponging, the occasional petty 'job' and—in west Stepney—acting as pimp, ponce or 'protector' for a girl. Failures by both conventional and criminal standards, evidence for retreatism lies in their mode of drift and withdrawal from any kind of adult responsibility. A group of 'yobs' in the Poplar caff embodied the fate of the aged 'corner-boy', socially incompetent and increasingly desperate as time brought no tangible reward or achievement:

X at one point looked around at the teenagers in the caff and said: 'Look at these kids, they can't be more than 16 or 17, can they?' He said: 'I'll be 24 next week,' as if he had only just thought of it. They were all 23–24, scruffy, down-and-out, unemployed, without even cigarettes. X invited Y out the following night: he had two 'bints' and no mate to take along. 'We'll get both ends up,' he said, clenching his fists and thrusting them in the air. 'One of 'em's married to a geezer who's in the nick. The other's engaged to a bloke who's in hospital. Fuck 'em, that's what I say.' . . . Y said he liked 'whip rounds' best, where you whip round just before closing-time for money to buy as many crates of beer as you can, take it somewhere and have a party. . . . X had been on probation for five years and 'inside' for a bit when he was 17. He mentioned a friend of his who was scared of singing in the street. 'He said, look out, there's a copper.' I said: 'Fuck that. Fuck the Law.' I was singing and I had a piss in a doorway as well. . . . Y, who had been moaning about life and threatening to throw himself in the canal, said he was looking forward to his 25th birthday, as he could have a party. But he was also worried about how old he was getting. He was recently back from looking for work in Liverpool and Leeds and travelling round the country. . . . He was threatening to beat up his brother-in-law, with whom he was living and who 'kept ordering' him about. X became enthusiastic and said: 'We'll get all the boys and go and

Delinquent Subcultures in Stepney and Poplar

> punch him up. All the boys.' Y said he wouldn't need anybody else, he could do it himself 'if I get just one word from him tonight.'

They came into the café less and less, and finally disappeared altogether. As the generations slot in behind them, their chances of breaking the pattern, of assuming some vestige of meaningful responsibility, dwindle. Their worst possible fate is the meths. and the bomb-site, or—as their despair grows—a crime of violence. Few groups are more in need of human agency. Equivalent cliques moved in the Maltese caffs on Commercial Road and the café-society of Cable Street. In West Stepney, they mingle more with those engaged in prostitution, drug-use and peddling, cater and act as carriers for seamen and 'tourists' from the West End who come slumming 'to see the vice'. Their participation in petty criminality increases their aversion to and suspicion of the police and any outsider. Content to degenerate in the vapid café-world of Cable Street and Brick Lane, they are more brutalised, and correspondingly more dangerous, than their Poplar counterparts. The Poplar 'yobs', however, were essentially 'local' boys; those in west Stepney had invariably drifted in from other parts of London and the rest of the country.

The definition of retreatism adopted by Cloward and Ohlin is much narrower than that devised by Merton, which is capable of subdivision:

> One prominent type of apathy is the loss of involvement in a previously sought cultural goal, such as occurs when continued striving results in persistent and seemingly unavoidable frustration. The loss of central life-goals leaves the individual in a social vacuum, without focal direction or meaning. But another crucial kind of apathy seems to emerge from conditions of great normative complexity and/or rapid change, when individuals are pulled this way and that by numerous conflicting norms and goals, until the person is literally disoriented and de-moralised, unable to secure a firm commitment to a set of norms that he can feel as self-consistent. . . .[17]

It is suggested that the affinities with retreatism of the 'yobs' is of the former type, those of the 'blacks' with the latter type.

[17] R. M. Williams, Jr., *American Society* (1951), pp. 534–35, quoted by R. K. Merton, *Social Theory and Social Structure* (1957), p. 190.

Informal Observation

Either way, the criminality of both groups is associated by male, working-class adolescents in general with downward mobility rather than desirable styles of life. This in part explains the lack of convergence between juvenile and adult crime rates noted in Chapter 6.

(*k*) *Integrated/Unintegrated Areas*

Central to the theorisation of Cloward and Ohlin is the distinction made by Kobrin between 'integrated' and 'unintegrated' areas as forcing-grounds for subcultural differentiation. While no part of Stepney or Poplar can be described as an 'integrated' area, western Stepney aligns almost exactly with the description given by Cloward and Ohlin of what constitutes an 'unintegrated' area:

> The many forces making for instability in the social organisation of some slum areas include high rates of vertical and geographic mobility; massive housing projects . . . and changing land use. . . . Forces of this kind keep a community off balance, for tentative efforts to develop community organisation are quickly checked. Transiency and instability become the over-riding features of social life. . . . The disorganised slum, populated in part by failures in the conventional world, also contains the outcasts of the criminal world. This is not to say that crime is non-existent in such cases, *but what crime there is tends to be individualistic, unorganised, petty, poorly paid, and unprotected.* This is the haunt of the small-time thief, the grifter, the pimp, the jackroller, the unsophisticated con-man, the pickpocket who is all thumbs, and others who cannot graduate beyond 'heisting' candy stores or 'busting' gas stations. Since they are unorganised and without financial resources, criminals in these areas cannot purchase immunity from protection. . . . Hence they are harassed by the police, and many of them spend the better part of their lives in prison.[18]

West Stepney, except for Wapping, has undergone, since the war, precisely this type of tremendous demographical upheaval, and has been left with a residue of slum housing, ethnic confusion and erratic population turnover. Its pervasive petty criminal elements lack all but the most rudimentary organisation, and there is little stable community life, except where pockets of the traditional Jewish community remain. Experience in many parts of west Stepney diametrically opposed the East End's reputation

[18] Cloward and Ohlin, op. cit., pp. 172–173.

for 'community' and 'hospitality' (which sprang from the old Jewish and Cockney neighbourhoods, now largely dispersed). For example, experience gained in census-taking (1961) in one pocket of Spitalfields tenementland produced the following impressions:

> The warren-like tenements were erected in 1889 and are now privately owned by a property company; accounting for over half the households in the tiny census-area. Rents are low, 8s. for a single room, unfurnished and without any amenities save the sharing of cold water and a latrine outside on the balcony. The flats are five storeys high, about 40 rooms to a balcony. There are no multiple households, and many families have three rooms, converted into a single flat by demolition of party-walls. Some interiors are, against all odds, quite affluent. Many have incorporated their own hot-and-cold, but few have a bath and none have sole use of a toilet. Key-money is frequently paid: several couples, mostly old, live together extra-maritally. Many single workmen and very poor, old women live alone, the latter recluse-like and unapproached except by welfare workers from the nearby Toynbee Hall. There is nothing approaching community spirit. There was little interaction between neighbours: 'We hardly see him/her' and 'You'll only catch him/her in early in the morning or after 11 at night,' etc. The typical household situations are (*a*) old man or woman living alone, (*b*) middle-aged or old couple, and (*c*) young couple with at least two children aged under 11. Very few teenagers were encountered. Age-structure is loaded with the old. The needs of several of these old people approach the desperate. . . . The population of 'the buildings' is ethnically varied. The hard core are Irish, with several Maltese, Cypriot and a few Jewish families. There are *no* West Indian or African immigrants, few of English descent. The Jews are mainly first-generation from Poland, East Europe or Russia. The Irish and English display a consistent insularity towards the rest throughout, often mixing up nationalities, e.g. 'They're Italian' or 'Greeks' for Maltese and Cypriots. With few exceptions, the occupational structure is uniformly unskilled and semi-skilled working-class. . . . Dislike of contact with officialdom and resentment of any kind of intrusion is automatic. People took time to overcome their suspicion of the census operation, but by the time for collecting the forms came, they were much friendlier and more hospitable. . . . Some passage-ways are completely blank in that they completely lack any interrelationship between neigh-

> bours. Other blocks in the area have more amenities than these tenements—e.g. indoor lavatory—and tenants less residual in the income-scale. They have more Jewish and English, more big families, more neighbourliness and less constriction. One couple with six children in two rooms was the extreme, well-kept and nicely-furnished as it was. . . . This is no 'teeming' slum of the Chicago-in-the-Twenties pattern. Few children played in the rubble, no gangs hung around. People 'kept themselves to themselves', and the huge forecourt was often deserted. The refusal and/or inability to be 'bothered' goes with the overall decrepitude of the property, the squalor of the 'amenities', the grey asphalt forecourt, the padlocked, silent doors. . . .[19]

The concept of the 'integrated' area simply does not apply, despite the existence in Spitalfields of several 'underworld' clubs (e.g., until 1960, the PEN Club on Duval Street) as there is little trace of any interdependence between the 'carriers' of criminal and conventional values. It is difficult to think of a London district, except perhaps Soho—largely non-residential—where such 'integration' exists. Many areas, including Stepney, feasibly contain bases for such integration on a supply-and-demand foundation, e.g. shopkeepers buying stolen goods, cigarettes, etc., as a regular transaction, but there is no overt institutionalisation of these links as in Whyte's 'Cornerville' or certain areas of New York.

Apart from West Stepney, therefore, Stepney and Poplar cannot be described as either 'integrated' or 'unintegrated' areas but simply as traditional working-class areas, combining the 'rough' and the 'respectable', but eschewing the overtly criminal elements. In the 'unintegrated' area of West Stepney, the criminal element is also frequently ostracised but community solidarity is too weakened to combat their influence in any systematic way. In an 'integrated' area, the syndicate itself and the police, however corrupt, would exert control over illegal violence and brutality. As Whyte observed: 'In Cornerville . . . the primary function of the police department is not the enforcement of law but the regulation of illegal activities.'[20] In an 'unintegrated,

[19] Audrey Harvey has done more than anyone to publicise the leprous state of much property, all privately-owned, in the East End, via articles in the *New Statesman* and in her *Tenants in Danger* (1964).

[20] W. F. Whyte, *Street Corner Society* (1955 ed.), Ch. 4, on 'The Social Structure of Racketeering.'

area, police strength is frequently outstripped by the sheer pervasiveness of such activities as prostitution and gambling, and the fragmentation of the community gives individual families no redress against 'the vice':

Mrs. B—— lived on a mean, near-derelict street between Commercial Road and Cable Street. She is married to a Polish builder's scaffolder. They have three boys, aged 3, 2 and 1, and live in one room on the ground-floor of a condemned three-storey block. 'I've never lived in a place as bad as this.' Next door is a brothel, whose working hours are 11–3 in the morning, and whose door-slams keep the children awake at night. Her 3 year-old boy keeps finding contraceptives on the door-step and in the back-yard. He thinks they're balloons, and sucks them. Five coloured people live upstairs, and he had spat at one the day before. 'He shouldn't have done that. Before we came here he never would have. He's picked that kind of thing up round here. Soon he'll be swearing. He fights his brother all the time now. He never used to. If we don't get away from here, I don't know what he's going to grow up like.' The Negro had threatened to hit the boy, had called Mrs. B—— a 'filthy whore' and a 'cunt'. Mrs. B— spelt out the second word, 'c–u–n–t'. They'd been in the room about 15 months. It was about 14′ by 12′ by 10′, was almost entirely filled by the double bed, the three cots and a wardrobe. 'When he hears them outside at night, he (the boy) gets scared and has to come to bed with us. That means we get no sleep.' The room was—incredibly—spotlessly clean. . . . She'd tried keeping the one lavatory which served for both houses clean, but it was impossible: the same with the yard, which was littered with newspapers and food-scraps the day after she'd scrubbed it out. The tenants upstairs threw rubbish out of the window. The doctor had confirmed that her health had suffered from living there: gastro-enteritis, her hair falling out through 'nerves', the doctor himself had told her this. She was mainly afraid of the children picking up disease. . . . A few weeks after they'd moved in, she'd answered a knock at the door. A man had asked if Maria was in. She told him he had the wrong house, and tried to shut the door. He wedged his foot in it, said Maria lived there. She said Maria must have moved, she lived there now. He said all he wanted was a short time, and she'd do. She somehow got the door shut. 'But they take you for just another one of them round here. I sensed it the first few days, people look at you in the street.' There were frequent incidents of violence between clients

Informal Observation

and the girls. . . . One night, they were awoken at about three in the morning by shouting and singing in the passage. Mr. B—— got up to ask them to quieten down. As he opened the door, a man burst in and hit him in the face with a bottle. Mrs. B—— got out of bed, and the man hit her in the face. The children were screaming. This time, the police were effective, the man got two years. Eventually, the B——'s struck it lucky. Mrs. B—— had said: 'I couldn't stand another winter here.' They moved round the corner to a two-roomed 'flat', but fewer people shared the lavatory, and the rent was the same, three pounds ten a week. . . .' They had, of course, tried all the usual ways of getting a flat, but landlords wouldn't take more than one child, and they'd only been on the Council list for four years. The house, although condemned, was not in a re-development area, so they stood no chance of being re-housed through demolition. They were afraid to move out of the area, as the husband might not have found as good a job.

The case of the B——'s illustrates the disorganisation of the 'unintegrated' slum area. The absence in this 'unintegrated' area of any approximation to an adolescent 'conflict' subculture is, however, of great relevance for the application of the Cloward-Ohlin hypothesis to the English situation.

(*l*) *Age-Level Integration*

Even taking generalised patterns of behaviour as analogous to adolescent contracultural structures, there appears to be little or no integration between those engaged in delinquent and criminal activities at different age-levels. This was to be expected from the Cloward-Ohlin theory, granted the absence in Stepney and Poplar of any 'integration' between legitimate and illegitimate opportunity structures. Delinquent adolescents in their late teens living locally typically avoided the 'unintegrated' adult crime areas of Cable Street and Cannon Street Road, Brick Lane, etc. As with the Poplar boys, their preference was for the exclusively teenage caff, though in Stepney, the great variety of youth clubs available eased the pressure of the adolescents' need for a café-life of their own. The Poplar boys occasionally interacted, but in no sense integrated, with the 'yobs' who used the caff, and who eventually 'didn't come in no more'. The boys sympathised, but never identified with them and, where the kind of criminality they represented was associated with 'the blacks', often displayed antagonism. As already stated, the 'yobs' seemed too inadequate and too redolent of failure to attract the boys. The Poplar boys avoided the notorious Stepney caffs:

> 'What, them on Cable Street? *They're too rough down there.* You get your throat cut down there.' Ray later went down Cable Street one night, and was genuinely disappointed: 'It's dead round there. Hardly any caffs. Nothing going on.'

The air of depression, the apparently boarded-up caffs, the few 'blacks' hanging around, had dissipated any expectation of glamour and excitement. But the Stepney boys, who knew the area better, shared this aversion. After the youth clubs closed, there was the Wimpy and little else, despite the restrictions this imposed:

> En route to the Wimpy, the group swelled to eight. They jostled each other all the way down Aldgate. A policeman stopped them after a bit, but they knew him, he came down to the club now and again, 'he's the only decent copper round here,' said Peter. 'That's because he's a City copper. The East London cops think they own the place.' The complaint was that they told the boys to move on for no apparent reason. At Gardiner's Corner, Peter pointed to two men, lounging in a shop doorway. 'Plain-clothes,' he said. 'You can smell 'em.' Apparently, they always wore the same clothes, blue sports shirt and sturdy black shoes. 'You can tell 'em a mile off.' And, in fact, as we hung around the Wimpy doorway, one of them came up: 'Police. Get inside or move away, we can't have you blocking the pavement.' The boys moved inside with studied contempt. On the pavement they could watch the girls, spot the cars and compare the scooters parked outside. Inside they had to sit, but they refused to buy a tea, all drinks being 1/- after 10 in the Wimpy, which, they asserted, was the only place they could go after 10. They never went in a workman's caff just up the road, 'it's never open when we can go in.' They went right to the back of the Wimpy and sat down, not one of them making a purchase. 'I'm not paying a shilling for a tea,' summarised Peter. . . . A stone's throw away were the all-night caffs on the Commercial Road and, a little further away, the Cable Street caffs. But they insisted there was absolutely nowhere else to go except the Wimpy. *They never 'went near' the Commercial Road or Cable Street caffs.*

The impregnation of west Stepney with a tremendous variety

of youth clubs means that delinquent male adolescents have a great deal of contact with conventional-world adults, who are frequently far from the image of the middle-class 'do-gooder', and are experienced, adult, working-class and local. This state of affairs is absent in other high delinquency areas, e.g. the Elephant and Castle in Southwark, where clubs are uniformly church or LCC-run, and where the 'unattached' resort by default to the few commercial caffs which are open at night, in one case a front for a brothel and gambling. The situation in Stepney ensures that even consistently delinquent boys have more contact with adults representing the values of the larger society, rather than the adult criminal world. Adolescents in the main Spitalfields Jewish club avoid even the Wimpy, as it is not kosher. Even in the Poplar caff, in an area which lacked the youth-club ethos, adult criminal role models were hardly in evidence, as the self-image of the boys as 'the Poplar hooligans' testifies. Also, as has previously been stated, criminals—in common with teachers, youth workers and policemen—are adults. This matters, when most adolescent delinquents are teenagers first, delinquents second.

(*m*) *Subcultural Integration*

As the patterns of behaviour—here used as analogous to delinquent subcultures—are aligned with age-levels, the same analysis applies as for age-level integration. This has had the beneficial effect so far of blocking adolescents from systematic drug-use.

Summary: Once West Stepney is clearly identified as an 'unintegrated' area, and the rest of the two boroughs as neither 'integrated' nor 'unintegrated', the theorisation of Cloward and Ohlin is negatively validated. The absence of a male adolescent 'conflict' contraculture is understandable in terms of the pressure of an adequate legitimate opportunity structure and a poverty-stricken illegitimate opportunity structure associated with downward mobility and ethnic 'out-groups'. Only for the young adult single coloured males who form the Cable Street area residuum is the legitimate opportunity structure clearly inadequate, but their numbers are too small for the emergence of any full-blown retreatist subculture.

(n) Status Frustration

The foregoing attempt at descriptive analysis leaves many questions unasked, as well as unanswered. The main question from both the Cohen and the Cloward-Ohlin viewpoints is: what response(s) does the male, working-class adolescent give to being accounted a failure—in middle-class terms—in the middle-class contexts of the school and the job-market? A corollary question is: irrespective of response, is the working-class adolescent at any time a victim of 'status frustration'? Answers are enormously difficult to provide, mainly because of the well-known circularity by which the answer is given in terms of the very behaviour one is seeking to explain, e.g. in this case, that the delinquent boy must experience status frustration since the delinquent group/gang provides him with an alternative source of status, thus enabling him to cope with his 'problem of adjustment'. But what criteria are available to assess whether or not the working-class boy typically meets with a 'problem of adjustment' at all? The following criteria leave much to be desired, but were used in a rough way in empirical research:

Evidence (past or present) for:

	No 'problem of adjustment'	*Experience of 'problem of adjustment'*
1.	Satisfaction with type of job.	Dissatisfaction with type of job.
2.	Tolerance/passive avoidance of middle-class people and institutions.	Active resentment/antagonism to same.
3.	No self-image as 'failure'.	Feeling of 'having failed'.
4.	No desire for change of membership-group.	Thwarted desire for such a change.
5.	Insulation from middle-class values.	Some internalisation of middle-class values.

Criteria 4 and 5 in particular are not presented as scientifically viable, but simply as indications of information sought.

With some exceptions, observation pointed on all criteria to the absence of any 'problem of adjustment' of the kind envisaged by Cohen in the lives of both the Poplar boys and those adolescents encountered in Stepney. There was an almost monolithic conformity to the traditional working-class value-system, and little discontent with working-class status, especially in the occupational sphere. This is not to say there were no economic dissatisfactions, but these are not peculiar to working-class adolescents: they permeate the working-class at all age-and skill-levels. The Poplar group showed—with the exception of Pete—no frustration over social status. Their self-image was not that of the 'failure' any more than it was that of a 'success': they did not think in these terms. The Poplar boys all had jobs: timber-shifter, lagger's mate, semi-skilled operatives, labourer; they earned roughly £8 a week. The highest status they could reasonably attain was chargehand or foreman. They 'chucked in' their jobs frequently, changing them for others bringing in fractionally higher wages or involving marginally different working conditions. Pete chucked in one job where he earned £8 for a 5½ day week for one where he earned £10 for a 7 day week, the first in a scrap-yard, the second as a lagger's mate. 'It's lousy, but better than before.' They were inactive politically, but traditionally claimed to be 'solid Labour'. They'd all left school at the age of 15—secondary modern—'to earn some money. . . . Everything depends on money round here.' They thought the school system was 'lousy' but wouldn't want to have been 'upper-class' and gone to college. In the absence of distinctive job-content, money is the sole differentiating criterion. They have access to a very narrow range of occupations, and work the changes between them without much sense of loss or gain. But most of them had a relative in the docks, who could get them into the 'closed shop' of dockland when they were 21. The boys were generally confident that adult status would bring high wages. Asked if any of the bunch had a car, Lennie replied: 'Yeah, several of our mates have got one. Ford V8, cars like that. I'll probably get one in a couple of years' time, when the money starts coming in.' (i.e. £11–12 a week at 18). Unless this group was completely unrepresentative, then a large stratum of working-class adolescents are still content to be 'workmanlike'.

The two exceptions in the Poplar group to the above pattern of status acceptance were Pete and Tony. Pete aspired to be something more than an expendable cog in a static and routinised industrial machine:

Delinquent Subcultures in Stepney and Poplar

He was 16½ and worked on the tugs, didn't like it much, but wasn't going to work in a factory. 'That's all there is around here, factories. I tried for the Merchant Navy but they turned me down. Too many jobs. Seven.' The Youth Employment was no good, they 'never gave you anything'. He'd leave Poplar if he had the money. He was one of a family of nine and was very despondent about money and life in general. 'I have to find two pound ten every week for my mother. I can't afford to lose my job.' Nevertheless, he changed his job at least twice in six months to bring his total to ten jobs in eighteen months since leaving secondary modern. He added: 'But what can I do? I can't spell or read or write. What's life anyway? You go to school at five, you leave at fifteen, get a job, leave at sixty-five and then die. That's life. What is it that teenagers are supposed to do.' Politics meant nothing to him. He wanted, if anything, to own his own business, a lorry of his own for haulage, but at that moment he was too young to drive. He viewed life as a dead end, like a job without prospects that you can't throw up. It was not only lack of money that depressed him: it was mainly the powerlessness and the routine degradation of the jobs to which he had access. At one point he was offered a job 'stacking sacks in a factory. They can keep *that*.' Pete 'chucked up' his job on the tugs, however, simply became 'fed up with it,' and got more money—£9 a week—working for a scrap-iron firm, as lorry-driver's mate. I asked him if there were any prospects at all in what he was doing. 'Prospects?' he said. 'What prospects? Don't make me laugh. How am I going to get a job with prospects?' He regarded even this kind of job as a bulwark against a delinquent career: 'If I ever run out of money again, I'm going to go out and do a job for some,' and 'I've stopped nickin' now, but if I'm ever out of a job again I'm going straight back to it.' He thought he might follow his father into the docks at the age of 21, but was still bitter about having been turned down for the other occupational escape-route for East End boys, the Merchant Navy.

If Pete stood apart from the group because of his sceptical appraisal of his own 'life-chances', Tony was never accepted as one of 'the boys' because of his decisively better 'life-chances'. Tony was that archetype, the grammar school boy in a 'black' secondary modern school area. About car-borrowing, Pete said:

'No, he wouldn't come in on anything like that. He does some things, but he's got an apprenticeship. *He's got something to lose.*'

Informal Observation

Tony had a 5-year apprenticeship as a technician lined up for him when he left school in a few months at 16½. 'It's only three quid a week till you're 21, but after that you get 15. I've got a cousin, he's a chief draughtsman for——, he gets 35 quid a week.' Tony liked his school, and the teachers, but was apprehensive about staying on, as he'd be too old for an apprenticeship after 17, and anyway he needed to be earning something. Lennie chipped in about his old school:

> 'They have an annual report. You know what was in the annual report last year? Nine pregnancies. That's the kind of school ours is.'

The group had an ambiguous attitude towards Tony, criticising him about behaviour which passed unnoticed in others. If he played badly on the pin-table, he was taunted, if only mildly: 'What you playin' at?', 'You never were any good at this, were you?' Tony said 'Fuck' more often than the others in a weird attempt to integrate, but they remained inconsistently friendly. Eventually he stopped coming in. Asked where he was 'these days', Lennie said:

> 'Don't know. Don't care about him. His father doesn't like him coming in here, or something. Oh, he comes in now and again, but we're not all that bothered.'

Attitudes in Stepney were broadly similar, though the adolescents there were encountered in youth-clubs as opposed to caffs and pubs, and no group's views were tapped over time. A feature of Stepney is its abundance of youth clubs of great variety and its possession of more grammar schools than are needed by available population, for much the same reasons that it is overcrowded with churches. Stepney grammar schools are largely filled by children commuting in from Essex. In some, local pupils are a minority. In one girls' grammar school, the local girls were a small, ostracised out-group. The large number of youth clubs—stratified into Jewish and non-Jewish, 'respectable' and 'rough' working-class—often attracted many users from other boroughs. Some clubs catered for the delinquent, 'unattached' boy who in other areas would typically have resorted to the caff. One such club was liked because 'there's no rules here'; but in fact a rough-and-ready discipline was maintained by adult helpers who had used the club in their teens and lived locally. These clubs were especially valued for dances in an area without dance-halls, the nearest being the Poplar 'Civic'. The process of selection in most church and LCC-run youth clubs left the 'rough' residue for this kind of club, which did not attempt to emulate their—at best—smooth organisation and well-run 'activities'. Throughout, only one example of vocal resentment about education and jobs was elicited (in a club where the helpers commented on the 'respectability' of the kids):

> 'I got an apprenticeship. What's that? At 19, I earn eight quid. . . . You get a second-class education and you get a second-class job with it. A pal of mine left school the other week and got a job as a lagger. A lagger. You can't get any lower than a lagger.'

Things were fixed against them in the East End, 'we can't possibly get a better job.' This isolated example of vehemence against the social structure came, significantly, from a boy in a skilled job, atypical because he articulated dissatisfaction with the type of job to which he had access, rather than with simply the job he had at the time. He vocalised the kind of resentment which was constantly looked for, but rarely found, in both boroughs.

Status-frustration, as portrayed by Cohen, appeared to be found in inverse, rather than direct, correlation with 'subcultural' delinquency. Discontent with role allotment, and resentment at structural blockage to upward mobility, seemed to be associated with lower-stream grammar and technical school, and upper echelon 'A' stream secondary modern school, boys—rather than the products of the typical 'black' secondary modern school. It must be emphasised that Cohen's theorisation stressed the occurrence of status-frustration at an earlier stage than late adolescence, and only research at the pre-school leaving stage in secondary moderns would supply any valid data on this point. Also, where status-frustration *did* occur in a lower unskilled and semi-skilled working-class context, it produced a degree of desperation which found some outlet—but no 'gang' status 'solution'—in delinquency. But the norm in this lower-class context appeared to be one of status acceptance. In this context, the 'renegade'—in Simmel's[21] sense—was not the delinquent boy

[21] G. Simmel, *Conflict* (1955), tr. K. H. Wolff, pp. 47–48.

Informal Observation

(unless the delinquency took violent form) but the 'college' boy, who sought a change of reference-group, either as skilled technical or white-collar salariat worker. The East End may be too atypical in this connection for any generalisation to be made on the basis of experience there. Its dockland especially has institutionalised the 'cult' of manual work, and—outside the Jewish population—all the cultural pressures are against the upwardly mobile child. The absence of any real pressure for upward mobility is in part explained by the lack of any tangible incentive to make any but the biggest upward climb. Full juvenile and adult employment are probably enough to make for status acceptance, in an area where wages are as high in many manual jobs as in most routine white-collar jobs, especially those involving academic qualifications, such as teacher, youth worker, probation officer—the middle-class representatives with whom the working-class boy comes into most frequent contact. In the docks and the markets, wages are appreciably higher—though much more erratic—than in office or low-prestige academic jobs. But Stepney and Poplar are not appreciably more conservative and hide-bound in class and occupational beliefs and values than are traditional working-class areas in many cities. The constrictions of the working-class value-system are still powerful enough to render technically low-status jobs acceptable. The working-class boys encountered typically measured themselves not against 'all comers', but against their own class-bound peer-group. The upwardly mobile working-class 'college'[22] boy is the 'renegade', and the delinquent gang is rendered unnecessary as a defence mechanism against status-frustration. This situation appears to have barely changed so far, but feasibly—as we expand our educational elites, recruit more from the lower working classes for our academically qualified technicians and administrators, and as the job-market for unskilled and semi-skilled labour contracts—the conservatism of the working-class value-system will weaken. 'The boys' still think in terms of 'Them' and 'Us' rather than in terms of 'Success' and 'Failure': the first implies a sense of group-affiliation and class solidarity; the second connotes the stress and strain of individual achievement: the first emphasises collective goals, fought for and won by union bargaining and strength; the second

[22] In this context, the grammar-school boy.

implies individual goals, to which access is controlled by exterior criteria. The more the situation changes from the first to the second configuration, the more prone working-class male adolescents will be to that specific 'problem of adjustment' which Cohen postulated as the core incentive to gang delinquency.

(*o*) *Alienation*

The concept of 'alienation' plays as central a role in the subcultural theorisation of Cloward and Ohlin as 'status-frustration' does in that of Cohen, and the largely negative findings for the latter apply even more forcibly for the former. There was barely any evidence to suggest that delinquent adolescents achieved any degree of alienation in the Cloward-Ohlin sense, i.e. 'withdrawal of attributions of legitimacy for conventional norms'. If the findings on 'status-frustration' were substantially correct, this is hardly a surprising conclusion: 'status-frustration' or profound disenchantment with available legitimate opportunities, is the stage in the delinquent subcultural sequence prior to the possible emergence of the alienated response. Alienation in this context means much more than a boy 'not liking' his job, or feeling at odds with the machine he operates. It means rejection of the normative system by which he was allotted the job, came to operate the machine, in the first place. Yet the jobs of the Poplar boys and—notoriously—of a disproportionate number of male delinquents, including the most recalcitrant, were of low status even by working-class standards. These boys were not impervious to the working-class image of 'the good job', the autonomy of the craftsman, the physical toughness of the stevedore, the offbeat glamour and on-shore independence of the Merchant seaman, the high wages and security awaiting the apprentice. Enough of their peers occupy these jobs for the contrast to be ever-present. To deny on their behalf any real degree of status-frustration and alienation is not to present a picture of boys who are happy to be laggers—'the lowest of the low'—van-boys, labourers, etc. What has been achieved, rather, is an opting-out of the joint middle- and skilled working-class value-system whereby work is extolled as a central life-issue, and whereby the male adolescent of semi- and unskilled origin is enjoined to either 'better himself' or 'accept his station in life'. To insulate themselves against the harsh implications of this creed, the adolescent in a 'dead-end' job, in a 'dead' neighbourhood, extricates himself from the belief in work as of any importance beyond the simple provision of income, and deflects what aspirations he has left into areas of what has been termed 'non-work' (rather than leisure).

This process has been best described as one of 'dissociation', as distinct from 'status-frustration' or 'alienation':

> Satisfaction from work and the significance attached to it will depend not only on the nature of the work, but also on the expectations which the individual brings to his job. These in turn will be the result of complex processes of selection and socialisation, which begin at 11 + with entry to the grammar or modern school, each of which carries its stream of children on to broad groups of occupations. . . . For the less able child in the lower forms of the modern school, the dominant picture that emerges is one of school as a source of boredom and frustration.[23] In many schools the imposition of dull, mechanical tasks, which lack any apparent significance or relevance to the life of the child, effectively train him to accept the routine demands of industry. The transition from school to work involves little more than a change of routine.[24] Many expect little from work and are satisfied with what they find, even though the work is repetitive and makes few demands. The secondary modern boy leaving school at 15 has received early training in dissociating himself from the demands which 'they' make upon him. *He simply doesn't care*. It is not surprising that psychologists have discovered that many are content to carry out routine tasks. Dissatisfaction is a measure of the gap between aspiration and achievement. *For many, no such gap exists—their expectations and aspirations are centred on the world outside the factory*.[25]

In school, the problem is not one of structured protest, defiance and rebellion against middle-class norms, but of pupil inertia, boredom and passivity, with periodic outbursts of what Webb termed 'spontaneity, irrepressibility and rule-breaking' as a reaction against the shackling of their individualism by the school as a legitimised agency of control. In this connection,

[23] See M. P. Carter, *Home, School and Work* (1962).

[24] See also Webb, 'Sociology of a School,' *Brit. J. Sociol.*, Vol. 13, No. 3, Sept. 1962.

[25] See S. Cotgrove and S. Parker, 'Work and Non-Work', *New Society*, Vol. 41, 11/7/1963, pp. 18–19.

the apology offered by the father of a Stepney boy who refused to be interviewed is of interest. The boy had previously reluctantly agreed to be interviewed, but on the date, had gone out to the pictures with his wife. The father simply offered 'They don't take to people with education' as a reason, a classic instance of dissociation, of evasion and withdrawal, as opposed to outright annoyance and anger at being pestered.

Cotgrove and Parker, in reviewing recent studies in industrial sociology, go a long way towards establishing a frame of reference for the analysis of the work situation as a main determinant of attitudes and values in areas of non-work. They complain that

> the sociologist, if he has looked outside the factory, has searched mainly for clues which would throw light on industrial behaviour. . . . The great weakness of such studies is their failure to sort out the components of the working-class situation and relate them to working-class culture, leisure and family life. . . . Short term hedonism, belief in fate, and the distinction between 'them' who decide and 'us' who passively carry out instructions . . . may well stem from the typical factory work situation, characterised by a lack of autonomy and involvement.[26]

'Extreme' occupations make the clearest impact on areas of non-work. The miner, for example, in particular the face worker,

> is deeply involved in his work and enjoys relative autonomy at the coal face. But it is dangerous and damaging work, demanding the closest co-operation . . . which makes its indelible imprint on life after work—the forgetfulness of alcohol in the long round of pub visits on Saturday and Sunday, wives left at home, and the deep significance of the trade union. . . .

The 'organisation man' is affected in a fashion equally commensurate with the demands and prospects of his occupation, which encourages the long view, the promise of deferred gratification, the blurring of the distinction between work and leisure.

> Yet although the effect of work on non-work activities is so marked . . . for the great mass of industrial workers, and for many white-collar workers too, *work is not a significant area of life*. . . . The activities most valued are found chiefly outside work.

[26] Cited here are: N. Dennis, F. Henriques and C. Slaughter, *Coal is our Life* (1956); C. Sigal, *Weekend in Dinlock* (1960); J. Tunstall, *The Fishermen* (1962).

Informal Observation

> The factory worker is seldom work-centred. Work for him is not something on which he centres his interests, his hopes and aspirations, nor even his worries.

Baldamus has shown[27] 'that the mental and skill demands made by the work task are of major importance' as determinants of 'involvement in work or dissociation from it'. The secondary modern 'drop-out', destined at 15 for the shallow range of unskilled and semi-skilled jobs, is already schooled to dissociation by the educational process.

> Those for whom work lacks intrinsic interest are likely to look elsewhere for satisfaction and achievement and to see work simply as a source of income. . . . In nine-to-five jobs, no obligations need encroach on leisure time. . . . Some, for whom work is not an area for free and meaningful action, turn to leisure as compensation. . . . Leisure . . . may be sought as an escape from the monotony of work, given over to such feverish pleasures as speedway and jiving. Withdrawal to home-centredness offers compensations of a different kind. Here, a man is boss of his own small world, and can engage in meaningful tasks of his own choosing. . . .

'The influence of work, however, is by no means confined to leisure activities. It may shape in a variety of ways political attitudes, family patterns, and even the 'world view' of the worker.' Lockwood[28] found the crucial pressures underlying the 'class consciousness' of the clerk, and his attitude towards unionisation, stemmed from the work situation—with its paternalistic relationship and sense of identity with the employer—rather than from market determined income. Cotgrove and Parker conclude that

> if, in fact, many of the components of working class attitudes and values spring from their position in the authority structure of industry or from the nature of the tasks they carry out, rather than from poverty and insecurity,[29] then affluence alone will not bring about the changes we might otherwise predict. The fact that work is not a central life interest for most has important

[27] W. Baldamus, 'Types of Work and Motivation', *Brit. J. Sociol.*, March 1951.

[28] D. Lockwood, *The Blackcoated Worker* (1958).

[29] E.g., if poverty, misery, insecurity and sheer generalised deprivation were the mainsprings of crime and delinquency, then the old age pensioners would be the most crime-ridden sector.

> implications. If we choose to concentrate on non-work satisfactions, we shall need to know much more about the extent to which work moulds leisure activities, and how far satisfying leisure can, in fact, compensate for alienating work. . . . What we can certainly say is that *work sets limits on the kind of leisure which are possible* and seem to be desirable, and profoundly influences non-work activities, beliefs and attitudes.

For 'the boys' in Stepney and Poplar, dissociation at work seemed to be coupled with dissociation in leisure. Granted the abundance of youth work in Stepney, the cause for surprise is not that this pattern has been broken down slightly, but that it has resisted such a variety of middle-class oriented blandishments. But it cannot be asserted that dissociation extends to the 'world view' of these adolescents, and it is this 'world-view' that affords least evidence of alienation in the Cloward-Ohlin sense. For example, the Poplar group showed firm loyalty to the monarchy, the government, etc. They disagreed with the way white Americans treated Negroes. Hatred of 'coppers'—'the boys'' sworn enemy—was not a manifestation of 'withdrawal of attributions of legitimacy from conventional norms', but rather a particularistic aversion to the kind of control enforced by the police. This was combined with an attitude verging on what Sykes and Matza termed 'techniques of neutralisation'—e.g. 'Coppers are a lot of cunts. They closed everything down, all the caffs. They stop us doing anything, always moving us along', etc.—i.e. 'accusing the accusers', though there is undoubted truth in their charge of differential victimisation. Police justification for this would be valid, however, as the groupings they break up and 'move on' are often ripe for trouble-making: removal of the causes which led the groups to form and 'hang about' in this way is not the police's concern. Yet hatred of the police is often suspended. The friendly cop is a rarity, but is enormously respected. Also, on one occasion, Ray listened in to a police car bulletin. He expressed no resentment, just excitement. The police, normally repressive, had for once *been* a source of excitement. 'Plain-clothes', however, are quite beyond the pale.

'Dissociation' for 'the boys' is generally from middle-class dominated institutions, rather than from the total non-working-class society. One of a group of 'ton-kids' who used the caff occasionally expressed this almost too articulately:

Informal Observation

> 'We go fast, but we watch it. We wait for straight stretches of road most of the time. *There's none of this defiance of society.* That's all in the newspapers and the newspapers are all wrong. They're just sensationalising to sell more newspapers. . . .'

Even about the Remand Home, the group showed clear preference for conniving dissociation from its aims rather than alienation from its norms:

> 'It's better "inside" than out here. Prison's alright. And places like Stamford House, that's just a holiday camp. You go there and behave yourself for a fortnight and they make you a prefect. Then you get more time to watch the telly, you don't have to do jobs, things like that.'

Interaction between middle-class 'helpers' and working-class 'delinquents' in youth-clubs provides many instances of confrontation producing friction, but antagonism resulted in dissociation rather than open conflict on the part of the adolescent. Overt hostility is rarely the consequence of such interaction, even where middle-class intrusion is resented. By analogy, the 'inverted snobbery' peculiar to the English working-class is the hall-mark of dissociation and its maintenance is an antidote to feelings of alienation.

(*p*) *Anomie*

Analysis so far has concentrated on what might be termed the consistently delinquent 'corner boy'—Cohen's clear-cut distinction between the 'corner' and the 'delinquent' boy appearing to be inappropriate at this juncture—and not on the working-class 'college' boy, the aspirant highly skilled manual and technical workers, or the conforming 'corner boy'. Also excluded are delinquent boys bent on pursuing a nascent professional criminal career—often on the basis of almost unbroken institutionalisation—and 'lone' offenders who commit delinquencies with no traceable pattern, e.g. those for whom delinquency is symptomatic of mental illness. It is still thought that the group delinquent 'corner boy' pattern accounts for the bulk of the major adolescent offences, i.e. the diversified activities of break-ins, car-borrowing, simple larcenies and theft from machines, rowdyism, receiving, weapon-carrying and—more atypically—vandalism and violence against the person. Yet these adolescents did not appear to be subject—or to have been subjected in the past—to any critical degree of status frustration or alienation. Interaction within middle-class institutions, and the experience of 'failure' in the context of both middle-class and upper working-class contexts, appeared to have evoked the response of dissociation from the ethic that work, and occupational status, were of crucial importance as a focal area for 'ego-involvement'. As a result, their reference- and membership-groups were pretty well aligned. This is not to deny that they were subject to a mild form of economic anomie, but this is not peculiar to the male working-class adolescent sector. It is built into the consumer economy as incentive for all classes and all age-levels.[30] But the strain towards anomie is not generated solely by frustrations encountered in monetary and occupational spheres. As Merton has repeatedly stressed:

> . . . the general theory of social structure and anomie is *not* confined to the specific goal of monetary success and of social restrictions upon access to it. . . . In terms of the general conception, *any* cultural goals which receive extreme and only negligibly qualified emphasis in the culture of a group will serve to attenuate the emphasis on institutionalised practices and make for anomie.[31]

Dissociation from the goal of occupational achievement—which feasibly occurs long before entry into the job-market—forestalls Cohen's issue of status-frustration: the 'problem of adjustment', consequent upon internalisation of middle-class values to at least some extent, never occurs. There is little merging: working-class and middle-class value-systems meet in head-on clash. As Merton, again, has stated:

> . . . the theory (of anomie) . . . sees the conflict between culturally defined goals and institutional norms as one *source* of anomie; it does not *equate* value-conflict and anomie. Quite the contrary: conflict between the norms held by distinct subgroups in a society of course often results *in an increased adherence to the norms prevailing in each subgroup*. It is the conflict between culturally accepted values and the socially structured difficulties of living up to these values which exerts pressure towards deviant behaviour and disruption of the normative system.[32]

[30] Cf. the discussion by T. H. Marshall, *Sociology at the Crossroads* (1963) pp. 317-318.

[31] R. K. Merton, *Social Theory and Social Structure* (1957), p. 181.

[32] Merton, op. cit., pp. 190–191.

Informal Observation

By acceptance of low job aspirations, the 'corner boy' is released from the pressures of upward mobility, and his view of the legitimacy of 'lower class culture' is endorsed. But dissociation—as has already been stated—means withdrawal of interest in work except as a source of income, and this has concomitant implications for his behaviour, with others similarly circumstanced, in areas of 'non-work'. Feasibly, the more debasing his job-content and the more dissociated he feels from work, the more the lower working-class 'corner boy' tries to recoup in leisure something of the freedom, achievement, autonomy and excitement he is denied in work. In other words, Cohen's concept of 'status frustration' might possibly apply in this country if 'status' is defined in the Weberian sense of 'style of life' and consumer behaviour, rather than in the narrower sense of occupational prestige and aspirations to middle-class orientated achievement.

(*q*) *'Subterranean' Values and Leisure Goals*

Sykes and Matza, by viewing 'adolescents in general and delinquents in particular as the last leisure class',[33] have attacked the conception that the values underlying the delinquent's behaviour constitute a deviant normative system. They assert that: 'A number of supposedly delinquent values are closely akin to those embodied in the leisure activities of the dominant society'. They hold that: (a) the values behind much juvenile delinquency are far less deviant than commonly portrayed, and (b) the faulty picture is due to gross over-simplification of the middle-class value-system.[34] Three major themes have emerged from the variety of classic accounts of delinquent behaviour and values, although consensus is limited to substance, and not interpretation: (i) delinquents are typically immersed in a restless search for excitement, thrills or 'kicks'; (ii) delinquents commonly exhibit a disdain for 'getting on' in the realm of work; (iii) delinquents characteristically accept aggressive toughness as a proof of masculinity.

[33] D. Matza and G. Sykes, 'Delinquency and Subterranean Values', *Amer. Sociol. Rev.*, Vol. 26, No. 5, Oct. 1961, pp. 712–719.

[34] In defending Cohen in particular against the charge that he 'grossly over-simplifies' the middle-class value-system, and 'reduces' the value-system of the whole society to that of the middle class, it can be asserted that this is precisely what the school sets out to achieve. Hence the strength of the postulated reaction against the value-system symbolised by the school context.

Delinquent Subcultures in Stepney and Poplar

(i) is not accommodated by legitimate outlets such as organised recreation, for the very fact that an activity involves breaking the law is precisely the source of excitement. In courting danger, provoking authority, etc., 'the delinquent is not simply enduring hazards: *he is also creating hazards in a deliberate attempt to manufacture excitement*'. The excitement that stems from danger and law-violation, e.g. especially in 'chicken runs' and 'rumbles', is not a by-product, but a—possibly the—motivating force.

(ii) places the delinquent firmly in the category of the unemployed, the casual worker, or the boy in the 'dead-end' job. Even where 'occupational goals involving the steady job or cautious advancement' are available, 'it takes deep faith—and naïveté—to believe that hard work at the lower end of the occupational hierarchy is a sure path to worldly success'. (In the words of a later-day 'courtesan', Mandy Rice-Davies, who began with a low-status background: 'Nobody ever made a bomb by plodding along in a dull job.' (paraphrase)).

(iii) is commonly interpreted as an index of the delinquent's alienation from the larger society, his aggression—whether verbal or physical—seen as an outlet for basic hostility, hatred, and the urge to injure and destroy. This may be so for atypical big-city 'structured' gangs. More typically, it expresses the delinquent's familiarity with the ethic that manhood is reached via an ability to 'take it' and 'hand it out'.

Far from taking this configuration of values as indicative of the delinquent's deviation from the dominant society, Sykes and Matza note its affinities with the code of Veblen's 'gentleman of leisure'. The emphasis on daring; rejection of the prosaic discipline of work; the flair for conspicuous consumption; the respect accorded to manhood demonstrated by force; all find a prototype in Veblen's leisured elite. Only the *mode* of expression—delinquency—is unfamiliar. '*The values are obscured by their context.*' But the context alone is not sufficient to account for the attribution of deviance to the delinquent's values. 'In our haste to create a standard from which deviance can be measured, we have reduced the value-system of the whole society to that of the middle class', and our portrayal of that value-system is grossly over-simplified. By an over-emphasis on the individualistic pursuit of work-goals, the Protestant Ethic and the deferred gratification pattern, and by a similar inflation of the ethic of reciprocity,

Informal Observation

belief in luck and short-run hedonism, we have polarised middle-class and working-class value-systems. Sykes and Matza compare these value-system portrayals to the now outmoded racial group portrayals, i.e. they amount to 'a distinct grouping of specific values unique to the social class in which they are found', instead of basing analysis on the 'distribution of frequencies', i.e.: 'Most values . . . appear in most social classes; the social classes differ, however, in the frequency with which the values appear'.

In any event, and whatever degree of distinctiveness is held to obtain between the value-systems of the social classes, Sykes and Matza argue that *all* classes accommodate certain 'subterranean values'—values which are in conflict or competition with other deeply held values, but which are still recognised and accepted by many.[35] 'These contradictions in values . . . may exist in a single individual and give rise to profound feelings of ambivalence in many areas of life.' They are akin to private as opposed to public morality, but they are not—*per se*—deviant.

Delinquent values, therefore, have their counterparts in the dominant society, most crucially in the upper and middle class sectors. But their expression is muted, confined to certain circumstances, such as holidays, sport, recreations, private conversation. Members of the middle class—and of all classes—seek excitement in gambling, parties, night-clubbing etc. 'Most societies provide room for . . . a sort of periodic anomie, in which thrill-seeking is allowed to emerge.' Indeed, 'the search for adventure, excitement . . . is a subterranean value that now often exists side by side with the values of security, routinisation, etc. It is not a deviant value . . . but must be held in abeyance until the proper circumstances for it arrive . . . In many cases, the delinquent suffers from bad timing.' Likewise, it can hardly be claimed that the dominant society is fully and unquestioningly

[35] Sykes and Matza fail to note that Cohen advanced much the same point, but regarded it as less crucial for an understanding of the middle-class value-system: 'The delinquent is the rogue male. His conduct may be viewed not only negatively . . .; positively it may be viewed as the exploitation of modes of behaviour which are traditionally symbolic of untrammelled masculinity, which are renounced by middle-class culture because incompatible with its ends, but which are not without . . . glamour and romance . . . They find their way into the respectable culture . . . only in disciplined and attenuated forms. . . . *They are not, however, allowed to interfere with the serious business of life.* The delinquent . . . is freer to divert these *subterranean currents* of our cultural tradition to his own use.' Cohen, op. cit., p. 140.

committed to hard work. The notion of 'pull' and 'contacts', the idea of the 'soft' job—for the working-class in England, the 'good skive'—are widespread. Riesman's 'inside-dopester', Whyte's 'organisation man' and Mills' 'fixer' are all concepts 'undermining the Weberian sociologists' affirmation of *the* work values of society'. In his disdain for the monotony of manual labour and his desire for 'easy' money, 'the delinquent is . . . in step with his time'. As for aggression, the dominant society exhibits a widespread taste for violence; books, magazines, films and TV jointly peddle fantasies of violence, from James Bond to 'Psycho', as well as acting as vehicles for the dissemination of criminal techniques. The actual use of aggression and violence in war and law enforcement provide further endorsement of the acceptance of aggression and violence on the part of the dominant social order. The equation between physicial toughness and virility is also widely accepted, though the use of aggression is surrounded by many prohibitions.

In brief, Sykes and Matza argue that, far from standing as an alien in the body of society, the delinquent may represent instead a dangerous reflection or caricature. By picking up and emphasising the subterranean part of the dominant value system, the delinquent serves to reinforce the overtly law-abiding in their tenure of its more respectable and publicly proclaimed values. 'These values bind the delinquent to the society whose laws he violates', and this sharing facilitates his 'reformation' with the coming of adult status. 'To the objection that much juvenile behaviour other than simply delinquent behaviour would then be analysed as an extension of the adult world rather than as a product of a distinctly adolescent subculture', Matza and Sykes reply that this is 'precisely their thesis'.

In approaching the relationship between delinquency and social class, however, the argument of Sykes and Matza comes to verge on the perverse. Because they have answered the question: 'What makes delinquency attractive in the first place?' exclusively in terms of leisure values, i.e. the values of what they term a 'leisure class', and because they assert these values apply to adolescents at all class levels, they are led to assert that delinquency is more or less evenly distributed throughout the social class structure. This argument is not only based largely on absence of evidence: it runs counter to the massive amount of evidence that exists. It is not enough to insist that the non-delinquent is a rarity. This is by now a criminological truism. Most evidence supports the view that group delinquency is more frequent, persistent, diversified and less amenable to control among male, working-class, urban adolescents than in any other sector. Moreover, this view is consistent with the theorisation of Matza and Sykes, provided that the concept of *differential access to leisure goals* is utilised, along with theorisation on the differential *distribution* and *functions* of leisure among adolescents.

Temporarily leaving out of consideration a small, moneyed, upper class élite, the distribution of leisure in adolescence by social class is clearly determined by educational allotment. At school, the non-secondary modern boy is subject to a rigorous academic time-table, home-work, and frequently school-sponsored commitments in sport and voluntary associations. Increasingly, this pattern of obligations—which eats into non-school activities —is unbroken till the age of 18, with the transition from school to higher education or training. The early leaver at 16 typically moves into a white-collar job, where he pursues an achievement-oriented career, frequently involving part-time or further education. Hence, the non-secondary modern school-boy is institutionally restrained from the most basic delinquency-producing situation of all: an abundance of 'free' time. The same applies on a lesser scale to a sizeable minority of upper stream secondary modern boys, who obtain apprenticeship, lower-grade white-collar jobs, or trainee skilled occupations, which involve either day release or evening classes. But for the substantial majority of secondary modern boys, both at and after school, few commitments encroach on leisure time.

Paradoxically, these adolescents—who have most leisure—also *need* it most, and ask more of it. Matza and Sykes have stated that all adolescents are alike in that 'they move in a limbo between earlier parental domination and future integration with the social structure through the bonds of work and marriage'. But for the grammar, technical and skilled working-class boy, it is not so much a limbo as a period of structured training for future role performance. Society has invested much more heavily in this type of adolescent than in the average secondary modern 'drop out' destined for the narrow ranges of numerous

Delinquent Subcultures in Stepney and Poplar

and interchangeable semi- and unskilled manual jobs. The strong likelihood of dissociation from this latter type of work has already been discussed, as have the consequences of dissociation for involvement in areas of non-work. Home-centredness is clearly unthinkable for most working-class male adolescents before their own marriage: numerous studies have pointed to the early age at which the working-class adolescent—quite distinctly from the middle-class boy—disentangles himself from parental domination. Similarly, the nature of his work appears to disincline him towards political and community activity. The only non-work area to which he is unequivocally attracted is straightforward, uncluttered leisure. Yet dissociation from the work situation, and from middle-class dominated authority contexts, has its corollary in leisure: the rejection of the youth club, except for those few which exert little discipline, do not insist on regular attendance, and do not intrude on the group's or the individual's autonomy. Hence the emphasis on commercial milieux, the caff, the cinema, the dance-hall. For work-oriented adolescents, no such prohibitions apply. School- and job-satisfaction often leave them self-sufficient in leisure: mere idleness, sheer relaxation, is enough. But the youth club, with its 'activities' and 'constructive' frame of reference, accommodates them if they feel the need for direction in leisure. Also, academically-oriented education has equipped them for individualistic leisure pursuits, such as reading, hobbies, etc. It is the 'corner boy'—who has most leisure, and lays most stress on it as the area for self-realisation—who has least resources at his disposal to use it positively.

It is in this situation that the adolescent 'corner boy' encounters blockage of access to certain leisure goals common to all adolescents. The concept of this group as a discriminated-against 'leisure class' involves little tampering with the formula proposed by Matza and Sykes. Leisure goals as a term is meant to subsume both 'subterranean values'—the search for excitement, the pursuit of aggression[36]—and certain leisure aspirations and expectations reflected in and perpetuated by 'teenage' culture—sophistication (clothes, wit), smartness, 'exploit', 'kicks'. Achievement in some or all of these areas might be said to constitute

[36] For Sykes and Matza, 'disdain for work' entailed apotheosis of 'the big score': this was jettisoned in an English context.

Informal Observation

'success' in leisure for adolescents. 'Teenage culture' stresses the possession of these attributes and the pursuit of these collective goals. It also lays special emphasis on certain artefacts and institutions: the fast car or motor-bike, the 'regular' girl, record-players, parties, etc. Rising expectations of leisure over the last decade have brought goals formerly within the reach of a minority into the purview of all: the holiday abroad, trips to the country, all-night 'raves', the kick of speed.[37] The genuinely leisured, upper-class adolescent has full access to these goals, as have most students. By contrast, the 'corner boy' is relatively deprived in access to arenas for this kind of 'exploit'. Law-breaking is the only area of excitement to which he has absolutely untrammelled access. 'Anything you get enjoyment from round here, you're breaking the law' and 'We did it for a bit of a giggle' or 'Just for laughs': these disavowals of malice are more than techniques of neutralisation: they are euphemisms for the absence of legitimate opportunities to realise leisure goals.

Observation in Stepney and Poplar gave some support for this view. A focal issue for the Poplar boys was what they termed the 'deadness' of the area, 'nothing going on', their aversion to the one institution—the youth club—which might have contained their 'periodic outbursts of anomie' (Matza and Sykes). Those with bikes had a valid outlet:

> 'We go fast, but we watch it. . . . There's none of this defiance of society. . . . *The bikes for us are mainly a chance.* We can get to places on the bikes we'd never get a sniff at without. We go to the Isle of Wight, Maidstone and so on. We can take the girls out on them. . . . There's a few nuts but not many. We never drink beer and I hardly smoke. We take good care when we're driving, even if we do go fast.'

Some did express the conventional 'ton-kid' persona, 'We go on "burn ups", playing "chicken" with each other . . . For the kick, the speed, *you* know', but the dominant attitude inclined to the former. The caff was virtually the only milieu for those without bikes (none had scooters, though Bill eventually bought a car for £20): apart from the cinema and dancing at the 'Civic',

[37] The Teddy Boy Movement can be seen, in part, as a response to the biggest single rise in adolescent leisure expectations of the last decade, i.e., the arrival of 'rock' and the full flowering of commercial 'teenage' culture; cf. Fyvel, op. cit., p. 70.

it was their only legitimate arena for excitement. Their behaviour in the caff was characterised by a milling restlessness, punctuated by long bouts on the pinball machine, the jukebox, etc. Strain was generated by the sheer absence of tension, the feeling that something ought to be 'going on'. Outside the area, they looked for the same framework: 'We go up the West End sometimes, go in those amusement arcades', and once came back tattooed, skull-and-crossbones, etc. on the forearm. Only work, sleep, the cinema and 'courting' took them outside the caff. They were interested in no music except pop, no sport, no reading except the *Mirror* every day and comics. They themselves viewed delinquency as a pretext 'for laughs'. a diversion from the long periods of boredom, constriction and inertia of the caff, whose ethos was in 'negative polarity' to the constructive, busy 'activities' of the model youth club.

It is not suggested that these boys constitute a 'leisure class', only that the analogy itself is suggestive. In the absence of work-orientation and job-satisfaction, and lacking the compensations accruing from alternative areas of non-work, such as home-centredness, political activity and community service,[38] the 'corner boy' attaches unusual importance to 'leisure'. There is no reason to suppose that the delinquent 'corner boy' does not share the more general, technically classless 'teenage culture', a culture whose active pursuit depends on freedom from the restraints of adult responsibility, but which reflects the 'subterranean values' of the conventional adult world. There is some reason to suppose, however, that the working-class 'corner boy' both lays greater stress on its leisure goals, and has far less legitimate access to them, than male adolescents differently placed in the social structure. This discrepancy is thought to be enough to provide immediate impetus to a great deal of group delinquency, limited in ferocity but diversified in content. The underlying sources, however, remain culture-conflict along class lines, school failure and subsequent dissociation from work-goals, and consequent non-involvement in desirable areas of non-work. This sequence appears crucial for the short-lived but intense emphasis on a particular set of leisure goals.

[38] Some boys achieve this, e.g., the Poplar 'Teenage Friendship Society' formed to provide help for the old age pensioners.

Informal Observation

(*v*) '*Sexual Deprivation*'
It has recently been suggested that Borstal boys have experienced less success than is normal for their peers in establishing heterosexual relationships, and that this contributes to recalcitrant delinquency, whether of a subcultural or individualistic kind.[39] It is more likely, however, that subcultural delinquency is a cause, rather than a result, of the inability to form a stable relationship with girls, although the continuing absence of such a relationship serves to perpetuate the delinquent response. Cohen has stressed that, in adulthood, the male's occupational achievements form the principal criterion of status for both husband and wife, and the chief moral responsibility for this achievement rests on the man. 'It follows that the man's success in the adult role is, as compared with the woman's, less dependent on whom he marries and more dependent upon his own achievements. *The woman has more to gain by "marrying up" and more to lose by "marrying down"*.'[40] For the adult male, status is ultimately determined by his own occupational success; for the woman, the functional equivalent is marriage to an occupationally successful male.

The more this axiom holds broadly true, irrespective of ethnic and social class subgroup variations, the more disadvantaged is the delinquent boy in his search for regular female company. That he wants such company can hardly be disputed, even if only for motives of sexual 'exploit' as distinct from the need for a stable, demanding relationship. Nor can it be disputed that, save for a minority, the delinquent's girl is a force for conforming behaviour, as opposed to acting as provocateur for delinquent activity. Hence the rigorous separation by delinquents of their 'courting' performance from the life of the peer group. 'Sex' might be a main collective leisure goal for male adolescents, but any relationship is typically maintained apart from the group, even though it might be sought for in group contexts—the dance-hall, the cinema, the walk-round. It is thought that, while the delinquent boy has dissociated himself from occupational achievement, the majority of working-class girls adhere to the necessity for marrying an occupationally successful male, albeit one who can give them 'a good time'. As early marriage becomes

[39] T. C. N. Gibbens, *Psychiatric Studies of Borstal Lads* (1963). See Ch. 6 and p. 107.
[40] Cohen, op. cit., p. 141.

increasingly the norm for female adolescents, an encouraging factor is that the disparity between the need for achievement and the delinquent reality is frequently resolved by a marriage of necessity, and enforced work-orientation and withdrawal into home-centredness and family-building. Where the delinquent either opts out of this solution, or rejects it in advance, he is correspondingly less of a proposition for the conformist-minded female, and resorts to the minority who are sexually accessible and/or promiscuous, but who can exert less control on the delinquent boy's future adjustment to adult responsibilities. Demographically, as well as structurally, the delinquent boy is more likely to have to resort to the promiscuous, or the younger and more inexperienced girl: simply numerically, there are fewer girls than boys available, and girls tend to marry older males. In Stepney and Poplar, in the 14–17 age-group, there are 4,964 males to 4,594 females. This figure in itself is meaningless, as no society has yet achieved a one-to-one male-female correlation. The figures for Stepney and Poplar for the 15–19 and 20–24 age-groups[41] are, however:

	15–19	*20–24*
Single	5, 614 males	3,945 males
	5,076 females	2,620 females
Married	107 males	1,777 males
	480 females	3,051 females

Even between 15 and 19, there are roughly 112 single males for every 100 unmarried females; between 20 and 24, however, there are roughly 3 single males for every 2 single women. While this discrepancy is swollen by the large influx of young adult, single, male immigrants, a minority of young adult delinquents are still likely to be deprived of that stable, marriage-oriented relationship which appears a crucial element in keeping others out of the courts after late adolescence.

The attitude of the Poplar boys was that, although they did not 'want' to get married 'for a long while', they felt that the dangers of non-marriage exceeded the restraints and responsibilities of the event itself. Hence they thought that marriage was best 'while you're young' as 'You have to before long or you get

[41] Census 1961, London, pp. 15, 17, 21.

like blokes who've waited too long, they just sit around moping.' Hence you 'have to' get married, whether you want to or not: the alternatives are too depressing. When Pete found a 'regular' girl, he became noticeably brighter, better-dressed, and strenuously played down the fact that he was going out with a girl: 'She's a nuisance, but going round with her's better than sitting around the caff'; on marriage, he said: 'I'd sooner take the kids for a walk than sit around stinking caffs all day.' While a great deal of cheerful obscenity was attached to 'courting', it brought out a kind of suppressed respectability in the boys, for as long as the date lasted. The more serious the relationship, the more the boy was kept away from trouble, out of the caff. This was expected and encouraged: the only losers were the boys who never made it.

(*s*) *Conclusion*

Informal observation among delinquent boys in mid- to late-adolescence supported the theorisation of Cloward and Ohlin that severe deprivation of access to the legitimate opportunity structure is a necessary basis for the emergence of delinquent contracultures, another determinant being the presence or absence of access to the illegitimate opportunity structure. Crucial in Stepney and Poplar was the existence of an adequate, if limited, legitimate opportunity structure, coupled with that of a petty and disorganised illegitimate opportunity structure, associated with downward mobility and ethnic out-groups. Neither is it thought that reactions to 'failure' in the context of middle-class dominated institutions are responsible for generating a sufficient degree of 'status-frustration' to produce a contracultural response. However, no attempt was made to assess these reactions in the principal such context, the school. Inferences were based on expressions concerning job-satisfaction, and occupational expectations and aspirations, subsequent to school-leaving. While a generalised pattern of delinquency resembling an extension through adolescence of Cohen's 'parent male subculture' was prevalent, the absence of any real degree of malice and negativism seemed to preclude a contracultural interpretation, although—again—study within the context of those schools containing the most deprived children would probably have yielded different behaviour patterns. Certain forms of acquisitive delinquency indulged in by male adolescents, e.g. miscellaneous larcenies, 'fiddling', etc., have their counterparts in the adult world at most class and age-levels, and merely serve to emphasise the subjection of the population as a whole to a condition of 'mild economic anomie'. Likewise, certain forms of violence committed by working-class male adolescents are paralleled in the lower sectors of the adult working class. Those forms of delinquent behaviour peculiar to male adolescents, however, the 'pointless' break-ins, take-and-drive-away, group rowdyism, are thought to originate in the process of dissociation from school and work areas, and a consequent over-emphasis on, combined with relative lack of legitimate access to, certain leisure goals common to the dominant society. Hence the existence of a delinquent subculture, as distinct from a delinquent contraculture, i.e. commonly situated delinquents hold to a set of norms and share a set of values and beliefs hardly markedly different from those characteristic of other sub-groups in the population, as distinct from holding to and embracing a 'contra' normative system hostile to, and formed by reaction against, that of the dominant, 'middle-class' society.

The principal qualifications to the above lie in the basic approach. Contacts throughout the seven months of observation numbered no more than 50, and of these, only about 10—those centering round the Poplar group—were pursued throughout the time spent in the areas. The rest consisted of on-the-spot conversations. Other contacts were made with youth workers, social workers and teachers in the areas, but observation consisted mainly of simply seeing what went on. Observation was rigorously limited to Stepney and Poplar, and an attempt was made to cover all parts of the borough, except possibly the Isle of Dogs. While it is by no means implied that the picture given applies to other parts of inner London or its vast suburbs, it is thought that most delinquency of a subcultural nature elsewhere in London represents either a dilution or an intensification of the above pattern, rather than a radical departure from it. That is, the basis for contracultures exists in the very possibilities for such intensification.

Summary and Conclusions

I SUMMARY

The use of the concept of the delinquent subculture by Cohen and—adapted—by Cloward and Ohlin is not wholly satisfactory since 'subculture' is too readily applied as a blanket term to any set of sub-group norms, values and beliefs that deviate from an 'ideal-type' dominant middle-class normative system. The distinction by Yinger between 'subculture' and 'contraculture' is thought to clarify the issue, though Yinger's assumption that 'contraculture' subsumes delinquent subculture is in advance of empirical validation. (Confusion re 'subculture' simply reflects the traditional confusion over—and multiple definitions of—'culture') (Chapter 1). Yet neither subculture nor contraculture necessarily apply only to the value-systems of gang delinquents, nor is the gang framework a sufficient proof of a contracultural value-system: this point is illustrated by reference to two empirical studies which embody this issue (Chapter 2).

The two major approaches to delinquent subcultural theorisation—those by Cohen (and Short) and by Cloward and Ohlin—have tended to be regarded as either mutually exclusive (as by Cloward and Ohlin themselves) or as essentially homogeneous (as by some empirical investigators, notably Clark and Wenninger.) Examination of their hypotheses in detail suggests that the points of difference which emerge in the exposition of their theories are due more to differential concentration on certain aspects of the 'five classes of questions' inherent in this theorisation, rather than to substantive differences. Moreover, after the differences due to differential exposition have been eliminated, the apparently

Summary and Conclusions

substantive differences remaining are seen to flow from Cloward and Ohlin's over-simplification of the Cohen-Short position on two variables: first, middle-class orientation; and second, the 'parent subculture'. These differences can feasibly be reconciled by the introduction of community-type and age-level variables, as utilised in part by Clark and Wenninger and Reiss and Rhodes, and despite the discarding of the latter by Cloward and Ohlin. These innovations would possibly accommodate also their disagreements over types of subcultural *process*. (Chapter 3).

The welter of critiques on the above subcultural theorisation can be classified into four main types: 'limiting', 'extensive', 'applied' and 'basic'. With the exception of one 'applied' study of values in gang delinquency, all critiques so far can be shown either to have internal inconsistencies, to have been anticipated by subcultural theorisation, to be compatible with the major hypotheses, or to enrich them. Despite this, subcultural theorisation is far from validation, and can likely survive only at the expense of considerable modification. Herein lies its promise, but the danger is that it will be applied recklessly to disparate phenomena. What is needed is a firm sense of the limitations of subcultural theorisation on delinquency. (Chapter 4). Such an example of recklessness might be the attempt to apply subcultural theorisation to the English scene, where delinquency in general is hardly a major social problem, where gang delinquency on the American model is non-existent, and where lack of research makes for difficulties not experienced by American investigators. What data exist, however, suggest the reality of subculture, if not contraculture, in large urban and metropolitan areas. The real research question emerges as being whether or not, or to what degree, the male working-class 'failure' is faced with a 'problem of adjustment' at all. (Chapter 5).

Statistical data on crime commission and delinquent residence (ages 8–25) in two East London boroughs, Stepney and Poplar, were used to test two limited propositions inferred from the theorisation of Cohen and of Cloward and Ohlin, on age-level differences and on between-area differences. A fairly distinct offence structure broadly characterised three age-levels: pre- to mid-adolescence, mid- to late-adolescence, early adulthood. Only the early adult offences differed between the boroughs; through adolescence, the regularities of delinquent behaviour appeared more striking than the between-borough differences, though a more distinct semi-'conflict' pattern emerged in Poplar than in Stepney. The data support Cohen's emphasis on age-level differences, and his concept of the 'parent male' subculture seems most relevant to the illegal behaviour involved. But the character of the West Stepney 'criminal' area makes comparative judgment difficult about the proposition inferred from Cloward and Ohlin. More generally, the data confirmed the absence of gang delinquency, although the group factor—declining in importance with age—is still important in late adolescence; also, accomplice rates varied very much by offence. Recidivism rates for all ages were shown to be heavier for the two boroughs than for the MPD generally. Lack of convergence between the delinquency rates for different age-levels by 'natural' area led to the conclusion that either age-specific delinquency and adult crime derived from distinct aetiologies, or the nature of habitual adult crime in the East End acted more as a repellent than a stimulus to young offenders. It was hypothesised that working-class adolescents associated adult criminality with downward mobility, rather than the reverse. Also (while about one-eighth of delinquents not in school had been unemployed for more than three months) the full-employment situation, in London and the South-East, probably crucially influences the mode of delinquent response. Hence, the pattern of delinquency is of a very different order to that emphasised by American sources. This pattern of offences peculiar to mid- to late-adolescents did not seem to be much affected by the presence in Stepney—but not in Poplar—of what the police term a 'criminal class'. (Chapter 6).

This picture was confirmed by informal observation in the boroughs, in particular with one group in Poplar, whose offences fitted the pattern shown by the crime data: petty break-ins, take-and-drive-away, minor rowdyism, various larceny offences. While their expressed norms, values and beliefs hardly differed markedly from those of the adult lower working-class, which are essentially conservative, their differential concentration on these norms, etc. in a specifically 'leisured' context warrants the use of the subculture concept, though not that of contraculture. Their illegal behaviour seemed to be due not to 'alienation' or 'status frustration', but to a process of dissociation from middle-class dominated contexts of school, work and recreation. This disenchantment provoked an over-emphasis on purely 'leisure' goals—sedulously fostered by commercial 'teenage' culture—rather than on other non-work areas. In a situation where he both needs to attain such goals, and cannot readily do so legitimately, the working-class boy is especially prone to illegal behaviour as a means of 'manufacturing' their ethos. Yet the working-class boy who has undergone this process, who has been hampered in school by his attachment to working-class values, reacts to 'failure' not by frustration, reaction-formation etc., but by the re-affirmation of the working-class value-system. Its social constraints still broadly apply, and the normative early marriage—with its family responsibilities, need for a steady job, need to 'get by' if not 'get on'—rob the leisure context of its attraction: alternative solutions have been provided. The need for 'exploit' is killed. This pattern of delinquency is to be distinguished from adolescent offences which characterise offenders of all age-levels generally, whose recent increases have been due, hypothetically, to an increasingly emphasised 'mild economic anomie'. It is also to distinguish it from delinquency springing from gross personal pathologies. It is thought that the pattern outlined above accounts for a serious proportion of group juvenile delinquency, and any general increase in 'dissociation' from the realms of school and work, and exacerbation of leisure goals as a consequence, will result in more delinquency of an 'exploit' variety. There is clearly room along this leisure dimension for goal-restriction severe enough and visible enough to generate contracultural, as distinct from subcultural, modes of adaptation. This may have already occurred in areas less traditionally working-class than the areas studied.

We are now in a better position to answer the question raised in Chapter 5; does the English 'corner boy', accounted a failure in school and work by middle-class standards, typically encounter any 'problem of adjustment' at all? From the evidence presented it appears that he may do, but not of the kind depicted by Cohen as facing his American counterpart. The English 'corner boy' successfully traverses the humiliations of school and job allocation by his re-affirmation of traditional working-class values. This is much what Cohen meant by saying that he 'revises his aspirations downwards'. But in one sphere, that of leisure proper, the old values have lost their potency, and it is to this sphere that the 'corner boy' displaces his search for achievement from the areas of school and work, and from other non-work areas. Beer and skittles, the darts match, the working men's club and the union have little significance for him. In leisure, therefore, the old solutions no longer apply; for the 'corner boy' with 'time on his hands' and 'nothing to lose', the palliated delinquent subculture is an attractive and functional solution to a most intensely-felt problem. This is not to say that non-delinquent working-class and middle-class youth face no 'problems of adjustment' in leisure: however, to echo Cohen's emphasis on the different distribution of problems throughout the social class structure, the working-class 'corner boy' is the only one to depend exclusively on leisure as the framework for 'exploit'.

II CONCLUSIONS

On the working basis that dissociation—not alienation—is the normative response of working-class male adolescents to semi- and unskilled work (and to no work at all), and that this is the primary source of much of the delinquency *peculiar* to male adolescents—the analysis should take into account possible preventive measures in three areas: work, school and leisure. Research should also be directed at the efficacy of various 'intervening variables' which operate to keep the delinquency-prone youth from delinquency, assuming that all working-class boys whose 'life chances' push them inexorably towards semi- and unskilled work are in a delinquency-promoting life situation. This is to reverse the conventional procedure, which is to assume that all adolescents are in a conformity-promoting life-situation, and which directs research towards 'intervening variables' which operate to make a boy delinquency-prone. The vast bulk of research in criminology has been directed along these lines in the search for factors which divert the boy from conformity to deviance: 'broken homes', maternal/paternal deprivation, family fragmentation, character-structure: even much sociological theory has implied that it is only when a crime-oriented 'lower class culture' wins out against the conformist conventional culture that a boy adopts deviant behaviour-patterns. However, if it is assumed that the working-class boy *starts out* in a delinquency-prone life-situation, these variables are seen as *aggravating*

Summary and Conclusions

rather than as intervening factors, and the researcher is freed to look for variables which keep the working-class boy *from* delinquency: 'college-boy' performance at school; stable middle-class-orientated or 'respectable' stable working-class family background; promise of skilled employment; political activity; community activity; home-centredness; stable courtship; legitimate leisure opportunities, etc. It is obvious that this approach involves research no less difficult than the usual approach: but at least its frame of reference appears more realistic. Instead of regarding the working-class delinquent as a deviant in a conformity-promoting society, it is possible to regard the working-class boy as born into a pre-ordained delinquency-promoting situation. Our task can only then be to change that situation, so that the bulk of working-class youth is freed from pressures to deviancy and heavy personal costs.

Of the three areas mentioned as in need of re-organisation, leisure is the most amenable and the most attractive proposition, but it is here argued that—as indicated in the previous chapter—the 'leisure' problem is at root a work and education problem. Were it not for our educational system's failure to engage the interests and energies of the average and below-average working-class boy, with its subsequent corollaries of dissociation from areas of work and school, his leisure problem would be far less acute. It is instructive here to contrast the dissociation-alienation reaction polarities between British and American youth, taking as a reference point a start made by Turner's distinction between *modes* of ascent through education.[1] Turner maintains that in any industrial society, the *mode* of upward mobility via education is just as crucially important as the *extent* of upward mobility. In Britain, elite status is *given* by existing elites on the basis of ability-linked qualities; in America, elite status is *won* by ability-linked achievement: the first Turner terms 'sponsored', the second 'contest' mobility. Here, one strand of Turner's argument stands out: that in the 'sponsored' system, final selection decisions are made as early as possible in the educational cycle, so that the process of acculturation can get under way; in the 'contest' system, final selection decisions are delayed as long as possible

[1] R. H. Turner, 'Modes of Ascent Through Education: "Sponsored" and "Contest" Mobility'. Ch. 12 in Floud, Halsey and Anderson, *Education, Economy and Society* (1961).

so that equality of opportunity is ensured. The central problem for the British system is thus refinement of the criteria for *selection*; for the American system, the development of incentives for *motivation*. In both, a core issue is the 'drop-out' (America) or the 'early leaver' (Britain), but here there are crucial differences in definition: the American 'drop-out' is any boy who refuses to finish high school and so qualify for college entrance; the British 'early leaver' is a boy who has already been pre-selected for higher education in the grammar school, but fails or refuses to stay the course. The point at issue here is that for the British boy, the educational contest is over by the age of 11 or, inferentially, by the age of 7–8 when 'streaming' begins;[2] for the American boy, the contest is technically open until the age of 17. Either way, the costs of failure are severe, but they differ in the reactions they evoke. For the British boy, dissociation is engendered and strengthened by the earliness at which selection (and rejection) takes place: the result is a certain fatalism towards the roles in school and work to which he has been allocated,[3] and an overt stress on fulfilment through leisure comes early. For the American boy, alienation is engendered and strengthened by the lateness with which final decisions are made, but rejection or inability to conform to ultimate criteria is anticipated, and an overt stress on protest comes early. Moreover, the American system lends itself more readily to the entertainment of unrealistic ambitions late into adolescence, so that rejection (in effect) comes all the more cruelly: the British adolescent has had no time and no incentives to nurture such ambitions. It is no surprise to find that the ambitions of British secondary modern pupils are not only firmly geared to their actual life-chances (Veness),[4] but are also much less prone to 'fantasy' aspirations than their American counterparts (M. D. Wilson).

[2] A point confirmed in J. W. B. Douglas, *The Home and the School* (1964).

[3] So much so that, in anticipation of rejection at 11+, the bulk of working-class boys in turn reject the 11+ ethic, *preferring* the secondary modern to the grammar school and opting out of the academic rat-race prior to selection procedures. This is truly subversive of meritocracy, and represents a refusal to be motivated to strive . . . etc. Unfortunately, this involves not only immense wastage of ability, but a premature cynicism about the role of education in their personal and social development which limits their scope for, and awareness of, *choice* in every sphere of life, not simply the occupational.

[4] T. Veness, *The School-leavers* (1962); Mary D. Wilson, The Vocational Preferences of Secondary Modern School-children,' *Brit. J. Educ. Psych.*, Vol. 23, 1953, pp. 97–113.

Summary and Conclusions

Hence, the working-class male adolescent's leisure problems originate in the school- and work-situations to which he is destined by socioeconomic role allocation. These connections are concealed, since his reactions to work-school are not in general of an alienation-status-frustration variety, but the relatively toned-down response of dissociation. Moreover, this propensity for dissociation from the semi- and unskilled job will feasibly worsen as the prospects for semi- and unskilled labour deteriorate. The process is well under way already, and automation will further erode the market- and work-situation of these levels of occupation, at the same time as it increases the visibility of the occupational rewards for skill and educational/technical qualifications.[5] If the situation of the semi- and unskilled young worker is not to deteriorate much further, radical re-organisation of the areas of school and work are basic, and must go further than 'revolutions' we have failed to at worst initiate and at best fulfil in the past.

(*a*) *Work and Education*

At present, much secondary modern education serves simply—and functionally—as a massive irritant on those to whom it imparts the meagre skills and discipline needed for recruitment as the unskilled and semi-skilled personnel of the future. In the U.K., prospects for even the manual working-class elite revolve around an outdated apprenticeship system and limited provision for further education. For those at the bottom of the heap', c. 25–30 per cent. of the age-group, there is only the 'dead-end' to which they become early resigned, and from which they early dissociate themselves. It is futile to say the opportunities exist for all when only a minority can be catered for: as long as 'dead-end' jobs persist, there will be a large minority who are not only beckoned into them, but who inevitably will have to take them. Their only recompense is being bought off for a few years by wages which are relatively high for adolescence. (This advantage soon disappears in adulthood). The problem here is partly one of 'social definition':[6] in the U.S.A. it is actually being implied

[5] At present, union strength and collective bargaining have gained some equivalence between much manual and white collar work in terms of income, if not in terms of status, security, 'fringe' benefits, etc., but see R. M. Titmuss, *Income Distribution and Social Change* (1962).

[6] R. A. Cloward, *Social Problems, Social Definitions and Social Opportunities*, pp. 47–48 (April 1963, *unpubl.*).

that, but for 'drop-outs', there would be no 'dead-end' jobs. 'Judging from the near-panic that drop-outs are creating in some circles, one might easily suppose that a precipitous rise in the rate of drop-outs had preceded the concern. Actually, the reverse appears to be true: that Americans of all classes and ethnic affiliations are more education-minded than ever before. As a consequence, rates of drop-out have been declining compared with earlier decades.

Why then the acute anxiety about drop-outs now rather than some years earlier? The answer is to be found in the economic structure. The school system has never adequately engaged and educated children from families at the bottom of our class structure. *In earlier years, this tendency aroused little concern because alienated adolescents could leave school and be absorbed into a vast unskilled and semi-skilled labour-force.* These manual labouring positions had to be filled; someone must always do the less pleasant work of the society. The school system helped to make the prospect of these less pleasant jobs more pleasant by *making education itself an irritant* for children from culturally different and academically unsophisticated families. Under the circumstances, only the most serious advocates of egalitarianism were likely to detect and decry the way in which the society was, through its educational enterprise, sifting and sorting children into manual and non-manual positions according to their social class rather than their basic endowment.[7]

Now automation has changed the picture; the need for manual labour has shrunk and will shrink much more. But educational practices remain much the same. No massive, genuine effort is made to engage the low-income child academically, and so he continues to drop-out: except that now he cannot be absorbed into the labour force. Hence the sudden tendency to define drop-outs as a 'social problem'.

But even if rates of drop-out were to diminish rapidly, we would not be appreciably better off: we would simply have a more sophisticated body of unemployed. For educated or not, we are faced with an occupational structure which is shrinking

[7] It is interesting that even Cloward here pinpoints wrongful *selection*, as distinct from vastly unequal status and rewards from manual/non-manual and unskilled/skilled employment; i.e. the U.S.A.'s basic unemployment problem blinds him to the deficiences of a full employment situation where job holding is vitiated by lack of status, autonomy, privileges, prospects, etc.

relative to the men it must absorb. Thus the streets of our urban slums are slowly filling with young men *who have no prospect of finding manhood through work*: who are coming of age in a society which neither wants them nor needs them.'

The relevance of this analysis to the English situation cannot be stressed too highly. Even in the present *status quo*, the young male unskilled and semi-skilled worker gets a raw deal: if automation is allowed to constitute the prospect of under- and unemployment in this sector, without adequate provision being made to revolutionise the school and further education systems, the raw deal will worsen into no deal at all. If the sizeable rump of non-skilled young male workers become convinced of their own expendability, their reaction in terms of delinquency could well be explosive, and assume fully-fledged contracultural proportions. (Other reactions are possible: high rates of mental illness, for example: crucial here are their definitions of the source of their frustrations). The least likely reaction is the most applicable to their needs: political activism (except for quasi-fascist irrationalism.) If the non-skilled young are to be denied the chance of engaging in building a technological society, as well as benefiting from its performance, the price they exact will be high.

Attempts to 'buy off' their discontent (bigger and better youth clubs) will not work; nor, if they offend by this refusal, will bigger and better borstals. Their root need is to engage in —and be rewarded adequately by—the society in which they live. They are at present humiliated by the subordinate role: likely they will soon be denied any role at all. The paramount need is for a revolution in comprehensive and further education paralleling that envisaged for the universities, and that already silently being effected in many branches of primary education. But for such a revolution to work, for it to engage the interests and energies of lower working-class boys, a restructuring of post-educational work-incentive is basic. Past and present attempts to invigorate secondary education have been and are being undermined by the antiquated structure of manual work. Continuing links between school and work until the early twenties, ways back in as well as ways to new skills and qualifications, are essential. The Crowther[8] and Newsom[9] Reports could be said to

[8] *15–18*, 2 vols., C.A.C.E., 1959.
[9] *Half Our Future*, C.A.C.E., 1964.

provide the blueprint for this kind of future: and in many respects, they do so. The Newsom Report, with its emphasis on the need to impart as much scope for *choice* as possible, both into the syllabus, and into the way the subjects are taught, at secondary moderns, is—in essence—a revolutionary document, which promises to a fully comprehensive system more than would be possible within an unreformed tripartite structure. In its recommendations for overcoming the problems of 'slum' schools, it goes far beyond mere re-building schemes. By its emphasis on 'pupil-centred' teaching, as distinct from the traditional subject-tied approach, it demonstrates how 'formal' education can be related to the personal and social development of children who have previously rejected 'school' or deemed it irrelevant to their lives. By raising the school-leaving age to 16 for all from 1971 on, it also commits the schools to a radical re-thinking of their teaching content and methods, since 'more of the same' would patently be a disaster, and merely raise the peak delinquency age from 14 to 15: school-leaving minus one.

In so far as Newsom's proposals succeed, however, pressure will be exerted on that section of the educational structure which is extremely ill-equipped to meet it: the further education sector. At present, according to the Henniker-Heaton Report[10] on day-release, only 28 per cent of boys aged 15–17 and not in full-time education were granted day-release. Provisional figures from a survey in Bethnal Green show a similar figure of 26 per cent, with another 19 per cent who have experienced some form of evening-only education.[11] Of 148 boys in this sample (aged 15–20) who had been to secondary modern schools, including a few who had been to comprehensives, 55 per cent had had no education since leaving school at 15. Moreover, these figures take no account of courses discontinued, failure rates, and non-attendance, especially severe in evening-only classes. Also, day-release courses are in general narrowly vocational in content, the willingness of the employer to consent to release varies enormously by industry, and type and size of firm, and—under the present voluntary system—incentives to take advantage of day-release facilities are in general limited to the apprentice

[10] *Day Release*, Ministry of Labour, 1964.

[11] To be published by the Institute of Community Studies. Figures quoted by kind permission of Peter Willmott.

or 'trainee', who is already *relatively* well catered for. The irony is that compulsion to undergo full-time education to the age of 16 has been introduced for those who would not have stayed on voluntarily: yet should the assumptions on which this measure is based turn out to be correct, and a vastly increased number of adolescents begin to entertain higher educational and occupational aspirations, no provision has been made to extend the framework of compulsion to part-time further education beyond the age of 16 to meet the demands that they will make. Moreover, since it seems desirable to adhere to Crowther's recommendations for a three-stage implementation of compulsory part-time further education for all—which allows for a five-year regional experiment and a phased extension to the rest of the country taking at least 4 years, all subsequent to the raising of the school-leaving age to 16—such a system appears uattainable before the 1980's, when the needs of Newsom demand that it should arrive by the mid-1970's. The only answer seems to be to begin the regional experiment in further education for all before, not after, the raising of the school-leaving age. Otherwise, for the first and most crucial decade of the Newsom reorganisation, the further education system will be inadequate in face of the expectations generated. The forces making for 'anomie' in such a context would be enormous: and the promise of the Newsom proposals would be needlessly threatened.

No claim is made for comprehensive and further education for all as automatic delinquency preventives, though—on the basis of this analysis—their establishment is a pre-requisite for any halt to rising delinquency rates. They are not recommended for therapeutic, but for the structural, reasons. Automation must bring redundancy in all routine work, so that adaptability and flexibility of skills must be integral to the socialisation of any adolescent in an urban, industrial society. Without automation, or with its postponement, economic stagnation and far worse problems than adolescent under-employment would be inevitable. In planning for automation, therefore, the question is not whether we should have a further education system within the framework of compulsion or not, but when it should arrive and what form it should take. Ideally, the comprehensive framework would be kept intact for all till the age of 18 by the evolution of an institutional form to accommodate sixth forms, technical colleges and all forms of part-time further education. Otherwise, stratification along meritocratic lines will develop as the system grows piecemeal. There should be no 'siphoning off' of early leavers to institutionally separate County Colleges. Also ideally, a regional experiment along these lines should be started by the late 1960's, in order to anticipate both automation and the age-group expansion of the 1970's, and to give the Newsom re-organisation as much support as possible in the further education field. Without these possibilities, the current secondary modern child's conception of the nature of school and work as marginally important only is unlikely to change very much.

(b) Leisure

Little can be done here to affect the situation radically, but even in the present context, much more provision could be made for the boys whose aversion to the present Youth Service sends them 'on the town'—which has correspondingly little to offer, but offers it without overtones of charity-authoritarianism. Such experiments as the Canteens, self-run clubs of the Leicester Youth Ventures kind, spontaneous provision for teenagers made by Tenants' Associations,[12] have proved viable, if hampered and often killed by lack of funds. (The duplicity to which many such schemes are reduced in the quest for money from orthodox fund-giving bodies is itself an area for study.) The desire for a visibly respectable end-product still vitiates the bulk of youth-service fund disposal. The point is not yet taken, despite Albemarle, that the boys at whom youth work should primarily be aimed simply are not willing to conform to success criteria based on 'activity participation'. Also, the machinery set up by Albemarle for the dispensation of funds to 'experiments' (two-thirds to follow if one-third is found) succeed only in diverting funds to already-established, or respectably-backed, ventures. This is not to attack provision for 'respectable' boys, simply to attack provision for them *exclusively*.

But in the absence of work- and school-satisfactions, in the absence of incentives to legitimate autonomy in the educational and occupational areas, it is doubtful if even the provision of full autonomy in leisure would be functionally equivalent.

[12] See G. Williams, in *Anarchy*, Vol. 30, August 1963, pp. 250–251, for a note on the provision made by Tenants Associations of a completely voluntary nature.

Summary and Conclusions

Only the radical restructuring of achievement means and goals in work and school will lessen the likelihood that the bulk of semi- and unskilled working-class male teenagers will attain their leisure goals in ways which are frequently delinquent. Hence, the implicit assumption of policy-making institutions that youth work with these boys is a waste of time is substantially correct: the source of their problem lies in the school and work systems, and leisure-time provision for them can be a palliative only.[13]

In conclusion, a paradox must be resolved. It has been proposed that status-frustration (in Cohen's sense) is not the source of the vast bulk of teenage male delinquency: but the very measures proposed to cut down on delinquency might seem to aim at promoting status-consciousness and—by inference—status frustration, thus providing the necessary base for the emergence of delinquent motivations on 'American' lines. By breaking down working-class conservatism, the main force for aspiration-control would be removed. In defence, it is suggested that an attack on working-class conservatism is not—despite the data of Jackson and Marsden—*necessarily* an attack on working-class solidarity, in so far as it impinges on the working-class teenager. Rather, it is thought that the tendency is for skilled workers to be more politically-oriented in a non-extremist way than for semi- and unskilled workers, whose political awareness and involvement is either low-level or extremist.[14] Alterations in the present school-work *status quo* would, far from merely invigorating delinquency from status-frustration sources, make for political awareness—which is ultimately the only alternative to delinquency for the stifled working-class adolescent, in the phase of non-attachment preceding home-centredness and the channelling of his aspirations into family life.

It could be argued that, even if no re-structuring takes place, delinquency in the late teens will still be curbed by the further juvenilisation of marriage, in itself the main check to the spread-over of delinquency into early adulthood. But even granted this association, delinquency in the early and mid-teens will continue to intensify and, but for early marriages, would hoist the rates of

[13] This assertion naturally excludes work with disturbed and handicapped youngsters.

[14] See R. Dahrendorff, *Unskilled Labour in British Industry* (1956), unpublished Ph.D. thesis, L.S.E.

adult criminality. Foreseeably, delinquency rates in late adolescence will increase exponentially only, *provided* the socioeconomic conditions for fruitful early marriage are maintained: but slump, unemployment or redundancy in this sector would have its effect on marriage-orientation and, unless resultant discontents were politically focused, would result in postponement of the transition from quasi-delinquent to conforming behaviour. In an a-political context, the automatic solution would be an increase in delinquent activity, feasibly of a nihilistic, contracultural type, the more so since an increasingly affluent society has endorsed rising expectations and aspirations among male, working-class adolescents who—unlike older members of the community—have had no experience of real adversities in the labour market.

[4]
Gambling as a Sociological Problem

There have been remarkably few sociological attempts to account for gambling – and this applies whether 'accounting' is taken in the sense of explanation, in the sense of understanding, or as covering both simultaneously. Whatever the reasons for this strange gap in sociological accounting – and the sheer absence of reasonably comprehensive empirical evidence may be among them – it should soon be filled by the re-emergence in fashion of carefully conducted small-scale ethnographic inquiries, and the growing availability of officially designed statistics and opinion polls. As things stand, the theoretical perspectives against which such data can be weighed may turn out to have been false starts, or of severely limited use. Nevertheless, they are all we have, and for their authors to have constructed them at all is a high contribution in a field otherwise bereft of all but polemic.

Gambling as play

In the most consummate attempt yet to give play its due in the creation of culture, Huizinga's *Homo Ludens*,[1] gambling is given short shrift as a parasitic, materialistic and entirely negative activity: the dark side of play. Huizinga was concerned to define play as exhaustively as possible and to link the 'play instinct' with institutions and activities hitherto conceived as embodying the antithesis of play: law, war and philosophy (as well as those conveniently viewed as closer to play: literature, art and music). By sheer force of protean example Huizinga seeks to convince us that 'civilization does not come *from* play like a babe detaching itself from the womb: it arises *in* and *as* play and never leaves it.' The less scope for play to flourish, the more its spirit is suppressed or eliminated in institutional life, the less scope also for civilization to survive. Huizinga could see regimented leisure as far more inimical to civilization than overwork in which the spirit of play was nevertheless alive.

It is on this basis that Caillois[2] seeks to build a sociology not merely *of* games but derived *from* games. He repudiates the view that games can be reduced to mere residues of former tradition, or childish imitations or substitutes for 'real' life. He defines play as (a) *free*, not compulsory or forced; (b) *separate*, circumscribed within limits of time and space, carved out from 'ordinary life'; (c) *uncertain*, as to its outcome; (d) *unproductive*; (e) *governed by rules*; and (f) '*make-believe*' – 'accompanied by a special awareness of a second reality, or of a free unreality, as against real life' (p. 10). He then distinguishes four characteristics as underlying the myriad forms assumed by play: *competition* (agon); *chance* (alea); *simulation* (mimicry); and *vertigo* (ilinx) – the names in brackets are the closest terms in classical or modern language to the ideal types Caillois wishes to distinguish.

The main contrast in which we are interested is that between agon and alea. Agon stresses the ability of contestants to surmount obstacles and opponents to achieve victory. Alea renders the outcome quite independent of the players. Both stress the equality of the contestants under the rules, but seek to bring this about in different ways: agon by handicapping or equalizing *skills* as far as possible: alea by compensating with profit as closely as possible to the risk involved. In agon the contestants rely upon their own abilities and seek to minimize the role played by chance; in alea 'it is the very capriciousness of chance that constitutes the unique appeal.' The player is active in the one, passive in the other.

> In agon, his only reliance is upon himself; in alea . . . he depends upon everything *except* himself. Agon is a vindication of personal responsibility; alea is a negation of the will, a surrender to destiny . . . Both, however, obey the same law – the creation for the players of conditions of pure equality denied them in real life (pp. 17–19).

Hence their natures are both oppositional yet complementary, a compatibility heightened by the battening of alea onto the uncertainty of outcome contrived in agon by the equalization of chances. In simulation, the escape from oneself to play the role of another, and in vertigo, 'the attempt to momentarily destroy stability of perception and inflict a kind of voluptuous panic upon an otherwise lucid mind' (p. 23), as in the whirling games of children and ecstatic dances, no such implication of equality occurs. The germ of Caillois's evolutionism emerges.

Each type contains the seeds of its own corruption: *agon* through professionalization, cheating, the ritualization of the means of victory over and above the point of the game; *alea* through the degeneration of the appreciation of impersonal chance into the belief in luck, destiny, superstitions, etc.; *simulation* through the *loss* of self in role-play, or (in modern societies) over-identification with fantasized hero-figures, as in fan-worship; and *vertigo* through the synthesizing or alteration of consciousness by resort to drugs.

Of the possible combinations of competition, chance, mimicry and vertigo, only two are truly compatible: competition–chance, and mimicry–vertigo. The latter are seen as typical of 'Dionysian' societies, ruled by masks, possession, shamanism and magic – Amerindian, Australasian, and African tribal societies exemplify this combination. The former are seen as typical of comparatively 'rational' societies – Chinese, Assyrian, Roman and Inca – in which order and merit are the basis for social cohesion. The latter are rooted in primeval fears of the unknown which they palliate by recourse to pantheism and ecstasy; the former have at least *some* notion of a *cosmos*, of a universe which can be ordered and perceived as stable in crucial respects. To Caillois, civilization can exist only in so far as the former displaces the latter as a principle of social organization.

Whatever one makes of Caillois's evolutionism, especially in the wake of Lévi-Strauss and the destruction of tribal cultures in large parts of both the American continent and Africa by civilizations which then consign their victims to the shanty town and the pursuit of alea, his central distinction seems valid, and leads him to pose the issue of the consequences for agonistically oriented societies of the stubborn persistence of the aleatory principle. Wealth/poverty, glory/obscurity, power/servitude are relatively constant polarities even in the most egalitarian societies. Despite reforms and even revolutions, most people are 'unable radically to change their station in life. From this arises the nostalgia for crossroads, for immediate solutions offering the possibility of unexpected success, even if only relative. Chance is courted because hard work and personal qualifications are powerless to bring such success about' (p. 114). Alea therefore seems, under these conditions, a necessary complement to and compensation for agon. Hence, while modern democratic societies may deplore alea and seek to eliminate it along with mimicry and vertigo, it remains tenacious and paradoxically compensates (as indeed do mimicry and vertigo) for the cruelties of merit.

Caillois cites one powerful instance of the importance of games of chance in the modern world, choosing – ironically in view of his evolutionary ideas – the Jogo de Bicho in Brazil. This lottery is played[3] by 60–70 per cent of the population, each spending *on average* 1 per cent of his monthly income *daily* on the game. All manner of corruptions are involved in its machinery and disposal of winnings, but for Caillois its main drawback is *economic*. 'The game practically immobilizes an appreciable part of disposable income by causing it to circulate too quickly. It is thus unavailable for the nation's economic development or for improving the standard of living of the inhabitants.' Once committed to gambling, capital is virtually immobilized, since winnings are usually reinvested. The Jogo de Bicho symbolizes the waste and unproductiveness of gambling.

In criticism of Caillois, two further points should be made:

1 His assessment of the aleatory factor in egalitarian societies does not cover the well-documented link between aristocratic life and gambling. If alea survives and even flourishes chiefly for compensatory reasons, why should the class most beneficently endowed with wealth and status be so clearly committed to upholding the 'Sport of Kings' and the green baize? Happily, the answer can easily be given from within Caillois's own model: those whose status is based on the aleatory principle of heredity will cultivate it at play.

2 A more serious criticism is that Caillois does not really convey the *meanings*, as distinct from the formal *essences* of different forms of games, and especially of gambling. He generally treats games as self-evidently attractive since victory or profit accrue from them, or as attractive in terms of distinctive attributes, e.g. they are free, spontaneous, etc., unlike the workaday world of everyday life. But this comes close to the very reductionism he sought to avoid at the outset. He analyses games in terms of their formal properties with great assurance; but we are left wondering why people really play them.

For illumination on that score, we turn to the work of Erving Goffman.

Gambling as action

Goffman's essay on games and gambling[4] is so beautifully structured that the argument is best put by condensation rather than by rearrangement of its parts. Analysing outwards from the archetype of two boys tossing a coin *for* the coin, he ends by rendering gambling intelligible in the context of a total culture. The culture in question is naturally that of the USA: but the range of application is universal.

In all games of chance or skill, the outcome is problematical, the odds ideally equal. The span of play covers four quite separate phases: 'squaring off' – in which the boys decide to toss for the coin; determination – in which it describes its parabola and lands; disclosure – in which the outcome is revealed; and settlement – the winner takes the coin, or the play is renewed. These phases inhere in any game, and also in most events in everyday life, But in marriage, for example, while the span can cover anything from a few weeks to a lifetime, it usually approximates to the latter rather than the former. 'The distinctive property of games and contests is that once the bet has been made, the outcome is determined and payoff awarded *all in the same breath of experience*' (p. 156). Everyday life is usually quite otherwise; it is the *uninterrupted* nature of the sequence which gives most forms of gambling their intensity, though the lengths of each phase and the pause between them are variables which differ from game to game.

It is in his discussion of the *consequentiality* of gambling that Goffman lays the foundations for an understanding of its career structures, the termini of which are occupied by the hardened or 'compulsive' gambler on the one hand, and by the professional gambler on the other. In general, the consequentiality of gambling – 'What winning allows and losing disallows the player later on to do' – is far more manageable than that of real life chance-taking. But what makes gambling consequential *at all* is the staking of money on the outcome of the bet, a practice conventionally held to originate in the human desire for gain. In a related essay,[5] however, Goffman allows a different view: that the purpose of the stake is to induce a correct seriousness in the attitude of players towards the game.[6] In common with Huizinga and Caillois, Goffman stresses that play and seriousness, far from being antithetical, eventually contrive to promote the most appropriate attitude-set towards games, which can only be enjoyed *to the full* if the players not only abide by the rules but do so with conviction. If players drift off the field halfway through a game, or play inattentively or absent-mindedly, the game is to a large extent spoilt for the rest of the players. As Huizinga first observed, it is the spoilsport, not the cheat, who is most inimical to the spirit of play. Moreover, play is not simply different from everyday life: the occasion, and often the setting for it, have to be *set apart from* everyday life, and this circumscription is not simply to facilitate the action – it is to maintain the boundaries between play and everyday life, boundaries which are fragile and have to be carefully contrived and sustained.

The stake is the player's commitment to *serious* play: it is also the prime determinant of its consequentiality. For play can become *too* serious and, as a result, increasingly consequential for the player. The greater the consequentiality, the more *fateful* the enterprise becomes. Over time, he may plunge too deeply, and what began as serious play becomes fateful action – as to why he might be drawn into such a spiral at all, we can only follow the path set out by Goffman.

The human condition is primordially fateful. The life of even the best actuarial risk is fraught with danger, both physical and psychic. Men have accordingly arranged their lives to minimize risk, and to reassure themselves. Even so, certain occupations persist which amount to 'practical gambles', shot through with problematic consequentiality and abnormally vulnerable to contingency: financially risky commercial roles; physically dangerous jobs; jobs whose holders operate against a tight margin of success and failure; performing jobs subject to switches of fashion; roles whose occupants man the boundaries of civil order – the police; the armed forces; criminal roles and professional sportsmen. Yet even in these roles, procedures and norms are developed which minimize risk and contingency as far as possible. By 'copings' (taking physical care, being provident) and by 'defences' (taking psychic care to anticipate eventfulness), men seek to ward off uncertainty and contingency.

Fatefulness cannot be entirely eliminated. But even if it could, ambivalence would persist about such 'safe and momentless living'. For, in Western society at any rate, and American society in particular, we still believe that the truest record of an individual's makeup is revealed in his reaction to fateful activities sought out *without obligation*. It is these activities which constitute *action*, a term which had its slang beginning in the gambling world, for 'gambling is the prototype of action'. The term has been diffused and commercialized far beyond these boundaries, perhaps because 'we have become alive to action at a time when – compared to other societies – we have sharply curtailed in civilian life the occurrence of fatefulness of the serious, heroic and dutiful kind' (p. 193).

Action of the former kind is now to be found in commercialized sports; non-spectator risky sports; commercialized settings for action – casinos, race-tracks, fairs, amusement centres, etc.; and arenas for 'fancy milling', resort to large, tightly packed gatherings which offer the promise of excitement, contingency and proximity to 'real action' performers. Brief penetrations into high living are increasingly commercially provided by casinos, restaurants, airlines, even pubs and filling stations with an overlay of glamorous service. Action is routinely available – at a price – for those who need it only transiently, irrespective of their social and psychological state (though it is much more appealing to men than to women).

Action celebrates self-determination via the revelation of *character* under stress. Certain properties of character (as distinct from those of skill, training and technical accomplishment) can emerge only during fateful events. The performer is judged, 'essentialized', against the showing he makes at such times, is accorded a 'strong' or a 'weak' character in terms of moral extremes. The principal attributes of character to which his performance can attain are courage; gameness; integrity; gallantry; composure; and presence of mind. 'Character' can be dramatically acquired or lost – hence the particular appeal of action. '*Character is gambled* . . . The self can be voluntarily subjected to re-creation' (p. 238). Even if material loss ensues, a real gain of character can occur.

Action, then, is not mere impulsiveness or irrationality, nor is the chief motivation to gamble the desire for gain. 'The possibility of effecting reputation is the spur.' Those who never risk never avail themselves of the opportunity to gain or lose 'character' in this way: they thereby lose direct connection with some of the values of society, though they may vicariously experience them via the mass media. Soap operas, thrillers, Westerns, what the French term 'histoires héroiques', re-establish and confirm our connection with values concerning character. Yet it is via gambling that men commonly struggle to achieve character in a society which has all but arranged action out of everyday life.

The force of Goffman's essay on gambling is that he lifts gambling out of the moral abyss into which successive generations of commentators and reformers have consigned it and renders possible a consideration of its meaning which is freed from *a priori* associations of a negative kind. It may well be that there is a hint of bathos in his insistence on seeing the rather drab routines of, say, fruit-machine players as even an attenuated pursuit of the heroic. But, without his analysis, we are reduced to a behaviourist model of a mindless automaton seeking profit from a machine which has been skilfully designed to minimize that eventuality. His analysis also makes sense of features of 'this sporting life' which would otherwise be inexplicable. In his social mapping of the world of the race-track, Marvin Scott[7] echoes Goffman in his characterizations of the jockey as the 'last in the line of "men of honour"', displaying attributes of coolness, gallantry and integrity most crucially when *under pressure*: 'risk-taking is an essential prerequisite for a jockey to "emerge"'.

Such doubts as arise from his essay relate not to his analysis of gambling, action and character but to the relations he draws between these phenomena and the encircling culture and social structure. Goffman depicts a culture composed of two diverse value patterns:

prudential and incremental coping (the Calvinist way) and action (what in another context have been termed the 'subterranean' values of toughness, excitement and disdain for routine work).[8] These systems can, as far as individuals are concerned, be treated in everyday life as straight preferences or as uneasy choices, which co-exist as alternative guidelines for behaviour.

Goffman does not allow himself to be drawn as to the likely distribution of such choices throughout the social system. 'Certain segments of each community seem more responsive than others to the attraction of this kind of action' (p. 200). 'Fatefulness, which many persons avoid, others for some reason approve, and there are those who even construct an environment in which they can indulge it' (p. 214). These are statements which give little help in assessing *for whom* action as he describes it is likely to be most attractive. He does suggest that lower-class street gangs – 'well organized for disorganization' – are most open to fateful activities of a physical danger kind because – in a circular vein – such action is relatively 'least disruptive' and 'most tolerable' for their members. The cult of 'masculinity' ascribed by Miller[9] to lower-class culture in general is also seen by Goffman as fatefully inclined, though he prefers to subsume 'masculinity' under the rubric of 'character', rather than the reverse.

Do we then ascribe the probability of choosing prudence or action to a straight class-based matrix of cause and effect? This is exactly the kind of prediction which Goffman wishes to avoid. How do we account for the co-existence of such apparently incompatible value systems? The answer is that society needs both. 'The individual allows others to build him into their own plans in an orderly and effective way. The less uncertain his life, *the more society can make use of him*' (p. 174). However, 'although societies differ widely in the kinds of character they approve, no society *could long persist* if its members did not approve and foster this quality [i.e. integrity]' (p. 219, italics supplied). Society can afford to license integrity-generating action because 'the price of putting on these shows is likely to provide an automatic check against those who might be over-inclined to stage them' (p. 238). Finally, Goffman slides away into an ambiguous quasi-functionalism:

> Social organization everywhere has the problem of morale and continuity. Individuals must come to all these little situations with some enthusiasm and concern, for it is largely through such moments that social life occurs, and if a fresh effort were not put into each of them, society would surely suffer. The possibility of effecting reputation is the spur. We are allowed to think there

is something to be won in the moments that we face so that society can face moments and defeats them (pp. 238–9).

The chief issues that remain to be explored within Goffman's own terms of reference might be set out as follows:

1 How do the puritanical manage to survive psychologically in an action-packed culture? While Goffman's analysis was of the exact opposite question, it inevitably raises its mirror image.

2 How did it come about that the spheres in which action is now centred, gambling and mass spectator sports etc., have displaced spheres in which fatefulness of the 'serious, heroic and dutiful' kind gained fuller expression? There is precious little reference to what has happened to political and religious definitions of character in Goffman's work.

3 Do those who undertake the 'practical gamble' of everyday life – men in physically dangerous jobs, etc. – find themselves more, or less, drawn to the pursuit of action in the sphere of sport and gambling, or is there no necessary connection between the two? This remains a central ambiguity of Goffman's analysis. Some of these issues are, however, clarified further by the third perspective, to which we now turn.

Gambling as strain

In a monumental, but unfortunately unpublished, work completed in 1949 Devereux[10] provides what is still the most rounded and comprehensive attempt to account for the nature of gambling in relation to the social structure of the USA, or indeed of any society, urban-industrial or otherwise. To an astonishing extent, he anticipated the themes later developed rather differently by Caillois and Goffman. A then graduate student of Talcott Parsons, he approached his theme within a rigorous structural-functional framework, and rarely has the strength of that method been better exemplified. Indeed, the charges commonly made against structural-functionalism as a doctrine seem rather irrelevant when, as here, its utility as an organizing conceptual framework paid such rich dividends. There is, of course, the customary due paid to equilibrium-maintenance – but the doctrinal trappings are fortunately detachable from the substantive argument, a separability pointed to elsewhere by Homans[11] and Gellner.[12]

It would be futile in the space available to attempt an adequate summary of the full range and complexity of Devereux's argument. Rather, we shall focus initially on his characterization of gambling as predominantly characterized by *strain*, and then on his attempts to answer the following questions:

1 What are the bases for the social disapproval of gambling; and why, in the face of that disapproval, does it persist?

2 What are the social determinants of gambling?

To Devereux, while gamblers *affect* the cognitive detachment of rational, economic man, as in the attention paid to odds and probabilities, and in the cold-blooded reaction to success or failure, the façade hides the fact that each stake placed at hazard subjects the gambler to a

> veritable emotional shower bath . . . to the flesh and blood gambler, the situation is full of promise, but it is also full of mystery, and danger, and meaning . . . it is also fraught with strain: the conflicting valences and ambivalences of hope versus fear, risk versus security, power versus helplessness, and faith versus doubt are playing complicated melodies within his consciousness. The result is an intolerable, but not necessarily wholly unpleasant, state of tension (p. 695).

Paradoxically, this tension is often deliberately heightened by gamblers, who clearly find it pleasurable as *strain*. But it remains intolerable, and the gambler seeks ways to resolve it. Real pleasure may also lie in tension-*resolution*, which is all the more heightened the greater the strain involved. Gambling is an ordeal which produces tensions which *ought* to be intolerable but are effectively managed by self-discipline:

> it seems obvious that whereas the gambler may 'enjoy' these tensions, he is still fundamentally ambivalent about them. Having once exposed himself to the situation, he takes extraordinary pains to make himself comfortable within it. . . . Although most of the mechanisms function as accommodation devices, permitting gamblers to make the most of a bad situation . . . many of them also figure positively among the basic motivational elements in gambling (p. 743).

Clearly Devereux is here near to formulating the view of gambling as the prototype of action, and what to him are techniques of accommodation are to Goffman 'copings' and 'defences' – the belief in luck, the resort to animism, the investiture of luck as an attribute of people and of particular objects; the mental 'writing-off' of a stake to reduce eventual disappointment; the equation of stakes with business investments or with recreational expenditures; the focus on *odds* (the stake: jackpot ratio) rather than *probabilities* (the number of prizes: number of players ratio) in lotteries; and the belief in 'systems' as distinct from rational calculation of probabilities. Devereux's insistence on the strain and ambivalence inherent in gambling, whilst very close in meaning to Goffman's emphasis on the revelation of character *under pressure*, matches his analysis of strains and ambivalences inherent in the dominant culture. To Devereux, the answer to the conundrum of why gambling elicits such powerful disapproval (to the point of remaining almost wholly illegal in the USA, except in the State of Nevada) and yet persists and even flourishes despite such disapproval, is best sought by analysis of 'fundamental cleavages and ambivalences' within a common culture rather than as the product of friction between conflicting groups and codes. Any adequate theory of gambling should provide *homologous* accounts of the dynamics of gambling as a phenomenon, the dynamic of the social reaction to gambling, both as expressed by different groups and as institutionally based, and of the relationship between the two phenomena. The account which Devereux provides takes him back to Weber's theory of the spirit of capitalism and its relationship to the Protestant ethic.

The structural features of capitalism: an 'open' market; a generalized money system; political order; some '*laissez-faire*'; the institution of contract; and the system of private property, cannot be sustained and operated without certain kinds of motivation on the part of the individual. A capitalist society will seek to standardize as far as possible certain ideal-typical characteristics in its citizens:

1 *Economic self-interest of a 'rational' kind* 'Money', 'profits' etc. are the clear goals of the economic system and should govern economic behaviour. But since men need 'non-logical rules to live by', the economic world must be institutionally separated from the larger social framework, and outside it, its values should not apply, e.g. wives are not to be treated as means to economic ends, judged impersonally, etc.

2 *Competition* For maximal efficiency, the economic system needs high levels of aspirations, effective channels for vertical mobility, ideological stress on equality of opportunity, and a visible correlation between effort and reward. At different stages of capitalistic growth, however, different motivations assume functional priority and are stressed accordingly:

> in the early stages of capitalistic growth, the stress on *thrift* ensures *accumulation*, and the build-up of wealth needed for capital formation;
> in later stages, the stress on *consumption* ensures expansion;

ISSUES IN THE STUDY OF GAMBLING

in all stages, the stress on work-discipline ensures stability of interaction.

3 *Institutional mechanisms* to bolster the economic system but *at the same time* to protect the broader systems from its potentially disruptive consequences. Devereux is here presumably referring to such institutions as the banking and credit systems, which service both producers and consumers with capital for expansion and consumption yet which operate on the basis of certain criteria whereby capital flow is processed in more rather than less 'functional' directions.

4 *Cultural definitions* to create and maintain appropriate motivations. These motivations find their origins in, and help regenerate, the Protestant ethic:

(a) as it derived from Calvin, it signalled the decline of the retreat from the world of monasticism, and the apotheosis of the Kingdom of God on earth;
(b) it promoted the study of science (cf. Merton's analysis of the seventeenth-century will to know God by his works);
(c) it stressed reason as God's gift to man;
(d) and of the individual conscience as productive of economic freedom;
(e) its stress on predestination incurred distrust of fellow men not visibly blessed by membership of the Elect;
(f) it promoted religious sanctification of work: the 'calling';
(g) it led to the sanctification of private property, as held in trust and 'stewardship' for God.

Not all of these elements were new: but Protestantism gave them coherence and divine sanction. (d), (f) and (g) in particular have become *residual values* central to American (to some extent, Western) culture. Sources of strain, however, are not difficult to pinpoint in this holistic system. It is not simply that strain originates from sources of conflict *extrinsic* to the system, as, for example, in the stubborn refusal of merit and reward to correlate, and in the ironical consequence that virtue has too often to be its own reward since few others are forthcoming, a state of affairs which would be more acceptable if the un-virtuous were not so visibly and numerously blessed instead; or in the strain exercised by the puritan ethic on the foundations of personality, where rationality vies with illogicality, and asceticism with hedonism. These strains could *ideally* be accommodated were the Protestant value system sufficiently institutionalized and intensively absorbed, though the cost in guilt, shame and anxiety over a wide area of human behaviour would probably be increased. It is, rather, in the sources of strain *intrinsic* to the role of the Protestant ethic in the rise of capitalism that conflicts more difficult to accommodate arise:

1 The system is inherently frustrating: it generates dissatisfaction in order to expand.

2 Some value-conflict is endemic in capitalism: thrift *v.* consumption; prudence *v.* risk-taking. This value-conflict is particularly acute as the transition is made from early capital-formation to full-blown consumer capitalism, in which the protestant 'vocabulary of motives' loses some of its functionality with regard to the economic system. Wealth as an end-in-itself is stressed far more, and the loss of the 'stewardship' motif leaves conspicuous consumption and status competition as *the* suitable criteria against which 'success' is to be judged. However, the core values of puritanism, whose decline has been prophesied since the 1660s, retain great power: even the irreligious or amoral feel impelled to 'get ahead' as a worth-while goal, irrespective of straight cash rewards; the fruits of success are increasingly suspect as the rise in GNP fails to provide any automatic 'pay-off' in terms of spiritual fulfilment – the hollowness of a purely materialistic success remains one of the great themes of our culture.

3 Some value-conflict is endemic between *capitalism and parent Christianity*: the affective neutrality of the economic order, with its stress on impersonality, self-interest, ambition and competitiveness, clashes with Christianity's central injunctions as to love, humility and self-sacrifice. This conflict is acted out in the dualism between work and the family, as for example in the conflict which arises when the values of the work-place are carried into the home, and vice versa.[13]

4 The development of capitalism towards 'rationality' – via machine technology, systematic economic analysis, scientific market information, bureaucratic business organization, etc. – and away from chance, bold, risk-taking entrepreneurship narrows the scope for initiative to activities defined as disruptive of established business norms and conventions. '*Risk has become a disutility, to be avoided, minimized, or insured against.*' Speculators, when successful, tend to be regarded as immoral, unworthy and *lucky*. However, ambivalence towards speculation rarely becomes hostility, since to attack it is very close to attacking the entire rationale of the economic system.

'Society' handles these conflicts by structural and symbolic differentiation and segregation. It is broken up into several differentiated sub-systems, each governed by norms appropriate to its own functional requirements. Segregation is comprised of the spatial and temporal separation of these sub-systems, and the symbolic definition of appropriate contexts. Barriers to communication and role segmentation keep these contexts separate. Finally, the overriding ethical conflict is resolved by ranking different sets of values in terms of some major scheme of allocation. Under this scheme, the major organizing imperatives of capitalism are officially defined as work, routine, thrift, prudence, conservatism, rationality and discipline. Such values as boldness, initiative, risk-taking and the pursuit of chance (shrewd or otherwise) are rated much more dubiously as necessary evils, which cannot be repudiated, but should only fleetingly be identified with, and are generally assigned to 'deviants', or specialists. Competing or threatening values are segregated contextually, 'ideal' values are confined to 'sacred' contexts. Dubious values may generate *sub rosa* contexts – in Devereux's view, this is most appropriate where the structural needs to be met are derived from and created in functional inadequacies and strain *within* the dominant system.

The disapproval of gambling centres around a basic theme: gambling rests on *chance*, and chance is a non-ethical (even *anti-ethical*) basis for the distribution of reward. Hence, its existence is a threat to the rationale in which work, merit and reward are supposed to go hand in hand, and even helps emphasize the extent to which they do not do so. Gambling is thus a threat to a properly ethical orientation, helps break down 'rationality', and fosters superstition and fatalism. In sum, gambling appears to be an *in principle* violation of capitalism. The nub of Devereux's thesis is that, in fact, the values deplored in gambling are by no means peculiar to it or foreign to the broader culture. They may in fact functionally relate to the legitimate economic system. Since these values cannot be attacked in their relation to the latter, it is only with regard to gambling, where the same values crop up in segregated contexts, where they *can* safely be attacked, thus safely 'grounding' the tensions and ambivalences they produce, and simultaneously reinforcing and bolstering the dominant system.

That gambling survives and even flourishes testifies to its meeting of needs, both social and personal, which are not, perhaps cannot be, fulfilled in other ways, at least in capitalist societies.

1 *The protest against budgetary constraints* Few gamblers realistically suppose that gambling will truly be for them a short-cut to wealth, though it is a convenient pretext for fantasy along these lines. Their gambles are on the whole far too petty and far too limited to be more than a minor break with their budgetary discipline. Yet this break is all-important – for what irks in everyday life are the constant reminders of the needs for budgetary control, of income limitations and the gap between even modest aspirations and reality. In this closed-circuit world, where no dramatic increases

in wealth are possible, the gambler can at least protest against the tyranny of the 'budget'. Winnings are usually 'blown' or perhaps rebet, though large prizes may be consumed via more solid purchases generally out of reach except to high income groups. Even if loss ensues, the pleasures of *anticipating* a win can be seen as worth the effort. A chance element is brought into the serious and orderly realm of earned income. But the break is usually carefully controlled, and the stakes kept small *relative* to income.

2 *The protest against rationality* Many gamblers ignore or choose to suppress even that element of rationality which does obtain in gambling. In such cases, a blow is struck against a rationality which is viewed with resentment as governing too many of life's pleasures, while leaving its central mysteries unsolved.

3 *The protest against ethics* Chance is non-ethical: its pursuit therefore entails *some* protest and escape from ethical constraints, especially puritanical ones. The guilt thus engendered, however, frequently involves the gambler in a great deal of self-mystification as to his motives, which he sustains by resort to symbolic refutation and disguise: 'All in fun', etc.

4 *Thrill-seeking* Gambling involves a cycle of tension accumulation and resolution. The respectable can experience the 'safe deviance' involved in acting out the counter *mores* of daring and risk-taking in a segregated setting, which renders its insecurities 'less real' than those of everyday life. It can thus alleviate anxiety and boredom.

5 *Competitiveness and aggression* In many forms of gambling, these motivations can be stepped up and indulged behind a 'playful' façade. In such games, rules and settings are provided in which what Goffman terms 'character contests' can be acted without any overlap into 'real life'.

6 *Problem-solving* Gambling, like crossword puzzles and chess (though with the additional contingency of the stake), provides artificial, short-term, miniature 'capsule' problems – and their resolution – for those who enjoy them, and who are either starved of them or who perhaps cannot face or solve them in real life. This particular motivation was amplified by Herman[14] in his analysis of horse-track betters as exemplars of displaced decision-making, compensating in gambling for work situations in which they lacked the scope for creative decision-making.

ISSUES IN THE STUDY OF GAMBLING

7 *Teleological motivations* Man imposes moral order on causal order, and generates legitimate expectations thereby. Chance events often run counter to legitimate expectations, dramatizing man's ultimate ignorance and helplessness, and raising anew the problem of meaning. Men are more imbued with legitimate expectations than women due to their far more intensive involvement in the rationalistic rhetoric of the work sphere. Women are thus more 'philosophical', 'intuitive', etc., *not* because inherently so, but because they are more cut off from the moral order of the economic sphere. Chance events, which can only be incorporated in science as symptoms of inadequate knowledge, nevertheless pose problems of meaning which men resolve by resort to transcendental schemes, as in religion, magic and superstition. In our heavily rationalistic culture, gambling is the *only* area in which permissive attitudes towards such notions as luck and superstition prevail. Gambling thus encapsulates the area of mystery diffused throughout life in general but culturally 'silenced' in most institutional areas. It becomes, therefore, a laboratory for probing the meaning and grounds of the self's relationship to things and nature. Since religion imposes a different teleology, based upon an inscrutable deity, gambling is not simply non-religious but *counter-religious.*[15] Gambling signifies a break in the moral closure of the dominant system. 'Am I lucky?' has a *cosmic* significance, but no final answer is possible: hence the gambler is forever 'testing' his luck.

8 *Extrinsic or contextual motivations*

(a) The wager always concerns an *event* with its own event–specific interests, e.g. football, horse-racing, etc. Intrinsic interest in the event may precede the desire to stake a bet on its outcome, and may be drawn upon to assuage any guilt feelings that would otherwise stem from gambling.

(b) All gambling takes place in some concrete *social setting*, which may attract in other betters for social reasons, a desire to be 'one of the boys', 'not spoil the fun', etc.; 'social gambling' may thus be compared with 'social drinking'. 'Charity' bets are also structured to drag in motivationally neutral players.

(c) *Associations* of a symbolic kind, e.g. racing as the 'sport of kings', and the link between cards and gaming and spas and 'high society' may appeal to players who would otherwise be neutral towards gambling. As Goffman has stressed, commercial entrepreneurs are well aware of the status passage thus provided.

In sum, 'most motivational themes woven into gambling do *not* stem from ... "human nature", but are (mainly) derived in a process of interaction with a particular social and cultural environment' (p. 986). To Devereux, the prime sociological determinant of gambling resides in where people stand in relation to this environment. In his view, the 'core culture' of American society remains the economic/religious/ethical synthesis of puritanism. And it is the challenge presented to that culture by secularization, the acquisitive materialism of the full-blown consumer capitalism to which it has given birth and the counter-mores it has thrown up, which accounts for the tremendous inconsistencies and conflicts of American culture.

The old puritan hegemony remains strongest in rural and small-town areas; among the lower middle class; and among protestants. It weakens the more one moves away, in *any* direction, from this centre of gravity. It has tremendous *staying-power*: it has been 'breaking down' since the mid-seventeenth century yet still constitutes the 'official' and approved set of values for modern America (and, for that matter, modern Britain). Its persistence can be attributed to its functional relationship to crucial imperatives of the social and economic structure. It will be most intensively 'carried' by those playing roles most salient for the *transmission* of that culture: not only churchmen, but magistrates, headmasters, and local government officials.

The clear implication is that gambling varies *inversely* with the sway exerted by this culture. Among the Protestant middle class, it is likely to be predictable, of very small scope, and within the permissible limits of recreational expenditure. It operates principally as a 'safety valve' which frees the individual temporarily from budgetary constraints. This pattern of occasional and petty gambling is also the norm for the majority, whose dominant patterns of life organization lie outside gambling, though its incidence will grow the more one moves away from the small-town middle-class Protestant matrix.

By contrast, 'heavy' gamblers – those who play with sufficient frequency and for sufficient stakes so that gambling becomes a major focal centre of individual life organization – have no sense of a 'budget'. The role is incompatible with middle-class norms and membership – it is hence a safe target for moralists to condemn 'excessive' rather than 'petty' gambling as 'demoralizing'. Gambling is more habitual the greater the absence of the traditional constraints of middle-class life: i.e. ties to job, family, neighbourhood, church, regular work and incremental income, satisfactory career lines, and *some* visible relationship between effort and reward. Since many of these constraints apply also to the 'respectable' working class, habitual gambling is a *slum* rather than *stable* working-class activity. Gambling of a habitual kind is also more likely in the criminal 'demi-monde', the upper class and the 'beau monde': in the first, 'windfall' spending has status-conferring power; in the second, it represents a ritualized affirmation of superiority; and in the third, where it often *is* excessive, it stems partly from the insecurities about the stability of one's *nouveau riche* status, and partly from the reassurance provided by reassertions of 'character' in fashionable contexts. In all except perhaps the upper-class case, it remains, however, fraught with strain and ambivalence, for 'the problem is not a simple matter of opposing groups and philosophies, and their relative positions of dominance within the community. Much more fundamentally, it is a problem of basic inconsistencies and ambivalences within a common culture, and of basic cleavages within the individual conscience' (p. 769).

Conclusion

There is a certain logical continuity in the three perspectives dealt with above. Caillois provides us with the notion that modern urban industrial societies, among others, have opted for the cultural matrix based on a combination of agonistic and aleatory principles and have largely shed or suppressed the principles of mimicry and vertigo. Goffman suggests that forms of action archetypically embodied in gambling have attained a salience they formerly lacked. And Devereux suggests a socio-historical model within which Goffman's analysis can to some extent be placed: a cultural dynamic in which puritanism vies with alternative world views in a society whose central imperatives are increasingly threatened by the force of their inner contradictions.

The work of Goffman and Devereux is explicitly based upon the relationship between gambling and the American social structure. However, British society shares perhaps the most crucial characteristic germane to Devereux's theorization: a rough similarity in the relationship between the Protestant ethic and the rise, and subsequent development, of capitalism. That immense dissimilarities also obtain between the two societies, and that these make comparative theorization very difficult indeed, should never be forgotten in the application of American-based theories to British society. But that should not serve as a blind to their relevance.

Gambling as a Social Problem

In his analysis of the history of the laws on vagrancy in England, Chambliss[1] showed the sensitivity of the relationship between the definitions accorded vagrancy, and the nature of its differentiation from other 'social problems', and changes in the social structure at different times from the early Middle Ages to the present day. In examining the history of gambling as a 'social problem' in England, it is helpful to adopt much the same perspective: that is, to attempt to relate changes in the legal definition of, and social response to, gambling to changes in the encompassing social structure, as well as the changes in gambling practices which were only partially independent of the socio-legal context which framed this operation. It should be stressed that any similarity between Chambliss's endeavour and our own is of approach rather than substance. Vagrancy, as Chambliss demonstrated, was never a unitary phenomenon, but a portmanteau term whose elasticity was very useful to law-makers and social controllers, a label which could be attached to measures against beggary or brigandry as the need arose. Gambling, collectively considered, does not – in contrast – appear on the statute book at all. Measures against gambling (with one exception) were aimed at specific forms of betting and/or gaming practice; and it is the *variation* in our piecemeal attempts at the control of specific forms of gambling that provides the substance for inferring structural implications.

The exception is a crucial one: the 1845 Gaming Act which rendered all gambling debts unenforceable by law. Rubner[2] asserts that this Act was the first in which the *moral* issue was paramount, in which the Puritan opposition to gambling on ethical grounds finally overcame the remnant of eighteenth-century licence, and whose main purpose was to dissociate the Victorian establishment completely from the adjudicatory role of the law in settling gambling disputes. There is certainly some force to his argument that before 1845 the character of anti-gambling legislation was *ad hoc* and instrumental, designed to combat extreme abuse, cheating or games (such as hazard) which gave flagrantly unfair odds to some players rather than others; or to seek to limit gaming, along with other forms of recreation, when these seemed injurious to the state – as in the famous 1541 Act banning the playing of a host of amusements whose pursuit was held to be detrimental to the practice of archery. The 1845 Act also strengthened the measures already in existence against gaming houses, and it is certainly the case that in the second reading of the Bill, the Home Secretary, Sir J. Graham, stated the purpose of the Bill as to 'put down gambling, which had lately very much increased in this country, and produced such pernicious and fatal effects'.[3]

It is more doubtful, however, whether the passing of the Act either constituted the *first* in which the moral issue was paramount, or indeed whether the moral issue *was* paramount in this particular case. The 1823 and 1826 Acts illegalizing lotteries, and bringing an end to the long run of state lotteries, begun under Elizabeth I and held at least annually throughout the eighteenth century, could be held to contain as strong a moral purpose as the 1845 Act – though no debates are reported in Hansard for these Acts, they stemmed originally from the 1808 Select Committee on Lotteries, which reported unequivocally against their being held, and uncovered a mass of corruption in their operation, and in the surveyance of the illegal insurances which had grown up around them.

> It has been represented to your Committee that the Lottery and the illegal insurances are inseparable; that the former cannot exist without the latter for its support; . . . In truth, the foundation of the lottery is so radically vicious that . . . under no system of regulations which can be devised . . . [can parliament] . . . adopt it as an an efficient source of revenue.

Efficiency and the amount of revenue collected were not their sole concern, however:[4]

> Idleness, poverty, and dissipation are increased [by the effect of the lottery] . . . truth betrayed, domestic comfort destroyed, madness often created, crimes are committed, and even suicide itself is produced. . . . And this unseemly state of things is to continue, in order that the state may derive a certain annual sum from the partial encouragement of a Vice, which it is the object of the law, in all other cases, and at all other times, most diligently to repress.

The language of the 1844 Select Committee is classically restrained by comparison.

This may simply serve as another example of Victorianism preceding Victoria, the high moral tone of the turn-of-the-century reformers paving the way for the massive restructuring of institutions of her reign. But in character, as well as in tone, the 1808 Select Committee Report appears far more moralistically concerned with the 'vicious' aspects of gambling than that of 1844. The 1808 Committee lambasted corrupt officialdom and recommended the outright abolition of the lottery (foreign lotteries and private lotteries were already illegal); the 1844 Committee expressly *denied* any intention of interfering with betting and sought only to suppress gaming houses, not gaming as such. They saw betting as on the decline from the excesses of the eighteenth century, and sought to rid the courts of the burden of settling gambling disputes, rather than seeking to suppress gambling by the removal of the legal context. Indeed, the main purpose of the 1845 Act seems to have been a clean-sweep systematization of the law on gambling along classical *laissez-faire* principles, rather than an onslaught on gambling *per se*:[5]

> At present, wagers are chiefly confined to sporting events, but the practice of Wagering is still deeply rooted ... and the practical imposition of pecuniary penalties for wagers would be so repugnant to the general feelings of the people, that such penalties would scarcely be enforced, or, if enforced, would be looked upon as an arbitrary interference with the freedom of private life.
>
> In the earlier periods of European civilization it was thought to be the duty of Governments to exercise a minute superintendence and control over all those private actions of the members of the community . . . and thence arose the laws on our Statute Book which prescribed to the different classes of the people what apparel they should wear, what Games they should play at, what amount of money they might win or lose, how their tables should be served . . . Such Regulations are out of date.

The Committee went on to recommend that wagering should be freed of such penalties as had become attached to it in the previous century (such as the Statute of Anne banning bets of more than a certain amount on games – the issue as to whether or not this should apply to horse-racing had never been settled in the courts) as well as rendered unenforceable by law. This brought English gaming law into line with that in Scotland and on the continent, and was justified by the Committee in terms of saving the courts' time from disputes which called for 'private settlement' rather than legal adjudication.[6]

The minutes of evidence of the 1844 Select Committee refer to examples of disputes which certainly verged on the ludicrous – one instance was of the court being asked to settle the outcome of a wager as to whether or not a man had jumped over a table backwards – but the witnesses called, and the questions put to them, revealed as much concern over the enforcement of the existing law on gaming houses as on the nature and extent of gambling in general, or on the consequences of involving the law in settling gaming disputes. It was clearly a matter of great concern to the Committee that gaming houses were flourishing in the West End much as illegal lottery and insurance transactions had flourished in the City before the abolition of the lotteries in the 1820s. (The City was relatively free from gaming houses, according to the evidence of Harvey, the Commissioner of the City Police Force.) The evidence of both Mayne (a Metropolitan Police Commissioner) and Baker (a Westminster Police Superintendent) stressed the disparity between the task the police were expected to carry out (the suppression of gaming houses) and the powers given them to do so – a familiar sounding complaint in modern terms, with a long ancestry. The police knew of at least fifteen gaming houses in Westminster alone, but could not proceed against them for lack of evidence: the police feared action for trespass; they could obtain warrants for entry only by a procedure – the sworn testimony of two householders that an establishment was used for gaming – which gave warning to the gamesters; they were not authorized to search the pockets of those found on premises that *were* raided, so that their only real chance of ensuring convictions was to catch the game in full spate. These restrictions, coupled with the neighbourly reluctance to inform, led not only to police fears of exceeding their powers, which might damage both their careers and the 'moral character' of the force; but also provoked suspicions that the gamesters were out to trap them into making false arrests, by setting up a fund for the purpose of bringing an action against the police once they had been lured into making a false raid on rigged premises (Mayne claimed that an action for trespass against a policeman could, if successful, 'effect his ruin').[7] Baker claimed to have been 'almost worn out' by the gamesters' ruses, who threatened revenge for police actions taken against gaming houses, followed him round, and so on. On balance, it needed only the sketchiest organization to avert the possibility of successful police action, and while the Committee appeared both surprised and alarmed by the lack of police success in closing the 'copper hells' under existing powers, they concluded by recommending stronger police powers, for instance, their authorization to search the persons of those found on premises suspected of gaming.

Two points emerge from the police evidence to the 1844 Committee: one, the police were already very skilful at presenting their case for greater powers (or more manpower, or both); two, the seeds of police ambivalence towards their role in regulating gambling were well and truly sown in their perception of the difficulties of prosecution where public collusion, either in the positive sense of active collusion, or the negative one of 'not informing', occurred with the deviants. Future Committees and Commissions were to express similar surprise and alarm at the reluctance and failure of the police to secure convictions against illegal gambling on anything other than a token scale. The 1923 Select Committee on Betting Duty could not understand why so few convictions had been obtained in Sheffield. Police reluctance to take the burden of upholding anti-gambling laws against street betting were an important factor in the legalization of (properly regulated) off-course cash betting in 1960. And Lord Kilbracken in 1968 expressed his criticism of police inactivity in prosecuting casinos which were contravening the 1960 Act by gaming for unequal chances. (The *ex parte* Blackburn case against the police actually forced them to prosecute clubs as the 1968 Act amending (and securing) their status was being debated.) Police–gambler collusion does not officially emerge as a factor of any significance; rather, it was the damage to the 'moral character' and standing of the force brought about by gambler–public collusion which, over a century, built up police reluctance to enforce the unenforceable, and lobby for the legalization of virtually all forms of gambling. But it is generally accepted that many policemen were bookies' runners: though how extensively and systematically so, and how far senior officers were involved, is a matter for further research.[8]

Other themes ran through the 1844 minutes of evidence which echo earlier concerns as well as presage later developments. One of these relates to what sociologists have come to term 'boundary maintenance', or that set of social processes to do with differentiating phenomena from one another in terms of acceptability and respectability.[9] In the eighteenth and early nineteenth centuries, Stock Exchange transactions were seen as far closer to gambling than is the case today. Perennial as the speculative element is in any stock market dealing, in the sense that certain variables cannot be allowed for,[10] in the period up to the mid-nineteenth century, a great many stock market transactions were illegal, stock dealings were poorly, if at all, regulated, and the overlap between stock market speculation and sheer gambling was openly admitted. Several exchanges in the 1844 Select Committee reflect this overlap. For example, the Commissioner of the City Police Forces is asked:

> Would not that [the question of the higher classes setting an injurious example to the lower] apply equally to those illegal [i.e. time bargain][11] speculations on the part of the large tenders [in the City] as it would to betting on the Derby on the part of gentlemen interested in the Turf?
>
> Precisely . . . but I think it is a matter of little importance to hear and to know that men of large fortune have transferred from one to the other £100,000; but I think it is a very undesirable thing that mechanics and persons engaged in industrious pursuits should be crowding around thimble-tables, and going into gamble-booths, and losing their money. *I think the moral and social inconveniences would be much greater from the latter.* At the same time, I admit that the evidence of the one palliates, and perhaps justifies the conduct of the other – and hence the undesirableness of both (para. 859, pp. 74–5).

This passage raises the other themes connected with the complex reaction to gambling in the nineteenth century and today: one, the concern over the 'example' set the poor by the profligacy of the rich; two, the perception, then tentatively expressed, that the latter mattered less, morally and socially, than the indulgences of the poor. The first attitude, that 'example' should be a major consideration in rich–poor relations, was put to several witnesses. For instance, Adams, the Chairman of the Middlesex Quarter Sessions, was asked:

> 'Is gaming encouraged by the example of "leading personnages" who game?'
>
> 'I do not think that one apprentice more or less would go to the copper hells because the first gentleman in the land did or did not gamble' (para. 616).

That the replies in general discounted the ill-effects of ill example (as did Lamb in his attack on this 'popular fallacy')[12] does not alter the extent to which the issue evidently preoccupied the Committee. The background of the gaming excesses of the eighteenth-century aristocracy and of the Regency period clearly mark these questions, a reminder that the anti-gambling legislation of the eighteenth century was chiefly aimed at the threat posed to large fortunes by excessive as well as crooked play. The reaction against the aristocratic style in gaming, as in dress, leisure and morality, heralded by Wilberforce, the Clapham Sect and ultimately by Utilitarianism and moral evangelism, was accompanied in the 1830s and 1840s by the political threat to the aristocracy by the new middle class 'The Middle Classes in the 1840s attacked the aristocracy through campaigns against the game laws, as well as against the Corn Laws.'[13] Less directly, much the same might be said of the new gaming law. The very raising of the issue drove home the extent to which the upper classes and royalty had not only put their fortunes at risk and set a bad 'example' – their excesses also gave radicalism its nearest equivalent to the pre-revolutionary *ancien régime.*

The related theme, that however reprehensible the gambling of the rich, that of the poor proved the greater threat, loomed larger as the century progressed. Clause 2 of the 1845 Act was levelled expressly against the gambling of the higher classes – namely, against hazard, roulette, and other games, where the bank was kept by the person to whom the house belonged, and where there was a dead pull against the player.[14] The object of the Bill was to 'protect the public, high and low, against *improper* Gambling' (italics supplied).[15] For some, detestation of gaming went with near veneration of betting. One Captain Rous who in the debate hoped that 'the first Conviction under it would be the Crockford Club House', stated before the Committee that 'betting is not offensive: quite the reverse. England would not be fit for a gentleman to live in if it were prohibited.'[16] (This did not prevent the banning of betting houses eight years later.)

To sum up, the first expression of predominantly *moral* opposition to a form of gambling to find legal expression was the banning of the State lottery in the 1820s, following the recommendation of the 1808 Select Committee, rather than the 1845 Gaming Act. Before the early-nineteenth century legislation had primarily been designed to check the excesses of upper-class gaming, as in the post-Restoration period, or to check gambling, along with other recreations, as injurious to the State. Preceding legal enactments, gambling was opposed and presumably held in check by the formal opposition of the Church. In a predominantly rural society, however, communities would exercise their own controls over excessive gaming, and it would only be in the eighteenth century, with its combination of stability and prosperity for the upper class, that the excessive gaming of a leisure class could develop into a style. Urbanization and industrialization were to alter the context of leisure for the working classes, and present the authorities for the first time with a formidable task: suppression, rather than reform, of emergent uses of leisure increasingly defined as *peculiar* to the working class. The withdrawal of the upper classes from popular forms of gambling in preference for the Stock Exchange strengthened this trend.

The Betting Houses Act of 1853 was passed without debate after a brief statement in the Commons by the Attorney General to the effect that 'the evils which had arisen from the introduction of these establishments were perfectly notorious and acknowledged upon all hands.'[17] The only need was to differentiate these houses, 'in which the owner holds himself forth to bet with all comers', from 'that description of betting ... which had prevailed at such places as Tattersall's, where individuals betted with each other, but no one ... held a bag against all comers.' The fine liberal sentiments prefacing the 1844 Report were absent from the Attorney General's speech, and the rather tentative opposition to both 'high and low' gambling of that Committee gave way to outright condemnation of the 'mischief arising from the existence of these betting shops ...' The problem was clearcut:

> Servants, apprentices and workmen ... took their few shillings to these places, and the first effect of their losing was to tempt them to go on spending their money, in the hope of retrieving their losses, and for this purpose it not infrequently happened that they were driven into robbing their masters and employers. There was not a prison or a house of correction in London which did not every day furnish abundant and conclusive testimony of the vast number of youths who were led into crime by the temptation of these establishments, of which there were from 100 to 150 in the Metropolis alone, while there was a considerable number in the large towns of the provinces.

Licensing would discredit the Government, and increase the problem rather than prevent it.

What had provoked such a stiffening in the tone as well as the character of anti-gambling legislation? In part, the situation in 1853 had been created by the Act of 1845. With wagering contracts unenforceable at law, and gaming houses facing stronger police powers, cash betting became the most economic form of wager for both punters and entrepreneurs. But this does not account satisfactorily for what was evidently a mushroom growth of betting houses: and since the 1853 Act set the pattern for gambling legislation for the following hundred years, it is worth looking for trends which the 1844 Committee had missed in their definition of the situation in largely eighteenth-century terms.

In the early-nineteenth century, the complex chain reaction set off by industrialization and urbanization involved recreational changes which in their turn were subject to the changing relations between the social classes. Brian Harrison[18] has cited W. Howitt's claim in 1838 that the decline in brutal sports represented a 'mighty revolution' in popular pastimes, and summarizes the processes underlying this decline: urbanization deprived working people of space, mechanization deprived them of physical exercise during working hours; both processes imposed economy in *time*, which came to be husbanded by codifying sporting rules and the abandonment or tighter regulation of games of uncertain duration, hunting and soccer for example. At the same time, middle-class notions of 'rational' and 'fulfilling' leisure as a *preparation* for work, instead of as an end in itself, gained over the old rural and aristocratic co-operation between the classes in unhealthy or dangerous blood sports. Arguably, gambling quickly became subject to the same degree of regularity and routinization. It was opportune that the sport of horse-racing and the growth in sophistication of horse-breeding had, by mid-century, progressed to the point where meetings and facilities were sufficiently developed to provide a calendar for racing which gave a routine to betting, and a structure for handicapping and the provision of odds.[19] But the chief developments in horse-racing had taken place in the eighteenth century. What gave it such impetus as a form for betting in the mid-nineteenth century on was chiefly the convenience it provided for those 'masses' of working people brought together, for the first time in history, and faced with a problem of leisure.

The 'problem' was self-created. As Burns[20] had stressed:

> the swamping of everyday life by industrialization has not been succeeded by a mere ebbing, or forcing back, of the flood. Social life outside the work situation has not re-emerged, it has been created afresh, in forms which are themselves the creature of industrialism, which derive from it and which contribute to its development, growth and further articulation.

Taking his cue from Chapman's thesis that 'the 10 Hours Act was by far the most important landmark in 19th century social history',[21] Burns argues that the working-class movement can be said to have 'created' leisure by successfully challenging the immersion of everyday life in industrial work in face of the power of industrial capital. But the leisure thus gained was won in terms of 'freedom from' labour, not 'freedom to' pursue other ends. The 10 Hours Act was fuelled by the hostility aroused by punitive working conditions and rules, excessive health risks and fatalities and the shackling of women and children to factory labour: the leisure that resulted was a vacuum 'which was largely filled, even to begin with, by the amusement industry.'[22]

In pre-industrial society, work and leisure were far less clearly demarcated. Equally important, most men were content with subsistence economy;[23] when that was achieved, work slackened or stopped altogether. The rhythm of work was set by the seasons and ritualized by the festivals and holidays of church and community. Time hung. Industrialization was as much a matter of breaking down the resistance to *routine* and *incessant* labour innate in such a psychology as it was about new techniques. The demand for leisure came only as the last vestiges of pre-industrial life were fast disappearing.

The upsurge of betting among the new urban working class, and the strong reaction against it, are fully intelligible only in the context of the newly created dualism between work and leisure. Thomas has argued that the triumph of industrialism came not by the force of economic or legal compulsion, but by 'the force of habit and even a sense of duty'. It is more likely that the latter took hold only when the former presented little alternative to working people than adaptation to the new regimes of work, or a revolutionary displacement of the economic and social arrangements which supported them. The early industrialists imposed a rigorous, even savage, labour discipline, with elaborate systems of fines, with campaigns against holidays and wages, and with sabbatarianism and allied attempts to check the violent forms of recreation to which the workers of the time were habituated. The old incentives to labour – subsistence, communal responsibility, craftsmanship – were wrenched aside to make way for the regimentation of the wage and the factory. While wage labour had become more predominant since the seventeenth century, Hill has conveyed the deep resistance to it in his remark that 'factory discipline must have seemed as irrational, as irrelevant to one's own interests, as unfree, as army discipline today.'[24] Both masters and men now regarded work as an imposition which only a strong constitution could bear. Idleness was the natural state: the habit of work had to be rigorously imposed upon recalcitrant material, and must not be allowed to break.

One of the classic, and mainly neglected, conflicts of capitalism (in England at least) is that between the attempt made on the one hand to control working-class leisure, largely by the suppression, or stringent regulation, of drink, gambling and a host of other amusements; and, on the other hand, the rush to cater for their tastes at a nice commercial profit. The situation was nicely summarized in the Wildean quip about newspapers fulminating against gambling on the front page whilst relying for their sales on the racing information given at the back. From the 1850s on, betting and horse-racing became increasingly interdependent and increasingly big business.[25]

> It is not a freak of language that the words 'bookmaker' and 'welsher' creep into popular speech in the early sixties. The old punting had been done inside the trade. Gully, prize-fighter, punter, race horse owner and member of parliament, and his like, had betted with their fellows. But now a public with leisure to enjoy desired to come in. . . . To assist it, a whole range of new publications came into existence. In 1859, *Sporting Life*, appeared as a weekly; in 1881, it increased to four days a week; in 1883 it became a daily . . .

In 1877 Henry James felt impelled to attend the Derby, so Festive had the occasion become, whose atmosphere he described majestically as one of 'gross plebeian jollity', in which 'the people that of all peoples is habitually the most governed by decencies, proprieties, rigidities of conduct, was for one happy day unbuttoning its respectable straight-jacket . . .'[26]

The double standard, whereby the rich gambled legally while the poor did so illegally, was by now thoroughly entrenched as an aspect of class warfare. For while, for the last several decades, thousands had flocked to the major races at Epsom, Ascot, Doncaster, etc. – Richard Baxter, who opposed all betting, had once been 'pelted' down the streets of the Yorkshire racing town[27] – millions cooped up in the cities and towns could bet only through the street bookmaker (since the 1853 Act), and local Watch Committees had made it their duty to outlaw such practices. So immense were the variations in local provisions, however, that parliament was repeatedly called upon to illegalize street betting nationally, which it duly did in 1906. The Bill was attacked by several members as 'class legislation of the worst type',[28] but these objections were brushed aside. To the Government spokesman, street betting was gambling 'in the most acute and urgent form'.[29]

It should not be forgotten that in the midst of the generally repressive and intolerant views taken of working-class gambling by the authorities and spokesmen for public morality, there was a vein of real humanitarian concern for the misery undoubtedly caused by excessive gambling, as by extensive drink and brutality. Mayhew had observed the costermongers' addiction to Sunday gambling, when at one fell swoop takings for the week, stock, cart and all would be lost.[30] Fifty years later Lady Bell wrote:[31]

> I would give a great deal to be furnished with some brief, plain, convincing argument against staking money on chance, which

> would seem to the man of small means a cogent reason for giving it up. To tell him that if he loses he will be ruined is not final, since he will reply that if he wins he will be enriched. And every now and again a working-man does win, and thereby acquires in one moment a lump sum of capital that would be accessible to him in no other way.

(She thought that the most feasible compromise was for public lotteries to be organized by the State, a solution favoured by Colquhoun in 1808[32] and Keynes in 1933;[33] on the premise that some gambling is ineradicable, both argued that a state lottery with a mass of small prizes would both provide revenue *and* keep gambling in check. Other forms of gambling could then be safely abolished. Keynes argued that the less 'pretence of skill' the better, and that 'gambling should be cheap, fair, frivolous and on a small scale. . . . I think it would add to the cheerfulness of life if punctually everyone in the country was to wake up each Sunday morning stretching out for the Sunday papers with just a possibility that they had won a small fortune. It is agreeable to be habitually in the state of imagining all sorts of things as possible.'[34] Premium bonds come nearest to meeting these suggestions, but without meeting the other assumption – that other forms of gambling would diminish.)

Victorian legislation survived in the main until 1960. Despite the rise in the twentieth century of new forms and strategies of gambling – principally pools betting and greyhound racing – the illegality of off-course cash betting was retained. By 1960 the law was a mare's nest of anomaly and contradiction. Governments had by then tried to tap betting for revenue – in the 1926–9 experiment which failed to produce anything like the returns expected. The 1932–3 Royal Commission had, in general, upheld the legislative *status quo*, whilst that of 1950–1 guardedly recommended the legalization, under strict control, of off-course cash betting facilities. It is nevertheless difficult to account adequately for why this position was eventually enacted in 1960. The establishment of premium bonds in 1957 may have been a precedent for the Government finally to accede to sporadic demands for the ending of the disparity between cash and credit betting off-course. But it could equally have been used as a reason for deferring such a move, arguing along the Keynesian line above. Certainly the Exchequer had an interest in the revenue that might eventually accrue from taxing off-course cash betting turnover: and the police had reiterated their reluctance to enforce the unenforceable. But these factors had been present for the past century – what tipped the balance? The answer probably lies in that peculiar openness to commercial suggestion which characterized the 'never had it so good' period of Macmillan's administration. The government which had introduced premium bonds and sponsored the creation of commercial television could with equanimity and an appeal to democratic principle end the proscription of what was, after all, the major form of gambling in Britain. The post-war experience of full employment, and the lack of any increase in gambling throughout the relatively prosperous 1950s, took the edge away from the opposition to the measure.

The immediate aftermath of the 1960 Act was of a sharp upsurge in the extent and variety of the forms of gambling legally available, and of moral unease at the scale of gambling apparently thus unleashed. Since the intention of the 1960 Act had simply been to legalize the existing volume of off-course cash betting, and to constrain inducements for the expansion of betting or facilities to encourage betting – betting shops were not to advertise, were to provide no services *other than* those for the placing of bets, etc. – the reaction was to be expected. The phrase 'a nation of gamblers' became a journalistic cliché. By the mid-1960s, however, most anxiety attached to the unanticipated side-effects of the 1960 Act – the loophole allowed by the so-called 'Vicar's Charter' (which allowed 'clubs' – the phrase was not defined, but was intended to cover mainly charitable organizations – to recoup their expenses by charging an entrance fee for the playing of games of equal chances) was exploited by the financial interests which had been waiting in the wings to develop the potential market for club gaming of a commercial type. A feature of the clubs and casinos which sprang up by the mid-sixties was their complete freedom from legal regulation as the result of poor parliamentary draftsmanship. Even so, the law was technically against the playing of games of unequal chance for profit, and a concerted campaign against them would undoubtedly have succeeded in closing them, or forcing them to conform to the law. As Kilbracken pointed out in the debate on the 1968 Bill intended to remedy this and other anomalies, thirteen out of the fourteen cases brought against casinos had upheld the law, and only police reluctance to prosecute a club for a second time (with far stiffer penalties) and to prosecute the large clubs, enabled them to survive. (It was left to a private citizen, Raymond Blackburn, to put legal pressure on the police to enforce the law – which was changed by the 1968 Act just in time to prevent acute police embarrassment.)

Police and governmental strategy appeared, however, to be evolving in response to innovations in the relationship between organized crime and the new gaming 'empires'. Fear that the easy and massive profits accruing from unregulated commercial gaming would capitalize the transformation of what had been small-scale and localized protection rackets into large-scale criminal syndicates along American lines were dramatized by the careers of the Krays and the Richardsons and their networks in the mid and late sixties. In retrospect, their strategies and organizations were still too 'underdeveloped' to benefit from the advice that Cressey maintains they were offered by American criminal organizations,[35] but their example certainly eased the passage of those clauses in the 1968 Bill which provided for the setting up of the Gaming Board, independent of the police and with its own inspectors, but with very considerable powers to uphold or rescind licences for gaming on grounds which amounted to suspicion of criminal involvement. It was assumed by 1968 that tight regulation and control was preferable to the attempt at renewed suppression, that to 'drive gambling underground', either by illegalization or over-taxation, would be to abandon its control to criminal entrepreneurs. The focal concern of legislation was no longer the formal suppression of gambling *per se*, but the calibration of social control mechanisms to prevent the unwanted side-effects of poorly regulated gambling, and to forestall the commercial promotion of inducements to gamble.

In conclusion, there are perhaps five periods in which the emergence and definition of gambling as a social problem can be related to changes in social structure. First, in the period up to the end of the seventeenth century, a basically agrarian society regulated gambling principally in terms of its nuisance value and occasionally in terms of its purely recreational threat to State interests. Second, in the eighteenth century, with the hegemony over social life exercised by the aristocracy and gentry, its regulation – in a flood of Acts between the late-seventeenth and mid-eighteenth century – was designed to protect the landed interest by enactments specifically against frauds, gaming with minors, and the legal enforceability of wagers over £10. Third, in the late-eighteenth to mid-nineteenth century, the differentiation of gambling transactions from capitalist transactions and the integrity of contract was ensured in the 1845 Act, whilst the City was freed from the burden of the contaminating side-effects of the State lottery in 1823. Fourth, from the mid-nineteenth to the mid-twentieth century, as Pizzorno has suggested,[36] the middle-class values of 'thrift, austerity and production were either adopted by, or "wished on to" the working class, but became obviously incompatible with their situation in industrial society', or rather, with their adumbration of a culture which was in many respects counter to that of the middle class. Fifth, 'in a society devoted increasingly to the values of leisure and consumption rather than to those of production, leisure presents itself as an alternative source of ethical values to those founded in production and work.'[37]

GAMBLING AS A SOCIAL PROBLEM

In a society whose economic structure and relative prosperity still depend very much on the latter, the rise of the former presents formidable problems of ethical strain and value conflict, both within individuals and between different groups.

Notes Gambling as a sociological problem

1 Johan Huizinga, *Homo Ludens: A Study of the Play Element in Culture,* Routledge & Kegan Paul, 1949; Paladin, 1970.
2 Roger Caillois, *Man, Play and Games,* Thames & Hudson, 1962.
3 Caillois refers to the situation in Brazil in 1958.
4 Erving Goffman, 'Where the action is', in *Interaction Ritual,* Allen Lane, 1972. First published 1967.
5 E. Goffman, 'Fun in games', in *Encounters,* Bobbs-Merrill, 1961.
6 For this and other crucial connections I am grateful to Richard Daventry.
7 Marvin Scott, *The Racing Game,* Aldine, 1968.
8 See D. Matza and G. Sykes, 'Delinquency and subterranean values', *American Sociological Review,* September 1962.
9 W. B. Miller, 'Lower class culture as a generating milieu of gang delinquency', *Journal of Social Issues,* 14 (3), 1958, pp. 5–19.
10 Edward C. Devereux, Jr, 'Gambling and the social structure: a sociological study of lotteries and horse racing in contemporary America', 2 vols, unpublished Ph.D. thesis, Harvard University, 1949.
11 George Homans, 'Bringing men back in', *American Sociological Review,* 1962.
12 Ernest Gellner, 'Concepts and society', in *Transactions of the Fifth World Congress of Sociology,* Washington, 1962, vol. I, pp. 153–84.
13 See, for example, R. M. Titmuss, 'Authoritarianism and the family', in *Essays on the Welfare State,* Allen & Unwin, 1958.
14 Robert K. Herman, 'Gambling as work: a sociological study of the race track', in *Gambling,* Harper & Row, 1967.
15 But see Jon Halliday and Peter Fuller (eds), *The Psychology of Gambling,* Allen Lane, 1974, for Fuller's introductory analysis of the different reactions to gambling of the Roman Catholic as distinct from the Protestant Church.

Notes Gambling as a social problem

1 William J. Chambliss, 'The laws on vagrancy', *Social Problems, 1964.*
2 A. Rubner, *The Economics of Gambling,* Macmillan, 1966.
3 Hansard, vol. 82, cols 793–6.
4 2nd Report from the Select Committee on Lotteries (1808).
5 Minutes of Evidence, 1844, Select Committee on Gaming, pp. v, vi.
6 Ibid., pp. 193–202.
7 Ibid., p. 16.
8 See James Mott, 'Popular gambling from the decline of the lotteries to the rise of the pools' in Raphael Samuel (ed.), History Workshop Series (forthcoming).
9 See in particular, Kai T. Eriksen, *Wayward Puritans,* Wiley, 1966.
10 The following letter from Professor A. L. Goodhart illustrates this well *(The Times,* 28 March 1972): Sir, In the spring of 1941, Maynard Keynes, Sir Wilfrid Greene and I were in Estoril on the outskirts of Lisbon, waiting for a sea-plane to fly us to New York. One evening we went to the local casino where Keynes and Greene, who were following a carefully planned system, seemed to be inexorably unsuccessful while I, a novice, recouped our depleted [sic] finances.

When we left, Keynes explained that a player's success depended more on intuition than on intelligence. He gave as an illustration his own reputation as an astute business man because he had made staggering profits both for King's College (Cambridge) and for himself by investing in the shares of a Chicago traction company.

For no particular reason he had sold these holdings two weeks before the stock market collapsed in the autumn panic of 1929. If he had not done so the College would have been in serious financial difficulties and he would have been wiped out. It was not reason but chance that had made him choose the crucial date. The fact that he was an economist, he said, was irrelevant.

11 A time-bargain was in the nature of a stock option today with the difference that failure to pay in the event of a loss could not then be enforced. In 1773, the City had petitioned the Commons to suppress the illegal lotteries, perhaps with the aim of reinforcing the distinction between Gambling and Commercial investment (Rat. 1933 Royal Commission). (Not, however, mentioned in C. L. Ewen, *Lotteries and Sweepstakes,* Heath, Cranton, 1932.)

12 Charles Lamb, *Essays of Elia,* Dent, Everyman, 1964.

13 Brian Harrison, contribution to discussion on 'Work and leisure in preindustrial society' by Keith Thomas, presented at 7th *Past and Present* Conference, 1964: *Past and Present,* no. 29, December 1964, pp. 63–6.

14 This was also the intention of the 1960 Act.

15 Graham, 1845 Games and Wagers Act Amendment, second reading.

16 Para. 3098, 1844 Minutes of Evidence.

17 Hansard, 3rd series, vol, 8718, col. 129.

18 Harrison, op, cit.

19 See Dennis Craig, *Horse Racing,* Penguin, 1944.

20 T. Burns, 'Leisure, work and the social structure', B.S.A. Conference Paper (unpublished), 1967.

21 Guy Chapman, *Culture and Survival,* Cape, 1940, p. 80.

22 Burns, op, cit., p. 8.

23 Wages were subsistence only, but their provision gave employers a total power which differed from the previous relationship between journeymen and craftsmen and the market.

24 *Past and Present* Conference, loco cit.

25 Guy Chapman, op. cit., p. 115: his chapters on the 'Delimitation' and the 'Exploitation' of leisure could not have been quoted here but for Burns's demonstration of their value in his 1967 paper.

26 Henry James, *English Hours,* Heinemann, 1905, p, 173.

27 See his evidence to the Select Committee on Gaming, 1844.

28 As by Clough, in the Committee stage: Hansard, 1906, vol. 167, col. 1162.

29 Ibid., col. 1164.

30 See P. Quennell (ed.), *Mayhew's London,* Spring Books, pp. 46–51.

31 Lady Bell, *At the Works,* 1906 (1911 edn, Nelson, p. 359).

32 Select Committee on Lotteries, 1808, Minutes of Evidence.

33 Royal Commission on Lotteries, 1933, Minutes of Evidence, 15 December 1932, 20th day.

34 The Commission did not take too kindly to the suggestion. For example: *Sir David Owen:* 'I do not quite know myself what an economist is. What is his function? Is it to add to the cheerfulness and frivolity of life?' – 'My object, I think, in this was to promote clear thinking on these matters.' – 'I should say you are a humourist.' 'All the expenses to be paid by the Sunday papers.' 'Everyone in the country waking up on Sunday morning stretching out for the Sunday paper.' What economic factor underlies that suggestion? – 'You would have to have some means of publication, and this would be a means whereby the profits of the State would be intact, without the subtraction of the expenses.' (7879–82).

35 Donald Cressey, *Organised Crime and Criminal Organisations,* Heffers, *1971; Criminal Organisation,* Heinemann Educational, 1972.

36 Quoted in Burns, op, cit., p. 12.

37 Ibid.

[5]
Promise and Performance in British Criminology

Twelve years ago, in this journal, Terence Morris wrote: 'There is no doubt that of all the specialized branches of inquiry into social behaviour, criminology has grown at a prodigious rate over the last decade.'[1] In 1976, Paul Wiles introduced Volume 2 of the book he first edited with W. G. Carson in 1970, by asserting: 'In the time that has elapsed since the first edition of this book appeared, British criminology has undergone a remarkable transformation . . .' and goes on to remark, 'The 1960s saw a renaissance in sociological criminology in Britain.'[2] Growth, transformation, renaissance, and—elsewhere—'paradigmatic revolution':[3] are these claims to be taken seriously, or are they symptomatic of delusions of intellectual grandeur? What advances in criminological knowledge have occurred to justify such claims?

The extent, direction and consequences of these trends can be characterized in diverse ways. The commonest is to see the trend as being a move from criminology to the sociology of deviance (and from penology to the sociology of control). The changes referred to in Morris's 1965 article are principally the establishment of the Cambridge Institute of Criminology in 1959 and of the Home Office Research Unit in 1957. But he also refers to the growth of sociological criminology in Britain, and welcomes the shift in the parameters of the field to take in such matters as 'the administration of justice, the exercise of police powers, and the definition and redefinition of behaviour as illegal or tolerable'.[4] By 1971, two further changes have occurred: one, the increasing polarization of criminology and the sociology of deviance: two, the very marked increase in the sheer number of practitioners of the latter persuasion in particular, a matching of the growth of sociology teaching and higher education in general. Two landmarks in this polarization were the article by Stan Cohen and the text by Michael Phillipson[5] which both sought to differentiate traditional criminology from the sociology of deviance in terms of key analytical problems which rendered the two approaches incompatible.

Since 1971, in this view, what has happened is the persistence of the break between 'traditional' criminology and the sociology of deviance, but its receding in importance to the point where a somewhat uneasy co-existence prevails. Displacing it in significance has been the growing variegation, fragmentation and schism within the sociology of deviance, between those favouring different perspectives and methods within it, increasingly differentiated by their practitioners into what Wiles has termed 'new criminologies', drawing from different paradigms within the sociological tradition, pursuing different purposes, and evolving distinctive projects to further them, united now only by a common antipathy to deterministic modes of discourse associated with traditional criminological approaches.

Another version of developments over the post-war period in British criminology tends to characterize them in terms of a move from conservative to liberal to radical approaches.[6] The first predominated in the immediate post-war and 'affluent society' period up to the mid-1960s; the second from the mid-'60s to the early '70s; the third is still emergent. The correlates are the political contexts of successive phases of British capitalism in its mixed economy, Social Democratic, Keynesian guise. In the first decade of post-war austerity and reconstruction, a tight consensus prevailed over the social problems field in which few forms of deviance other than crime and delinquency surfaced, and these were identified almost wholly with one form of pathology or another, usually cast in clinical or at any rate individualistic terms, but sometimes taking a 'social factor' form. The second decade, the decade of Macmillan, affluence and 'You never had it so good', corresponds to the consensus coming under strain. Problems that should have disappeared, like poverty, or that should have been diminishing, like crime and delinquency, didn't. The search was on for theories that told us why, and criminologists began to look further afield for suitable models and theories, finding an untapped reservoir in the USA, where sociological explanations had flourished since the Chicago School of the 1920s. This made for a partial break with the orthodoxies of medico-legal individualism, but the break was carried through more decisively only when the imported perspectives collided headlong with the most basic axiom of traditional approaches: that deviance, for all main purposes, was *prior to* social control. The third decade revolves around the turbulence created by the reversal of that proposition, which neatly coincides with the first real signs of crisis in the economy, and the growth of a series of challenges to the dominant control culture from newly politicized 'deviant' groupings—the women's movement, gay liberation, claimants' unions, black power (in a suitably fragmented British form), et al. As the third decade wore on, however, the model of explanation which began the break, labelling theory, fell apart under the weight of demands being placed on it, was seen to be thoroughly inadequate for all but very limited purposes, and has now been displaced by, and incorporated in, the 'new' 'critical' criminology, which aims to wed the traditions of European macro-sociologies to the possibilities offered by American methodologies. This version also tends to discard the deviancy concept for a more stringently criminological one, thus returning, in one respect at least, to the more orthodox terrain that preceded the break.

A third version, and perhaps a more pessimistic one, from a chauvinistic standpoint at least, is to characterize developments as the results of successive borrowings from American sociology, sharply scrutinized for their relevance to the British experience, and readily modified and adapted for their British context, to be sure, but essentially borrowings, nonetheless. Credit for pioneering this gambit should really go to Terence Morris, whose *Criminal Area: A Study in Social Ecology*, published in 1957, constituted the first systematic haul from American sources.[7] Drawing on the work of the Chicago School, Morris noted some correspondences with nineteenth-century British social statistical studies of crime, and tested the relevance of the area study concept on crime data for Croydon, finding the model seriously deficient in terms of British processes of urban development. Before then, American sociological theory had been astonishingly absent from British criminology, though Jephcott and Carter tacked on a link with anomie theory to their neighbourhood study of delinquency in a mining town.[8] Since 1957, however, layer after layer of American theory is chronologically discernible in British work: subcultural theory in the work of Downes (1966) and Hargreaves (1967); labelling theory and interactionist approaches in the work of Stan Cohen and Laurie Taylor (1971 and 1972), Paul Rock (1973), and Jock Young (1971); control theory in the work of Steven Box, and so on. Even the 'new' criminology of Ian Taylor, Paul Walton and Jock Young (1973) arguably has its source in Gouldner's critique of labelling theory (1968).[9] A few important exceptions should be noted. John Mays' 1954 study of delinquency, *Growing Up in the City*, which viewed delinquency as an outcome of key working class values colliding with middle class authority, anticipated much that was to come, and even launched the concept of subculture, though the term was used descriptively rather than analytically; and Leslie Wilkins' theory of 'deviation amplification' emerged simultaneously with labelling theory but independently of it.[10] Otherwise, the distinctively British criminological tradition was much as Stan Cohen described it: a particular brand of pragmatic eclecticism, which had as its scientific ideal a kind of clinical positivism, as its ends the exact prediction of criminality, and as its solutions purely legalistic and administrative reforms.[11] A later exception is the Birmingham School, which draws far more heavily on European Marxist than American sociological sources for inspiration. But the primary debt is still to non-British sources. This tendency is irrelevant to the quantity and quality of the sociological work produced by British criminologists (using that term in its broadest sense): it matters only insofar as the key analytical innovations have been imported, for the continuance of fruitful work might then depend on the continuing supply from external sources of seminal ideas and concepts. And the main source of these, the US, has currently dried up. The great innovators of the '50s and '60s—Al Cohen, Cloward and Ohlin, Becker, Lemert, Matza, Cicourel, Goffman, and Gouldner[12]—have settled for refining their original ideas, or have moved on—after Genesis, Exodus. The most worrying feature of contemporary British criminology, therefore, is—insofar as it has been parasitic on American developments—to what extent will it now run inexorably down, since the process of refining and modifying American insights inevitably yields diminishing returns? Fresh sources of inspiration, Marxism *à la* Gramsci or critical theory of the Habermas variety, and the prolific studies of the Scandinavians, especially the work of Thomas Mathiesen,[13] afford some relief, but the key question remains: what are the prospects for a burst of originality from British criminologists which transcend the re-cycling of theories from elsewhere?

On closer examination, none of these versions of post-war British criminology seems wholly satisfactory. The first, the 'from conjecture-and-refutation' to 'paradigmatic revolution' approach, has difficulty in dealing with the extraordinary eclecticism that characterizes the sociological, as well as (though of a differing kind) the more orthodox criminological, perspectives. The move to a deviancy, as distinct from a purely crimonological perspective, has never really transcended the heuristic phase. Definitions of what constitutes deviancy abound, and Michael Phillipson embodied the dilemma involved in embracing the concept as a step forward from criminology, whilst finding it wanting as a coherent foundation from which analysis can proceed. In the same year, 1971, he published a book advocating its adoption, and gave a paper avowing its impossibility.[14] Different attempts to resolve the problem of just what constitutes deviance have arguably led to the fragmentation referred to above, with interactionists, such as Paul Rock, making the most spirited case for its adoption as the core concept in the discipline, whilst phenomenologists tend to have abandoned it as beyond redemption, and Marxists tend to by-pass or actively reject it. Moreover, in an allied field, that of social history, a profusion of work has been carried out over the past decade which converges in many respects with the interests of sociologists of deviance, but which can hardly be said to emanate from the same intellectual origins—indeed, many regard sociology as antithetical to history.

The second version, the knowledge-as-ideology approach, which shares with the first version a certain Whig Interpretation of History flavour, suffers from quite different defects. The key issue here is: is the series of developments in British sociological criminology best viewed as the adoption of positions by individual theorists in line with ideological preferences, or as attempts at what Lakatos has termed 'progressive problem shifts'?[15] In the former case, the emphasis is on theoretical innovations as corresponding, rather too neatly, with 'stages' in post-war capitalist crises. In the latter case, traditional criminology was found wanting in terms of its capacity to deal with the social and cultural contexts in which crime and delinquency were formulated; subcultural theories of a 'zero-sum' variety could not cope with middle-class deviance and the 'crimes of the powerful'; labelling theory expanded the range of study enormously, and aimed at a faithful rendition of the processes of becoming deviant; its failure to encompass the political economy within which deviance and control were engaged led to the adoption of a Marxist synthesis, and so on. Much of the debate within British criminology at present concerns the extent to which this attempt at a progressive problem shift has paid off or not, for a great many problems have been dissolved rather than resolved *en route*.

The third version, the 'British as parasitic on American break-throughs' model, is deficient more for what it implies than for what it describes. It is the case that the key analytical developments in the field have been produced by American sociologists. But that does not mean that British sociology has suffered from their productivity, or that they have been inert in applying and modifying their theories in fruitful ways. Not least, some fine ethnographic work has come from the generally emancipating effects of American example. It would have been surprising if any other relationship had obtained, since only when the post-Robbins expansion of higher education in Britain got under way in 1964 did the number of career sociologists in this country exceed the number that could have been absorbed by one of the larger departments of a single American university. Not that it is a simple matter of numbers; and, as the 1970s wore on, the broad parallelism between developments in the US and Britain has certainly been somewhat eroded.

In sum, none of these versions of changes in British sociological criminology seems really adequate as a characterization of developments over the past 15 years or so. The closest approximation seems to me to flow, instead, from applying Lakatos' concept of 'progressive and degenerating problemshifts' to the field, despite the problems involved in relating a model of scientific growth primarily geared to the natural sciences to what he designates as the 'underdeveloped' social sciences, and despite his cavalier dismissal of Marxism and Freudianism. The main propositions of relevance are that 'sophisticated' as distinct from 'naïve' methodological falsificationism consists of appraising

> series of theories rather than isolated theories. . . . A series of theories is theoretically progressive (or 'constitutes a theoretically progressive problemshift') if each new theory has some excess empirical content over its predecessor, that is, if it predicts some novel, hitherto unexpected fact. Let us say that a theoretically progressive series of theories is also empirically progressive . . . if some of this excess

> empirical content is also corroborated, that is, if each new theory leads us to the actual discovery of some new fact. Finally, let us call a problemshift progressive if it is both theoretically and empirically progressive, and degenerating when it is not. . . . Progress is measured by the degree to which a problemshift is progressive, by the degree to which a series of theories leads us to the discovery of novel facts. . . . The time-honoured empirical criterion for a satisfactory theory was agreement with the observed facts. The idea of growth and the concept of empirical character are soldered into one.[16]

This articulation of the nature of scientific change seems to correspond most suggestively to both the spirit and the achievements that have occurred in British criminology over the period concerned, though practitioners, particularly those most concerned to disassociate themselves from the 'ideology' of objectivity in the social sciences, may be disinclined to accept the concept of 'fact' at any level of discourse. But, particularly in association with Lakatos' ideas of paths of research to avoid (negative heuristic) and paths to pursue (positive heuristic); with his argument that 'such series of theories are usually connected by a remarkable *continuity* which welds them into *research programmes*'; and with his view that these are characterized by a 'hard core' of postulates which must be shielded from attack by a 'protective belt' of 'auxiliary hypotheses', we have arguably a superior model for explaining what has been attempted; for what has been achieved; and for the spirit that has animated the shifts in the field. There is, of course, a slightly ludicrous aspect to applying a model illustrated *inter alia* by the victory of Newtonian physics over Cartesian theory to the divergences between the Institute of Criminology and the National Deviancy Conference. But at least the issues involved are not negligible.

Using this model as the basis for assessing developments in British criminology, there are two major, and two minor attempts, at effecting a 'progressive problemshift', in relation to the earlier predominance of 'naïve falsificationism' in the field. The two major attempts have generated extensive research programmes, though the term must be used in a looser sense than may be implied by Lakatos. Though Lakatos also implies that 'research programme' and 'naïve falsificationism' are incompatibles, the continuing researches of criminologists who are indifferent or hostile to these attempted problemshifts seem to warrant the use of the term. Thus five programmes can be discerned, as follows:

(1) work in the orthodox criminological tradition, as it is in general carried on in different centres, but notably at the Cambridge Institute of Criminology, focusing on testing particular theories, or sets (rather than series) of theories and/or propositions concerning crime, delinquency and the efficacy of different penal measures. Far from diminishing in volume, this tradition has accelerated its output: for example,

the Home Office Research Unit has produced at least thirty reports since 1970, compared with the seven or eight published in the 1957–70 period;

(2) sociological work in the ecological-anomie-subcultural theories vein, which largely petered out in the late 1960s;

(3) sociological and social psychological theories of deviance, deriving from labelling theory, and focusing on social reactions to deviant behaviour, utilizing processual and interactionist approaches to social behaviour: it was on the basis of providing a forum for theory and research based on this and allied perspectives that the National Deviancy Conference was inaugurated in 1968;

(4) a somewhat abortive foray into the phenomenological approach to deviance;

(5) sociological work in the Marxist traditions mainly deriving from Gramsci, but alluding to Habermas, aiming to link crime, delinquency and conflict (rather than deviance) to the political economy of capitalism, and to the dynamics of class conflict—the former pre-occupying the 'new' or 'critical' criminologists, the latter the Birmingham School. This approach tends to have dominated the N.D.C. for the past few years, but is to be distinguished from Althusserian Marxism, whose exponents forbid analysis (though not discussion) of deviance and allied concerns.[17]

The 'stocks of knowledge', modes of discourse and social purposes of these various research programmes are diverse, and often mutually antipathetic. There are also complementaries, but these tend to be played down in pursuit of inter-group differentiation, and intra-group cohesion. What follows is an attempt to convey the distinctive characters of these programmes, the progression of problemshifts and programmes being linked by the belief of the innovators that they are engaged in moving the dynamics of criminology into closer and more faithful alignment with the dynamics of crime and its control. However, it is by no means the case that the innovators of one problemshift merely become its custodians in face of the challenge from the next. They are as likely to seek to incorporate it into the pre-existing programme, or to build linkages between the programmes which make for syntheses.

I. ORTHODOX CRIMINOLOGY

The variety of topics documented, and the arrays of propositions tested, by criminologists over the past 20 years have been impressive. Radzinowicz's history of the criminal law, Walker's work on crime and insanity, Hood's sentencing research, the close examination by McClintock and others of the epidemiological yield of official statistics, the longitudinal study of the correlates of delinquency by West and his colleagues: these testify to the capacity of mainstream criminology to document and appraise the development of medico-legal responses to crime and delinquency, and to catalogue their incidence in relation to a wide range of attributes, social, environmental, and psychogenic.[18]

Despite the excellence of much of this and allied work in its own terms, sociologists increasingly, in the 1960s, drew attention to the limitations of those terms, at both explanatory and observational levels of theorization. At the explanatory level, criticism for much of the time was along the same lines as C. Wright Mills' onslaught[19] against 'abstracted empiricism' in sociology in general. Despite all its inter-disciplinary talk, criminology tended to eschew the sociological in its search for the appropriate inter-disciplinary blend. But even if the sociological level *had* been incorporated, little would have been gained, for the 'multi-factor' approach which accrued from each discipline being combed for aetiological leads meant the aggregation of data on individual cases stripped of the linkages with social and political contexts which alone gave those data meaning. And at the observational level, criticism of the excessive reliance on official criminal statistics grew alongside a concern to pay far more attention to the process of their construction and to the accounts of their motivations offered by deviants themselves.

Were this the only divide between criminology and sociological approaches to crime and delinquency, it would merely reproduce the divisions that inhered in other fields of study, that between psephology and political sociology, for example, or industrial relations and industrial sociology. But another dimension in criminological work gave added edge to the growing opposition to that tradition among the self-styled sociologists of deviance: criminological findings could lend legitimacy to innovations in and extensions of the realm of social control. For example, the concern with predicting crime and delinquency had gone largely unchallenged in the 1950s, both in the US and the UK. But with the advent of Eysenck in the early 1960s,[20] the idea that one could leave the matter of predicting delinquency to the safety of I.S.T.D. Summer Schools had to be abandoned. Before Eysenck, no clear idea had emerged of what might be inflicted on 'pre-delinquents', should an adequate predictive instrument be devised, a seemingly remote possibility in any case; after Eysenck, the implication that aversion therapy might just be round the corner lent force to the critique of criminology as essentially correctionalist. That his theory has, in the intervening period, been far more frequently refuted than corroborated is no great comfort, since the USA has in the same period escalated its armoury of penal control techniques based on conditioning theory.[21] Also in the same period, we have learnt that we can predict delinquency surprisingly well, in selected samples, and it doesn't make any contribution to the task of explaining it in general. Jackson Toby[22] found dependence on public relief (i.e. poverty) a surprisingly accurate predictor—a finding reproduced by West in London: but by this time, the observational theory on which such predictions were based (police statistics) were regarded as topic rather than resource.[23]

2. SOCIO-CULTURAL THEORIES

The first attempt at a problemshift in British criminology was orthodox enough: an attempt, from a variety of standpoints, to re-insert the primacy of social context into criminological explanation. Astonishingly, Mays' (1954) was the first systematic attempt to do so since Mayhew (1854, or thereabouts), a testimony to the medico-legal-psychiatric hegemony over the field. Mays was the forerunner of things to come in several respects: his use of the interview (nobody since Mayhew had bothered to talk with delinquent boys, as distinct from subjecting them to clinical tests); his use of the term subculture to describe the normalcy of delinquency in working-class urban neighbourhoods; and his finding that delinquency was almost universal, barely tapped by official processing of police and courts. Morris applied American ecological theory to the task of explaining the social distribution of crime and delinquency in an English urban context, and the concept of inmate culture to accounting for socialization in the prison. The former, area study, was also applied by Bottoms and Baldwin in their study of variations in crime rates in Sheffield. The work of Downes and Hargreaves derived more from the subcultural variants of anomie theory. After 1967, allied work either merged with or was superseded by the labelling perspective, and broke virtually completely with the anomie tradition, though Young stressed their complementarities.[24]

If the introduction of these perspectives into Britain did not, as had been the case in the USA, lead to substantial research programmes, it was largely because their comparative yield seemed quickly exhausted, and because their application came relatively late, coinciding with the challenge to their positive and negative heuristics by labelling theory. What this began, however, was the move from naïve to sophisticated falsificationism, with its purpose of generating the capacity to account for 'some novel, hitherto unexpected fact'. The variable traditionally addressed had been the fact of delinquency or non-delinquency: the more elaborate versions might allow for degrees of seriousness, but little more. The socio-cultural theories ultimately displayed great ingenuity in elaborating a series of theories designed to explain the social characteristics and distribution of delinquency, especially the group delinquency which seemed to belie economic rationality, around a 'hard core' postulate provided by Merton's goals-means schema. The break with individualistic theory that ensued was never complete, and despite a concern with meaning as well as causal adequacy, no fresh observational theories were developed to complement the innovations in explanatory theory. The trends suggested by the official statistics were assumed to hold good, as was the unproblematic nature of the law as a basis for consensus. The problemshift came to be seen as degenerating when the 'hard core' came under attack, when its 'protective belt' of auxiliary theories suffered excessive schematization, and when facts it had failed to predict, such as middle class deviance, assumed a novel visibility.

3. LABELLING THEORY

The second problemshift was also stimulated by American work, though of generally more recent vintage, and led to a much more extensive research 'programme'. The shift occurred at both explanatory and observational theory levels, and also entailed a simultaneous extension of the field of enquiry and a break with orthodox causal imagery. Particularly influential was the work of Becker, Cicourel, Goffman, Lemert and Matza: and the series of theories which they generated were collectively labelled—ironically enough, in view of later dissensus about their precise meaning—by a variety of terms (processual/societal reaction/transactional/interactionist/labelling). But the major catalysts, as far as British work was concerned, were the following statements by Becker and Lemert respectively: 'The deviant is one to whom that label has been successfully applied: deviant behaviour is behaviour that people so label';[25] and 'Two kinds of research problem exist: (1) how deviant behaviour originates; (2) how deviant acts are symbolically attached to persons and the effective consequences of such attachment for subsequent deviation on the part of the person.'[26] The term 'deviance' came to displace that of 'crime' as the focus of inquiry, and was taken to include such phenomena as crime, delinquency, mental illness or disability, sexual activity of a sanctioned kind, and proved elastic enough to accommodate stuttering, nudism, blindness, and other phenomena subject to the processes of the subtlest forms of stigmatization and rejection. Onto this shift was also grafted, at least early on, the theorizing of Leslie Wilkins on 'deviation amplification', which defined adverse social reaction as a critical variable in the crystallization of deviant commitment. The initial work of British sociologists influenced by labelling theory, such as Stan Cohen and Jock Young, was focused on the ways in which social control could generate more deviancy than would otherwise have existed, and this proposition was elaborated in the spheres of delinquency and drug-taking.

If labelling theory had meant no more than this, it would scarcely have amounted to more than a focused version of Merton's 'self-fulfilling prophecy'.[27] But this was only one in a series of theories which came to be evolved from the labelling perspective. Its impact on observational theory stemmed from the postulate that the very process of defining behaviour as deviant, and of applying that label to some persons rather than others, was problematic. The long-standing but diffuse scepticism about official statistics was given systematic shape in Cicourel and Kitsuse's work,[28] which Box applied to the British context in an attempt to discern the contours of systematic bias along class lines in criminalizing processes; a consolidation of Chapman's earlier work.[29] A concern with the most prominent (but hitherto ignored) features of deviancy also gave point to the pursuit of methods on the margins of criminological acceptability. The sanction of *ban* in particular and control in general makes for deviousness, covert practices and a blending of 'accounts' to fit acceptable meanings: only a form of participant observation can cope at all adequately with the task of getting beneath the surface of such phenomena; and only sustained observation can cope with their subjects' capacity to *change* either their attitudes and beliefs, their behaviour, or both. Two of the most outstanding pieces of ethnography in the field have used this approach, Parker's *The View from the Boys*, and Ditton's *Part-Time Crime*.[30] The sheer amount of time spent documenting the different phases of the Boys' involvement with their chosen form of craft crime (car radio theft), or gaining access to the forms of fiddling and pilferage through sustained interaction with the participants, was in each case a precondition for being 'faithful' to the phenomena under study. Other research of note carried out in the spaces won by applying a 'sceptical' view of deviancy and an extensive use of interactionist methods have covered the experience of long-term imprisonment (Cohen and Taylor); the making of a delinquency area (Owen Gill); the process of debt-collection (Rock); safety legislation enforcement in factories (Carson); homosexual role-taking (Plummer); police work (Cain, Holdaway); industrial sabotage (Taylor and Walton); courtroom procedures (Carlen, Tomlinson); halfway hostel's work with ex-patients (Sharp); the impact of detention on first offenders (Ericson); and the construction of media bias (Chibnall). The adoption of the deviancy perspective has elicited linkages with other fields (e.g. Wallis, and the sociology of religion); the stress on formalism has led to more sensitive depictions of criminal careers (McIntosh); and the strengths of the interactionist approach have been evident in the capacity of its practitioners to transcend (and refute) simple labelling theory (Damer; Parker; Ericson).[31]

Labelling theory has many novel facts (and facets of phenomena) to its predictive credit: but they are not the ones which appeared to emanate from the approach as it was first announced. Hence, those assailing its 'hard core' for a form of reverse determinism (social control *causes* deviant behaviour) have found its practitioners surprisingly resilient in disclaiming that novelty in favour of a 'hard core' of 'sensitizing concepts' around which are grouped a series of auxiliary hypotheses concerning power, social distance, motivation, visibility, etc., as variables mediating the interplay between deviance and control. Such critiques as those of Akers; Taylor, Walton and Young; West and others; and Scull, have focused on the naïve aspects of labelling theory as unable to account for the active appropriation of the deviant role by those (arguably the majority) fully aware of its definition and consequences; for, in Gouldner's dictum, 'treating the deviant as "man on his back", not "man fighting back"'.[32] Those who oriented their work around the 'social control leads to deviance' approach now tend to stress the metatheoretical and axiomatic strengths of the parent theory, symbolic interactionism. Assailed from both above and below, so to speak, by the radicals who insist that a political economy of crime must frame interactionist pursuits, and by the alternative 'micro' sociologies of phenomenalist and ethnomethodological casts who have whipped the rug from under 'deviance', labelling theorists nonetheless have a developing body of work to their credit.

4. PHENOMENOLOGICAL AND ALLIED APPROACHES

The critique mounted by these approaches of theory and research into deviance and control in general focuses on what Lakatos would term the inadequacies of their observational theories. The whole burden of their attack, and the purpose of the alternative methodologies they recommend, is to lay bare the flimsiness of the observational foundations on which grand theories of deviance and control (or, more generally, of society and social action) are erected. Their own output, in the British context at least, is slender. One can point to little more than the work of Phillipson and Coulter, and work in related fields by Keddie and Hargreaves: but the time scale involved is, as with the recent work in the Marxist tradition, so short that little substantive work has had time to emerge. The element of unison between the theorists concerned (who otherwise differ quite profoundly about method) is that there is no warrant for proceeding with explanatory theories at all in the face of the basic inadequacies at the level of observational theory. The interactionist approach is found just as wanting here as the structural theories. To say 'deviance is that which is so labelled', etc., is to presume that we know (*a*) what constitutes deviance (or schizophrenia, in Coulter's case), (*b*) that we are familiar with the procedures whereby deviancy ascription is accomplished, and (*c*) that observational 'data' can be documented and communicated within a shared set of understandings about what constitutes knowledge. On all three counts, existing approaches are found seriously inadequate, and preliminary work has focused on negative heuristic—what to avoid—rather than on positive heuristic—what to pursue (and how to do it), of which Keddie's work is perhaps the most accessible example. Its practitioners' severe censure of all existing theories and methods have provoked counter-critiques which point to the precarious nature of knowledge claims restricted to the realm of linguistic performance.[33]

5. MARXIST APPROACHES

As late as 1970, if one had been asked to identify a Marxist criminology, one would have been able to cite the work of Wilhelm Bonger, a few ironical flourishes about crime as functional to capitalism by Marx and Engels, and just possibly rope in the historical work of Hobsbawm and Rudé.[34] There seemed little scope for a Marxist criminology beyond the categorical assertions that capitalism is essentially criminogenic, and socialism is (potentially) not so. Its fate in Soviet bloc societies was consignment to Institutes far more positivistic than anything in the West.[35]

The transformation wrought over the past seven years has been remarkable enough to constitute a progressive problemshift in the direction of a Marxist political economy of crime (though Lakatos would have seen such a characterization as self-contradictory). The research programme which has flowed from this shift is in some senses continuous, and in others intermittent, depending on the source of the shift. Three main sources can be discerned: first, the developing body of social historical work, as conducted by Hobsbawm, Rudé, Thompson, Samuel, Stedman Jones and others;[36] second the work of the 'new' or 'critical' criminologists, Taylor, Walton and Young, whose alignments were initially to Goulder but latterly to Habermas and the Frankfurt School tradition; and third, the work of Stuart Hall and his colleagues at the Birmingham Centre for Cultural Studies, who have so far built chiefly on the insights of Gramsci to link the themes of social structure, deviance and conflict with the study of youth cultures and delinquency.[37]

The conjunction between the social historical and the criminological development is more coincidental than the result of longstanding interdisciplinary 'cross-fertilization', though the analytical yield for criminology has been considerable. (There are, however, some mutual links stemming from the New Left of the '60s.) The upsurge of interest in 'history from below' parallels the growth of a concern with 'appreciative' studies in criminology, to give the 'authenticity' of deviant phenomena their due in opposition to reductionist and determinist accounts (an approach that comes under strain when the movements concerned are of the Right rather than the Left). The most obvious pay-off for criminology has been to remind practitioners that much of their work is totally a-historical, and that context without history is as thin as action without context. The kindling of historical approaches to crime has also re-animated interest in comparative work, which had tended to wither in the face of the priority accorded capture of the fleeting and evanescent meanings informing multiple deviant realities. Scull, for example, argues that the nineteenth-century counterparts of labelling theorists made no headway against institutional solutions to crime and mental illness not because their arguments were less formidable, but because the capitalist political economy of their day found prisons and asylums useful, unlike their contemporary equivalents.[38] McIntosh treats historical materials as central to an understanding of the organizational forms appropriate for different criminal enterprises.[39] The Hobsbawm/Thompson analysis of the rationality and instrumentality of dissent and conflict that lay beneath the surface of 'irrational action', as in the case of the machine-breaking of the early nineteenth century, is the model for Pearson's decipherment of the meaning of 'Paki-bashing'.[40] The salience of law as an element in the consolidation of a dominant consensus by which ruling class control is maintained during rapid change, the theme of Thompson's *Whigs and Hunters*, is also the theme of the Birmingham School's *Policing The Crisis*.[41] The main difference between the historical and contemporary work is that the phenomenalist problem—being and becoming deviant, as distinct from 'situated' deviance—weighs far less heavily on the historian.

The New Criminology is perhaps the boldest attempt at a progressive problemshift of those here considered. Taylor, Walton and Young argued that only the axiomatic acceptance of Marxist methods could fill the 'blank spots' left by other attempts to construct social theories of deviance. The main gap was a political economy of crime. Once that was established, the strengths of the previous approaches could be incorporated into a 'fully social theory of deviance'. Aspects of the anomie and labelling theories could be retrieved from their degenerative phase and meshed with the only theory adequate to cope with the criminogenic potential of capitalism. Moreover, theory and practice must be related to the task of bringing nearer the possibility (masked by functionalist inevitabilism) of a crime-free society based on 'socialist diversity', opposed to correctionalism and criminalizing processes. A second book, *Critical Criminology*, treated the whole history of criminology as little more than a run-up to the decisive break in 1973. It is far too soon to say what kind of research programme will emerge from so grand a synthesis. But the whole weight of reconceptualization tends to be thrown on explanatory levels of theory, as distinct from observational levels. As a result, the most critical issues left unresolved by the problemshifts of the 1960s remain unexplored or even short-circuited. The interactionist critique of 'reified' constructs, Matza's strictures against over-prediction, the problems involved in deviance ascription (not resolved by calling it diversity): these were untouched. If present pointers serve, and Frank Pearce's *Crimes of the Powerful* and Young and Greenwood's *Abortion on Demand* are virtually all there is to go by, the 'new' criminology is settling for a functionalist version of Marxism.[42]

The promise of the new criminology can only be retained if its perfectly legitimate call for the insertion of a political economy into criminological work is uncoupled from the doctrinal baggage of

Marxism. To adapt Sklair's verdict on functionalism: 'It is essential to evaluate the Marxist method in the sense that it suggests to us where we might look in isolation from the Marxist doctrine that tells us what we will find there.'[43] Sumner's work on social sanctions is a beginning in this direction, as is the Glasgow University Media Group's documentation of the filtering of news.[44]

The approach of the 'Birmingham School' is best captured in Issue No. 2 of their house journal, Working Papers in Cultural Studies. The cover shows a bike boy in full regalia, metal-studded leather gear, etc., astride a powerful machine sprouting hardware of image-making intent. Paul Willis's article on the bike as a symbol of action and autonomy for a group of working class boys exemplifies the approach he later develops in *Learning to Labour* and *Profane Culture.*[45] In the subcultural vein, but using that concept in ways quite distinct from its role in strain theories, he draws on semiotic and existential discourses to decode and interpret the symbolic purposes of style. The same issue carries perhaps the most wholly original theorizing on post-war youth cultures: Phil Cohen's bending of Gramsci, Freud and Bernstein to the analysis of subcultural innovation among working class youth.[46] Disconnecting subculture from its origins (in strain theory) as solutions to problems set by the dominant (shared) culture, connecting it instead to the parent culture of the working class, where it performs much the same role, the shift has been made to reading subcultural styles as attempted symbolic solutions to problems set by the dynamics of class conflict in post-war Britain. Ecologically (the dismemberment of working-class community), familially (the dispersal of the extended family), occupationally (the erosion of the inner city industrial base), the working class parental generation have faced, but failed to resolve, a crisis of culture and personality. Youthful styles are an attempt to appropriate lost space, retrieve past symbols of solidarity and express both unity with and differentiation from the parental generation. 'They are an attempt to resolve, albeit "magically", the contradiction of their situations and . . . if there is a circularity about their attempts, it is because subcultural solutions can never transcend the limitations inherent in that situation'. This model has been adapted with great adroitness to serve as a framework within which styles of dissent and differentiation more generally can be analysed; and in *Resistance through Ritual* Stuart Hall and his colleagues collate their findings under a title that expresses the transition from strain to conflict perspectives. They are aware of the dangers involved in giving too media-centric and too ideological a set of readings to deviance and dissent: it remains to be seen how far the research programme that is well under way avoids them. If their work is to transcend plausible historical reconstruction, the series of theories that inform it should be more clearly detached from their 'hard core'.

CONCLUSIONS

This attempt to apply Lakatos's model of scientific development to British criminology can be no more than suggestive. Its strengths are that criteria are offered by which to indicate 'progressive' and 'degenerative' problemshifts, and the quality of closure in Kuhn's alternative model is avoided. Even so, as Giddens remarks, 'he offers no indication of how the criteria of what is to count as a "progressive problemshift" are themselves to be grounded epistemologically'.[47] It is indeed difficult to avoid an end-of-term report flavour creeping into the evaluative task involved: 'Made a good start, but is now slacking badly', 'promises well but must watch his fieldwork', etc.

Even with so flexible a model, there are research programmes and 'one off' studies which do not fit neatly into the scheme of things adopted. The work of Halloran and his colleagues in media research is one, though their excellent case study *Demonstrations and Communication*, on the media treatment of the 1968 anti-Vietnam War March, has strong affinities with the Birmingham School approach. Steven Box's work attempted a linkage of labelling and control theories. James Patrick's book on the Glasgow gangs was a brave challenge to sociological orthodoxy.[48]

Perhaps the major problem in applying the Lakatos model is that the criterion of novelty in the prediction of new *facts* has proved less illuminating in assessing the character of problemshifts than the capacity of theories to permit new *facets* of phenomena to become integrated in both explanatory and observational theories (the two types of theory can never be prised apart entirely). New facts are legion. The problem is to sift them theoretically: though one colleague, after a decade of coping with a succession of theories, regarded these as far more prolix and easy-to-come-by than established facts. The danger of experiencing too great a succession of so-called paradigmatic revolutions, without any concomitant intervals of normal science, is a sense of toppling into a metaphysical swamp. Hence, the pattern is of overlapping and competing attempts at accomplishing progressive problemshifts, rather than any one model winning out by the criterion of a superior research programme adequately monitored by sophisticated falsificationsim.

Nonetheless, immense gaps remain in both theory and research. The blank spot or 'silence' on the subject of the deviance of women is now itself the subject of a study by Carol Smart.[49] Apart from Lambert's study, little has been done on the experience of deviance and control among ethnic minorities.[50] Crimes of the powerful in Britain remain largely unresearched.[51] It may well be that more empirical work on these phenomena will not resolve any of the key outstanding analytical issues. But it would be surprising if no contribution to their resolution emerged from such work, given the specialized division of criminological labour, and corresponding scope for a vigorous eclecticism that now exists. One worrying feature of the past decade is the uncomfortably high contribution to innovation that flows from higher degree work, in part a reflection of the extent to which, as the stress on field studies and participant observation has grown, career academics are badly placed to conduct salient research in the interstices of teaching and administration. Hanging onto higher degree work becomes a pre-condition for scientific growth in such circumstances.

David Downes
Department of Social Science and Administration
London School of Economics

NOTES

1. Terence Morris, 'Crime and Criminology', *Brit. J. Sociol.*, vol. XVI, no. 4 (December 1965), p. 358.
2. Paul Wiles (ed.), *The Sociology of Crime and Delinquency in Britain. vol. 2: The New Criminologies*, London, Martin Robertson, 1976, pp. 1, 14.
3. Steven Box, review of Hood and Sparks, 'Key Issues in Criminology', *Brit. J. Crim.*, vol. 11, no. 3 (July 1971), p. 298.
4. Terence Morris, loc. cit., p. 364.
5. Stanley Cohen, 'Criminology and the Sociology of Deviance in Britain: A recent history and a current report' in Rock and McIntosh, *Deviance and Social Control*, London, Tavistock, 1974; Michael Phillipson, *Sociological Aspects of Crime and Delinquency*, London, Routledge & Kegan Paul, 1971.
6. This version is a somewhat free distillation of propositions advanced in Ian Taylor, Paul Walton and Jock Young, 'Critical Criminology in Britain: review and prospects', in their (eds) *Critical Criminology*, London, Routledge & Kegan Paul, 1975; but also draws on John Clarke et al., 'Subcultures, Cultures and Class: A Theoretical Overview', in their (eds) *Resistance Through Rituals*, Birmingham University: Working Papers in Cultural Studies, nos. 7/8, Summer 1975, and London, Hutchinson, 1976; and in Graham Murdock and Robin McCron, 'Youth and Class: The Career of a Confusion' in Mungham and Pearson, *Working Class Youth Cultures*, London, Routledge & Kegan Paul, 1976.
7. Terence Morris, *The Criminal Area: A Study in Social Ecology*, London, Routledge & Kegan Paul, 1957. See also his (with Pauline Morris) *Pentonville: A Sociological Study of an English Prison*, London, Routledge & Kegan Paul, 1963.
8. Pearl Jephcott and Michael Carter, *The Social Background of Delinquency*, University of Nottingham, 1954, unpublished.
9. David Downes, *The Delinquent Solution: A Study in Subcultural Theory*, London, Routledge & Kegan Paul, 1966; David Hargreaves, *Social Relations in a Secondary School*, London, Routledge & Kegan Paul, 1967; Stanley Cohen (ed.), Introduction to *Images of Deviance*, Harmondsworth: Penguin, 1971; *Folk Devils and Moral Panics*, London, MacGibbon & Kee, 1972; Laurie Taylor, 'The Significance and Interpretation of Replies to Motivational Questions: The Case of Sex Offenders', *Sociology*, vol. 6, no. 1 (January 1972); reprinted in Paul Wiles (ed.), 1976, op. cit; Stanley Cohen and Laurie Taylor, *Psychological Survival: The Experience of Long-Term Imprisonment*, Harmondsworth, Penguin, 1972; Paul Rock, *Making People Pay*, London, Routledge & Kegan Paul, 1973; *Deviant Behaviour*, London, Hutchinson, 1973; Jock Young, 'The Role of the Police as Amplifiers of Deviance' in S. Cohen,

1971, op. cit.; *The Drugtakers: The Social Meaning of Drug Use*, London, MacGibbon & Kee, and Paladin, 1971; Steven Box, *Deviance, Reality and Society*, London, Holt, Rinehart and Winston, 1971; Ian Taylor, Paul Walton and Jock Young, *The New Criminology: For a Social Theory of Deviance*, London, Routledge & Kegan Paul, 1973: Alvin Gouldner, 'The Sociologist as Partisan', *American Sociologist*, vol. 3, 1968, pp. 103–16; reprinted in his *For Sociology*, London, Allen Lane, 1973.

10. John Mays, *Growing Up in the City*, University of Liverpool Press, 1954; Leslie Wilkins, *Social Deviance*, London, Tavistock, 1964.

11. Stanley Cohen in Rock and McIntosh, 1974, op. cit.

12. See in particular: Albert K. Cohen, *Delinquent Boys: The Culture of the Gang*, Glencoe, The Free Press, 1955; Richard Cloward and Lloyd Ohlin, *Delinquency and Opportunity*, New York, The Free Press, 1960; Howard Becker, *The Outsiders*, Chicago, The Free Press, 1963; Edwin Lemert, *Human Deviance, Social Problems and Social Control*, New York, Prentice-Hall, 1967; David Matza, *Delinquency and Drift*, New York, John Wiley, 1964 and *Becoming Deviant*, New York, Prentice-Hall, 1969; Aaron Cicourel, *The Social Organisation of Juvenile Justice*, New York, John Wiley, 1968; Erving Goffman, *Asylums: Essays on the social situation of mental patients and other inmates*, New York, Doubleday, 1961; *The Presentation of Self in Everyday Life*, New York, Doubleday, 1959; *Stigma: Notes on the Management of Spoiled Identity*. New York, Prentice-Hall, 1963; Alvin Gouldner, 1968, op. cit.

13. In particular, his *The Politics of Abolition*, London, Martin Robertson, 1973.

14. Michael Phillipson, op. cit., 1971; and (with Maurice Roche) 'Phenomenology, Sociology, and the Study of Deviance', paper delivered at the British Sociological Association Conference on Deviance, 1971, published in Rock and McIntosh, op. cit., 1974; and reprinted in Paul Wiles, op. cit., 1976.

15. Imré Lakatos, 'Falsification and the Methodology of Scientific Research Programmes', in Lakatos and Musgrave, *Criticism and the Growth of Knowledge*, Cambridge University Press, 1970.

16. Lakatos, op. cit., pp. 118–19.

17. Most articles and sources relevant to this debate are contained or cited in Ian Taylor et al., *Critical Criminology*, 1975. See also the review by Paul Hirst of *The New Criminology*, and the authors' reply, in *Brit. J. Crim.*, vol. 13, no. 4, 1973, pp. 396–8, and 400–3.

18. Leon Radzinowicz, *A History of English Criminal Law and its Administration from 1750*, 1948–68, Stevens, 4 vols.; Nigel Walker, *Crime and Insanity in England*, Edinburgh University Press, 2 vols., 1968–73; Roger Hood, *Sentencing in Magistrates' Courts*, Stevens, 1962; Roger Hood, *Sentencing the Motoring Offender*, Heinemann, 1972; McClintock, F. H. (with Evelyn Gibson), *Robbery in London*, Macmillan, 1961; McClintock, F. H., *Crimes of Violence*, Macmillan, 1963; McClintock, F. H. (with N. H. Avison), *Crime in England and Wales*, Heinemann, 1968; D. J. West, *Present Conduct and Future Delinquency*, Heinemann, 1969; D. J. West (with D. P. Farrington), *Who Becomes Delinquent?* Heinemann, 1973; D. J. West (with D. P. Farrington), *The Delinquent Way of Life*, Heinemann, 1977. See also Hermann Mannheim, *Comparative Criminology*, 1965, Routledge & Kegan Paul, 2 vols. The focus in this article is on the criminological rather than the penological literature, too voluminous to cite here. Though the trends referred to embrace both spheres, the more positivist studies exert greater sway in the penal and institutional sphere. Partly for reasons of access, partly because of the censorship attached to settings covered by the Official Secrets Act, sociological penetration of the control sector remains negligible. Visiting American sociologists regularly confess surprise at the restrictions imposed upon academic research in this sphere. See also, regarding restrictions on research in schools and into legal processes, M. J. Power et al., 'Neighbourhood, School and Juveniles Before the Courts', *Brit. J. Crim.*, vol. 12, no. 2 (April 1972), pp. 111–32, and the Editorial, ibid.; and John Baldwin and

Sean McConville, *Negotiated Justice: Pressures on Defendants to Plead Guilty*, London, Martin Robertson, 1977.

19. C. Wright Mills, *The Sociological Imagination*, 1959, Oxford University Press. It should be stressed that much of the criminological literature, particularly the socio-historical work, comfortably eludes such strictures.

20. H. J. Eysenck, *Crime and Personality*, London, Routledge & Kegan Paul (rev. ed.). Eysenck's theory has been integrated with social factors by Gordon Trasler, *The Explanation of Criminality*, Routledge & Kegan Paul, 1962; and the critical evidence is summarized by R. Cochrane, 'Crime and Personality: Theory and Evidence', *Bulletin of the British Psychological Society*, vol. 27, 1974, pp. 19–24. It should be stressed that Eysenck is opposed to the use of such techniques in the prison context.

21. Wayne Sage, 'Crime and the Clockwork Lemon', *Human Behaviour*, September 1974, pp. 16–25.

22. Jackson, Toby, 'An Evaluation of Early Identification and Intensive Treatment Programs for Predelinquents', *Social Problems*, Fall, 1965, 13, 2, pp. 160–75.

23. The crucial work remains that of Aaron Cicourel in (with J. I. Kitsuse), 'A Note on the use of Official Statistics', *Social Problems*, 1963, 11, 131–8; and *The Social Organisation of Juvenile Justice*, John Wiley, 1968.

24. J. B. Mays, op. cit.; Henry Mayhew, *London Labour and the London Poor*, 1851; T. P. Morris, see note 7; John Baldwin and A. E. Bottoms, in collaboration with Monica Walker, *The Urban Criminal: A Study in Sheffield*, Tavistock, 1976; D. M. Downes, op. cit.; D. Hargreaves, op. cit.; Jock Young, 'New directions in subcultural theory' in John Rex (ed.), *Approaches to Sociology*, Routledge & Kegan Paul, 1974.

25. Howard Becker, *Outsiders: Studies in the Sociology of Deviance*, The Free Press, 1963, p. 9.

26. Edwin Lemert, *Human Deviance, Social Problems and Social Control*, Prentice-Hall, 1967, p. 17.

27. Robert K. Merton, 'The Self-fulfilling Prophecy' in his *Social Theory and Social Structure*, The Free Press, 1957, 2nd rev. ed.

28. See note 23.

29. Steven Box, op. cit.

30. Howard Parker, *The View from the Boys*, David and Charles, 1974; Jason Ditton, *Part-Time Crime*, Macmillan, 1976.

31. Stan Cohen and Laurie Taylor, op. cit.; Owen Gill, *Luke Street: Housing Policy, Conflict and the Creation of a Delinquency Area*, Macmillan, 1977; Paul Rock, *Making People Pay*, Routledge & Kegan Paul, 1973; W. G. Carson, 'White Collar Crime and the Enforcement of Factory Legislation', *British Journal of Criminolgy*, 1970, 10, pp. 383–98; Ken Plummer, *Sexual Stigma: An Interactionist Account*, Routledge & Kegan Paul, 1975; Maureen Cain, *Society and the Policeman's Role*, Routledge & Kegan Paul, 1973; Simon Holdaway, 'Changes in Urban Policing', *British Journal of Sociology*, 1977, 28, 2, pp. 119–39; Laurie Taylor and Paul Walton, 'Industrial Sabotage' in Stan Cohen (ed.); *Images of Deviance*, Penguin, 1971; Pat Carlen, *Magistrates' Justice*, Martin Robertson, 1976; Penelope Tomlinson, *Structure and Process in the Juvenile Court*, L.S.E., unpublished Ph.D. thesis, 1975; Victor Sharp, *Social Control in a Therapeutic Community*, Saxon House, 1976; Richard Ericson, *Young Offenders and their Social Work*, John Wiley, 1975; Steve Chibnall, *Law-and-Order News*, Tavistock, 1977; Roy Wallis, *The Road to Total Freedom: A Sociological Analysis of Scientology*, Heinemann, 1976; Mary McIntosh, *The Organisation of Crime*, Macmillan, 1975; Sean Damer, 'Wine Alley: The Sociology of a Dreadful Enclosure', *Sociological Review*, May 1974, 22, 2; reprinted in Wiles, P., op. cit., 1976; Howard Parker, op. cit.; Richard Ericson, *supra*.

32. Ronald Akers, 'Problems in the Sociology of Deviance: Social Definitions and Behaviour', *Social Forces*, 1967, pp. 455–65; Ian Taylor, Paul Walton and Jock Young, *The New Criminology*, ch. 5, 1973; D. J. West and D. P. Farrington, *The Delinquent Way of Life*, ch. 7, 1977; Andrew Scull, 'Social Control and the Amplification of Deviance' in R. Scott and J. Douglas (eds), *Theoretical*

Perspectives on Deviance, Basic Books, 1972; Alvin Gouldner, op. cit., 1968.

33. Michael Phillipson, op. cit.; Jeff Coulter, *Approaches to Insanity*, Martin Robertson, 1973; Nell Keddie, 'Classroom Knowledge' in Michael F. D. Young (ed.), *Knowledge and Control*, Collier-Macmillan, 1971; David Hargreaves, Stephen Hester and Frank Mellor, *Deviance in Classrooms*, Routledge & Kegan Paul, 1975; Sheila Hillier, 'Anyman Goes Mad', *Sociology*, 1975, 9, 2, pp. 323–8; and Coulter's reply in *Sociology*, 1976, 10, 2, pp. 317–20.

34. Wilhelm Bonger, *Criminality and Economic Conditions*, 1916, Little, Brown & Co.; reprinted in abridged form, edited by Austin Turk, Indiana University Press, 1969; Eric Hobsbawm, *Primitive Rebels*, Manchester University Press, 1959; George Rudé, *The Crowd in History*, John Wiley, 1964.

35. Peter Salomon Jr., 'Soviet Criminology—Its Demise and Rebirth 1928–63', in Roger Hood (ed.), *Crime, Criminology and Public Policy*, Heinemann, 1974.

36. See note 34, but also: E. Hobsbawm, *Bandits*, Weidenfeld and Nicolson, 1969; E. Hobsbawm and G. Rudé, *Captain Swing*, Allen Lane, 1969; E. P. Thompson, *Whigs and Hunters: The Origins of the Black Act*, Allen Lane, 1975; Raphael Samuel, *Village Life and Labour*, Routledge & Kegan Paul, 1975; Gareth Stedman Jones, *Outcast London: A Study of the Relationship between Classes in Victorian Society*, Oxford University Press, 1971.

37. John Clarke, Stuart Hall, Tony Jefferson and Brian Roberts (eds), *Resistance Through Rituals*, Working Papers in Cultural Studies, nos. 7–8, Summer 1975; also Hutchinson, 1976; Stuart Hall, et al., *Policing the Crisis*, Macmillan, 1978.

38. Andrew Scull, *Decarceration*, Prentice-Hall, 1976.

39. Mary MacIntosh, op. cit.

40. Geoff Pearson, 'Paki-bashing in a North East Lancashire Cotton Town: A Case Study and its History' in Geoff Mungham and Geoff Pearson (eds), *Working Class Youth Culture*, Routledge & Kegan Paul, 1976.

41. Andrew Scull, op. cit., 1976.

42. Ian Taylor et al., op. cit., 1973 and 1975; David Matza, *Delinquency and Drift*, John Wiley, 1964, ch. 1; Frank Pearce, *Crimes of the Powerful; Marxism, Crime and Deviance*, Pluto Press, 1976; Victoria Greenwood and Jock Young, *Abortion on Demand*, Pluto Press, 1976. For a more eclectic view of the sources of 'critical theory', see Geoff Pearson, *The Deviant Imagination: Psychiatry, Social Work and Social Change*, Macmillan, 1975.

43. Leslie Sklair, 'The Fate of the "Functional Requisites" in Parsonian Sociology', *British Journal of Sociology*, March 1970, 21, 1, pp. 30–42.

44. Colin Sumner, 'Marxism and Deviancy Theory' in Wiles, P. (ed.), op. cit., 1976; Glasgow University Media Group, *Bad News*, Routledge & Kegan Paul, 1976.

45. Paul Willis, 'The Motorbike Within a Subcultural Group', *WPCS*, 2, Spring 1972, pp. 53–70. See also his *Learning to Labour*, Saxon House, 1977; and *Profane Culture*, Routledge & Kegan Paul, 1978.

46. Phil Cohen, 'Subcultural Conflict and Working Class Community', *WPCS*, 2, Spring 1972, pp. 1–51.

47. Anthony Giddens, *New Rules of Sociological Method*, Hutchinson, 1976, p. 141.

48. J. D. Halloran, P. Elliot and G. Murdock, *Demonstrations and Communication: A Case Study*, Penguin, 1970; Steven Box, op. cit., 1971; James Patrick, *A Glasgow Gang Observed*, Eyre Methuen, 1973.

49. Carol Smart, *Women, Crime and Criminology: A Feminist Critique*, Routledge & Kegan Paul, 1977.

50. John Lambert, *Crime, Police and Race Relations*, Institute of Race Relations/Oxford University Press, 1970.

51. Frank Pearce's book dealt chiefly with American anti-trust laws violations, and the role of the rackets in buttressing corporate power. Journalism is way ahead of sociology in this respect. See, for example, Charles Raw, Bruce Page and Godfrey Hodgson, *Do You Sincerely Want to be Rich? Bernard Cornfield and IOS: An International Swindle*, André Deutsch, 1971.

[6]
Praxis makes Perfect
A Critique of Critical Criminology[1*]

For the past fifteen years or so, the trend has been for the dominant 'model' of sociological thought — composed of a more or less deterministic, explanatory and quantitatively researched set of assumptions — to give way before the attacks mounted against it by sociologists of a more or less voluntaristic, interpretative and qualitatively minded persuasion. Three articles signalled the decisive break as far as American sociology was concerned: Dennis Wrong's 'The Over-socialised Conception of Man' (1961), George Homans's 'Bringing Men Back In' (1964) and Everett Hughes's 'Race Relations and the Sociological Imagination' (1963).† In substance, these articles were less radical in the alternatives they preferred than in the dramatic challenge to orthodoxy implied by their titles. Wrong's trenchant attack on the 'over-socialised' conception of man as a counterpart to the 'over-integrated' view of society led to a plea for the reinstatement of Freud in sociological theorising. Homans's dissection of the incongruity of structural-functionalism and historical change must be seen in the context of the limitations of his own brand of social behaviourism. And Hughes, in his laying of the blame for American sociology's failure to foresee a sharp deterioration in race relations at the door of 'abstract empiricism', did little more than echo C. Wright Mills.[2] But all these papers were addressed to the American Sociological Association: all duly appeared in the *American Sociological Review* between 1961 and 1964. In sum, they were an acknowledgement, from the most senior platform in the discipline, that sociological theory was ill-equipped to cope with the most pressing social and intellectual problems. Gouldner's 'coming crisis' (Gouldner, 1970),[3]

*Notes on the text will be found at the end of each paper.

announced somewhat late in the day, had already come, and it is clearly still with us.

Ultimately, two attempts at resolving the crisis have attracted most following (though even now it is doubtful whether more than a minority of sociologists on either side of the Atlantic subscribe — in any thoroughgoing sense — to either; they either lack any firm theoretical anchorage or opt for a safe Weberian harbour.) These attempts emanate from Mead and the symbolic interactionist tradition,[4] and from Marx — and the 'humanistic' early Marx in particular.[5] For a time an uneasy alliance between the two prevailed. The case was made anew for regarding man as a subject rather than an object: for causality as mediated through men as active agents, rather than as passive receptors; and, more tentatively, for sociology as a practice attuned to social conflicts and the open advocacy of radical means of resolving them, rather than as an upholder of the *status quo,* with a veiled advisory role in the making of social adjustments. But this compromise proved provisional only. For if the most penetrating work in sociology in the sixties went on at the micro-sociological level, it was because the issue of determinism at the level of the individual and interpersonal relations was pursued at the expense of the issue of determinateness at the institutional and macro-sociological level. The pull to Marx has been a move to 'bring society (or political economy) back in'. And events which shook American society in the late 1960s and 1970s prised the two approaches even further apart.

In criminology these developments were more dramatic, chiefly because the initial gap between the mode of explanation favoured in criminology and the revived aspirations for a more humanistic sociology of deviance was even greater than in sociology in general. The dominance of the medico-legal approach to explanations cast in terms of structural and cultural 'forces' and 'patterns' had given criminology a marginal status as far as sociologists were concerned. Even so, the vogue for regarding criminology as a sort of unique backwater in the social sciences has been overdone. In the sociology of education, in demography, in political sociology and in industrial sociology, similar rigidities prevailed. What gave peculiar force to the trend away from positivism in criminology was the conjunction between the more general reassertion of the claims of interpretative sociology and an unusually forceful rejection of the philosophical grounds for the existence of criminology as a subject in its own right.

The grounds on which criminology existed as a subject have never been adequately appraised or even satisfactorily outlined, but the distinctiveness of the criminal sanction is implicitly assumed to lend credence to the study of those found guilty of legal infraction. As it evolved, criminology paid little attention to how and why the criminal sanction came to be invoked against certain kinds of behaviour and not others, or against certain individuals and not others who engaged in similar infractions. This omission was seen as crucial by those who preferred a different and more inclusive deviancy framework for the study of crime and delinquency. Because the law is the outcome of processes of definition which emanate primarily from the powerful, and as a result is so cast as both to secure their interests and minimise the likelihood of their incrimination, it cannot be taken for granted as a neutral arbiter of conforming and aberrant behaviour. Moreover, many laws are almost wholly declaratory, 'more honoured in the breach than the observance', e.g. the 30 m.p.h. speed limit in built-up areas; by contrast, many quite legal activities are both viewed as morally opprobrious and arouse an intense emotionality and hostility of response, e.g. homosexual exhibitionism. The assumption that the criminal sanction is somehow unique palls before the sheer variability of its definition and enforcement. In criminology, as a result, Becker's publication of *Outsiders* (1963) was an event of much greater significance than the articles by Wrong, Hughes and Homans in sociology. His central organising principle — 'Deviant behaviour is that which is so labelled' — superficially a banal and even trivial assertion, caused an explosion in the petrified forest of criminology. It signalled a major reorientation from a position which assumed the virtual unchallengeability of studies which took the legal code and the manner of its enforcement for granted to one which treated these processes as problematic. The scope of enquiry was widened from law infraction to rule- and norm-infraction. The mode of inquiry was shifted from the statistical to the interpretative. The social reaction to deviance became as central to inquiry as the deviance itself. In the process, the sociologist was required to take account, as never before, of the deviant's view of himself and the world. One aspect of this concern was a redefinition of praxis: the sociologist was to be partisan in his defence of the underdog (deviant) in the face of the attack mounted against him by social controllers (police, social workers, welfare bureaucrats). Arguments for decriminalisation and an active reassertion of liberal pluralism followed in train.

It was primarily to this aspect of the new sociology of deviance that Gouldner addressed himself in his critique of Becker and others in 1968. Donning the mantle of C. Wright Mills, Gouldner was at pains to point out that, to mix mythological metaphors, having helped to slay the minotaurs of objectivity and structural-functionalism in sociology, he did not intend standing idly by whilst new dragon's teeth were sown in the shape of subjectivism and relativism which lacked all semblance of regard for social structure. In a by now hallowed phrase in the annals of critical criminology, he stated: 'Becker's school of deviance thus views the underdog as someone who is being mismanaged, not as someone who suffers or fights back . . . [It] is directed at the caretaking institutions who do the mopping up job, rather than at the master institutions that produce the deviant's suffering' (Gouldner, 1968, p. 39). To Gouldner, the deviant's version of events and himself, ironically, can only reproduce that of the master institutions whose definition of reality has been stamped upon him. While this is in itself questionable, the way forward for radical, as distinct from liberal, sociologists is to be the study of the deviance of 'overdogs', whose power not only to grasp but to *shape* the machinery of control also enables them to shape the worlds in which both deviants and caretakers move and interact. 'The Sociologist as Partisan' provided the point of departure for those who sought to differentiate a radical criminology from a liberal sociology of deviance. It is in this spirit that *The New Criminology* (Taylor et al, 1973a) and *Critical Criminology* (Taylor et al, 1975a), as well as *Crime of the Powerful* (Pearce, 1976) should be approached.

As critical criminologists lay great emphasis on purposes, my own should be alluded to. Since the appearance of *The New Criminology,* but especially since that of its successor volume, *Critical Criminology,* teaching the subject to a wide variety of students in higher education, further education and training courses has had to take account of a challenging new approach. Long moribund, Marxist criminology has been revitalised by these books (whatever the Althusserians might say). Some effects have been entirely to the good: students can now be directed (in the case of the first of the books) to what is still the most comprehensive and succinct coverage of virtually the entire criminological studies field; certain issues — for example, the contribution of Durkheim to the study of crime and deviance — have been freshly explored, and the 'crimes of the powerful' issue has been rediscovered. But some effects have been more negative: notably, the difficulties encountered, in my own case at any rate, in examining the issue of just what the 'new' or 'critical' criminology is *for.*

This may seem obtuse, in that the authors concerned have stated their aims with great apparent clarity as being 'to argue for a criminology which is normatively committed to the abolition of inequalities of wealth and power' and 'to attempt to create the kind of society in which the facts of human diversity are not subject to the power to criminalise' (Taylor et al,

1975a, p. 44). Where, then, is the difficulty?

The core of the problem lies in their relation of theory and practice (praxis), and it is best conveyed by quotation:

> The point about theoretical praxis, for us, is that it is concerned to encourage the changes specified by the precepts of its own radical theory, and to develop research procedures relevant to that project... It has to develop methodologies for the realisation of the societies its own critique would necessitate, for, as David Harvey puts it, 'a revolutionary theory . . . will gain acceptance only if the nature of the social relationships embodied in the theory are actualised in the real world.' (Taylor et al, 1975a, p. 24)[6]

In other words (a) the answers to the questions that matter are already known; (b) it is not, however, possible to specify what these answers amount to in advance of their actualisation.

In my view, these axioms serve ultimately to constrain rather than liberate, to fetter rather than free; because they commit their authors to precepts and purposes which are inherently self-confirming, their work seems to present insurmountable difficulties to sociologists who may otherwise be in sympathy with their aims.

One of the most striking criticisms that Gouldner makes of Becker's 'Whose Side are We On?' (1967) is that Becker never makes explicit his answer to this question. While in both that address (to the American Society for the Study of Social Problems) and in *Outsiders,* Becker implies throughout that we should be on the side of the underdog deviant who is 'more sinned against than sinning', nowhere can Gouldner find an explicit assertion to that effect, a discovery that leads him to some dark reflections on the difficulty that liberals would find themselves in both professionally and financially if they had the courage of their convictions.

In a similar spirit, the collected writings of radical criminologists can be searched in vain for what one might take to be the central premise on which their project rests: a statement of the properties which a truly socialist (and crime-free) society would possess. Now this omission is of a far more fundamental character than that attributed by Gouldner to Becker, for, in the latter case, whether or not Becker made an explicit personal commitment to the underdog makes not one jot of difference to the intellectual strengths and weaknesses of his position. But in the case, as it has so far been stated, of critical or radical criminology, the entire intellectual construction rests on the postulates that capitalist society is essentially criminogenic, and that only by the total repudiation of the ethic of possessive individualism on which it rests can 'true' equality and

6 *Deviant Interpretations*

'socialist diversity' — the prerequisites for a 'crime-free' society — be attained. As it may be argued that these propositions are quite independent, that is, that we may accept the one without *ipso facto* needing to accept the other, the authors concerned might appear to be making things unnecessarily hard for themselves by linking the two. Yet this is what they appear to do.

> The processes involved in crime-creation are bound up in the final analysis with the *material* basis of contemporary capitalism and its structures of law . . . Critically, we would assert that it *is* possible to envisage societies free of any material necessity to criminalise deviance. Other controls on 'anti-social' behaviour (and other definitions of what that might constitute) can be imagined, and, from the point of view of a socialist diversity, would be essential. (Taylor et al, 1975a, p. 20)

On this last point, the reader is then referred to Young's essay, 'Working-class Criminology', (1975) which asserts the need for working-class control of deviance in working-class communities (on which, see below). This aside, nowhere is any attempt made to lay bare for analytical inspection the properties which would characterise a truly socialist society. Frequently invoked, it serves as a rhetorical foil against which to highlight the evils of capitalism. This kind of argument by affirmation reaches a pitch of absurdity in the statement 'A socialist conception of man would insist on the unlimited nature of human potential in a *human* society' (Taylor et al, 1975a, p. 23), where the italics are in some fashion intended to carry the full weight of philosophical argument to sustain the assertion.[7]

Were this simply a matter of parenthesis, of a stylistic flourish or embellishment to the major issues at stake, it would hardly be worth pursuing. But all the indications are that, far from serving merely to decorate the argument, the invocation of a crime-free socialist diversity is the very core of the argument. It enables the authors to dismiss all or almost all that has gone before as so much 'conservative' or 'liberal' mystification, the former (knaves) actively supporting, the latter (fools) indirectly reinforcing, the structures of capitalist political economy. The sharpest analysis and the deadliest invective are indeed applied to mere 'social-democrat reformism', particularly of the Fabian variety. Any attempt to reform capitalism from within, by recourse to the institutions of bourgeois democracy, is to be rejected. The idea that considerable variations exist *between* capitalist societies, in the extent to which the welfare state, for example, has made inroads upon the market economy, is held in particular scorn. By definition, such interventionism can only serve to prop up the essentially exploitative nature of capitalism. That state socialist societies have not only found it necessary to develop a welfare state apparatus, but have also experienced a set of social problems comparable to those in social democratic societies is not regarded as much of an obstacle to this line of argument, though a growing literature attest to this — *The Case-Worker* by George Konrad (1975) is the most impressive recent example from Eastern Europe.[8] In common with the New Left, the answer to this would doubtless be that these societies are not truly socialist, but rather state capitalist. As to how it came about that state capitalism was the outcome of socialist praxis, there is a massive apologetic literature concerning the 'wrong road' or whatever taken by the socialist societies in the main. But the twin themes that recur in that literature, betrayal from within and capitalist encirclement, are increasingly threadbare. Socialists would greet with derision the argument that capitalism had taken the wrong road because its leaders had betrayed it, or because of feudal or precapitalist encirclement. The sad truth is that, as increasing proportions of the world's population come to experience one or other variations of the state socialist theme, the relevance of Marx diminishes and that of Weber increases in almost geometric progression. But the authors of *Critical Criminology,* and the New Left in general, rarely feel obliged to resolve these questions. Next time, they say, it will be different.

Now the conception of praxis which is brought into play at this stage has several crucial functions. It enables the 'radicals' to postpone indefinitely the need to examine analytically the nature of the socialist alternative to the capitalist system; to insist that, because the future is unknowable, no time need be wasted on the likely institutional configuration that would render socialist diversity more than a nominal possibility; to ignore the substantial differences and variations that exist between capitalist societies in the light of the experience gained of different 'mixtures' of private and public sectors of the economy and welfare services; and, finally, to minimise the relevance of the experience of state socialism in resolving the very problems they discern as essentially bound up with capitalism. Praxis becomes a means for suspending awkward theoretical issues and stubborn historical constraints. The ideal of freeing men from the tyranny of causality by endowing them with knowledge gained by sociological theorising is undermined by the insistence that its tentative and ambiguous character should be rejected in favour of clear-cut Marxist presuppositions about the world. Attempts to translate the latter into practice have, moreover, a familiar authoritarian ring to them (see Stan Cohen's 'It's All Right for You to Talk' (1975)) 'We Know Best' is not the only possible outcome of this epistemology but it is the one historically shown to be

8 *Deviant Interpretations*

most likely, especially when concepts like 'false consciousness' can be employed to bridge any gaps between theory and actuality.

The search for what in *The New Criminology* was described as the 'total interconnectedness' between crime and the political economy of capitalism too easily leads to a revival of the 'seamless web' approach to social phenomena. An example of the latter is Jock Young's argument that

> Cultures which threaten work discipline, sexual behaviour which undermines the nuclear family, adolescent hedonism are all subject to legal prosecution and distorted coverage in the mass media. Thus when the state of California spends $73 million in 1968 on marihuana control, when more is spent on Social Security prosecutions than has even been obtained illegally from the State, when supposedly scarce police resources are utilised in the persecution of gays, and when legislation denies women the right to choose whether to give birth or not — all this seeming ruling-class irrationality contributes enormously to the maintenance of bourgeois institutions. (Foreword to Pearce, 1976, p. 18)

Doubtful as it is whether or not such 'irrationality' does indeed contribute to the 'maintenance of bourgeois institutions', the point about this argument is its circularity. If marihuana use is prosecuted, then that is because it threatens capitalism. If the penalties are drastically reduced, or if they are abolished altogether (as is in prospect in several U.S. states), then that is presumably because capitalism no longer fears it. (This is not, however, the case with Greenwood and Young's study of abortion (1976), where more careful consideration is given to the 'ruling-class interests' variable.) None of which should detract from the importance of seeking to establish what connections obtain between crime and its control and the 'master institutions' of any society, capitalism included. But it is even more important to forestall a resurgence of functionalism in the process, even if it is linked with humanistic Marxism. As Sklair concluded in his review of Parsonian functionalism: 'It is essential to evaluate the functionalistic method, in the sense that it suggests to us where to look, in isolation from the functionalist doctrine, that tells us what we will find there' (Sklair, 1970, p. 40).

The most depressing accompaniment of this form of praxis is the foreclosure it threatens on theorising. The premise that crime derives from the material facts of life in propertied societies rests on a set of unexamined assumptions about crime and its control, assumptions which have been subjected to the most searching criticism over the past decade. Not that such a premise lacks plausibility: just that it begs all the most fruitful methodological, analytic and theoretical questions raised by the critics of positivist and consensual approaches in criminology. Praxis brings the wheel of consensus full circle, back to an unproblematic view of the world. The premise ignores the possibilities that alternative sources of crime exist which are not reducible to propertied inequalities: notably, that the division of labour in advanced industrial societies of both capitalist and socialist societies of various kinds may play a causal role. Neither does the premise begin to make sense of the vast differences of crime and its control in societies with rough equivalence in properties inequality; for example, such differences hardly account for the variation in homicide rates that exist between the U.S.A. and Britain. In one society, China, there is a correspondence between the absence of propertied inequality and a (from all accounts) negligible crime rate, but the fate of political deviants, and the possibility of diversity (the phrase is never expanded upon) must await further documentation than has so far been available even to sympathetic Western observers. This is not to say that the present range of human societies exhausts the full range of human possibility. But the experiences of the post-1917 period should be enough to be going on with, without acting as if socialist praxis has never been tried before. Theorising may not have to end with what exists, but should at least take it into account. As it is, critical criminologists too often write as if imperialism was monopolised by capitalist societies, as if the tanks had never rolled into Prague or Budapest, as if people in capitalist societies were utterly dehumanised (except where they are struggling heroically against the bosses).

Such comments may seem invidious, particularly when the authors elsewhere clearly display an acute consciousness of the repression endemic in state socialist regimes — as in Ian Taylor's review of Connor's book on crime in Russia (1973a), and Young's reference to Soviet labelling of political dissidents as mentally ill (Foreword to Pearce, 1976, p. 12) (though the Soviet regime goes far beyond mere labelling in the last case). However, the comments do seem appropriate in the context of such absolutist statements as: 'It is not that man behaves as an animal because of his "nature" (under capitalism): it is that he is not fundamentally allowed by virtue of the social arrangements of production to do otherwise' (Taylor et al, 1975a, p. 23). Such a statement is simply bizarre when set beside such a record as *The Gulag Archipelago* on the one hand, and against the humanistic achievements of Western societies ('under capitalism') on the other. In general, however, it is not that they are asking unimportant or wrong questions about capitalism: it is that they allow such questions to *stop* at capitalism, as if oppression and corruption, of a systematic and regularised nature, did not present issues of any great analytic interest when they occur under nominally socialist systems. In one passage only (Taylor et al, 1973b, p. 401) do they state that crime is not specific to capitalism, i.e. that capitalism is distinctively criminogenic, not uniquely so. The issue is treated as 'true' (but 'obvious'): no more need be said than a reference back to the incompatibility of criminalisation with socialist diversity.

The usual reply to this kind of criticism is that existing forms of state socialist society are not to be equated with *true* socialism, that it is ludicrous to expect a blueprint for a truly socialist society, when its possibilities have only ever been glimpsed, and when praxis is by definition a process of open-ended struggle, rather than the ushering in of a preformulated framework. It is certainly the case that a blueprint is the last thing we want. The ideal of a perfectly planned Utopia has proved as abhorrent to twentieth-century writers in the dystopian tradition — particularly Zamyatin and Huxley — as it was to Marx. But avoiding prediction at all costs is no solution to the Utopian dilemma. What is needed is not a blueprint, but an ideal-typical sketch of the kind of society summoned up by the phrase 'socialist diversity'. How is it envisaged that we move away from a society based on propertied inequality without becoming a state capitalist society? How would people be allocated to jobs — by merit, by rota, or what? How will political life be conducted? These questions could be postponed in the not-too-remote past, when a capitalist ruling class was unquestionably dominant, when class differences resembled a caste-like massification, and before any substantial attempt had been made to remove basic industries and services from the private to the public sector. The first can hardly retain credibility when a Tory government has been trounced from office after a humiliating confrontation with the miners. The second has given way to a far more complex structure in which class inequalities still obtain but are increasingly measurable only by resort to relative rather than absolute indicators of difference. The third has reached the point where approaching one-third of productive industry and two-thirds of all transfer payments are state owned and managed. In other words, we have reached the point at which the days of modern consumer capitalism *could* be numbered, in Britain at any rate, if the political will to despatch it matched the evident and already mobilised strength of the forces which oppose it ideologically, yet actually operate to keep it in existence. (Its days are ultimately numbered anyway, since — as *The Limits to Growth* spelt out, with data that may be problematic but on principles that surely aren't — the constant fostering of the propensity to consume, by which capitalism has sustained itself these last fifty years, cannot outlast the limits on that consumption set by the eco-system; see Meadows et al, 1972, and Hirsch, 1977.) But the system is still actively kept in existence, if only in a negative and inert way, by the very movements which oppose it, in part at least because no specifiable alternative to it has been shown to exist, or has been adequately proposed as a potential alternative by the various groups on the Left. A few exceptions should be noted. The work on workers' control by Ken Coates is one; the writings of André Gorz on political democracy are another (see Coates, Gorz in Anderson and Blackburn, 1965). But in the main, the Left has concentrated on sheerly polemical fulmination against the existing system or endless analyses of the contradictions of capitalism, with all of which we are by now wearisomely familiar.

It is to this impasse that the conception of praxis which appears in the work of radical criminologists and others on the Left has helped bring us. By equating specifiable and documented proposals for change with 'mere' reformism, by — indeed — dismissing the ideal of gradual and therefore reversible change as contemptible, they may convey the *grounds* on which the socialist diversity they invoke is preferable or superior to the liberal capitalist-cum-social democratic society they reject, but we are left without any clue as to what practices might constitute its character (see, for example, Titmuss, 1970). In seeking to transcend *all* aspects of contemporary practice, in asserting the need to change the *status quo out of recognition,* they create a vacuum which is to be filled by . . . what? Since they not only fail but make a positive virtue of *refusing* to specify those institutional features which might serve as the basis for socialist diversity, they should not be too surprised if the response is guarded caution.[9] As Orwell pointed out even thirty years ago, the British people have a great deal more to lose than their chains.

In one instance, though, an attempt has been made to outline an alternative to present institutional practice. In his 'Working-class Criminology' (1975), Jock Young asserts the need for the working class to wrest control of its own communities from 'external policing agencies'. The implications of this position (which lacks any accompanying strategy) can at least be subjected to some sort of sociological scrutiny, in sharp contrast to the foreclosure of any possibility of validation that characterises the critical perspective in other respects. This said, Young's brief allusion to this issue is more remarkable for what it leaves unexplored than for what it actually states. It rests on the assumption that external policing agencies simply or mainly act to enforce the law of the bourgeoisie, in a

12 *Deviant Interpretations*

manner and on principles which are at odds with working-class interests. (Needless to say, this is quite different from the Fabian position, which is broadly that considerable consensus exists about the law, but structured inequalities exist in relation to its mobilisation on behalf of those — still the majority — who lack the means to afford its practitioners' services.) It assumes that the working class overwhelmingly resides in homogeneous communities which share a distinctive consensus, at odds with the middle class, about the scope, range, aims and methods of policing. It implies that working-class communities would benefit from internal policing, in the face of the considerable conflicts and fissures that exist *within* such communities. It implies that working-class deviants would fare better under class-specific rather than constitutional safeguards — but no differentiation is made between types of justice, which run the gamut of possibility from authoritarian and arbitrary lynch law to the most subtle forms of mutual aid. All the dilemmas of due process vs. executive, legalistic vs. welfare and restitutive vs. deterrent forms of justice and control are ignored. In sum, it raises the most important issues only to duck them. The most likely result of implementing Young's ideas would be a reversion to the chaos that prevailed in London before the Metropolitan Police Act of 1829. It would leave the poorer and more vulnerable sections of the working class far worse off than now, reproducing a state of affairs that already prevails in the worst American ghettoes. It would herald the rapid expansion of private security forces, the costs of which would be heaped regressively on the poor — unless, of course, all this hinges on the prior attainment of a state of 'socialist diversity'. In which case, the adoption of a class-based form of control will be redundant.

Linked with Young's argument is the view that the criminal statistics are most fruitfully interpreted as an index of 'the credibility of a propertied society at particular periods of its development — the extent to which the distribution of property is latently accepted or rejected amongst certain sections of the working population' (Taylor et al, 1975a, p. 42). The fact that we *can* 'read' them this way, by extension reading into the rise in crimes against property a growing rejection of the ethic of possessive individualism, in no way overcomes the formidable problems involved in 'reading' the criminal statistics any way at all, or of choosing between this 'reading' and the equally plausible alternative that a rise in propertied crime entails an *increase* in attachment to possessive individualism. For one of the striking findings of the recent rash of studies of victimisation has been the extent to which the victims of crimes against property are those people without any (relatively speaking, that is). For example, field studies carried out for the 1967 President's Commission on Law Enforcement and the Administration of Justice in the U.S.A. were summarised as showing that 'the risk of victimisation is highest among the lower-income groups for all Index offences except homicide, larceny and vehicle theft; it weighs most heavily on the non-whites for all Index offences except larceny' (Ennis, *Challenge of Crime in a Free Society,* 1967 p. 39). Moreover, even the larceny finding relates only to sums of $50 or more: if all larcenies had been included, that finding too may have tallied with the other offences in its distribution of victims, since the lower one's income, the less one is likely, presumably, to be in possession of sums of over $50. Indeed, this is partially borne out by figures showing median net property losses by income group, which for whites shows the average for those whose incomes were under $6,000 was $34, while for those whose income exceeded that sum it was $30, a result that could have occurred only if the lower-income group experienced a far higher rate of larceny of sums under $50 than the higher income group (see Ennis, 1967, tables 8 and 14). The point, however, is that only by the most tortuous reasoning can a rejection of the ethic of possessive individualism and the current distribution of property be culled from such evidence. For what such figures show is not a Robin Hood-like robbing of the rich to serve the poor, but a massive infliction of misery on those least able to protect themselves. These results hardly tally with the often-quoted denial of local victimisation by delinquent boys; though the most fiercely held loyalties may be respected, this does not necessarily protect those of the same status living on the next block. What this evidence points to is an affirmation of possessive individualism *come what may,* what Robert Merton some forty years ago termed 'innovation', as opposed to its alternative, 'rebellion'. It may well be that such predatory activity represents the final, seedy triumph of 'bourgeois' culture: but it is possible to test this proposition against the resurgence of similar forms of victimisation in non-capitalist societies only if we abandon approaches which limit analysis to capitalism alone.

All the issues debated here are of ancient lineage. Their reinscription, their resurfacing at this stage is perhaps a sign that sociology has come full circle, that its potential as an escape route from time-worn philosophical constraints is at an end. I would prefer to believe that those constraints are illuminated and modified by sociological theorising and research, that the grounds on which certain positions are advanced can be clarified by sociological work, but that such a perspective bears fruit only if certain ground rules are respected. As Giddens has argued, '... those conditions in which human beings appear as objects to themselves ... may be altered by "self-knowledge" which is false just as much by that which is valid' (Giddens, 1976, p. 154). To foreclose the issue at the outset, on the strength of a world view that takes in only half the world, can only pre-empt all possibility of criteria that hold the terms of the debate open. If, on the other hand, you choose to operate on the view that capitalism is the source of nothing but evil, that no accommodation with it can be reached short of revolutionary action, that state socialist societies are really state capitalist societies and thus are not admissible as models of the likely outcomes of socialist praxis — a species of 'convergence' theory just as unacceptable as the orthodox kind — then you can indeed reel off the connections between crime, delinquency and capitalism as the central causal matrix.

Ironically, the adoption of this form of socialist praxis makes the advocacy of socialist diversity unnecessarily difficult. For the intellectual 'self-denying ordinance' that true socialism can be known only by negation, dialectically, rather than empirico-deductively, by tangible documentation, removes debate altogether from the realm of the known or knowable to that of sheer speculation. Not that such an alternative is easy, but it at least offers certain safeguards against absolutist conceptions, such as the comparative assessment of one system against another in terms of certain agreed-upon criteria, rather than resisting such scepticism as incompatible with immaculate theoretical conceptions. It is the mode of analysis shared by both social-democratic reformism, whose record is hardly as contemptible as critical criminologists make out, and latter-day anarchists, whose mauling at the hands of the state in both capitalist and socialist societies has lent a certain defiant modesty to their proposals. The most significant of these is an insistence that freedom, equality and justice are not remote abstractions to be realised only in some future and essentially unknowable society, but tangible realities to be grasped here and now in the many-sided forms of praxis that exist in education, housing, industry and family relations. It is the difference between a specifiable mode of praxis, in which it is possible to document the more from the less human, and a transcendental form of praxis, in which the contrast is made between an utterly inhuman and deformed present and an immaculate future and unknowable Utopia.

Marxists, especially those of the New Left, are fond of referring to social democratic theory in disparaging terms connoting theoretical vacuity, emptiness, intellectual void, etc. Most typically, Perry Anderson's diagnosis of British culture as 'bourgeois' culture was based on his view that intellectual life in Britain lacked the centre that in other European societies was formed by Marxism and the dialogue with Marxism (Anderson, 1968). Yet this notion of the 'absent centre' seems to apply with equal force to Marxist theory itself, for at the very centre of Marxist theory there is indeed a void: the nature of the 'classless' society. That that void has since been filled in by two major possible structures, Stalinism and Maoism, is no great comfort, since we know far too much about the former and far too little about the latter to be able to take them as corresponding to what theorists might mean when they invoke the classless society as their ideal. What is missing is any developed analytic treatment of the distribution of power and the division of labour that would match the attainment of 'classlessness' in an advanced industrial society. For, as Parkin and Giddens have made clear, it is upon the power relations that ensue from the *fusion* of control over the polity and the economy that the most oppressive features of state socialist societies are built (Parkin, 1972, especially ch. 6; Giddens, 1973, especially ch. 15).[10] In this perspective, even the deformed split between these two bases of power under modern capitalism afford their citizens some measure of freedom from total 'dehumanisation'.

NOTES

1. My thanks to Ernest Gellner, Paul Rock, Stan Cohen and Laurie Taylor for helpful comments on an earlier draft of this paper.
2. Mills's classic onslaught against 'grand theory' and 'abstracted empiricism' in *The Sociological Imagination* (1959) began what these and a host of other writers later consolidated.
3. The ultimate consolidation of Mills's critique.
4. See Matza (1959) for the most elegant summary of this tradition.
5. See Gouldner (1970) for a summary of these developments in the sixties. The most influential exponents in Britain were to be found in the New Left.
6. Their reference here was to Harvey (1973), p. 125.
7. The references are to *Critical Criminology* (Taylor et al, 1975a), in which these issues loom distinctly larger than in *The New Criminology* (Taylor et al, 1973a). The passage quoted is aptly met by Passmore's argument that:

   > One ought to regard with an initial suspicion such expressions as 'truly human' and 'dehumanising' . . . Cruelty and envy are peculiarly human forms of behaviour; to assert of someone who is cruel or envious that he is not 'truly human' is undeservedly to compliment the human species. It takes a human being to be a Marquis de Sade, to construct the concentration camps at Auschwitz, to wage war, to lie, to betray, to hate. Man is never less an animal than in the depths of his depravity. To describe a state of society as 'dehumanising' merely because it encourages men to deceive, to lie, to be cruel is, on the face of it, arbitrarily to admit as human only what is good. (Passmore, 1970, p. 279-280.)

8. This novel is both by, and portrays the life of, a social worker in Budapest.
9. The work of Thomas Mathiesen is of special relevance here, particularly his *The Politics of Abolition* (1974). One critic of the 'critical criminologists', Stan Cohen (in Bailey and Brake, 1975), finds Mathiesen's strategy of the 'unfinished'

16 *Deviant Interpretations*

preferable to one recipe for praxis floated by Ian Taylor. The strategy of Mathiesen, however, which is basically to avoid incorporation at all costs (whilst taking his role as an academic sufficiently seriously to struggle for abolition long-term and general reforms short-term) by means of a refusal to specify alternatives, is difficult to distinguish from sheer pragmatism. It is a pragmatism inspired by a passionately real commitment to work for a (wholly unspecified) socialist society, but that does not rescue us from the impasse of being asked to work for a future about which we are not allowed to theorise (at least in public). For an astringent view of the consequences of abolition in practice in the USA, see Scull, *Decarceration* (1977).

10. Both of these authors argue for the continuing relevance of Marx's concepts of class and class conflict as essential for an understanding of societies based on market economies. But the importance of their work is their avoidance of an acceptance *a priori* of the Marxist mode of analysis, their subjection of Marx's theories to the critical perspectives offered by other modes of analysis and their extension of the scope of inquiry to a comparative assessment of neo-capitalist and state socialist societies. It is this kind of approach, which seemed immanent in *The New Criminology*, from which *Critical Criminology* represents a turning away.

[7]

Abolition: Possibilities and Pitfalls

The ultimate penal reform is abolition. Thinkers as diverse as Shaw and the Webbs, William Godwin and the anarchists, and H. J. Eysenck and the aversion therapists would at least agree on that. An unlikely consensus, but one which may be a pre-condition for ultimate reforms of the abolitionist kind: the abolition of capital punishment gained this kind of consensus as a goal in the post-war period. But two barriers ordinarily stand in the way of the realisation of such ultimate reforms: first, the route to the reform; second, the alternative(s) to the system which is to be abolished. It is against these two barriers that the energies of penal reformers are spent; it is on the issues they entail that debate customarily centres; it is in the answers reformers give to the questions involved that the sharpest conflicts and disagreements are revealed. For Mathiesen (1974) these barriers constitute the major dilemmas of penal reform. The first classically revolves around the reform versus revolution issue (which has its correspondences in radical politics in general): should short-term considerations take precedence over long-term aims in the struggle for change? Penal reformers typically opt for the former, thereby losing sight of the latter (the counterpart is gradualism in politics). The second entails not only a degree of omniscience and prescience about possible futures rarely if ever granted mere mortals, but also implicitly snares the reformer into an acceptance of system goals: the alternative must meet the same goal as the system it aims to replace. Both have their Catch-22 aspect: the first, by improving the system, reinforces it; the second, by insisting that alternatives be shown to meet system goals in advance of their actualisation, sets impossible tasks for reformers. In combination, and given that the bureaucratic power of the authorities ensures that they are the arbiters in evaluating the case for reforms, the stage is set for penal reformers to end up hopelessly compromised with the system, on the one hand, or condemned to the 'irresponsible revolutionary' role, on the other.

The immense appeal of the work of Thomas Mathiesen on the

'politics of abolition' lies in his redefinition of the problems involved, and the solutions that emerge, in and from these dilemmas. In line with a great deal of philosophical work, he does not solve or resolve these dilemmas: he dissolves them. The first dilemma, reform versus revolution, he dissolves by insisting that *both* goals must be pursued. To make this more than sheer word-magic, a certain strategy must be followed, which involves distinguishing between reforms which at least do not strengthen the system — and which therefore can be pursued without detriment to long-term aims — and those which do — which must as a consequence be foregone. The second dilemma is dissolved by refusing to be drawn on the question of alternatives. Activists should press for abolition in its own terms and without becoming implicated in the system demand for a *quid pro quo* outcome. Alternatives are emergent properties of abolition rather than a prerequisite for it. Taken together, these are the theoretical elements in the 'politics of abolition'. The practice is to be catalysed by prisoners themselves. They are to be the prime movers in the struggle for penal reform, and their neutralisation and/or elimination from that process has been the result of previous strategies playing into the hands of the Establishment. They alone can preserve a reform movement from sterilisation. By their influence on reformers outside the walls, who must maintain a sensitivity to their demands, a form of action theory can be evolved which avoids both immaculate theoretical conceptions on the one hand, and token administrative 'practical' changes on the other. The whole strategy is termed by Mathiesen the 'unfinished', a dynamic, open-ended form of praxis which has as its components only the insistence on the need to move towards abolition, and to do so in combination with the 'expelled' themselves.

We are indebted to Mathiesen for providing so full and so personal an account of how he came to evolve this strategy, which coincides with that of KROM, the Norwegian prison reform movement, of which he was chairman throughout its formative years. He (and KROM) began in 1968 to construct a perspective on penal reform little different from that embraced in many respects by the Howard League and many other penal reform organisations in the western world. Its policy was basically treatment-oriented and humanitarian, and it was only when several prisoners (the 'group of nine') contacted them for information about their activities, that the long haul towards radicalisation began. For the authorities refused to allow any contact between KROM and those it aimed to serve, and whose participation it sought. This began a series of confrontations with the authorities over the rights of prisoners to participate in outside organisations of the KROM type, and by implication of their rights to contact with 'outside' on a whole series of fronts, including visits, furloughs, home leave, mail censorship and rights to telephone in privacy, issues which incidentally reveal by comparison the as yet relative mildness of equivalent demands by prisoners in British jails. The keynote to this stage is the relationship between KROM and the authorities, with the prisoners as victim, and the prison staff as the villain of the piece.

The longest single sequence in the book is, however, a record of the Swedish counterpart of KROM and its role in the 'negotiations' which followed the prison strikes of 1970 that emanated from Osteraker. From a stance implying that real concessions would be the outcome of their work, a working group was set up composed of an equal number of representatives from the prisoners and the authorities, with the Swedish KROM allowed a strictly limited advisory role 'backstage' for the prisoners. The tactics of the authorities are conveyed as a masterly exercise in 'divide and rule', with above all their insistence that 'negotiations' (from which results might flow) were in reality 'talks' (from which nothing might come), and with their insistence on the inability of the talks to go beyond strict adherence to possibilities within the current legal constraints. Despite their inexperience in the art of administrative psychological warfare, the prisoners' representatives nevertheless managed to emerge with a few proposals of significance. The package was then put before a large working party, where the inexperience of the prisoners' representatives in drafting proposals was cruelly exposed, and exploited, to whittle down the eventual settlement to one minor change regarding the dates at which prisoners of different kinds became eligible for furloughs. The whole episode, which was born of the gravest risks being run by prisoners in hunger, and in some cases, thirst striking, had been successfully protracted and eventually emasculated by the authorities (with the representatives of the staff vetoing a few concessions that even the authorities had allowed). For Mathiesen, and increasingly of course for those who share his views, this is the type-case of how authorities behave, with the utmost, callous indifference to the interests of prisoners (and the 'expelled' in general): whatever their skills in wrapping it up may be, the reality is one of effectively totalitarian power confronting total powerlessness.

It is important to understand how Mathiesen came to develop his view on the tactics of reform, for — as he makes clear at the outset — it could have been otherwise, if the authorities had reacted differently early on to absorb the reform group by acceptance rather than rejection. For Mathiesen, the emergent quality of the politics of abolition is a paradigm for the emergent properties of abolition itself. Mike Fitzgerald (1977), in his account of the origins and development of PROP (the British prisoners' union), and his analysis of the context in which that took place, makes much the same point.[1] Both go on to locate the crisis in the penal system within the class nature of capitalist (and state-capitalist) society. In such a society, prison is not simply an anachronistic and muddle-headed 'wasteful' response to crime: it is part and parcel of the system, and plays crucial functions within it. Hence, liberal exposés and moral indignation will do little more than patch up glaring excesses: a radical critique is needed to make the connections between prisons and class conflict. In line with Gouldner's (1973, ch. 2) critique of labelling theory, the conflict is not simply between prisoners and prison authorities and staff (the 'caretakers' of the system): it is ultimately between the 'expelled' in particular, and the working class in general; and an implacable State which serves the interests of a capitalist ruling class. Logically, as the crisis in the system deepens, crime rates, and imprisonment rates escalate; sentences get longer; the costs of labour-intensive staffing lead to cutbacks in amelioration; *ad hoc* solutions to stem the tide make matters worse (e.g. parole); and covert repression surfaces in bureaucratised form (e.g. control units). Things can only get worse: the only break in the expansion and intensification of penal control can flow from the struggle of the prisoners themselves, aided by outside organisations.

The appeal of Mathiesen's strategy for two groups in particular should be clarified: these are what one might term the 'liberal radicals' and the 'radical liberals'. The 'liberal radicals' are those who are committed to a form of libertarian socialism which aims to retrieve Marxist analysis from more monolithic interpretations. For them, the 'expelled' (dismissed as the lumpenproletariat in conventional Marxist terms) *do* have a role in the class struggle, and should not be dismissed as dangerous allies. Orthodox Marxism has tended in many respects to converge with conservative positivism in regarding 'deviants' in general, and criminals in particular, as the 'pathological' products of forces over which they have no control. For libertarian socialists, such as Mathiesen, Fitzgerald, and the 'new' criminologists (see Taylor *et al.* 1973, 1975), the struggle of deviants to achieve political voice for their authentic demands is just as valid as that of other subordinate groups. Hence, a strategy which links the two more specifically is to be welcomed. For 'radical liberals', those who do not embrace the Marxist analysis in general, but who regard more radical measures as essential if liberal values are to be activated for more than a minority, the more salient aspect of Mathiesen's work is his notion of the 'unfinished'. Thus, Stan Cohen views this strategy as ruling out the kind of subtly coercive élitism he discerns in Ian Taylor's interpretation of radical praxis (Cohen 1975). Both groups view the stated insistence on opposition to State power as basic to any strategy on behalf of and including the 'expelled'. Indeed, it is the 'State as enemy' theme which lends Mathiesen's linkage of the politicisation of the 'expelled', and the adoption of an open-ended strategy which is immune to incorporation, its peculiar force.

All of which should make one scrutinise with especial care this notion of the 'unfinished'. Mathiesen's main concern coincides with what Michels (1911) termed the 'iron law of oligarchy', the built-in tendency, as he defined it, for any organisation to stratify, as it expands, to the point where a self-perpetuating oligarchy come to run things, and define the situation their way, increasingly indifferent to the true interests of their mass membership. To avoid this, Mathiesen sees some escape as possible via the process of transition itself, in the metamorphosis from pre-political to organised movement, in the course of which 'negative' reforms should be pursued, i.e. 'changes which abolish or remove greater or smaller parts on which the system in general may depend', e.g. the abolition of forced labour in Norway for vagrants. The converse is to avoid any foreclosing of future possibilities by settling for a fixed plan of an alternative scheme, or by strengthening the system by 'positive' reforms, e.g. adopting 'treatment' strategies. Ultimately, the only alternative lies in the pursuit of abolition itself, 'in an ever-widening circumference' (pp. 198 ff.). The pressures *against* such politics are, as Mathiesen makes clear, immense. They emanate from — *inter alia* — prisoners who think they will benefit from short-term reforms, but who neglect their illusory nature; system representatives who press for 'alternatives'; the whole ethos of our social system, which also demands 'alternatives' of a positive kind; and which as a result of promulgates 'seeming' negations, e.g. the matching of greater internal freedoms by greater perimeter security. Only the constant unmasking of system interests, and the avoidance of system-strengthening reforms, will resolve the dilemma of how to combine short-term with long-term interests.

Possibilities

The possibilities opened up by the adoption of an abolitionist strategy in Britain are perhaps best illustrated by the Scandinavian experience, since the two main attempts to organise on such lines in this country have been so far somewhat abortive by comparison. PROP — as Fitzgerald (1977) describes — was hamstrung for most of its brief history by internal disagreements over strategy, and by a consequent over-selling of its capacity to deliver. RAP has concentrated its energies entirely on the very question of alternatives that in Mathiesen's view should be avoided, and has regarded issues internal to prisons as outside its scope.[2] Assuming, however, that some *rapprochement* is achieved along Mathiesen's lines, what results might follow (assuming more active political and intellectual-cum-academic support than PROP and RAP have achieved so far)?

(i) A much more focused attack on specific targets, which might be expected to attract more widespread support from established reform organisations. In Norway, KROM developed a three-pronged strategy of attacking *existing* controls (e.g. the vagrancy laws and the system of forced labour for vagrants), *defending* such abolitions once they were pushed through, and *resisting* projected controls in their formative stages (e.g. a detention centre planned for young offenders along the lines of the British centres). Also, a 'protectional' school for school-age child offenders was closed down, and a proposal to abolish the entire youth prison system in Norway gained the support of the Norwegian Advisory Council on the Penal System. Pressure for abolition in the adult sector has met far tougher resistance (apart from the vagrancy acts etc.), but the (putative) gains so far are impressive. A similar campaign in the U.K. would probably take as high priorities the abolition of the youth prison sector that has developed as an unanticipated side effect of the 1969 Act, if not the 1969 Act itself; the forcible use of psychotropic drugs in prisons; and resistance to any attempt to introduce new, tougher measures against 'soccer hooligans' and allied forms of youthful delinquency. Ironically, the most spectacular abolitionist case has recently been made out for virtually the entire Borstal system by N.A.C.R.O. (1977a), though whether its recommendations will be actively lobbied for, or quietly shelved, remains to be seen.[3]

(ii) Central to Mathiesen's strategy is the situation of the 'expelled' as a whole, though prisoners as a particular 'group' constitute his main focus so far. A long, visionary passage from a book by Jörgen Eriksson (1970) prefaces his chapter 'Organisation among the expelled', in which the bad and the mad, the vagrant and the forgotten tribes of the elderly lead a surrealist assault on the powerful, wielding bayonets and crutches — the defences of the weak? The organisational principle which Mathiesen recommends is the 'horizontal' linkage of these groups to higher status allies who lack one element in common with the expelled — power. In Britain, the list of the expelled would be even longer, including for a start the immigrant minorities. But the list of putative allies is also longer, producing an embarrassment of riches. What could a British KROM achieve that the N.C.C.L. for example, could not already claim to have achieved or be attempting for such groups (many of whom have their own pressure groups anyway)? The answer presumably would lie in the attempt to connect the expelled by the abolitionist strategy, rather than taking up their individual troubles piecemeal. And certain groups, e.g. dossers, have tried and as yet failed to initiate their own political movement (PROD

— Protection of the Rights of Dossers), an outcome which may have differed had a British KROM been in existence.

(iii) A third possibility is the constructing of more systematic links between PROP/RAP/KROM and the labour movement, a strategy already in process in Norway, but as yet in embryo in Britain. Even quite minor gains here might pay off quite disproportionately in terms of political militancy among prisoners. There would also be the prospect of greater gains for what Mathiesen terms 'positive' organisation in an 'upwards' direction, i.e. the making of a greater economic contribution in terms of prison industry, which yields a built-in contribution which prisoners can withdraw strategically. Mathiesen regards this with some disfavour as a system-strengthening manoeuvre, but on balance seems to come out in favour of it. So far, as Fitzgerald has stressed, British unions have maintained a stony indifference to the situation of prison labour, even when prisoners are used in strike-breaking! *Any* advance here should be an improvement, abolition aside, as prison work remains the most under-developed aspect of the penal system.

(iv) The fourth possibility is that far more pressure would be exerted in the direction of securing certain rights for prisoners as legally guaranteed, rather than as at best somewhat arbitrary privileges, and at worst as non-existent. Both Mathiesen (1974) and Fitzgerald (1977) (and Cohen and Taylor (1978)) as individuals, and KROM and PROP as organisations have produced exhaustive catalogues of what such a 'Prisoners' Bill of Rights' should include. If, as Sparks (1971), McConville (1975) and others have stressed the treatment era is over, and 'humane containment' is (abolitionists apart) the best to be hoped for, then such a strategy seems the minimal denominator common to all reform groups. Greater realism in thrashing out an agreed list of rights for inclusion would be the most appropriate next step.

(v) The work of Mathiesen, Fitzgerald, Cohen and Taylor *et al.* brings sharply into focus, usually as the villain of the piece, the prison staff. The staffing of prisons is almost entirely neglected as an abolitionist issue, presumably because it is assumed that there is no point in attempting to 'improve' a system in need of abolition. But this neglects the process of abolition as a long-term transition, the very point these authors are at pains to emphasise in other respects. It is almost as if the present situation, in which the social system of the prison resembles some colonial outpost, with a District Commissioner, a missionary and a bunch of squaddies holding the natives at bay, is viewed as promoting abolition, since the contradictions of the system are overt and blatant. Crude as this picture obviously is in many respects, the theme that recurs in much of the critical literature is the correlation between the rise in political consciousness of inmates and staff alike. Indeed, a major irony is the denunciation by radicals of industrial action by prison staff, such as work-to-rules, which would be applauded in other industries — naturally, prisoners are the victims of such action. However, unless the prisoners are going to suffer even more as a result of growing militancy activating counter-militancy by staff (and we have Albany, Parkhurst etc. as well-documented instances), then rather greater investment in better trained, paid, even 'treatment-oriented' staff seems a possible implication of the abolitionist strategy.

Pitfalls

It may well be that a strategy evolved in Scandinavia has little hope of successful transplantation to the larger and more heterogeneous societies such as Britain and the U.S. Whilst in the latter there have been dramatic instances of prisoners organising collectively within particular jails, or networks of jails in the case of the U.S., the outcome of the struggles has tended to be tragic and explosive, lacking the steady growth of an abolitionist framework along the Norwegian and Swedish line. KROM claims a membership of almost one-third of the prisoners in Norway. The 1972 prison strikes in Sweden and Britain led Fitzgerald to note that 'the Swedish protests involved over 60 per cent of the prison population; PROP had had the support of less than 25 per cent' (Fitzgerald 1977, p. 158).

Major differences of relevance may be the very position of academics like Mathiesen in small, social-democratic societies, possessing a status not easily imaginable in Britain or the U.S. (The relative cohesiveness of the academic criminological community there, and its stature in the social sciences generally, should also be noted.) And if criminology looms smaller in Britain and the U.S. than in Scandinavia, crime looms arguably far larger, appears both more baleful and intractable a problem, and presents a correspondingly more difficult task for abolitionists. These arguments, however, do not undermine the abolitionist case. They strengthen it: for the larger the prison population relative to the population as a whole, the greater the number of prisoners serving lengthy sentences for relatively serious crimes, the greater the challenge for abolitionists. The pitfalls of abolitionist strategy seem to be of a different order to the sheer *scale* of the task they confront, and have to do with their analysis of that task, and the way they define it.

(i) The abolitionist strategy, by equating 'treatment' with covert control and oppression, and defining it as system-strengthening (by legitimising control measures as medically or therapeutically necessary etc.), may rule out too much. For example, the development of the special unit at Barlinnie Prison, arguably the most promising innovation post-war, comes at a time when 'treatment' and 'rehabilitation' are being written off as useful goals for the penal system. Yet the prisoners selected for Barlinnie were among the most violent in Scottish jails: the concept of a 'therapeutic community' was at the core of the thinking that made the creation of the special unit possible; and the initiative for its establishment came from within the Scottish prison service (see Johnston and MacLeod 1975). Eloquent testimony to the flexibility and willingness to experiment with democratic procedures within the unit has been provided by Jimmy Boyle (1977), himself sentenced to life imprisonment for murder, and scarred by having spent four of his six years in prison in solitary confinement. Subjected to a barrage of criticism for relaxing too many rules, the Unit has not only survived for six years, '. . . it evolves in unforeseeable ways, calling for changes in the behaviour and feelings of prisoners, in the regime of the wider prison service, and in the attitudes of the public at large' (Donnison 1978). The experience of growing trust between inmates and staff, the gradual extensions of freedom within the unit, led Boyle (1977) to describe it as a 'rebirth': 'This is the only place I know of that is offering any realistic hope for guys serving long sentences, or short ones for that matter' (pp. 247, 253). No professional psychiatric or psychological expertise was involved in this transformation, but the 'treatment' umbrella still provided the broad justification for the experiment. Boyle's principal fear is that the political pressures to warp the work of the unit will eventually succeed, and its character will be emasculated as a result, thus demoralising both staff and inmates, and providing grounds for closure. Would abolitionists help fight such pressures, or welcome them as system-weakening? To be placed in the position of opposing or ignoring such developments by virtue of a commitment to abolition seems an unacceptably high price to pay for resolving a dilemma.

(ii) The implication of a great deal of abolitionist writing is that prisons are functional for the survival of a class society, and cannot simply be argued out of existence by superior liberal rhetoric, or substantially reformed or run down by State action. It is difficult to square this analysis with the dramatic reduction in imprisonment in the Netherlands in particular, though a trend towards 'decarceration' more generally has been detected by Scull (1977). Admittedly, it does seem to be the case that rates of *entry* to prison in Holland have not diminished: but that is in the context of their daily population falling to as low as 3,280 in 1971, a rate of 25.4 per 100,000, compared with 37 in Norway, 62 in Sweden and 81 in England and Wales. The figure for the U.S.A. is far higher, 208, but that was in 1965, before the trends analysed by Scull accelerated (see Van Hofer 1975; Cohen 1972; Heijder 1975). The most encouraging inference to be drawn from the Dutch experience is that the decreasing resort to imprisonment, *via* reductions in the average length of sentence, in the 1950–72 period, seem not to be associated with any greater increase in crime rates than had occurred in other countries which did not pursue these policies. 'The increase in reported crime . . . was *lower* in Holland than in Sweden despite the fact that Swedish sentences are traditionally longer, and have experienced a slower rate of decrease in average length during the last twenty years' (Van Hofer 1975, p. 135). There are obviously immense problems involved in interpreting these official data, especially comparatively between societies. But the Dutch experience does seem a heartening one from the abolitionist point of view, if on terms which do not readily lend themselves to the analytical assumptions of the more radical abolitionists. For the prime movers in Holland have been the judiciary, partly facilitated by the powers given to the public prosecutors to waive prosecution (see Heijder 1975; Bishop 1974). In sum, there is a danger of abolitionist strategy ignoring the potential for substantial moves to be made towards abolition by means other than militant forms of praxis.

(iii) For Andrew Scull (1977) also writing from an avowedly 'radical' perspective, the trend in institutional policies towards the 'bad' and the 'mad' is towards decarceration, the converse of, for example, Fitzgerald's view, and at considerable odds with Mathiesen's. Scull discerns the watershed in penal policy as coming in the 1950s, with the capitalist economies facing increasing difficulties in *funding* institutional solutions to crime and mental illness. *Inter alia*, the costs of replacing the prisons and asylums built in the heyday of Victorian expansionism; the growing costs of unionised, labour-intensive staffing; and the escalation in rates of crime and mental illness, combined to push the State towards decarceration. However, the rationale was malign rather than benign: sheerly financial considerations outweighed all else, though the State was quick to latch onto labelling theory and 'community care' as legitimating ideologies. Scull's depiction of the results of decarceration resemble that culled from Norwegian newspapers after the ending of the vagrancy laws (which Mathiesen quotes disapprovingly): the streets and parks 'fill' with derelicts and deviants; deviant 'ghettoes' are created in the inner city to which the decarcerated gravitate, in part because the communities which are held to 'care' mobilise to expel them; the rate of mortality among the 'released' psychogeriatrics exceeds that of those left in hospitals. . . . Scull is scathingly critical of a major abolitionist 'victory', the closure — virtually overnight — of the juvenile reformatories in Massachusetts. The much-vaunted claims made on behalf of this and the related programmes in California are shown by Scull to be at best rhetorical and at worst designed to mislead. The tremendous financial gains (in the U.K., the cost of a prison place is 15 times as high as probation) are not offset against the 'hidden' costs to the community: the uneven and regressive cost of welfare etc. falling on families; the resort (in Massachusetts) to private agencies as dumping grounds for the worst cases; the ghettoisation of deviant populations as respectable communities squeeze them out.

There are many criticisms that can be made of Scull's markedly polemical critique. His case is far stronger for the mad than the bad. In Britain, he notes that imprisonment has *fallen* relative to the increase in indictable crime, but neglects the increasing length of sentences (and the fall is not that marked, a ratio of 25% to 18% of admissions to indictable offence convictions). Nor is his evidence for the malign effects of decarcerating the 'bad' nearly as strong as that for those of the 'mad'—a few excerpts from the *New York Times.* His *forte* is exposing the most overblown aspects of the abolitionists' case especially in the U.S. (Mathiesen's work and the cases of Norway and Holland are not embraced by his analysis). Neither Scull nor Mathiesen addresses himself to the immense variations in the use of imprisonment in capitalist societies, or to the often far more repressive system in nominally socialist states.

It may well be that the forms of decarceration attacked by Scull are quite different from the processes of abolition implied by Mathiesen. But there is little in the latter's work to suggest where those differences might lie. The one point of major agreement between the two is in their argument that modern capitalism is creating and coming to depend on a sizeable 'under-class' for whom it increasingly cannot afford decent welfare in conditions of burgeoning crisis. The burden of Scull's argument is that they are not necessarily helped by abolition, and their plight is conceivably made worse.

(iv) Martin Wright (1975) has noted that 'To demand abolition without proposing alternatives, as advocated by Mathiesen, may well be the best method in some cases; but the tactics he advocates, using the example of abolishing imprisonment for vagrants, would not necessarily apply to offenders who are perceived as presenting a greater risk to the public' (p. 93). The public tend to get short shrift in the abolitionist literature, largely because — one suspects — that reified spectre 'public opinion' is so relentlessly exploited by the authorities to veto practically any suggestion for reform that might make headlines of the 'Prisons getting too soft' or 'Residents say no to hostel plan' variety. This does not mean, however, that public reactions can simply be brushed aside. As Scull has made clear, community reactions to deviants are frequently hostile, and abolitionists neglect at certain of the latter's peril that neglected function of imprisonment, the protection of the offender.

(v) Mathiesen's work displays an overriding concern with the dangers of reforms strengthening the legitimacy of the system. Hence, part of the appeal of arguing for *rights* (particularly those of political and industrial bargaining), since this is seen as weakening the power of the system. However, it is not at all clear that the effects of granting rights *will* be to weaken the power of the State, or the system. Arguably, the granting of 'rights' is the ultimate legitimation of the system. If this is so, then a great deal of the energies that abolitionists would expend arguing the 'rights' versus 'improvements' issue could be better spent on pursuing reforms and long-term aims more straightforwardly.

(vi) In the end, Mathiesen's dilemma is the anarchist's dilemma: how far can an organisational framework based on negation be pushed before it adversely affects the structures which guarantee its abolitions? Stray references to the 'cultural revolution' in China and Albania hardly constitute an answer, as Mathiesen himself is obviously aware. The process of metamorphosis cannot be indefinitely prolonged. Either the 'unfinished' means little more than being pragmatic and flexible (which does not rule out resistance to incorporation, the pursuit of abolition, and the alliance with the 'expelled') or it implies working to bring about a society about which one is not allowed to theorise. Suppose one *had* an alternative: should one keep quiet about it? Mathiesen seems to invoke a species of guilt-by-association in his attitude towards alternatives. Because the system makes a great deal of the need to specify them as a delaying tactic, therefore they become a bad thing in themselves. Ultimately, the 'unfinished' can become the nebulous in a profoundly anti-democratic way, since alternatives are never formulated clearly enough for people to make rational choices between them.

Conclusion

In the intractable field of penal reform, the abolitionist strategy of Mathiesen has immense appeal (though ironically, if Scull is right, capitalism is working in the same direction). Its strengths are the refusal to be polarised into either short-term or long-term, reform versus revolutionary, stances; the commitment to abolition tempered by (some) humanitarian reforms; and the centrality of the alliance between inmates, ex-inmates and diverse outside agents. Its weaknesses lie in the obsession with system-strengthening, and remaining 'unfinished' to the point of ruling out 'alternatives', which obscure and even endanger these strengths.

NOTES

1. PROP stands for 'Preservation of the Rights of Prisoners'. PROP was officially launched in May 1972, and called a 'national prisoners' strike' on 4 August 1972. The events of that summer are chronicled in Fitzgerald (1977, ch. 5). Subsequently, PROP split into two locally-based splinter groups, in London and Hull.
2. RAP stands for 'Radical Alternatives to Prison'; it was formed in 1971 out of the remnants of the Prison Reform Council, with which many of those imprisoned during the 1960s anti-nuclear marches had been associated. RAP has been financially linked to Christian Action for most of its history, but is itself not a specifically Christian organisation. For the story of RAP see now Ryan (1978, ch. 5).
3. N.A.C.R.O. is the National Association for the Care and Resettlement of Offenders, formed in the 1960s. It is in receipt of substantial Home Office grants for various hostel and crime prevention projects, and, like the Howard League for Penal Reform (with whom it shares premises) it is generally regarded as a 'reformist' rather than 'radical' organisation, in contradistinction to RAP and PROP.

REFERENCES

Bishop, N. (1974) 'Aspects of European penal systems', in: L. Blom-Cooper (Ed.), *Progress in Penal Reform*, Oxford, Clarendon Press.

Boyle, J. (1977) *A Sense of Freedom*, London, Pan Books.

Cohen, D. (1972) 'Out of jail', *New Society*, *20*, 234–5.

Cohen, S. (1975) 'It's all right for you to talk', in: R. Bailey and M. Brake (Eds.), *Radical Social Work*, London, Edward Arnold.

Cohen, S. and Taylor, L. (1978) *Prison Secrets*, London, Radical Alternatives to Prison and National Council for Civil Liberties.

Donnison, D. (1978) 'Special unit', *New Society*, *43*, 60–1.

Eriksson, J. (1970) *Revolt i Huvet*, Stockholm, Bonniers.

Fitzgerald, M. (1977) *Prisoners in Revolt*, Harmondsworth, Penguin.

Gouldner, A. (1973) *For Sociology*, London, Allen Lane.

Heijder, A. (1975) 'The recent trend towards reducing the prison population in the Netherlands', *International Journal of Offender Therapy and Comparative Criminology*, *18*, 233–40.

Johnston, J. and MacLeod, C. (1975) 'Barlinnie's approach', *New Society*, *34*, 482–3.

McConville, S. (1975) 'Future prospects of imprisonment in Britain', in: S. McConville (Ed.), *The Use of Imprisonment: Essays in the Changing State of English Penal Policy*, London, Routledge and Kegan Paul.

Mathiesen, T. (1974) *The Politics of Abolition*, London, Martin Robertson.

Michels, R. (1911) *Political Parties* (Eng. trans. 1949, Glencoe, Free Press).

Scull, A. (1977) *Decarceration: Community Treatment and the Deviant — A Radical View*, Englewood Cliffs, Prentice-Hall.

Sparks, R. F., *et al.* (1978) *Surveying Victims*, Chichester, Wiley.

Taylor, I., Walton, P. and Young, J. (1973) *The New Criminology: For a Social Theory of Deviance*, London, Routledge and Kegan Paul.

Taylor, I., Walton, P. and Young, J. (Eds.) (1975) *Critical Criminology*, London, Routledge and Kegan Paul.

Van Hofer, H. (1975) 'Dutch prison population', *Kriminologi* (Scandinavian Research Council for Criminology), No. 17, 104–50.

Wright, M. (1975) 'Tactics of reform', in: S. McConville (Ed.), *The Use of Imprisonment: Essays in the Changing State of English Penal Policy*, London, Routledge and Kegan Paul.

[8]
Law and Order: Theft of an Issue

"We are now in the middle of a deep and decisive movement towards a more disciplinary, authoritarian kind of society. This shift has been in progress since the 1960s; but it has gathered pace through the 1970's and is heading, given the spate of disciplinary legislation now on the parliamentary agenda, towards some sort of interim climax." Stuart Hall's "interim climax", invoked in his 1979 Cobden Trust Human Rights Lecture, has been and gone. It occurred on the streets of Brixton, Toxteth, Manchester and other urban centres in 1981. It produced a humane interim response in the form of the Scarman Report of that year. But its more durable legacy lies in the extended police powers, and lack of concession in the realm of citizen defence against those powers, of the 1983 Police and Criminal Evidence Bill. Although that Bill lapsed with the calling of the General Election, the indications are that it is to be re-introduced substantially unchanged. The "drift" towards a 'Law and Order Society' has gathered pace since Hall's coining of the phrase four years ago.

One decisive step had already been taken before that point: the success with which the Conservative Party had appropriated the 'law and order' issue in the General Election campaign of 1979. Before the 1979 election, Labour and Conservative Paries alike had not chosen to contest their records and policies on that particular ground (Morgan, 1981). Indeed, some of the build-up to the situation analysed by Hall had taken place under Labour Governments. Despite policy clashes over specific pieces of legislation, in particular the 1969 Children and Young Persons Act, which the Tories implemented only in small part, a bi-partisanship prevailed in relation to the 'law and order' issue.

As the 1970's wore on, however, that bi-partisanship came under strain: it evidently occurred to the Tories, at the time of the Grunwick dispute, if not before, that Labour were vulnerable to attack on the 'law and order' flank of their industrial relations record. From that point, it was a short step to the association of Labour with rising crime rates and falling moral standards. Thus, Margaret Thatcher could assert in March 1979: *"A trade union leader had advised his members to carry on picketing because they would act in such numbers that the authorities would need to use football stadiums as detention centres. That is the rule of the mob and not of the law, and ought to be condemned by every institution and minister in the land. The demand in the country will be for two things: less tax and more law and order"* (Daily Telegraph, 29 March 1979, quoted in Ian Taylor, 1981).

This passage contrives to link several positives – law and order, national institutions and government, and the rule of law – with the Conservatives and 'less tax'; and several negatives – mob rule, detention centres, defiance of the law – with picketing, trade unions and Labour.

The strategy appears to have played a crucial role in the return of a Conservative Government in 1979. An Independent Television News research survey, reported

An Independent Television News research survey, reported on election night after the closure of the polls, indicated that 23% of voters who had switched allegiance to the Tories did so on law and order.

on election night after the closure of the polls, indicated that 23% of voters who had switched allegiance to the Tories did so on law and order, compared with 22% who switched on trade unions, 26% on prices and 13% on taxation. If these and similar findings (see Taylor, 1981) can be relied upon at all, then a significant, if not decisive, number of voters were swayed to support the Tories by the belief that they could be relied on to maintain law and order, while Labour could not.

The Post-war Record

Since the 'law and order' issue has been thrust by the Conservatives into the centre of political debate, the question naturally arises: do the Tories have a 'better' record on crime control than Labour? The answer is simply 'No'. There is no warrant for the view that the Conservatives have dealt with crime more effectively than Labour. Though the official criminal statistics are a most unsatisfactory way of charting crime trends (see Bottomley and Coleman, 1981, Walker 1971, Box 1971) it is the only conceivable basis for the Conservative claim to superiority in the field of criminal policy. No other trend data exist. When we come to examine the post-war trends in crime, there is no discernible connection between the party in government and crime rates:

'Serious' Crimes Known to the Police

Rate per 100,000		Per cent annual change	Party in Govt.
1945/50	1,134/1,094	−1	Labour
1950/1	1,094/1,255	+15	Labour
1951/55	1,255/1,040	−4	Conservative
1955/59	1,040/1,586	+13	Conservative
1959/64	1,586/2,463	+11	Conservative
1964/70	2,463/3,221	+5	Labour
1970/74	3,221/3,994	+6	Conservative
1974/79	3,994/4,833	+4	Labour
1979/82	4,833/6,227*	+10	Conservative

(* = estimate from number of offences)

One obvious point to emerge from these crude totals is that the first three full years of Mrs. Thatcher's Government have been accompanied by a steeper rise in crime than the five preceding years of Labour Government. Nor does the picture change at all greatly if trends in the number of offenders found guilty are considered, or specific crimes, such as the more serious crimes of violence. Theorising about *why* these trends have occurred is too complex a question to be entered into here. We can speculate that the trends mirror in some broad sense changes in *expectations,* on the one hand, and *social reality* on the other. When these relate to each other in some semblance of equilibrium, crime changes only negligibly, as in the immediate post-war period of 'austerity' under Labour. When social reality actually exceeds expectations, a fairly rare ocurrence, as in the lifting of post-war restrictions by the Tories, crime actually falls. With the era of the 'revolution of rising expectations', roughly from 1955-70, crime rises sharply as social reality fails to match hopes. The era of the 'revolution of falling expectations' of the 1970's sees the rise in crime slowing down somewhat. The recent sharper rise does not fit this pattern, since expectations have fallen even lower and crime has risen faster, but it makes nonsense of the view that the Tories have any claims over Labour in the realm of crime prevention and control. Indeed, so many factors affect these figures, not least the number of police employed, which one major study (Carr-Hill and Stern, 1979) found to be the major correlate with crime rates, that it would be fatuous for any Party to claim superiority in crime control.

Crime in Perspective

The paradox about crime trends is that they are both better and worse than the picture that emerges from the official statistics. First, the good news: the rise in crime over the past decade may have been much less steep than the official figures indicate. Using a different indicator, answers to questions about burglary and theft from dwellings included in the General Household Surveys of 1972, 1973, 1979 and 1980, Home Office researchers concluded that such offences had increased between 1972-80 at an average rate of only 1% a year, compared to the rise of 4% a year recorded by the police. "The larger increase in those offences recorded appeared to have been due mainly to an increase in the *proportion* of such offences which were recorded." (*Criminal Statistics,* 1981,) Among the reasons which might account for the difference are a greater tendency to report such offences to the police for insurance purposes, combined with the spread of property insurance.

The bad news is part of the same picture. By definition, only a proportion of crimes committed come to be notified to the police: the so-called 'dark figure' of crime. The size of this figure varies greatly by type of offence, social attitudes towards offences, the settings in which they occur, and so on. The Home Office estimate burglaries to be 1½-2 times greater in number than are officially recorded. What occurred over the past decade is an apparently greater rise in recorded burglaries than in actual burglaries. The 'dark figure' shrank, so that the official trend appeared more serious than the actual trend. But the 'dark figure' is far greater in general the less serious the offence. Victim surveys indicate that the actual volume of crime is some 4 times greater than recorded crime. The first *British Crime Survey,* conducted in 1981, (HMSO, 1983) concluded that "hidden crime was generally less serious than that which appeared in *Criminal Statistics,* though some relatively serious offences were not recorded and many fairly trivial ones were." (p.32) Victim surveys are a useful supplement and corrective to the

Criminal Statistics, but they too have their limitations: shoplifting, employee and corporate offences, and institutional victims, for example school vandalism, are not tapped by this approach.

The main point about the 'hidden' crime picture is that it is nothing new. Without trend data, we have no way of establishing how far rises in 'hidden' crime mirror those in the *Criminal Statistics* (with the exception of the burglary example). We are now alerted to the way in which 'crime waves' can be 'manufactured' by even quite negligible increases in public reporting and police recording of offences that were formerly 'hidden'. The bulk of even quite 'serious' crimes has been shown to be trivial: for example, over half the burglaries disclosed by the Victim Survey were attempts (39%) or involved losses of under £5 in value (16%). Financial loss is not of course the sole effect of crime. For victims of violence, social and emotional adverse effects were longer-lasting and more serious than financial loss, in general (Shapland, 1983). By any reckoning, serious crimes *have* risen markedly over the post-war period, and there are correspondingly more people whose lives have been significantly damaged in some way as a result. Within this overall picture, however, there are some features which have been unduly exaggerated, and others relatively obscured. It is to these we now turn.

Crime and its control amount to a regressive tax on the community.

Crime and Social Class

Crime and its control amount to a regressive tax on the community. The defining characteristic of a regressive tax is that it falls disproportionately heavily on the poor. Our knowledge about the social distribution of criminality has of late had to be revised. The traditional association of crime with 'rough' working-class neighbourhoods can be sustained only if attention is focussed almost entirely on certain crimes against property and 'street-crimes'. These are the offences that bulk largest in the *Criminal Statistics* and the media. In the case of robbery, they dramatise crime in its most immediately threatening and predatory form. But once the focus is broadened to take in less sensational offences, the correlation between class and crime practically disappears. 'Fiddling' at work is a major preoccupation of many who regard themselves as upright citizens (Ditton, 1977). The 'hidden economy', now estimated to be "only" 7% of the Gross National Product, represents tax evasion on a scale so massive that it dwarfs all but the most sensational standard crimes against property (Ditton, 1983). Frauds, corporate crimes and economic offences concerning currency and share transactions combine with these somewhat shadowy forms of deviance to cast profound doubt on what was previously assumed to be, on the whole, a direct connection between crime and 'deprivation'. 'Crime in the suites' is emerging as just as formidable a problem as 'crime on the streets' (Henry, 1979; Mars 1982; Clarke, 1981).

The costs of victimisation do not, however, fall evenly on all citizens alike. From victim surveys, it would appear that 'the poor pay more' in this as in other respects. They are just as likely to be victims, more so in some cases, than the better off. But in addition the costs of crime prevention and losses in such cases as shoplifting, where higher prices result, are regressive in their effects. While the less well-off may benefit from the 'hidden' economy, the better-off arguably benefit more. And the cutbacks in public services that result in part from this sort of insular tax-haven affect the poor most directly.

'Street-crime' is therefore more rigorously monitored than occupational deviance or corporate crimes.

But it is in the realm of control that the poor arguably suffer most. First of all, police powers are at their maximum on the streets, at their minimum in the suites. 'Street-crime' is therefore more rigorously monitored than occupational deviance or corporate crimes. Secondly, the courts tend to deal more severely with 'working-class' than with 'middle-class' offences. For example, in 1979, 404 people were sentenced to immediate imprisonment for Social Security offences, compared with 5 for offences against Revenue laws. Yet the scale of tax evasion far exceeds that of Social Security fraud – some £4,000m. a year compared with £200m. a year. This is not to say that courts deal inequitably with working-class and middle-class offenders, once guilt is proven. But, thirdly, differences are likely to occur in the extent to which defendants from different social backgrounds can mobilise legal services of high quality and cost on their own behalf. The operation of Legal Aid for poorer defedants is notoriously varied from court to court and area to area (Hansen, 1982).

The Tory Government response to these issues since 1979 has been to tighten the screw on Social Security offenders (losses of £4 million and 576 prosecutions a week) and tone down measures against Revenue offenders (losses of £80 million and 2 prosecutions a week) (1981 figures). The size of the Social Security inspectorate has been increased (an extra 1,000 investigators hired at an extra annual salary cost of £3 million) while the size of the tax inspectorate has been reduced. The scale of the sums involved in tax evasion can hardly be accounted for by odd-job 'Moon-lighting' – the so-called 'Black and Decker' brigade who perform useful services for reward in cash or kind. When the Inland Revenue ran checks on 0.25% of companies in 1979, 82% were found to have understated their profits. Nor was this a fluke: "The 87% of cases examined which disclosed under-statement of profits represented a slight increase over 1980, but more serious cases – involving penalties and interest – had increased from 17% in 1980 to 24% in 1981. The Department told us that they had no evidence that the increasing coverage of their selective examination was bringing into play the law of diminishing returns: the results suggest that this point was still a long way off." (22nd. *Report of the Committee of Public Accounts,* 1982, Cmnd. 339, p.v, para. 3.)
The Conservatives clearly intend it to remain 'a long way off'. It would be difficult to conceive a more regressive form of crime control than that which emerges from these trends.

Crime and Unemployment

A recent review of the problem concluded: *"There is extensive evidence, mainly from research in the United States but also from research in Britain, that unemployment is a factor contributing significantly to crime and delinquency, so that high levels of unemployment can be expected to contribute to higher levels of crime and delinquency and to an increase in the prison population."* (Hakim, 1982, also Tarling, 1982).

A study drawing on evidence from a variety of countries concluded that unemployment combined with urbanism (taken together with indicators of GNP and the comprehensiveness of data collection) "achieved the highest levels of explanation" of rates of ordinary crime-sanctions. (McDonald, 1976). The character of the links between unemployment and crime are by no means direct, however, and one study would deny *any* connection (Carr-Hill and Stern, 1979). It is a mistake to argue from such findings that higher crime rates are directly attributable to the unemployed themselves. What *can* be asserted on balance is that any government which precipitates increasing unemployment also risks associated increases in crime, particularly crimes against property. Endemic unemployment in the inner-city seems integral to the worst gang delinquency in the United States (Miller, 1976).

The links between unemployment and imprisonment are much more pronounced than those between crime and unemployment.

The links between unemployment and imprisonment are much more pronounced than those between crime and unemployment. One American study concluded: *"The results showed that the unemployed rate alone explains 54% of the variation in the prison population sentenced during the years 1952-74...After considering sentencing practices, one per cent increase in male unemployment results in 1,395 additional prisoners in Federal penal institutions."* (Yeager, 1979)

There is strong agreement that the link between unemployment and imprisonment exceeds that which can be ascribed to changes in the crime rate. The connection remains an open question, but studies of sentencing suggest that employment is a crucial mitigating factor which judges and magistrates take into account in deciding upon a sentence of imprisonment. Those who have "nothing to lose" are on this basis more likely to be imprisoned than those who have a stake in employment. Given that rates of unemployment are significantly higher among young males, particularly from working-class or minority group backgrounds, the main increase in the use of imprisonment would predictably affect these groups most: and this trend is clearly in evidence over the past ten years in Britain (Baldock, 1980).

The connection between imprisonment and unemployment may be strengthened in two other respects. Firstly, historically and now, sentencers have displaced imprisonment mostly by fines. However, persons considered *ineligible* for fines are more likely to be imprisoned, which may explain in part why the proportion of persons fined fell, and those imprisoned rose, during periods like the 1970's when unemployment rose (Softley, 1978). Secondly, this will continue to be the case until fines are more closely related to means (Morgan and Bowles, 1981).

Given the nature of Tory rhetoric about law and order, it is clearly a major problem for the Government to dissociate itself from responsibility for generating the very conditions most strongly associated with crime and disorder, let alone the prison conditions which the former Home Secretary William Whitelaw has himself described as "an affront to a civilised society". Commenting on the Brixton riots, Mrs Thatcher said: "Nothing can *justify* this kind of violence" (Emphasis added). She chose her words carefully. In one sense, nothing can. But the substitution of the word "explain" for "justify" would have brought to the surface those very connections between crime, unemployment, racism and inner-city decay from which she most wishes to distance herself and her government.

Unemployment is not the sole or even the major cause of crime, nor crime the major consequence of unemployment. Other effects attributable to unemployment, such as physical and mental illness, apathy, impoverisation and marital breakdown are just as, if not more serious than crime and delinquency. (Hakim; Tarling; and Sinfield, 1981). Two phenomena are often cited by those sceptical of, or who wish to deny outright, any link between crime and unemployment: the lower rates of crime and civil disorder that accompanied the depression of the 1920's and 30's; and the rise in crime during the period of full employment in the 1950's and 60's. In considering these questions, it is worth remembering that employment and unemployment are not utterly distinct situations, but end-points of a continuum. At one pole, a minority enjoy secure, lifelong, diverse, well-rewarded and rewarding full employment; at the other pole, a minority endure chronic, long-term unemployment unalleviated by part-time jobs or casual work. In between, the majority vary immensely in their experience of an array of different work situations. Even in times of 'full' employment, the jobs of most semi- and unskilled young manual workers are 'dead-end', routine and unrewarding secondary labour market jobs. It was in that job context that delinquency rose in the 1960's. As for the 1930's, comparisons between then and now generally ignore the extent to which unemployment then was experienced in many communities as a shared class experience, affecting all generations in a way that at least left working-class institutions intact (Bakke, 1933). In the 1980's , that is arguably much less the case: unemployment, especially in the inner cities, is taking place in more fragmented communities, is hitting the young especially heavily, and is complicated by institutionalised racism. The return to the full-blown pursuit of 'private affluence and public squalor' has weakened the controls that working-class communities could themselves exert against crime and delinquency, even in times of high unemployment.

The Fear of Crime

It is often said that the fear of crime is worse than crime itself, that more people imprison themselves in their homes for fear of crime than are imprisoned for actually committing offences. The 'fear of crime' may affect the quality of life adversely: and may make crime more likely by turning cities at night into empty, forbidding places. The 1981 Crime Survey sensibly distinguished between 'fear of crime' and 'concern about crime', the first being equated with people's fears of victimisation, the second with a more general anxiety about crime that does not necessarily have to do with personal risk. The authors also point out that 'fear of crime' embraces worry on behalf of family or friends becoming victims of crime, and is not limited to fears solely on their own behalf. Nor need the 'fear of crime' be strictly rational, in that people may not worry at all despite a relatively high risk of victimisation; others may become preoccupied with becoming a victim of a very rare crime in the full knowledge of its rarity.

The risk of actually being victimised is far greater (7%) among young men than among elderly women (1%).

The 'fear of crime' is far more prevalent among women, the elderly and those in inner cities than among other groups. For example, among those surveyed, only 1% of men in areas other than the inner city felt anxiety for their personal safety, compared with 60% of women aged over 60 in inner city areas. Yet the risk of actually being victimised is far greater (7%) among young men than among elderly women (1%). Part of the difference is due to the greater exposure to the risk of crime of young men. But "victimisation among the elderly was low even for those who lead an active life: taking only those who went out four or more evenings a week, the rate of 'street crime' victimisation for those aged 60 or under was three times that of older people". Clearly, it would be wrong to jump to the conclusion that where 'fear of crime' exceeds the actual risk, such fear is irrational. Age, physical vulnerability, and other factors, such as whether or not one lives alone, can influence the meanings different victims attach to the 'same' offence. "Nevertheless, in some areas fear of crime appears to be a serious problem which needs to be tackled separately from the incidence of crime itself.".

Perhaps the best way to reduce the fear of crime is to improve the quality of information generally available. It may not necessarily allay all anxieties to be told that, in 1981 terms, the 'average' person over 16 can expect to be robbed only once every five centuries, assaulted with at least slight injury only once a century, have their car stolen only once every 60 years, and their house burgled once very 40 years: but it does provide a framework within which to place the more lurid crime profile that emerges from the media. Such 'averages' can mislead, and depending on circumstances, risks can be higher or lower. But at least it is good to have the *right* average, instead of one that exaggerates the risks of crime to the point where myths take over completely. A recent BBC programme on penal policy showed a magistrate at a training session on sentencing justifying a prison sentence for a first offence of burglary because "...there's a rather horrific statistic I've heard recently that if in the Metropolitan area you're standing in a crowd of sixteen people, waiting to go home at night, one of those sixteen will find when they get home that their house has been burgled." (*Panorama*, 22.2.82). The daily chance of being burgled in London is not one in sixteen but one in eleven thousand.

There are many quite specific findings from such surveys that suggest how crime can be prevented in rather more mundane ways than imprisonment which, it is argued below, has only a marginal role in crime prevention at best, and at worst operates to aggravate the problem. Much crime is trivial and opportunistic, and can be prevented by relatively trivial technical means: better home security, car steering locks, entry-phones and the like. Some would generate employment: rates of vandalism on one-man operated buses are several times greater than on those with a conductor. Free telephone installations for the elderly who are unable to afford them would allay some of their worst anxieties about intruders. More caretakers on large housing estates would stem much petty vandalism. Such measures are naturally unattractive to a Government and to Conservative Councils which are dedicated to cutting public expenditure: they prefer to spend far larger sums on increased prison building programmes.

The Tory party has by now developed a very considerable stake in the law and order issue.

Crime as an Issue

"People ask me whether I am going to make crime an issue at the next election. The answer is no. It is the people of Britain who are going to make it an issue."
Mrs Thatcher, Conservative Party Annual Conference, 1977).

The Tory party has by now developed a very considerable stake in the law and order issue. It helped to put them in power in 1979 and, though dispensed with as an issue by the Manifesto in 1983, many local candidates gave it prominence. It trades on a sense that people have quite understandable fears about crime, and that a sizeable majority believe it can only be dealt with by tougher measures of policing and imprisonment. A rhetoric of 'law and order' has been orchestrated by the Government to capitalise on those fears and beliefs. But that rhetoric is a double-edged weapon. Should the Conservatives fail to deliver the goods, should crime continue to rise, and tougher measures fail to stem that rise, then the problem of accounting for that failure will have to be addressed. Experience suggests that this will be accomplished by the 'breastplate of righteousness' technique. Despite our best efforts, crime continues to rise. Crime must be dealt with by even tougher measures. The police must have even stronger powers. The prisons must be expanded. Civil liberties will be further eroded. The constituent elements of a 'police state', which have already been assembled, will be further consolidated.

Most crime is probably fiscal and occupational: it is almost invariably dealt with informally or by negotiation rather than by the police and the courts.

The reality of crime is more complex and less sensational. It merits an informed rather than an inflamed response. Most crime is probably fiscal and occupational: it is almost invariably dealt with informally or by negotiation rather than by the police and the courts. We choose to ignore it and to concentrate almost exclusively on a relatively narrow band of offences whose predatory character is more visible. The perpetrators and victims of these offences tend to be working-class rather than not, and to be in certain localities associated with ethnic minorities. The rise in these crimes has been exaggerated, and the police and the media have chosen a dangerous course in so heavily overemphasising one crime – robbery, in one area – Lambeth, in which one ethnic minority is heavily implicated – young blacks. At the same time, every effort is made to deny any possible connection between that one form of deviance and the very social and economic conditions that, in several societies, have been shown to be strongly associated with it: high unemployment in the context of racial discrimination. As Scarman showed, such distorted stereotyping leads to false diagnoses of the problem; and thus to seriously flawed solutions in the form of punitive policing and severe sentencing. The result is the scapegoating of one particularly vulnerable section of the community to allay the genuine concern about crime, the character of which is far more widespread and pervasive.

2. Socialism, Crime and the Labour Party

Labour's record as a party of radical legal reform has not been matched by its record on law and order in general. For a party with major reforms to its credit in the 1960's (notably the abolition of capital punishment, and homosexual and abortion law reform) its thinking on crime control has been largely orthodox. The governing assumption has been that long-term social and economic changes are needed to diminish crime, and that until such changes 'pay off', crime and delinquency must be dealt with along largely traditional lines. The major exception to this rule was the acceptance of rehabilitation as a principal alternative strategy, especially in connection with delinquency. But as the evidence for the success of rehabilitative strategies failed to materialise, a policy vacuum developed, fresh alternatives were not evolved, and the drift to more authoritarian measures enhanced. Labour thus got the worst of both worlds: a 'soft' image combined with a 'hard' policy.

The ultimate justification for the 'hard line' is that people *want* law and order, and that any Government which fails to seek to promote it is not only failing in its duty towards them, but also courting electoral suicide. 'Law and Order' as a slogan implies that there are simple recipes for the delivery of law and order in reality. It is a political commonplace to refer to the myth of 'law and order'; that if only we were not so squeamish, and got really tough with offenders, the problem would at least be curbed, if not resolved. No amount of evidence to the contrary seems to weaken this belief. Yet there are signs that 'public opinion' is not so wedded to a policy of massive retribution as is usually implied by politicians and policy-makers. It may be that 'public opinion' is not such a major obstacle to reform, but is used as a resource by those who wish to justify the extension of 'hard-line' policies. The evidence gathered by the Prison Reform Trust (1982) indicated that people's views on appropriate penalties are far more diverse, and equivocal, even in connection with more serious offences, such as burglary, than had been assumed. It is no longer permissible, therefore, to dodge the issue on the grounds that 'law and order' at all costs is what the public want and so, reluctantly, we have to go along with that (see also Maguire, 1982).

The hostile reactions of many professional groups to the subsequently withdrawn clause in the (1983) Police and Criminal Evidence Bill which would have permitted police scrutiny of confidential files is a sign of dawning awareness that the requirements of 'order' exist in considerable tension with those of 'law' and 'liberty'. Our aversion to the 'Police State' is that it buys 'order' at the expense of 'law'. Compliance is exacted from the people at the cost of basic freedoms. Civil liberties are set aside to promote greater efficiency in crime control. In principle and practice, once the goal of 'order' is taken to be the over-riding priority, nothing is sacred. It then becomes 'obvious' that the police should be armed, the jails expanded, regimes toughened, in short, the repressive arm of the State apparatus extended, and the scope of civil liberties contracted. 'Law' under such conditions quickly becomes a mere counterfeit of justice and 'order' a forced regimentation.

Britain has arguably the sternest sentencing policy in Europe.

A socialist policy towards criminal justice should be based on a realistic acknowledgement of these tensions, as well as of people's desire for civil peace and protection from criminal victimisation. How might the traditional socialist ideals – of equality, liberty and fraternity – best be translated into criminal justice terms? Even a fairly narrow interpretation yields some strong policy leads. Equality as an ideal applied to the administration of justice shows a glaring discrepancy between social class, gender and ethnicity on the one hand, and an almost exclusively upper- or upper-middle-class white, male judiciary on the other. Immense obstacles stand between the formal principle of 'equality of opportunity' and equality in practice in terms of recruitment to both the judiciary, the legal profession, and the magistracy (Labour Campaign for Criminal Justice, 1983). Liberty as an ideal spells the minimum use of liberty-depriving penalties, when in reality Britain has arguably the sternest sentencing policy in Europe. And fraternity connotes a degree of participation in criminal justice, and of democratic controls, which we are only now beginning to explore in relation to police accountability. In the very running of prisons, borstals and detention centres, the only mention of the term is ironical: 'criminal fraternity.'

The larger sense in which a humane socialism can operate in criminal justice terms must be sought in a re-thinking of restitutive rather than retributive principles. Paradoxically, these operate at their fullest in the realm of economic and fiscal offences most associated with occupational deviance. In cases of tax evasion, infringements of health and safety legislation, both in industry and public health fields, social control is very largely a matter of negotiation and protracted settlement, rather than prosecution and retribution. (Carson, 1971, 1982; Paulus; Chapman, 1963) In part, this may stem from the implication of productive activity in the enterprises concerned. But the major reason seems to lie in the consequences for society of too stringent a tightening-up and formalisation of the controls. For example, a major crackdown on tax evasion would alone swell the prison population even further. Socialists face a dilemma on this score. Do we think prison wrong for the bulk of those who are currently inside only because others (tax evaders, motoring offenders, currency speculators) should take their place,or because it is wrong in itself? If we reject the latter choice, then we merely reproduce the penal crisis under a different ideology. But if we reject the former, it is then consistent to demand a policy which extends to the bulk of those currently imprisoned for largely non-violent property offences the same concern for the avoidance of stigma, excessive damage to their personal and economic prospects and care for their eventual re-entry into society that we now reserve for those committing a better class of crime. To leave things as they are is to reinforce the widely held view that there is 'one law for the rich, another for the poor'.

In other words, it is more consistent with humane socialism to redress the balance by extending restitutive principles of justice to the great majority of cases now handled retributively. The most serious offences – murder, rape, armed robbery, major frauds – would still be dealt with severely. But in all cases, the principles framing the operation of due process should incline towards the restitutive rather than to the retributive. As we examine the implications of such a shift for the major control agencies in turn, it should be clear that such an approach would enhance, rather than detract from, the social processes most germane to law and order.

3. *Policing*

More effective policing was one of the principal ways in which the Conservatives claimed 'law and order' could be improved. In the past five years, the police have been singled out by the Tories as a relatively favoured group in the general toll of public sector cutbacks, both in terms of pay and personnel. On the face of it, this strategy seems perfectly sensible: the police are, after all, the major agency responsible for crime control.

But the simplicity of the objective is largely illusory, and in many ways does the police a dis-service. It begs the question of methods, of just *how* the police could best improve their effectiveness; and it over-emphasises the role of the police as 'crime-fighters' holding the line against a rising tide of lawlessness. Inflated expectations have been aroused which the police have found it impossible to fulfil. The danger now is that they ascribe that failure to inadequate powers, personnel, technological resources and crime-fighting hardware, instead of to an unrealistic set of expectations of the role of the police in a complex and all too conflict-ridden society.

The Limits to Policing

Policing emerges from recent research as surprisingly limited in relation to crime control (Clarke and Hough, 1980; Heal and Morris, 1981). It has been established by victim surveys that at least 80% of crime goes unreported, and this figure is almost certainly a gross under-estimate, since the surveys do not tap such realms as occupational deviance. Of the 20% of the total volume of crime that, for the sake of argument, *does* become classified as 'crimes known to the police', some 60% or more (over 80% in the Metropolitan area) is not 'cleared up': that is, at most, 8% of the total *is* 'cleared up'. Of that 8%, around 75% is solved relatively routinely and very quickly or not at all, on the basis of victim reportage and suspect identification, or as crimes 'taken into consideration' in connection with a principal offence. In other words, in at most only 2% of crime control work are police skills of any developed order called for. This is not to denigrate the skills in so-called 'routine' police work, but to point out the limits within which they are exercised. It is glaringly obvious, and certainly well-known to the police themselves, that significant short-term improvements in their effectiveness could flow only either from a spectacular increase in public reportage (which would send the crime rate soaring) or the most draconian extension of police powers and presence to hitherto private realms of social and economic life.

Both strategies would, if put into practice, prove hopelessly counter-productive. The first would increase the 'fear of crime' and swamp the police with a mass of largely minor offences. The second would not only debase civil liberties, but would also lead to a spiral of deviousness that would poison social and economic life, and bog the police down in a morass of secondary conflicts with the custodians of institutional and corporate interests. The way to tackle corporate deviance is by changing the distribution of power, not by blanket extension of *police* powers.

Community Policing

The police have long known that formal social control is largely bluff. Social order is overwhelmingly the outcome of *informal* social work by people in families, schools, work and leisure. Policing, at least in a democratic society, has to be by consent, and has to be based on a shrewd acknowlegement of its limitations. It is ironical that the police are being encouraged, by the exploitation of the 'law and order' issue, to over-step these limits just when researchers are exposing them in some detail.

Yet the best possible hope for crime control flows from building grounds for more confidence in the police, and co-operation with them, by the public. More serious crime might be reported, but more importantly, more information leading to clear-up would be given. Greater police powers lead to those very conflicts which undermine public willingness to co-operate. At the end of that road lies Northern Ireland.

In introducing a recent review of some 20 years' study of the police in Britain and the USA, John Croft, former Head of the Home Office Research Unit, wrote: "First, the authors suggest that the police exercise a limited control over crime. Second, although the police may be less effective in controlling crime than traditionally supposed, they have a range of other important tasks to fulfil, including the education of the public in how to avoid crime, the reduction of fear in the community, and the support of those who have recently become victims"(1981). In a similar review of the evidence on police effectiveness, Michael Zander wrote: "*The evidence so far suggests that adding police does not have the expected pay-off in terms of more good arrests, let alone any reduction in the total level of crime. One reason is that so small a proportion of a policeman's time is spent in the pursuit of criminals. "Service" functions such as traffic duties, attending to accidents and fires, crowd control, tracing missing persons, intervention in domestic disputes, and the like, accounts for the bulk of police time. When police numbers are increased, the service functions go up in proportion*" (Zander, 13/12/79).

This distinction, between "crime control" and "service" policing, is at the heart of debates about the role of the police. The police are practically the only public service (along with hospital emergency departments) available 24 hours a day, seven days a week, every week of the year. People turn to the police for aid and advice on a host of matters, some not strictly to do with crime control or prevention at all (Manning, 1977). Two distinct philosophies of policing have emerged, one the "crime-fighting", the other the "peace-keeping", which bestow very different priorities on the two kinds of activity. The 'fire-brigade' conception would strip away the servicing aspects and intensify the core crime control aspects of policing. The 'community policing' conception views the two as inseparable, since the 'service' aspects of the job provide the basis for the consent without which the public become alienated from the police.

The evidence suggests that the 'community policing' view is the more correct. There is some evidence that concentrating police resources on specific targets pays off to a limited extent, but the effect is temporary, some crime is 'displaced' to adjacent areas, and "such a strategy may incur costs in the form of public alienation from the police, or rivalry between one group of officers and the next". (Heal and Morris, 1981,) At worst, more convictions are bought at the cost of heavy casualties, as in the notorious Detroit 'decoy' plan to combat street robberies, in which "eight offenders were killed by police officers and 38 police officers were wounded, one fatally". The 'Swamp '81' strategy in Brixton came perilously close to reproducing this state of affairs in Britain. (Scarman, 1981).

Mutual paranoia will continue to flourish until the issues of complaints against the police, and a democratic framework for police accountability, are settled.

Police Accountability

'Brixton also brought to the fore the issue of police accountability: "*Accountability is . . . the key to successful consultation and socially responsive policing. Exclusive reliance on 'voluntary' consultative machinery will not do, as the Brixton story illustrates. It must be backed by law*" (Scarman, 1981).

At present, and especially in London, which lacks a Police Authority other than the office of the Home Secretary, the system of police accountability is a recipe for mutual paranoia to flourish in police-public relations. As with much paranoia, there is a grain of truth in both points of view. The police view civil libertarian 'watchdog' groups as excessively anti-police, eager for any instance of 'police brutality' on which they can pounce. The 'watchdog' groups, such as the National Council for Civil Liberties, the GLC Police Committee, and the Lambeth Working Party into Community/Police Relations tend to view the police as authoritarian, closed to alternative views, often racist and hostile to informed criticism. Mutual paranoia will continue to flourish until the issues of complaints against the police, and a democratic framework for police accountability, are settled.

It is vital they are settled in a framework that prevents too close a link between local politicians, professional criminals and senior police, the formula for the successful emergence of organised crime in the USA. Similarly, it is important to avoid too rosy a view of community policing: "*At the simplest level, where the police work for a greater degree of collaboration between themselves and local authority agencies, they are in danger of being criticised for stepping beyond their conventional role and usurping the role of others; while on those occasions when the police urge the public to recognise, accept and act upon those aspects of crime to which they may be contributing, a position may arise in which the public find themselves accountable to the police.*" (Heal and Morris, 1981).

There is no one system of policing which will fit all problems and all communities. Too bureaucratised a form of community policing would fit only too well the Poujadism of Mrs Thatcher's Government. There are forms of specialist crime which simply cannot be tackled by community policing methods. But the bulk of minor offences are local, often opportunist and best dealt with by police who have local knowledge and some sensitivity to the diverse groups who compose the community. The 'no stone unturned, no orifice unexplored' brand of policing should be consigned to perdition.

The question of democratic control of

the police has been brought into sharp focus in recent years by increased specialisation and use of technology; by the increased arming of the police; by the growth in size, and reduction in number of local authorities appointing Police Authority Councillors; by disquiet over certain deaths in police custody; by the lack of any independent machinery for investigating complaints; by tactics in policing political demonstrations (in particular, the course of events surrounding the death of Blair Peach); and the increasingly overt nature of political campaigning by police organisations (which recently included the call by the Police Federation for the reintroduction of capital punishment).

The feebleness of existing democratic controls is summarised by Stuart Hall's remark that he searched the pages of Hansard in vain for the days when the "momentous move" to create the Special Patrol Groups "was debated by those to whom senior policemen insist they are ultimately accountable." Yet Police Authorities, mainly composed of elected councillors, do have power to monitor and take part in formulating police policy, (Regan, 1983) if only by pressing for more detailed information and regular meetings. Even so, "the evidence suggests that many local police authorities have a most unsatisfactory approach to their responsibilities. They display a tentativeness which in some cases amounts almost to passivity" (Regan). Flicking over the pages of the Complaints Book at the end of the quarterly meeting, and rubber-stamping increases in establishment and equipment, are hardly rigorous forms of monitoring. How can a more active form of ensuring accountability, let alone control over policing, be accomplished?

There are already certain developments in train which would improve the situation. Mandatory consultation via police-community liaison committees, outside the police committee of the local authority, was one positive feature of the Police and Criminal Evidence Bill. Lay visitors to police stations with access to the books and interviews are no mere sop to ward off full democratic control, but a valuable way of exercising such control. Other reforms are clearly called for: in particular, the elimination of Justices of the Peace from Police Authorities, and the creation of a Greater London Police Authority. However, before we can contemplate the full control of policing by such reconstituted Police Authorities, we must be clear about the character of the independence that must be left to the Chief Constables; reserved issues over which they would have authority without recourse to the elected Authority. At a minimum, these should include the investigations of individuals; appointments and promotions below the rank of Superintendant; and the discipline and disposition of particular officers. Appointment and dismissal should still be subject to Home Office ratification.

England and Wales are among the few countries in the world where the police not only investigate a crime but also prosecute the suspect.

Prosecution

England and Wales are among the few countries in the world where the police not only investigate a crime but also prosecute the suspect. The case for separating these two processes has been amply made by the Royal Commission on Criminal Procedure, which has recommended the establishment of a public prosecutor system for England and Wales. There is no particular merit, however, in the Commission's view that the prosecutor should be accountable to the local police authority committee. The latter should determine the policing policy for the area and should not be involved in individual prosecutions. The general lines of the Scottish system offer a better model, and would put the prosecutors under the ultimate control of the Attorney General. Prosecutors should have sole control over the decision to prosecute in individual cases, leaving the Attorney to establish the general guidelines. In England, about a third of the cases tried at the Crown Court are currently dismissed before they go to the jury. Indpendent prosecution should lead to fewer miscarriages of justice, less time spent awaiting trial, less expense and more public confidence in the criminal justice system. Prosecutors should also have the power to inquire into the content of particular investigations.

The police should support such reforms, for they have a stronger stake than they might realise in the success of democratic community policing. For when 'fire-brigade' policing fails, as it must, to deliver the goods, the next Tory policy option is privatisation. The model is already familiar: guard dogs and armoured transit vans, for those who can afford them. 'Securicor' strategies will be hailed as the solution to 'law and order' problems which other parties cannot reach.

4. *Sentencing*

Apart from strengthening the police force, the other main theme of Conservative policy on 'law and order' has been to reassert the value of punishment as a means of deterring criminals. The much-heralded and now enacted intention to experiment with more rigorous detention centres set the tone of recent penal policy. However, on assuming office, the former Home Secretary, William Whitelaw, to his credit, was quick to express his view that conditions in too many of our prisons are "an affront to a civilised society". He sought to persuade sentencers to be more sparing in their use of custodial sentences, and in 1981-2 was on the point of acting to reduce the appalling over-crowding in our prisons by introducing a supervised release scheme for short-term prisoners. The hostile reaction of both the senior judges, and his own Party at Conference, led him to abandon the proposal.

The 1982 Criminal Justice Act as a result was a much watered-down version of earlier liberal proposals, and a re-assertion of a basically punitive philosophy. The sentence of imprisonment was finally abolished for soliciting and vagrancy, but against this liberal measure, a form of curfew was introduced for young offenders on supervision, and the partially suspended sentence for adult offenders. Both are likely to aggravate the numbers entering custody, the first by responses to a breach of curfew, the other by sentencers using partially suspended sentences instead of non-custodial sentences. But the main point about the Act is its massive irrelevance to the fundamental need for sentencing reform.

Sentencers continue to make far too extensive use of imprisonment.

The Case for Sentencing Reform

Why is sentencing reform needed? The principal reason is that sentencers continue to make far too extensive use of imprisonment at a time when it has become increasingly clear that this measure is not only largely futile and costly, but also tends to deform rather than reform offenders. (Ashworth, 1982) Throughout the 1970's, a string of reports rammed this message home. The Advisory Council on the Penal System reported *"Neither practical experience nor the results of research in recent years have established the superiority of custodial over non-custodial methods in their effect upon renewed recidivism"* and the Home Office itself said *"No evidence has been found that longer sentences or longer periods of incarceration produce better results than short sentences"* (Sentence of the Court, 1978).

These conclusions stem from sources which are hardly associated with rash or radical statements. And there are signs that sentencers, especially magistrates, are making some attempt to be more sparing in the use of custody as a result. But their efforts are too little and too late, and the conditions in prison, especially local prisons, continue to deteriorate.

A basic problem is that crime continues to rise and, as long as sentencers resist a fundamental re-thinking of the traditional responses to it, the prison population is bound to rise also, despite parole, suspended and partially suspended sentences. It can of course be argued that, if people knowingly commit crimes, they *deserve* the punishment of imprisonment even if it *is* futile, costly and deforming. But it then becomes difficult to establish just how much prison is deserved, and *for whom*? Why do we single out not only murderers, rapists and armed robbers (who amount to less than 10% of the prison population) but also petty persistent offenders against property of certain kinds – mostly burglars and those guilty of minor larcenies – and avoid almost altogether the use of imprisonment, and even prosecution, for tax evaders, violators of health and safety legislation and the like? Why is a sentence of 9 months imprisonment appropriate for an incompetent shop-breaker with one distant previous conviction? Why not 6 months, or 3 months? Why prison at all? As long as this degree of incoherence reigns in sentencing philosphy and practice, the sentencing process will remain "a disgrace to the common law tradition" (Ashworth).

There remains the argument for the sheer incapacitation of offenders – locking them up longer prevents them from committing offences while they are inside (forgetting, for the sake of argument, those they may commit inside). But the impact on the total level of crime is marginal, since there are so many others who remain free. We should have to imprison far more people for far longer to make a difference of even a few per cent to the crime rate in general, though for highly specialist professional crimes, the impact is slightly greater (Brody and Tarling). The acid test of that proposition is what happens in other societies with a higher prison population than our own. Here we are moving towards wonderful penal company. The only comparable societies with higher prison populations than the United Kingdom are the USA, the USSR, South Africa and Austria West Germany. The first is notorious for its problems of organised crime and high levels of violence; the second for its 'darkness at noon' repression of political and intellectual dissent; the third for its appalling institutionalised racism; in the fifth there are trends to reduce the prison population below our own. Countries with far lower prison populations incude Japan, Holland, the Scandinavian countries and Australia: in none do crime trends compare adversely with ours, though their prison populations are *per capita* between 25% to 400% lower:

Daily Prison Population in 1979 (per 100,000)

Holland	22
Norway	43
Sweden	52
Denmark	58
Australia	68
England and Wales	86
West Germany	89
U.S.A.	250
South Africa	320

The policy of punishment and its variations have no effective influence on the rate of crime.

It would appear from comparative crime and prison population trends that prison has a far more peripheral impact on crime levels than traditionally imagined. This conclusion was reached nearly half a century ago in one of the most celebrated analyses of the data then available for several European countries: "The policy of punishment and its variations have no effective influence on the rate of crime. Changes in penal praxis cannot seriously interfere with the operation of the social causes for delinquency" (Rusche and Kircheimer 1939). Current research has strengthened rather than weakened the force of this contention.

Why, then, do sentencers remain so attached to the sentence of imprisonment? To answer this question is difficult, since judges in Britain have blocked attempts to inquire into their working philosphy. To say that they simply interpret the law is nonsense: the law does little more than prescribe a (usually very high) maximum penalty for broadly defined offences. But it helps to understand how judges and magistrates become locked into a custodial frame of mind if we examine the practical dificulties they face in their job.

The most formidable difficulty is that, as Ashworth stresses, "society is expecting sentencers to perform daily what even the great moral philosphers cannot achieve in a lifetime, that is, to reconcile satisfactorily the diverse factors of varying strength in each case, and to express the result in the form of a sentence which is regarded as fair." Does a first offence involving violence merit sterner measures than the fifteenth routine offence against property? What are the mitigating, and what the aggravating, factors? How should they be weighed? In this morass, sentencers rely heavily on two principal guidelines: *seriousness* (the extent of the injury, the amount stolen *etcetera*), and *consistency* (keeping sentences in line with similar cases in the past (Van Dijk, 1981). One problem is that sentencers tend to be informed only about what they and their immediate colleagues have done in the past: sentencing practices vary widely from area to area. Even Court of Appeal judgements make a limited and probably increasingly inconsistent impact (Thomas, 1982). So, if consistency and seriousness are the overriding guidelines, the prison population is bound to rise roughly in line with the crime rate. Only the most searching review of sentencing principles and practices could change things widely enough for the effects to be felt in terms of a *reduction* in the prison population.

It tends to be axiomatic for sentencers to accept the need for custody to be treated as the "last resort", especially as wide publicity has been given to prison over-crowding (though judges reject the view that this factor should be allowed to influence their sentences). Despite this widely shared assumption, certain competing assumptions routinely over-ride it. Once a prison sentence has been given, it is most unlikely for a non-custodial sentence to be passed if a person re-offends. So the factors governing *first* custodial sentences start people off on what is likely, given the high rates of recidivism among ex-prisoners, to be a penal career ended only in old age after several spells inside. Here the move to a shorter sentence, rather than to no custody at all, can be counter-productive. On the assumption that a short, sharp shock will "nip in the bud" a burgeoning criminal career, or that the "clang" of the gates will produce a momentous deterrent effect, many could be sentenced to short spells in custody who should have received a fine or supervisory sentence such as probation.

Persistent Offenders

Ashworth sees the nub of the prison problem as the petty, persistent offender: "thus in 1981 about half of the sentenced custodial population were persons convicted of burglary, theft, fraud or forgery who had three or more previous convictions". In these cases, it is persistence rather than seriousness which leads to a clustering of sentences around the '18 months to 3 years' range. There is no evidence that the stepping-up of sentence lengths to punish persistence has any deterrent effect, either on the individual concerned or generally. A modest theft, break-in or car-theft should not entail a custodial sentence even if persisted in for "the fifth, tenth or fifteenth time". There are non-custodial measures available, and those of a restitutive character could actually benefit the victim far more than custody (where the only conceivable benefit to the victim is vicarious pleasure at the offender's pain) (Wright, 1982). The only alternative to grasping this nettle is to accept a tariff for persistence which doles out swingeing penalties for petty crimes to such cases as *Gilbertson* (1981) – 12 months' imprisonment for two crimes of theft from shops, to a total value of under £10, by a woman with 14 previous convictions for similar offences; or *Harrison* (1979), 3 years imprisonment for a single failed burglary in a dwelling-house by an offender with a long record of previous offences (Ashworth). In Holland, such offenders may well have received a prison sentence, but its length would have not exceeded one or two months.

The moral issue is clear: do we choose to continue sentencing such offenders to years of custody in prisons at least half of whose inmates live in conditions recently described as "cattle-pens" by John McCarthy, who resigned as Governor of Wormwood Scrubs having expressed his disgust at the situation in which staff and prisoners had to work and live? Or do we live with the fractionally increased risk of the petty crimes that those we do not incarcerate for so long might commit if left free? For the basic issue is moral rather than environmental. Even if a sum of Falklands War proportions were spent on prison-building, it would still be wrong to deprive people of their liberty for relatively minor offences, albeit in clean, well-lighted places. If custody really is to be the "last resort", it should be treated as a last resort even if over-crowding, squalor, clogged sewerage and staff shortages were eliminated. It is for this reason that many penal reformers regard the ambitious Home Office plans for new prison building with keen anxiety: more capacity tends to spell more prisoners. What we need are fewer, refurbished prisons for a much reduced prison population rather than more, 'purpose-built' prisons for a much greater number.

Obstacles to Reform

The major obstacles to this objective are not only those to do with sentencers' acceptance of a logic that penalties should escalate for persistence as well as seriousness. This logic is girded about by other assumptions, and myths, which are invoked to justify its perpetuation. Firstly, there is the standard reference to 'public opinion' as "calling for" harsher penalties. 'Public opinion', however, tends to be tapped in only the crudest way, by broad opinion poll questions about 'crime' or 'violence'. More searching questions yield more subtle and flexible responses. Maguire's study (1982) of 300 burglary victims found that only 29% thought that the person who had committed "their" offence should receive a custodial sentence. Yet when the same people were asked about the sentencing of burglars in general, they gave far more punitive answers. The most likely explanation is that in the latter case people are drawing on stereotypes of burglary, of a kind that are heavily influenced by media presentations. For example, it is widely believed that many burglaries are accompanied by major damage and even soiling of domestic property. In fact, such damage occurs in only a few per cent of burglaries, and the British Crime Survey did not find one such case. Reliance on 'public opinion', therefore, undermines the very basis on which sentencing should rest: an informed consideration of the case in as impartial a manner as possible, freed from the kinds of hearsay and opinion which the law is constructed to exclude.

A second major obstacle is the myth that sentencing policy should be exclusively the preserve of the judiciary. "There is no constitutional rule or convention which prevents the legislature from restricting or removing judicial discretion in sentencing: the simple fact is that Parliament has taken little interest in the matter and has rarely legislated so as to impinge on the discretion of the courts to impose any sentence beneath the statutory maximum. The judiciary has acquired a central role by default...The Court of Appeal has, it is true, striven hard to develop principles to guide sentencers in the exercise of their discretion, but the senior judiciary has no constitutional claim to this policy-making role and seems to lack both that understanding of sentencing practice at all levels and that appreciation of broader issues of penal policy which are necessary in order to fashion realistic guidance for sentencers in lower courts. The judiciary seems to believe that it has the right to determine sentencing policy, and for that there is neither constitutional nor pragmatic justification." (Ashworth).

The judiciary seems to believe that it has the right to determine sentencing policy, and for that there is neither constitutional nor pragmatic justification.

The third obstacle is the form that arguments against the use of custody have taken, both by reformers and the Home Office, whose advocacy of a greater use of non-custodial measures tends to be resented by the judiciary, particularly when such arguments are cast in mainly economic terms. Judges in particular have stoutly maintained that sentencing should not be influenced by such matters as prison overcrowding. The moral arguments against prison tend to be undermined by this kind of economism, for it can then be argued that we should spend our way out of penal crisis. The main arguments against custody are basically moral: that deprivation of liberty should be used as sparingly as possible, as it constitutes the strongest claim that authority can make over the freedom of the individual; that no evidence exists for its effectiveness as either a special or general deterrent; that most other comparable societies make far less use of imprisonment without discernible adverse effects on their crime rates; that conditions in prison have now deteriorated to the point where it amount to a more severe sentence than in the recent past; that it deforms rather than reforms an offender's character; and that by stigmatising offenders it aggravates rather than ameliorates the problems they face on release.

Because sentencing is the key to the whole character of criminal justice and the penal system, it is of the utmost importance that a framework is devised to reform sentencing with the above considerations in mind.

The Case for a Sentencing Council

Because sentencing is the key to the whole character of criminal justice and the penal system, it is of the utmost importance that a framework is devised to reform sentencing with the above considerations in mind. The immense difficulties involved in formulating guidance and stimulating research into sentencing rule out any attempt at a complete system of highly specific sentencing guidelines: sentencing by computer, as it were. At the same time, the Court of Appeal is rightly too concerned with the purely juridical element in sentencing to take on the task of comprehensive sentencing reform. The best proposal is that of Ashworth, for a "middle way which builds upon the best of existing principles and practices, whilst improving the system so as to provide sentencers in the Crown Court and in magistrates' courts with a fuller and more consistent guidance". He proposes a Sentencing Council, chaired by the Lord Chief Justice himself and producing recommendations which would be issued as Practice Directions. Its membership should draw on persons with considerable experience of the penal system, from magistrates, to a Circuit Judge sitting in second and third tier centres, to a Probation Officer, a Prison Governor, a Home Office official, an academic, and – it should be added – a serving police officer and Prison Officer, an ex-prisoner, a victim and a citizen or two with no claims to specialist knowledge. Such a body would represent expertise from all levels of the criminal justice system with the sentencers as 'primus inter pares' but no group excluded. The work of the Sentencing Council would be to prescribe maximum sentencing levels for common types of offence, and to "tackle the more urgent issues of general principle, notably the proper approach to sentencing persistent offenders". Much as some sentencers distrust central direction of any kind, if they recognise that the Sentencing Council is fully conversant with their problems, respect for its recommendations should be increased both by sentencers and the public. To ensure that its recommendations are translated into practice is still problematic, however, and the only weak link in Ashworth's case is what measures might be needed to guarantee that they are not simply shelved. He avoids the explicit mention of legislation, but this must surely be essential at some stage if the Practice Directions are widely ignored. However, "at best, and with proper support from the judiciary, the introduction of a Sentencing Council should provide the basis for a system in the 1980's and beyond which is properly sparing in its use of custody".

5. Prisons

There are several crises, not just one, afflicting the British prison system (Fitzgerald and Sim). There are crises of numbers (too many), conditions (too squalid), objectives (what should prisons be for?), authority (among staff as well as prisoners), and secrecy (what goes on, how is it monitored, why so much censorship?). By comparison with most other Western societies, imprisonment in Britain is nasty, brutish and long. But the crises do not afflict all sectors of the prison system equally. There are major respects in which the experience of prison is far worse in the local adult prisons than in the training and juvenile prisons. The solutions to these problems have been reiterated time after time, and in a cost-effective way: what is lacking is the political will to put things right.

Even if the best scenario prevails, and custodial sentences are reduced to produce in the medium to long-term a prison population of roughly half the present size (which would still be relatively twice as high as that in Holland), we would still have about 20,-25,000 prisoners in the jails, and in youth custody. That would relieve the pressures of overcrowding, and allow for more humane containment. But what kind of regime should be followed? How should resoures be allocated? Most crucially, what should happen in the short-term when numbers remain as high as they now are? (Even this is an optimistic scenario: Home Office plans now assume a prison population of 53,000 by 1990).

Security was tightened at the expense, both financially and socially, of all other objectives.

Minimum Use of Security

The case for the minimum use of custody has been made above. For those who are imprisoned, two further policies should be implemented: the minimum use of security; and the normalisation of the prison (King and Morgan, 1981). The first refers to the extent to which, following the Mountbatten Report of 1966, security was tightened at the expense, both financially and socially, of all other objectives. The cure proved worse than the disease, for since then our prisons have been plagued by riots, lockdowns (prisoners being cell-bound for 23 hours a day), staff discontents boiling over into strike action, work-to-rule and task refusals, and several worrying cases of non-accidental deaths. Was it really worth it? Were all our lives suddenly more grieviously at risk because of the escape of George Blake to Russia and Ronald Biggs to Brazil? Heavy sentences again are implicated: would either have bothered if they had faced 5 or even 10 years instead of 30? Would, for that matter, the use of firearms in robberies have risen so greatly if sentencers had not imposed so long a set of sentences for the Great Train Robbery, in which firearms were not used? Compare Blake's sentence with that of Anthony Blunt, to the Keepership of the Queen's Pictures.

Mountbatten was a man of immense practical wisdom who certainly cannot be blamed for what followed his *Report* (1966, HMSO). He advocated a policy of *concentration* (a perhaps unfortunate term for its connotations) of high security risk prisoners, some 1% of the prison population, in one or possibly two maximum security prisons. He argued that all of our jails were under-secure for this tiny proportion of prisoners. Concentrating them in one or two maximum-security prisons would enable the rest to maintain relatively relaxed custodial regimes. Unfortunately, as it has turned out, the Home Office then appointed a Committee, headed by Sir Leon Radzinowicz, to enquire into the feasibility of this proposal. The Radzinowicz Committee (1968, HMSO) rejected the policy of concentration in favour of one of *dispersal*. They feared an Alcatraz effect, in which a pressure-cooker atmosphere would be created in a prison housing the criminal elite, to which staff would be difficult to attract, and which would heighten the risk of a mass 'springing' of prisoners by well-financed outsiders. Dispersal was reckoned to be both safer and more humane, since several jails, and not just one, could take the worst security-risks, and mix them with the more manageable prisoners. The arguments were convincing at the time, and accepted by the Prison Department of the Home Office.

Events since then have done much to undermine the force of the arguments for dispersal. We now have 4,000 prisoners under conditions of maximum security, instead of the 400 for whom it would be appropriate. The classification system proposed by Mountbatten of Category A, B, C and D has tended to silt up, with long delays in re-categorisation condemning prisoners to maximum security for far longer than necessary. The dispersal prisons have tightened their regimes, and reduced the mixing of Categories C and D with A and B to such a point that, in effect, we have 7 concentration prisons instead of just one or two (with one more already built). Dispersal prisons such as Albany, Hull, Wormwood Scrubs, Gartree and Parkhurst were the settings for major disturbances in the 1970s. Only Long Lartin and Wakefield have so far avoided them, partly because major control changes were made in the light of the disturbances elsewhere, partly because of unusually enlightened Governorship. But these pressure-cooker establishments cannot always rely on 'scenting the wind' and talented administrators. If the system is badly conceived, the pressure will blow in time.

The tragedy is that we now have a model of how a concentration principle *could* work, and it is not Alcatraz, but Glasgow's Barlinnie (Boyle, 1977). The Special Unit at Barlinnie, generously staffed, democratically run, open to a more generous flow of visitors than elsewhere – though there are signs that this is now under threat – and with an enviably violence-free record by contrast with units and wings for long-termers elsewhere, could be the basis for similar developments throughout maximum-security prisons. It is expensive, but its costs have never been adequately compared with equivalent contexts. And in a scaled-down, more efficiently run prison system, its costs would bring tangible benefits. Boyle is one prisoner who has rehabilitated himself, but that would not have been likely in an authoritarian setting, without staff whose finest and most humane attributes were given free rein in the right atmosphere. There may be limits and problems to extending the Barlinnie model. But these cannot be known until the right initiatives are taken.

The main arguments against concentration, which could begin tomorrow by the rolling back of the spread of the dispersal system, are that high-risk prisoners could not be moved on if at risk from other prisoners; that terrorists would be grouped together; that 'en masse' springing could occur; and that too many Category B prisoners also present formidable security risks for them to be taken out of maximum security. The first two points can be met by the same facilities that now exist for most terrorists, who are in Special Wings outside the dispersal prisons; the third applies to the dispersal prisons just as strongly; and the fourth, apart from making a nonsense of categorisation, makes it difficult to explain why the ratio of category B's to all inmates varies so extensively in the different regions.

As Morgan has argued (1982), such variations as that between Midland Region (11.6% of prisoners in security category B in 1981) and South West Region (29.3%) owed far more to the type of accommodation available than to objective security needs. With no adverse security risks, a general lowering of security categorisation to Midland Region level would alone save the Prison Department £25 million in staffing costs, a sum that could be spent on redeploying staff resources to guarantee minimum standards of work, recreation and education elsewhere in the system.

The second major aspect of prison organisation which is increasingly difficult to defend is the distinction between local and training prisons. This rests intellectually on the idea that distinctive training regimes have been established to which medium- and long-term prisoners can be directed after classification and evaluation. But the training is largely either standard – and should in principle be available for all prisoners – or illusory – and should be exposed as such. The distinction has immense resoure implications, however, for the training prisons are shielded from the worst effects of the prison crises by the maintenance of higher standards of cell allocation and amenities. The worst overcrowding in the local prisons, 2 or 3 to a cell, is to some degree preventible by spreading the prison population more evenly between the two sectors. A comprehensive network of local prisons is in principle superior to the local/training dichotomy, since training should be available to all prisoners, and many local prisoners never see the inside of a training prison anyway, despite classification-allocation, due to shortage of space and staff under the present rules.

Normalisation

"People are sent to prison *as* punishment, not *for* punishment" (Alexander Paterson).

Paterson's meaning should be clear enough: deprivation of liberty is *the* punishment, not simply the pre-condition for a series of extra punishments to be inflicted on prisoners. Yet prisons in Britain mock Paterson's words. No senior administrator, Governor, judge or criminologist would be likely to disagree with him. Indeed, the new strategy for warding off hostile criticism of the prisons is to agree with every word. William Whitelaw agreed that many of our prisons are "an affront to a civilised society". The former Director-General of the Prison Department has reiterated that view. Representatives of prison staff concur, as do prisoners. Why, then, do prisons continue to be run like "cattle-pens"? The answer is only partly to do with resources. It is far more to do with the heavy load carried by the term 'security'.

To 'normalise' the prisons would be to make them, as far as possible, resemble life on the outside. The standards of life inside, the amenities, facilities, services, rights and standards that prisoners should experience should be linked to the standards that prevail in the outside community. Otherwise, people are sent to prison for far more punishment than the deprivation of liberty.

The obsession with security, however, blocks this clear and simple precept at every point. Because of 'security', for example,it is argued that prisons must have their own medical staff. Independent medical advice is difficult for prisoners to obtain.

Despite some notable and well-publicised successes, such as prisoners gaining Open University degrees, work and educational opportunities in prison are severely limited, and among the first casualties of staff shortages and disciplinary action. Prison wages remain an insult, and education accounts for a tiny proportion of the total prison budget. For example, in 1981, education, training and recreation accounted for only £20 million in a total expenditure of £455 million in England and Wales. In recent years, a welcome liberalisation has produced some excellent television exposure of life inside to the public gaze. Yet journalists and researchers entering prisons for reporting purposes are likely to find themselves severely restricted in terms of what they can see and who they can meet. Researchers face the additional strait-jacket of the Official Secrets Act, as do all those who work in prisons. Censorship of letters and restriction on their numbers are still practiced. Prisoners cannot vote. They are denied heterosexual relations – and any other kind will hardly be approved of by the authorities. Prisons are constructed and administered in Britain to design out normality. It does not have to be so, as other countries in Western Europe have shown.

In May 1981, about 4,900 prisoners were living three, and 11,000 were living two to cells certified as suitable for one man: "*If any reader unfamiliar with the prison system finds it difficult to picture the squalor in which many inmates of local prisons are expected to spend their sentence, let him imagine himself obliged to stay in an hotel so overbooked that he has to share his room with two complete strangers. The room itself is so cramped that there is little space for his clothes or personal possessions, and if he wants to walk up and down, the other occupants must first lie on their beds. Worse, the hotel management insists that guests remain in their rooms for all but an hour or so each day and must take their meals there. As a result, the atmosphere rapidly becomes fetid, especially since neither the reader or his room mates have been able to take a bath for some days. But not only is there no basin or bath available, there is no lavatory either, and the reader and his companions are faced with the prospect of relying for the foreseeable future upon chamberpots thoughtfully provided by the management. If the reader does not conclude that such an experience lasting several days would be degrading and brutalising, he is being less than honest with himself: how much worse would it be after several weeks?*" (Report 1981).

Or, HM's Inspector of Prisons might have added, for several months, or even years. In many ways, the prison staff also experience much of the squalor of the prisoners' lot. Their facilities and conditions of work are often appalling. The danger is that they and the prisoners become brutalised and apathetic. Now that the public have seen several reasonably accurate and pointed documentaries about prison life, the danger is that they too become acquiescent about the system. After all, if those actually running the system can throw up their hands in civilised horror at the degradation of it all, what can be done by the rest of us?

The least we can do is reject the hypocrisy that there is nothing to be done. Quite a lot of money is spent on the prisons: £500 million in 1982-3. Apart from basic manpower costs, quite a lot of it goes on refurbishing worn out buildings, building new prisons, feeding guard dogs (at a greater cost than feeding prisoners, per capita), endless escort duties (popular with staff, since they break the monotony and pile up overtime): all in all, expenditure on the penal estate has risen at a faster rate than that on health services or education over the post-war period. Much of it is mis-directed, since a great deal goes on forms of security that are unnecessary, eroding that very capacity for responsibility on the part of prisoners that they will need if they are to survive socially on release. We still tend to forget that prisoners re-enter the world, usually significantly worse off, in every respect, than when they left it.

A Prisoners' Charter of Rights

What we *can* do is legislate a Prisoners' Charter of Rights guaranteeing to each prisoner:

- access to all rules and regulations dealing with prison life, except those relating explicitly to security;
- a statement of specified standards relating to food, drink, cell-space, recreation, clothing, laundry, sanitation, visits, earnings, work, possessions, and the like, which are the minimum a prisoner should have the right, admissible in law, to expect;
- access to all files, dossiers, case records and other information about him, except those explicitly relating to security, with the right to appeal to an independent body if they are withheld.

Normalisation of prison life could begin to be built piecemeal on such a foundation. Some prisons already exceed many of the minimum standards that would be entailed in such a charter (Cohen and Taylor, 1978).

Four other reforms demand urgent passage. They are:

- the enactment of the 1975 Jellicoe Report recommendations that Boards of Visitors be re-constituted along genuinely independent lines as a body to deal with prisoners' requests and complaints. A separate independent body should be established to deal with all adjudications.
- the lifting of restrictions on the numbers of letters written or received by prisoners, and the abolition of all censorship of letters, unless for reasons of security that should be subject to appeal to the Board of Visitors.
- prisoners should be granted the vote in both national and local elections (a provision important in itself, and one that should encourage more politicians to visit their local prisons) and
- rapid use of the funds already provided for the regional secure psychiatric units recommended as an urgent priority by the Butler Committee on Mentally Abnormal Offenders in 1974 (Kilroy-Silk, 1983).

Such a programme by no means exhausts the catalogue of reforms that are needed to begin to ensure some congruence between standards of life on the inside, and those in the outside world. As things stand, there will be few voices raised in protest if Mrs Thatcher decides to privatise the prisons, 'hiving off' their more profitable industries to the private sector, to which all that cheap labour should prove attractive. After all, a government which has retraced its steps to the mid-nineteenth century for its economic ideas should find no difficulty in returning to the middle of the eighteenth century for its penal policy.

Juvenile Justice

Juvenile justice is in many ways the saddest area to survey after the high hopes of radical change invested in the 1969 Children and Young Persons Act. The intention of that Act was to divert young offenders as far as possible from custodial regimes. For the Act to have had a chance of working as intended, extra resources had to be made available to local authority Social Service Departments, borstal and detention centres abolished for the under 17's, and the age of criminal responsibility raised to 14. The difficulties involved in implementing the Act were greately compounded when the Conservative Government of 1970 chose not to activate the last two provisions, and by the time of the return of a Labour Government in 1974, the rehabilitative philosophy on which the Act rested was increasingly under fire. The policy remained one of drift throughout the 1970's, with the following results:

Young Offenders aged 14-16

	Guilty or cautioned			Receptions under sentence		
	male	*female*	*total*	*male*	*female*	*total*
1971	69,000	11,100	**80,700**	3,032	34	**3,066**
1981	94,900	18,800	**113,700**	7,535	52	**7,587**
% change	+36	+69	+41	+149	+53	+147

(Crime figs. slightly reduced for 1981 due to changes in counting rules in 1978; indictable offs. only; sources, CS 1981 p.107; PS 1981 p.61)

Even taking bare numbers (the rise in the crime *rate* for this age-group being markedly lower) custodial sentences for 14-16 year old boys (who make most impact on the figures) rose by **over 4 times the rate** at which the number of offences rose, a rise that is almost entirely due to a tripling of the numbers sentenced to detention centres, whose failure rate, in terms of recidivism is over 70%. That for borstal is on average over 80% for this age-group. The moral and practical bankruptcy of this policy should be by now abundantly clear.

Custodial sentences for juvenile offenders were boosted in the 1970's by the uneasy jostling of welfare and custodial ideas (Taylor, Lacey and Bracken, 1979). 'Care' orders have been shown to have played a major role in the unexpectedly large jump in custodial measures for this age-group, since the breach of a 'care' order leads in many cases to Detention Centre or Borstal, and 'care' orders were made too readily too low down the tariff (Thorp, 1981). The three criteria used for research into 'care' orders – danger to self or others; no home; and special educational or psychological requirements – were shown in a study of 6 areas to be applicable in only 14% of 537 cases (that is by any *one* of the criteria). In other words, well-intentioned legislation, confusingly implemented, has had a net-widening effect which quickly fed through to the custodial end of the system.

The 1982 Criminal Justice Act has replaced Borstals by the idea of Youth Custody, and clearly is aiming to reduce the reformative element in such regimes. Their nature is not yet apparent, since so much emphasis is being placed on the new, shorter, tougher Detention Centre Orders. But a swing back to custody of a punitive nature is hardly likely to improve on the past.

A Labour Government must make one of its first priorities a thorough and critical examination of what has happened in the realm of Juvenile Justice since the 1969 Act. As a start, it could do much by implementing the proposals made by Taylor, Lacey and Bracken:

- Extension of the use of the caution, which has not increased proportionately since the early 1970's, to cases which at present lead to court appearances; the reduction of the present differences between police authorities in cautioning.
- The abolition of re-labelling of assessment centres in recognition of their actual functions as 'containment' centres.
- A halt to the construction of 'secure units', which DHSS studies have shown to be taking increasingly less serious

offenders, and the immediate examination of their current role and impact on children (Cawson, 1975).

- An immediate inquiry into the use of medication for control purposes in juvenile institutions.
- The establishment of a Care and Control Test for all children subject to 7(7) care orders, that is that (a) the child should present a danger to himself or the community; (b) should be literally homeless; (c) have medical, educational or psychological needs that can only be met in an institution.
- The establishment of a National Children's Legal Centre.

In other respects, the arguments put forward in connection with sentencing adults to imprisonment should be equally applicable to children: custodial sentences for the under 17's are even more out of alignment with practice elsewhere in Western Europe than is the case with adults.

Parole

The argument for parole is that it has an important role in reducing the amount of time served by medium- and long-term prisoners. The working of the Parole Boards has been fruitful in linking the judiciary in at least one respect to the broader penal framework. However, the case against parole is now well made in several respects: that parole played a role in the lengthening of certain forms of sentence; that it is a form of 're-sentencing'; that it introduces an element of executive discretion, and rehabilitative thinking, which is unaccountable; that prisoners are granted no right of Appeal, and are not informed of reasons for the withholding of parole; that it exerts unwarranted strain on prisoners; and that for these and other reasons, some 5-10% of prisoners never apply for parole (thus failing to benefit from any notional extra element in their sentence length due to the existence of parole in the first place (Hood, 1974; West and Thomas, 1974; Morris 1981). Parole cannot be reformed to take account of these criticisms without secondary conflicts arising within prisons, since staff opinions are crucial to parole outcomes. Parole should therefore be abolished, at a phase when the Practice Directions for sentencing are established.

Alternatives to Prison

It is widely believed that the existence of various alternative measures to imprisonment has had a significant effect in limiting the use of custodial sentences. The official figures on sentencing show that this has not been so:

Percentage of indictable offenders who received various sentences

	1971	*1981*	*% change*
Absolute/Conditional discharge	13	12	−1
Probation	8	7	−1
Supervision order	5	3	−2
Fine	48	45	*−3*
Community Serv. Order	*	5	*+5*
Attendance Centre Order	2	3	+1
Detention Centre Order	2	3	+1
Care order	2	1	−1
Borstal	2	2	0
Suspended prison	7	7	0
Immediate prison	9	10	+1
Other	1	1	0

Source: Criminal Statistics, 1981
* = not available

The overall impression left by these figures is of consistency and continuity, rather than any sharp break with the established pattern of custodial sentencing. Room has been made for the major new alternative to custody of the 1970's, the Community Service Order, not so much by a reduction of the use of custody, which has actually increased, but by a reduction in the use of other alternatives to custody. The adumbration of yet more alternatives to prison is unlikely to break this pattern: they are more likely to be alternatives to alternatives than to prison itself.

All very frustrating, since waiting in the wings are fresh ideas for alternatives to prison, not least that of *restitution*, the case for which has been most convincingly put by Martin Wright (1982). He argues that the current system of criminal justice is singularly punitive towards the offender and notably useless to the victim. By agreeing to make restitution to the victim, and by the victim agreeing to accept such restitution, the offender is arguably brought to a sharper realisation of the harm done, and given an opportunity to expiate his guilt more fully than by feeling himself victimised by imprisonment. There is also scope for victim and offender *reconciliation*. There are obviously many cases to which restitution could not apply, but in the USA in particular some experience has been gained, in both crimes against property and the person, that suggest such schemes can be surprisingly successful. There are obvious ways in which the idea could be explored further, by comparative research, and we could begin by making restitution permissible in, for example, minor cases of theft.

The drawback to such a scheme, as to other alternatives to prison, is in their breach:

Offenders Breaching Orders as a % of Offenders Sentenced (1981)

Suspended sentence	27
Community service	19
Probation order	14
Cond. discharge	10

Source: Criminal Statistics, 1981

In the case of suspended sentences, a further conviction brings not only a fresh penalty, but the activation of the suspended sentence – in some 80% of breaches in 1981. Whilst the use of imprisonment for the breaching of other non-custodial penalties is much more sparing, clearly there is a risk that the use of alternatives instead of the fine (whose rate of reception into prison for non-payment is just over 1%) will increase the prison population unduly by default.

This question is of the utomst importance to people on low incomes, especially those on Social Security, who are most at risk of imprisonment due to the sentencing assumption that they cannot by definition be eligible for fines, since a subsistence income excludes that option. Yet Department of Health and Social Security (DHSS) norms have been set up to enable arrears of rates, fuel bills *etcetera* to be paid by those on Social Security which involve low payments spread over time. Similarly low maxima could be devised for fines. Such re-thinking of the structure of fines, which are imposed in almost half of serious, and the great majority of non-serious cases, is urgently required. The day-fine system, which takes capacity to pay into account far more systematically than is currently the case, provides the most suitable basis for removing from the poor the unwarranted risk of imprisonment for poverty rather than criminality. (Morgan & Bowles 1981).

The simplest answer is to make breaches non-imprisonable. That, however, may lead sentencers to desert the use of such alternatives even more than now. The idea is worth exploring, however. In Holland, the recommendation to probation is, at the insistence of the probation service, entirely voluntary. If an offender does not keep up links with the probation officer, the fact is noted should he be re-convicted for a further offence; but there is no penalty for the breach itself. To detach these alternatives from prison altogether would at least make them more authentic alternatives, though it would rob social work students of the staple essay theme of 'punitive' versus 'welfare' roles in the client relationship.

Probation could be more widely used without any risk of increased crime or recidivism.

Brody (1976) concluded his review of the 'effectiveness of sentencing' by stating: "two studies, one in Britain and one in America, arrived at the same conclusion – that probation could be more widely used without any risk of increased crime or recidivism." We may not have much idea what to do to cope with the crime problem, but at least that leaves us with every incentive to adopt the most humane options.

The Home Office have chosen this moment to reduce the Community Services share of their Budget from a derisory 0.68% in 1981-2 to 0.60% in 1983-4 (£23 million out of a total 'Law and Order' Budget of £4,013 million). So much for hostels, Intermediate Treatment schemes and the like. A major saving has, however, been made by lopping £300,000 (0.007% of the same) off the salaries of trainee Probation Officers.

We could also do much more, relatively

cheaply, to *prevent* crime. Like the medical profession, we seem to prefer expensive and highly technological cures (though in the case of crime, they don't work) to cheap and labour-intensive prevention. The authors of the British Crime Survey suggest that "in a sense it is the motor car which is the 'villain of the piece' when it comes to explaining the growth and prevalence of crime...Though opportunities do not *have* to be acted upon, a number of researchers have demonstrated that increases in crime often go hand in hand with increases in opportunity...Methods of making cars more difficult to get into, drive away and vandalise seem urgently needed..." As things stand, "somewhere in excess of one quarter of households who kept their vehicles on the streets of the inner city suffered some sort of theft of or from them annually." (pp. 19, 34-5). More manpower on buses, transport, in parks, on housing estates, would reduce unemployment and curb opportunistic crime, as well as provide community services.

Victim compensation is the other major way of curbing the 'fear' and ameliorating the effects of crime. At present, compensation schemes exist for victims of crimes of violence: these schemes could be extended, and made more generous. Victims also seek something more than the purely passive role they play in the criminal justice system. (Shapland, 1983) It is in these kinds of ways that we should seek to deal with crime and its aftermath, rather than pursuing the will o' the wisp custodial cure-all. In the process, however, we must avoid permeating society with a network of surveillance and monitoring that makes a prison of society itself Cohen (1979). Nor must we blur the line between freedom and control by *ad hoc* alternatives to custody that widen the net to those allegedly 'at risk' of delinquency, or technically 'free' but perpetually and indefinitely liable to 'recall', as is the case with 'lifers' released from prison. The Labour Party should regard such forms of open-ended control as an affront to natural justice.

6. Conclusions

Law and order, in the narrow sense of a preoccupation with rates of crime, is a Pandora's Box of an issue, traditionally and wisely avoided by politicians as a partisan problem. Ironically, for the myth is patriarchal, it is Mrs Thatcher who has chosen to open it. Exploiting people's fear of crime, which is real enough, and claiming that the appropriate answer to it lies in stronger policing and sterner punishments, which they are not, she has ignored the paradox at the heart of the law and order issue.

That paradox is the ease with which the law can be subverted to counterfeit justice, and be wrenched into the shape required by 'order'. The Police and Criminal Evidence Bill was the beginning of that process. The 'order' that results is a regimented and repressive variety, not what people have in mind when they demand law and order, by which they generally mean what Orwell meant when he talked about the English people's belief in 'common decency'. The more honest approach is by no means to fob people off, to claim that crime is actually falling, or no worse than it was.

It is to acknowledge that the problem has worsened, but to provide the fullest information to enable people to put crime into perspective, and to counteract media sensationalism and bias, whilst encouraging the media to do what they do best – investigative, critical reportage. That means the abolition of the Official Secrets Act and its replacement by a Freedom of Information Act. In the end, however, we need a yardstick against which to measure the quality of reforms, since so many well-intentioned measures have back-fired or proved unexpectedly coercive. That yardstick can only be 'natural justice', which demands fairness, openness, and reasoned decision-making on grounds and evidence that are publicly available. A humane socialism, which means the practice of such principles in social and economic terms, holds out the only hope of reducing both crime and punishment.

References

Ashworth A: "Reducing the Prison Population in the 1980's: The Need for Sentencing Reform," Noel Buxton lecture, NACRO, 1982.

Bakke E W: *The Unemployed Man: A Social Study,* 1933.

Baldock, J C; "Why the Prison Population has Grown Larger and Younger", *Howard Journal* 19, 1980.

BBC: 'Panorama', 22.2.82, transmission recording transcript.

Biles D: "Crime and Imprisonment: A Two-Decade Comparison between England and Wales and Australia," *British Journal of Criminology.,* April 1983.

Bottomley K and Coleman C: "Understanding Crime Rates," in Clarke, R V G and Hough, J M (eds.) *The Effectiveness of Policing,* 1980.

Box S: *Deviance, Reality and Society,* 1971 (rev., 1982).

Brody S and Tarling R: *Taking Offenders Out of Circulation,* Home Office Research Study No 64, 1980.

Brody S: *The Effectiveness of Sentencing,* Home Office Research Study No 35, 1976.

Carr-Hill R and Stern N: *Crime, The Police and Criminal Statistics,* 1979.

Carson W G: "White-Collar Crime and the Enforcement of Factory Legislation," in his (co-ed) *Crime and Delinquency in Britain,* 1971.

Carson W G: *The Other Price of Britain's Oil,* 1982.

Cawson P: *Referrals to the Units and Behaviour Prior to Referral,* DHSS, Research Division, 1975.

Cawson P and Martell, M: *Children Referred to Closed Units,* DHSS 1979.

Chapman D: *Sociology and the Stereotype of the Criminal,* 1963.

Clarke M: *Fallen Idols: Elites and the Search for the Acceptable Face of Capitalism,* 1981.

Clarke R V G and Hough J M (eds.): *The Effectiveness of Policing,* 1980.

Cohen S: "The Punitive City", *Contemporary Crises,* 1979.

Cohen S and Taylor L: *Prison Secrets,* 1978.

Cox B, Shirley J and Short M: *The Fall of Scotland Yard,* 1977.

Ditton J: *Part-time Crime,* 1977.

Ditton J: "How did the black economy do in 1982?" *Assessment: Newspaper of the Inland Revenue Staff Federation,* Feb. 1983.

Ditton J: *Controlology,* 1979.

Downes D M: "Origins and Consequences of Dutch Penal Policy", *British Journal of Criminology.,* October 1982.

Fitzgerald M and Sim J: *British Prisons,* 1979.

Hakim, C: "The Social Consequences of High Unemployment", *Journal of Social Policy.,* October 1982.

Hall S: *Drifting into a Law and Order Society,* 1979.

Henry S: *The Hidden Economy,* 1978.

Hood R: *Tolerance and the Tariff,* 1974.

Hough M and Mayhew R: *The British Crime Survey,* Home Office Research Study No 76, 1983.

HMSO: Criminal Statistics, England and Wales, 1947, 1962, 1979 and 1981.
Prison Statistics, England and Wales, 1981.
Report on the Work of the Prison Dept., 1981.
Public Expenditure Estimates, 1983-4/85-6, Cmnd. 8789, 2.
Report of H.M. Chief Inspector for England and Wales, 1981.
Report of the Inquiry into Prison Escapes and Security, (*Mountbatten Report*), 1966, Cmnd. 3175.
The Regime for Long-Term Prisoners in Conditions of Maximum Security, *(Radzinowicz Report)*, Advisory Council on the Penal System, 1968.
Kilroy-Silk R: "Scandal of the Missing Millions", *Sunday Times,* 1 May 1983.
King R and Morgan R: *The Future of the Prison System,* 1980.
Labour Campaign for Criminal Justice: *A Survey of the Recruitment of Labour Party Members to the Magistracy"* 1983.
Levenson H: *Democracy and the Police,* Labour Campaign for Criminal Justice, 1980.
Maguire M: *Burglary in a Dwelling,* 1982.
Manning P: *Police Work,* 1977.
Mars G: *Cheats at Work,* 1983.
McDonald L: *The Sociology of Law and Order,* 1976.
Miller W B: "Youth Gangs in the Urban Crisis Era" in Short J F (ed), *Delinquency Crime and Society,* 1976.
Morgan R and Bowles R: "Fines: the Case for Review", *Criminal Law Review* April 1981.'
Morris P and Heal K: *Crime Control and the Police,* Home Office Research Study No 67, 1981.
Morris T P: "The Parole System: 'Executive' Justice", in *Criminal Welfare on Trial,* Social Affairs IUnit, No. 1, 1981.
Paulus I: *The Search for Pure Food,* 1975.
Prison Reform Trust: *The People's Justice,* 1982.
Regan D: *Are the Police Under Control?* Social Affairs Unit, Research Paper 1, 1983.
Rusche G and Kirchheimer O: *Punishment and Social Structure,* 1939.
Scarman Report: *The Brixton Disorders, 10-12 April 1981,* Penguin 1982.
Shapland J: "Victim assistance in the criminal justice system", forthcoming, 1983.
Sinfield A: *What Unemployment Means,* 1981.
Softley P: *Fines in Magistrates' Courts,* Home Office Research Study No 46, 1978.
South Africa: Annual Report of the Commissioners for Prisons, 1978-9.
Tarling R: "Unemployment and Crime", *Research Bulletin No 14, Home Office Research and Planning Unit, 1982.*
Smith D E: "Strategies for diversion and decarceration", paper given at International Conference on Psychology and Law, British Psychological Society, Swansea, 1982.
Taylor I: Law and Order: Arguments for Socialism, 1981.
Taylor L, Lacey R and Bracken D: *In Whose Best Interests?: The Unjust Treatment of Children in Courts and Institutions,* 1979.
Thomas D A: "Appellate review and sentencing decisions," paper given at Kings College, London, 4 Dec. 1982.
Thomas D A and West D J (Eds.) *Parole,* 1974.
Thorp D and others: *Out of Care,* 1981.
Thorp D: "The Making of a Delinquent", *Community Care,* 26/4/79.
Van Dijk J: *Sentencing Process,* Ministry of Justice, The Hague, 1981.
Wright M: *Making Good,* 1982.
Wright M: "Reparation", *Abolitionist,* 1982 (3).
Yeager M G: "Unemployment and Imprisonment," *Journal of Criminal Law and Criminology,* 70, 1979.
Zander M: "What is the evidence on law and order?", *New Society,* 13 Dec. 1979.
Yeager M G: "Unemployment and Imprisonment," *Journal of Criminal Law and Criminology,* 70, 1979.

[9]

Theories of Decarceration: Problems of Accounting for Sentencing Trends in The Netherlands

On the assumption that the reality of the trends dealt with in Chapter 2 have been established, and that they cannot be explained away in terms of crime rates, clear-up rates, or hidden sanctions, the problem remains of accounting for them at all adequately. The problems are particularly acute in the Dutch case, since the rough parallelism between crime rates and rates of custodial sentencing in England are more in line with the canons of consistency and seriousness imputed to sentencers by research into sentencing process. That is not to say that the levels at which consistency and seriousness have come to operate in England are not in themselves problematic. It is that the problems of explanation in the Dutch case are compounded by their evident departure from such canons, despite an operational commitment to them. Nor is it readily apparent that commonsense accounts (which social scientists, if we can use such a pejorative term, are exhorted by politicians to emulate) do the job for us. Both English and Dutch sentencers tend to say alike that they use prison as a 'last resort', avoid it in 'trivial' or 'first offences' wherever possible, and disregard the availability of prison places as a factor in their sentencing. Such affirmations would predict similarity in sentencing trends, rather than the distinct differences that have obtained in the post-war period.

Several theories, or broad ways of explaining the trends, have been derived, either from the criminological literature on penal changes, or from interviews with members of the Dutch judiciary and specialists in allied fields. They are by no means mutually exclusive but, in assessing their merits, it seems essential to ask of each in turn not only how well they fit the facts of the case in The Netherlands, but also how well they do so for England and other comparable societies. A good explanation would also suggest the processes whereby so-called 'causes' are mediated through the human agencies, in this case primarily the judiciary, who accomplish their apparent effects. Having reviewed the strengths and weaknesses of each theory, the somewhat artificial process of separating out the elements of each in isolation can be abandoned, and the best possible combination sought.

The economics of decarceration

In his book *Decarceration: Community Treatment and the Deviant*, Scull (1977) argues that trends towards the de-institutionalization of both punishment and treatment (i.e. of responses to the 'bad' and the 'mad') are increasingly marked in capitalist societies, mainly for reasons of gathering economic stringency rather than from any substantial humanitarian concern or profound therapeutic breakthrough. In the same vein as O'Connor (1973), he sees 'welfare capitalism' as increasingly beset by fiscal crises, as the costs of manning burgeoning welfare institutions outpace economic growth. Morever, the labour-intensive character of welfare institutions forbids more than marginal gains in productivity to offset these costs. Hence the new-found enthusiasm of governments for the panacea of 'community care', though the cheapskate, cost-cutting versions they espouse bear little resemblance to the model of heavily subsidized community support promulgated by the earlier critics of institutions (see, e.g. Townsend 1963, Morris 1969).

Scull's case was based chiefly upon trends in the United States and England, in both of which prison populations had fallen relative to the growth of crime rates in the two decades before the mid-1970s. This definition is the weakest of the relative measures of decarceration, which in stronger form can be based on the proportion of the sentenced population which is imprisoned. An absolute definition would pivot on actual falls in the prison population, unless such reductions were less than falls in either the crime rate or the proportions receiving other disposals. Some critics of Scull's thesis (e.g. Chan and Ericson 1981) have seen decarceration only in absolute terms. However, even in its weakest sense the thesis was quickly overtaken by events in the United States, where the overall prison population doubled in the decade 1975—85, far outstripping growth in the crime rate. In England too, the proportion of offenders[1] sentenced to immediate custody rose steadily from 15 per cent in 1974 to 20 per cent in 1984, though historically, as Bottoms (1983) has reminded us, this remains well below the 29.1 per cent imprisoned in 1959 and the

---

1 The reference is to adult offenders.

33.3 per cent in 1938. On the other hand, his argument retains much force in relation to the mentally ill. Rates of mental illness are perhaps considerably higher than they were in the 1950's, notably in connection with the greater numbers surviving to the age of onset of psycho-geriatric illnesses: but mental institution populations have plummeted in both England and the United States. In relation to offenders, the most striking example remains the case of Massachusetts, where juvenile reformatories were closed down virtually overnight (Rutherford 1986).

By any definition, The Netherlands is a classic example of decarceration in the penal sphere. It does not appear, however, to have conformed to the theory of fiscal crisis. If anything, it has conformed to the reverse. The major reductions in the prison population, both in terms of average daily populations and in relation to the rise in crime rates, came from the mid-1950s to the early 1970s, when The Netherlands was experiencing an unprecedented growth in prosperity and a relative absence of fiscal crisis. Conversely, plans are now in train for a doubling of penal capacity from its 1975 level by 1990, at a time of considerable economic anxiety. 'Between 1950 and 1960 public expenditure accounted for about a third of the national product, rising to about half in 1970. It now accounts for about 70%. All growth in the national product during the seventies went into public spending, the greatest rise in expenditure being on social security' (SCPB 1984: 28). Morever, even in relation to the mentally ill, the predictions one might make from fiscal crisis theory have not been fulfilled. Mental institutional care has survived in The Netherlands to a much greater extent than in either England or the United States. 'The present Social and Cultural Report is again forced to note that the desired shift from institutional to non-institutional care has not taken place. The proportion of costs accounted for by the latter even dropped from 31% in 1972 to 28% in 1982' (*ibid* 28). However, the desire was correctly predicted, and with public sector expenditure at 70 per cent of national product, it may be simply a matter of time before some shift towards its fulfilment is discernible.

It may be worth noting in passing that some rough correspondence does seem to hold, in at least the three cases mentioned, between trends in penal and mental institutions. In the United States and, more sluggishly, England, the decanting of very large numbers of patients from institutions to the community has been followed by rising prison populations. In The Netherlands, the relative stability of the mental hospital population has accompanied a fall in that of the prisons. It is, however, unlikely that these two populations are substantially interchangeable, though at the margins there is undoubtedly some possibility of substitution. It would not account at all significantly for the trends, important as the issues involved undoubtedly are. For example, on 30 June 1977 some 769 prisoners in England were defined as potentially transferable to mental hospitals under the terms of the 1959 Mental Health Act, a figure which had fallen to 240 in 1987 (Hansard Col. 1, 25.1.88). (See also pp. 77–81.).

The carceral society and the dispersal of social control

There is one sense in which Scull's approach, with its emphasis on the tilting of control away from the prison and the asylum to the spurious blessing of community corrections or care, chimes with that of theorists who, in the last two decades, have discerned the lineaments of the 'carceral' society in new forms of penality (Garland and Young 1983). In particular, Foucault (1977) and Stanley Cohen (1979, 1985) view the prison as likely to become less prominent (though still held in reserve for the dangerous and recalcitrant) as a focus for formal control in advanced capitalist societies. Instead, a web of control institutions will permeate civil society in an ever-tightening mesh of state regulations. People in general, not only those designated deviant, will come under systematic surveillance. The ideal of the 'carceral society' would in principal render the prison superflous, achieving perfect social control by other means: Foucault's 'hundreds of tiny theatres of punishment', each a 'perfect arithmetical representation of the bourgeois social contract' (Cohen 1985: 85). In a notable metaphor, Cohen (1979) viewed contemporary trends in social control as subject to processes of 'blurring', 'net-widening', 'mesh-thinning', and 'penetration'. With the best of intentions, penal reformers have contrived to blur the distinctions between what is, and what is not, regarded/defined as punishment (e.g. creative definitions and extensions of licence, conditions, half-way houses, etc.) The scope of the control nets have consequently been widened (e.g. those previously defined as non-deviant may be recast as 'at risk'; those previously informally warned may now be brought into the control system by a formal caution — see e.g.

Pratt 1986). The mesh becomes finer to control more intensively the greater number who are hauled in, e.g. by more searching inventories of their personalities. Finally, the whole system of formal control thus refined and enlarged penetrates more deeply and extensively into the public and private realms of civil society. The ultimate irony is that, despite the origins of these developments in the attack on the prison as outdated and inhumane, these measures come to supplement and not replace it. We end up with the worst of both worlds: an unreconstructed *ancien régime pénal* and a new-style carceral society.

This undeniably gloomy view of modern developments in social control is not without its critics. Bottoms (1983) has made the fundamental point that the post-war growth in the use of the fine, an essentially non-disciplinary penalty in Foucault's sense, is the reverse of what one would have logically expected from a 'carceral society' standpoint. It is of course the case that, before World War I, the majority of prisoners were in custody for the non-payment of fines, and in the past five years the use of fines has fallen relative to other measures of a non-custodial but penal character (i.e. entailing the supervision of a 'penal agent') such as community service. But the fact remains that it is the fine and not probation or community service which has displaced imprisonment over the past two to three decades most significantly. The same holds to a lesser extent for The Netherlands. Garland (1985) has questioned the whole basis of Foucault's case, and implicitly that of Cohen, by conceptualizing modern developments in the individualized treatment of the offender as no simple outgrowth of the disciplinary framework of the prison in its Victorian form, but as requiring a 'discursive' transformation of penality, a transformation that was wrought in the period 1890 to 1914. Garland takes much the same view as Cohen about the character and implications for control of these changes, but sees them as fundamentally discontinuous with the carceral discipline of Foucault.

The problem in evaluating these visions of social control is that they each have considerable merit, not least that of lifting the debate above sheer administrative reformism of the one hand and blanket condemnation of capitalist society on the other. The difficulty lies in finding indicators of what might constitute 'carcerality' or disciplinary forms of penality that are relatively uncontentious. What interests us here is how far this approach may account for the differences in sentencing trends in The Netherlands and England. If The Netherlands is simply 30 years ahead of England in some key respects connected with the dispersal of social control, or if it always was a more 'carceral' society than England in the above sense, then that could account for the disparities we have documented. Take a notion such as 'regulation of whole groups and classes of persons', on which practically everyone agrees as a regulatory trend of a non-penal sort (Mathiesen 1983, Cohen 1985, Bottoms 1983), such as the use of TV monitors in large stores and supermarkets. Short of an inventory of such devices in both countries, it is impossible to say which bristles with them the more. They are about the same in this respect, but it is difficult to see what would be proved by showing that one or the other had more or less, except perhaps that shoplifting and the like were viewed as more of a problem. Another example might be traffic regulations. The typical Amsterdam street is festooned with signs and symbols concerning traffic (of the wheeled variety), but that is largely due to the cycling phenomenon in The Netherlands. The cyclists, a formidable lobby, have gained certain rights which are upheld by large amounts of street markings and furniture. Clearly, regulation in this sense — the by-products of consumer rights and technological developments — need to be distinguished from regulation in the interests of the extension of state control. Absence of regulation may be more detrimental than its presence, as the power of the road lobby in this country shows.

In the penal sphere proper, it seems unlikely that the Dutch were more advanced for a time on the road to the dispersal of social control. Chronologically, the development of probation in The Netherlands roughly matched that in England, though probation in The Netherlands was never a servant of the court in the sense that came to prevail with its formal establishment in England in 1907 (Garland 1985). Dutch judges had the choice of suspended and partially suspended prison sentences, the former in combination with the fine, which itself could be partially or wholly suspended, from the early 1920s. But the introduction of some of these variations in England in the 1960s and 1970s hardly staunched the use of immediate imprisonment. Indeed, it is a by-word among penal reformers that non-custodial sentences in English courts are used interchangeably rather than as alternatives to custody. In other respects, attendance centres were introduced in some areas in

England following the 1948 Criminal Justice Act; and community service was introduced — indeed originated — in England in 1973, in The Netherlands only in the 1980s. In short, it is difficult to see The Netherlands as a *prima facie* carceral society in contradistinction to England. The waiving of prosecution has been consciously developed by the Dutch in major diversionary ways for filtering out the more routine cases. But, with a few exceptions, that process lacks a continuing penal element, and other countries which share the formal system, such as West Germany, do not use it in a way that helps to shape a reductionist penal policy.

There are some pointers to possible sources of differences in penality between the two societies in the work of Garland. The emphasis in England on the principle of 'less eligibility' (i.e. that institutional life should be less preferable than that of the poorest in the community) is seen by him as crucial for the entire character of the prison, not only in its Victorian form, but also in the transformation which allegedly occured in the 1890–1914 period as a major obstacle to the full implementation of educational and welfare programmes in prisons. 'In the face of recommendations that suggested reformative and educational regimes for offenders, the customary arguments for deterrence and less eligibility presented a strong line of opposition, which was deployed by men such as Anderson, Tallack, and Du Cane, as well as a variety of official reports' (Garland 1985: 164). Writing in 1939, Hermann Mannheim saw the principle of less eligibility as *the* major obstacle to penal reform. It is possible that Garland understates its all-pervasive miasmic grip on the prison system even today. No trace of such a principle survives in the attitudes or policies of contemporary Dutch prisons or welfare institutions in general, and it is difficult to see how its influence would have disappeared so completely if it had been as institutionalized as in England.* Here the periodization of the industrial revolution seems a crucial factor. Nineteenth-century Dutch society lacked so developed an industrial working class. However, the response to beggars and vagrants seems to have been just as, if not more repressive, in The Netherlands than

* For an authoritative account of Dutch penal history, see Herman Franke, *Twee Eeuwen Gevangen* (Two Centuries of Captivity), 1990, Utrecht: Het Spectrum. See also his 'Dutch Tolerance: Facts and Fables', *British Journal of Criminology*, Winter 1990, pp. 81–93, and my Response, pp. 94–6.

in England. Penal labour colonies took the place of the English workhouse, for those not provided for by the denominations or voluntary aid. Whether conditions in these 'colonies' were better or worse than in the prisons is difficult to ascertain. Howard had praised the late eighteenth-century prisons in The Netherlands in quite fulsome terms: 'Prisons in the United Provinces are so quiet and most of them so clean, that a visitor can hardly believe he is in a gaol' (1784: 44). The numbers in the penal colonies, however, exceeded those in the jails, and as late as 1905 held some 75 inmates per 100,000 inhabitants, compared with rates of 35–40 in prisons and 20 in the houses of detention. They were phased out as late as the 1970s; in Belgium they continue to account for about a third of the daily institutional population, though in The Netherlands after 1955 their daily average population barely exceeded 100. The variation in continental practice may have lacked the clear formulation of 'less eligibility' that was institutionalized in the English workhouse, but marginal populations were nevertheless clearly subject to punitive treatment (Spierenburg 1986). Hence, one can hardly alight on 'less eligibility' as the crucial differentiating factor in accounting for the greater humanity of the Dutch in post-war policies of imprisonment and penal administration.

Drawing on the work of Donzelot (1979), Garland has also stressed the power of 'welfare state' agencies to exercise a form of sanction which 'takes as its object not a citizen but a client, activated not by guilt but by abnormality, establishing a relation which is not punitive but normalising' (Garland 1981: 40). In at least two major respects, the Dutch welfare system differs from that in England: first, the levels of income maintenance and social security are set at much more generous levels in relation to average incomes: and secondly, the psychological testing and profiling of children is far more comprehensively developed. There is not, however, any indication that this 'soft machine' has developed, in its regulatory mode, any further or faster in The Netherlands than in other societies with a far greater investment in more traditional carceral establishments. The field of welfare sanctions is little explored in contemporary comparative research, but France and West Germany, both societies with relatively high prison populations, are reported to deploy them relatively punitively, reacting to often minor infractions by, for example, the sequestration of goods and the cutting of benefits at source. Such sanctions offer perhaps the clearest indicators of 'carceral' control techniques.

In sum, there is an all too apparent sense in which the 'punitive city', 'carceral society', or 'dispersal of control' model fits The Netherlands. But as it fits other advanced industrial societies equally well, of both capitalist and state socialist varieties, it does not appear to offer an adequate basis for explaining decarceration in The Netherlands. Indeed, much of the theorizing rests on an assumption that the rhetorics and labels of so many of the agencies concerned are translated into practice. What one wants to know is whether the pedlars of 'social control talk' so tellingly catalogued by Cohen (1985: Ch.5 and App.) make the same sort of impact on people's lives as the 'cruelty man' (officers of the National Society for the Prevention of Cruelty to Children) in late Victorian and Edwardian England. In many respects, however, the growth of the machinery of regulation is real enough: the growth of both public and private security, the proliferation of quasi-judicial state agencies in the sectors of economic and administrative control, and the tendencies to substitute executive for judicial power in a growing number of respects even in the criminal justice system: in these kinds of ways, the 'carceral' society has taken quite substantial hold. There are, however, many respects in which this awesome machinery of control limps behind the growth of phenomena which it can barely chart, let alone constrain: the informal economy, tax evasion, corporate crime and occupational deviance are tolerated more because of the dispersal of their victimization than its magnitude (Ditton 1977, Box 1983). It sometimes seems as if the only people in gaol, apart from the occasional spectacular gangster, are those unemployed or marginal workers who lack routinized access to occupational crime. But it is hardly to The Netherlands' discredit to have acted on that insight more than other comparably developed societies. It is difficult to impute to the Dutch, in other words, a more developed 'carceral' society than that in other countries with far higher prison populations.

The limits of penal capacity

Broadly stated, this theory maintains that it is penal capacity which determines penal population levels in any given society, rather than the reverse. A general statement of this view is contained in Blumstein and Cohen's (1973) theory of the 'stability of punishment'. Drawing on the axioms of the functionalist tradition of Durkheim (1895) and Erikson (1966), they maintain that societies exert formidable constraints against undue variations in the amount and type of resource they are prepared to employ on formal social control. This rather deterministic view of societal self-regulation in the penal sphere is subject to the endemic problems of functional theorizing in general, not least a circularity of argument which accounts for changes in penality with reference to rather poorly specified changes in social structure. It is difficult to see how the approach can adequately account for the doubling of the American prison population in the space of ten years. Nor is it entirely clear what is being explained: the amount of punishment, the rate of punishment, or its forms.

If the amount of punishment is the problem, then The Netherlands certainly provides a startlingly durable example. Van Ruller (1981), has provided a well-documented basis for the examination of this approach: 'The suggestion implicit in the rates is that the existing penitentiary infrastructure strongly determines the degree to which the prison sentence is used in The Netherlands.' Van Ruller shows the astonishing longevity of the trend towards a reduction in the average prison population relative to that of the population as a whole in The Netherlands. The reduction is traceable back virtually to the 1840's and is broken only by short-term increases during the crisis periods of the two world wars and their immediate aftermaths, after which the progressive decrease is resumed. By contrast, the penal capacity (excluding the nineteeth-century beggar colonies and their successors, the state labour colonies, which retained separate but diminishing populations until their abolition in the 1950s) remained relatively stable over the entire period at 4,000–6,000 places. Its decline to below that figure in the early 1970s produced a crisis of sorts over penal capacity which was only temporarily resolved by the mass pardons of 1975. Recent plans to increase the capacity to 7,000 by 1990 have of late been pruned by the government to some 6,000 places. In short, if penal capacity is assumed to be constant, then the reduction of the prison population relative to that of the population as a whole is inevitable, given the steady growth of the latter (the size of the Dutch population has quintupled since 1840), irrespective of the crime rate. So marked a trend does indeed call out for explanation.

The main question which this approach begs is just *why* a certain level of penal capacity should come to be adopted by a society over so extensive a period of time. The solution is almost a restatement of the problem: penal capacity is the way it is because it has always been so. Van Ruller (1981) essays an answer to this problem, but in terms which raise a fresh set of issues of quite different character: 'The opinion that prison does not solve social problems, and that prison is rather such a social problem itself, and that it should be repudiated, is rather widely propagated in The Netherlands.' The assertion that what has occurred is not so much a passive acceptance of the *status quo* but an active repudiation of the penal sanction, implies that policy choices have been made all along the line. Other societies, England and the United States in particular, have found other remedies for limited penal capacity: building more prisons. And where the resources for such building cannot be found or politically justified, though the courts continue to send more people to prison regardless of capacity, the English have evolved another remedy: overcrowding. In short, to view penal capacity as the major determinant of penal policy is to reify that capacity as the major phenomeon *sui generis* that somehow transcends the will to change, expand or transform institutional infrastructures. If, on the other hand, the problem is put in Van Ruller's second form, — 'What is it that leads the Dutch to treat penal capacity as a constant, as a key element in penal policy?' — then we move onto a different terrain.

Even in these terms, however, there are difficulties in placing such an emphasis on penal capacity alone. Not only does it fail to address the issue of why some societies and not others seem to stabilize that capacity: it also leaves unexamined the mediation of cause and effect. It is, in a sense, the criminological equivalent of monetarism: a fixed resource somehow promotes desired ends. But the question of why those ends should be sought in the first place, and how they are in practice accomplished, is left unanalysed. This is also a problem for those who, like Andrew Rutherford (1984) favour reductionist policies in which the limitation or reduction of penal capacity is viewed as a fundamental precursor to reductions in the prison population. As he acknowledges, limiting change to that one variable alone would arguably lead to such unwanted side-effects as even greater overcrowding, unless other related strategies were pursued to divert people from prison or equivalent institutional disposals. For the links between penal capacity and policy are far from clear. For example, one would expect Dutch judges to pay marked attention to penal capacity in their sentencing. However, in interviews, they almost all denied that they often do so on strong grounds of principle.

Nevertheless, it may operate as a background factor to which they pay some regard. If so, there is a far from exact fit between sentences of imprisonment and actual capacity, as the build-up of waiting prisoners in the 1970s testified. Also in the early 1970s, a situation of overcapacity developed, in which penal closures were effected. A strict theory of penal capacity would entail the filling of all available places. Such anomalies point to the inadequacy of this theory as it stands, even for The Netherlands.

If we regard the second of the two approaches as the more fruitful (*i.e.* 'What is it that leads the Dutch to treat penal capacity as a constant?'), the post-1945 period presents a particularly interesting context in which to attempt an answer. First, the progressive fall after 1955 in the penal population was even greater if we include those detained in state labour colonies. Secondly, concern about the crime rate could take numerical form only after 'crimes known to the police' were published after 1950, so that reductionist effects were wrought within the context of a known rising crime rate. Thirdly, the most striking differences between England and The Netherlands only emerged in the period from the mid-1950s onwards. In the inter-war period, the prison population in England was relatively low and stable. In the pre-World War I era, it had fallen, with some fluctuations, from the 1870s , so that in terms of penal trends England in the period from 1870 until the early 1950s was in parallel with rather than divergent from The Netherlands. Yet from the mid-1950s, the rise in the prison population in England was so marked that proportionate increases in the penal budget came to exceed those in the fields of health and education. (King and Morgan 1980)

In both societies, therefore, penal capacity was a constraint, but it was a constraint overcome in England by progressive overcrowding and fresh prison building. The increase in overcrowding was particularly pronounced, but this has been little explored by penal analysts. 'During the first forty years of this century, placing more than one prisoner in a cell designed for one person was virtually unknown. In 1950 some 2,500 prisoners, 12 per cent of the prison population, were sharing cells and by 1980 the number of prisoners sharing cells exceeded 17,000, 40 per cent of the prison population' (Rutherford 1984: 53). Given that prison overcrowding is the major target of penal reform groups in Britain, particularly when combined with over-flowing chamber pots, this development has remained surprisingly absent from theories of penal history. It is rare in comparably developed countries and is only marginally necessary in Britain. 'It is important to note that 12,000 persons were required to share cells in 1973, despite the near-equivalence of total capacity of the prison system and average daily population' (Rutherford, 1984: 100). King and Morgan have repeatedly drawn attention to the policy decison that local prisons should bear the brunt of overcrowding, whilst 'training' prisons should be maintained at or under capacity (King and Morgan 1980). Hence, two of the elements noted by Garland as crucial for an understanding of British penal policy seem to be implicated in the practice: first, the legacy of less eligibility preserves intact the legitimacy of treating prisoners as undeserving of standards that obtain in the rest of society. And secondly, the rhetoric of 'treatment and training' borne of the post-Gladstone Report era is institutionalized in the double standards which operate in local and training prisons. The result is that, lacking any stringent guidelines to govern minimum standards or prisoners' rights, there is in England no impediment whatsoever, other than the pragmatic, to limit overcrowding to its present levels. If three to a cell is possible, why not four? Or five?

By contrast, in The Netherlands, from the Fick Commission of 1947 onwards, far more attention to conditions and amenities has been based on the stringent proscription against exceeding the limits of one prisoner to a cell. This is not to say that the physical environment is basically superior to any marked degree: 'almost three-quarters of the cells in closed prisons in Holland remain unsewered and without running water' (Vinson 1985: 6). It is the social and not the bare physical aspects which distinguish Dutch prisons so sharply from those in England and many other countries (see Ch. 6 below). But the strict mandate to accept into prison only as many as can be accommodated on a one-to-a-cell basis makes the 'limits of penal capacity' a more compelling theory for The Netherlands. The sources of that self-imposed constraint are not, however, at all apparent.

The question of sources becomes even more compelling when the notion of the 'limits of capacity' is applied to the criminal justice system as a whole. For the limits of capacity apply not only to the penal sphere, but also to the judiciary and the police. The numbers of public prosecutors and judges in the penal chamber in The Netherlands are relatively small. Although they have doubled in the past 25 years, most of that increase was in the past five years, and the number of cases processed by the public prosecutors rose at least fourfold over the period from 1960 (Netherlands Ministry of Justice 1985c: 130, Table 6). The workload of judges rose far less markedly, largely due to the sharp increase over that period in waiving prosecutions. The point of maximum pressure, therefore, was at the public prosecution stage, and increased waiving was in part at least explicable in terms of overload. The objective of waiving is to filter out the routine and less serious cases: but in the process much time is saved, by the avoidance of dossier production and court appearance by the prosecutor. Policing also doubled in strength over the past 25 years, but again this increase in manpower fell far short of the eightfold increase in recorded crime, the result being a much reduced clear-up rate. (see Ch. 2) The cumulative effect of growing constraints and overload throughout the entire criminal justice system logically operated to facilitate a stabilized prison population. Yet the question remains as to why so high a premium was and is placed on minimizing the resort to prison, not only among the judiciary, but also at governmental and ministry levels, as well as among opinion-makers in the media.

The culture of 'tolerance'

A more straightforward theory is that penal sentencing policy and practice in The Netherlands is a manifestation of Dutch 'tolerance', a term which connotes a long tradition of relative leniency towards, and acceptance of, deviants, minority groups, and religious dissent, and which grants a respectable hearing to views which elsewhere would be dismissed as extreme or eccentric. Evidence of the reality of what amounts, in this view, to a culture of tolerance is a matter of impressive historical record. Indicators are, for example, the low rates of execution in The Netherlands in the eighteenth and nineteenth centuries by comparison with other European societies and in the early abolition of both capital and corporal punishment (1870 and 1854 in The Netherlands, though the abolition did not extend to Dutch colonies, and was superseded in wartime and for collaborators tried in the immediate post-war period). This is not to say that periodic measures of great harshness were absent: 531 members of the robber bands called 'Bokkenrijders' were tried during the period 1741–78. After the mass trials of the 1770s no less than 243 of them were hanged or broken on the wheel'. (Diederiks 1980: 157). In the early 1730s, at least 75 persons were executed by strangulation for the crime of sodomy, an episode which led the editor of the *Free Briton* to compare the Court of Holland with the Catholic Inquisition. By contrast, however, executions in Amsterdam were far fewer than in London: four a year on average, whereas in London, in an admittedly unusually savage phase, some '348 personss died on the gallows in the five years after 1783' (Ignatieff 1978:87). Diederiks argues (1981), *contra* Ignatieff, Rothman, (1971), and Foucault (1977), that the use of custody in The Netherlands as a penalty, rather as a transit camp for those awaiting execution, transportation or for debt, predated the end of the eighteenth century and contributed to a humanization of punishments somewhat earlier. Most notable as an acid test of tolerance was the very low number of wartime collaborators who were lynched in The Netherlands after the war: a total of six by comparison with other occupied countries such as Belgium (400-500) and France (3,000–4,000) (Mason 1952). This culture of tolerance can be said to operate on two mutually reinforcing levels to produce a relatively low prison population: first, directly through the judiciary, who make the actual sentencing decisions; secondly, through the relative absence in The Netherlands of authoritarian 'public opinion' which in other countries, both as articulated through the media and as directly expressed in everyday life, plays upon the judiciary to enforce harsh penal sanctions. The interplay between sentencing and public opinion was seen as one of mutual influence by Barbara Wootton:

> What ranks as a long sentence . . . is largely a matter of convention. In Holland, for example, sentences have been steadily reduced over a considerable period until 2 years' imprisonment has come to be regarded as a relatively severe sentence. Moreover, these conventions are seen to be based ultimately on public opinion, and that opinion may itself be, and indeed has been, in its turn modified by changes in sentencing practice. (Wootton 1978: 65)

A comparison of attitudes towards the death penalty nevertheless shows striking differences between the two countries. In The Netherlands, 37 per cent in 1970 and 39 per cent in 1983 favoured its reintroduction (it was abolished, as we have seen, as long ago as 1870). In England, over two-thirds of the population continue to favour its reintroduction, a figure virtually unchanged since its abolition 20 years ago (SCPB 1984: 296; and Jowell, *et al.*

1986: 160–1). Clearly, the influence of legislation and sentencing upon public attitudes is highly variable. Abortion, for example, has become less subject to moral disapproval than was the case two decades ago. However, if attitudes towards the death penalty are any guide, the Dutch remain markedly more tolerant in relation to the most heinous crimes than the British, though there has been a marked loss of support for the view that 'criminals should be changed not punished' (down from 73 to 49 per cent between 1970 and 1983) and that 'sexual offenders should be cured not punished' (70 to 40 per cent) over the same period. The grounds of Dutch 'tolerance' in this sphere may therefore by shifting, if not diminishing.

Similarly, maximum sentences for the offences of varying seriousness are sigificantly lower in The Netherlands than in England (Appendix 4.1). Though maxima are usually greatly in excess of normal sentences (see ACPS 1978), the disparities between the two sets of maxima reflect corresponding differences in actual sentencing to some extent. For example, simple theft in The Netherlands carries a maximum sentence of four years' imprisonment, in England ten years. Robbery in England carries the liability of life imprisonment, as does rape: in The Netherlands, the maxima are 9 and 12 years respectively. Although largely symbolic, these marked differences may indicate levels of tolerance which are possibly translated by the judiciary into normal sentencing practices. However, since in The Netherlands they have been in force since the Penal Code of 1886, they are unlikely to explain trends which have occurred in the past 30 to 40 years.

Dutch tolerance is particularly well documented in the sphere of religious and racial 'pluralism'. Bagley's (1973) study of race relations in The Netherlands also provides useful comparative material with British attitudes and practices towards immigrants. The greater tolerance of the Dutch enables them to turn what was in all respects a more difficult situation to better advantage than has been the case in Britain.

The proportion of coloured immigrants in The Netherlands is similar to the proportion in Britain. The Netherlands is a much more crowded country than Britain, and in comparison with this country has an acute housing shortage. Immigrants to The Netherlands arrived, moreover, in much heavier concentrations than immigrants to the United Kingdom. Despite these facts it appears that the Dutch express markedly less prejudice than their English counterparts, and practise markedly less racial discrimination. Social policy on behalf of immigrants has been, moreover, markedly more generous and systematic than social policy in Britain. Such policy was carried through in a country with (then) somewhat less national wealth per head than Britain. (Bagley 1973: 246)

Events since 1973 serve to reinforce Bagley's thesis, in particular his prescience on the likelihood of violent responses to indigenous racism in Britain, and continuing good race relations in The Netherlands, with the stated exception of the Moluccans. Though the Surinamese arrivals of the mid-1970s generated more tensions than earlier migrants and the Indonesians (see Ch. 5), they have not been goaded into such riots as in inner-city Britain since 1979.

Dutch tolerance in not a simple blanket acceptance of all manner of behaviour and opinion. It is rooted in a society 'marked by kindly authoritarianism, deference to one's elders and those in positions of authority, with particular respect for the moral dogmas of Christianity' (Bagley 1973: 171). In this sense, 'Dutch emigrants to South Africa have been deviants from Dutch life, the extreme Protestants for whom any kind of compromise with other religious groups, including reformed Calvinists and Roman Catholics, was unacceptable. It is possible that this emigration of extremists from The Netherlands has indirectly contributed to the stability of Dutch society' (ibid. 173). Moreover, 'tolerance is extended only to the extent that the minorities conform to the Dutch *verzuiling* rules of restrained and deferential inter-personal behaviour' (ibid. 171). Over the past 15 years perhaps the most formidable and sustained challenge to the tolerant cast of Dutch government and administration has come from the squatters in particular, and youthful radicals in general, groups who explicitly repudiate these rules.

In Bagley's view, the sources of this form of tolerance reside in two major characteristics of Dutch social structure and colonial history. First, drawing on Lijphart's analysis (2nd edn. 1975), the rules for overcoming *verzuiling* (the 'pillarization' of Dutch society) stress decorum, negotiation, accommodation and pragmatic tolerance (by no means the same as sympathy) for the interests and values of other groups. Equality of consideration and the proportional distribution of power mean that minority groups avoid the fate of endless subordination that has so disastrously characterized Northern Ireland's Catholic population, the working class in Britain, or minority groups in Britain more generally. (Bagley perhaps overdoes his thesis here, for autonomous institutions of socialization and communication do exist among Catholics in Northern Ireland, though these have not, of course, brought them any share in effective power. Also, as he acknowledges, some minority groups in Britain, the Jews outstandingly so, have been integrated without any particularly pronounced loss of their identity.) Secondly, colonialism in the Dutch case did not rest so heavily, for largely religious reasons as well as by the export of *verzuiling*, on the assumption of racial superiority which has so poisoned the post-war experience of coloured immigrants to Britain, an absence also accounted for by the fact that miscegenation was far more characteristic of Dutch than British colonialism. In Bagley's view, this absence of prejudice, relatively speaking, can be explained in functional terms. Dutch society does not need to cohere around the scapegoating of coloured or any other minority groups, since it has evolved its own institutional devices to promote social integration out of diverse social groupings: the inter-élite 'politics of accommodation' of the different religious and secular blocs. By these means, class conflict (horizontal stratification) is diffused by cross-cutting bloc allegiances (vertical stratification). In other societies, e.g. the United States, this pattern of fragmentation has not minimized conflict, since the blocs have not materialized or become articulated politically.

To the extent that Bagley's theories have substance, much the same analysis could be made in relation to crime. Marxist criminology in Britain has recently focused on the integrative role played by crime and its 'control' in the context of an otherwise class-ridden and structurally divided society (e.g. Hall *et al.* 1978). Lacking the basis for integrative institutions to form on lines of religious allegiance (to Bagley, Britain is a 'non-Christian' society by comparison with The Netherlands), crime has operated as a basis on which the ruling class can impose the legitimacy of its claims to hegemony. The rhetoric of 'law and order' is the justification for punitive sentencing. By contrast, The Netherlands has never engaged at this level in the 'war on crime' around which all can unite; it has not needed to invoke such grounds for a solidarity which it already possesses by other means.

This approach has considerable plausibility. It seems to account for the relative mildness of Dutch reactions to crime, though it allows for occasional outbursts of hostility to groups which either reject or have yet to accept the 'rules of the game'. It is chiefly lacking in a detailed application to the sphere of crime and its control, that is, in the specification of the mediating processes at work whereby 'tolerant' outcomes are accomplished and, in particular, why tolerance as expressed in sentencing has apparently actually increased at a time of rising crime in the post-war period. It also leaves unclear the reasons why 'religion has been so important to the Dutch nation in the first place' (Bagley 1973: 248), though the most obvious explanation seems to lie in the crucial symbolic role played by religion in the very formation of Dutch nationalism in the sixteenth and seventeenth centuries.

The politics of accommodation

Lijphart's ([1967], 1975) concept of the 'politics of accommodation' has been explicity linked with the reduction of the lengths of prison sentences in The Netherlands by Johnson and Heijder (1983). The distinctive quality of the politics of accommodation is that of bargaining and pragmatic compromise between the élites which stand at the apex of the four 'pillars' of Dutch society. The process of inter-élite negotiation turn to advantage a denominational structure which elsewhere, notoriously in Northern Ireland, would be the basis for endless and unproductive conflict. Catholics, Calvinists, secular liberals and secular radicals each form their own constituency, to which their élites are responsive, and which therefore possess by proxy a stake in the system. The major price, so to speak, for such an arrangement is that the élites, both in and outside government and Parliament, are relatively insulated from criticism, unless in exceptional circumstances. As long as they produce results, the negotiations whereby those results are reached are not of immediate public interest. Delays in the post-electoral formation of governments which in Britain would herald a major constitutional crisis are a normal feature of political process in The Netherlands.

Johnson and Heijder's argument is that, in the crucial post-war period, the law and order issue was effectively neutralized politically by the interlocking character of party coalitions. Quoting van Weringh, they assert that:

> issue-oriented bargaining among political parties, none of which hold absolute power . . . have been crucial to criminal justice policy . . . because the long-term rejection of prison by the Social Democrats

became politically significant in this bargaining among political parties . . . The Christian Democrats are inclined towards a 'law and order' policy in dealing with abortion, homosexuality, pornography, drug abuse, and similar issues because of religious conviction. The Liberals share economic conservatism but do not agree with the Christian Democrats on moral issues. So the Liberals make accommodations with the Social Democrats in support of tolerant policies. (Johnson and Heijder 1983; 7–8)

Socialists presided over the major changes in penal policy for 12 years after the war, which ushered in such major reforms as the 1951 Act which contained the principle of rehabilitation.

Within this setting, the criminal justice system operates, as it were, its own politics of accommodation. 'The setting of criminal justice policy operates largely detached from public monitoring . . . A small professional élite, with a fringe of complementary groups, dominates practice in the field of criminal justice. Shared training, position, norms, and values provide an effective boundary-maintaining system shielding the operations of criminal justice from public opinion.' (Johnson and Heijder 1983: 10). No neat consensus prevails, but the system affords a diverse array of flexible devices for achieving solutions to problems as they arise. The various pressure groups lock into the politics of penal reform, and even advocates of extreme positions, such as abolitionism, take the business of participation seriously, avoiding the polarization so evident in Britain. Criminologists like Bianchi and Hulsman, whose views on criminal justice would tend to exclude them from advisory roles in Britain or the United States, have served on commissions of enquiry, are quoted by quite orthodox members of the judiciary as holding views that deserve to be taken seriously, produce 'green' papers as alternative policy proposals that are published along with official policy statements by the government, in short, operate perhaps to shift the axis of debate to more radical positions of compromise than would otherwise occur. Informed criticism by the Coornhert-Liga (the radical Dutch penal reform group) since the early 1970s almost certainly stiffened resistance to the swing away from reductionist policies. The flexibility of the system is such that precedents can be invoked for extensions of such devices as 'waiting' for places in prison; for the large number of pardons granted (to judicial objections) in 1975; or the increase in the proportions of cases waived by public prosecutors in the 1960s and 1970s. Freedom of the professional judges and prosecutors from the need to work with lay colleagues or juries was quoted to me many times in explanation of the direction sentencing policy had taken since the war. It tends to be assumed as a matter of course that any involvement of the public is bound to introduce a degree of unwarranted emotionalism into the process of sentencing and prosecution. The Dutch criminal justice system approximates to the Fabian ideal of small, highly trained élites getting on with their jobs without undue public interference (though with a due regard to public opinion and the public interest).

There is considerable evidence for the view that the media have generally exerted a far more restrained stance towards penal policy in The Netherlands than in Britain or the United States. The sensationalism of crime reporting so endemic in the latter societies is, with the generally cited exception of *De Telegraaf*, notably absent in The Netherlands. Comment tends to be more informed and more inclined to present liberal policy sympathetically, though a concern about rising crime is now becoming commonplace. The police do not act as a pressure group lobbying for tougher measures along the lines of the Police Federation in Britain (which indeed is showing every sign of taking the Dutch example as a threat to English sentencing policy: see, for example, the strongly critical editorial and article on Trends in Dutch penal policy in *Police*, March 1981). Police evaluations emerged as quite close to those of prosecutors concerning the seriousness of offences in a study by Buikhuisen and van Dijk (1975), with the public ranking offences generally, through not too markedly, as more serious than either group. With the media, the police, the politicians, and the administrators taking much the same line as the judiciary, a well-entrenched defence of the policy seems guaranteed. Even so, the last decade has seen an upturn in the proportion and numbers of sentences of over a year in length, and there are indications that the period of sentence shortening is finally over. It still seems unlikely, however, that any wholesale abandonment of the generally lenient tariff is imminent. The recommendation of Van Hijlkema Commission that the penal capacity be increased by 1,300 additional places over the 1981–85 period stimulated prompt and informed criticism (see, e.g. Soetenhorst 1981). Since that point, a further 2,000 places have been planned. Pardoxically, reductionist policies can be pursued yet 'recarceration' eventuates if the crime rate rises sufficiently steeply.

Whether or not the two trends are at all connected, the last two decades have also seen the undermining, if not collapse, of the 'pillarized' structure, and the accompanying 'politics of accommodation' that Heijder and Johnson regard as the essential context for Dutch leniency in sentencing. Lijphart, in the 1975 edition of his book, views the period of 1965–75 as that of its disintegration. Bryant (1981) asserts the emergence of social class as a more potent source of allegiance in this period than denominational loyalties. Undoubtedly some realignments of a politically crucial nature have been going on: it seems premature, however, to infer the demise of the 'politics of accommodation' from this realignment. What remains lacking in the approach outlined above is as yet any clear analysis of precisely what connections in the political sphere led to the changes in sentencing policy with which we are concerned. After all, sporadic attempts in England on the part of the Home Office to persuade judges and magistrates to reduce the length of sentences to prison have in general met with signal lack of success. Given the independence of the judiciary in both societies, why should judges and prosecutors in The Netherlands either accede to or even initiate more lenient policies in line with ministry thinking, when in England no such alignment occurred?

Confluence

The view that Dutch sentencing trends are the outcome not of any systematic policy but of a confluence of largely unanticipated prior social developments is put most vigorously by Hulsman:

> The considerable measure of de-escalation in penal matters during the past decade in The Netherlands and the general situation of the criminal justice system are less the results of deliberate policy (demands for which have only become clear or clamorous in recent years) than of a development evolving more or less fortuitously from the interplay of the factors outlined above. (Below, in this case: Hulsman *et al.* 1978: 377)

After disposing of two previous myths often invoked to explain the relative mildness of Dutch sentencing, i.e. the 'masking' of institutionalization (see above) and the alleged homogeneity of Dutch society (which is not necessarily a synonym for its degree of integration), Hulsman singles out five 'environmental' factors that have combined to produce the situation: (a) the comprehensive range of social services; (b) the extensive network and character of youth centres; (c) the multiplicity and client-orientation of welfare and social service agencies; (d) the mass media as integrative and destigmatizing agencies (could this statement be made of the mass media in any other country?); and (e) the pressure group activities on behalf of penal reform by the social service agencies (including the probation service). Some of these factors extrinsic to the criminal justice system also operate within it (e.g. the probation service) in a 'de-escalating ' manner; and some factors alluded to above, e.g. the limited manpower of the judiciary, also serve to promote an economical use of prison. Other factors not mentioned in this context by Hulsman also seem to be most compatible with this approach, e.g. the often-quoted argument that the experience of internment by hundreds of thousands of Dutch people, including members of the élites, during the Second World War, led to a widespread association of prison with oppression and an intense awareness of the costs of the deprivation of liberty.

There is much to be said for this approach, not least because it takes account of the oldest sociological truism that 'social facts are the product of human actions, not human designs'. But it is exceptionally difficult to gauge the extent to which any or all of the above developments are in some way responsible for the mildness of Dutch sentencing, or are themselves products of the same causal matrix. War-time internment, for example, was also the experience of hundreds of thousands of Belgians and French: but their penal policies are relatively harsh. A comprehensive range of social services and youth clubs is available in Britain, albeit perhaps to a less adequate level (or at least was, until the past decade's mounting toll of cut-backs in social service expenditure): again, without a similar pay-off. Nor does there seem to be any marked correlation between the proportion of GDP spent on welfare and the prison population. As Table 3.1 shows, the relatively high spenders on welfare — The Netherlands, Belgium, and West Germany — include both the lowest and highest prison populations. Conversely, the lowest spenders — Ireland, the United Kingdom, and Italy — include one of the lowest, the second highest, and a country intermediate in terms of prison population. The correlation is no stronger when health care or psychiatric personnel as a ratio of the population as a whole are considered (Table 3.2).

It should be stressed that the amount spent on services is not to be equated with their quality, and is but a poor guide to the quality of

TABLE 3.1 *Social expenditures as a percentage of GDP and prison populations per 100,000 inhabitants*

	Health care		Social budget [a]		Prison population	
	%	Rank	%	Rank	Rate	Rank
Belgium	6.4	8	30.2	2	79	3
Denmark	6.9	7	29.3	4	58	7
France	9.3	2	27.2	5	67[a]	5
West Germany	8.2	4	29.5	3	92	1
Ireland	8.2	4	22.0[b]	9	38	8
Italy	7.0	6	24.7	7	60	6
Luxemburg	9.5[b]	1	27.1	6	74	4
Netherlands	9.1	3	31.7	1	25	9
United Kingdom	5.9	7	23.5	8	85[c]	2

Source: Adapted from Mangen (1985: 10, Table 1.1) and Pease (1980: 10, Table 1).

Note: Prison population data are for 1978, health care for 1981, social budget for 1982, expect where indicated. The fact that the social expenditure data do not pre-date the prison population data is of negligible significance given the stability of the rank order of prison populations over the past decade.

[a] The 'social budget' comprises all forms of public services in the fields of health, welfare, housing, education, etc., as well as social insurance and social assistance expenditure and tax concessions.

[b] Data for 1980

[c] England and Wales only.

TABLE 3.2 *Mental health care per 1,000 and prison populations per 100,000 inhabitants*

	Beds in psychiatric hospitals		Psychiatrists[a] per 100,000		Prison population in (1978)	
	Rate	Rank	Rate	Rank	Rate	Rank
Belgium	2.6	3	12.7	1	79	3
Denmark	2.1	5	8.3	2	58	7
England and Wales[b]	1.9	6	7.6[c]	4	85[d]	2
France	2.6[e]	3	5.1	8	67[e]	5
West Germany	1.9	6	8.3	2	92	1
Ireland	4.1	1	5.3	7	38	8
Italy	1.5	9	2.1	9	60	6
Luxemburg[b]	3.6	2	6.6	5	74	4
Netherlands[b]	1.9	6	6.1	6	25	9

Source: Mangen (1985: 21–4. Table 1.2, 1.3); *q.v.* for full details of problems of enumeration and interpretation.

[a] Various dates 1977–84

[b] Including beds in psychiatric units in general hospitals.

[c] England only.

[d] 1980.

[e] 1977.

social relations that pervades them. (The supreme exemplification of this elementary truth remains, and is likely to remain, Richard Titmuss's *The Gift Relationship: From Human Blood to Social Policy,* 1970.) All that can be noted here is the absence of any obvious relationship between the average prison population rate and the level of welfare provision by certain gross indicators. It may be emhasized in passing that, whatever may be held to have caused Britain's economic decline relative to European competitors, the level of expenditure on the social budget can hardly be among them.

Perhaps the most interesting of the above developments is the character of *reclassering* agencies in The Netherlands. Founded in the early nineteenth century, closely allied from the mid-nineteenth century with the judiciary, and fiercely independent of state or court control (despite the total financial dependence on the state), the *reclassering* agencies in The Netherlands do seem to have played a more influential role in penal policymaking and its implementation than the probation service has in England. The most obvious means whereby their agents influence actual sentencing is their recommendation to the court on the social background and situation of the defendant. The balance of opinion among members of the judiciary was that it was a factor, no more, in the trend towards greater mildness. Until the links can be established with greater precision, it seems impossible to say that the developments listed by Hulsman were any more than an accompaniment to sentencing trends rather than in any way causative.

The culture of the judiciary

A pervasive theme in many interviews was that judges and prosecutors in The Netherlands have evolved a distinctive occupational culture, central to which is the strongly negative value placed upon imprisonment, which is viewed as at best a necessary evil, and at least as a process likely to inflict progressive damage on a person's capacity to re-enter the community. It should therefore be minimized as far as possible. The strength of this negative evaluation is a central feature of legal training, in which lawyers are introduced to criminological teaching and research, including that of abolitionists, which expose them to the weight of evidence against prison as a penalty. For example, several members of the judiciary mentioned in interview Rijksen's book (1958) on the psychological damage wrought by prison, a book based on prisoners' accounts, which the Ministry of Justice originally sought to suppress. By contrast, a few also mentioned a more statistical study by Steenhuis (1977), in which a controlled comparison was made of the blood alcohol levels of drivers from areas in west and east Netherlands. In the former custodial, in the latter non-custodial sentencing tended to be the norm for offenders of drunken driving. No significant differences emerged from these spot-checks of blood alcohol concentrations in the two samples, from which it was inferred that fines should replace imprisonment as the standard sentence. It is difficult to imagine a similar degree of awareness of criminological literature among English judges and magistrates. On the other hand, it does not seem to have deflected the extensive use of custody in such cases (Steenhuis, 1986). This core concern is reinforced when judges enter the penal chamber (i.e. when judges assume responsibility for criminal as distinct from civil cases, by a system of rotation), and especially when they act in more serious cases with two other judges. Their professional activities can also involve them in greater and more complex contacts with non-jurists who share an anti-penal view, and their likelihood of actually visiting prisons is far higher than is the case with their counterparts in England. (Almost every prosecutor and judge whom I interviewed had visited prison at least once, and several had made numerous visits in different capacities, to different types of prison and to TBR clinics). The strong commitment of the judiciary to this aspect of their role was exemplified by one instance in Amsterdam. Some 20 judges and prosecutors spent a Saturday morning along with psychiatrists, viewing a film on TBR. A minor event, perhaps, but on top of the heavy judicial workload and outside the run of formal conferences, it testified to the seriousness with which judges in The Netherlands approach their job. It is difficult to conceive of the same event occurring in London.

Another much-quoted element is the reduced social distance between judges and defendants in The Netherlands compared with the situation in England. In The Netherlands some judges questioned whether they were members of the 'upper ten'. Though it seems to me they were too modest on this score, there is no doubt but that in England judges belong to the 'upper one'. (Even England's magistrates, for whom there is no Dutch counterpart, are drawn predominantly from the upper-middle class. This reduced social distance enables judges, so it is said, to establish more rapport with defendants under the relatively straightforward rules of Dutch court procedure. By contrast, the ritual and ceremonial aspects of the trial are far more pronounced in England. As we have already seen, 'We are judging the person rather than the facts' was a statement made on quite a few occasions in interview. The Dutch trial process is not conducted on the full-blown adversary model of the Anglo-Saxon tradition. It is more a review of evidence gathered before the trial takes place, evidence assembled in dossiers which judges already know. Victims are rarely present, witnesses have already made their depositions. In the report of the *reclassering* officer, the defendant's needs are given full attention. The prosecutor has to recommend a specific sentence, and as it is his function to represent the 'public interest' while nevertheless, taking other parties (victim, defendant, their families, etc.) into account, judges tend to treat his recommendation as an upper limit within which to exercise their own discretion. Consensus is by no means automatic, but the role attributes are firmly drawn, as the following example suggests. One judge recalled the case of a young man who tried to rob a shop by holding a knife at a woman's throat. The judge, who had not tried the case, was actually 'shocked' by the leniency of the sentence, which had been one month's imprisonment and four month's probation. Because the offender had been the son of a professional, she suspected an element of 'class justice'. She felt strongly enough about it to ask the judge why he had given so lenient a sentence. 'Well', he replied, 'the public prosecutor did not ask for more'. She then asked the prosecutor the same question. 'He was very angry that I asked at all, but replied, 'Well, it *was* a five-month sentence and a first offence'.

Data for 1973–76 indicate that the sentence was the same as the requirement in fully one-third of all cases at the district courts, and that the average difference in the remainder amounted to actual sentences of 12–20 per cent less in length than the prosecutors' recommendations in cases of rape, robbery, burglary, manslaughter, and extortion (Zoomer 1979: 45, 51–4). (Actual sentences were higher in cases of murder and attempted extortion.) But the overall concordance is remarkable. In short, a shared community of values does seem to underpin the scheme of sentencing and the adoption of a certain tariff. The directives and guidelines issued by senior prosecutors are by no means capable of yielding a precise set of sentences and though they are adhered to in general, variations obviously exist. Current attempts at a greater degree of co-ordination of sentencing would doubtless iron out some of the extremes, but in the case of some offences these (to an outsider) do not seem to be at all remarkable, being in general a matter of months rather than years. For burglary, for example, the range by district is from 5.3 to 8.1 months imprisonment, though the dispersion is larger for other offences (Zoomer 1979: 41).

The character of the 'culture of the judiciary' in The Netherlands, as elicited by questions about the attitude to imprisonment, is conveyed by such replies as:

I have to tell you that a sentence of a year or more is, in our opinion, in our custom, already a long sentence. (prosecutor)

The police may feel frustrated as they notice a case takes them more time than the offender has to spend in prison, and that is what you are often hearing. I think, however, it is a matter of habituation, for after a while you would hear the complaints, even if we start to punish four times higher than now. The experience of what is long, what short, is very subjective. Those kinds of remarks are not very rational. I do not think that there will change a lot if we would start to follow a completely different policy. For also in much harsher regimes than Holland people are saying: the judges are too mild . . . Nevertheless, we have to take care for extremities . . . the hard core . . . to keep that group as small as possible. (judge)

In a certain way, we think that giving one a prison sentence of several years will not solve the problem of handling the criminality. The only thing you can say if you put someone in prison five years is that in these five years he cannot do anything wrong. But unless you have the death penalty or the life imprisonment, every prisoner will at a certain time return in our society. And I think that is a remark that everyone here in this country has in his head. (senior prosecutor)

If really necessary, I would be able to deviate from the prosecutor's recommendation. On the other hand, I keep in mind that, especially in juvenile cases, the difference between one month and two months is enormous. So, in general, I do not go over the requirement. (Juvenile Court judge)

One of the books that made a great impression on me was the 'green' book of Professor Rijksen . . . For most people, the only time that really counts are the first weeks, the first months in prison, and the first *time* they are in prison, and every other time doesn't make any difference. So why should we do it when it costs so much to put them in prison? (judge)

The problem in making such excerpts from often long and complex interviews, conducted in what for the interviewees, whatever their facility, was a second language, is the danger of ironing out the nuances, qualifications, and genuine ambiguities which inhere in attempts to answer such conundrums as why and how sentencing trends have taken a certain path. For example, in one interview, a judge stated that the changes 'start at the universities where they all come from. I do not think there is one special side of it. It is not only the prosecutor, not only the judge, but also the *reclassering* and people writing about it.' Asked if that amounted to a 'general consensus', the reply was affirmative. Later in the interview, it became evident that any such consensus could not be neatly assigned to criminological training, 'because the training was not really a criminal training. You had a general training and then criminal law was not my main subject. It was more like a subject you were doing and you needed it because of exams. We had a very fine professor, but not really ideological, more the rules. She went to court with us once, but there was not so much attention paid to what prison means, and so on. It was not very much criminological. No, I think more of it came when I was a lawyer. Well, I think then you lived with the people. And you saw what happened to them [defendants]. And you felt with them what it [prison] meant.

A few members of the judiciary spoke in quite analytical terms about the various influences that had helped to shape the trends in criminal justice over the past thirty years or so. One prosecutor, for example, saw a two- or even threefold set of overlapping influences: the concern about the 'human impact of imprisonment' of the Utrecht school; the 'functional' approach of such figures as Enschedé, who stressed the need to formulate a clearer relationship between the goals and means of sentencing policy; and the indirect influence of Hulsman, not so much for the 'abolitionist' view, but in his emphasis on the scope for referring the offender back to the community and the victim in a restitutive sense.

It was more common, however, for responses to stress the importance of 'on the job' factors, the constraints of time, resources and the judicial division of labour. The only real common denominators were a marked antipathy to long-term imprisonment; acceptance of shorter terms as a minimum requirement lest people 'take the law into their own hands'; and a preparedness to accommodate changes that could be justified in justicial as well as system terms.

Whether or not this pragmatic liberalism is sufficiently rooted to withstand the strong pressures for yet tougher measures remains to be seen. The first five years of the 1980s not only produced a sharp rise in crime of over 50 per cent (though it should be stressed that the rise in England was almost as steep), but a rise also in the welter of demands made of the criminal justice system. A senior prosecutor emphasized the rapidity with which the insulation of the judiciary had broken down in the face of such changes as a more vocal and critical media; demands for stiffer sentencing from, *inter alia*, feminist and minority groups in relation to offences involving sexual aggression and racial discrimination; organizations such as the National Association of Shopkeepers publically calling for tougher measures against shoplifters; uprecedented questions in Parliament about judicial recommendations for sentence; newspapers which ten years ago hardly ever named judges or prosecutors now quite commonly doing so. 'The signals from society are cumulatively very strong and impossible to ignore.' English judges, long accustomed if not inured to the buffetings of the media whenever a sentence approaches the lenient end of the spectrum, might be forgiven a wry smile. Stolwijk cites a number of additional developments as undermining the status quo: the rising salience of a politics of law and order; the pruning of the social services; and the loss of faith in rehabilitation. 'The hostility to custodial sentencing is vanishing. The emphasis on alternatives to reduce imprisonment is disappearing . . . It seems that the ideological base of the alternative movement has gone . . . If there is one lesson to be learned from the period of alternative sanctions, it is the lesson that without a convincing ideology, it is impossible to reduce the use of custody' (Stolwijk 1986: 290–1).

Real as many of these tendencies may be, this tone seems too apocalyptic. The same prosecutor who cited the pressures above also said that nevertheless 'what remains is still a feeling of some community within the judiciary, some common background'. It is not so much an ideology, a neat consensus, and it is doubtful if it ever was: it is more a shared outlook, with some considerable resilience, on the futility of inflated penal expectations. As Stolwijk himself admits, 'it should be noted that the insistent calls for heavier sentences as a means of combating crime have failed to produce a response' (Stolwijk 1986: 289). Yet if the Dutch judiciary were no more than pragmatists, they would long before now have revised their penalties upwards for the sake of a quiet life. That they have resisted this course so far suggests both a principled stand against expansionism, and a marked scepticism about where it would lead. On this interpretation, the expansion of penal capacity is neither simply an 'end to decarceration' (in van Ruller's phrase, 1985) nor a capitulation to 'neo-conservative' penal philosophy (de Haan 1986), but a means of pursuing reductionist aims in what, for The Netherlands, is an unprecedentedly expansionist climate.

Hence, this shared outlook does not preclude change, and in recent years sentences to prison have been stiffer, though they remain mild by English standards. There does not seem to be any marked generational effect involved in this development. A reformed system of judicial recruitment and training, introduced in 1971–72 to broaden and systematize these processes, has if anything strengthened the exposure of younger recruits to the anti-penal influences mentioned above. The problem of accounting for the anti-penal character of the culture of the judiciary in terms of these features, however, is that in different circumstances they would equally well support a pro-penal ideology. For example, English magistrates are not necessarily less penally minded than English judges, despite being closer socially to their defendants. In a salutary demonstration that greater professionalism and criminological training do not necessitate milder sentencing, Stanton Wheeler revealed in one American study that the better-trained judges doled out longer sentences, since their acceptance of a rehabilitative ideology led them to accept the need for more exposure to such influences in reformatories (Wheeler *et al* 1968). In that case, the nature of the criminological training was heavily influenced by psychiatric thinking. How has this linkage been avoided in The Netherlands, where perhaps the most influential post-war school of thought was the 'Utrecht School'? The interplay between the theories and institutional outcomes of some of that School's thinkers perhaps supplies a missing element in the explanation of the trends under scrutiny (Bianchi 1975, Moedikdo 1976).

The rise and fall of rehabilitation

For a relatively brief period, from the late 1940s until the mid-1960s, the rehabilitative ideal was accepted in The Netherlands by the judiciary to an extent unknown in England, where its sway (despite the strong rehabilitative emphasis of the 1895 Gladstone Committee) was always more muted among judges and magistrates. The inter-war period in The Netherlands had seen a pronounced move towards the acceptance of psychoanalytical models for the treatment of a small minority of offenders, and the introduction of TBR in 1928 went beyond any equivalent tendency in England. However, in both countries, treatment of the individual offender by casework methods was regarded as progressive in social work and probation circles. After the Second World War, however, there emerged in the work of the so-called 'Utrecht school' a small group of distinguished professors — Baan, Kempe, and Pompe — whose advocacy of rehabilitative measures, and whose opposition to penal measures, went far beyond that of any comparable group in Britain. The establishment of several clinics of a largely non-custodial kind in the 1950s in The Netherlands was matched in England only by the lone establishment of the Henderson Hospital. The fact that by 1955 a third of all 'prisoners' serving over a year, and a third of the average daily population in liberty-depriving institutions, were in TBR, indicates the extent to which judges in The Netherlands were prepared to invest considerable faith in these measures. By contrast, in England compulsory admissions to mental hospitals were a far smaller fraction of the long-term and average daily population. By 1966, the peak of attempted psychiatrization was reached with the Hustinx Committee recommendation in The Netherlands that all defendants facing sentences of one year or more should be subject to psychiatric reports, and that to undertake this task clinics were needed in all five High Court areas. These recommendations were never implemented, and shortly afterwards the reaction against TBR set in. From a number of disparate standpoints — prisoners' rights, the indeterminacy issue, the flaws in clinic security — attacks were mounted, not least by the judges, against the over-use of TBR. Its use was progressively curtailed from that point, though it remains a fairly standard sentence in combination with prison for aggressive offenders. Its status and procedures have been reviewed by the Mulder Committee (Netherlands Ministry of Justice, 1983) and its role for this much-reduced minority of offenders is secure. The proportion of cases in which psychiatric reports were called for fell from 15 per cent to 7 per cent between 1971 and 1981 in the most serious cases (tried by three judges) and from 0.7 to 0.2 per cent in the less serious (SCPB 1985: 225). Nevertheless, the commitment to treatment remains, relatively speaking, substantially higher than in England in the 1980s — though in the 1950s it was remarkably higher.

How can we account for this contrast? First, the energies and evangelistic zeal of the chief members of the Utrecht school were obviously formidable. As Frank Kuitenbrouwer, a journalist specializing in criminal justice policy, put it in an interview: 'They spoke all over Holland, they wrote newspaper articles, they hammered at the Establishment to be more humane. Pompe made the link between the reform of prisons and the reform of sentencing. He had immense moral authority and a very strong personality. And he was teaching lawyers.' Secondly, the talents of the group were complementary: Baan provided psychiatric expertise, Pompe the legal and criminological linkages, and Kempe the concept of the 'dialogue' between therapist and client which lent philosophical lustre to the mental health movement and the professional social workers. *Reclassering* gave strong support to the ideals of the school. Thirdly, the anti-penal critique implicit in their approach reinforced the pre-existing antipathy to imprisonment that had already been fostered by war-time experience. It seems likely that, even when in the 1960s the judiciary abandoned the high hopes that treatment would have discernible positive effects on offenders, they retained their acceptance of the school's rejection of prison for its negative impact on them. This is not to say that the school was the sole source of anti-penal thinking, merely that it reinforced it at a critical period. Nor is it to deny that the school's treatment orientation was strongly opposed from the outset by certain leading criminologists, such as Nagel, who none the less endorsed the anti-penal strand in their thinking.

By contrast, in England, despite the attempted innovations of the 1959 Mental Health Act, judges have never really been swayed from their belief in the need for the fundamentally punitive and deterrent functions of prison, though a minority perhaps placed some faith in the notion of prison as a context within which rehabilitation could occur. The designation of so many establishments in Britain as 'treatment and training' prisons testifies to the lack of serious Establishment opposition to the very compromise that the Utrecht school rejected: that punishment and treatment could be rendered compatible.

There was in some cases sharp disagreement in interviews with the view, expressed most forcibly by Bianchi (1975: 53–4), that the Utrecht school's impact in The Netherlands was 'enormous', and that they 'converted' the authorities to their views. Also, the nature of the commitment of Baan, Kempe and Pompe to the medical model varied considerable (Moedikdo 1976). They did, however, share an anti-penal, anti-retributivist, and in some respects existentialist philosophy of treatment that was unique; and they occupied the plurality of roles necessary for them to mediate their views at all levels of the control system, from the Ministry of Justice and Supreme Court down.

It is difficult to be more assertive than this about the influence of the Utrecht shool. Certain moments stand out as clear indicators of the shift from a relatively strong and clear advocacy of treatment and rehabilitation, in the early and mid-1950s, to the greater stress on the damage wrought by over-long imprisonment of the early 1960s. In the first wave of ministerial and judicial enthusiasm for rehabilitation, a quite remarkable degree of co-ordination prevailed at senior levels. Dr A. M. Roosenburg (in an interview on 27 June 1985, subsequently clarified by personal communication) outlined the twofold role of the Psychiatric Observation Clinic in Utrecht. First, it had to advise courts requesting a psychiatric report before trial. Secondly, it advised the Ministry of Justice on special problems with people serving long-term or life imprisonment, for instance, whether or not it would be safe for society to pardon them.

The essence of Baan's achievement was that he did not restrict the role of the Psychiatric Observation Clinic to advice on statements on imputability. Instead, he tried to conceive constructive ways, within the boundaries of the Dutch legal system, for dealing with people who were under observation because of their 'dangerous' behaviour. Yet his advice could often not be acted upon: first, because of insufficient resources within both prisons and treatment institutions; and secondly, because the practice of the Ministry of Justice was to 'more or less administratively and routinely allocate patients to institutions instead of the reverse: adapting institutions to patients' and community needs'.

A high degree of co-ordination between people at senior level developed *because* of this impasse. Baan, psychiatrist and lawyer, felt the need to discuss such difficulties with everybody involved with policymaking: the head of the Prison system, the head of the TBR system, the head of the Probation Service, the Utrecht University professors of penal law (Pompe) and criminology (Kempe), as well as the directors of the several treatment institutions. 'Every six weeks, Baan called them together and Roosenburg prepared two or three cases for discussion. Then the prisoner or 'patient' was called into the already crowded room and every participant could say and ask what was on his mind. So the files began to live for them'.

These meetings, which testify to the extraordinary sway exerted, by the Utrecht school, went on until 1957, as long as Baan was the head of the Psychiatric Observation Clinic; afterwards they were discontinued. It was in this context that in 1955 some 263 offenders were committed to unsuspended TBR, and 353 to suspended TBR, of whom perhaps 20–30 per cent would have the measure activated due to a subsequent offence. Almost a third of the long-term institutional population (sentences of a year or more) were then detained under TBR regulations: some 1,478 compared with a prison population of just over 3,000. So marked a conversion to the treatment model was never apparent in England, or indeed in Britain as a whole.

This degree of psychiatrization had never been without its critics and, as the problems it entailed became apparent, the judiciary began to question its use for other than the most serious sexual and aggressive offenders. A standard remark in interviews was 'In the 1950s, you could get TBR for bicycle theft'. Its relative decline was most marked in cases against property (see Table 3.3).

> In fact the shift is even greater than shown in the above table . . . If account is taken of all violent offences committed before admission (including offences against morality and property including violence) it is found that 22 per cent of the patients admitted in 1955–6 and 84 per cent of those admitted in 1975–7 committed at least one violent offence. (van Emmerik 1982: 19)

In TBR institutions as a whole, the decline in property offenders,

TABLE 3.3 *Admissions into the Van der Hoeven TBR Clinic by type of offence 1955–1977 (percentages)*

	1955–6	1957–62	1963–69	1970–4	1975–7	Total
Offences against property	75	68	60	46	38	59
Violence	8	9	20	25	42	19
Morality	14	22	19	25	16	20
Other	2	1	1	4	4	2
Total no. of offences	117	142	156	133	79	627

Source: van Emmerik (1982: 19)

both in numbers and as a proportion of the whole, was even more marked (Netherlands Ministry of Justice 1977: 7).

The case against the view that the Utrecht school influenced the judiciary significantly in the growth of milder sentencing was made most notably by Nagel, Enschedé, and Moedikdo, prominent respectively as criminologist, jurist, and analyst of the school's theory and practice. Interviewed in May 1981, Nagel enumerated three points which he saw as limiting their influence: first, they were too diverse to be a 'school', and did no research to test their approach, a point also made by Enschedé (at an interview in the same year); secondly, he had opposed their teaching concerning rehabilitation, despite liking them personally. In 1951, he had said at a meeting at the Ministry of Justice concerning TBR: 'If I commit a crime, I would stand upon my rights to be punished for it, and not to be cured by you, Baan.' He thought prison for up to two years would be bearable, but to be perpetually 'aroused' by doctors intolerable. Thirdly, Baan's successor as medical director of the Van der Hoeven Clinic, Roosenburg, had been too extreme in rejecting due process of a legal character and propagating indeterminate treatment as an alternative to imprisonment, an approach which 'upset the lawyers in training in her lectures.' Hence he demurred from the idea that TBR had weaned judges from imprisonment, seeing penal capacity as more central to the shortening of sentences. Enschedé put forward a more comprehensive explanation of the capacity argument, viewing the workload of public prosecutors in particular as critical for the sharp increase in the waiving of the prosecutions in the 1960s and 1970s (see pp. 68–9 above). Moedikdo

(1976) has given the most sympathetic distillation of the work of the Utrecht school but later (interview, 23 Apr. 1982) also resisted the view that the 'school' had much influence on trends in penal policy. A more likely source of such influence, in his view, was M. P. Vrij (1895–1955), Professor of Law and Criminology at Groningen University, whose work introduced elements of sociology into the study of criminal law (see, for example, Vrij 1956), and who in 1947 became a member of the Supreme Court. His influence can be discerned in the making of the Economic Offences Act of 1950, which was mainly the creation of A. Mulder, whose doctoral research on the theme of economic criminal law had been conducted under Vrij's aegis. Vrij and his pupils (the latter are still united in the 'colloquium Prof. Mr. M. P. Vrij' that holds conferences once or twice a year) were linked by their interest in criminal law as a just but efficient instrument of criminal justice policy. The more effective integration of the latter was the main interest shared by his ex-students, several of whom attained high office, notably Mulder, who as chairman of the senior prosecutors in the mid-1960s initiated the extension of the subject-matter of their fortnightly meetings from public order to criminal justice policy as a whole (interview, Enschedé, 1982) as well as Van Veen, his successor at Groningen and chairman of the Appeals Council that deals with prisoners' complaints (see also below, pp 97–8). Insofar as 1965 was a crucial year for the 'making of a rational criminal justice system' (Enschedé), of a sort which does not and cannot exist in England (as the constitutional basis for it is lacking), considerable significance must attach to the intellectual formations which made such developments possible.

Taking these points in turn, it is, first, difficult to see the diversity of the Utrecht school as a weakness. Its diversity was its strength, much as that of the so-called 'Chicago school' resists easy assumptions of uniformity of outlook or method (Rock 1979; Bulmer 1985). The research point is most telling for the later period of disenchantment with the more radical psychiatrization of Roosenburg; but even Nagel did not criticize Kempe and Rijksen on this score. The nature of their research was (to employ a perhaps outworn distinction) qualitative rather than quantitative, exploratory rather than evaluative, and of a case study/life history form rather in any way positivistic. Pompe was by no means anti-empirical, but his work was juridical rather than research-oriented. However, the influence of their *form* of research was clearly marked. Their main appeal was philosophical: a form of existentialist and phenomenological reinstatement of the offender as a human being with individual rights, against which the penal system was seen as imposing an authoritarian and often unjust, as well as counter-productive, and unnecessarily oppressive, regime. In the aftermath of the German occupation, one can readily apppreciate a not unreceptive climate of opinion for such an approach, put forward as it was with immense conviction and persuasive power by men who, like Pompe, had emerged from the war with much credit. His Catholicism led him to the notion of requital, or reconciliation, between offender and authority, a notion with a strong confessional element. But a punishment which embitters the punished and disgraces him in the eyes of others not only misses its target but is also unjust. The ideal of requital is the voluntary expiation on the part of the guilty themselves. In 1956, the Criminological Institute of Utrecht organized lectures on the long-term prison sentence. Pompe compared the ruining of people by long-term imprisonment with human sacrifices in honour of Moloch (Moedikdo 1976). He argued for the implementation of the reduction of the parole threshold to one-third of the sentence, a recommendation that was never taken up. But his major theme remained, with subtle shifts over the course of his long career, for the possibilities of requital, undertaken by the offender accepting moral responsibility for his offence, to be as unimpeded as possible by the character of punishment. Indeed, ideally the nature of the penalty would enhance the possibilities of requital, by granting trust to the prisoner and strengthening his legal rights. 'In fact he proposed the juridication of the prison community with clear rights and duties for all participants' (Moedikdo 1976). This position involved much tension with the advocacy of treatment by Baan and Kempe, but their views of rehabilitation took account of similar concerns.

As Moedikdo comments, it is to the credit of the working group behind the Utrecht school that criminology there both broke with traditional (orthodox legalism) ways and yet did not collapse into Social Defence, which considers the criminal as an identifiable type to be institutionalized until cured or for life (Radzinowicz 1966: Ch.2). Kempe's work in the areas of social inquiry reports and *reclassering* led him to formulate the concept of the dialogue between the social worker or psychiatrist and the offender. The main task of the investigator was to accept the act as a meaningful expression which can only be revealed by the offender himself in the dialogue/meeting with the investigator. Whilst the latter should avoid moral judgment, he must not simply empathize with the offender, but somehow situate the act in the context of the latter's existential reality. To do otherwise is either to objectivize the offender as a criminal in the Lombrosian way, or as a social product in the more sociological sense. Both in pre-sentence reports and in after-care, however, without taking the authorities' part, the investigator should, on the basis of his knowledge, mediate the insights gained to them. Baan took a similar view from a more psychiatric standpoint. The two differed in the role they would accord the investigator in sentencing and parole decision-making: for Kempe, that was to be the responsibility of the judge; for Baan, the psychiatrist should have an equal say with the judiciary in those matters. The lines of future conflicts were laid down in these differences, with Roosenburg pushing Baan's views somewhat further, whilst Pompe, Kempe and later the 'new' Utrecht school, of Kelk, Peters, and others adhered to fundamental legal procedures, rights and duties. This later became the entire project of the 'new' Utrecht school, who came to distance themselves somewhat from the world of the clinics: while accepting that they have a role to play with a small minority of seriously disturbed offenders, they have tended to focus on extending and clarifying prisoners' and patients' rights (Kelk 1983, Koenraadt 1983).

It would be a great mistake, however, to reduce the project of the 'old' Utrecht school to a purely psychiatric mission, on the one hand, or to a semi-mystical existentialism on the other. (The standard joke about the latter is that guards were to be trained to unlock doors as 'encounteringly' as possible.) The achievement of the Utrecht school was not only to mount a critique and adopt a coherent philosophy: it suggested many practical alternatives, some of which were actually realized. And even in the work of Roosenberg, who is usually cast as the most extreme advocate of psychiatrization, the methods were psychotherapeutic, not behaviouristic. TBR should involve as much contact with the community as possible, both intramurally and via conditional release and extra-mural projects. It was not an advocacy of brain surgery and ECT.

It was only with the work of Rijksen, however, that the Utrecht school made a direct impact on the judiciary. The publication of his *Prisoners Speak Out* in 1958 was clearly an event of major importance in the history of Dutch post-war criminal justice. Thus far, the concern of the members of the school for the human dignity of the offender as a legal subject and a responsible person has always been mediated through their therapeutic and scholarly concern.

In 1958, a collection of letters was published in this spirit. These letters, written on request by prisoners, covered their experiences of the administration of criminal justice. Most contained considerable criticism of judges and public prosecutors, but also of lawyers and probation workers. The result was a storm of public indignation: the different functionaries were, for the first time, confronted with the implications of their own actions and, for a while, their self-confidence seemed to be shaken. What had been achieved in any case, was the first piercing of the hermetically closed prison situation. For the first time, prisoners could let their voices be heard from captivity. (Kelk 1983: 158–9).

The Ministry of Justice first tried to suppress the book, thus perhaps guaranteeing an even greater impact. Even 20 years after its publication in a fresh edition in 1961, judges and prosecutors named this more than any other book as the source of their belief that too long a sentence of imprisonment would embitter and damage prisoners, both socially and psychologically. The attempted suppression, incidentally, seems to qualify the commitment of the Ministry of Justice to taking the initiative in reducing the prison population, though its opposition to the book's publication may have been due more to a fear of such issues becoming openly debated issues rather than to any rooted objection to the policy message. However, it is also significant that the author and his colleagues did not 'go public' on the issue of attempted censorship: though critical of the Dutch 'Establishment', they were also very much in and of it. It is also significant that, faced with perhaps the closest English equivalent some ten years later, Cohen and Taylor's *Psychological Survival* (1972), published in strict breach of the Official Secrets Act, the Home Office decided against prosecution, prompted no doubt by the publicity it would have stirred. Judges and magistrates are not known to have led the rush for copies, though the message was much the same as Rijksen's, albeit in more sociological terms.

As a result, the pre-war work of Pompe on requital, and the

impediments to it embodied in the criminal justice and penal system, and the post-war work of Kempe and Baan on the need for dialogue with a fully human subject found perfect expression in Rijksen's elicitation of prisoners' experiences of such barriers. It completed the paradigm. By comparison, it is difficult to see so coherent a philosophy in reductionist terms emerging from the work of Vrij (as discussed in Sharples 1972: 172–3) who *inter alia* argued for sterner measures against prostitution and a notion of 'subsociality', which entailed a measure of account being paid analytically to public opinion in the criminal justice process. Such views may be expected to have had expansionist implications for the penal system, though it may well be that his influence was felt in other respects, notably in the attempts to promote a more integrated system from 1965 onwards.

Vrij suggested that in addition to guilt and unlawfulness, a third condition for criminal liability or culpability should be what he termed 'subsociality'. An act should not count as an offence unless some damage or disturbance to the social order could be established. Four levels at which such disturbances might be discerned fanning out from the infraction concerned the victim(s), the witnesses or spectators, the community, and the larger society. The notion of 'subsociality' was later revised by his followers, prominent among whom have been van Veen, A. Mulder, G. E. Mulder, R. de Waard, and Enschedé, to refer not so much to the *offence* as to *prosecution*. Discernible here are criteria for operating the principle of expediency which minimize the recourse to prosecution unless the public interest can be shown to be served by it. 'With this doctrine Vrij carried penal science into the field of social politics, thereby introducing a de-juridicating element into penal law' (Remmelink 1980). The crucial linkage here, however, was also made by Pompe (1959), who 'did not see *het subsociale* as constituting either a third element of the offence or any independent condition for imposing punishment. He considers that its significance consists in providing guidance for operating the expediency principle and for meeting out punishment. From this standpoint, the negative condition of *subsocialiteit* take a place quite different from unlawfulness and guilt' (Sharples 1972: 173; Pompe, 1959: 77–80). While it would be an oversimplification to see the Utrecht school as supplying the direction of reductionist policies, and that of Vrij the functional framework for their accomplishment (their influences holding sway in the 1950s and 60s respectively), it is in their interpenetration that much of the cast of post-war penal policy in The Netherlands must be sought. (See also p. 121 below)

What then can be made of the varying views put forward on the influence of the Utrecht school on reductionist policies? First, it has to be acknowledged that 'many of the milder tendencies in penal practice might just as well have occurred without the Utrecht school' (Moedikdo 1976). For example, the Fick Committee of 1947, which initiated the long-term fall in the prison population in particular and the institutional population in general, recommended a wide-ranging series of humanizing reforms to penal regimes, notably the opening up of prisons to community living and association within walls. They reaffirmed but did not initiate the concept of one prisoner to a cell, which was already standard, albeit in terms which amounted to solitary confinement. 'One-to-a-cell is more constitutional than the Constitution' (Kelk, interview, May 1983). Also, though the war-time experience of several of the Committee members, and of scores of thousands of Dutch people, may have facilitated liberalization, it may have also encouraged rehabilitation even more. Similar experiences of mass internment and occupation in Belgium and France did not lead to reductionist penal policies. But the equation may have been drawn between the pains of imprisonment and mental disturbance: would anyone in their right mind ever risk imprisonment? The 1951 Act codified such tendencies, but again, similar acts of rehabilitative intent in Britain and elsewhere, e.g. the Children and Young Persons Act 1969, have been preludes to increases in the prison population rather than the reverse. It is mainly in the maintenance of the impetus towards reductionism in the 1950s and 1960s that the influence of the Utrecht school should be sought.

One must also pose the question of where the offenders committed to TBR actually were. From the late 1940s through to the early 1970s, with peaks in the mid-1950s and mid-1960s, between several hundred and 1,500 people were assigned to TBR at any one time. But they were not necessarily in the clinics, whose capacity rose to 500 or so only relatively late in the 1950s. So they were either on conditional furlough, home leave, or elsewhere in the mental hospital system, or they were *passanten* in the houses of detention (remand), waiting for a place in the Selection Clinic. Indeed, the opening of the Van der Hoeven Clinic was accelerated by legal steps on the part of a group of *passanten* to activate their TBR orders! Before 1960, that wait could be measured in years, rather than months. Hence, one major effect of rehabilitative policies was to load on to the prison system hundreds of offenders who were indeterminately sentenced, which must have made at times for severe capacity problems even in a prison system which overall was running at a capacity to population ratio low enough to enable prison closures to take place. This could have been one substantial reason for the growing disenchantment with TBR among judges which took several forms: first, the indeterminacy issue, particularly over routine property offences. Though judges had the decisive voice concerning release, they had to pay due attention to psychiatrists' recommendation. Secondly, the process of graduated release was felt to be too risky: several scandals erupted over offences committed by paroled patients. Thirdly, the clinics were thought to be insufficiently secure (with one exception: the Mesdag). And fourthly, the capacity problem put pressure on the staff to release (though only conditionally) even risky cases (de Smit, interview June 1981). The power of the psychiatric experts was too entrenched for any direct challenge. However, as judges could only gradually move away from the psychiatric model, and were indeed still convinced of its value for the most serious cases of sexual and aggressive crimes, they could compensate by becoming even milder for the non-psychiatric cases. The strength of the conversion to rehabilitative policies in the 1950s, partly inspired by anti-penal convictions, may as a result have accelerated sentence-shortening for other cases. De Smit has written of the 'babylonic confusion between psychiatry and criminal law' (1976)—and, by this point, TBR was being used less readily, and with reductions in the average length of 'sentence': though a move to limit TBR to six years, reviewable annually after two, has so far been delayed. The rise and fall of rehabilitation may therefore have contributed to reductionism, both directly—through the work of Pompe, Kempe and Rijksen in particular—to the shortening of prison sentences, and indirectly—through judicial moves to compensate for the unanticipated side-effects of indeterminacy. Such considerations would, however, matter only among groups who were already committed to anti-penal sentiments, and who adhered to high standards of social relations for those in custody.

Conclusion

Adequate tests of theories in the social sciences are in far more parsimonious supply than the theories themselves. Use of the comparative method, however, suggests that the first two approaches have considerable shortcomings in their starkest form. Economic constraints are unlikely to account for reductions in the resort to imprisonment at a period of unprecedented economic prosperity in The Netherlands. Countries similarly placed, or even experiencing greater economic stringencies, failed to match the Dutch example of relative decarceration. For much the same reason, penal capacity does not seem, even allowing for inertia, to account for the trends under scrutiny. What happened pre-war did not prove much of a basis for predicting what occurred post-war in any society except in The Netherlands. Progressive declines in penal population occurred from around the 1880s to around the eve of the Second World War in Britain, France, Germany and Belgium, a trend that Rusche and Kirchheimer (1939: Ch 9) attribute to improvements in economic conditions and falls either in the incidence or the rate of increase of crime from the alarming levels of the early and mid-nineteenth century. If, however, the limits of penal capacity are extended to the criminal justice system in general, then a substantial (though by no means the major) part of the phenomenon can be accounted for by the progressive filtering out of potential inputs by (*a*) the sharp decline in the clear-up rate, (*b*) an increase in the proportion of offences not brought before the prosecutor even though they have been cleared up, and (*c*) an increase in the proportion not passed on to the court by the prosecutor.

Some of these trends can be accounted for by policy considerations. The 'principle of opportunity', whereby the public prosecutor may waive prosecution for reasons of public interest, provides the constitutional imprimatur for considerable flexibility. The progressive waiving of prosecutions may thus be linked with the shortening of prison terms by judges. Explanations in terms of a generalized 'culture of tolerance' operating within the context of a 'politics of accommodation' help explain *how* the élites concerned were enabled to carry their policies through without eliciting fierce opposition and public hostility. The context of an unusually generous welfare state which gave high priority to the assimilation of minority groups would also ease the task of justifying such measures. But the main burden of accounting for the trends seems to fall ultimately on variables closely connected with the actual accomplishment of sentencing by the prosecutors and judges themselves; and here the manner of judicial training and socialization, and the character and timing of the brief ascendancy of rehabilitative policies, seems to be crucial in ways which have yet to be analyzed at all adequately. What is incontestable, however, is that rehabilitative policies, in the Dutch context, were clearly compatible, if not causally connected, with the striking reduction in the prison population.

The Depth of Imprisonment: An Exploratory Study of The Netherlands and England

They treat you like a human being. They say, 'Enjoy your meal', 'Good morning'. They treat you like a man, they let you do things the way you like, they're not always looking up your arse for drugs, they don't guard you when you see the governor, with two warders either side. Even when you go to solitary, you take yourself there. You think, 'It can't be true, there must be a catch.' But there isn't. I just can't believe they don't despise you because you're a criminal. In England, they punish you for being a criminal. Then they punish you while they're punishing you. Then you're punished for the rest of your life. (English prisoner in a Dutch closed prison)

Dutch prisons are much better, especially at thinking how to bring prisoners back to the normal life. There is home leave every weekend or so—here there is no way you can get that experience. If they realize that you are not a thoroughgoing criminal, they will do their best to re-establish you in society. Here there is no real attempt to do that, and for the English prisoners that is very bad. He goes out to nothing, so he goes back to crime . . . (Dutch prisoner in English training prison)

Penal reformers, from John Howard onwards, have long preferred the Dutch penal system to that of England. Prisons in The Netherlands have traditionally been smaller, cleaner, and run in a more humane fashion than in England. That, at least, is how it appears from the vantage point of concerned middle-class inquiry. What remains an open question, however, is how far that view is shared by the prisoners themselves. Is the actual experience of imprisonment in the two systems as distinctively different as penal theory implies?

To go some way towards answering that question, and as part of the broader enquiry into post-war Dutch penal policy, I interviewed a small number of prisoners in each system, some of whom had experience of *both.* Interviews were carried out in June and July of 1985 with 12 British (and one Irish) prisoners in 5 Dutch jails, and 14 Dutch prisoners in 4 English jails. This was about a third of the number available in each system coming from their respective countries. Seven of the British and six of the Dutch prisoners interviewed had also been imprisoned in their own countries. Their experience is not necessarily representative, but it would be surprising if those not interviewed felt significantly at odds with the views expressed, for on certain issues there was near unanimity—above all, on the strong preference expressed by both British and Dutch prisoners for the Dutch penal system. This was despite the fact that none of the four prisons selected by the Prison Department for interviews with Dutch prisoners in England was a local prison, where problems of under-staffing and over-crowding are at their most unrelieved.

It is probable that the Dutch prisons chosen for interview were more representative of the system than those selected for me in England. Permission to conduct the interviews was granted initially from the Prison Department of the Home Office in England, and the Prison Department of the Ministry of Justice in The Netherlands. It was then sought and granted by the governors of the prisons concerned. In England, the Prison Department assembled the list of four prisons where Dutch prisoners were held in custody, and it was left to me to contact the appropriate member of staff to arrange the most appropriate time. Prisoners were asked, in advance of my arrival, if they wished to take part in the interviews and none refused. In The Netherlands I was allowed to contact *any* prison at which British prisoners were held, and asked to write a letter to the prisoners outlining the purpose of the interviews, though in practice only a few of the prisoners actually received the letter. None refused an interview when permission was sought at the outset, however. The number of interviews in other prisons could have been extended in The Netherlands once official permission had been granted. Only constraints of time precluded interviewing more than 13. There was only one prisoner whom I was refused permission to interview. In England, if more interviews had been possible, I would have had to re-apply for official permission afresh. Another difference in the interviewing lay in the constraints which governed the time they could take. In the Dutch prisons, once entry had been gained, there was no particular time limit set to the interview beyond the interviewee's own wishes. In English prisons, strict time limits—usually those of the hours of visiting—were adhered to in all but one case. All interviews in The Netherlands were in private, and in all but one prison in England this was also the case. Interviews were tape-recorded with the prisoners' permission, except for three refusals in The Netherlands and two interviews in England which could not be taped because they took place in general visiting conditions.

In The Netherlands permisssion to inspect prisoners' files would have been needed from the prisoners themselves, but no such constraint applied in England. Cross-checking details of offence and sentence were carried out in three cases of Dutch prisoners in England, and prisoners' and file accounts tallied in all main respects. Convergence was also the case on occasions that prisoners had been convicted jointly. Otherwise, I had no marked inclination to cross-check that which had already been conveyed in confidence. The interviews were of a frankly exploratory nature. The main focus was explicitly on the prisoners' experience of the criminal justice system in general and of imprisonment in particular, and it was thought useful to ask for such perceptions even where they had no experience of their own system. Where they had such experience, they were asked about the similarities and differences between the two systems, again in terms of their own experience.

The contrast between the British and Dutch penal systems is usually drawn in terms of the *length* of sentences of imprisonment. The average Dutch sentence—three months or so—is far shorter than the average British sentence of roughly ten months, a difference which principally accounts for the much smaller proportionate size of the Dutch prison population relative to that of Britain. The two sets of prisoners interviewed were, however, closer to each other in terms of sentence length than the average. The British prisoners in Dutch jails were typically in prison for hard drug offences, mainly dealing and trafficking in cocaine, and in three cases for heavy crimes of violence: armed robbery, attempted murder, and murder. Their average length of sentence of 25 months was several times the Dutch average, compared with an average sentence of 39 months for the Dutch prisoners in English jails, which is still four times the average for this country. The principal offence committed by the Dutch prisoners was 'soft' drug smuggling, typically large consignments of cannabis, though in five cases cocaine or heroin was involved. In practice, parole etc. would reduce each average term by one-third, to 16 months for British prisoners in The Netherlands and 26 months for Dutch prisoners in England.

Important as this magnitude of difference is for the individuals concerned, and for the operation of the system as a whole, the main contrast in the interviews between the two systems was couched in terms of the *depth* rather than the length of imprisonment.[1] In a variety of ways, some gross, some nuanced, prison in The Netherlands is experienced as a far less damaging and repressive phenomenon than in Britain. Another way of putting it is to say that even the less unpleasant end of the prison system in Britain holds few positive features for the prisoners. The main impact of the system here, even the training prisons, is to blunt sensibilities rather than—as in the Dutch system in general—making some attempt to preserve or even sharpen them. This sense of a contrast in terms of psychological invasion by the prison was expressed on a variety of levels: relations with staff; relations with other prisoners; rights and privileges; material standards and conditions; and a sense of the overall quality of life which the prison regime made possible or witheld.

Relations with staff

As the first of the accounts implied (p. 163) relations with staff were among the more unexpected as well as welcome features of prison life in The Netherlands, particularly for prisoners who had experience of the British system. With the exception of open prisons in Britain, whose atmosphere corresponds most closely to that in the majority of Dutch prisons, British jails were regarded as unnecessarily oppressive. Some saw this difference as lodged in system and broader societal terms:

> The main difference is the attitude of your fellow prisoners and staff . . . In Wormwood Scrubs, . . . the staff are not particularly friendly—that's a polite way of putting it—and the system is unnecessarily degrading. Whereas in Zutphen [a Dutch remand prison] you didn't have to do anything that wasn't common sense; there was nothing that was done completely pointlessly, just to punish you . . . The whole atmosphere was different. The staff seemed to treat you as a human being, whereas

[1] The 'depth of imprisonment' is one of those familiar sounding phrases which strike one as obvious but which have not been coined before. It was first used, to my knowledge, by Mr T. Robinson, an adult educationist with long experience of the Dutch penal system, at the 1985 Abolitionist Congress in Amsterdam. It is not to be confused with the 'depths of imprisonment', a more literary phrase connoting the hidden miseries and squalor to be found in the recesses of Victorian prisons—but not, for that reason, unknown today.

the staff in Britain would treat you as, well 'animal' is too strong a word, basically with a lack of any humanity. The way that going to the toilet is arranged, the lack of showers, the way staff would shout at people continually, that wouldn't work in Holland, they'd go on strike or something. It's basically alien to the Dutch character to have that sort of divide between people.

Others prisoners were less constrained in describing their experience of the British local prisons in particular: 'barbaric', 'inhuman', 'degrading', and 'makes you an animal because it treats you like one' were commonly employed. Even the least critical made such points as 'guards here are more human, you can joke with them; in England, guards are much more strict'. The Dutch attitude was summed up by one English prisoner: 'They've got your liberty and that's enough. They don't have to make your life complete hell.'

Three points emerged, or were made, that undercut some of the more common objections to staff–prisoner relations assuming too 'normal' or sociable a form. Firstly, the lessening of what one prisoner called 'physical and mental control' did *not* entail more indiscipline and risk to staff safety. It was asserted that staff were trained to spot trouble coming, and to deal with it quickly and without animosity, using verbal rather than physical means to defuse potentially violent situations. Secondly, what King and Morgan have termed the 'normalization' of the prison is much enhanced by the presence of women staff. Women both serve as guards in men's prisons in The Netherlands and as governors, social workers, and secretaries, as well as psychologists and teachers: their presence is now taken for granted. They are abused neither physically nor verbally: 'nobody has ever tried anything on'. Indeed, their presence is said to lower the aggressive atmosphere that builds up in all-male environments: 'If there are men and women in prison, you relate to them as human beings. If there are only men, you relate to them only as men', as one prisoner put it. A women deputy director stated that until a few years ago, the Ministry of Justice's fear that sexual attacks would occur inhibited such appointments as her own; but there have been no 'incidents' of any kind over the two-year period of her employment. Not least, 'they can speak about emotional problems as they can't with a man.' Under the impact of equal opportunities legislation, similar developments have occurred in England, so that by 1988 there is no type of male penal establishment in which women are not represented at governor grades. Though few have as yet been recruited as prison officers in male prisons, this is an encouraging trend. Thirdly, the view is often expressed, both by and on behalf of prison officers in Britain, that the presence of social workers and other 'caring' staff in jails strips the prison officers of their welfare roles, and reduces them to mere turnkeys (J. E. Thomas 1972). The Dutch experience shows that this need not be so.

The experience of Dutch prisoners in English training prisons was not a symmetrical mirror-image of their counterparts in Dutch prisons. There were no accounts of physical brutality or sadistic mind control. But, despite several accounts of acts of individual kindness by particular officers, the picture that emerged was of an absence of humanity or normal human relations. Both staff and prisoners were said to be caught up in a deadening routine imposition of 'niggling' and 'silly' rules. Three of the 14 Dutch prisoners had landed favourable jobs within the system, such as probation orderly and library work. These jobs meant friendlier staff relations, and some small freedoms which made doing time without extra problems more feasible. But the theme which recurred most frequently was the all-pervasive character of being pinned down within walls by what Cohen and Taylor (1978) have called 'rules-within-rules-within-rules'. These could be both opaque and varied from prison to prison. 'It is very hard and impersonal here. Rules here are very complicated, even the guards don't know them.' Even in the prison that was least 'closed' in character, examples were given of 'silly rules' entailing such penalties as loss of seven days' remission for going to the dining room at the wrong time; certain common toiletries were not allowed to be purchased; lying outside on the grass instead of going to gym was sometimes okay, and sometimes not. 'A cup of tea under a tree—not even that is allowed on a summer's day—just silly walking round in circles.' When asked about the chief difference between prisons in England and The Netherlands, one prisoner summed them up in terms reminiscent of Alexander Paterson's remark that 'prisons should be *as,* not *for,* punishment':

> The most important comparison is that you are in prison to be taught how to behave in society. So, in The Netherlands, they take your freedom, but that's it. You work, to teach you how to be in society as a normal working man. People who work in prisons there treat you as a human being, not as a child or as a mental patient. Here, it's so different . . . It's so difficult for us, they expect you to behave yourself. Okay—so

then they should treat you as a grown man, not as a child, coming at you with children's rules. For example, you're supposed to wear slippers on the Wing, and a shirt. A week ago, there is a library visit once a week, some still had shoes on from work. They had to wait for an officer to go for a shirt, since they only had a T-shirt on. Little things. To write a letter, you have to ask for a letter. In Holland, you buy 15 envelopes and stamps from the shop and write as many letters you like. Here two letters are impossible. Buying two letters and stamps leaves no money for tobacco.

In such examples, staff–prisoner relations are clearly determined by the fine mesh of institutional rules. It is by such minute particulars that the depth of imprisonment is partly to be plumbed. Censoriousness, in terms of an appeal to the yardstick of the rules of equity in society at large, was seen by Mathiesen (1965) as one of the principal 'defences of the weak'. It was notably absent, however, from British prisoners' accounts of their experience in Dutch jails.

Relations with other prisoners

Relations with other prisoners were not, in general, experienced as a problem by British prisoners in Dutch jails. The one-to-a-cell system made for privacy when it was wanted, and the relatively generous amount of time allowed for association and recreation did not make isolation the other side of the coin. Dutch prisoners in English jails tended to feel under constant pressure from the conflicts arising in part from the deprivations of prison life, in part from over-crowding even in the less congested end of the penal system. Only one British prisoner in The Netherlands, in a remand prison, felt cell-sharing was less onerous than enforced privacy, for the company it provided. The rest, who often called their cell their 'room', valued the one-to-a-cell arrangement. British prisoners in British jails were seen as 'tougher, more out to prove themselves . . . Discipline is more severe in England. They don't like violence at all here, it leads to quick transfers, which are not so much in England unless it's real bad.' Another British prisoner in a Dutch jail recalled that one of Scotland's more notorious jails was very strong in the ' "hard man" gang thing'. Dutch jails are hardly trouble-free, but the prisoners there felt that trouble could be avoided relatively easily. By contrast, the Dutch prisoners in British jails felt the restrictive discipline was counter-productive, generating tensions and making it more difficult for them to mix with prisoners they liked and to avoid those they did not. 'Here, not a minute, not a second, privacy—never.' Relations with other prisoners could hardly be easy and relaxed where substandard rights and conditions made for 'nervousness' all round. For one prisoner at least, the combination of restrictive discipline and a turbulent inmate culture that was as inescapable as the prison itself proved almost unbearable: 'Here, it is a nightmare when you wake. Only when you go to sleep you live again.'

Rights, privileges, and conditions

Rights, privileges, and conditions were almost overwhelmingly regarded as far superior in Dutch prisons by comparison with those in England by both sets of prisoners. The major exception to this picture concerned remand prisoners at the pre-trial, or at least the investigative, stage of their confinement in police and prison cells. 'What was not so good was that after arrest I was kept incommunicado in Zutphen for three months, and for a few weeks my wife and family didn't know where I was.' Another prisoner saw the pre-trial remand system in Britain as '10 times better' than that in The Netherlands: 'Here they do things in reverse: you get real privileges in England on remand until proven guilty, your own clothes, food, visits every day, lager, cigs. and so on . . . here they deny you all privileges, no visits and for two months no letters were either sent or received. My brother actually came over from England but was denied a visit.' This young prisoner said he had attempted suicide, 'but that didn't change things.' Things only changed when his plea changed, otherwise he could have been kept in isolation for up to 106 days. The Dutch authorities were seen as using isolation as a weapon in the investigative process. 'You're treated like an animal before conviction, even if you're innocent, then you get all the privileges afterwards. Seems the wrong way round to me.' Another prisoner commented: 'If you're remanded in custody in England, you can see your family every day, they can bring you food and so on[2], but here you can be held in isolation. They start the punishment straight away . . . Underneath the nice, liberal facade in Holland, I think suspects are dealt with far more severely, initially.'

[2] The right of remand prisoners to have their own food and drink sent in was ended on March 1, 1988.

In this one major respect, however, it is doubtful if the differences between the two systems are as pronounced as the prisoners maintained. In their study of remand prisoners in Winchester local prison, King and Morgan (1976) concluded that 'the special provisions for the protection of unconvicted persons in custody, which are valuable but slender enough in theory, mean very little in practice' (p. 39). 'In our wider comparative study of prison regimes there was a good deal of evidence to suggest that unconvicted prisoners experienced more constraining regimes than convicted prisoners . . .' (p. 40). Nor is solitary confinement, for periods far longer than those reported by the prisoners in Dutch jails, unknown in comparable cases in England. 'Arrested some nine months ago, my client is still in custody awaiting trial . . . Since his arrest—except for periods totalling 10 days—he has been held in solitary confinement as a Category A prisoner. The regime in which he has been held consists of 23 hours a day cellular solitary confinement, no association with other prisoners and exercise for the remaining hour each day' (Letter to the editor, *Guardian*, 12 Sept. 1987, from James Butler, Offenbach & Co.). The provisions protecting the rights of unconvicted prisoners are grounded in the presumption of innocence, but that is 'tempered by a second principle, namely, that the course of justice must proceed unhindered by the activities of those who would seek to subvert it' (King and Morgan 1976: 32). In practice, therefore, the English presumption of innocence affords little more protection than the European convention that any case not proven falls. At the investigative stage, therefore, there is less to choose between the two systems than the above accounts asserted. Nevertheless, the right to visits, under however inhibiting a set of conditions, and letters, does remain inviolate in the English system at this stage, and in that signal respect it is superior to the Dutch.

There are, however, worrying instances of that right being curtailed in practice by sudden transfers for security reasons (as in the case of McAvoy, 1984, on which see Richardson 1985: 57) or for reasons arising from conflicts over staffing levels (Ballantyne 1988).

What all prisoners agree upon is that, once the investigative stage is over in The Netherlands, things dramatically improve for the prisoners; and once conviction is secured in Britain, things rapidly change for the worse.

Accommodation

Accommodation provides the basis for much that differentiates the two systems' standards. With one exception, all the British prisoners preferred the one-to-a-cell system which the Dutch have placed a high premium on retaining. (It is made possible by the system of prisoners 'waiting' for a prison place and will be further facilitated by a planned expansion of penal capacity that, if implemented, will double the number of places from 3,683 in 1980 to 7,070 by 1990.) The commitment to the one-to-a-cell rule was sharply expressed by a senior member of staff in an Amsterdam prison who was willing to resign if it was abandoned: 'If two to a cell, I go.' The closed prisons allow for more individualization of cell furnishing and decoration than is the case in the remand prisons, where even convicted prisoners may have to wait several months for a place in the closed prisons to become available. But even there cells are usually open from 7.00 in the morning until 9.30 at night, with prisoners not otherwise on work duties or under discipline being allowed to leave their cells or not as they wished. TV can be rented at a cost well within the weekly pay budget, floors can be carpeted, 'one man even has an aquarium in his cell'. 'Here you can control the lighting system in your room, so you can read [at night] if you want to—that's not so in England—very small things make a big difference.' By contrast, even in the less-congested 'C' category training prisons in England, accommodation is often shared, in dormitories with three, four, or five prisoners in one space. Far more time is spent in the cells, and less scope exists for private effects to be there. In only one of the Dutch remand prisons did conditions verge on the British, with confinement to cells being the norm except for work and an hour's recreation a day, with two hours additional recreation every other evening. Staff shortages at night also involved slopping-out, as in England. In no Dutch prison, however, were the prisoners 'locked down' for 23 hours a day, or anything like it.

Food and clothing

Clothing was left to the prisoners' choice in The Netherlands, not so in England: few chose to comment on this, but those that did preferred choice, and it is clearly the most visible signifier of prisoner status. Food elicited varied responses, which differed more by prison than by country. The greater preference shown by some British prisoners for the fresh milk, fruit, and yoghurt that was more frequently available in Dutch prisons was offset by that of others for the cooked (rather than cold, buffet-style food) which was the norm in British prisons. The food in Dutch jails seemed more varied. In one, a barbecue for all the prisoners was being prepared with three different kinds of meat for different religious groupings. The festival of Ramadan was the occasion for Turkish prisoners being allowed to prepare their own food in the kitchens. In England, food was 'dumped on disgusting plastic plates'; real plates were used in The Netherlands. Washing and toilet facilities were clearly superior in the Dutch prisons. Prisoners could have four showers a week, and could in general leave their cells to use the toilet where cells had no integral flushing toilets. One Dutch prisoner who had been in Wandsworth called it a 'real hell. Eighty persons for four toilets, one shower a week, mice, cockroaches, you had to sleep fully clothed, you were 23 hours in a cell.' (On the continued postponement of integral sanitation in Wandsworth Prison, see Stern 1987: 182:) Training prisons in England were not so bad, but some still had no access to toilets during the night in shared cells.

Work and pay

Work and pay are basic determinants of the experience of prison. Work offers a break from the cell, a chance to socialize, and at best some form of training that offers a marketable skill on release. The two systems were not so very different as far as foreign prisoners were concerned, though Dutch prisoners in Dutch jails were said to have better training opportunities than British prisoners in British jails. Pay, however, differed greatly between the two systems, with the prisoners in The Netherlands earning roughly £12 a week, compared to a *maximum* £2.98 a week in England. The effect of this extremely low rate of pay was seen by Dutch prisoners in English jails as much needless friction and pointless deprivation. 'You get at most three packets of cigarettes. So if they buy [extra] letters, something happens in the family, then they can't buy the tobacco. So they feel bad, they get things out of proportion, then trouble breaks out without reasons.' Tobacco is the mainstay of prison life, but prison pay does not stretch to more than three packets a week—a source of constant haggling when soap, toiletries, extra letters, confectionery and so on have to come out of wages. 'Two stabbings over a quarter-ounce of tobacco—I can't believe it.' Dutch prisoners were also keenly aware that tobacco for roll-ups was four times as expensive in England as in The Netherlands—in effect a tobacco allowance ratio of 1 : 16, since wages there are four times as high. A further irritation was that even if one had the money, the discretion allowed to prison governors meant that, for example, the sale of toiletries could be severely restricted—in one jail to powdered toothpaste. 'They take everything here. They take your freedom but they also take your smokes.' 'At the end of the week, people come to you for dog-ends. At first, I thought it was to do with a dog!' 'A lot go down over Rule 43 due to debt over dope and tobacco.' By contrast, in The Netherlands the wages enable prisoners to buy extra food: 'In the canteen here you can get everything you can in a supermarket outside—muesli, yoghourt, cans of fruit. You can live decently.' The low rates of pay were seen by Dutch prisoners in England as derisory for work that was often both long and demanding. 'One girl did 35 metres of tasselling a week and she got £2.67. Kitchen work is very demanding, no time off, a 7-day week from 6.00 in the morning until the evening.' 'The wages are really stupid. My family can't believe it.' Ironically, the less the prisoners earned, the higher the premium attached to wages. 'There is education here . . . but few go. It takes time off work, so you lose money from earnings.' Yet educational provision was one of the few features of the English system praised by the Dutch prisoners.

Communication with the outside world

The depth of imprisonment is most graphically conveyed by the rules governing letters, phoning, and visits. It is here, for foreign prisoners ineligible for home leave, that the differences between the two systems were most starkly inscribed. 'Prisons are certainly more comfortable here [in The Netherlands] than in Britain. But comfort is beside the point—the main thing is more letters, visits, and so on. There is no reason to deny any number of letters. But in England I had to ask my girl-friend to write fewer letters.' In Dutch prisons, there is no limit to the number of letters prisoners can write or receive. There is random censorship, but it is not a pretext for limiting correspondence. Postage has to be paid for, but the more generous wages mean this is no problem. In English prisons, there is one free letter a week; the number of additional letters that prisoners can buy varies between prisons. Some are limited to one, others more—but affording envelopes and stamps out of prison wages becomes a major obstacle. The Dutch prisoners complained in one or two cases about unexplained delays in receiving mail, and censorship was cited as more prevalent than in The Netherlands. At the remand stage in Britain, however, prisoners can write as many letters as they like, at their own expense.

Use of the phone could vary even more between the two systems. In The Netherlands it was taken for granted that prisoners have the right to make at least one free foreign call a week, two or possibly more by permission of the governor on welfare or other grounds. One prisoner stated calls within The Netherlands could be made daily 'to encourage personal contact'. In England, phoning was unusual, either abroad or domestically. It is very much a privilege, to be granted only on application to the governor. It varied from prison to prison on a discretionary basis: 'one call every six to seven weeks', 'one after application to the governor', 'one call a month but had to wait three months for her first call', 'no phoning was allowed at all in Holloway', 'possible with governor's permission, but costs too much, so I have only made one', 'no phoning at all here' and so on. The picture was of a sparely given privilege for which the prisoner had to mobilize considerable welfare support.

Visits are the most fundamental of prisoners' rights, the main way in which the prison's hold over the prisoner is temporarily reduced by the presence of family, friends, or other contacts from the outside world. But even here the prison can and does intrude via the host of variables that make up the context in which visits take place, the degree of monitoring that pervades them, the length of time they are allowed to last, and so on. The character of visits is therefore a prime determinant of the depth of imprisonment. At its most developed, in the long-term closed prisons, the Dutch system allows three visits of up to three hours weekly, plus one 'private visit' a month, with extra visits if the case can be made. In remand prisons, convicted prisoners could receive visitors twice a week for up to two hours each, but facilities did not exist for private visits. The frequency of visits in English training prisons was markedly less, one visit of up to two hours being allowed only once fortnightly. Some prisons are more flexible than others, and where families found difficulty in visiting from abroad, daily visits were in one case arranged for three days running. However, for prisoners remanded in custody, visiting arrangements are more generous in English than in Dutch prisons. (They may, however, be of very short duration; daily visits for prisoners remanded in custody in Holloway last only quarter of an hour.)

Both British and Dutch prisoners argued that private visits should be introduced into British prisons, though the likelihood in the foreseeable future is, to put it mildly, remote. Their arguments go to the heart of the debate about whether imprisonment should be as, not for, punishment. The main argument was ' . . . that relationships are kept alive. You have sexual contacts and they keep you alive.' The result was seen as less dependence on drugs, less homosexuality, and less violence—in prisons and after release. It was argued that in British prisons, as in British society, 'people are too controlled, so they go mad when they get out'. Another prisoner made the point that private visits were not only or mainly for sex, but allowed an intimacy and self-expression not possible on a routine visit: 'Sometimes we just cuddle each other and weep.' Another prisoner linked the significance of the length and depth of imprisonment: 'They don't put people away here for 12, 15, 18 years, when your marriage breaks down, you come out, you've got nothing. Here, you can have private visits, you can have sex, you can plan a family, you've got something to come out to.' Others affirmed that family relations had been kept together by the visits. Such visits are not possible in British prisons, and their introduction is opposed by the Prison Officers' Association, partly because they may be subject to abuse. One reply to this criticism by a Dutch prison deputy director was that such abuses as, for example, drugs being brought into the prison, exist as a possibility with *any* visiting. In both systems, body searches can take place after visits as a check against illicit substances or weapons being brought in from the outside. And the British prisoners were emphatic that both soft and hard drugs were as prevalent in the British as in Dutch jails. What *is* apparent is that the Dutch authorities regard the benefits of such visits as outweighing the costs.

While visiting arrangements have improved in English jails over the past few decades, the Dutch prisoners in English jails seemed to have had fewer visitors than their counterparts in The Netherlands. The difference may in part be due to the British prisoners having more settled relationships in The Netherlands, in part because the size of the country means it is possible for visitors from abroad to reach even the more remote prisons without the extensive travel needed to reach British prisons outside the East Coast and the Home Counties from The Netherlands.But the main conclusion must be that the incentive to undertake such long and costly journeys is seriously diminished when the visiting arrangements are too restrictive. Even when family visit periods had accumulated over three to four months, for example, one Dutch prisoner stated that the visit could still last only one and half to two hours. Rules vary, and elsewhere allowance had been made to extend the number of visits to allow to some extent for previous non-take-up. The arrangements another prisoner had made with his girl-friend had to be cancelled due to a missing Visiting Order slip. The picture is of sparse and relatively inflexible visiting arrangements, occasionally modified on welfare grounds but generally not. The setting in which the standard visits take place is not so very different between Dutch and English training prisons—in both, several visits take place simultaneously in rooms where guards are in general out of earshot. Refreshments may be available, and the atmosphere can be relaxed. The glass screens that one Scottish prisoner remembered between prisoners and visitors in Barlinnie in 1983 seem exceptional even for Britain. But the relative infrequency and lack of privacy in visiting arrangements in British prisons combined with the much more restrictive rules governing letters and telephoning markedly diminish the prisoners' social bonds with the outside world, and correspondingly deepen those within the world of the prison.

Welfare

Welfare considerations loom larger in the Dutch than in the British system. When asked about the chief differences between the two, one English prisoner in The Netherlands replied that it lay in a 'lot of emphasis on rehabilitation', though (as discussed below) this was regarded as applying mainly to Dutch rather than to foreign prisoners. 'If you want rehabilitation, they will do anything for you.' By 'rehabilitation' or 'resocialization' was implied a set of helping strategies akin to Bottoms and

McWilliams's (1979) 'non-treatment paradigm': work training facilities that can be tailored for the individual, generous educational provision, ample time and facilities for sport and recreation, minimal discipline consonant with security, and ease of access to social work and specialist assistance. 'The main asset here is the resocialization. Children aren't ashamed to come here. Welfare payments are kept up . . . whereas stigma in England is very powerful. I had friends who refused me permission to see their children after I'd been in prison for cannabis . . . In England, the attitude is "once a criminal, always a criminal". Here, they think maybe next time you'll be different.'

The situation in English training prisons is not simply the obverse of that which exists in The Netherlands. Educational provision in two of the prisons was singled out for praise by Dutch prisoners, and library facilities were seen as adequate. One prisoner stated: 'What is very good here is education, better than Holland. You can even transfer between prisons here for educational reasons. Here they have a school—I do English, typing, and mathematics. Nothing else is better here than in Holland.' These best practices were not referred to in the two other prisons where interviews took place, though in one the scope for hobbies such as photography and computing were seen as very good; sport and keeping fit in the gym were also stressed as important outlets. If only for reasons of the time allotted to these activities, however, they came across as more marginal to prisons in England than in The Netherlands, despite the fact that they were cited as the best features of the prison life here.

Discipline

Discipline was clearly more severe in English than in Dutch prisons, and less subject to rights of appeal. 'There is no democracy inside the prison [in England]. Every prison officer is like God. No complaints are possible. In The Netherlands, if the governor says no, and you think you have a right, you can appeal to a Commission one of whom has to be a jurist, and you might get your right.' Punishments were seen (sometimes exaggeratedly) as heavier in England than in The Netherlands. 'I'm on three days' punishment [solitary] for having a bit of hash . . . In England, you'd get three more months on your sentence for that.' A parallel case cited by a Dutch prisoner in England had actually cost him 14 days' remission—not three months—but the disparity in punishment was still marked, in part perhaps a reflection of the greater tolerance towards 'soft' drug use in The Netherlands in general. But even legal drug use is penalized in England more than in The Netherlands: 'Going on report here can be just for giving another prisoner tobacco . . . You can get on report so easily here.' 'A £6 fine could do for you if you are a smoker.' Nor can money and tobacco be sent in from the outside quite legally, as it can in The Netherlands. Tobacco baroning is relatively unknown there: the depth of imprisonment and the strength of inmate hierarchy built on scarce resources and their illicit distribution are no doubt correlated to some degree. The contrast in disciplinary terms is that of constraints within constraints as the pattern of prison life in England, many of which are seen as both unnecessary and arbitrarily imposed, 'just to remind you you are a convict, not a human being' (Dutch prisoner in English jail). In The Netherlands, the constraints are more acceptable not simply because they are less severe, but because they are recognized as kept to a minimum consonant with security and good order.

Quality of life

The quality of life was not explicitly addressed as a theme in the interviews, but implicitly linked the otherwise uneven perceptions of the prisoners that a marked difference obtained between the two systems. It was evidently just possible, given a level of self-control none too common in the world at large and not noted for its presence among those officially cast as deviant, to do time quietly in English training prisons. Keeping one's nose clean—avoiding illicit drugs, spinning out the tobacco, making the most of the few hours a day allotted to education, work, and leisure, and keeping on the right side of the staff—would with luck see one through without extra penalties. But it remained an ordeal, an assault on the self to be survived, time out of life. In Dutch prisons, the rupture is not so marked, the passage of time less prolonged, the sense of social distance from society less acute, and the problems of psychological survival less chronic. Allusions to such differences occurred repeatedly in such statements from both sets of prisoners as: 'In Britain, you *always* know you're in prison. Here, you can for a time forget about it . . . Here, you are a person, not just a number in the system.' 'Here there is much more to do, time goes much quicker here. You are only locked in your rooms at night.' 'Here they *want* you to take advantage of what's offered. You have more chance afterwards.' 'There's a chance to keep a bit of your own life going.' 'You are still a member of society.' When asked what features of the Dutch prison system should be introduced into England, British and Dutch alike responded both in holistic terms—'the whole attitude', and so on—and in terms of specific points, ranging from fresh fruit and milk to friendlier and better trained officers, to home leave and more frequent visits. By contrast, the reverse question, on which features of the English penal system should be introduced in The Netherlands, almost invariably produced a strong negative: 'Not a thing from here should be introduced in Holland.' 'England has nothing to offer the Dutch, just to mind their own fucking business.' 'It's not just bull shitting for Holland. The prisons there really are better—stay in there for two days or so and you'll see.'

The near-unanimity among both sets of prisoners on the comparison between prisons favouring the Dutch was in sharp contrast to the much more disparate responses to questions about policing and the criminal justice sytem in general. There, answers were more in line with a belief in the superiority of one's own system, or on there being no substantial difference at all. It is especially disturbing that the comparison between the two prison systems would have been even more marked if interviews with Dutch prisoners had taken place in the more congested local prisons. The only exception was the greater stated preference for the English system in the early stages of remand in custody, though women prisoners who had been at Holloway did not share this preference.

Double punishment? Prisoners abroad

What makes the generally favourable response of British prisoners to Dutch prisons even more notable is that, as foreign prisoners, they felt relatively more discriminated against, by comparison with Dutch prisoners, than did Dutch prisoners in the English system with their English counterparts. Their perceived discrimination—along with other foreign prisoners—began with the sentences they received and extended to the withholding from them of such major rights as home leave and 'interruptions' to sentence. As these latter rights do not exist anyway in the English system, except in very limited respects in the small number of open prisons, the Dutch prisoners in our jails had fewer grounds on which perceptions of discrimination could arise in the first place. In their case, the sense of discrimination was largely limited to the operation of parole.

Though a research project conducted by Jongman, Bosma and Tildemans of the University of Groningen[3] did not in general support the view that foreign offenders were more severely sentenced than Dutch nationals, the usual assertion by British prisoners was that on average foreigners were subject to sentences of imprisonment roughly double the length of those passed on nationals. The great majority of the British prisoners interviewed were imprisoned for hard drug offences, mainly smuggling or dealing in cocaine. As the Dutch authorities have been under strong domestic and international pressure to toughen sanctions against hard drug offenders in particular, this claim is not altogether implausible, and Jongman's team did not include drug offences in their research coverage of the issue. Moreover, drug offenders in The Netherlands were liable to find themselves assessed for hefty tax bills and sequestration of assets. For example, one British prisoner sentenced to three and a half years' imprisonment for dealing in and possession of 215 grams of cocaine had a tax bill for 87,000 guilders (about £20,000), and possessions such as TV and video taken from his house in part payment. When the maximum sentence for an offence is greater than six years, such prisoners are liable to instant deportation on release. It is difficult to sustain the image of The Netherlands as soft on hard drugs in the light of this kind of penalty. If was felt that foreign drug offenders were particularly liable to such additional penalties, since welfare workers would have intervened on behalf of Dutch nationals to forestall such actions. Nevertheless, resentment at such perceived differences of sentence were largely offset by the conviction that comparable sentences in England would have been far stiffer. For example, a prisoner convicted of smuggling 200 grams of cocaine and sentenced to 18 months' imprisonment reckoned he would have received at least five years in England. Another prisoner

[3] Summarized in an interview by one of the participants, Mr Tildemans, as showing for male larceny cases a greater chance of custody for non-Dutch first offenders but the reverse for recidivists (interview, 14 Jan. 1985).

sentenced to four and a half years in prison for armed robbery thought he would have received a 15-year sentence in Britain. Estimates of the difference were roughly in the range of English prison sentences being three times as long.

By contrast, Dutch prisoners in England tended to feel a rough parity with English prisoners on sentence length, though they also felt that in The Netherlands their sentence would either have been non-custodial or for a far shorter term, especially for the cannabis-related offences. They did, however, feel discriminated against in terms of parole, an issue which did not arise for English prisoners in The Netherlands, where parole is more akin to remission, being both automatic (for all sentences of over nine months) and not subject to licence and recall in the same way. 'There is no way foreigners can get parole [in England]. Even for good behaviour, you can't get out earlier.' Another prisoner, jailed for two years for smuggling cannabis and a recent recipient of a parole 'nodback' (refusal), was told by his probation officer not to waste his time asking for a review as 'drugs offenders never get parole anyway'. This statement may reflect one consequence of the then home secretary Leon Brittan's withdrawal of parole rights for—in effect—all drug offenders imprisoned for over five years. This restriction may have become informally extended to all drug offenders regardless of the length of their sentence. Dutch prisoners were uncertain whether or not to attribute the cause of their 'nodbacks' to being foreign or being drug offenders or both. But whatever the reasons—and the prospects of supervizing foreigners so close to home as the Dutch may be among them—the withholding of parole was experienced as a major form of double punishment, particularly as in half the cases the type and length of sentence were felt to be far heavier than would have been incurred in The Netherlands.

Discrimination against foreign prisoners in The Netherlands by their denial of home leave and interruptions to sentence must be seen in the context of the far more extensively developed system of such forms of 'time out' by comparison with Britain. The system of home leave and allied forms of time out is largely confined to the long-term prison population, roughly half the overall prison population in that country, who are Dutch by birth or adoption, or who, as foreigners, have five-year residency permits. As roughly one-third of this sector have foreign nationality, of whom only a small number have the necessary residency, the exclusion of this group from home leave arrangements is clearly of quite major significance. At least one of the British prisoners intended to challenge the exclusionary workings of this rule. Nevertheless, the system was otherwise seen and praised by them as *the* cardinal feature of the greater commitment of the Dutch system to prisoners' welfare: 'There is a striking amount of home leave for the Dutch, and this is a good thing. I was never allowed out at Leyhill even when near the end of my sentence. Here, they let you go out for home leave so you have something to go out to. There, you are completely cut off [in England]. Here, you are still a member of society.' It is normal for 60 hours' home leave to be granted every eight weeks in the long-term institutions. In addition, 'interruptions' may be allowed, that is, breaks in the sentence for welfare reasons but which, unlike home leave, do not count as time served.

Another issue in terms of relative deprivation is the refusal of the relevant Dutch authorities to allow foreign prisoners the alternative sanction of TBR—indefinite stay in the closed mental hospitals for offenders which offer therapeutic regimes of varying sorts. Biennial reviews are mandatory for offenders kept in TBR institutions. The main reason given for the general exclusion of foreign offenders from TBR is that therapy would be unduly inhibited by lack of mastery of the Dutch language. None of those interviewed had sought TBR but the case of Alan Reeve (1983) was cited as an example of a prisoner who might more appropriately be placed in such an institution. (Reeve was the only British prisoner in The Netherlands whom I was informally refused permission to interview. The extent to which his then recent hunger strike was connected with that decision, and with the TBR issue, is unknown.)

The imprisonment of women could not be contrasted in the same way as that of the men. There were no British women prisoners in Dutch jails at the time of the interviews. One Irish woman prisoner, who had no prior experience of the criminal justice system in any country, stated that the situation for women differed for the worse from that for men since her entire sentence had to be served in the only closed prison for women in Amsterdam. Also, whereas key decisions about such issues as home leave were taken locally for men, and only exceptionally referred to the Ministry of Justice in The Hague, in the case of women the site of decision-making was much more likely to be The Hague. Four Dutch women prisoners were interviewed in an English training prison, and their views on the similarities and differences between the two systems corresponded broadly with those of the men.

Recidivism and deterrence

Considerations of recidivism and deterrence loom large in the minds of those concerned with criminal justice policy, in part because 'public opinion' and political representatives alike tend to make a commonsensical link betwen harsh penalties and effective deterrence. Such considerations tend to have been more prominent in Britain than in The Netherlands until the very recent past. As stated above (pp. 118–19), direct comparisons of recidivism rates are not possible, since such data are not routinely available in The Netherlands. (60 per cent is the rate given for the whole sample, 66 per cent for the sample excluding those convicted of serious traffic offences; see van der Werff 1978: 10, 28). This one comparison, however, suggests that Dutch reconviction rates are no higher, and may be lower, than those for England.

Crime rates offer a problem-strewn check on the effectiveness of penal policy for reasons which are by now amply documented (see, for example, Bottomley and Coleman 1981; Carr-Hill and Stern 1979). Victim surveys do confirm the official statistical view that crime has increased in the post-war period, though they provide a cross-check only for the past 12 years in The Netherlands and the past 3 years in Britain (van Dijk and Steinmetz 1980, Hough and Mayhew 1985). But they usually chart both a far greater incidence of crime than the official figures, along with a slower rate of increase, in part due to changes in public reporting and police recording practices. Raw crime rates show a broad parallelism in trends between the two countries over the past three decades, with that in Britain rising relatively faster in the first half of the period, that in The Netherlands 'catching up' in the second half. The great bulk of both rates remain petty property crime. It may be that drug and drug-related offences have contributed to the relatively greater increase in standard crime rates in The Netherlands than in England, though the situation in England may have changed significantly in that respect over the past four or five years; whereas serious offences against public order have been relatively more marked in the recent past in England by comparison with The Netherlands. Again, however, it would be rash to link the trends in crime to differences in sentencing severity and penal harshness.

The easy assumption that longer sentences necessarily spell more deterrence was challenged by one young British prisoner, who argued in effect for the view that long sentences entail 'prisonization' and subsequent recidivism, whereas shorter sentences do not automatically mean painless confinement:

> Twenty-one months is enough for me. Just not having your freedom, just being away from your wife and kids, it's killing me. More than 5, 10 and so on, it's giving no-one a chance. So it's well and truly enough for me—I don't want to be locked away again. It's completely cured me, and it's humane here. In an English prison, I'd probably be full of hate and want to get back at the system. Here brings it home to you even more. Three in a cell in England, there's no way you can think, it's just down to survival. Here I've got a cell to myself, all the comforts of home *except* your family and freedom—that really brings it home to you. When I ring home, I just want to crawl down the phone. Dogs barking, kids shouting—it brings it all home to you.

Despite the elements of overstatement in that account, it manages to specify how tough measures can simply lead to desensitization, and so-called soft measures to a more acute sense of the fundamental reality of imprisonment, the loss of liberty and personal relationships. Nor are the measures that keep such relationships alive all that costly: the annual costs of the prison system per capita (of the population) are estimated to be 114 per cent higher in England than The Netherlands, and 144 per cent higher as a proportion of the GNP (Netherlands, Ministry of Justice 1984*b*: 77).

Finally, an attempt was made to tap reasons for British offenders in The Netherlands, and Dutch offenders in Britain, having come to commit their offences abroad. The Netherlands may have come to experience, in the criminal justice sphere, some of the problems associated with 'socialism in one country'.[4] How far does its relative leniency in punishment, especially in the drug

[4] The reference is to the debate associated with Stalin and Trotsky in the 1920s: Stalin argued that 'socialism in one country' was possible despite capitalist encirclement, Trotsky that the first priority was that revolutionary struggle in other countries should be actively promoted, or the gains of the Revolution would be undermined by such encirclement. Needless to say, Stalin won.

field, attract career criminals from other countries? When asked why they had come to The Netherlands in the first place, not one prisoner replied in terms of instrumental planning for lighter sentences. They had come looking for work, had stayed on, and had subsequently become involved in the drug scene; or they had come to The Netherlands to buy drugs for use and/or sale in England, but without knowing that sentences may be lighter; in one case, fear of reconviction for cannabis use in England led to the move; in another case, the prisoner had left Britain having skipped bail and needed to stay abroad. In some cases, an initial attraction to the general ambience and drug scene in Amsterdam played a role; but in no case did penal policy as such figure explicitly in the process.

The Dutch offenders, who were all in prison for smuggling drugs into Britain, had not been deterred by the tougher sentencing. In some cases, they had not realized sentences *were* tougher; the rest thought the risk had been worth it. Two women had been arrested at Heathrow Airport where they had simply been in transit to Schiphol with a large consignment of cannabis intended for The Netherlands. Quite what we are doing hauling Dutch nationals off Schiphol-bound planes instead of wiring suspicions to the Dutch Customs at their destination is an open question. But as one was a single parent with two children under 18 (one only 10), for whom imprisonment outside The Netherlands was singularly cruel, it seems an aspect of policy long overdue for change. It is also clear that drug traffickers target novices to do their dirty work for them, people without a record whom they hope will be waved through at Customs. The pool of such novices is vast, and it would need truly draconian sentences to filter through to that level abroad with any deterrent effect.

Discussion

The experience of imprisonment varies in terms of depth as well as length. Comparative work on the subject has tended to concentrate on length, in part because it lends itself to quantitative analysis. Recent work on social control trends has focused on its *breadth*, ways in which the 'carceral society' is generated by the permeation of disciplinary modes of supervision by 'penal agents' throughout non-custodial community-based forms of correction (Foucault 1979; Garland and Young 1983; Cohen 1985). The bleakest view of the future of social control is offered by Cohen's depiction of a remorseless increase in the extent of and correlation between the length, depth, and breadth of imprisonment.

The difficulties of comparing whole societies in terms of their 'carcerality' has been discussed above (Ch. 3). However, the extent of the penetration of penal control into civil society may be more concisely addressed in terms of such indicators as the numbers and percentages of ex-prisoners recalled to custody for breach of parole; the volume and character of conditions attached to parole; the scale of imprisonment for breach of non-custodial penalties, such as the fine or probation; and the extent to which penal agents continue to exercise supervision over the lives of those released from custody above and beyond normal limits, e.g. over 'lifers' released on licence in England. Though no attempt has been made here to contrast the two systems in terms of such indicators of the 'breadth' of imprisonment, and even allowing for the extension of control implicit in the 'call-up' system of awaiting a prison place, it is most probable that penal control in The Netherlands is less constraining in these respects than is the case in Britain in general, or England in particular.

The Netherlands has traditionally offered an alternative way forward, one which embraced a 'reductionist' approach to all forms of penality (Rutherford 1984). Recent developments in The Netherlands, however, suggest that even there the early 1980s have been something of a watershed in penal policy. Sentence lengths are creeping up; the prison population is likely to double in the decade 1980–90, and prison capacity is being increased to accommodate it (though the latest official projections, as shown in Fig. 1.1, suggest a lower increase, to 5,900 rather than 7,000 by 1990); staffing ratios are being reduced, implicitly threatening the relatively humane character of the regimes; and Community Service Orders have been introduced to divert offenders from custody, a measure which in Britain has tended to supplement rather than displace imprisonment for a significantly large proportion of offenders. It remains the case, however, that on the three indicators of length, breadth, and depth, The Netherlands, even by 1990, on present trends, will remain substantially less carceral a society than Britain and the great majority of other industrial societies.

In conclusion, all prisoners interviewed expressed a clear and strong preference for the Dutch system over that of England and (where it had been experienced) Scotland. The only exception to that opinion concerned a reversal of preferences at the pre-charge stage of remand in custody. The depth of imprisonment in The Netherlands is markedly shallower than that in Britain; the length of prison sentences is substantially shorter (Tulkens 1979, Hulsman, *et al.* 1978, Downes 1982) and the breadth of imprisonment remains prima facie less developed than that in Britain. If the prisoners' voice counts for anything in the debate on crime and punishment, it is at one with those who argue that the benefits of reductionist policies tangibly outweigh the as yet undemonstrated costs.

References

BAGLEY, C. (1973). *The Dutch Plural Society.* Oxford: University Press.

BALLANTYNE, A. (1988). 'Warning of Violence at Remand Centre', *Guardian,* 9 Jan.

BIANCHI, H. (1975). 'Social Control and Deviance in The Netherlands', in his (co-ed) *Deviance and Control in Europe.* London: Wiley.

BLUMSTEIN, A., and COHEN, J. (1973). 'A Theory of the Stability of Punishment', *Journal of Criminal Law and Criminology* 64: 198–207.

BOTTOMS, A. E., (1983). 'Neglected Features of Contemporary Penal Systems'. in Garland, D., and Young, P. (eds.) 1983.

BRYANT, C. G. A. (1981). 'Depillarisation in The Netherlands', *British Journal of Sociology* 22:56–74.

BUIKHUISEN, W. and DIJK, J. J. M. van (1975). *Official Police Reporting of Criminal Offences.* The Hague: Research and Documentation Centre, Ministry of Justice.

BULMER, M. (1985). *The Chicago School.* Chicago University Press.

CHAN, J. B. L., and ERICSON, R. V. (1981). *Decarceration and the Economy of Penal Reform,* Toronto: University of Toronto, Centre of Criminology Research Report 14.

COHEN, S. (1979). 'The Punitive City', *Contemporary Crises* 3: 339–63

COHEN, S. (1985). *Visions of Social Control.* Cambridge: Polity Press.

COHEN, S., and TAYLOR, L. (1972). *Psychological Survival.* Harmondsworth: Penguin.

DIEDERIKS, H. (1981). 'Punishment During the Ancien Regime: The During the Ancien Regime: The Dutch Case', in *Criminal Justice History:* An International Annual, Vol. 1. New York.

DONZELOT, J. (1979). *The Policing of Families.* London: Hutchinson.

DURKHEIM, E. ([1895],trans. 1952). *The Rules of Sociological Method.* London: Routledge and Kegan Paul.

EMMERIK, J. L. van (1982). *Detained at the Govemment's Pleasure.* The Hague: WODC.

ERIKSON, K. (1966). *Wayward Puritans.* New York: Wiley.

FOUCAULT, M. (1977). *Discipline and Punish,* Harmondsworth: Penguin.

GARLAND, D. (1981). 'The Birth of the Welfare Sanction', *British foumal of Law and Society,* 8: 29–45.

GARLAND, D. (1985). *Punishment and Welfare: A History of Penal Strategies.* Aldershot: Gower.

GARLAND, D.. and YOUNG, P., eds., (1983) *The Power to Punish.* London: Heinemann.

HAAN, W. DE. (1986). 'Abolitionism and the Politics of Bad Conscience', 157–77 in Bianchi, H., and van Swaaningen, R. (eds.) *Abolitionism: Towards a Non-repressive Approach to Crime.* Proceedings of the Second International Conference on Prison Abolition. Amsterdam: Free University Press.

HULSMAN, L. H. C., BEERLING, H. W. R., and DIJK, E. van (1978). 'The Dutch Criminal justice System from a Comparative Legal Perspective', in Fokkema, D. C., *et al* (eds.) *Introduction to Dutch Law for Foreign Lawyers,* Netherlands: Kluwer.

IGNATIEFF, M. (1978). *A Just Measure of Pain: The Penitentiary in the Industrial Revolution 1750–1850.* London: Macmillan.

JOHNSON, E. H. and HEIJDER, A. (1983). 'The Dutch Deemphasise Imprisonment: A Sociocultural and Structural Explanation'. *IntemationalJoumal of Comparative and Applied Justice* 7: 3–19.

JOWELL, R., WITHERSPOON S., and BROOK, L., eds. (1986). *British Social Attitudes: The* 1986 *Report.* Aldershot: Gower.

KELK, C. (1983). 'The Humanity of the Dutch Prison System and the Prisoners' Consciousness of their Legal Rights', *Contemporary Crises* 7: 155–70.

KING, R., and MORGAN, R. (1976). *CA Taste of Prison: Custodial Conditions for Trial and Remand Prisoners.* London: Routledge and Kegan Paul.

KING, R., and MORGAN, R. (1980). *The Future of the Prison System.* Farnborough: Gower.

KOENRADT, F. (1983). 'Forensic Psychiatric Expertise and Enforced Treatment in The Netherlands', *Contemporary Crises* 7: 171–82.

LIJPHART, A. (1975). *The Politics of Accommodation* (2nd. rev. edn.) Berkeley and Los Angeles: University of California Press.

MATHIESEN, T. (1965). *The Defences of the Weak.* London: Tavistock.

MATHIESEN, T. (1983). 'The Future of Control Systems: The Case of Norway', in Garland, D., and Young, (eds.) 1983.

MOEDIKDO, P. (1976). 'De Utrechtse school van Pompe, Baan en Kempe', in Kelk, C. *et al.* (eds.), *Recht, Macht en Manipulatie.* Utrecht and Antwerp: Uitgeverij Het Spectrum.

MORRIS, P. (1969). *Put Away.* London: Routledge and Kegan Paul.

NETHERLANDS, MINISTRY OF JUSTICE (1977). *Detention at the Government's Pleasure: Treatment of Criminal Psychopaths in The Netherlands.* The Hague: State Publications.

NETHERLANDS, MINISTRY OF JUSTICE (1984). *Interimrapport van de Commissie Kleine Criminaliteit* (Interim report of the Committee on Petty Crime). [The Roethof Committee Report.]. The Hague: State Publications.

NETHERLANDS, MINISTRY OF JUSTICE (1985c). Structuurplan Penitentiaire Capaciteit: Rapport van de projectgroep ingesteld bij beschikking DD. 8. Nov. 1984 van deStaatssecretaris van Justitie (Plan for the Construction of Penal Capacity: Report of the project group established on 8 Nov. 1984 on behalf of the Secretary of State for Justice). The Hague: State Publications.

O'CONNOR; J. (1973). *The Fiscal Crisis of the State.* New York: St Martin's Press.

RADZINOWICZ, L. (1966). *Ideology and Crime: A Study of Crime in its Social and Historical Context.* London: Heinemann.

RICHARDSON, G. (1985). 'Judicial Intervention in Prison Life', in Maguire, M., Vagg, J., and Morgan, R. (eds.), *Accountability and Prisons.* London: Tavistock.

ROCK, P. E. (1979). *The Making of Symbolic Interactionism.* London: Macmillan.

ROTHMAN, D. J. (1971). *The Discovery of the Asylum,* Boston, Mass.: Little, Brown.

RULLER, S. van (1981). 'Het aantal gevangenen in Nederland sinds 1837: Een analyse van 140 jaar gevangenisstatistieken' (The number of prisoners in The Netherlands since 1837: An analysis of 140 years' imprisonment statistics), *TijdschriJt voor criminologie* 23: 209–23.

RUSCHE, G. and KIRCHHEIMER, O. (1939). *Punishment and Social Structure.* New York: Columbia University Press.

Rutherford, A. ([1984] [1986a]) *Prisons and the Process of Justice.* London: Heinemann and Oxford: Oxford University Press.

Rutherford, A. (1986b). *Growing out of Crime.* Harmondsworth: Penguin.

Scull, A. (1977). *Decarceration: Community Treatment and The Deviant.* Englewood Cliffs, N. J.: Prentice-Hall.

Sharples, K. S. (1972). *The Legal Framework of Judicial Sentencing Policy.* Amsterdam: University Press.

Spierenburg, P. (1986). 'Deviance and Repression in The Netherlands: Historical Evidence and Contemporary Problems', *Historische socialforschung* 37: 4–16.

Steenhuis, D. W. (1977). *General Deterrence and Drunken Driving.* The Hague: Research and Documentation Centre, Ministry of Justice.

Stern, V. (1987). *Bricks of Shame: Britain's Prisons.* Harmondsworth: Penguin.

Stolwijk, S. A. M. (1986). 'Alternatives to Custodial Sentences', in Dijk, J. J. M. van *et al* (eds.), 1986.

Townsend, P. (1963). *The Last Refuge.* London: Routledge and Kegan Paul.

Vinson, T. (1985). *Impressions of the Dutch Prison System.* The Hague: WODC.

Wootton, B. (1978). *Crime and the Penal System.* London: Allen and Unwin.

Zoomer, O. (1979). *Sanctioning in Cases of Serious Offence.* The Hague: Research and Documentation Centre, Ministry of Justice.

[10]
Employment Schemes for Offenders

1. Introduction

The research upon which this report is based was commissioned by Manchester University and funded by the Home Office Police Research Group, to investigate public violence and its prevention on two local authority housing estates – one in London and the other on Merseyside. The focus of the research was on the prevention of repeat violent victimisation. As the work progressed, racial attacks emerged as requiring urgent attention on the London estate whilst domestic violence was a pressing problem on Merseyside. As a consequence, ideas on the prevention of 'street crime' which this report addressed were not developed. This report is the first part of a longer study of the two estates which may be published on completion of crime prevention projects now underway in those areas.

Its basic themes are long familiar to criminologists from the work of anomie and subcultural theorists between the 1930s and the 1970s (see, in particular, Cloward and Ohlin, 1960; and Downes, 1966). However, the basic idea underlying this report drew on the work of Elliot Currie in the United States who traces the social sources of crime from the 1920s onwards and relates them to contemporary violence and argues, on the basis of existing research, that imaginative and comprehensively conceived programmes of social and economic change can, and have, lowered levels of violence (Currie 1985). Innovative employment schemes at a local level are one such strategy. There is a general and growing interest in employment schemes for offenders and it was thought helpful to make this report more widely available.

The first section of the report describes the relationship between crime rates and trends and employment variables, and establishes that there is a link, be it complex and indirect rather than simple and direct. The dynamics of crime–employment relationships are still, basically, far from clear. Nevertheless, enough is known to make these relationships deserve far higher priority than has previously been the case. The second section identifies the possible crime reduction constituents of employment schemes based on fieldwork undertaken in 1990/91 which examined some employment schemes for offenders operating at that time.

2. Employment and crime

The relationships between crime and employment have been researched in a number of ways. The standard approach is to test for positive links between *un*employment and crime rates. Such studies have led to conflicting conclusions: some have observed no crime–unemployment links whilst others claimed to have established a clear causal relationship. Another, and perhaps more promising approach is to relate crime to the *quality* of employment and neighbourhood factors. This research has mainly taken place in America and shows that the type of work, the dynamics of the local labour market and the social and economic infrastructure are better predictors of the crime–employment relationship. These two types of studies will be discussed in greater detail below.

Unemployment and crime

The standard approach in relating crime in general to employment variables is to test for positive links between *un*employment and crime rates. Three types of analysis have been adopted: cross–sectional, relating crime and unemployment rates across areas at the same point in time; trend data, using time series for one or more countries or other geographical bases; and individually based data, comparing the behaviour of particular persons when in and out of work. All three sorts of evidence have yielded seemingly inconsistent results, though the overall tendency is for *some* sort of link to be found between crime and unemployment. For example, Steven Box concluded a cross–sectional survey in England with the statement: 'Since these results are lagged, ie measuring unemployment at the end of the year preceding the one in which these crimes were recorded, there is a temporal sequence built into the analysis, and this supports the view that unemployment is causally linked to crime levels.' (Box, 1987, p.85). The strongest correlations were between unemployment rates and rates of burglary and violence against the person, both of which were statistically significant,[1] suggesting a rough equivalence in impact even on such different types of crime.

By contrast, in a time series analysis, Simon Field (1990) found striking differences between the two major types of crime, those against property and against the

[1] The level of statistical significance used throughout this paper is 5%.

person, and consumption growth rates (rather than unemployment). During periods of rapid personal consumption growth, property crime tends to grow relatively slowly, or even fall, whilst crimes against the person grow relatively quickly, and vice versa. For example, rising consumption, drinking in pubs and clubs, and violence are plausibly strong correlates. Field's work shows personal consumption to be a better predictor of crime trends than unemployment; it sharpens our understanding of why full employment is no panacea for violence – that the 1960s as well as the 1930s were periods of rising crime rates; and that we need to dig deeper if we are to grasp the complex relations between crime, including violence, and unemployment.

The work of David Farrington (1986) and others exemplifies the third approach based on an analysis of individual cases. Data from the early 1970s showed that youth were significantly more involved in delinquency when out of work than in work. Though the basis for linking crime and unemployment emerges clearly, the context of the times was one of relatively full employment. Dropping in and out of work was then a more voluntary activity than in more recent times of endemically high rates of youth unemployment, which could prove more criminogenic.

Why this might be so is well documented in the work of Parker, Bakx and Newcombe (1988) and Geoffrey Pearson (1987). During the 1980s, 'hard' drug use began to pervade the most socially deprived areas. Parker's team established beyond reasonable doubt that a 'new to crime' group had resulted from the need to finance heroin use which, combined with the prolonged and intensified criminal careers of already delinquent users, accounted for higher rates of property crime. 'The "extra" crime the Wirral has experienced in recent years appears to be closely related to the community's heroin 'epidemic'" (p.104). The exceptionally high rise in the crime rate in the Wirral of 113% between 1979–86, compared with 46% for Liverpool as a whole and 40% for England and Wales, is linked with the drugs problem by the especially high rates of acquisitive crimes such as burglary and theft from cars. Since a survey of known users revealed that 87% relied on illegal means of financing the habit, the causal links between heroin use and crime could hardly be more graphically established.

Though heroin use was by no means confined to the inner cities, or uniformly present there, experience in such areas as the Wirral on Merseyside and declining manufacturing centres such as Bradford confirmed the view that 'high unemployment serves to foster drug use' (Parker *et al*, p.25). The ten townships in the Wirral with the highest rates of known opioid use (av. 0.7%) had a mean unemployment rate of 20%. The nine with a zero opioid problem had a much lower unemployment rate of six per cent (p.19). The 'new' heroin users of the 1980s were typically young, aged 16–18, unemployed, usually male, single, living with their families in a socially deprived neighbourhood, with few or no qualifications, on a 0.25 to 0.5 gram a day habit costing £20–£35 a day (mid–1980s prices), and smoking rather than injecting the drug.

Whilst the above studies have found *some* sort of link between crime and unemployment the links are more likely to be various, mediated and indirect than simple and direct. Indeed one study found no connection (Carr–Hill and Stern, 1979). As Brake and Hale (1992, pp. 112–13) point out, this work, based on sophisticated techniques, has been influential in refuting the links between crime and unemployment. Census data were combined with other cross–section information for the years 1961, 1966 and 1971, and econometric techniques were used to estimate an independent model of crime rates and police activity. However, Hakim (1982) re–analysed the data and found that 'the results .... confirm the association between crime and unemployment, and suggest it has been increasing over time' (p.453). The reason for the conflicting conclusions is because:

> a careful reading of this study (Carr–Hill and Stern) shows that the authors never carried out the test in question .... but instead test the contribution of unemployment to explaining the number of police *per capita* in each area. In effect the authors reject the hypothesis about unemployment contributing to crime on theoretical (or subjective) grounds, but they imply that they tested it fully. However, they are unable to sidestep the results that show that areas with a high proportion of young men aged 15–24 years and a high proportion of the working class have significantly higher crime rates – both these groups have the highest levels of unemployment experiences.
>
> (Hakim 1982: 452)

Carr–Hill and Stern were also concerned to establish that the orthodox use of officially recorded crime rates confounded the relationship between unemployment and crime, since the unemployed are more at risk of police attention, and since police numbers are highly correlated with high crime rates.

However, at least one study based on victim survey data – which avoids this problem – has found that the probability of burglary and household theft victimisation increased with the rate of local unemployment (Sampson and Wooldredge 1987). In sum, there are decreasing grounds for regarding the Carr–Hill and Stern study as a conclusive refutation of the linkages between crime and unemployment. Much more work is, however, clearly needed to explore what forms and sequences of unemployment are most likely to generate increasing crime. Little work exists on *types* of unemployment and specific forms of victimisation. Long–term youth unemployment and 'never having been employed' may be far more criminogenic than short–term intervals between high quality jobs.

The quality of employment, neighbourhood factors and crime

American work by Elliot Currie (1985), Richard McGahey (1986) and Mercer Sullivan (1984, 1989) suggests there is a *triple* effect of unemployment on crime: firstly, high rates of long–term unemployment in particular undermine and destabilise communities, weakening informal social controls against crime; secondly, desistance from crime is strongly associated with finding stable jobs of sufficient income and quality to support a family, and unemployment adversely affects all these processes; and thirdly, unemployment opens up a void in people's lives that facilitates a drift into delinquency and drug use, which in turn demoralise communities further.

Given the potency of these processes, why is it that far stronger and more consistent correlations have not been found to link crime and unemployment? The answer lies partly in the vagaries of what officially constitutes unemployment (those concerning crime are far better known). Unemployment may be short, medium or long–term; it may be voluntary or enforced; it may hide considerable undeclared economic activity (Henry, 1978) – though most studies suggest that it is the employed and more affluent who benefit from the 'hidden economy' (Pahl, 1987). Similarly, jobs may be short–term, 'dead–end' and badly paid; or jobs may flow from explosive commercial and industrial developments which strain communities. For these reasons, the main links with crime are to be found in the quality of work and under–employment rather than official unemployment rates (Currie, 1985, Ch 4). Currie (1985), McGahey (1986) and Sullivan (1984, 1989) all suggest a direct link between unemployment and crime is less clearly established than important indirect relations between the extent and *quality* of employment and the extent and severity of income–related crimes (for example, street robbery) for various groups.

In one of the rare studies to examine such relationships in a quantitative way (Allan and Steffensmeier, 1989), labour market effects on arrest rates are shown to differ for juveniles and young adults, groups which are usually clumped together for such statistical purposes. The *availability* of employment produces strong effects on juvenile arrest rates: full–time employment is associated with low arrest rates, *un*employment with high arrest rates. In the case of young adults, by contrast, high arrest rates are associated with *low quality* employment, as measured by inadequate pay and hours. The authors stress that correlation does not equal cause at an individual level (the ecological fallacy), ie. these findings should not be taken to imply that under–employed young adults are necessarily the ones committing crimes or being arrested. Rather, the labour market 'climate' establishes conditions that may be conducive to law–abiding or criminal behaviour in the population at large.

The important implications are that, for juveniles aged 14–17, for whom work is part–time, voluntary activity to provide largely recreational goods and services, *any* job will do. However, by the age of 18–24, work of *some* quality is the main requirement for self–support let alone that of a family. Providing more dead–end jobs is *not* the answer for this group, who will only 'mature out of' delinquency if they have a reasonable prospect of decently rewarded work to aim for. 'The most viable policy is one that produces more jobs for teenagers while simultaneously providing better paid, higher quality jobs for young adults.' Our failure to do so goes far towards explaining the lack of success in many training and job–provision schemes for offenders which lack this progression.

The difference between holding a succession of dead–end, secondary labour market jobs and having a stable, primary labour market job is a principal reason for the imperfect relationship between crime and unemployment. High quality employment also reduces income inequalities, a major correlate of high crime rates (Braithwaite, 1979), and buttresses family and community cohesion. 'Poverty itself is less clearly significant as a factor in high crime rates than is inequality between the races and between the affluent and the poor...Harsh inequalities in living standards in both 'developing' and developed countries are closely associated with high levels of violence' (Currie and Skolnick, 1988). In his analysis of the results of one of the best conceived and executed studies of crime and economic conditions, the massive Vera Institute of Justice ethnographic work in three lower–class New York neighbourhoods, McGahey (1986) draws on the work of Sullivan (1984, 1989) and others to document how central the local labour market is to an understanding of the economy and character of crime in Brooklyn. The core of his analysis is that white youths had access to work in primary labour market jobs through family networks. Lacking family members with such contact, black and hispanic youths lost out in the competition for high quality employment. As a consequence, the delinquent careers of the white youths were shorter lived and less predatory than those of the non–whites, who resorted more frequently to robbery and drug dealing for income support.

While informal networks may help determine who gets which job in a given local labour market, they do not generate *more* jobs. Moreover, although better and more employment may be a pre–condition for lasting community crime reduction, it is clearly not the whole story. Especially in the worst hit areas, which have tipped from moderate to severe levels of crime, the erosion of stable employment of any sort not only promotes but is exacerbated by the weakening of key social institutions. The reality and fear of crime can drain communities of jobs, through the loss of retail shops, small firms and the impoverisation of services. Sullivan (1984, 1989) documents the rapidly dwindling commercial sector in a high–crime Brooklyn neighbourhood. In a review of federally sponsored programmes to prevent violent juvenile crime in a number of high–crime, inner–city areas across the US, Fagan (1987) concluded that social and institutional factors were as crucial as economic conditions in the three (out of six) areas where violence was reduced.

Some 10 years ago, Roger Tarling (1982) concluded a rigourous review of the evidence on crime and employment as follows:

> Since crime goes up during periods of low unemployment and many crimes are committed by people in employment or of school age, it is clear that unemployment is not the sole determinant, or even the major determinant of crime. Against this, and despite the caveats that can be made in connection with the aggregate studies discussed, some evidence of a relationship persists, suggesting that unemployment is a factor in the causation of crime, although it may not be a major factor; furthermore it appears to be inter–related in some complex way with other aspects of economic disadvantage or social deprivation.

> It seems unlikely that additional aggregate studies would clarify the issues. The studies of individuals, on the other hand, are more promising but such studies are few and in their infancy ... (p.32)

Although a handful of later aggregate studies *have* clarified the central issues, Tarling has proved prescient in emphasising the main direction fresh research would take. Ethnographic studies, mainly in the USA but also in Britain, have greatly increased our understanding of the causal links between labour markets, crime and inequalities of employment. Practical steps to resolve the problems thus raised are more the exception than the rule, and it is to those that we now turn.

3. Employment schemes for offenders

Neal Shover's study of *Aging Criminals* (1985) found two critical career points in typical offender life cycles: first, the transition from late adolescence to early adulthood, at which the decision to move from the excitement–oriented phase of delinquency to a more risk–laden commitment to adult crime is taken; and secondly, the onset of middle age, at which failing powers might prove decisive in dropping out of crime for which nerve and strength are essential. At both stages, argues Shover, a more or less rational weighing–up of the costs and benefits takes place. It is at these points that offering offenders tangible benefits for desistance should have maximum potency.

Employment training schemes might well be of tangible benefit to offenders, either in these two age groups or in general. Yet, despite the best efforts of such helping agencies as NACRO and APEX, and a small number of probation services around the country, no coherent policy or framework appears to exist to promote such endeavours in relation to offenders. It may well be that, as Crow and others point out, the often inconclusive nature of the evidence linking crime and unemployment, and the negligible evidence of success in reducing reconviction where such schemes have been mounted, feeds into the 'nothing works' perspective which has dominated criminal justice studies since the mid–1970s.

Three studies which reinforced these views were those by Soothill (1974, 1981) and that by Corden, Kuipers and Wilson (1978). In his carefully controlled study, Soothill found almost identical reconviction rates for both a group assisted by APEX in finding employment and a group who were not. He concluded that 'It is the exception rather than the rule for the finding of employment *in isolation* to modify an ex–prisoner's subsequent criminal pattern ..... What this study means in a wider framework is that one should abandon a belief in a single or simple solution for the after–care of prisoners.' (*op.cit.*, pp.25/29, quoted in Haines, 1990, p.21, emphasis added). A later study of white–collar offenders proved less pessimistic, though limited reductions in reconvictions for those helped in job placements were offset by the costs in time and resources of finding jobs for just over a third of the sample – the rest did not ask for Apex help or could not be placed. The study by Corden, Kuipers and Wilson (1978) found that 53% of ex–prisoners studied found no work at all and, of the rest, the great majority did so with help from friends, family or previous employers rather than from the Department of Employment, or intervention from probation officers – and this at a time of growing but far lower rates of unemployment than today. They concluded that 'the Probation Service and Prison Welfare Officers should concentrate on helping prisoners to maintain these informal links during their sentence, since they seem to be so much more successful than official agencies in this sphere.' (*op.cit.*, p.42) These studies provided an understandable rationale for the low priority accorded by probation officers to assisting offenders in the search for employment in the 1980s.

The positive aspects of these studies therefore emphasise the importance of social networks and the community context if the employment prospects of offenders are to be enhanced. The importance of the social situation or community to which the released prisoner returns is further demonstrated by contrasting programmes which aim to reintegrate prisoners into society with those which do not have such an aim. Programmes which are essentially institutionally focused, i.e. they make no attempt to change the social situation of the offender and do not build on links with the wider community, for example, Fowles (1978) on prison welfare treatment, Hood (1966) on after–care pre–planning and Sinclair and Snow (1971) on hostels, all fail to show any positive programme effects in terms of reduced levels of offending (but see Shaw, 1974). Whereas programmes which are essentially community focused (Bernstsen and Christiansen 1965; Fair 1988; Le Clair 1988; and Miller 1964) are able to demonstrate 'clear programme benefits of reduced recidivism.' (Haines, pp. 35–6). In the present context of higher rates of unemployment, it is even more vital to generate community–level employment training and job creation schemes which help sustain the social networks on which offenders rely so heavily, and to foster such links for those who experience social isolation.

There are, however, fewer employment–related schemes for offenders than might be supposed, especially after a decade of pioneering work by NACRO, APEX and other agencies in establishing and developing them in the 1980s. Between 1984 and 1986, NACRO ran 150 schemes for some 20,000 people (Crow *et al*, Ch 4). Yet employment is far less of a priority for most probation services than is conventionally assumed. Crow states that probation officers were sufficiently opposed to the nature of the national Youth Training Scheme (YTS) and the

Community Programme (CP) for adults to reduce referrals even to the 'user–friendly' NACRO versions. 'Referrals originating from probation and social services staff declined consistently over a period of years... Probation referrals fell from 33% during YOP (the earlier Youth Opportunities Programme) in 1982–3 to 14% during 1985–6' (pp97–8). This led to a reduction in the proportion of young offenders among those joining the schemes from around 70% in 1983–4 to under 60% in 1985 to under 50% in 1986. It is now even more likely that probation staff will oppose referrals, since the very features of the YTS and CP schemes which they disliked – the loss of flexibility in the programmes which shut out the more disadvantaged and difficult entrants – seems to have been reinforced by the current move to shift what since 1988 has been called Employment Training (ET) to the employer–led Training Enterprise Councils (TECs) (Jackson, 1991).

Training managers most involved with schemes for offenders have voiced anxieties about the likely impact on existing programmes. John Lowe, of Beaver Workshop, stated his growing concern as follows: 'Basically there has been a 30% reduction in funding but this has meant about a 40% reduction in places. The whole of the TECs' funding is now inclined towards those who are of employed status or "training ready" (ie well–motivated and with basic literacy, numeracy and communicative skills). This means that the programme is both reduced and not aimed at the long–term unemployed of which offenders (in the main) are part' (Lowe, personal communication, 4 February 1991). Programmes which have succeeded in establishing strong links with a sceptical probation service, the main source of their referrals, will thus face increasingly stringent criteria for funding.

Such pressures come at a time when the widespread lack of enthusiasm in the probation service for training programmes may be giving way to a readiness to explore options anew in principle if not in practice. This may develop further as a result of increasing encouragement by the Home Office for probation services to work in partnership with other agencies. The reasons for that lack of enthusiasm are complex. In the only systematic study of the issue, of the Hereford & Worcester Service, Diana Fulbrook (1990) concluded: 'The main finding was that probation officers do not engage with employment issues, seeing it as an area of role discretion rather than a prescribed priority. Whilst recognising the effects of unemployment on their clients, the tend to define problems in other ways, such as relationships, which they feel more comfortable with. There was a tendency to label clients as unemployable and to work reactively on the issue.' (p2). From interviews with several of the more experienced probation employment specialists in the country, in Nottingham, Birmingham and South–East London (a good scheme also reportedly exists in Northumbria), it is clear that this approach is not confined to Hereford and Worcester. No mention of employment was made in the statement of its aims and objectives by the Inner London Probation Service, for example. Yet the Service remains utterly central to any employment–related strategy for offenders released from custody as well as those subject to community–based sanctions.

None of which should be taken to imply that individual officers are simply indifferent to the employment needs of their clients; rather that such issues tend to be crowded out by the myriad pressures, such as the top priority given to social inquiry reports for the courts, that shape their work. So many offenders have chaotic and disorganised lives that the main priority in supervision is often to sort out accommodation and benefit problems and to address family and personal issues. Employment needs rank low, especially in an economy which, even before the current deep recession was running an unemployment rate of over three million in the mid–1980s. Yet where good local schemes exist, run by NACRO, APEX or other agencies, some officers will refer clients to them. The issue then becomes: what do the schemes have to offer the clients? What are their outcomes? And what examples of 'best practices' can be built on in the future? The following are among the more notable projects and agencies visited in the course of this research:

i. *Beaver Workshop, Nottingham*; founded in 1977, the scheme is funded by Nottingham Probation Service, and offers a 1 + 11 weeks initial assessment and multi–skills and employability training course based on woodworking. Almost entirely catering for probation and post–release referrals, some evaluation dating from the early 1980s (carried out by Nottingham University, Department of Social Administration) found that for a group whose average predicted reconviction rate was 67%, the actuality was 56% after a two–year follow–up. Almost all of the success rate was accounted for by under 21 year olds who completed the one–week assessment, but all groups performed slightly better than predicted despite the groups which went on to the full course having significantly greater problems.

The scale of the problem is shown by the far worse unemployment rate of 60–70% among clients, and over 80% among the 336 referrals to Beaver in 1990 compared with 10% for Notts as a whole. Over half, 55% in 1987, go on to jobs or further training, which is 'quite a high degree of success' given many have been written off as 'unemployable'. Also, any who start on probation with a job on offer would usually be encouraged to take it by officers and forgo training, despite the scheme's stress on employability rather than employment. But any job, even a dead–end one, would be pragmatically and practically defensible as a choice, not only for income reasons but also to break the long–term unemployment sequence. The Beaver scheme, however, sees probation officers as still too negative about training. Many referrals come from only one or two sources within a probation team. The crux of the scheme is to assess practical and basic educational skills and levels, mechanical knowledge and conceptual ability which produces greater motivation for basic training and the components for an individually–based skills programme, either in Beaver or in ET. It is a course with strong links to local training agencies and colleges of further education and would offer scope for up to 5 more full–time officers to be employed, especially in connection with post–release training. Its strength also lies in its stress on the 'personal touch', avoiding a 'processing' impersonality. This feature was picked up by the Nottingham University study which showed the whole experience had mattered to many; some still had Beaver materials with them after two years and valued them.

ii. *Rochdale Rework* is a scheme based on training in cabinet–making, upholstery and furniture restoration with an impressive record of training and crime reduction for heavy drug users. Rework began in the early 1980s as a probation–inspired community programme scheme sponsored by the Health Authority. Early attempts to work with drug users only, and on a drug–free basis, were soon changed to a mixed group, roughly half of whom were long–term unemployed non–drug users, and with a harm reduction methadone programme for users. The changes worked well. They stabilised the group and brought home to the drug users how many problems those *not* on drugs had got and avoided ghettoising them. Evaluation was limited to reconvictions during or soon after leaving or being dismissed from Rework. In 1987 of the 36 drug–takers in the project, 30 had previous convictions (15 with four or more convictions), and only seven reoffended. Since, at this stage of the project, regular urine testing took place, there were strong grounds for linking the low rate of reoffending with the much reduced heroin use (Council of Europe, 1987, p6). "Those who have completed the programme have avoided re–offending and only one trainee has so far offended whilst on the project" (Hyland and Underdown, 1988, p145). For a group whose violence was 'implosive' and who were so heavily damaged socially, the small workshop and training programme provided a unique facility, and one that encouraged a high level of input from probation officers. Special factors at this stage of the project were (a) the regular urine testing, and (b) its resource–intensive facilities and (c) its wages. Also, the therapeutic workshop enabled a group literally to reconstruct their own lives, even making their own furniture which, given their marked debts and poverty, they often lacked.

In 1989, the project closed due to Rochdale Council's objections to the changed structure of Employment Training and was restarted only when joint management by the Rochdale Training Association and Turning Point, a charity in the drugs and mental health field, was arranged, with funding from Safer Cities. The philosophy and approach is much the same, but as yet, fewer drug users than before are on the programme. Nevertheless, nine long–term users have been trained since late 1989, four with previous convictions. Generally a very non–violent group, their histories of car–theft and shop–lifting are impressive enough to show that the high–risk groups have not been abandoned. For example, a young adult female trainee, referred to the scheme by the Community Drugs Team (CDT), who have replaced probation as the main referral source, had been on over a gram of heroin/day, over a £100 a day habit, which led to her stealing a car a day; 40,000 cars were stolen in Greater Manchester in 1989, the highest rate for this offence in Europe! Her career at Rework had brought her off heroin via methadone, on a script so she no longer stole, and her children were properly looked after due to the project arranging a £50 a week child–minding grant. Another trainee, male aged 35, had become a supervisor–instructor at Rework; a long–term drug user since 22, multi–drug but mainly heroin, he had lost a good career in the furniture trade as the habit built up. Thieving out of desperation and physically unable to work, he was referred to Rework by the CDT. 'This place has done me a lot of good and has probably saved my life. I never thought I'd work again'. Time after time, in talking with offender trainees, the prime need to gain or recover the *self–confidence* to work, a point which is worn cliche–thin in texts and conferences, takes on real meaning; but only *after* experience on the right kind of programme, which includes exposure to genuine workshop life, can such inner confidence be restored or created.

iii. *Rhodes Probation Centre, Oldham* is a good example of a probation team which gives high priority to employment–related skills and problems, and is developing its own workshop resource for clients as well as pursuing inter–agency and job networking contacts, for example, by being represented on the Equal Opportunities Committee of the TEC. Only 33% of clients are in full–time work or training. An employment module has been developed as an option within the 30–day programme for unemployed clients on a 4(b) requirement. Forty went through the programme in 1990, of whom 19 found mainly unskilled jobs of a short–term kind, though only 4 are still in work and 3 in ET, which is unpopular in general, not just with offenders. It would be premature to judge the success of the programme on these results, which tend to reproduce a short–term, unskilled work pattern since the full programme is still being developed. A setback has been the closure of open courses in, for example, car repair and sheet metal work which the local Technical College ran until late 1990. Now Technical Colleges are so geared to higher skills levels that access for clients is difficult, even where they have had good skills training before. Hence the need to build up on–site facilities to provide workshop skills, as well as tackling self–presentation and confidence in chasing and retaining jobs. It is too soon to say how far the Oldham team can make good the lack of provision elsewhere in a high unemployment area, but what can be learnt from Oldham is the potential for assembling the making of an impressive training programme even in a hostile economic climate.

iv. *Selcare/British Telecom Initiative, Manchester* is a training agency specialising in clients referred from probation and CDTs, mostly males aged 18–25. Underway for a year, results so far are promising: the project director stated that only six out of 250 trainees had re–offended during the 13–week training and assessment period, and none had dropped out. (Another 250 who made appointments did not show up, a kind of pre–entry drop–out rate. However, this is an unknown factor with all projects.) The programme comprises two weeks' initial assessment followed by skills training in one of two centres plus work tasters from 35–40 options with local employers, mostly small firms. The incentive for employers is that STEP (Selcare Pre–Employment Training Programme) pays the £2–3 hourly rate. One worker monitors each trainee's employer relationship and experience to guard against the 'cheap labour' danger. So far, 10% have gone into full–time jobs, 50% to ET for 12 months and 15% to Further Education or job clubs. Wages for ET are £28 for under 25s, £38 for over 25s + £10 + travel. The intake is from or via probation and it is estimated that four out of five trainees are offenders. Numeracy, literacy and computer and communicative skills etc are taught at the Victoria Park Centre, after which trainees progress to the Manley Park Centre for more focused training. Four out of five need some basic and social skills training which are important for 'employability'; for example, punctuality, self–presentation, self–discipline, and so on. The crux is to tailor the whole pre–employment programme to individual abilities and potential. Selcare is just the sort of well–conceived and yet caring training scheme now under severe pressure from the new changes in ET. The grant used to be paid if trainees went on to ET; work was a bonus. Now the Training Agencies have changed that and will pay STEP only if they get them into jobs!

> They count getting a job at MacDonalds as a success. We used to count a success as getting the right job for the individual, but we are being pushed into counting *any* old job as a success – like the old probation order used to stress the worst unskilled manual work as a job, coke shovelling, etc, which they would leave after four weeks. Unfortunately, legislation and the new TECs are pushing us back to what we are trying to get away from. Doing the right job reduces the anger, frustration and even violence offenders may produce if forced into the wrong work. We have got to change government thinking since we cannot survive on ET income (the British Telecom grant pays all the extras) and would have to move away from low achievers, our whole purpose.... Government should recognise the value of our work, the length of time it takes to pay off. The Training Agency is trying to cut us down to 6 weeks, and we are talking about people without any skills at all, whose years of education have basically failed, and the idea we can bring all this back in 6 weeks is just not on! ... Government money is moving up to those with skills who *can* get jobs, so it will be an easy success in numbers terms but at the expense of those at the bottom who are a much more difficult proposition... A lot of our people *have* been on schemes and not completed, roughly *half*; yet they stick with our scheme, and get on to ET schemes which they've walked out of before. But now we know from informal contact when they come back to see us that they've stuck them out for the full 12 months (worker).

v. *Hexagon Community (Liverpool)* is one of 60 Training Managers in Merseyside. Hexagon serves the Liverpool estate areas and offers training courses of a wide range for the long–term unemployed: computers/desktop publishing; admin/clerical; joinery/furniture making and restoration/french polishing and upholstery; painting and decorating; bricklaying; catering; floristry (one of only two courses in the North of England); industrial sewing; and warehousing, storage and distribution. It is currently training 225 men and women aged 18 and over, but cuts will reduce that to 190. The new ET performance funding was expected to force a greater selectivity in 1992 due to the high costs of training the 70% or so who are slow achievers.

> But when I talk of slow learners and low achievers, I am still talking about people with good practical skills who *can* get to the job stage with time. Hexagon takes all comers, including referrals from probation: they may have records, but we don't even ask (worker).

In over three years only two trainees have been barred for fighting – behaviour on the job is the only criterion, especially involving any threat to safety in workshops. The huge two–storey building had been converted by the trainees and was rented cheaply from GEC who had recently pulled out of Liverpool at the cost of ten thousand lost jobs. Hexagon offered a more realistic craft training than colleges of Further Education (FE), for example, painting and decorating training took place in a full–size mock–up set of rooms to teach speed and team coordination, whereas in the college, only a small space could be allotted. The overall standard and atmosphere was impressively efficient and yet warmly personal. Even so, the likely result of the cuts, less severe here than elsewhere on Merseyside, is that one or other of two senior managers will have to leave, breaking up a team that has built Hexagon up from scratch in under three years. As for YT for 16–17 year olds, the Liverpool estate badly needs a project–based training centre locally. G Force operated there from 1984–8, its intake rose from 30 to 300 in that time, and it had a 30% job provision rate for a group containing many offenders with drug problems, 'mainly people nobody else would touch'. It may be that Hexagon could act as a core base for a satellite YT in that estate.

vi. *Hoxton Impact Centre (APEX)*: the aim of the Centre, which has now closed, was to provide under one roof a host of community services, including training for offenders. Over the past five years in particular, Apex have pushed employment for the 'at risk' long–term unemployed and offender field forward in several ways: through the mounting of schemes which target specific mismatches between the supply and demand for labour in particular areas, as, for example, in their joint agreement with British Rail for the recruitment and selection of trackmen *(On The Right Tracks*, 1989); through exploring and disseminating knowledge about employers' responses to hiring offenders (see, for example, *Breaking the Cycle*, 1988; and *The Hidden Workforce*, 1991); by seeking to re–negotiate the constricting performance funding criteria of the new TECs, to include relevant indicators for entry into FE, National Vocational Qualification (NVQ) in literacy and numeracy or holding down a job placement for 3 months – 'this would be a very positive outcome for a 27 year old who had never held down a job in his life'. It was hoped that the Impact Centre approach would diversify sources of income away from the over–reliance on government funding. Cuts in ET led to 200 redundancies and the scrapping of a major project evaluation scheme which had taken immense pains to set up, which would have analysed outcomes and destinations of all Apex schemes' trainees, and tracked the sources of the falling offender ratio, probably due to growing disillusionment among probation officers with the new ET courses. An 18 rather than 12 month generalised skills training course was envisaged.

Various other APEX projects have been developed and while real evaluation is lacking, demonstrable success is claimed for the Peckham job club. Another project in Seacroft, Leeds has reportedly reduced crime substantially by employing LTU's and offenders on a community industry project. The Birkenhead project based on a skills mismatch analysis of the local labour market in clothing manufacture led to an even more striking apparent outcome, a reoffending rate of under 1% during the two–year period over which the project had been running. (*Breaking the Cycle*, pp28–30). A training audit was carried out in 1989 for the proposed joint Bellway/Brent Council redevelopment initiative on the Stonebridge Estate. The hope is to learn from the mistakes of the Docklands Redevelopment which was insufficiently geared to local community needs (Church, 1991). A pre–release, prison–based training scheme has just been started in Pentonville Prison. In sum, Apex has generated a host of fruitful ideas in the offender/employment field, based on their conviction that offenders are an important and grossly neglected part of the labour market. Rigourous project evaluation is as yet, as with all other schemes in the 1980s, unavailable.

vii. *The work of NACRO*: the pioneering work of the National Association for the Care and Resettlement of Offenders has already been cited above, and figures prominently in the study of the field by Crow and others.

NACRO's work programmes are more training than employment–based, some 70 centres in 1991 for roughly 11,000 adults and 1,500 youths per day. Provision in 1992, including Employment Action, is substantially reduced, for some 5,000 adults and 1,400 youths, largely due to the TEC changes, which militate against long–term unemployed people and for quick, hi–tech trainees. NACRO training is weighted towards basic skills: 50–60% have real literacy/numeracy and/or communicative problems. NACRO provides schemes covering a very wide range of training areas including construction and administrative skills, as well as motor mechanics, printing, hairdressing, horticulture and community care, among others. Between a third and a half of all trainees have recent convictions. No rigourous evaluation exists to confirm outcomes regarding reconvictions, but schemes in general bear out the crime reduction view sufficiently well for their continuation and development. London has proved an especially difficult area in which to mount projects, trainers of high quality are tougher to recruit, premises more expensive, and agencies and offenders more suspicious of what schemes actually offer. One exception to this rule appears to be the Peckham printing workshop, which feeds into a number of small printing firms locally.

viii. *Probation employment specialisms*: the idea for such specialisms was first aired at a joint Home Office/ACOP/NACRO conference in 1987, at much the same point as the conversion of the Department of Employment to accepting custody as unemployment eligibility for Community Programmes. Of 55 probation areas, about two–thirds have set up employment specialisms, with great variations as to their status, role and organisation. The most advanced are generally seen as those in Northumbria, Nottinghamshire and West Midlands. They are the most tangible sign that probation officers' awareness of employment issues is growing, that it is no longer enough just to refer clients to mainstream ET or – if one is available – projects run by NACRO or APEX. Mike Quille, who is both Secretary of the Offender Employment Forum and of the ACOP Committee responsible for developing employment links for offenders, as well as being West Midlands Employment Specialist Officer, sees the background to the low priority accorded employment in probation circles as stemming from the near–total absence of such issues in professional social work training and in the historical pattern by which after–care was tacked onto probation in 1966, when the tendency was for the officer to link the client to the job agency and leave it to them to take things further. These factors, combined with high inner–city unemployment, cynicism about employment training as a device to get the unemployed off the registers, and generally over–stretched resources, mean that probation officers who will take pains to set up counter–offending behaviour groups and alcohol education programmes still baulk at doing the same for employment. Nor, unlike accommodation, has the Home Office ever played any direct role in employment funding for offenders because it is funded by the Employment Department.

Things do seem to be changing partly because the stress is now more on the *quality* of work and skills assessment, and partly because NACRO in particular has done a considerable amount of work in showing the potential for offenders of the pre–ET Community Programmes – being 'on the NACRO' became a form of self–description. Also, the Hereford and Worcester research showed that clients felt they *were* benefitting from such projects. The big reductions in the numbers on such projects due to the funding changes mean that probation officers are now, having had their consciousness raised about employment and employability, becoming more positive on the issues. Interest in partnership schemes is growing. The Employment Service has a real interest in setting up employment preparation schemes even in the poorest inner city estates, and could fund, in combination with the probation service, job–clubs for small groups of offenders following restart and ET. The main problem is that the Employment Service will support such schemes generously only if attendance is guaranteed, which means high levels of engagement by both officers and clients. In London, where the probation service is still jaundiced about such prospects following the demise of the Bulldog programme in the early 1980s, there may be special difficulties; Bulldog provided full–time but mainly low–grade work for clients with substantial criminal records within the rehabilitative context of probation training. It lacked both a structured programme of skills training and post–project job finding supports. Though its 'clients gained little in terms of improved employment, there were tangible gains nevertheless' (Pointing, 1986, p.109). Though post–programme rates of reconviction and seriousness of new offences showed only marginal improvement, reoffending while participating in the programme was 'comparatively rare' (p.112). Despite these gains Bulldog was also reportedly hampered by an over–ambitious profitability condition that restricted the type of work taken on, thus actually narrowing employment opportunities rather than the reverse, at a time of gathering economic recession. Failure under these circumstances should not mean, as Pointing argues, that we abandon such schemes in periods of recession. In his view 'any such scheme either needs to employ people permanently or give them the means to work independently on leaving ... Another approach to encourage independent working could be pursued through community development. Environmental and housing improvement in areas of particular deprivation (such as those occupied by Bulldog clients) could be undertaken by community based organisations and organised by them rather than public bureaucracies', a model more common in the USA than in Britain (p.127). Such schemes need to be placed, he concludes, on the political agenda. And a few such schemes *are* starting to spring up, such as Southwark's Probation Partnership Project and the joint Probation/Youth Service/FE Drop–in Centre being set up in the Isle of Dogs. It is an important feature of such schemes that they take on all comers, not simply offenders.

To summarise; the central paradox has been defined by Crow *et al* (1989) as stemming from the clear evidence of links between long–term unemployment and reconvictions, on the one hand, and only negligible overall success in employment schemes for offenders reducing reconvictions, on the other (see also Soothill, 1974). Resolving the paradox may flow from the view that long–term unemployed (LTU) offenders are adversely labelled and subjected to undue levels of methodical suspicion by the police, and/or that employment schemes are usually short–term only and do not lead to high quality jobs. There are, however, some notable successes, and the community dimension seems to be a crucial factor. If local networks are so crucial for linking offenders to worthwhile jobs after training, then the community employment context of those networks needs to be sustained and enhanced.

Unfortunately the evaluation of schemes is in general unsatisfactory especially so in relation to the *quality* of employment[2]. Part of the problem is that realistic funding is hardly ever built into schemes for evaluation purposes.

However there seem to be a number of important elements to schemes which may assist in the reduction of crime. These are

* the opportunity to learn literacy and numeracy skills (NACRO)
* scope for learning individually–based skills tailored to individual abilities and potential (Beaver Workshop and Selcare)
* provision for personal attention (Beaver Workshop and Selcare)
* provision for training slow achievers (Hexagon)
* small workshops, wages, child support and regular urine testing for drug addicts (Rochdale Rework)
* development of own workshop resources and pursuing job networking contacts (Rhodes Probation Centre)

[2]. There are crucial problems, not touched on here, concerning the difficulties even well–trained offenders face in the disclosure process when seeking work. However, all training agencies visited in the course of this research asserted very strongly that offenders were treated equally on their own programmes, behaviour on the job being the only grounds for the rare exclusion of a trainee. Offenders are also given specific help by agencies on how to present their records to prospective employers.

* taking into account local needs by specifically targeting skills training to any mismatch between supply and demand in the local job market (APEX)

* build realistic funding into employment schemes for evaluation purposes.

4. Summary

It can be concluded from a number of studies in both Britain and North America that employment variables are causally linked with crime rates and trends, though the relationships are uneven, imperfect, and complex rather than simple and direct. The links are more clear–cut in relation to acquisitive crime, though robbery, drug–related crimes against the person and the most entrenched forms of gang violence are also at their height in *some* inner–city areas with long–standing patterns of unemployment across the generations (Miller, 1976). Sharp inequalities of wealth and income and a sense of powerlessness form the context within which joblessness results in crime.

A number of employment schemes for offenders were visited and local monitoring and research suggested that many of these led to reduced repeat offending. However there has been no thorough or detailed evaluation so that their real potential for crime reduction cannot be fully established.

Neighbourhood level factors are seen as the 'missing link' in both kinds of conventional employment policy programmes, which either focus exclusively on individuals, as in most training programmes, and thus do not address the local and situated character of most youth employment; or aim in macroeconomic terms to 'create more job opportunities for the poor (along with everyone else) through general economic growth' (McGahey, pp 257–8), thus failing to specify how broad economic changes can be translated into specific improvements for poor communities.

So what should the main elements of a local employment programme be? High calibre skills which are marketable across a range of occupations should be the first priority. First, 'efforts must be made to increase stable employment among adult residents of poor communities' (McGahey, p 260). If traditional training programmes are not appropriate in so many circumstances, what is? One promising alternative is for supported work programmes that offer graduated exposure to the world of work along with social supports. Some success is claimed in crime reduction among certain groups, especially ex–addicts. (In Britain, two such schemes with some convincing success along these lines are Rochdale Rework and the Beaver Workshop in Nottingham – see above). A second avenue is the more effective delivery of basic competencies in schools – literacy, numeracy, language and computer skills head the list but equally crucial are craft, design and technology and interpersonal skills for which art and drama offer great potential (see, for example, Johnston 1993). For adults and teenage dropouts, argues McGahey, competency programmes should be tied to work experience in a cooperative fashion. (The Selcare scheme in Manchester, described above, offers a good model along these lines.) A third set of measures are needed for youth still 'in' school but in practice not 'of' it – the 'bunkers off' who voluntarily exclude themselves, and the disruptive pupils who are officially excluded. While school transfers or home tuition are available and sometimes work towards reintegration, good resourcing of schools in terms of staffing for the learning support of such pupils, combined with support work aimed at re–entry into the school for temporarily excluded children seem to be important. Such measures should also help reduce the growing numbers of pupils who are permanently excluded.

All these proposals would integrate rather than exclude, and support rather than punish those who have offended and victimised others in the process. Despite its complexities, the weight of the evidence suggests that real progress in crime prevention and reduction cannot be made any other way. The problem is that far more resources and thought are put into the exculsionary than into the integrative processes. Until that imbalance is addressed we are unlikely to stem either the rise in crime or the growing seriousness of its character.

Acknowledgements

My main debt of thanks is to Alice Sampson of the Home Office Police Research Group (formerly Crime Prevention Unit), whose expertise and encouragement were invaluable in the shaping of this report.

In a study of this kind it is difficult to thank all of those individuals who spent time discussing views or sharing information with me, but I am very grateful to them all for their help. More specifically I would like to thank
Apex Trust: Nick Flynn
Birmingham Probation Employment Specialism: Mike Quille
Elliott Currie, University of California at Berkeley;
Peter Dubery: South East London Probation Service Employment Specialism
Chris Hale, School of Business Management, University of Kent
Inner London Probation Service: Steve Stanley, Research and Intelligence
Manchester Probation Service: Cedric Fulwood and John Stafford,
Manchester Selcare: Alex Calverley and Colin Nuttall
Nottingham Probation, Beaver Workshop: John Lowe and Tony Raban
NACRO: Fiona Lea–Wilson and Clem Hendrickson
Rochdale Rework: Stephen Abbott and David Edwards (Turning Point Area Manager and Regional Officer); Rachel Sweeting, Co–ordinator; Sheila McEvally. Community Drugs Teams; Clive McCormick, supervisor–instructor
Oldham Probation Service: Helen Allen and Andrew Underdown
Safer Cities: David McFarland (Tower Hamlets); Ron Tench (Rochdale)
Southwark Probation Employment Advice and Training: Jan Roberts

David Downes
Department of Social Administration
London School of Economics

References

ALLAN, E.A. and STEFFENSMEIER, D.J. (1989) 'Youth, Underemployment and Property Crime: Differential effects of job availability and job quality on juvenile and young adult arrest rates.' *American Sociological Review*, 54, (February): 107 – 123.

APEX TRUST (1988): *Breaking the Cycle: Crime, Employment and Ex–Offender – The Employer's Perspective*. London: Apex Trust.

APEX TRUST (1989): *On The Right Tracks: A Report on the Recruitment and Selection of Trackman for British Rail (Southern Region)*. London: Apex.

APEX TRUST (1991): *The Hidden Workforce: Employing Ex–Offenders – Recruitment Policy and Practice*. London: Apex.

BERNSTSEN, K. and CHRISTIANSEN, K. (1965): 'A Resocialisation Experiment with Short–Term Offenders'. In: Christiansen K (ed) *Scandinavian Studies in Criminology*. Vol.1. London: Tavistock.

BOX, S. (1987): *Recession, Crime and Punishment*. London: Macmillan.

BRAITHWAITE, J. (1979): *Inequality, Crime and Public Policy*. London: Routledge.

BRAITHWAITE, J. (1989): *Crime, Shame and Reintegration*. Cambridge University Press.

BRAKE, M. and HALE, C. (1991): *Public Order and Private Lives: The Politics of Law and Order*. London: Routledge.

CARR–HILL, R. and STERN, N. (1979): *Crime, the Police and Criminal Statistics.* London:Academic Press.

CHURCH, A. (1991): 'Urban regeneration, economic restructuring and community response in London Docklands'. *London and New York: Cities in Decay* Conference at Michael Harrington Centre, Birkbeck College, 25.1.91–27.1.91 Mimeo unpubl.

CLOWARD, R. and OHLIN, L.E. (1960): *Delinquency and Opportunity.* Glencoe: The Free Press.

CORDEN, J., KUIPERS, J. and WILSON, K. (1978): *After Prison.* University of York: Department of Social Administration and Social Work.

COUNCIL OF EUROPE, POMPIDOU GROUP (1987): 'The Rework Project, Rochdale, England'. Strasbourg: mimeo.

CROW, I., RICHARDSON, P., RIDDINGTON, C. and SIMON, F. (1989): *Unemployment, Crime and Offenders.* London: Routledge.

CURRIE, E. (1985): *Confronting Crime: An American Challenge.* New York: Pantheon.

CURRIE, E. and SKOLNICK, J. (1988): *America's Problems: Social Issues and Public Policy* (2nd ed) Glenview Scott, Foresman.

CURTIS, L. (1990): *Youth Investment and Community Reconstruction: Street Lessons on Drugs and Crime for the Nineties* Milton S Eisenhower Foundation. Final Report. Washington D.C.

DITTON, J. (1977): *Part–time Crime.* London: Macmillan.

DOCKLANDS FORUM (1990): *Employment in Docklands.* London: Birkbeck College.

DOWNES, D.M. (1966): *The Delinquent Solution*. London: Routledge and Kegan Paul.

FAGAN, J. (1987): 'Neighbourhood Education, Mobilization, and Organisation for Juvenile Crime Prevention'. *Annals of the American Academy of Political and Social Science* 494, November, 54–70.

FAIR, M. (1988): *The Massachusetts Department of Correction's Community Reintegration Program*. Massachusetts Department of Corrections.

FARRINGTON, D.P. et al (1986): 'Unemployment, school–leaving and crime'. *British Journal of Criminology* 26, 4, 335–356.

FIELD, S. (1990): *Trends in Crime and their Interpretation*. London: HMSO.

FOWLES, A. (1978): *Prison Welfare: An Account of an Experiment at Liverpool.* Home Office Research Study No. 45, London:HMSO.

FULBROOK, D. (1990): *Long–term Unemployment and the Probation Service*. Bath University, unpubl, M Phil thesis.

HAINES, K. (1990): *After–care Services for Released Prisoners: A Review of the Literature.* Cambridge: Institute of Criminology.

HAKIM, C. (1982): 'The social consequences of high unemployment.' *Journal of Social Policy* 11, p433–467.

HENRY, S. (1978): *The Hidden Economy*. Oxford: Martin Robertson.

HOBBS, D. (1988): *Doing the Business: Entrepreneurship, the Working Class and Detectives in the East End of London.* Oxford: Clarendon Press.

HOOD, R. (1966): *Homeless Borstal Boys*. London: Bell.

HYLAND, J. and UNDERDOWN, A. (1988): 'Drug abuse: community sentencing needs community teamwork'. *Probation Journal* 35, 4, 144–7.

JACKSON, M. (1991): 'Shotgun match of ideology and pure necessity'. *Times Educational Supplement* 15 March. p.10.

JOHNSTON, C. (1993): 'Behind the mask and the motive'. *Guardian 2.* Society Supplement, 10 February 1993, p. 13.

LE CLAIR, D. (1988): *The Effect of Community Reintegration on Rates of Recidivism: A Statistical Overview of Data for the Years 1971 Through 1985.* Massachusetts Department of Corrections.

McGAHEY, R. M. (1986): 'Economic conditions, neighbourhood organisation and urban crime'. In A J Reiss, Jr and M Tonry (eds) *Communities and Crime.* Chicago University Press.

MARRIS, P. and REIN, M. (1972): *Dilemmas of Social Reform*. Harmondsworth: Penguin.

MILLER, D. (1964): *Growth to Freedom*. London: Tavistock.

PAHL, R. E. (1987): 'Does jobless mean workless ? Unemployment and informal work.' *Annals of the American Academy of Political and Social Science* 493, (September) 36–46.

PARKER, H., BAKX, K. and NEWCOMBE, R. (1988): *Living with Heroin*. Milton Keynes: Open University Press.

PEARSON, G. (1987): *The New Heroin Users*. Oxford: Blackwell.

POINTING, J. (1986): The Failure of Supported Work: The Bulldog Programme. In Pointing J. (ed.) *Alternatives to Custody*. Ch.7, 106–129.

SAMPSON, R.J. and WOOLDREDGE, J.D. (1987): 'Linking the micro and macro levels of lifestyle – routine activity and opportunity models of prodatory victimisation'. *Journal of Quantitative Criminology*, 3,371–393.

SHAW, M. (1974): *Social Work in Prisons*. London: HMSO.

SHOVER, N. (1985): *Aging Criminals*. London: Sage Publications

SINCLAIR, I. and SNOW, D. (1971): *Explorations in After–Care.* Part 11. Home Office Research Study No.9. London: HMSO.

SOOTHILL, K. (1974): *The Prisoner's Release: A study of the employment of ex–prisoners.* London: Allen & Unwin.

SOOTHILL K. (1981): 'Employing White–Collar Ex–Offenders: A five–year Criminological Follow–up'. *British Journal of Social Work,* 11, 77–87.

SULLIVAN, M. L. (1984): *Youth Crime and Employment Patterns in Three Brooklyn Neighbourhoods*. New York: Vera Institute of Justice.

SULLIVAN, M. L. (1989): *'Getting Paid': Youth Crime and Work in the Inner City.* Ithaca: Cornell University Press.

TARLING, R. (1982): 'Unemployment and Crime'. *Home Office Research and Planning Unit Research Bulletin* No. 14, 28–33.

[11]
Mitigating the Social Effects of Unemployment

EVIDENCE ADDITIONAL TO THE CONTENTS OF *EMPLOYMENT OPPORTUNITIES FOR OFFENDERS* (1993) by David Downes (Professor of Social Administration, London School of Economics)

1. The best *summary* report on the state of the evidence on the unemployment/crime rate relationship remains that of Theodore Chiricos (1987). Chiricos challenged the (then) conventional wisdom that the relationship was "inconsistent", "insignificant" and "weak" on the grounds that previous summary analyses had been limited to at most 18 U-C studies, all but 7 of which used pre-1970s data. His own analysis reviewed the findings of 63 U-C studies, "40 of which involve data from the 1970s when unemployment rose dramatically".

Chiricos demonstrates how the U-C relationship is "conditional" on a number of factors, though it is rarely other than positive and often extremely strong, far more so than the "consensus of doubt" that had built up around it allowed. Those factors include the time-period involved, eg 1960s, 1970s; the level of data gathered, eg time-series or cross-sectional; the specificity of the data, eg total crime, or specific types; and the method of statistical analysis used. It is hardly surprising that varying the data and methods in different combinations by different researchers, especially given the vagaries of measuring the key variables of crime and unemployment themselves, have led to varying results. What *is* surprising is that these variations have been treated by so many commentators not as *complex and cumulative* but as *conflicting and inconsistent*, even though they preponderantly point in the same direction, albeit with different emphases.

Chiricos concludes that property crimes, 1970s data, and sub-national levels of aggregation "produce consistently positive and frequently significant U-C results". "While the U-C relationship under *these* conditions contradicts the "consensus of doubt", there are *other* conditions that do produce the "inconsistent" and "insignificant" U-C relationships described by that consensus: (p 199). Even so, there is little evidence of a *negative* U-C relationship. Property crimes, over 80% of all crimes, may be linked *motivationally* to sharply rising unemployment, But post-1970, all violent crime also relates positively to unemployment rates, though less strongly than property crimes. Sub-national data produce more consistently positive results than national data perhaps because - especially in so vast and heterogeneous a society as the United States - national data "wash out" important differences in crime and unemployment that characterise different sections of cities.

In sum, as Chiricos concludes with due caution, what Wilson and Herrnstein (1985) dismissively referred to as "... this now well-plowed terrain" of unemployment and crime should not be abandoned to the "consensus of doubt". "The evidence favors the existence of a positive, frequently significant U-C relationship. This is especially true since 1970 for those property crimes making up about 90 percent of the Uniform Crime Reports Index total. This suggests that rational policy addressing the problem of "street crime" should recognise that work and crime are the principal alternatives for most people to generate an income... Efforts to increase the availability and value of work can be expected to have some depressing effect on the value of property crime as an alternative. And, while the relationship between unemployment and crime is far from perfect, it is sufficient to put jobs back on the agenda for dealing with crime." (p 203)

2. The findings of David Dickinson (1993) on crime and unemployment in England and Wales are remarkably consistent with those of Chiricos. Acknowledging that the links between total crime and unemployment rates over long periods of time are relatively weak and inconsistent, Dickinson disaggregates pre- and post-1970 trends; unemployment rates for males aged under and over 25; and rates of burglary compared with other crimes. He also allows for the changes in the proportion of reported burglaries recorded by the police, though this makes little difference to the findings.

The principal difference to emerge from the study is the marked contrast between the crime-unemployment rates relationship in the 1955-69 and 1970-90 periods. In 1955-69, there is little or no relationship between crime rates and the very low, largely frictional unemployment rate. After 1970, and especially between 1977-90, a much closer relationship obtains. From 1977-90, specific unemployment rates for males aged under 25 show a "close and contemporaneous relationship" (p 23) with rates of burglary. Figure 7 (p 24) amounts to a virtual 'double helix' of burglary and unemployment rates for under-25 year old males. The same relationship for males aged over 25 was marked but less symmetrical. The possibility that police bias against unemployed youth with known records accounts for this close relationship over time is discounted by Dickinson. "In only 11% of primary detections (at or near the crime scene) was the suspect arrested by patrolling officers interviewing those 'acting suspiciously' - a method in which possible prejudice against young unemployed men might be expected to play a part" (p 27, citing Burrows 1986).

Dickinson concludes that, while it cannot be maintained that unemployment is the sole cause of crime, since much crime is committed by those not in the labour market or who are in work, nevertheless - given the prevalence of crime among young men - the importance of unemployment as a cause of crime should not be under-estimated. Males aged between 17 and 25 accounted for almost 50% of all convictions and cautions for burglary in 1990, and for almost 70% of all adult convictions and cautions. Clearly, any cause of crime which particularly influences this group's propensity to offend will have a multiplier effect on the crime rate quite disproportionate to their numbers.

Dickinson's final conclusions are worth quoting in full: "No claim is made that there is a simple relationship between unemployment and crime, but unemployment must be regarded as a major factor motivating crime. While unemployment alone may not be sufficient to result in criminal behaviour, it may well be the catalyst for those having least educational and economic opportunities and who are, as a result, least affected by social restraints. Worryingly, unemployment may erode those social restraints where they do exist.

By allowing mass unemployment to continue, and letting young men shoulder a disproportionate burden of this (their unemployment rate is twice that of over 25's), we condemn ourselves (and them) to rising crime now and create criminals for the future." (p 32)

3. Many studies have been carried out on delinquency using the self-report method, usually on in-school populations. To the bemusement of sociologists who have conducted field studies of delinquency, these self-report studies often find negligible differences in delinquency by social class or even gender. An obvious reason for at least part of this mismatch between self-report and field study findings is that the most 'at risk of delinquency' groups, school drop-outs and homeless youths, are not available for in-school self-reports of their misdeeds.

An important study in Toronto by Hagan and McCarthy (1992) extended the self-report method to teenage runaways, contacted via shelters and drop-in centres. For every 20 youths in school in Toronto, there was one on the street (40% from Toronto, 60% from elsewhere - London similarly acts as a magnet for homeless youth throughout the UK). Using various measure of property crime, street youth were found to be substantially more delinquent than school youth. For example, "the greatest absolute difference is in frequency of theft, with street youth scoring 32.61 on this scale (since leaving home) and school youth scoring 5.59 (ever)" (p 544). Controlling for background risk factors, more than half of the difference in theft involvement between street youth and school youth remains attributable to the exigencies of street life. Moreover, "our findings demonstrate that children of surplus population (unemployed) families are more likely to take to the streets and that streetlife itself increases serious delinquency" (p 555). In other words, unemployment doubly compounds the likelihood of involvement in delinquency, first due to the greater likelihood of youth from unemployed families leaving home, and secondly due to the "truly adverse consequences for youth who are on the street" and jobless,.

4. These three studies reinforce the conclusion that, whatever the ambiguities of the evidence on the links between crime and unemployment before 1970, since that date - both in North America and Britain - the relationship has become far more pronounced. In the 1970s in the USA, and in the late 1980s and early 1990s in Britain, high endemic rates of unemployment among males aged 15-25 are arguably linked with not only crime rates rising unduly sharply but also a growing seriousness in the character of street crime, not least due to the huge increase in illegal drug use and trafficking, itself in part a produce of unemployment (Parker et al, 1988). Our response to this situation has been to become hyperactive in individual risk management (by private insurance, domestic security etc) and situational crime prevention (by 'target hardening', electronic surveillance etc) but to remain curiously inactive in collective risk management (by protecting families and communities from sudden social and economic dislocation) and social crime prevention (by bolstering job training for the long-term unemployed, including offenders; or by investing in special needs education for those at risk of school exclusion).

5. It is often said that 'Mass unemployment in the 1930s did not lead to massive increases in crime'. This is undeniably so, though it is worth noting that crime rates more than doubled in the 1920s and 30s in England and Wales (see Mannheim, 1940, pp 42-3) and the New Deal in the USA arguably staunched a crime explosion. As Currie argues (1985, pp 123-7), "conservatives have seized on the apparent failure of crime to rise during the Great Depression as evidence against any connection between economic hardship and crime..... It's often forgotten...that the Roosevelt administration launched, in addition to widespread public relief, the largest program of public employment in the nation's history. One of its most important components was the Civilian Conservation Corps (CCC), which between its inauguration in 1933 and the coming of World War II put over *2.5 million* poor young men to work - between a quarter and a third of the young, poor men in the entire country - mainly in national and state forests and other public-works projects. No sophisticated evaluation of the CCC's role in reducing crime was ever carried out, but contemporaries (including Roosevelt himself) widely thought it had one..."

It is also worth remembering that material aspirations in the 1930s were far more modest than today. In the intervening half-century, goods which were once luxuries for the few have become necessities for the many. Items such as cars, TVs, refrigerators, foreign holidays, and the like, which would once have been fatalistically accepted as out of reach are now taken for granted expectations. Their denial constitutes relative deprivation. The advertising industry has taken a quantum leap from the mild stimulation of appetites to an array of frontal and sophisticated assaults on them. It is hardly too surprising if, as more than one generation of sociologists have argued, social restraints begin to dissolve in the process.

6. The evidence from an impressive number of comparative sources suggests a crime-unemployment relationship which is becoming closer and more serious in its implications. The relationship hinges on the 'revolution of rising consumer expectations' coinciding with de-industrialisation and the collapse of opportunities for stable, income-generating work that sustains families, communities and a sense of self-worth. More is at stake, however, than a simple formulation of 'blocked opportunities' suggests, since the context is one of growing inequalities and social polarisation. The time seems ripe for another New Deal, sufficiently comprehensive and imaginative in scope to address these problems in all their complexity.

References

Chiricos, T.G. (1987) "Rates of crime and unemployment", *Social Problems*, Vol. 34, pp. 187–211.

Currie, E. (1985) *Confronting Crime: An American Challenge*, New York: Pantheon.

Dickinson, D. (1993) *Crime and Unemployment*, mimeo, Cambridge.

Hagan, J. and McCarthy, B. (1992) "Street-life and delinquency", *British Journal of Sociology*, Vol. 43, 533–62.

Parker, H., Bakx, K. and Newcombe, R. (1988) *Living With Heroin*, Milton Keynes: Open University Press.

Mannheim, H. (1940) *Social Aspects of Crime Between the Wars*, London: Allen and Unwin.

Wilson, J.Q. and Herrnstein, R. (1985) *Crime and Human Nature*, New York: Simon and Schuster.

[12]
Dumping the 'Hostages to Fortune'? The Politics of Law and Order in Post-War Britain

(*with Rod Morgan*)

For the purposes of this chapter we take the term 'the politics of law and order' to mean the public contestation of the dynamics of crime, disorder, and their control. The key players in this matrix are: the major political parties, in particular successive Home Secretaries and their ministerial and Opposition teams; senior civil servants who, despite their non-political role, bear crucial advisory responsibilities; pressure and interest groups in the criminal justice field; and the mass media. The private, off-stage, often confidential and even secretive processes of discussion, negotiation, and exchange, which provide the ingredients of public utterance and action, remain implicit rather than spelt out in what follows. Further, when we employ terms such as 'the Conservative Party' or 'the Labour Party' we do not mean to propagate the fallacy of misplaced concreteness: these terms are necessary abbreviations for the welter of possible responsibilities for actions and policies that may be the work of many thousands of individuals. Nor, in quoting the words of ministers or other politicians, do we assume that perfect comprehension can be achieved—if it ever can be—without much more detail about timing, context, multiple purposes, encoding and decoding artfulness, and much else. We assume that our readers will grasp that a limited purpose is pursued in making quotations and examples, namely, to demonstrate a point rather than to convey some total reality.

Compared with the contested party politics of the economy, foreign affairs, defence, health, housing, and education, those of 'law and order' are of remarkably recent origin: they emerged in the mid-1960s, but came decisively to the fore only with the 1979 election. This longstanding absence from party political discourse and contention is remarkable. Law and order are highly emotive and fundamentally political issues. Few topics can routinely arouse such passionate debate. That law and order were relatively insulated from the realm of party politics for so long testifies perhaps to the strength of belief that crime, like the weather, is beyond political influence; and that the operation of the law and criminal justice should be above it. This is not to deny that criminal law reform has long been regarded as the prerogative of Parliament. But once laws are enacted, the liberal doctrine of the separation of powers holds that their enforcement is the preserve of the police and the judiciary. Hence, bipartisanship has been the rule rather than the exception in the twentieth century on such matters as the response to crime, the nature of policing, sentencing policy, and so on. Even at the fringes of political life, few challenges were made to so profound a consensus.

The nature of and the reasons for the change from a broadly bipartisan to a sharply contested politics of law and order are central to our concerns in this chapter. But the prelude to that change was not without deep significance because the nature of the consensus itself was both complex and far from apolitical. This was, however, a politics more of nuance and inflection than of explicit difference. Also, the politics of law-breaking are not necessarily those of order-defiance (Elder, 1984), and the latter has a far more developed history, particularly in the realm of industrial conflict (Dixon and Fishwick, 1984). Friction over public order legislation and its enforcement has throughout the period been far more evident than that concerning straightforward criminality. It was the achievement of 'Thatcherism' to blur the difference between the two and even to fuse them symbolically to political effect. And the consequences of the change have been more than a simple matter of the major parties taking up starkly opposing stances across the range of relevant issues. Despite new, overt differences, a species of second-order consensus has emerged to replace former orthodoxies. Moreover, the politics of law and order are not confined to the party sphere. Extra-parliamentary processes have often been more vigorous than those within the confines of Westminster, and developments at local government level, or formulations by pressure groups and lobbies, have frequently been the stimulus for national attention. Finally, the eruption of particular scandals and concerns, via a rapidly changing media framework, have consistently proved catalysts for changing policies. In what follows, we shall address these topics in turn.

BRITISH GENERAL ELECTIONS AND 'LAW AND ORDER', 1945–1997

In 1945 Britain 'was a society both exhausted and exhilarated' (Morris, 1989: 13). The awesome task of post-war reconstruction led the three main parties to contend overwhelmingly about the priorities of rebuilding the economy and constructing the 'welfare state'. Despite fundamental ideological differences, out of this period was evolved a form of consensus, usually known as 'Butskellism',[1]

[1] 'Butskellism' was a word coined in the early 1950s to convey the similarity and continuity of economic policy between the outgoing Labour Chancellor of the Exchequer, Hugh Gaitskell, and the new Conservative Chancellor, R. A. Butler (see Marwick, 1990: chapter 6).

which set limits to the scope of political conflict. Full employment, core welfare rights in health, housing, income and maintenance, and education and economic growth based on Keynesian assumptions, were broadly accepted as shared goals, as was a mixed economy—though strong differences persisted over the nature of the mix. Crime and criminal justice were minor, taken-for-granted aspects of this consensus.

Our analysis of trends in the salience of 'law and order' as an issue in British politics is heavily reliant on manifestos for, and campaigning during, the relatively short (generally three-week) run-up to general elections. The method has obvious advantages. Such material provides a time series of supremely public character which has enabled political analysts to chart the changing complexion of party policies and their intended and actual appeal. The work of David Butler and his colleagues has furnished a thorough guide to the complexities and problems of interpretation. Against this view, it can be said that manifestos are formal exercises in party rhetoric which are little read and, as such, provide highly problematic guides to party thinking and influence. Such a view seems to us too dismissive. Manifestos are highly accessible documents and they play a major part in the process of democratic accountability. After elections they are constantly referred to by opponents of the government, and the notion of a mandate to pursue policies is heavily dependent on their prior legitimation by majority (or winning minority) vote by an electorate which has, in principle, had prior warning of party thinking and intentions. That electoral promises are far from sacrosanct does not alter the basis on which they rest: that voters have had the chance to assess the worth and credibility of party strategy.

In the first part of this section we describe and compare the way in which successive post-war manifestos and campaigns developed 'law and order' issues; we then attempt to discern the underlying reasons for the distinctive pattern that emerges.

The Post-War Manifestos and Campaigns

Not until 1959 did any party mention in a manifesto anything to do with topics of law and order, though in both 1955 and 1959 issues of legal aid and betting and gaming legislation were raised. In 1959, the new note struck by the Conservatives was simply 'to review the system of criminal justice and to undertake penal reforms which will lead offenders to abandon a life of crime. A scheme for compensating the victims of violent crime for personal injuries will be considered' (Conservative Party, 1959). In 1964, the Conservative manifesto extended its coverage to include: strengthening the police; the (abortive) Royal Commission on the Penal System; tougher measures against hooliganism; and supporting family ties to counteract delinquency. The Liberal Party implicitly attacked the inadequacy of the government's record by switching the emphasis on combating crime to prevention and rehabilitation (Liberal Party, 1964). Yet even in 1964, after thirteen years of continuous Conservative government, the Labour Party said nothing about law and order, or the government's record in the face of crime rates which had risen steeply since the mid-1950s. This self-denial was all the more noteworthy because in 1963, in the run-up to the coming election, Harold Wilson had convened a study group on crime and criminal justice under the chairmanship of Lord Longford. Though the group's report, *Crime—A Challenge To Us All*, became available only as Labour was taking up office in 1964, it was presumably known in advance that its members were 'breaking new ground' (Morris, 1989: 114), mainly on penal reform, the treatment of juveniles and capital punishment.

In 1966, however, after two years in government, the Labour Party for the first time devoted as much space to 'law and order' policy as the Conservatives. The preamble to its pledge to strengthen the police, reform juvenile justice, and modernize the prison system was implicitly critical of the Conservatives: 'For years Britain has been confronted by a rising crime rate, overcrowded prisons and many seriously undermanned police forces' (Labour Party, 1966). The Conservatives were also keen to 'beat the crime wave' in 1966, announcing policies which differed from Labour's only in that they favoured the formation of larger police forces and greater use of compensation orders by the courts. On one issue, however, they signalled a disagreement with Labour that was to persist for many years. Whereas the Labour reforms, drawing on the report of the Longford Committee, envisaged the end of juvenile courts and their powers, by contrast the Conservatives would 'preserve the juvenile courts and expand the methods available for dealing with the problems of young people' (Conservative Party, 1966). It should be stressed that, as previously, no party manifesto suggested that the level or form of crime was itself attributable to the politics of the party in government.

All that changed in 1970. In ways that mark this election rather than that of 1979 as the real watershed in the policies of 'law and order', all three major parties devoted more space than ever before in their manifestos to these issues. Moreover, the Conservatives, albeit in restrained fashion, argued that 'the Labour Government cannot entirely shrug off responsibility for the present situation'. The 'situation' was 'the serious rise in crime and violence' and increased fear of both (Conservative Party, 1970; for contemporary examinations of the nature of these problems see Downes, 1966; Cohen, 1972; Hall *et al.*, 1978). While the Conservatives laid this situation at the door of the Labour government, pointing to their having restricted 'police recruitment at a critical time' (a contentious argument, since full employment in the whole post-war period had bedeviled police pay levels and their effects on recruitment—see Bottoms and Stevenson, 1992), 1970 also saw them draw a clear connection between crime, protest, and disorders associated with industrial disputes. The law, the Conservative manifesto proclaimed, 'needs modernising and clarifying and needs to be made less slow and cumbersome, particularly for dealing with offences—forcible entry, obstruction and violent offences connected with public order—peculiar to the *age of demonstration and disruption*' (Conservative Party, 1970: 25, emphasis added). Against this thinly veiled linkage of issues of law-breaking and order-defiance that had hitherto been quite distinct in political discourse, Labour asserted its recognition that it was 'the first duty of government to protect the citizen, against violence, intimidation and crime', and undertook to prosecute vigorously . . . the fight against vandals and law breakers'. However Labour decried the breakdown of bipartisanship about crime: 'Nothing could be more cynical than the current attempts of our opponents to exploit for Party political ends the issue of crime and law enforcement' (Labour Party 1970). Indeed, the Labour manifesto sought to reassure the electorate that 'the streets of our cities are as safe today as those in any throughout the world. They must remain so' (*ibid.*: 26).

The chords struck in the 1970 election campaign persisted and grew more insistent in those of 1974 and 1979. In that of February 1974, the Conservative Party further increased the amount of space devoted to law and order issues in its manifesto, claiming some success during their period of office in reducing crime (the rate had barely risen between 1970 and 1973, though it was to soar in 1974). These 'encouraging signs' were attributed to the growth in police manpower, tougher penalties for offences involving firearms and vandalism, and the ability of the courts to impose compensation orders. More of the same types of measures were promised if the Party were re-elected (Conservative Party, 1974*a*). By contrast, the Labour Party, back in opposition, said nothing on law and order: it promised nothing and said nothing about the government's record (Labour Party, 1974*a*). The Liberal Party also said nothing though, continuing its well-established tradition, it advocated a Bill of Rights (Liberal Party, 1974).

The outcome of the February 1974 election—a narrow Labour victory with a hung Parliament in which the Labour government depended on Liberal support—led to a second election in October 1974. Once again the Labour Party said little about law and order and what it did say was couched in generalities and promised no specific measures (Labour Party, 1974*b*). By contrast the Conservative Party again devoted a substantial part of its manifesto to law and order issues. It vigorously pursued the approach of attacking the government's record, but with a significant difference. On this occasion, it was the government's integrity rather than its policies and priorities that was condemned. Following the traditional defence of the need for law and the protection it affords the weak against the strong, they continued: 'But recently the law has been under attack and these attacks have all too often been condoned and even endorsed by members and supporters of the present Government' (Conservative Party, 1974*b*). This veiled reference to the support given to the National Union of Mineworkers, in its successful deployment of mass picketing in 1973, by Labour MPs and key members of the then Shadow Cabinet, such as Tony Benn, gave the Conservative Party a crucial opening. The Clay Cross affair, in which the Labour government failed to prosecute Labour local councillors who had refused to increase rents in line with Conservative legislation during their period of office, was another lever to be deployed in prising apart the image of Labour and the wholehearted, not selective, support for the law without which there could be no freedom. A detailed array of specific policies were put forward in relation to policing, young offenders, and crime prevention, including the commitment to amend the Labour government's Children and Young Persons Act 1969, 'to deal more effectively with persistent juvenile offenders—for example, soccer hooligans—and the range of available institutions must be improved' (*ibid.*).

It is apparent, therefore, that by the mid-1970s it had been established that law and order issues could assume as much prominence in major party election manifestos as, for example, housing, transport, and urban renewal policy. However, while 'law and order' was not a question on which only the Conservatives pronounced, the manner in which the major parties dealt with the issues was increasingly different. The Conservatives were refashioning their traditional claim to be the natural party of government, representing the order of established authority (Honderich, 1990), a claim which had lost much credibility as a result of the Conservative defeats in the 1974 elections, following the huge loss of face involved in the miners' strike of 1973. By emphasizing respect for the law, the Conservatives—now under the leadership of Mrs Thatcher—were laying claim to a clear moral and practical ascendancy in this field. By contrast, Labour was experiencing difficulties in mounting a convincing counter-attack and, in the two 1974 elections, in effect ducked the issue. Since Labour nevertheless won those elections, that strategy seemingly paid off. The clear difficulty for Labour was the success with which the Conservatives were fusing the issues of law-breaking and order-defiance in the industrial relations field. Labour felt inhibited from unequivocally condemning disruptive and at times aggressive strike-related actions by its principal constituency, trade unionists. During the late 1970s, following the forced loan from the International Monetary Fund and especially during the strike-ridden 'Winter of Discontent'[2] of 1978–9, it seems probable that a number of anxieties symbolizing national decline came to be associated with Labour government: lack of economic competitiveness; fear of crime; fear of inner-city decay; fear of an explosion of black criminality; fears of youthful extremism (embodied in both the brief rise of the punks and far-right street demonstrations that culminated in the murder of Blair Peach at Southall[3]); and fears that the authorities could not cope with the array of problems thus presented. It was at this time that many an editorial was written on the 'ungovernability' of Britain. It was out of these ingredients that the major

[2] In autumn 1978, it was widely predicted that the Labour government, then with a much reduced majority, would call an election. It was not called. But a plethora of strikes ensued, notably in the health and other public services. The number of days lost from work rose above those recorded during the General Strike of 1926 (see Marwick, 1990: 261).

[3] On 23 April 1979 the National Front held a meeting at the Town Hall, Southall. It was a deliberate provocation to the predominantly Asian local community. An estimated 3,000 anti-National Front demonstrators gathered to protest, and approximately 4,000 police were drafted in to confront them. During the mêlée that ensued a white teacher, Blair Peach, was killed, possibly after having been struck by a member of the Metropolitan Police Special Patrol Group (see Marwick, 1990: 221).

differences between the parties on 'law and order' assumed their most polarized form in the 1979 election.

In 1979 the Labour government knew, because the Conservative Party had long signalled the fact, that its record in office was to be attacked on this front. In its manifesto, Labour devoted space to 'law and order' issues but dealt with them *within* the context of its objective of creating 'one nation' by eliminating the evils of inequality, poverty, and racial bigotry (Labour Party, 1979). It invoked the need to 'fight against crime and violence', protect citizens' rights and liberties, and continue to back the police more strongly than the Tories had done. Its focus was on attacking 'the social deprivation which allows crime to flourish'. Labour's 'law and order' policy was therefore implicitly to be found elsewhere in the manifesto, in its social and economic policies, though it gave such specific, if low-key, undertakings as to provide more law centres and extend legal aid and help for victims. By contrast, the Conservatives made restoring the 'rule of law', which they claimed that the Labour Party 'in government as in opposition . . . have undermined', one of their five major tasks; and they undertook to do so by implementing specific 'law and order' policies (Conservative Party, 1979). First, they would 'spend more on fighting crime even while we economise elsewhere'. Secondly, they would improve the pay and conditions of the police and, in particular, 'implement in full the recommendations of the Edmund-Davies Committee', which the Labour government had said it would implement in two stages rather than at once.[4] Thirdly, the police would be relieved of many non-crime-fighting duties. Fourthly, provision would be made for more effective sentencing, 'tough sentences . . . for violent criminals and thugs'; but also 'a wider variety of sentences' should be available for those offenders for whom 'long prison terms are not always the best deterrent'. Such measures would range from experiments with 'short, sharp shock' regimes in detention centres to making more compulsory attendance centres available 'for hooligans'. Finally, MPs would be given an early free vote on the restoration of capital punishment. Two other aspects of note were, first, in a substantial section on trade union reform, a proposal to revise the law on picketing to prevent 'violence, intimidation and obstruction'; and secondly, eight specific undertakings were given to achieve 'firm immigration control' which was said to be 'essential for racial harmony'. The 1979 Conservative manifesto brought 'law and order' to the fore as a major election issue and dispelled any lingering trace of bipartisan consensus.

By 1983, the party political battle over 'law and order' had been firmly joined. The Conservatives listed their achievements in office (all inputs as opposed to outputs) as: giving the police 'every possible backing'; revising police powers (in the Police and Criminal Evidence (PACE) Bill); giving the courts 'tougher and more flexible sentencing powers'; and embarking on a major

[4] The Edmund-Davies Committee of Inquiry (1978) had been set up by the Labour government primarily to advise on problems of low police recruitment and high wastage. The Committee recommended, *inter alia*, that police pay be increased and thereafter index-linked.

prison building programme (Conservative Party, 1983). Finally, broadening the scope of any 'law and order' discussion, and widening responsibility for it, they pronounced: 'Dealing with crimes, civil disobedience, violent demonstrations and pornography are not matters for the police alone. It is teachers and parents—and television producers too—who influence the moral standards of the next generation. There must be close co-operation and understanding between the police and the community they serve.'

The law and order issue was thus extended to embrace not only law violation and order-defiance, but also present and future morality.

Labour's 1983 manifesto (Labour Party, 1983) was the longest it had ever produced and twice as long as the Conservatives'. It devoted more space than ever before to law and order issues, spelling out a detailed programme of reform for reducing the prison population by non-custodial measures; for improving prison conditions, regimes, and prisoners' rights; and for enabling citizens to activate their rights under the law. Though stressing the need for support for the police, Labour pledged to repeal the PACE Act and replace it with a framework for police accountability which would 'protect the rights of individual suspects' and create elected police authorities.[5] Labour's programme made no reference to punishment, deterrence, or particular categories of heinous offenders. The policies they advocated were directly at variance with the existing and predicted programme of the Conservative administration. Otherwise, the Labour manifesto maintained the 'one nation' perspective and focused on 'healing the wounds' brought about by unemployment and cuts in public expenditure.

Both major parties displayed a greater realism and restraint in the 1987 election. The Labour Party manifesto (Labour Party, 1987) said nothing about the much amended Police and Criminal Evidence Act 1984, nor about the penal and criminal justice systems. Though elected police authorities figured once more as a pledge, police responsibility for 'all operational matters' was guaranteed. Social crime prevention schemes in the community were massively endorsed. However, for the first time in any but the most glancing way, the Labour Party shaped up to attack the Conservative 'law and order' record: 'eight years of rising crime, of greater insecurity on the streets and housing estates and in the home'. Labour attributed the continued steep rise in recorded crime directly to Conservative policies (though not necessarily those on 'law and order').

The Conservative manifesto (Conservative Party, 1987) was no more con-

[5] The first PACE Bill was widely held by the left (civil liberties groups and the Labour Party) significantly to increase police powers without providing adequate safeguards for suspects. Following the inner-city public disorders in St Pauls, Bristol, in 1980 and Brixton and elsewhere in 1981 (see Scarman Report, 1981), increased police use of paramilitary equipment and tactics, without that use having been sanctioned by public debate in either Westminster or police authority fora, led to major disputes between some police authorities and their chief constables. This in turn led to calls from the left for the full democratization of local police authorities and the empowerment of police authorities to determine general policy (see Christian, 1983; Spencer, 1985; Downes and Ward, 1986; Lustgarten, 1986; Reiner, 1992).

frontational than Labour's for the first time since law and order emerged as an electoral issue. Though making no concessions to the structural inequalities typically cited by Labour as producing crime, the Conservatives no longer implicitly claimed that their own policies would readily lead to lower crime rates or safer streets. Instead, responsibility for fighting crime was—in line with the 1983 manifesto—extended to 'all of us'; and the worsening crime rate was a problem 'not just in Britain but in most other societies too'. Its origins lie 'deep in society' (a rarc reference to this hitherto taboo collectivity), though *not* in any form of social differentation such as wealth or income inequalities: rather, in poor parental support; in poor school discipline; and in the glamorization of violence and the attack on traditional values. The mobilization of communities to support the police by such schemes as Neighbourhood Watch, and tough measures against, *inter alia*, drug traffickers in the envisaged Criminal Justice Bill, betokened a persistently resolute stance against crime. Control of drug abuse and immigration—topics perhaps unfortunately discussed in adjacent sections of the manifesto—were priorities.

The Liberal/SDP Alliance produced the most radical law and order manifesto of 1987 (Liberal/SDP Alliance, 1987), after two elections in which the Liberals had adopted a position either compromising between Conservative and Labour (1979) or little different from the latter (1983). They advocated a Bill of Rights incorporating the European Convention of Human Rights; the establishment of local 'Crime Crisis Areas'; a Ministry of Justice; a strengthened Judicial Studies Board to lay down sentencing guidelines; a Royal Commission on Violence in the Media; and a requirement on local authorities to set up Crime Prevention Units.

The period immediately before the election of 1992 suggested the likely and lively engagement by the opposition parties with the government's record on law and order. The Labour Party produced a criminal justice policy document, *Seven Steps to Justice*, which represented its most ambitious thinking since the 1964 document *Crime—A Challenge to Us All* and seemed likely to provide much of the material for the law and order part of the Labour manifesto. The Conservative government produced a flurry of measures to tackle 'bail bandits' (Morgan and Jones, 1992), car theft, and 'hotting',[6] and teenage crime in general was addressed by 'work camps'. The Home Secretary, Kenneth Baker, termed Labour 'soft and flabby on crime'. His Shadow, Roy Hattersley, persistently called for more police strength (in part to neutralize that attack), and invoked social measures to stem the unprecedented rise in the crime rate. A sign that the Conservative Party may, for the first time, have been vulnerable on the law and order front was to be discerned in opinion poll findings that showed little difference between the two major parties on these issues. This presumably reflected two consecutive years, 1990 and 1991, during which recorded crime rose by an unprecedented and much-publicized 36 per cent. Whether or not

[6] The fashion for racing stolen cars around local estates. A related craze for 'ram-raiding', using stolen cars as battering rams for forcing entry into shops and even houses, also caused much concern during the period (see Webb and Laycock, 1992; Light *et al.*, 1993).

these rises were 'real', they are generally regarded as indicating gross trends (see Maguire, this volume). As such, they may be seen as 'real' in their political consequences.

In the event, somewhat anti-climactically, Labour chose to fight the 1992 election on a smaller front and fewer issues than any since 1945. Its manifesto (Labour Party, 1992) devoted only one half-column in a document of over twenty pages to law and order issues, focusing on crime prevention involving local authorities (who had been marginalized on this front by Conservative governments) and on implementing the Woolf Inquiry recommendations on prisons (see below). It was a recipe for reform that could have been culled from the eighteenth-century works of Henry Fielding and John Howard. By contrast, the Conservative document (Conservative Party, 1992) devoted five of its fifty pages to 'Freedom Under Law', siting crime prevention in 'communities', Neighbourhood Watch schemes, and community policing, without mention of local authorities; listing a number of modest reforms in each criminal justice field, and making the claim to have 'reversed the Labour Party's neglect of the prison service in the 1970s'. The Liberal Democratic Party's manifesto (1992) brought rising crime rates and soaring expenditure on police and prisons together in dramatic montage, listing reforms such as the creation of a Ministry of Justice as necessary for a more coherent policy-making process. The most striking feature of the campaign period, however, was Labour's disengagement from this whole terrain: even more strikingly than in 1983 and 1987, it was a clear case of 'the dog that did not bark'.

Election campaign analysis substantially bears out these trends. According to the Nuffield studies, 'law and order' topics (that is, if broad industrial relations issues are excluded) did not figure at all in the elections of 1945, 1950, 1951, 1955, and 1959. In their exhaustive scrutiny of election broadcasts, leaders' speeches, and press coverage, as well as constituency election addresses, there is not a single reference to a law and order topic—crime, policing, or immigration—by any of the three major parties (McCallum and Readman, 1946; Nicholas, 1951; Butler, 1952, 1956; Butler and Rose, 1960). Neither the 'race riots' in Nottingham and Notting Hill in 1958 nor the Street Offences Act of 1959 impinged on the 1959 election campaign. Even in that of 1964, with the notable exception of the campaign at Smethwick, where exploitation of the fear of immigration led to the defeat of Patrick Gordon Walker, Labour's Shadow foreign affairs spokesman, by Peter Griffith, who 'almost invariably linked immigration with violence, crime and disease', such issues were surprisingly marginal and all three party leaders were keen that it should remain so (Butler and King, 1965). Despite rising crime rates, and heavy media coverage of the youth cults of the day and the disturbances in which they regularly engaged, there was no attempt by the party leadership to exploit either law and order or immigration as an issue with which to attack the opposition.

'Law and order' emerged as a clear Conservative issue in 1966, more so in the campaigns than in the manifestos: 40 per cent of Conservative addresses mentioned crime, compared with none for Labour and only 2 per cent of

Liberal addresses (Butler and King, 1967). Yet immigration appears to have been less of an issue in 1966 than in 1964, perhaps due to Labour's acceptance, in a White Paper in August 1965, of the need for immigration control: only 11 per cent of Conservative addresses mentioned it compared to none among both Labour and Liberal addresses. It is not clear why such a high proportion of Conservative election addresses mentioned crime in 1966 when, according to the Nuffield studies, none had in any previous post-war election. However, the most plausible explanation is that substantial media coverage of youth cults and organized crime—1964–6 marked the climax of the notoriety of the Kray and Richardson gangland 'empires' (see Hobbs, this volume)—led to a groundswell of concern that was translatable into Conservative, though not Labour and Liberal, discourse.

Whatever the explanation for the party differences in 1966, they were amplified in 1970. In that year the Conservatives decided, for the first time, to attack the Labour government's 'law and order' record. There was incident enough on which the Conservatives could draw: 1968–9 saw, *inter alia*, the great 'permissive society' debate on homosexual and abortion law reform; the end of censorship by the Lord Chamberlain; the Paris and UK student demonstrations and occupations; the Rolling Stones drug furores; Enoch Powell's 'rivers of blood' speech against immigration (and for repatriation); anti-apartheid demonstrations (during the election campaign itself) against the South African rugby tour; and a spate of strikes which led to the abortive Labour government response of *In Place of Strife*.[7] It is not too surprising, therefore, that 'law and order' appears to have figured for the first time in the media coverage of an election. But the Nuffield analysis of constituency election addresses shows a clearly marked difference between the parties: 60 per cent of Conservative addresses compared to only 15 per cent of Labour mentioned law and order questions. 'Law and order' was now sixth in the Conservative 'top ten' of topics: it did not figure in the Labour top ten (Butler and Pinto-Duschinsky, 1971). The Conservatives won a handsome majority, an outcome hardly expected until, late in the campaign, opinion polls registered the decisive shifts.

The trend set in 1966 and 1970 continued in the two elections of February and October 1974. In that of February, the industrial relations crisis led the Conservatives to fight on a 'Who Governs?' front (Butler and Kavanagh, 1975*a*). When the narrow win by Labour left them without an overall majority, they went to the country again in October. Once more, 60 per cent of Conservative addresses mentioned 'law and order' compared to only 2 per cent of Labour and 7 per cent of Liberal. Although the Conservatives lost more heavily, Labour policies on immigration and defence were rated by polling

[7] *In Place of Strife* (Cmnd. 3888, 1969) was the White Paper discussion document aimed at curbing the trades unions' right to strike by proposing a commission to look at disputes; a secret ballot before a strike could be called; and a cooling-off period of up to two months between a strike threat and its implementation. Resistance from the trade unions led to the withdrawal of the proposals and, arguably, to Labour's unexpected defeat in the 1970 election.

respondents more negatively than those of the Conservatives (unfortunately, the parties' popularity on 'law and order' was not examined: see Butler and Kavanagh, 1975*b*).

It is apparent, therefore, that the seminal and much-analysed 1979 election represented the heightening of a trend in relation to 'law and order' issues which was already well established. In 1979, the Conservatives successfully promoted their positive public image on law and order, and all the evidence suggests that they did so to the great detriment of Labour. Nor was this lead simply a matter of the wounds inflicted on Labour by the 'Winter of Discontent' of 1978–9. 'Maintaining law and order' moved from sixth to fourth in the list of 'biggest failures of the present government' in the regular Gallup polls during 1975–8 (Butler and Kavanagh, 1980: 37–8). Across a range of policy issues tested by MORI polls between August 1978 and April 1979, *no* policy placed the Conservatives so far ahead of Labour as 'law and order': a thirty-point lead compared with eleven points for 'unemployment' and little difference for 'prices/inflation' and even 'industrial relations/strikes' (*ibid.*: 131). One third of Labour voters and almost half of Liberal voters expressing a clear preference on the issue thought that the Tories had a better 'law and order' policy than their own parties (*ibid.*: 163).

The salience of the 'law and order' issue for the Conservatives was heightened during the election period itself by a number of events and developments, such as the killing of a leading Conservative MP, Airey Neave, by an IRA bomb in the Palace of Westminster; the Southall Riot in the wake of a march by the National Front; and a number of statements by leading 'law and order' figures, such as Robert Mark, the then recently retired Commissioner of the Metropolitan Police, and Lord Denning, Master of the Rolls, asserting respectively that the unions enjoyed a Nazi Party-like immunity from the law and were 'almost above the law' (quoted in *ibid.*: 187). Press coverage, mostly in support of the Conservative Party, boosted the issue more than ever before. 'Law and order' emerged, not surprisingly, as a favourite topic in Conservative candidates' election addresses: an astonishing 87 per cent issued tough calls for action. By contrast, 66 per cent of Labour addresses were silent on the subject and those that did take it up argued that only social reform could tackle crime (*ibid.*: 297). Moreover, 35 per cent of Tory addresses mentioned the death penalty, compared to none among Labour (*ibid.*: 297). During the campaign, the Nuffield analysts conclude, the growth in Tory support on this issue was greater than for any other issue. 'Law and order' had become what political scientists term a 'valence issue'; that is, party and voters alike agree on the objectives, but doubt whether the party has the capacity to affect the issue. The voters of 1979 judged that the Tories put 'law and order' first, of which they overwhelmingly approved: they doubted whether Labour did so. Labour lost a substantial degree of its traditional working-class vote and got only half the trade unionists' vote. The Conservatives won a sizeable majority.

By 1983, law and order had begun to assume a less prominent role, but it remained a central card in a way in which, until the 1970s, it never had been.

No party could afford to cede this ground to the opposition, and all parties felt obliged to address it in some way during the campaign. By 1987, a kind of second-order consensus had been evolved whereby all parties asserted their support for the police and the need to increase their effectiveness; all parties agreed that crime prevention and victim support were priorities; and all parties accepted the logic of 'bifurcation' (Bottoms, 1977), according to which extended custodial sentences are appropriate for the most serious offenders, but an enhanced range of non-custodial measures for the less serious should be used. By 1987, 65 per cent of Labour, 74 per cent of Conservative, 74 per cent of Social Democrat, and 65 per cent of Liberal addresses mentioned the topic. Yet significant differences remained in the manner in which they dealt with an issue which all now felt obliged to discuss. Substantial minorities of Conservative addresses called for tougher sentences (30 per cent) or capital punishment (19 per cent), or claimed that Labour was anti-police (14 per cent). By contrast, Labour Party addresses talked of the crime which pervaded a divided society, a Britain divided by the Tories' social and economic policies. In 1987, the local election addresses comprehensively mirrored the presentational stances which, throughout the 1980s, had been developed in the national manifestos. It was a configuration that seemed likely to play a prominent role in the election of 1992. But in the event Labour chose to remain content with the neutralization of the issue, rather than its contestation, a strategy which arguably left the Conservative Party in a position of inert supremacy as the guardians of law and order. In spite of continued rising crime in the face of substantially increased expenditure on 'law and order' services, Labour made nothing of the topic during the 1992 campaign (Butler and Kavanagh, 1992; King, 1993). The opinion poll evidence suggested that the Conservatives still inspired greater confidence on this issue and six weeks before the election the Party capitalized on the fact by unveiling a poster depicting a policeman with one hand tied behind his back. The accompanying slogan was: 'Labour's soft on crime'.

Explaining the Trends: Images, Philosophies, and Constraints

Frank Parkin argued over two decades ago that the principal strength of the Conservative Party was its capacity to claim oneness with the bastions of traditional British sovereignty: the monarchy, the aristocracy, property, the armed forces, the ancient universities, the land, and the law (Parkin, 1967). The only countervailing force to this ruling-class ideology was that offered by the Labour Party as representative of the working-class labour movement and its trade union organization. Yet this constituency was always deviant with respect to the core values and most cherished allegiances of British traditionalism. The Labour Party could flourish only in direct relation to movement away from their sites, most typically in a single-occupation, one-class urban area like a mining town. Against the Tory Party's keystone value of what Macpherson (1962) termed 'possessive individualism', the Labour Party rests on an appeal to the alternative morality of redistributive social justice and community.

These ideological differences translated readily into quite distinct policy choices in the post-war period. The Conservative preference for owner-occupation in housing has contrasted sharply and successfully with Labour's emphasis on municipal rented accommodation. On the other hand, Labour's development of the National Health Service could still command such widespread support that the Conservatives strove to resist the claim that their policies amounted to privatization. In taxation, Labour supports progressive direct taxation of income and wealth; the Conservatives favour regressive indirect taxes on spending. The choices are fairly distinct. Yet issues of 'law and order' do not lend themselves to such clear-cut articulation along party lines. This asymmetry is not due to the absence of sharp differences between the parties in their *explanations* of the underlying causes of crime. For Conservatives, these inhere in the realms of individual pathology and/or lax authority whether imposed at parental or institutional level. For Labour, they derive far more from social and economic realities: inequality, deprivation, marginalization, and outright poverty. For Labour, the task of political persuasion is therefore to make connections between crime and public issues, such as trends in employment and welfare. For the Conservatives, the task is to *disconnect* them, to contest, indeed, the very act of making such connections as inimical to law and order maintenance (Downes, 1989*a*). In Conservative rhetoric, 'explanation' amounts to 'excuse', an equation Labour has failed to challenge at all effectively. Throughout the 1980s, Mrs Thatcher successfully deployed this philosophically unacceptable elision by using the rhetoric of moral outrage. Thus, her statement that rioting can never be 'justified by unemployment' (or poverty, or racism, or police malpractices) always overrode the logical objection—rarely voiced—that nevertheless such realities may help to explain it. Edged by such tactics into appearing to be 'soft' on crime, Labour reacted not by challenging the image but increasingly by claiming equal toughness to—if not greater toughness than—the Conservatives.

An attempt to resolve this impasse appeared in a speech given in February 1993 by Tony Blair, then Labour Shadow Home Secretary. Addressing public anger and unease following the abduction and murder in Liverpool of a two-year-old boy, James Bulger, Blair set out Labour's policy on law and order as being 'tough on crime, tough on the causes of crime'. As yet, in the run-up to the 1997 general election, it is the first part of this formula that has received most attention: the need to provide more secure places for serious juvenile offenders; the proposal that lengthy periods of imprisonment be available for breach of 'community safety orders' made on the testimony of police or local government officers against persons engaging in 'chronic anti-social behaviour'—nuisance, noise, and so on—not necessarily criminal or for which there may be insufficient evidence to bring a prosecution (von Hirsch *et al.*, 1995); and the endorsement of 'zero tolerance' policing on the fashionable New York model. It remains to be seen if and how the second part of the policy will be developed, but given the Labour Party's commitment not to increase personal taxation if elected, the prospects for any radical attack on the economic inequalities and social deprivations of contemporary Britain seem poor.

In the 1993–6 period, Labour produced a flurry of policy papers, several of which focused explicitly on the alleged causes of crime. *Tackling the Causes of Crime* (1996) linked crime, somewhat baldly, with problems of parenting, schools, and truancy, drugs and alcohol misuse, unemployment and recession, care in the community, homelessness and the youth service, and suggested forms of best practice at both local and national level to address them. Another paper, *Parenting* (1996), took the parent–child relationship to be the 'crucial factor' in youth crime and made extensive proposals for parental education and support. The main running, however, was made in terms of criticisms of the criminal justice system under the Conservatives, especially the falling conviction rate and delays in juvenile justice.[8]

These are all important issues, and Labour clearly feel they have fashioned a telling response to the Conservatives by focusing on flaws in the latter's chosen ground: the criminal justice system itself. The irony is that the Criminal Justice Act 1991 was the climax to a decade of policy-making which had reduced the proportionate use of imprisonment by use of enhanced community sanctions (in 1991–2, the prison population fell to 40,600 from a peak of 50,000 in 1988—see Morgan, this volume). At the same time, due largely to the economic background of deep and lasting recession, the crime rate rose by over 40 per cent. It was ideologically impossible, however, for the Conservatives to accept that link, so that after 1992 they resorted to the U-turn in penal policy associated with Michael Howard (see Ashworth and Morgan, this volume). The economy gradually recovered as a result of the forced devaluation of 1992, and with it the crime rate stabilized, despite the disarray of the criminal justice system. That Labour have focused so heavily on criminal justice rather than economic and social causes—though they have kept that ball in play—is a sign of their determination to wrest this ground from the traditional dominance of the Conservatives, even at the expense of fears that they are flirting with new forms of authoritarianism in the process.

It follows that party policies on law and order can be related only tenuously to their ideological foundations. Image—associations of ideas and mythology—lent the Conservatives weight as *the* party of 'law and order'. No warrant for this assumption can be found in any indicator of actual performance. If anything, the reverse holds true, since periods of Labour government have seen lower rises in the recorded crime rate, both relatively and absolutely, than have

[8] *Protecting our Communities* (1996) recommended Community Safety Orders and composite offences. *Breaking the Vicious Circle* (1996) proposed new treatment and testing programmes in relation to drug-related crimes. *Tackling Youth Crime: Reforming Youth Justice* (1996) urged, in particular, use of a Final Warning to replace cautioning. And *Honesty, Consistency and Progression in Sentencing* (1996) recommended, *inter alia*, a form of indeterminate sentencing for rapists, and argued for explicit progression in sentencing, i.e. opposing, without acknowledgement, the 'just deserts' principle of the 1991 Criminal Justice Act.

Conservative administrations (Downes and Young, 1987; Downes, 1989*b*; Young, 1992). Despite the similarity or even superiority of Labour by comparison with the Conservative record on law and order, Labour have nevertheless proved vulnerable on this front due to various hostages to fortune derived from their association with, and implicit need to defend, several key constituencies.

These hostages to fortune on the left are bound up integrally with the origins and continuing role of the Labour Party as the parliamentary voice of the trade unions, on the one hand, and as the major vehicle for progressive intellectuals of a non-Marxist, socialist persuasion, on the other. The uneasy alliance between the labour movement and intellectuals of both Fabian and the more left-wing *Tribune* group persuasions is the chief strand in the story of the Labour Party, each involving the party in a set of distinctive concerns on the 'law and order' front which have exposed it to accusations from the right of undermining the 'rule of law'. Paradoxically, though the right also bears hostages to fortune in distinct (though fewer) respects, these can be handled in ways that strengthen rather than weaken their association with the forces of law and order.

Trade Unions and Labour

The labour movement both launched and proved the main ballast of Labour Party history, but in the period 1978–85 arguably almost sank it. This is no place to essay analysis of the long and tangled history of the relationship between the Party and the movement. The major point is that the struggle to win basic labour rights, from assembly to picketing to the very process of unionization itself, of a kind now accepted as legitimate in all democratic states, entailed a great deal of order-defiance and law-violation. In the immediate post-war period, however, the dominance of the right wing within the labour movement lent it a new respectability. Two pivotal factors eventually led to the situation whereby, in the late 1970s and 1980s, trade unionism could be equated with hooliganism and violence.

First, the electoral, though not numerical, defeat of the Labour government under Attlee in 1951 ushered in a period during which Britain, unlike any other Western European country, enjoyed the fruits of post-war prosperity under a right-wing government. The association of ideas between Toryism and prosperity has proved lasting. Despite intervening periods in office, Labour appeared to be the party of the austerity years, with union links that could 'threaten' economic growth. By contrast, trade unions in Scandinavia and West Germany were seen as playing an essential part in the process of economic recovery and expansion.

Secondly, the peculiar nature of capitalist law in Britain (and the USA) places unique emphasis on the overriding priority to be accorded the rights of shareholders in company development. Again by contrast, such rights in West Germany, Japan, Scandinavian, and other industrial societies are tempered by the requirement to give far more consideration to two other entities: the community and the employees (see e.g., Dore, 1992, on Japan; Schneider-Lenné, 1992, on Germany). Rights, conditions, amenities, and wage levels which were granted relatively smoothly by a process of negotiated settlements in these countries were in Britain too often wrung from reluctant employers by protracted conflict involving strike action. The litany of protracted industrial conflict in Britain embraces manufacturing industries in historic decline as well as light industries in the ascendant after the Second World War. In the 1970s, the left in Britain came to associate success in industrial conflict with militancy, a strategic choice which heightened the linkages made by the right between the labour movement, violence, and lawlessness. The eventual climax to this sequence of events was the 'Winter of Discontent' of 1978–9 (see note 2 above), which led to the downfall of the Labour government and ushered in the Thatcherite era.

The unions at times colluded in the process. For example, the print unions presided over the notorious Fleet Street ghost worker scandal, whereby workers who were already relatively well paid also drew wages for non-existent employees (see Martin, 1981). Perhaps the most tragic instance was the misconduct of the National Union of Mineworkers in 1983 in embarking on a national strike without the legally prescribed ballot of members. This tactic split the miners' otherwise united front, legitimized the government's pursuit of the union's funds by sequestration, and neutralized the likelihood of open Labour Party support for the strike. These factors arguably led to the miners' defeat after eighteen months of bitter strike action, in which the union was hauled through the courts, hundreds of miners were unwarrantedly harassed or victimized by the police, and the strikers' cause was marred by occasional acts of outright criminality and, in one case, manslaughter. The fact that the dire predictions by the NUM leadership, under Arthur Scargill, of pit closures and mass redundancies have been cruelly vindicated by events, with a labour force of 220,000 in 1983 reduced to 41,000 in 1992, does not nullify the association of ideas between trade union militancy and law-violation that resulted.

The unexpected defeat of the Labour Party in the 1992 election was widely ascribed to the success with which the Conservatives and the right-wing tabloid press revived fears of the 'hostages to fortune'. 'Tax and spend' policies, renewed union powers, immigrants 'flooding' into the country, and even more unemployment featured heavily in the campaign (Linton, 1995). (Crime was largely absent from this catalogue, reflecting the previous three years' rise of over 40 per cent in the official crime rate.) The consequence is that Labour has since further redefined its relations with the trades unions, distancing itself from the militant wing and nurturing links with more 'responsible' leaders. In 1993 John Smith, then Party leader, succeeded in extending the franchise within the Party, giving majority voting rights to constituency members and MPs and reducing the block-voting powers of the unions, a tradition seen as inimical to the Party's claim to represent broad public interests. Under the present leader, Tony Blair, the Party Conference has voted to abolish Clause 4 of its constitution, which since 1920 had committed the Party, in principle if not in practice, to wholesale public ownership. Pre-strike secret ballots and the ban on secondary-picketing are to remain and the trade unions are no longer to sponsor MPs. And no commitment has been made to restoring to the public sector those industries and utilities privatized since 1979.

> Fifteen years after the Conservatives' election [in 1979] the scope of labour reform exceeded even the wildest dreams of the New Right of the 1970s. There was no regulation of working time; no legally protected conditions for labour hired under fixed-term contracts; no minimum wage legislation; minimal employment protection; and employees had no legal right to representation at the workplace. The OECD, compiling a composite list of these measures, could, by the summer of 1994, rank Britain at zero—the lowest, apart from the US, in the industrialised world. (Hutton, 1995: 94)

Apart from the position of fixed-term contract labour, which the Conservatives would review, Labour is committed to restoring or strengthening all these rights, either by legislating or by joining the EU Social Chapter. In sum, the thrust of 'New Labour' has been to diminish union influence within the Party and to distance the Party further from any lingering association with union militancy, without losing union support or funding in the process. Even so, the right-wing tabloid press is reluctant to abandon so well-worn a hostage to fortune. 'Blair "all ready for sell-out"' (9 December) and 'Blair in "battle to death" with Unions' (27 December), were two headlines in the *Sun* on Labour–TUC relations at the end of 1996.

The New 'Underclass'?

The concept and formation of a new 'underclass' is vigorously contested (see e.g. Abercromble and Ward, 1988; Dahrendorf, 1987; Macnicol, 1987; and, on the USA, Jencks and Peterson, 1991; Wilson, 1996). What is not disputed is that de-industrialization has fractured the links between steady manual work and the stable communities which it once sustained. Further, the official statistics attest to the fact that the least wealthy half of the population now holds a lower proportion of overall wealth than it did a decade ago and that income differentials between households have grown. The rich have become richer, the poor poorer. To the extent that there can be said to be an 'underclass', it comprises groups as diverse as impoverished single parents; discriminated-against minority groups; the long-term unemployed; the never-have-been-employed youth of the poorer housing estates; and, as ever, those who, as Henry Mayhew (1862) put it, 'will not work'. The old working class has decayed. High, endemic unemployment and non-employment rates have provided the tinder from which—from 1980 onwards—riots have been kindled by policing which may have been insensitive but was rarely outlandish: the real cause lies in the economic marginalization and political exclusion of disadvantaged youths in particular, whether black, white, or both (Lea and Young, 1984). Relations between 'underclass' and authority are inherently conflict-ridden at any time, since the lot of the socially excluded is to be under-protected and overcontrolled.

The key problem for the Labour Party is unfortunately much the same as that for sociologists; how to connect private troubles with public issues (Mills, 1959). When riots as vicious as that at the Broadwater Farm Estate in North London in 1985 flare up, and a police officer is hacked to death, the best way to make the connection is hardly to announce that 'the police got a good hiding'. This remark by Bernie Grant, the local black Labour MP for a constituency with a large black population, was perhaps the biggest single hostage to fortune handed to the Conservatives by a left-wing source. The 1987 Labour strategy on policing was watered down from a policy of local accountability (strongly opposed by the police) to one of local consultation (little different from Conservative policy), due to fears that this and similar 'anti-police' remarks by left-wing sources would otherwise be quoted endlessly by the Conservatives in their campaigning: much the same backing-off process arguably occurred in 1992. However, Mr Grant did have a problem: how to supply a soundbite at the scene and under pressure which, by putting the events in context—that of racism, unemployment, and the oppressive policing resulting in the death of Mrs Groce, a West Indian mother of a black male suspect in a minor case of car theft, that had triggered the riot—did more than simply condemn the rioters. That he got it so resoundingly wrong in the event is in part a testimony to the massive difficulties in transcending sheer condemnation and moving on to explanation and constructive action. Given the constituencies involved, this was far more of a problem for Mr Grant and the Labour Party than for the Conservative government.

It is on this front that 'New Labour', and especially Jack Straw, Shadow Home Secretary in 1995–7, has moved most decisively to eliminate a potential 'hostage to fortune'. A series of policy announcements from 1994 onwards exorcised any trace of special pleading for socially disadvantaged offenders and even those guilty of no more than 'incivilities'. In 1995, Straw proposed a crackdown on 'squeegee merchants'—mostly youths who washed windscreens at traffic lights in return for small change, at times without clear consent from the 'captive' motorists. Shortly thereafter the Party published a consultation document *A Quiet Life* proposing that there be introduced a 'community safety order' for dealing with anti-social neighbours, the terms of which order outraged the civil liberties lobby. A further proposal was to enable local authorities to impose curfews on 10-year-olds out on the streets after 11 p.m. All these measures broke strikingly with 'Old Labour' thinking, which stressed broad social and economic measures and welfare support to control minor deviance. Straw's proposals also reflected enthusiasm for the apparent success of the policing methods of Bratton in New York. Indeed, the USA has been the role model for both Tory and Labour policy-makers in the 1990s, despite the fact that levels of homicide and violence in general remain several times higher than in Europe, a paradox explicable only in terms of the popularity of such 'tough on crime' policies with electorates.

It has, however, been by his broad acceptance of Michael Howard's U-turn on penal and sentencing policy that Jack Straw, Shadow Home Secretary, most clearly signalled his break with past Labour policy. The government's U-turn (see Ashworth and Morgan, this volume) was explicable as a response both to sharply rising crime rates and to the loss of the Conservative lead over Labour on 'law and order'. Howard clearly aimed to 'smoke Labour out' as a Party essentially 'soft on crime', by adopting a strong 'prison works' policy and by adopting a modified form of the 'three strikes and you're out' mandatory custodial sentencing policy embraced by President Clinton. Straw's decision to take a broadly bipartisan approach to such measures effectively neutralized this strategy, with seeming popular success: an ICM poll in August 1996 showed Labour to enjoy roughly double the support accorded the Conservatives on 'law and order' (*Guardian*, 7 August) without jeopardizing his position within the Party—his vote for the National Executive Committee by constituency members rose in autumn 1996. Moreover, in January 1997 Tony Blair, in an interview with the magazine for the homeless, *The Big Issue*, endorsed the 'zero tolerance' policing policy being pursued in the Kings Cross area of London, a policy which has reportedly involved sweeping the streets of homeless beggars. The fact that these much-publicized stances create fresh 'hostages to fortune' of a different kind post-electorally is clearly seen as a price worth paying to spike Conservative guns on this front. As a result, opposition to such measures has been displaced from the Labour Party to the Liberal Party, civil liberties and penal pressure groups, and the judiciary itself.

Though in their writings Labour leaders stress that their intolerance is focused on the causes of homelessness and other deprivations, their well-publicized public utterances emphasize first priority acceptance that public nuisance be cleared away and order restored. Such disorders have waxed as stable employment and the strength of the labour movement have waned. Working-class trade unionists demonstrate and take industrial action in pursuit of recognizable, collective ends, in ways—such as mass picketing—which may verge on or constitute law-violation under certain circumstances. Denied employment, the new 'underclass' is incapable of such organizational feats, though some remarkable examples of community action (see, for example, Campbell, 1993) give the lie to the view that the socially excluded are a 'new rabble' (Murray, 1994). However, riot and criminality may conceivably be interpreted as impoverished routes to these ends, but they are hardly recognizable or shared, and explanation in these terms all too easily sounds like special pleading. In short, the more the organized labour movement and the trade unions are pushed off the stage by endemic mass un- and non-employment, and by rapid technological change, the more the emergent underclass presents the Labour Party with a massive problem of translation. For example despite widespread and articulate opposition across the social spectrum, even the poll tax presented the Labour opposition with a particularly nasty version of the 'law and order' paradox, whereby the iniquitous character of the law would only be changed by strong public reaction, including non-compliance (since compliance would be taken by the government as confirming public acquiescence).[9] However, for the opposition to support non-compliance would have been denounced as inciting people to violate the law, an accusation that was indeed levelled against several Labour MPs who advocated it despite official Labour policy on the issue. Non-compliance would also have deprived Labour-controlled local authorities of essential income.

Civil Disobedience

Civil disobedience has been a substantial and generally honourable strand in the history of the Labour Party. The inter-war period was notable for such events as George Lansbury's imprisonment in 1921 for leading the non-payment of local precepts by Poplar Council in protest against the burden placed on local government to provide poor relief, the 1926 General Strike, and the 'hunger marches' of the 1930s Depression years, all of which were actively supported by Labour MPs (see Mowat, 1955). It might have been expected that, as Labour formed the government for seventeen of the post-war years, old habits would have died and indeed, for the first decade after the war, that seemed to be so. However, the Suez Crisis of 1956 revived the tradition, and the Campaign for Nuclear Disarmament, formed in the same year, founded the annual march to London from the first American forces' nuclear base at Aldermaston (see Taylor, 1988). Left-wing Labour MPs were prominent figures on these demonstrations which, although eminently peaceful, were increasingly drawn into association with extra-legal activities, such as the exposure by an Anarchist group on the 1961 march of the hitherto secret Regional Seats of Government bases. The formation of the Committee of 100 in 1961 brought a new repertoire to civil disobedience: the systematic violation of the law by leading and usually left-wing intellectuals to focus attention on the nuclear disarmament cause.

The Vietnam War from 1964 onwards provided the target for a rising crescendo of demonstrations which, with the rise of the student movement in the USA and its spread to Europe in the mid-1960s, added site occupations to the armoury of protest. Labour, which formed the government from 1964 to 1970, pursued a policy of damage-limitation with respect to the policing of such forms of protest. Media coverage of the October 1968 Grosvenor Square demonstration, however, lent a new imputation to reportage: the expectation that the potential for violence implicit in any mass movement would be realized. As Halloran *et al.* (1970) pointed out, the press greatly exaggerated such violence as did occur on that march.

[9] The so-called 'poll tax', or community charge, introduced by the Conservative government in 1988 to replace local authority rates, levied the same tax *per capita* regardless of income, wealth, or size of property. The only major exemptions concerned people on income support and students, who were charged 20 per cent of the tax.

After Grosvenor Square, and the student demonstrations in Paris in May 1968 which almost led to the collapse of the French government, the die was cast. No left-wing cause had street credibility without a march, demonstration, or occupation. The Clydebank occupation of 1972 firmly associated industrial militancy with key figures in the Labour Party following the much publicized conversion of Tony Benn to the merits of such direct action. The case of the 'Shrewsbury Three' in 1974 embodied the ease with which direct action by pickets could turn ugly and involve criminal prosecutions.[10] It was also in 1974 that the newly elected Labour government's Director of Public Prosecutions failed to prosecute Labour councillors in Bolsover who had refused to raise rents in accordance with the previous Conservative government's Rent Act. Another *cause célèbre* was the Grunwick strike and several months' long mass picket of 1976–7, which even right-of-centre Labour ministers such as Shirley Williams felt the need to attend, in solidarity with a workforce largely composed of Asian women who had been denied the right to unionize by their employer. The 1970s were characterized by a plethora of such events, the policing of which was frequently contentious and costly, and at times tragically counter-productive.

In the 1980s street protest turned sour. The symbolism had become devalued to the point where the absence of a demonstration or march against a measure was taken for popular compliance with it. The threshold for media coverage was raised to the point at which, unless a demonstration involved violence, little reportage could be expected. The poll tax riots of 1989–90 were the climax of these developments. By this juncture, however, the 'freedom of the streets' had been greatly constrained. Thereafter the strategy brought diminishing returns of publicity and, in the face of disruption and traffic congestion, of public support and interest. Bans on marches by the extreme right had been extended to all unless stringent criteria of stewardship and route-taking were met. In the 1992–6 period, civil disobedience was conducted on largely non-partisan lines on single-issue causes, such as the sustained opposition to new motorways (the Winchester and Newbury by-passes, the M11 link through Wanstead, etc.) and to the export of live animals. There was less call for Labour to take a position on these events; and fading memories of the halcyon days of civil disobedience tend to be associated with 'Old' rather than 'New Labour'.

If the increasing frequency and size of demonstrations heralded the eclipse of a Conservative government in 1974, their decreasing salience and vigour have marked the ascendancy of the neo-Conservative regimes since 1979. In so far as Labour is associated with both the decline and the unwanted side-effects of taking to the streets, its image as upholder of law and order is at risk. Only when the politics of the street are actively welcomed as a symbol of peaceable and healthy democracy is such a risk neutralized. Without them, the arena for the legitimate expression of views is greatly reduced.

[10] This *cause célèbre*, which involved sentences of imprisonment, arose out of a strike in the building industry and the use of 'flying pickets' (see Wallington, 1975).

Libertarian Criminal Law Reform

Though Labour Party history has been marked by a libertarian strand which has surfaced from time to time, the late 1960s witnessed a sustained programme of criminal law reform under a Labour government: the decriminalization of male homosexuality and abortion; the substantial relaxation of the censorship laws; the abolition of capital punishment; and the resolution of key problems threatening the legalization of casino gaming. The last of these stemmed from the sweeping legalization of gaming carried out by the Conservative government of Harold Macmillan in 1960 and 1963; a government which also decriminalized attempted suicide in 1963. It was left to a Labour Lord Chancellor, Gerald Gardiner, systematically to push the reform through, however. Two decades later, the entire period of liberalizing achievement by both Conservative and Labour was to be derided by the new right of Thatcher and Tebbit as the 'permissive society', having achieved nothing more than a slackening of authority and an unwanted release of baser passions. What was, by most standards, a major period of reform promoting greater tolerance and freedom of expression came to figure in the popular press and in rightwing ideology as the source of unprecedented rises in criminality in the 1980s.

What had been a relatively clear-cut battle between the 'progressive liberals'—who in the 1960s had migrated to the Labour Party to a much greater extent than before or since—and the forces of reaction, had in the 1980s become more complex, however. First, certain forms of backlash arose from unexpected quarters. For example, radical feminists, including such leading Labour MPs as Clare Short, and leading traditionalists, such as Mary Whitehouse, ranged themselves, albeit for different reasons, against pornography and the exploitation of women as exemplified on page three of the *Sun.* The porn merchants had made far narrower and more profitable use of the new-found liberties of expression of the 1960s than the exponents of liberalization had ever predicted. The average suburban newsagent carried a far greater spread of female nudity in the 1980s than the average Soho pornshop in the 1950s. Secondly, gay militancy had found forms of political expression which included material for primary schools. The resulting backlash included legal constraints such as section 28 of the Education Act 1988, which expressly forbade the inclusion of family imagery in school material other than that connoting the heterosexual nuclear family.

In sum, once basic freedoms had been won, the complications to which their extension gave rise tended to saddle Labour with the worst of both worlds, able neither to defend such developments as 'gay' schoolbooks nor to define where the line should be drawn afresh. Such defensiveness left such minorities as gays feeling betrayed, on the one hand, and the 'silent majority' feeling that Labour had allowed too much scope for deviant viewpoints, on the other. Conversely, Labour spokespersons who opposed such phenomena as the 'page three nude' could be castigated as killjoys. One notorious election-day ploy in the *Sun* (9 April 1992) was the substitution for the usual page three model of a stereotypically reverse image, a flabby parody of coquettishness. The caption read: 'Here's How Page 3 Will Look Under Kinnock.' Labour could be blamed for both the unwanted developments of libertarianism and the negative aspects of the selective backlash against them.

Since 1992 Labour has reacted more selectively to issues that might cause embarrassment on this front. First, by reverting strongly to its image as the Party of 'the family', Labour registered its disinclination to defend, let alone promote, the interests of such groups as single parents and gays, as actively as in the recent past. In 1996, for example, Labour abstained in the House of Commons vote to exclude homosexuals from the armed forces. Secondly, on issues such as the clauses in the 1996 Police Bill, which endorse phone-tapping and house searching on warrants issued by Home Office-appointed commissioners, with the role of the judiciary recast as a retrospective sample check, Labour's stance only belatedly changed from barely qualified active promotion to critical opposition. Labour has also abandoned its traditional opposition to the annual renewal of the Prevention of Terrorism Act. Thirdly, Labour has even ruled out debate within its ranks on certain sensitive issues. In 1996, for example, Clare Short, a Shadow cabinet member, was slapped down for expressing the view, following the proposal by some chief constables, that debate on the possible decriminalization of small-scale cannabis possession be reopened.

In the face of wide-ranging attacks on the potential for order-defiance and law-violation of several of its key constituencies Labour has reacted defensively, content to neutralize the appeal of the Conservatives wherever possible as *the* party of law and order, but backing away from outright contention on the issues involved. The scope for Labour to turn the tables on the Conservatives on these terms was limited by the simple 'rule of law' principle to which the latter adhered quite uncritically. Thus, the law-violations of the extreme right, or those endemic in the operations of the commercial-financial world of the City of London, or those emanating from flawed police procedures, could always be explained in terms of individual pathology, a 'few bad apples'. The kind of challenge to the very terms of the debate which Labour had mounted in some respects in the 1960s was increasingly foregone as anxieties about the electoral liabilities of the hostages to fortune rose.

By any objective standard, the period of Conservative government since 1979 has been a conspicuous failure in crime control terms. In spite of a host of crime prevention initiatives[11] and real increases in spending on the so-called 'law and order' services, increases greater than in any other branch of government expenditure—more police, better paid and with more powers; more courts with an increased range of penalties at their disposal; more prisons and more prisoners in them—the fear of crime has increased, there have been larger than normal rises in recorded crime, and a sequence of urban disturbances has

[11] These have included the development of Neighbourhood Watch and numerous other Watch schemes, the Safer Cities initiative, and the encouragement of multi-agency schemes of various types: see Pease, this volume.

occurred unprecedented in their ferocity this century. And yet, the polls suggest that until the early 1990s, the Conservative Party retained its supremacy as the party of 'law and order'. It managed to persuade a large section of the electorate that the rising tide of crime was not to be explained by the widened divide between rich and poor, the undermining of public goods and services, the emasculation of local government, and the lauding of competitive individualism to the detriment of collective responsibility. Rather, crime is to be ascribed to evil individuals or persons; generally young persons, subject to insufficient control by parents who have a duty to police their behaviour. Either way, criminals are to get their just deserts, punishment proportionate to their culpability and the harm they have caused. Explanatory references to structural forces—poverty, unemployment, discrimination, oppression, social and economic hopelessness, and alienation—are castigated as damaging to the ethos of personal responsibility on which the maintenance of law and order is said ultimately to depend. The question at stake is whether the hegemony of the philosophy of individual pathology, a philosophy closely allied to the paramountcy of the market in Conservative economic policy, can be sustained in the face of further increases in crime and disorder, and whether the Labour Party will continue to adopt a defensive law and order policy on the terrain that the Conservative Party has mapped out; or whether the tide will turn and the opposition successfully call into question the moral basis of the political economy which current law and order policies are designed to support.

In the event, the Labour Party chose to adopt an aggressive law and order policy on the very terrain mapped out by the Conservatives, refusing to be upstaged by the increasingly punitive policies of the Home Secretary, and even pre-empting certain ideas—curfews, the control of incivilities, and more rapid juvenile justice—overlooked by the government. Electronic tagging and mandatory sentencing were swallowed by Labour with barely a public hint of indigestion and the privatization of prisons, though initially opposed, seems now to be accepted. As a result, the mantle of opposition to such measures fell even more heavily on the Liberal Party, the liberal press, the Probation Service, the penal pressure groups and—at least in connection with mandatory sentencing and some aspects of prisoners' rights—the judiciary. The result appears to have been to neutralize Michael Howard's attempt to wrest back the image of the 'Party of law and order' to the Conservatives, though at considerable cost to Labour's credibility as the upholder of humane standards in criminal justice and penal policy.

In one respect, Labour was greatly aided by a change in Conservative fortunes from an unexpected quarter. In October 1992 Britain's exit was forced from the Exchange Rate Mechanism, at the cost of several billion pounds in a few days' attempt to prop up sterling, following a spate of financial scandals in the City of London. Given widespread unease about the moral 'state of the nation', the Prime Minister, John Major, attempted to reassert the government's standing by, *inter alia*, launching a 'Back to Basics' campaign on morality. This exercise backfired badly as the tabloid press homed in on the involvement in extra-marital affairs of several Conservative MPs, and a Minister, David Mellor. Over the next few years, Ministers were roundly criticized for their role in the earlier Thatcher administration's handling of arms sales to Iraq (by the Scott Report); two Conservatives MPs were accused of having taken 'cash for questions' in Parliament on behalf of lobby group interests (condemned by the Nolan Report, which set up new procedures for monitoring potential conflicts of interest); and the *Guardian* newspaper criticized a Minister of Defence, Jonathan Aitken, for allegedly accepting hospitality from Arab businessmen with arms trade connections. Several grisly murders, from that of James Bulger to the mass slaughter of sixteen school children and staff at Dunblane in Scotland, and the street killing of a London headmaster, Philip Lawrence, by a knife-wielding youth, led to a national debate. Though *some* aspects of the reactions could be defined as 'moral panic', the dignity and raw grief of the victims' closest kin commanded a respect which ensured a serious hearing for their campaign for a complete ban on the sale and ownership of handguns. The Labour and Liberal Parties were able to wrongfoot the government by supporting a total ban, whilst the Home Secretary was compelled by internal Party and interest group pressure to retain .22 weapons.

The result amounted to a moral inquest on an era in which the pursuit of economic salvation had visibly damaged social cohesion. It led to an institutional anxiety about incipient *anomie*: the breakdown of a recognizable moral order. The media were awash with debates, discussions, dialogues, and documentaries about every nuance of social pathology, from weapon control to the effects of media violence, though rarely in any decently informed, as distinct from sound-bite, fashion. For a time at least, the government appeared to have lost any convincing claim to integrity, competence, and expertise. For once, the Conservatives, accustomed to travelling lightly on the high moral ground of personal responsibility exercised in a social vacuum, and without the burden of 'hostages to fortune', were suddenly afflicted by a welter of illicit arms deals, hypocrisy in family affairs, serious frauds, and the antipathy of almost all branches of the criminal justice system to which they appealed for the 'rule of law'. In short 'sleaze' became the disease to which the Government seemed increasingly prone and, under these circumstances, the opposition parties could for once enjoy a certain *Schadenfreude*. It remains to be seen how far this issue can be turned to Labour's electoral advantage.

PRESSURE-GROUP AND INTEREST-GROUP POLITICS

As Bottoms and Stevenson (1992) argue, the fundamental variable in any assessment of 'What went wrong?' in post-war criminal justice policy and practice is the inexorable rise of the crime rate. From the mid-1950s onwards, this almost unbroken increase in crime of 5–6 per cent annually beggared explanation in terms of simple poverty and deprivation, as both were manifestly on the decline. With the rise in crime despite the rise in welfare and increasing prosperity came rises in criminological and pressure-group activity, attempts respectively to account for crime and to improve the nature of responses to it. The proliferation of pressure groups was not unique to the law and order field but was a trend in British politics as a whole in this period. Electoral behaviour was more capable of being altered by short-term single issues which could 'only with difficulty be forced within the straitjacket of the old, class-based, two-party system. A new political agenda centred on Europe, disarmament, the environment, quality of public and private services, and citizenship rights has already become well established in many countries of the European Community' (Gamble, 1990: 353).

Perhaps because law and order issues had never fitted that straitjacket to any marked extent, pressure groups in this field often bore pedigrees going back to before the Thatcher decade, though some—notably Inquest (founded 1981) and the Prison Reform Trust (founded 1982)—are of very recent origin. The oldest, the Howard League for Penal Reform, emerged in 1921 from the amalgamation of the original Howard Association, founded in 1866, and the more militant Penal Reform League, formed in the wake of the suffragette movement in 1907 (see Ryan, 1978). It has counterparts in many Commonwealth countries. Until the foundation of the National Association for the Care and Resettlement of Offenders (NACRO) in 1966, it had no real contenders in the field of penal reform. From the late 1960s, however, new pressure groups flourished: Radical Alternatives to Prison (RAP) in 1969; the Legal Action Group (LAG) in 1971; and, within the Labour Party, the Labour Campaign for Criminal Justice in 1978. JUSTICE had, however, preceded even NACRO: founded by Tom Sargent, it was a remarkably successful pressure group in its highly focused pursuit of legal reform. On occasion, alliances between two or more of these groups enhanced their effectiveness, as with the battle of the Howard League, JUSTICE and NACRO to expunge certain classes of ex-offender records in the Rehabilitation of Offenders Act 1974 (*ibid.*: 60–3).

The concept of the campaigning consortium was successfully adopted between 1978 and 1983 when New Approaches to Juvenile Crime—a grouping of NACRO and the principal social work and probation practitioner organizations, did much to generate the climate of opinion which led to the dramatic decline in the use of custody for juvenile offenders in the 1980s. The group used all the informational techniques which have made NACRO a force to be reckoned with: briefing papers and associated press releases were regularly produced; deputations to ministers were arranged; meetings with magistrates were held; and regular parliamentary briefings were organized. It was Lady Faithful, the group's organizer, who, against Government wishes, introduced amendments to the Bill which became the custody criteria for young offenders in the Criminal Justice Act 1982, section 1: this measure led to greatly reduced use of custody. Moreover, though cause and effect can never precisely be established, there seems little doubt that New Approaches to Juvenile Crime did much to counter the rhetoric of the early 1980s in support of the experimentally punitive 'short, sharp shock' regimes in detention centres—the courts used these centres less rather than more—and helped to lay the foundation whereby the DHSS funded more than 100 Intermediate Treatment programmes from 1983 onwards.

A more recent pressure grouping is the Penal Affairs Consortium, a lobbying collective which comprised thirteen organizations when it was formed in 1989 and which now comprises thirty-one, ranging from the Prison Governors' and the Prison Officers' Associations to NACRO, the Prison Reform Trust, the Howard League, and Liberty—a previously unthinkable combination. Some single-issue pressure groups, such as the National Campaign for the Abolition of the Death Penalty (1955), rise and fall as the issue around which they are built waxes and wanes. The extent of pressure group activity in 1990 can be gauged from the (by no means exhaustive) catalogue of such groups listed as having given evidence to the Woolf Inquiry into the prison disturbances of April that year. They ranged from the Aids and Prison Consortium Project to the Mental Health Foundation to Women in Prison and included some sixty-five groups in all, as well as professional associations, public service unions and ministries, and agencies of central and local government.

The sheer proliferation of such groups is striking, but less salient than the impressive professionalization of the major organizations in the field, particularly NACRO, the Prison Reform Trust, and the Howard League. Before 1970, the date assigned by Bailey (1987) to the final break-up of the post-war consensus on delinquency, pressure-group activity metaphorically sought to influence policy by a well-informed word in the ministerial ear. From that date, reformers increasingly began to beat on the ministerial door in a far more public, confrontational way, albeit one which was, if anything, even more highly informed. Douglas Hurd, Home Secretary from 1984 to 1988, remarked that such clamour was counter-productive. However, this metaphor should not be allowed to obscure the growth, especially in the 1980s, of myriad links between the Home Office and the pressure groups. In conferences, media debates, seminars, and the regular call for expert evidence on penal matters in particular, opportunities abounded for pressure groups to inform penal policy-making processes. None of these processes, either singly or in total, however, equalled the kind of unforced access that the Howard League enjoyed in its heyday of close informal as well as formal contact with the Home Office (see Ryan, 1978) or the strong role for criminological expertise provided by the Advisory Council on the Penal System (ACPS, 1966–80) and its predecessor the Advisory Council on the Treatment of Offenders (ACTO, 1944–64). The abolition of the ACPS in 1980 signalled the end of the inside track enjoyed by the more Establishment academic liberal reformers, adding to the scope for group activity. That inside track had, of course, carried the danger that research might uphold punitive measures, and inhibit strong contestation of government policy, as in the example of Max Grunhut's long gestation of a project which eventually reported in favour of detention centres, to the detriment of the Howard League's stance on the issue (Ryan, 1978: 83–4). Further, in its final years, the ACPS produced more and more lengthy reports—on *Young Adult Offenders* in 1974 and *Sentences of Imprisonment* in 1978—which attracted critical academic judgement as well as ministerial impatience (see Morgan, 1979). In the 1980s the government largely replaced advice from Royal Commissions and standing advisory bodies with official inquiries set up whenever a need was perceived.

It was this decline in government reliance on officially organized advice that stimulated the emergence of more professional pressure groups, most of them of recent origin and, even when beneficiaries of government funding—as NACRO has always been—more or less critical of government policy. The pressure groups have generally favoured: explanations of crime which stress social and economic inequality and individual vulnerability; use of social policy in general rather than criminal justice policy in particular to prevent or control crime; scepticism about the value of police powers and punitive methods (particularly imprisonment) as crime-control measures—indeed, they generally stress the discriminatory and unjust consequences of such methods for repressing already oppressed minorities (Ryan, 1978, 1983). Thus though there are substantial differences between these groups regarding their ideological commitments, constitutional form, access to policy-makers, and credibility with government, they have a good deal in common. They are generally perceived as left of centre, generally have allegiances with Liberal or Labour rather than Conservative politicians (though NACRO and the Prison Reform Trust are always careful to involve politicians of all parties on their councils), and tend, in spite of the consortia arrangements referred to above, also to have fragile relationships with the practitioner sectional groups, such as the Prison Officers' Association, the Police Federation, the Association of Chief Police Officers (ACPO), and the Magistrates' Association. The latter tend to adopt policies emphasizing the 'thin blue line' and the importance of their members' powers to safeguard the community from crime.

Given these dissonances, it is notable how much interchange occurred between the groups and the government in the 1980s. In other fields of social policy, such as education, where pressure groups of comparable expertise are largely lacking, ideologically driven changes since 1979 arguably met with less resistance, despite strong interest-group and practitioner unease or hostility. Given the immense imbalance of power between the groups and the Home Office, the latter could be said to have little to lose and much to gain from such contacts. The pressure groups provide positive feedback services for governments in furnishing early warnings of probable trouble, in canvassing feasible reforms, and in heightening the legitimacy of the governmental process itself. In a complex society, pressure-group and interest-group activities are the major avenues for active citizen participation in democratic decision-making. In the 1980s, pressure groups also fitted the ideological predispositions of the Thatcher administrations to accord client-based and consumerist agencies a better hearing, albeit at the expense of local government (which still harboured socialist residues) and the trade unions. Quangos and Royal Commissions were seen as stifling government and citizen initiative. The Woolf Inquiry of 1990 was a model of democratic participation by an informed citizenry (by comparison with, say, the average Royal Commission), holding seminars at which the views and evidence of different groups were debated rather than simply presented *seriatim*—though the views of prisoners were separately canvassed and, to that extent, somewhat devalued (Morgan, 1991; Sim, 1993). This consultative model was subsequently adopted by the Committee of Inquiry into Complaints about Ashworth Hospital in 1991–2, with similarly radical impact (Blom-Cooper Report 1992; see also Richardson, 1993).

Nevertheless, the huge imbalance of power remains a political reality. When 'pressured', the Home Office can brush aside any protest, as exemplified by the recent acceleration of prison privatization, a policy opposed vehemently by all the groups cited as well as the Prison Officers' and Prison Governors' Associations. The Conservative government in its drive to cut the cost of public services and expose them to the allegedly beneficial rigours of market competition has increasingly viewed the practitioner-representative organizations as little more than vested interests resisting any challenge to the inefficient monopolistic services within which they shelter. Thus the consultative instincts of senior judges, like Woolf, asked to undertake official inquiries, have seldom characterized ministerial policy initiatives. The early 1990s, for example, saw a series of initiatives regarding policing policy in which real consultation was lacking. Changes in the rank structure and proposals radically to alter the basis of police pay—changes recommended by the 1992 Sheehy Inquiry—and major amendments to the constitutional framework for the governance of the police—amendments first set out in the 1991 White Paper on *Police Reform* and implemented in the Police and Magistrates' Courts Act 1994—were taken speedily and *in spite of* the views of practitioners, local government associations, and the overwhelming majority of informed commentators.

The government's drive to effect change in law and order services in the face of practitioner opposition has prompted the Labour Party to move closer to the slighted practitioner organizations and distance themselves from the pressure groups whose liberal credentials and 'soft' image have themselves become hostages to fortune in the struggle for the political middle ground. As a consequence the pressure groups have not enjoyed the direct contacts and influence with the world of either Whitehall or Westminster in the 1990s which they achieved in the 1980s. To compensate for the deficit, the pressure groups have deployed their expertise in two respects: media influence and the appeal to comparative criminology.

Media influence is important to the pressure groups for the impact it may enable them to bring to bear on policy-making *and* for its sheer publicity value. The higher the profile the groups achieve the more members they may gain and the more they may be able to persuade public opinion to take note of the problems facing such unpopular groups as ex-offenders (see Schlesinger and

Tumber, 1992: 190–1). The Home Office and the police are not immune from pursuing the same strategy. Greater openness by police and prison staff is often inspired by the demand thus generated for more resources.

Comparative criminology has increasingly been used by the pressure groups to highlight the extent to which prisoners in Britain are both relatively more numerous than in virtually all other Western European countries and often held in worse conditions. The NACRO league table of numbers of prisoners per head of population (drawing on Council of Europe data) has been a feature of their briefings for the past decade. Analyses comparing Britain's current penal conditions unfavourably with those of the Netherlands (Tulkens, 1979; Downes, 1982, 1988). West Germany (Feest. 1988), the Netherlands, and Japan (Rutherford, 1984), and those of Britain in the recent past (King and McDermott, 1989, 1995) were drawn on by the pressure groups, as well as by criminologists in general, including those working within the Home Office Research and Planning Unit (Graham, 1988). The Woolf Inquiry (1991) broke new ground by interviewing British prisoners abroad, in Spain, the Netherlands, and West Germany, as well as drawing on comparative evidence for the second part of the Report. In 1989 Prison Reform International (PRI) was formed with, significantly, Vivien Stern, then Director of NACRO, as its Secretary General. PRI currently has an expanding membership drawn from almost fifty countries: the information pooled by that membership is providing an increasingly international backcloth to the shape of penal pressure-group politics in Britain.

The micro-politics of law and order are intimately bound up with the processes whereby the goals and agendas set by ministers are translated into policies and specific directives by civil servants. They are also creatively authored in key respects by senior civil servants, whose briefings and policy formulations have a distinct part to play in formal policy-making. As Rock (1990) has shown, policy formation within the Home Office is typically a matter of written argument developing creatively. For example, the 1991 Criminal Justice Act was the outcome of a lengthy, decade-long process of casting about for the most appropriate means of reducing the level of the prison population without either eroding the independence of the judiciary or offending the more reactionary wing of the Conservative Party. David Faulkner was a Deputy Under-Secretary at the Home Office from 1982, and for much of the decade he pursued that brief with the *imprimatur* of the Permanent Secretary, Sir Brian Cubbon. In the context of the demise of the rehabilitative policies that dominated the progressive field up to 1970, to be replaced by the 'just deserts' model pioneered in the USA (see e.g. American Friends Service committee 1971; von Hirsch, 1976; Martinson, 1974), Faulkner sought a compromise which would respect judicial independence and yet persuade sentencers to reduce their resort to imprisonment. The provision of *more* non-custodial measures had failed to achieve this effect in the 1970s. They had simply tended to be used as alternatives to *other* alternatives to custody. The major reason always given by sentencers for this result was that the existing alternatives were 'too soft'. Logically, tougher versions of existing community measures, especially probation, might succeed where the provision simply of extra alternatives had failed. That informed guesswork was incorporated, after much sounding and debate, in the 1991 Criminal Justice Act. In the event, core ingredients in the Act were soon reversed (by the Criminal Justice Act 1993, see Ashworth, this volume) but the legislation testified to the active working through of such measures by civil servants still stereotyped as passive bureaucrats. By their creation of a 'symbolic environment' (Edelman, 1971), by their active refinement of current issues, and by their deployment of arguments culled from gatherings as diverse as international conferences and informal discussion groups, it is possible, even in Britain, for senior civil servants such as Faulkner and, in an earlier period, Morrell (in connection with the Children and Young Persons Act 1970) to energize the field (see Rock, 1986, 1990; Bottoms, 1974; Rutherford, 1996; King and McDermott, 1995: chapter 1).

It would, however, be mistaken to assume that the benign hand of some concerned civil servant is always to be found behind major legislative and policy-making processes, or that policy initiatives are the outcome of an increasingly open and well-informed discussion between ministers and their advisers on the one hand and experts and practitioners working with a growing array of penal pressure groups on the other. Just as important, if not more commonplace, is the process of masterly inactivity or just plain drift. For example, analysis of the history of one penalty, the senior attendance centre order, has found little by way of cumulative rationality or systematic planning in its development (Mair, 1991). Other relevant processes at work can be found in the Select Committee stages of drafting legislation. The often painstaking scrutiny involved in this stage of a Bill's enactment can be the means for its profound amendment or effective termination by delay. For example, the Police and Criminal Evidence Act 1984 was a vastly different affair from the 1983 Bill which lapsed on the calling of the 1983 general election, after a clause-by-clause challenge to its composition by the opposition parties (see Ryan, 1983 for a searching analysis of parliamentary processes in this field). Such major transformations as a result of detailed parliamentary scrutiny are, however, increasingly the exception rather than the rule. Within four months of the implementation of the Criminal Justice Act 1991, the then Home Secretary, Kenneth Clarke, conceded, in the face of criticism from the judiciary and magistracy, that some of the detail within the legislation required amendment: critics argued that the Bill had received altogether too little parliamentary scrutiny.

Since 1993 and the advent of Michael Howard as Home Secretary, criminal justice policy-making has become dominated, to quite an unprecedented extent, by the politics of law and order. The lengthy process of gestation, consultation, and re-drafting which went with the decarceration policy of the 1980s was abruptly thrown into disarray by the 'Prison Works' U-turn of 1993. The Home Office has been turned away from the:

> once standard processes of internal consultation, from committee meetings, briefings and circulating files, towards procedures that are more fragmentary, centrifugal and loosely bounded. Portions of criminal justice policy-making have become somewhat less cohesive, coherent, controlled and centralized as they come under the sway of devolution, 'contracting out', Next Steps Agencies and external consultants. . . . The newest modes of policy making are themselves the fruits of a new politics of populism, moralism and the market (Rock, 1995: 2).

The result is a prison population carcering out of control, a penal estate seething with discontent and the resort to measures, such as the importation of a prison ship from the United States, which symbolizes desperate remedies.

By contrast, some policy innovations emerge out of the blue because of a minister's personal enthusiasm, or are the product of almost haphazardly won concessions granted during the committee stage of a bill, or are adopted following various lobbying by small groups of backbenchers, sometimes with the support of one or another of the Select Committees of the House of Commons. For example, section 58 of the Criminal Justice Act 1991, which provides for parents to be bound over if the court is satisfied that to do so would be desirable in the interests of preventing the commission of further offences by a young offender, would almost certainly not have been included in the Bill had it not been for the enthusiasm, against the tide of practitioner and pressure-group opinion, of John Patten, then a junior minister in the Home Office. Mr Patten originally proposed a much more drastic measure in order to ensure parental control of their children, a prophylactic he considered lacking. In March 1989 he proposed that it should be made a criminal offence for parents to fail to make reasonable efforts to prevent their children from committing offences. This proposition encountered considerable opposition and was dropped. The bind-over provision of section 58 was the barely acceptable substitute.

The enthusiasms of backbench MPs and peers may also carry the day, if they are backed by influential groups. We have already noted the example of Baroness Faithful backed by the Juvenile Justice lobby. A contrasting example is to be found in section 84 of the Criminal Justice Act 1991. This provides for the contracting out of the management of prisons and could in principle mean that every prison currently run by the Prison Service might be turned over to the private sector through the affirmative resolution procedure of section 84(5). This is an astonishing provision given that, as recently as 1987, the then Home Secretary, Douglas Hurd, informed the House of Commons that he did not 'think that there is a case, and I do not believe the House would accept that there is a case, for auctioning or privatising the prisons, or handing over the business of keeping prisoners safe to anyone other than government servants' (Hansard HC, 16 July 1987, vol. 119, col. 1299). The about-turn is explained by the fact that in 1986–7 the Select Committee on Home Affairs produced a brief report (1987) in which the majority of the Committee recommended that there should be experimentation on contracting out the management of prisons. By skilful lobbying (see Ryan and Ward, 1989, for background detail) various members persuaded a reluctant government to insert a clause providing for the contracting-out of remand prisons, a restrictive provision arrived at after consultation following a Green Paper on the question (Home Office, 1988). However, a backbench Conservative MP introduced an amendment to the Bill during the report stage, permitting the contracting-out of *any* existing or future prison, and the amendment was carried. Though the government maintained that it would not consider contracting out any prison other than the new remand prison at the Wolds, until that experiment had been carefully evaluated, the management of three more prisons was contracted out before any independent evaluation of the Wolds was commissioned and published (Bottomley *et al.*, 1997). The additions to section 84 are radically changing the shape of the penal system.

This discussion suggests, gratifyingly perhaps, that Parliament is frequently the site of innovatory discussion and intervention on aspects of criminal justice and penal policy. Unfortunately, many aspects of policy development receive remarkably little parliamentary scrutiny or debate. It needs to be emphasized that, because so much contemporary legislation (the Prison Act 1952, for example) is permissively diffuse, granting ministers and thus departments substantial discretionary powers, many important policy developments are preceded by virtually no public debate, Parliamentary or otherwise (see Richardson, 1993). Much policy is made by stealth or is announced as a *fait accompli,* challengeable only *ex post facto,* if it is challenged at all. For example, in 1983 the then Home Secretary, Leon Brittan, was able fundamentally to change parole policy without consulting either Parliament or the Parole Board and, in the event, his power to do so was upheld by the House of Lords following judicial review. In response to what he saw as growing public concern about the rise in violent crime, Mr Brittan announced in a speech to the Conservative Party Conference that he intended to use his discretion to ensure that certain classes of prisoners—serving sentences of five years or more for drug-trafficking or violence—would not get parole. Moreover, certain categories of murderer would in future serve at least twenty years. Needless to say, Mr Brittan's speech was well received by his immediate audience though it caused much controversy elsewhere, not least because some prisoners, already transferred to open prison conditions with the expectation that they would soon be released, fell foul of the new guidelines and were sent back to closed prisons. Two such prisoners challenged the new policy by way of judicial review but the House of Lords ruled, contrary to a first instance opinion, that since the Home Secretary had taken account of the relevant considerations of deterrence, retribution, and public confidence, he was under no obligation to consult even the Parole Board before making the changes *(Re Findlay* [1985] AC 318).

Policing provides a much broader example of the absence of parliamentary debate. Policing policy arguably underwent a sea-change in the early 1980s, with increased reliance on mutual aid between forces, sometimes under the direction of the National Reporting Centre (Spencer, 1985; Lustgarten, 1986); the deployment of new paramilitary equipment and techniques (Jefferson, 1990; Waddington, 1991); and the adoption of neighbourhood crime-prevention strategies (Bennett, 1990; Rosenbaum, 1988), without the benefit of research or public debate. Again, when police authorities sought to challenge some of these policies by judicial review, the High Court upheld the power of chief constables and the Home Secretary to make such far-reaching decisions. Or, to take a more recent example, the Criminal Justice Act 1991 incorporates no definition of a 'serious offence', yet on the court's interpretation of that term substantially hangs the future size and complexion of the prison population!

It is precisely because so much policy is made and implemented without adequate public debate of its implications that many analysts of criminal justice and penal policy insist that statutes should in future state more precisely what objectives agencies should pursue and what specific powers decision-makers should have, and provide for procedural rights for those citizens—suspects, prisoners, and mental hospital patients—caught up in the system (Richardson, 1993). Ideally, accountability should begin with Parliament and end with the day-to-day answerability of practitioners.

MATTERS OF SCANDAL AND CONCERN

The remaining variable is the unpredictable realm of scandal and concern. For all their pretensions, both parliamentary and extra-parliamentary groupings can be utterly outpaced by events which explode in such a way that unusual responses are called for by 'public opinion'—a phenomenon for which media attention is often taken to be the proxy. In the penal realm, for example, two types of events seemingly dwarf all others in their impact on the 'public': escapes and riots. The escapes of Ronald Biggs and George Blake in 1965–6, and the high security break-outs from Whitemoor and Parkhurst in 1994–5, radically changed the emphasis on security in the Prison Service. The rioting at Strangeways, Manchester, and other prisons in 1990 led to a major inquiry conducted by Lord Justice Woolf, the outcome of which appeared, initially, to set a new agenda for prisons but which the security lapses of 1994–5, combined with a rising prison population, have in turn knocked off course (see Morgan, this volume). In the realm of public order, the riots in Brixton (1981; see Scarman Report, 1981) and on the Broadwater Farm Estate (1985; see Gifford Report, 1986) far transcended other disturbances in their evocation of profound unease. Lord Scarman's Report on the events at Brixton led to the development of formal police community consultation (see Morgan, 1992). In 1993, in the wake of the horrific murder of two-year-old James Bulger by two juveniles, and a sustained police campaign regarding offences committed, particularly by juveniles, while on bail (see P. Morgan, 1992; Morgan and

Jones, 1992), custodial measures were introduced for serious juvenile offenders which contravened principles only just implemented in the Criminal Justice Act 1991 and which research suggested were ill-advised (see Newburn, this volume). Or, to take the most dramatic recent example, the massacre by Thomas Hamilton of schoolchildren and their teacher at Dunblane in 1996 stimulated the Government and Opposition literally to vie with each other over the extent to which gun control and, subsequently, control over other offensive weapons, should be tightened, a parliamentary competition still being played out as we write in January 1997.

However, not all scandals translate into calls for reform or change: for example, the so-called Moors Murders of the early 1960s, in which several children were fatal victims of sadistic sexual practices, were the source of heightened moral fears, but also of sheer bafflement. As Bottoms and Stevenson argue:

> It is a fact well known to students of social policy that reforms of the system often take place not so much because of careful routine analysis by ministers and civil servants in the relevant Department of State, nor even because of a critique or exposé by an outside journalist or pressure group, but because one or more individual incident(s) occurs, drawing public attention to some underlying imperfections of policy in a dramatic way which seems to demand change. Very often an inquiry is set up after such incidents, and it is the report of the inquiry that sets the agenda for subsequent reforms; but the reforms would not have taken place without the public attention created by the original incident [1992: 23–4].

It is worth embellishing this point a little. Such incidents tend to generate change only when they discredit institutions so drastically and dramatically that their credibility and effectiveness—and, by extension, those of the government and the state—risk serious erosion unless changes are made. The damage is not simply symbolic, a matter of reputation and belief, though declining public confidence carries grave implications for the agencies of control and the caring professions. The authority of the modern state rests heavily on its claims to expertise (Giddens, 1984). Practical effects include the predictable increase in, for example, escape attempts in the wake of successful breakouts, and increasing dismissal rates in courts where juries no longer unquestioningly accept police evidence. As the latter point suggests, scandals can and should result in improved policy and practice. The abolition of capital punishment is arguably an example of 'things going right' in criminal justice and penal policy after a series of executions that caused public disquiet. Much hinges on the character of the response; and, we argue below, the trend has recently been towards specific and limited rather than wide-ranging and searching modes of inquiry. Nor are scandals randomly scattered throughout the system: the police and the prisons have produced far more than, for example, probation and after-care.

Prisons: From Mountbatten to Woolf to Learmont

The prison escapes of 1965–6 transformed the prison system. Until the mid-1960s, little was thought to be awry with the prison system, apart from its legacy of Victorian architecture and authoritarian regimes. R. A. Butler's famous White Paper, *Penal Practice in a Changing Society* (1959), seemed to have set the agenda for the next few decades. But the escapes made a 'public laughing-stock' of the Prison Department (Bottoms and Stevenson, 1992: 25) and the Labour Home Secretary, Roy Jenkins, felt that anxieties could be assuaged only by a rapid inquiry. This was conducted by Lord Mountbatten (1966) and resulted in a tough but perceptive report which discerned the major problem as a combination of insufficiently secure provision for the tiny minority of high-escape-risk prisoners and over-security for the great majority. The measures taken in the wake of the Mountbatten Report heightened security across the system, prioritized control and surveillance at the expense of other objectives (such as work, training, education, recreation, and better rights and conditions), and, in combination with the impact of adverse research findings, halted the spread of therapeutic regimes while leaving intact the differentiation between local and training prisons based upon that ideology (see King and Morgan, 1980, for a detailed inventory; also Morgan, this volume).

The growth of what Rutherford (1984) has termed 'high-cost squalor' in the penal system advanced most dramatically in the 1970s and 1980s, mainly because the new strategy was both labour-intensive and overly security-based. Conflicts between prisoners and staff, and staff and Prison Department officials, became endemic. The May Committee was appointed to resolve a pay dispute but widened its brief to look at the overall context. Its report (May Report, 1979) led to only one innovatory gain, an inspectorate independent of the Prison Department. The prisons continued to fester, conditions deteriorating on virtually all fronts (King and McDermott, 1989), locked into a logically endless drift borne of rising numbers and costs in a policy vacuum. When it came, however, the frequently predicted climax of two decades of often serious outbreaks of prison unrest took even informed observers by surprise in its scope and ferocity. Strangeways Prison, Manchester, the largest in the land, was completely taken over and gutted by its inmates, an occupation lasting three weeks that became a media event as prisoners humiliated the authorities by their rooftop defiance. One death, a host of injuries, and the terrorization of sex offenders occurred. Several other prisons erupted in a sequence of less sustained rioting.

The Woolf Inquiry into these disturbances broke new ground in several respects. It was completed in two stages: the first covered the disturbances, and addressed questions of responsibility and culpability; the second, with the then Chief Inspector of Prisons, Judge Stephen Tumim, examined the causes of so signal a system failure. This process enabled them to look in depth at the massive mismatch between needs and resources in the system; at the myriad ways in which containment fell far short of the humane; and at remedies in the short and longer terms (Woolf Report, 1991). Unusually, as mentioned above, evidence was gathered from prisoners at home and abroad. Uniquely, five public seminars were held at which specialists from government, the Prison Service, academic research, pressure groups, and other bodies debated key issues. The Report was widely acknowledged to have advanced the most comprehensive agenda for radical change in the penal system since the Gladstone Report of 1895. It pioneered a process for democratic accountability and debate on urgent problems that should serve as a model for inquiries in all fields, not simply penal affairs.

Nevertheless, the Inquiry was debarred by its terms of reference from exploring one subject of utmost relevance to the topic, namely the judicial framework of sentencing policy. In one sense, the Prison Service is correct in stating that it cannot be held responsible for all aspects of its performance, since one key variable—that is, the number of prisoners it is called upon to contain—is largely beyond its control. That responsibility lies with the judiciary, and the prisons are under a statutory obligation to accept all those who are sent there by the courts. Unlike other institutions, and prisons in a few other countries such as the Netherlands, no legal limit is placed on the numbers any prison can be called upon to hold. Certified Normal Accommodation (CNA) is a formal baseline that is regularly exceeded. The power of the judiciary to stand aloof from the entire debate about penal policy is perhaps the most salient feature of the politics of law and order, since all agendas for reform must bow to their refusal to take part in any such process. This refusal, justified by the judicial elite in terms of the essential independence to embrace not simply their judgment of cases—where indeed it is vital—but the entire conspectus of sentencing trends and practices—where it is not—forces all other components of the criminal justice system to adjust to their often ill-co-ordinated actions. This feature of the system has led many to see better co-ordination as an end in itself—Woolf, for example, recommended the formation of the Criminal Justice Consultative Council (CJCC) and area fora, now in operation—the attainment of which will automatically bring improvement. But unless some agreed objective, such as a reduction in the numbers in prison, is laid down, this co-ordination is simply a means without an end. It is around these issues that the arguments for and against some version of a Sentencing Council have been made (Ashworth, 1983; Cavadino and Dignan, 1992: chapter 4), but the judiciary has so far largely insulated itself from the policy process. It is noteworthy that some commentators now see the CJCC, in which the judiciary has learnt to sit alongside key decision-makers from the other criminal justice agencies, as a vehicle for resuscitating the idea of a Sentencing Council (Ashworth and Hough 1996).

In September 1994 and January 1995 the Prison Service was again prey to security breaches—the escape of category A prisoners from Whitemoor and Parkhurst high security prisons—which led to high profile inquiries (Woodcock, 1994; Learmont, 1995), and, ultimately, to the sacking of the

Director-General (for details see Lewis, 1997). These events consolidated a trend already well established since the Home Secretary's pronouncement at the Conservative Party Conference in October 1993 that 'prison works' and that prison regimes should be 'austere'. The Woolf reformist agenda was effectively dislodged. The prison population rose steeply and continues to do so. The Woodcock and Learmont recommendations legitimated, on security grounds, the more punitive and restrictive climate in prisons. And Woolf's emphasis on justice in prisons was no longer mentioned. Talk of prisoners' rights gave way to a focus on incentives and privileges (for more detailed discussion, see Morgan, this volume).

Policing: Dixon to Robocop

The conventional wisdom about policing tends to the apocalyptic. Things have fallen apart since the Golden Age of policing in the 1950s, embodied in the folk hero, PC George Dixon, the linchpin of the community in the long-running TV serial *Dixon of Dock Green*. Nowadays, in Reiner's vivid contrast, the image of the police constable is more like *Robocop*, a barely human presence in a technological armour, holding a seething mob at bay with advanced weaponry (see Reiner on the police, this volume). The real story is more complex and less sensational. The Golden Age of policing was a myth based upon blind faith in authority and ignorance of actual police work at a time of relatively harmonious community relations. Declining public confidence in the police is due to rates of crime that have soared for social, economic, and cultural reasons that affect but hardly originate in policing; the exposure of forms of corruption that were customary rather than novel; and the growth of problems such as terrorism and drug trafficking which are unparalleled this century in their scale and viciousness. We are only now coming to grips with age-old problems that defy short-term solutions. The police are almost certainly now in a healthier state than before, but look worse because far more is known about their shortcomings, thanks to a mixture of fly-on-the-wall media exposure, scandals, research and the gradual move towards more stringent forms of both legal and political accountability (Morgan, 1996).

The three cases which came to dramatize public concerns about policing most vividly were those of the Guildford Four, the Maguire Seven, and the Birmingham Six. In all three cases, Irish suspects were convicted of causing explosions that killed multiple victims. Outrage as expressed through the media placed immense pressure on the police to get 'results'. Sentences of life imprisonment were accompanied by recommendations that at least twenty years be served in several cases. Fifteen to seventeen years later, after tireless campaigning, the verdicts were declared 'unsafe' and the prisoners freed. These and other cases of similar magnitude so eroded public confidence in the police and the courts, as shown by opinion polls, that a Royal Commission on Criminal Justice was appointed in 1991, the first Royal Commission for fourteen years, to inquire into the procedural issues involved and suggest remedies.

These cases exemplify the tendency for matters of notoriety to originate in taken-for-granted practices that are exposed as a result of unusual degrees of pressure or modes of scrutiny, rather than being exceptional instances of individual pathology—a 'few bad apples'. 'Constructing the suspect' by embellishing the evidence against him or her and ignoring countervailing evidence is standard police practice (McBarnet, 1981; McConnville, Leng, and Sanders, 1991). Once socialized into an occupational culture which affirms such practices as a necessary evil and a professional skill, designed ultimately to secure conviction in the ornate adversarial exchanges in open court, it is a small step for the police officer to fabricate evidence and 'lose' counter-evidence. The appeal of such procedures is the greatest when the suspect has 'previous' and is 'overdue' for conviction. The logic of methodical suspicion casts certain groups more readily into the suspect role than others. The moral economy of police work reinforces these images of deviance, certain groups being seen as 'slag', 'rubbish', and 'police property' (Reiner, 1992). If such variables as age, sex, ethnicity, demeanour, degrees of co-operativeness with the police, and the reputation of areas are consequential in routine offending, how much larger they loom when intense pressures for a 'result' are generated. Another example of unusual modes of inquiry bringing new focus to established practices was Roger Graef's 1982 TV documentary series on the Thames Valley police. The public outcry at the merciless grilling by officers of a female rape victim led to rapid changes in the procedures for the processing of similar cases. The impetus had also led to the heightened awareness and changing practices in cases of domestic violence (see Stanko, 1990; Dobash and Dobash, 1992; Levi in this volume).

Northern Ireland and its Impact

The context for the most notorious recent miscarriages of justice is of course the political quagmire of Northern Ireland and its ramifications for the control of terrorism in Britain. Since 1969, 'nearly 3,000 people have died because of political violence in Northern Ireland. The conflict has often spilled outside the borders of the region, leading to the deaths of approximately 200 people in Great Britain, the Republic of Ireland, and sites elsewhere in Europe, ranging from Gibraltar to Western Germany' (O'Leary and McGarry, 1993). Three thousand dead may seem a relatively small toll over two decades. 'However, scale matters. The population of Northern Ireland in the 1981 census . . . was estimated as 1,488,077. If the equivalent ratio of victims to population had been produced in Great Britain in the same period some 100,000 people would have died, and . . . in the USA . . . over 500,000, or about ten times the number of Americans killed in the Vietnam War' (*ibid.*: 2). Comparatively speaking, 'the death-toll in Northern Ireland alone made the UK absolutely the most violent liberal democracy during the same time-span' (*ibid.*: 4). Close to one in fifty of the population have suffered serious injuries over the period. The costs in law enforcement, paramilitary measures, compensation, and legal processes have been huge. One audit in 1985 estimated the annual direct costs of violence in Northern Ireland at £1,194 million *per annum* (*ibid.*: 22). The costs in terms of negative effects on public trust in British political institutions have been incalculable. The granting of strong emergency powers to the legal authorities under the regularly renewed Emergency Provisions Act in Northern Ireland and the Prevention of Terrorism Act throughout the UK has meant that departures from traditional English legal procedures have become normal in Northern Ireland and spill over into aspects of crime control in Britain (as, for example, in the short-lived 'control units' for recalcitrant prisoners in two English prisons in the 1970s, whose regimes paralleled forms of sensory deprivation used in Northern Ireland). 'Since 1973 no-jury single-judge courts have presided over cases arising from "scheduled offences", i.e. "terrorist offences", on the grounds that jury-trials are not safe from perverse verdicts or the intimidation of jurors and witnesses. Confessions are admissible as the sole basis for conviction on charges "of this kind"' (O'Leary and McGarry, 1993: 24). The rise and discrediting of 'supergrass' evidence in the 1980s (Greer, 1994); the abandonment of the 'right of silence' in 1988; the regular delay of several years in holding inquests on persons killed by the security forces (Amnesty International, 1978); and the violation of the European Convention on Human Rights on a number of fronts concerning interrogation and time held in custody; have all severely eroded the belief, both nationally and internationally, in the impartiality of British justice. They also provided the context within which routine police practices for constructing the suspect escalated into 'the greatest twentieth century crisis of confidence in the administration of justice in Great Britain' (*ibid.*). In the event the 1991–3 Royal Commission proved unequal to the task of tackling such deep-rooted problems.

Forms of Official Inquiry

The appointment of the Royal Commission (Runciman, 1993), and the unusually open and searching nature of the Woolf Inquiry, went against the grain of the trend, especially notable during the Thatcher years, increasingly to use the *ad hoc*, highly specific, departmental inquiry as a policy-making mechanism. Such inquiries were internal, as when HM Chief Inspector of Prisons was asked to consider the prison disturbances of 1986 (HMCIP, 1986); or external, conducted either by a committee, as in the case of the Prior Committee on prison discipline (Prior Report, 1985), or by an individual, usually a judge, as in the case of the Woolf Inquiry. The latter embrace both statutory inquiries, as in the cases of Lord Scarman's investigation of the Brixton disturbance in 1981 under section 32 of the Police Act 1964 (Scarman Report, 1981) or Sir Louis Blom Cooper's investigation of Ashworth Special Hospital 1991 under section 125 of the 'Mental Health Act 1988 (Blom-Cooper Report, 1992), and not statutory inquiries, as in the case of the Woolf Report.

Such inquiries may be resorted to for a variety of political reasons (see Morgan, 1991) but, unlike statutory or even non-statutory standing consultative bodies and Royal Commissions, they have the merit for ministers of being focused, relatively short-term, and manageable. Their terms of reference are precise and often, though not invariably, narrowly technical. By contrast, standing bodies, like the Advisory Council on the Penal System, are liable to take a robust view of their terms of reference; and Royal Commissions tend to be wide-ranging and long-lasting. Which mechanism is resorted to depends on the seriousness of the incident(s), the degree of loss of public confidence, and whether ministers have a clear objective, wish to distance themselves from a potentially unpopular solution, or play for time. What is clear is that straightforward assumptions about the political methodology likely to be adopted in relation to one mechanism or another can no longer be made. The Woolf and Blom-Cooper Inquiries were unusually open and consultative in their methods. It was widely anticipated that the 1992 Royal Commission on Criminal Justice would be the same, particularly since Sir John May's inquiry into the 'Guildford Four' miscarriage of justice (an inquiry eventually incorporated by the Royal Commission) had indicated his readiness to hold public seminars. In the event, the Royal Commission, though it took oral evidence in the usual manner and commissioned a good deal of research, was relatively orthodox: it held no seminars. The 1992 Sheehy Committee on police ranks, structure, and conditions of employment held one seminar, but under conditions of excessive secrecy (Sheehy Report, 1993). The 1990s have so far been characterized by a highly managerial and undemocratic strategy for developing 'law and order' policy. The second-order consensus alluded to above has proved short-lived.

CONCLUSIONS

The politics of law and order in the post-war period have been shaped by the nature of responses to the continuous rise in rates of recorded crime and to the unforeseen explosion of politically inspired terrorism and illicit drug trafficking. Three phases can be discerned in the party political sphere. First, until 1970 a consensus prevailed whose terms, heavily influenced by 'liberal progressive' ideology, implicitly rested on the non-partisan character of crime and on the merit of gradual shifts towards rehabilitative policies for its control. This consensus was not shared, other than for a range of juvenile offenders, by the judiciary who continued to adhere to broadly retributive and deterrent principles of sentencing, except for a small minority of clinically diagnosed mentally ill offenders. Governments of both left and right shared a strong reluctance to intrude into the judicial realm. The 1970 election was a watershed which, by 1979, had swept away the main supports of non-partisanship. The second phase, of sharp and growing contention between the parties for the 'law and order' terrain, saw the Conservative Party emerge relatively unscathed from Labour's tentative attempts to link rising crime with the social and economic effects of growing inequality and unemployment: the 'hostages to fortune' which the Labour Party, traditional attachments to the trade unions and to libertarian causes entail, initially led its leaders to seek to neutralize, rather than sharply contest, the Conservative hegemony on this issue. Since the 1992 Election a third phase appears to have begun. The Conservatives, bent on the further restructuring of public services to achieve cuts in public expenditure whilst simultaneously pursuing tough populist penal measures, have prejudiced their traditional support base with the judiciary, the police, and prison personnel. Meanwhile 'New Labour' has distanced itself from the trades unions, the penal pressure groups, and libertarian causes, particularly those entailing street protests. Labour has also been coy about opposing Conservative 'law and order' legislation. Indeed, Labour has on several occasions sought to out-tough Conservative legislative proposals. In the run-up to the 1997 general election the opinion poll evidence suggests that this populist strategy is paying off for Labour. The Party now enjoys greater public confidence regarding 'law and order' than do the Conservatives. Conservative hegemony on this issue appears to have been undermined and Labour's 'hostages to fortune' forgotten or receded.

Though the elements of a 'second-order consensus' remain in some respects—bifurcation, the need to reduce prison overcrowding, victim support, and crime prevention are all examples—the routes to those ends have often differed. The Labour Party, for example, has always placed greater emphasis on the role of local authorities as the linchpin of crime prevention initiatives of a social (rather than a purely situational) kind, and this continues (Labour Party, 1995). The Conservatives have stressed a host of alternative frameworks—Neighbourhood Watch, Safer Cities, and crime prevention through environmental design (see Clarke and Mayhew, 1980; Bottoms and Wiles, this volume)—which bypass local authorities rather than engage them in community crime prevention schemes: indeed, they have founded an independent organization, Crime Concern, to evangelize their approach. The stress on 'active citizenship' and the 'community' was evolved in the mid-1980s as a form of recognition by the government that reliance on the 'rule of law' alone was no longer serving as a credible strategy (Reiner and Cross, 1991). Crime rates and public disorder alike were reaching new heights. These new watchwords and strategies were intended to signify fresh thinking and active concern, on the one hand, and a refusal to countenance the role of social and economic variables, on the other. The irony is that the Home Office under the Conservatives has, since 1979, assembled a criminal justice and penal policy which, however unevenly, shares broad cross-party support. Yet the government struggled to put that policy into effect in a context rendered peculiarly unfavourable in crime control terms by the impact and character of their social and economic policies.

For the Labour Party the real Conservative enemy in crime-control terms is not the Home Office but the Treasury, the Department of Trade and Industry, and the ethos embodied in successive leaders (notably Mrs Thatcher) who deny the existence of 'society' and state that—as far as offenders are concerned—'we should understand less and condemn more' (Mr Major in 1993). In other words, it is not so much that the Conservatives have tightened the screws on civil liberties and citizenship rights (apart from trades unions); in some ways they have even formally extended them. It is rather that they have effectively excluded far larger numbers of people from any conceivable activation of those rights—by doubling unemployment, quadrupling homelessness, increasing inequalities of wealth and income, and draining local authorities of both power and resources (see Stewart, 1992; Brake and Hale, 1992). The problem for the opposition parties has been that they have found it difficult to find ways of convincing the electorate that these connections exist and can be influenced by political decision-making in the medium to long term. The signs are that 'New Labour' has begun to persuade the electorate that a greater measure of equality of opportunity, a collective sense of social justice and the provision of good quality public services, is connected with the incidence of crime and the deepening sense of public insecurity that fuels fear of crime. But the Labour Party has had to sacrifice many of its traditional allegiances in order to build this platform of electoral credibility and it is not at all clear that the Labour Party, if elected in 1997, will pursue a markedly less punitive policy than that embarked on by the Conservatives in the first half of the 1990s.

Selected Further Reading

There have been few studies of the part played by 'law and order' in British political life. Philip Norton's *Law and Order and British Politics* (Aldershot: Gower, 1984) and Mike Brake and Chris Hale's *Public Order and Private Lives: The Politics of Law and Order* (London: Routledge, 1992), the latter a highly critical account of the Thatcher years, are exceptions. David Downes' edited collection, *Unravelling Criminal Justice* (Basingstoke: Macmillan, 1992), contains relevant essays, particularly those by Bottoms and Stevenson on the extent and difficulties of the liberal consensus, and McBarnet on the burgeoning field of tax avoidance and evasion. Roger Hood's collection, *Crime, Criminology and Public Policy: Essays in Honour of Leon Radzinowicz* (London: Heinemann, 1974), provides detailed scrutiny of the public policy issues of the mid-period, and Terence Morris' *Crime and Criminal Justice in Britain since 1945* (Oxford: Blackwell 1989) covers the entire period with shrewd political insight. Brendan O'Leary and John McGarry (*The Politics of Antagonism: Understanding Northern Ireland*, London: Athlone, 1993) are sure guides to the complexities of Northern Ireland, without which some key developments are lost. In *Beyond Law and Order: Criminal Justice Policy into the 1990s* (Basingstoke: Macmillan 1991) Robert Reiner and Malcolm Cross have collected a set of papers on most of the key aspects of criminal justice policy with their editorial chapter spelling out the political context. Finally,

Mick Ryan (*The Politics of Penal Reform*, London: Longman, 1983) is a political scientist in criminology who documents the micro-politics of penal reform in the wider political economy of Britain.

REFERENCES

ABERCROMBIE, N., and WARDE, S., eds. (1988), *Contemporary British Society*. Cambridge: Polity.

ADVISORY COUNCIL ON THE PENAL SYSTEM (1969), *The Regime for Long-term Prisoners in Conditions of Maximum Security*. London: HMSO.

AMERICAN FRIENDS SERVICE COMMITTEE (1971), *Struggle for Justice*. New York: Hill and Wang.

AMNESTY International (1978), *Report of an Amnesty International Mission to Northern Ireland*. London: International Secretariat, Amnesty International.

ASHWORTH, A. (1983), *Sentencing and Penal Policy*. London: Weidenfeld and Nicolson.

—— and HOUGH, M. (1996) 'Sentencing and the Climate of opinion', *Criminal Law Review*, 776.

BAILEY, V. (1987), *Delinquency and Citizenship: Reclaiming the Young Offender, 1914–1948*. Oxford: Clarendon Press.

BALL, A. B., HUFF, C. R., and LILLY, J. R. (1988), *House Arrest and Correctional Policy: Doing Time at Home*. Newbury Park, Cal.: Sage.

BENNETT, T. (1990), *Evaluating Neighbourhood Watch*. Farnborough: Gower.

BLOM-Cooper REPORT (1992), *Report of the Committee of Inquiry into Complaints about Ashworth Hospital*, Cm 2028. London: HMSO.

BOTTOMLEY, A. K., JAMES, A., CLARE, I., and LIEBLING, A. (1997), *Monitoring and Evaluation of Wolds Remand Prison*. Home Office Research and Planning Unit. London: Home Office.

BOTTOMS, A. E. (1974), 'On the Decriminalization of English Juvenile Courts', in R. Hood, ed., *Crime, Criminology, and Public Policy*. London: Heineman.

—— (1977), 'Reflections on the Renaissance of Dangerousness', *Howard Journal*, 16: 70–96.

—— and STEVENSON, S. (1992), 'What Went Wrong?: Criminal Justice Policy in England and Wales, 1945–70', in D. Downes, ed., *Unravelling Criminal Justice*. London: Macmillan.

BRAKE, M., and HALE, C. (1992), *Public Order and Private Lives.. The Politics of Law and Order*. London: Routledge.

BUTLER, D. (1952), *The British General Election of 1951*. London: Macmillan.

—— (1956), *The British General Election of 1955*. London: Macmillan.

—— and KAVANAGH, D. (1975*a*), *The British General Election of February 1974*. London: Macmillan.

—— and —— (1975*b*), *The British General Election of October 1974*. London: Macmillan.

—— and —— (1980), *The British General Election of 1979*. London: Macmillan.

—— and —— (1988), *The British General Election of 1987*. London: Macmillan.

—— and —— (1992), *The British General Election of 1992*. London: Macmillan.

—— and KING, A. (1965), *The British General Election of 1964*. London: Macmillan.

—— and —— (1967), *The British General Election of 1966*. London: Macmillan.

—— and PINTO-DUSCHINSKY, M. (1971), *The British General Election of* 1970. London: Macmillan.

—— and ROSE, R. (1960), *The British General Election of 1959*. London: Macmillan.

CAMPBELL, B. (1993), *Goliath: Britain's Dangerous Places*. London: Methuen.

CAVADINO, M., and DIGNAN, J. (1992), *The Penal System. An Introduction*. London: Sage.

CHRISTIAN, L. (1983), *Policing by Coercion*. London: GLC Police Support Unit.

CLARKE, R. V. G., and MAYHEW, P. (1980), *Designing Out Crime*. London: HMSO.

COHEN, S. (1972), *Folk Devils and Moral Panics*. London: MacGibbon and Kee.

CONSERVATIVE PARTY (1959), *The Next Five Years*. London: Conservative Party.

—— (1966), *Actions not Words*. London: Conservative Party.

—— (1970), *A Better Tomorrow*. London: Conservative Party.

—— (1974*a*), *Firm Action for a Fairer Britain*. London: Conservative Party.

—— (1974*b*), *Putting Britain First*. London: Conservative Party.

—— (1979), *The Conservative Manifesto*. London: Conservative Party.

—— (1983), *The Challenge of Our Times*. London: Conservative Party.

—— (1987), *Our First Eight Years. The Next Moves Forward*. London: Conservative Party.

—— (1992), *The Best Future for Britain*. London: Conservative Party.

CRAIG, F. W. S. (1975), *The British General Election Manifestos 1900–1974*. London: Macmillan.

DAHRENDORF, R. (1987), 'The Underclass and the Future of Great Britain', lecture delivered at Windsor Castle, 27 April.

DIXON, D., and FISHWICK, E. (1984), 'The Law and Order Debate in Historical Perspective', in P. Norton, ed., *Law and Order and British Politics*. Aldershot: Gower.

DOBASH, R. E., and DOBASH, R. D. (1992), *Women, Violence and Social Change*. London: Routledge.

DORE, R. P. (1992), *Japanese Capitalism, Anglo Saxon Capitalism: How will the Darwinian Contest Turn Out?* London: LSE Centre for Economic Performance Occasional Paper no. 4.

DOWNES, D. M. (1966), *The Delinquent Solution*. London: Routledge and Kegan Paul.

—— (1982), 'The Origins and Consequences of Dutch Penal Policy since 1945: A Preliminary Analysis', *British Journal of Criminology*, 22: 325–62.

—— (1988), *Contrasts in Tolerance. Post-War Penal Policy in the Netherlands and England and Wales*. Oxford: Clarendon Press.

—— (1989*a*), 'Only Disconnect: Law and Order, Social Policy and the Community', in M. Bulmer, J. Lewis, and D. Piachaud, eds., *The Goals of Social Policy*. London: Unwin Hyman.

—— (1989*b*), 'Thatcherite Values and Crime', *Samizdat*, May/June.

—— and WARD, T. (1986), *Democratic Policing*. London: Labour Campaign for Criminal Justice.

—— and YOUNG, J. (1987) 'A Criminal Failure', *New Society*, 13 May.

EDELMAN, M. (1971), *Politics as Symbolic Action*. Chicago, Ill.: Markham.

EDMUND-DAVIES REPORT (1978), *Report of the Committee of Inquiry on the Police*, Cmnd. 7283. London: HMSO.

ELDER, N. C. M. (1984), 'Conclusion', in P. Norton, ed., *Law and Order and British* Politics. Aldershot: Gower.

FEEST, J. (1988), *Reducing the Prison Population: Lessons from the West German Experience?* London: National Association for the Care and Resettlement of Offenders.

GAMBLE, A. (1990), 'The Thatcher Decade in Perspective', in P. Dunleavy, A. Gamble, and G. Peele, eds., *Developments in British Politics*, iii. London: Macmillan.

GIDDENS, A. (1984), *The Constitution of Society*. Cambridge: Polity.

GIFFORD REPORT (1986), *The Broadwater Farm Inquiry. Report of the Independent Inquiry into Disturbances of October 1985 at the Broadwater Farm Estate, Tottenham*. London: Karia Press.

GRAHAM, J. (1988), 'The Declining Prison Population in the Federal Republic of Germany', *Home Office Research and Planning Unit Research Bulletin*, 24: 47–52.

GREER, S. (1994), *Supergrasses*. Oxford: Oxford University Press.

HALL, S., CRITCHER, S., JEFFERSON, T., CLARKE, J., and ROBERTS, B. (1978), *Policing the Crisis: Mugging, the State, and Law and Order*. London: Macmillan.

HALLORAN, J. D., ELLIOTT, P., and MURDOCK, G. (1970), *Demonstrations and Communications*. Harmondsworth: Penguin.

HER MAJESTY'S CHIEF INSPECTOR OF PRISONS (1987), *Report of an Inquiry into the Disturbances in Prison Service Establishments in England between 29 April and 2 May*, HC 42. London: HMSO.

HOME AFFAIRS COMMITTEE (1987), *Fourth Report on Contract Provision of Prisons*. London: HMSO.

HOME OFFICE (1988), *Private Sector Involvement in the Remand System*, Cm 434. London: HMSO.

—— (1993) *Police Reform*. Cm 2281, London: Home Office.

HONDERICH, T. (1990), *Conservatism*. London: Hamish Hamilton.

HUTTON, W. (1996), *The State We're In*. London: Vintage.

JEFFERSON, T. (1990), *The Case against Paramilitary Policing*. Milton Keynes: Open University Press.

JENCKS, C., and PETERSON, P. E., eds. (1991), *The Urban Underclass*. Washington, DC: Brookings Institution.

KING, A. (1993), *Britain at the Polls 1992*, New Jersey: Chatham House.

KING, R. D., and MCDERMOTT, K. (1989), 'British Prisons 1970–97: The Ever-Deepening Crisis', *British Journal of Criminology*, 29/2: 107–28.

—— (1995), *The State of Our Prisons*. Oxford: Clarendon.

—— and MORGAN, R. (1980), *The Future of the Prison System*. Farnborough: Gower.

LABOUR PARTY (1959), *Time for Decision.* London: Labour Party.

—— (1966), *Time for Decision.* London: Labour Party.

—— (1970), *Now Britain's Strong—Let's Make it Great to Live In.* London: Labour Party.

—— (1974*a*), *Let Us Work Together—Labour's Way Out of the Crisis.* London: Labour Party.

—— (1974*b*), *Britain Will Win with Labour.* London: Labour Party.

—— (1979), *The Labour Way is the Better Way.* London: Labour Party.

—— (1983), *New Hope for Britain.* London: Labour Party.

—— (1987), *Britain Will Win.* London: Labour Party.

—— (1992), *It's Time to Get Britain Working Again.* London: Labour Party.

—— (1995), *Safer Communities, Safer Britain.* London: Labour Party

LEA, J., and YOUNG, J. (1984), *What Is to Be Done About Law and Order*? Harmondsworth: Penguin.

LEARMONT REPORT (1995), *Review of Prison Service Security in England and Wales and the Escape from Parkhurst Prison on Tuesday 3rd January 1995,* Cm 3020. London: HMSO.

LEWIS, D. (1997), *Hidden Agenda.* London: Hamish Hamilton.

LIBERAL PARTY (1964), *Think for Yourself: Vote Liberal.* London: Liberal Party.

—— (1974), *Change the Face of Britain.* London: Liberal Party.

LIBERAL DEMOCRATIC PARTY (1992), *Changing Britain for Good.* London: Liberal Democratic Party.

LIBERAL/SDP ALLIANCE (1987), *Britain United: The Time Has Come.* London: Liberal/SDP Alliance.

LIGHT, R., NEE, C., and INGHAM, H. (1993), *Car Theft: The Offender's Perspective,* Home Office Research Study no. 130. London: HMSO.

LINTON, M. (1995), *Was it the Sun Wot Won It?.* Oxford: Nuffield College.

LUSTGARTEN, L. (1986), *The Government of the Police.* London: Sweet and Maxwell.

MCBARNET, D. (1981), *Conviction.* London: Macmillan.

MCCALLUM, R. B., and READMAN, A. (1946), *The British General Election of 1945.* Oxford: Oxford University Press.

MCCONVILLE, M, LENG, R., and SANDERS, A. (1993), *The Case for the Prosecution.* London: Routledge.

MACNICOL, J. (1987), 'In Pursuit of the Underclass', *Journal of Social Policy,* 293–318.

MACPHERSON, C. B. (1962), *The Political Theory of Possessive Individual.* Oxford: Oxford University Press.

MAIR, G. (1991), *Part-Time Punishment.. The Origins and Development of Attendance Centres.* London: HMSO.

—— and NEE, C. (1990), *Electronic Monitoring: The Trials and their Results,* Home Office Research Study no. 120. London: HMSO.

MARTIN, R. (1981), *New Technology and Industrial Relations in Fleet Street.* Oxford: Oxford University Press.

MARTINSON, R. (1974), 'What Works?—Questions and Answers about Prison Reform', *The Public Interest,* 35 (Spring): 22–54.

MARWICK, A. (1990), *British Society since 1945.* London: Penguin.

MAY REPORT (1979), *Report of the Committee of Inquiry into the United Kingdom Prison Services* (Chairman, Mr Justice May), Cmnd. 7673. London: HMSO.

MAYHEW, H. (1862), *Those That Will Not Work,* vol. 4 of *London Labour and the London Poor (1851–62).* London: Griffin. Repr. ed. P. Quennell, *London's Underworld,* London: Spring Books, 1955.

MILLS, C. W. (1959), *The Sociological Imagination.* New York: Oxford University Press.

MORGAN, P. (1992), *Offending While on Bail: A Survey of Recent Studies,* Home Office Research and Planning Unit Paper no. 65. London: HMSO.

MORGAN, R. (1979), *Formulating Penal Policy: The Future of the Advisory Council on the Penal System.* London: National Association for the Care and Resettlement of Offenders.

—— (1991), 'Woolf. in Retrospect and Prospect', *Modern Law Review,* 54: 713–25.

—— (1992), 'Talking about Policing', in D. Downes, ed., *Unravelling Criminal Justice.* London: Macmillan.

—— (1996), 'Custody in the Police Station: How do England and Wales Measure Up in Europe', *Policy Studies,* 17: 55–72.

—— and JONES, S. (1992), 'Bail or Jail', in E. Stockdale and S. Casale, eds., *Criminal Justice under Stress.* London: Blackstone.

MORRIS, T. P. (1989), *Crime and Criminal Justice in Britain since 1945.* Oxford: Blackwell.

MOUNTBATTEN REPORT (1966), *Report of the Inquiry into Prison Escapes and Security by Admiral of the Fleet, the Earl Mountbatten of Burma,* Cmnd. 3175. London: HMSO.

MOWAT, L. W. (1955), *Britain between the Wars, 1918–1940*. London: Methuen.

MURRAY, C. (1994), *Underclass: The Crisis Deepens*. London: Institute of Economic Affairs.

NICHOLAS, H. G. (1951), *The British General Election of 1950*. London: Macmillan.

O'LEARY, B., and MCGARRY, J. (1993), *The Politics of Antagonism: Understanding Northern Ireland*. London: Athlone.

PARKIN, F. (1967), 'Working-Class Conservatives: A Theory of Political Deviance', *British Journal of Sociology*, 18/3: 278–90.

PRIOR REPORT (1985), *Report of the Departmental Committee on the Prison Disciplinary System* (Chairman, Mr Peter Prior), Cmnd. 9641. London: HMSO.

REINER, R. (1992), *The Politics of the Police*, rev. edn. Brighton: Wheatsheaf.

—— and CROSS, M. (1991), 'Introduction', in R. Reiner and M. Cross, eds., *Beyond Law and Order: Criminal Justice Policy into the 1990s*. London: Macmillan.

RICHARDSON, G. (1993), *Law, Custody and Process: Prisoners and Patients*. London: Hamish Hamilton.

ROCK, P. (1986), *A View from the Shadows: The Ministry of the Solicitor General of Canada and the Justice for Victims of Crime Initiative*. Oxford: Clarendon Press.

—— (1995), 'The Opening Stages of Criminal Justice Policy Making', *British Journal of Criminology*, 35: 1–6.

ROSENBAUM, D. (1988), 'A Critical Eye on Neighbourhood Watch: Does it Reduce Crime and Fear?', in T. Hope and M. Shaw, eds., *Communities and Crime Reduction*. London: HMSO.

RUGGIERO, V. (1991), 'Public Opinion and Penal Reform in Britain', *Crime and Social Change*, 15: 37–50.

RUNCIMAN REPORT (1993), *Report of the Royal Commission on Criminal Justice*. Cm 2263, London: HMSO.

RUTHERFORD, A. (1984), *Prisons and the Process of Justice*. London: Heinemann.

—— (1996), *Transforming Criminal Policy*. Winchester: Waterside.

RYAN, M. (1978), *The Acceptable Pressure Group-Inequality in the Penal Lobby: A Case Study of the Howard League and PAP*. Farnborough: Saxon House.

—— (1983), *The Politics of Penal Reform*. London: Longman.

—— and WARD, T. (1989), *Privatization and the Penal System*. Milton Keynes: Open University Press.

SCARMAN REPORT (1981), *The Brixton Disorders 10–12 April 1981*. London: HMSO.

SCHLESINGER, P., and TUMBER, H. (1992), 'Crime and Criminal Justice in the Media', in D. Downes, ed., *Unravelling Criminal Justice*. London: Macmillan.

SCHNEIDER-LENNÉ, E. R. (1992), 'Corporate Control in Germany', *Oxford Review of Economic Policy*, 8: 11–23.

SHEEHY REPORT (1993) *Inquiry into Police Responsibilities and Rewards*. Cm 2280, London: HMSO.

SIM, J. (1993), 'Reforming the Penal Wasteland? A Critical Review of the Woolf Report', in E. Player and M. Jenkins, eds., *Prisons After Woolf*. London: Routledge.

SPENCER, S. (1985), *Called to Account*. London: National Council for Civil Liberties.

STANKO, E. A. (1990), *Everyday Violence*. London: Unwin Hyman.

STEWART, J. D. (1992), *Accountability to the Public*. London: European Police Forum.

TAYLOR, R. K. S. (1988), *Against the Bomb: the British Peace Movement 1958–1965*. Oxford: Clarendon Press.

TULKENS, H. (1979), *Some Developments in Penal Policy and Practice in Holland*. London: National Association for the Care and Resettlement of Offenders.

VON HIRSCH, A. (1976), *Doing Justice: The Choice of Punishments*. New York: Hill and Wang.

——, ASHWORTH, A., WASIK, A., SMITH, A., MORGAN, R., and GARDNER, J. (1995), 'Overtaking on the Right', *New Law Journal*, 145: 1501–16.

WADDINGTON, P. A. J. (1991), *The Strong Arm of the Law*. Oxford: Oxford University Press.

WALLINGTON, P. (1975), 'Criminal Conspiracy and Industrial Conflict', *Industrial Law Journal*, 4: 69–88.

WEBB, B., and LAYCOCK, G. (1992), *Tackling Car Crime: The Nature and Extent of the Problem*,Crime Prevention Unit Paper no. 32. London: Home Office.

WILSON, W. J. (1996) *When Work Disappears: The World of the New Urban Poor*. New York: Knopf.

WOODCOCK REPORT (1994), *Report of the Enquiry into the Escape of Six Prisoners from the Special Security Unit at Whitemoor Prison, Cambridgeshire, on Friday 9th September 1994*, Cm 2741. London: HMSO.

WOOLF REPORT (1991), *Prison Disturbances April 1990: Report of an Inquiry by the Rt Hon. Lord Justice Woolf (Parts I and II) and His Honour Judge Stephen Tumim (Part II)*, Cm 1456. London: HMSO.

YOUNG, J. (1992), 'The Rise in Crime in England and Wales 1979–1990'. Middlesex Polytechnic: Centre for Criminology.

[13]
The *Macho* Penal Economy: Mass Incarceration in the United States – a European Perspective

Abstract

The rise of mass incarceration in the USA is related to the historic character of American exceptionalism and the abandonment, over the past few decades, of policies of rehabilitation and radical social reform. The components for a compararable penal expansion are, with the exception of high rates of lethal violence, in process of assembly in some European societies: rates of serious property crime surpassing those in the USA; a shift in the politics of law and order towards 'governing through crime' and populist punitiveness; and rising anxieties about risk and insecurity, in particular relating to ethnic minorities and crime. The distinctive character of social democratic societies, which has so far shielded them against mass incarceration and which already face challenge due to globalization, face further adverse comparison with the more deregulated US economy in terms of unemployment rates which are significantly distorted by the size of the American prison population. Economic debate should be better informed of the unprecedented extent to which the penal factor has come to exert a hidden influence on cross-national images of socioeconomic success and failure, and of the costs and benefits of social-democratic relative to more deregulated market economies.

Key Words

comparative penal policy • Europe • USA

INTRODUCTION

American exceptionalism in deviance and control, for most of the 20th century, consisted of exceptionally high rates of serious crime, notably homicide, robbery, hard drug dealing and gang violence in both its juvenile and organized crime forms. Theorizing about crime, especially in the *anomie* tradition, has been massively influenced by this major contrast with the general run of European experience. So there has been a certain experience of cognitive dissonance as, over the past two decades, crime rates in the USA have levelled off and recently fallen, whilst those in some European countries have risen, in the case of serious property crimes, to surpass the US rates. Moreover, these trends have occurred despite a sharpening of the contrasts between the USA and Europe[1] in the alleged root causes of crime: the extent of inequalities of wealth and income, poverty and the apotheosis of the winner/loser culture (James, 1993). An aetiological crisis (see Young, 1986), due to crime trends spinning out of alignment with predictions drawn from the major social theories, was avoided only by the phenomenal growth of the US prison population. Even powerful causes can be over-ridden by so devastating a penal response, though there are the awkward facts that state by state increases in imprisonment correlate only weakly with crime rate fluctuations, especially crimes of violence (Currie, 1998).

The aetiological crisis may, however, simply have been displaced to another site. Social theorists have long maintained that the criminal justice and penal systems are poor guarantors of crime prevention and reduction. Structural and cultural variables are seen as far more potent in explaining and predicting trends in crime and their variations. But the US penal explosion, which has now persisted for over two decades, eluded both prediction and convincing explanation. Why, in short, did nobody see this coming? An earlier generation of sociologists had been taken to task by Everett Hughes for failing to foresee the scale of racial conflict in the late 1950s and early 1960s, due to their attachment to Parsonian systems theory. It may well be that the 1970s' equivalent was the assumption that governments would respect the view, shared by most criminologists, that deterrence and incapacitation would not, except at an unacceptably high human and financial cost, serve significantly to reduce crime. The argument that the price was worth paying (Wilson, 1975, is the *fons et origo* of this case) was a paradigmatic break. Sufficiently pursued, the penal route, it was claimed, *does* pay off. A decade or two later, the American example's appeal to governments elsewhere, especially those of a New Right persuasion, is that prison does indeed 'work'. And it works not just by keeping vast numbers of offenders off the streets. It also works by showing how a deregulated capitalism can have its cake and eat it: a market economy can produce a market society without a rocketing crime rate.

No comparable democratic society has embraced what Leon Radzinowicz (1991) termed 'penal regression' with remotely equivalent fervour. Of the other high imprisonment societies, China remains pre-democratic, and Russia, the former Soviet bloc countries and South Africa, are – for very different reasons – in transition from massively oppressive regimes. In the 1980s, by contrast, a New Right Britain did the opposite, to everyone's surprise. It was only in the 1990s, clearly influenced by the American example, that the appeal of a 'prison works' strategy was seen as ideologically more palatable, politically advantageous and also cheaper than crime reduction bought by substantial increases in employment and welfare services. And in The Netherlands, a high-cost welfare society, imprisonment also came to be seen as the only resort where welfare and lesser punishments had failed. The Netherlands too has quintupled its prison population over the past two decades, albeit from a far lower base and, as yet, to no more than the European average.

There are, however, several examples of resistance to this trend (Stern, 1998). The Scandinavian countries have maintained very high welfare spending with relatively low and, in the case of Finland, striking falls in imprisonment levels. France and Germany have maintained a steady state despite rising crime rates. Closest to home, Canada has preserved roughly stable crime and imprisonment levels for two decades,[2], an achievement that is rarely mentioned in Anglo-American debate on penal policy. And, of course, there are some states within the USA which have bucked the trend in significant respects (Kuhn, 1999; Tonry, 1999).

A great deal rides on whether or not, and the extent to which, the USA is an exceptionalist outlier in the penal sphere or both a prefiguration and a driver of things to come. If the era of global capitalism is both highly criminogenic *and* punitive, as Nils Christie (1993) has so forcefully argued; and if, as his colleague Thomas Mathiesen (1990) has proposed, the more developed societies resort heavily to penal innovations in periods of rapid changes in their political economy – as in the late 16th, late 18th and now late or post-20th centuries – then we can expect the latter course to be followed. Global capitalism is not necessarily 'late' capitalism. 'We are still in the early stages of capitalism. Our lives are still shaped on all sides by pre-capitalist residues, though they are under assault as never before' (Collini, 2000).[3] It may be better seen as its belated onset, in the sense that capitalism until now has been much constrained by its context. Nineteenth-century capitalism was still subject to pre-capitalist encirclement. Second, it was constantly pressured by diverse socialist movements from within and, after 1917, State socialism from without. It consequently adapted Bismarckian welfare defences to ward off revolution and civil strife. It is only now that it is off the leash. Third, imperialism may have exported capitalism on a global scale, but it was not global capitalism. It was mainly British, French, or Dutch, and these countries tended to fetter capitalist development for nationalistic or paternalistic reasons. It is only now, in the post-communist, post-colonial era that a more purely global capitalism holds sway, albeit largely of an American model.

There is a fourth and arguably more fundamental characteristic of this new, purer form of capitalism. Until now, capitalism has been not only constrained but also facilitated by traditional, massively taken for granted social values and forms of conduct. Emile Durkheim may, as David Greenberg (1999) has argued, have proved a poor predictor of penal trends. But his dictum that contract rests on 'non-contractual elements' of trust and co-operation, born of social solidarity, summarizes acutely how capitalist successes so far have rested implicitly on forms of social relations which it is now in the process of dissolving. To John Gray (1998) and Richard Sennett (1998), global capitalism is corrosive of both social cohesion and the bases of character. Karl Marx would not have been surprised by this analysis. Ironically, far from being eclipsed by the fall of communism, Marxism has never looked so good, though it is Marx the diagnostician of capitalism rather than the prognosticator of communism who appears to be back on track (Hobsbawm, 1998). None of which explains why, well in advance of the fall of communism and with a far from negligible public sector, the USA switched to so immense an investment in imprisonment.

AMERICAN EXCEPTIONALISM: CAUSE OR CONSEQUENCE?

In his review of possible explanations for the trends towards mass incarceration in the USA, Michael Tonry (1999) classifies current theories into five types: empirical (crime-led);

psephological (public opinion-led); journalistic (media manipulation of crime as a 'wedge' issue, political (what Jonathan Simon has termed 'governing through crime' in the context of issue fragmentation); and historical (a cycle of tolerance and intolerance towards key forms of deviance). Tonry concludes that no factor taken alone can account for so gross a development as the quintupling of the US prison population over 25 years, but that the historical approach may provide a basis for the other factors to weigh in. He rejects most of the theories on comparative grounds: other countries, with far lower prison numbers than the USA have also experienced the empirical, psephological, journalistic and political shifts concerned and, it might be added, also have their own versions of swings between periods of tolerance and intolerance. American history is indeed unique, but less for its cyclical patterns than for the culture that shapes them.

In short, American exceptionalism in the penal sphere must be related to American exceptionalism itself, as a broad, unifying mythology that stretches back, with remarkable cultural continuity, to the Puritan settlement. As Melossi and Lettiere note, quoting Thomas Dumm

> 'the emergence of the penitentiary in the United States was a project *constitutive* of liberal democracy. That is, the penitentiary system formed the epistemological project of liberal democracy, creating conditions of knowledge of self and other that were to shape the political subject required for liberal and democratic values to be realised in practice . . .' . . . We could in a sense say that the American penitentiary was erected by the Founding Fathers of the Nation as an imposing and monumental Gateway to the Republic. (1998: 24–5)

Though the origins of the penitentiary lay in 17th-century Holland, it was only in Jacksonian America that 'it became the task of the prison to do nothing less than ensure the future safety of the Republic' (Rothman, 1995: 115).

In similar vein, Deborah Madsen (1998) traces the extraordinary extent to which the founding notions of the 'federal covenant', the 'saving remnant' and the 'elect' or 'redeemer nation' continue to animate, and set the terms for, current political and cultural discourse. America as the 'city on a hill' was charged with a divine mission to build a model society on earth – the New World – which would, by force of example, serve to purify the Old World they had left behind, but not abandoned. Especially relevant for deviance and control are the concepts of 'declension' – the falling away from the high ideals of the original 'errand' – and the 'federal covenant', whereby any moral backsliding by a community would threaten the salvation of the whole. Drawing on the work of Perry Miller and others, Madsen traces American exceptionalism as the animating force in Benjamin Franklin's self-exemplification of American virtues; in the 'American Renaissance' of Emerson, Hawthorne, Melville, Thoreau and Whitman; in the mythology of the western genre in cinema; in the abolitionist case against slavery, most notably by prominent slaves themselves; in the legitimation of the annexation of former Mexican and Caribbean territories; and in the case for promulgating war in Vietnam. The notion of the American Dream, so beloved of anomie theorists, captures only limited aspects of American exceptionalism – the stress on individualism and the right to happiness through virtue – and neglects its other components – the dangers of and penalties for declension, and the injunction for America to be 'not only a model nation, but also the world's guardian, regulating the conduct of other nations, and representing the world's last and best chance of salvation' (Madsen, 1998: 38).

Suitably secularized and modernized, American exceptionalism furnishes a vocabulary of motives for mass incarceration to be viewed as an inescapably utopian mission. It may have been pragmatically punitive in its origins. In *Thinking about crime* (1975), for example, James Q. Wilson argued 'for a sober view of man and his institutions that would permit reasonable things to be accomplished, foolish things abandoned, and utopian things forgotten' (quoted in Rutherford, 1996: 25–6). But in its rapid politicization and development beyond all comparable limits, it has become a utopian experiment: a social cleansing by penal means. That appeal, along with its popular accreditation for crime reduction, helps account for its widespread acceptance and lack of effective opposition, especially by the judiciary, whose discretionary powers have been greatly weakened by mandatory sentencing. It also provides an *imprimatur* for its export on a global scale. And, like many utopias, it has become dystopia, a cataclysm for those most adversely affected by its realization.

Against this view, it can be said that American exceptionalism may account for the Salem witch-hunts of the late 17th century but hardly for the sudden shift to mass incarceration in the late 20th century. As a constant, if evolving, foundation of American culture, it ran for over 300 years without producing this effect. Yet it has only been in the late 20th century that American exceptionalism ran out of, or rather ruled out, alternative options with regard to deviance and control. Two such options have, until the recent past, been the rehabilitative ideology and radical social reform. A third, the prospect of new frontiers, has – Madsen argues – been self-cancelling, as the exceptionalist drive of the pioneers ceded to settlement. New frontiers are now – following the fall of communism – new markets and technological means of penetrating them.

Rehabilitative movements have flourished both long and extensively, both within prisons and outside them, in the USA; and greater claims arguably have been made for their success than elsewhere (Rothman, 1971, 1980; Melossi and Lettiere, 1998). The use of the indeterminate sentence in California was a particularly florid example of its penal expression. It was perhaps only to be expected, therefore, that in the post-Martinson, 'Nothing Works' era after 1974, the movement to overthrow the rehabilitative agenda would have its greatest impact in the USA. This movement reached much further than psycho-analytically or psychiatrically based approaches. It seemed to wipe out the political will to experiment adequately with social and economic approaches to crime prevention and reduction. Hence, the major argument of Elliott Currie, Jerome Miller and other critics of penal expansionism – that the alternative to prison is not doing nothing, it is spending equivalent amounts on well-resourced community alternatives – met with the same 'nothing works' response.

Second, what David Garland (1996) has termed the 'solidarity project', the post-Enlightenment ideal of extending full and active citizenship to all subjects, was effectively dispensed with by the Reagan Presidency. Before then, the New Deal, and the Great Society and War on Poverty programmes had held open the possibility that the United States would move towards a 'welfare state' along European lines. Even in the 1970s and under Richard Nixon, affirmative action and the extension of Head Start projects perpetuated that hope. But the advent of 'Reaganomics', and the Bush and Clinton years, have effectively removed all but a vestigial welfare safety net for most and, for some (e.g. unwed mothers in certain states) not even that. Between 1981 and 1993, there was no increase in the proportion of GDP (21 percent) spent on welfare in the USA (Hills,

1997: 10). This was not due, in the richest nation on earth, to the 'limits of welfare' being reached, but to the perception of the economic leadership that welfare undercut market disciplines (Parenti, 1999).

A related aspect is supplied from academe – the repudiation, notably by James Q. Wilson and Charles Murray, of the search for 'root causes' of and the affirmation of penal incapacitation as the sole sure remedy for crime on the streets. If individuals are entirely responsible for crime, structural and cultural theorizing is inadmissible. Prisons are not in themselves a utopian device, as in earlier eras, such as Jacksonian America (Rothman, 1971). Rather, utopia consists in the removal of criminals from American society by penal means.[4] It rests on exclusion and banishment rather than inclusion and hopes of reform (Young, 1999). Human warehousing (Cohen, 1985) rather than normalization (King and Morgan, 1980) or minimal 'just deserts' (Von Hirsch, 1976) is all that is required. Roy King's study of 'Supermax' prisons in the USA (King, 1999) confirms that they, in particular, are an over-used facility antithetical to both humane containment and rehabilitation. Nor is there evidence to suggest that their expansion has 'freed up' the rest of the system for more humanitarian and constructive regimes.

A COMPARATIVE PERSPECTIVE ON PENAL FUTURES

In their comparative analyses of incarceration trends, both Tonry and Kuhn rightly stress the unique scale of US incarceration and the extent to which it 'dwarfs' that in comparable European societies. As noted above, Tonry goes on to reject certain much-touted 'causes' of the American phenomenon due to their co-existence with the far lower prison populations of Europe, Australasia and Canada. But that logic holds only as things currently stand. If these 'causes' are weighed in terms of their future potential rather than their current impact, then it may be only a matter of time before they begin to exert more influence in these countries too. The cliché that what happened in California yesterday is happening in the rest of America today, and will happen in Europe tomorrow, cannot be lightly dismissed. The challenge is to assess how far the recipe for the US mass incarceration is in embryo in European and other societies. In addition, having gone this route alone, the US is actively exporting it, and key groups in comparable societies are eager to adopt it. It may be more, not less, difficult for other societies to resist its appeal when the USA is both its role model and its advocate, both in the 'law and order' and in other political and economic respects.

Crime is not the problem?

Zimring and Hawkins (1997) have convincingly shown the extent to which crime rates in the USA, with the single exception of lethal violence, are now relatively normal compared with several European societies. It is a peculiar irony of American exceptionalist mythologizing that the right to bear arms, which harbour the potential for instant lethal violence, is regarded as sacrosanct, while the right to bear drugs, whose potential is rarely so, is regarded as taboo. Hence 'crime is not the problem' as a cause of US mass incarceration, as only a quarter of admissions to prisons are for violence (Tonry, 1999: 8).[5] But the fact that European crime rates have reached US proportions, while it may be reassuring from an American perspective, is disquieting from a European vantage-point. Signs of relative normalcy to the one may portend the advent of pathology to the other.

Burglary and car theft may be non-lethal offences but they are still profoundly unsettling, especially when experienced as repeat victimizations. It may well be, as Katharine Beckett (1997) has shown, that public anxieties about crime register most strongly after media and political campaigns rather than rises in crime rates or drug use. As Chambliss (1999) argues, politicians and criminal justice agencies typically quote the worst trends for the most serious crimes, even if they are plea bargained away! But rising crime rates still set the context within which such campaigns resonate. And, once in train, penal expansionism gains the credit when crime rates fall, even when other explanations, such as falling unemployment and rising prosperity, may be more plausible reasons.

The most damaging crime phenomena are those periods in which a quantum leap in crime rates coincides with allied sequences of events yielding a virulent symbolism of social breakdown. Thus, the mid-1960s to the mid-1970s in the USA combined steep rises in crime with a doubling of the homicide rate; the assassinations of John and Robert Kennedy, Martin Luther King and Malcolm X; major urban riots, both racial and anti-war; and extremist political violence. There were elements of 'la grande peur' of revolutionary France in the atmosphere of the times. In Britain, the 1980s saw a doubling of the crime rate and, especially in 1989–92, when the crime rate rose by 50 percent, in a context of rioting and high unemployment following deindustrialization, the sense of a breakdown of social order was very strong. The murder of a 2-year-old boy, James Bulger, by two older boys, provided the climax to a decade of growing fear of crime that symbolized a sense of social changes spinning out of control. In The Netherlands, the rising crime rate during 1979–84 resembled a cliff face compared with earlier trends. Combined with fears about hard drug use and drug-related crime, it provided conditions ripe for a toughening of criminal justice and penal policy. In all three countries, but to very different degrees, the scene was set for prison populations rising to unprecedented heights.

The definition of the problem, heavily influenced by political and media agendas, seems crucial in explaining whether structural or punitive measures are deployed in response. In the USA and to a lesser extent in Britain, the most influential explanation imputed rising crime and riots to a newly jobless marauding underclass (Taylor, 1999). In The Netherlands, 'depillarization', the erosion of the institutionalized bases of informal social control in the family, denominational groupings, the school and the community, was seen as the principal cause in the influential *Society and crime* report (Ministry of Justice 1985). This explanation probably did more to arouse anxieties than to allay them, and the publication of the first International Victim Survey in 1987, showing The Netherlands to be apparently the most crime-prone nation surveyed, compounded such fears. Other Western European countries to have experienced such trends have avoided or resisted so penal a response, though several – e.g. Italy, Spain, Portugal – have raised their prison populations markedly (Ruggiero et al., 1995). In others, – e.g. Austria, France – politically fascistic parties have gained ground.

Crime thus holds the potential to symbolize social breakdown in ways which mobilize popular and elite support for punitive formal controls to be stepped up to previously impermissible heights and lengths. Seismic shifts can occur in the regulatory character not only of the criminal justice field (Feeley and Simon, 1992) but across the entire culture of control (see Garland, forthcoming). As a result, even when crime has ceased to be *the* problem, changes have been set in motion which are immensely difficult to modify and may be impossible to reverse. In this welter of disturbing change, imprisonment offers one touchstone of secure social order. Prisons are the guarantee that *ultimately* law and order will be enforced or restored. Modes of punishment are profoundly expressive (Garland, 1990), and the symbolic potency of imprisonment in particular offers politicians endless dramaturgical possibilities, conveying multiple messages to different audiences (Sparks, forthcoming). It is *the* sign that governments are prepared to do whatever it takes to wage war on crime. In some penal climates it attains a kind of fiscal benefit of clergy, as an experiment that cannot fail – if crime goes down, prisons gain the credit; but if it goes up, we clearly need more of the same medicine whatever the cost.

The politics of law and order

With some allowance for time-lags, Tonry rightly sees much common experience between the USA and European societies on this front. In Britain, crime control emerged as a partisan issue only in the 1970 General Election, then even more resoundingly in 1979 (Downes and Morgan, 1997). In the USA, it first surfaced with Goldwater in 1964, in The Netherlands 20 years later. In France, Germany and the Scandinavian countries, it remains much less prominent, despite highly visible episodes of youthful disorder and growing drug use. Though variation persists, two trajectories are discernible. The first is that, once embarked on a course of 'governing through crime', with the heightened emotionalism and bidding-up of punitive measures that this entails, no society has managed to find a way of extricating itself from that upwards spiral. Part of that pattern is at least *some* convergence between the USA and Europe at the ideological level. It may well be that Americans have given less weight than Europeans to social and economic factors in offending behaviour (Kuhn, 1999: 19), but rehabilitation also connotes self-improvement aided by counselling and treatment, a long-established if now marginalized American practice. At the European end:

> analogous to the conversion of the welfare state since the 1980s into . . . a 'market economy', diminishing the responsibility of the state to its citizens and heavily emphasising individual responsibility, causes of criminal behaviour are no longer seen as lying in the criminal's social background, life situation and the circumstances of the offence, but in the moral fault of the actor resulting in acts of free will for which he is fully responsible. (Junger-Tas, 1998: 19)

The second is that economic growth in the richest countries has in part depended on inflows of migrant workers, has fostered immigration from former colonies and prompted refugees to seek haven on a scale not easily accommodated without conflict. The problems involved in integrating diverse culturally distinctive groups into highly unequal societies can all too readily be translated into crime control terms.

In Britain, only since 1992 have both major parties engaged in 'populist punitiveness' (Bottoms, 1995). The Tories had long contrived to cast Labour as a party neglectful of the police, 'soft' on crime and tolerant of public disorder born of industrial militancy. Labour had pursued the alternative case that rising crime was largely due to social and economic inequalities (Downes and Morgan, 1994). As Shadow Home Secretary during 1979–92, Roy Hattersley also pressed a Rawlsian case, the need to combine social justice with civil liberties (Bowling, 2000). Between 1989–92, Britain experienced a major recession, with male unemployment rising to 15 percent; a prison population falling from 50,000 to 42,000; and a crime rate that rose by almost 50 percent. For the first time in over 30 years, the Conservative lead over Labour as the party best able to guarantee law and order vanished. Labour pressed home their advantage, not by emphasizing the links between economic factors and rising crime but by stressing the leniency of sentencing. Tony Blair's celebrated sound-bite on the need to be 'tough on crime, tough on the causes of crime' nicely allowed for both, but the sub-text, being 'tough on criminals', was what emerged in policy terms (Pease, 1998; see also Ryan, 1999). This strategy owed much to the American Democratic Party's approach to avoiding a repetition of the Dukakis debacle of 1988. Clinton was 'smart' as well as 'tough' on crime (Rutherford, 1999). To neutralize Michael Howard's 'Prison Works' policy, Jack Straw, both in Opposition and in government, formulated policies (some enacted in the 1998 Crime and Disorder Act, some either still forthcoming or meeting resistance) which Labour would hardly have countenanced before 1992. These include

- activating minimum mandatory penalties for burglary, drug-dealing and violence (authorized by a statute passed by the outgoing Conservative government);
- the creation of Anti-Social Behaviour Orders which, inter alia, blur the distinction between criminal and civil law burdens of proof (see Ashworth et al., 1998);
- local authority powers to impose curfews for juveniles;
- renaming the Probation and After-Care Service the 'Community Punishment and Rehabilitation Service' (a measure to which 85 percent of Chief Probation Officers are opposed);
- reducing the threshold for returning probationers to court from three breaches to two (a breach being such conduct as failing to attend a meeting with the officer at the agreed time); and automatic withdrawal of social security benefits for up to six months for a second breach;
- the extension of privatized prison management from three prisons to 14;
- the ending of *doli incapax* (the presumption of lack of offending awareness) for offenders under the age of 14;
- the replacement of Social Security payments by subsistence vouchers for asylum seekers;
- the prosecution of 'squeegee merchants' and beggars;
- drug testing of arrestees at police stations;
- extending disclosure to employers of previous convictions to all offences.

Much of this catalogue is inspired by the American example of 'zero tolerance' policing and prosecution. The effect is that both major parties have engaged in raising the punitive stakes, and the prison population in England and Wales rose from 42,000 to 65,000 in six years.

There are, it must be said, compensating liberal components to offset the generally punitive drift of these measures. For example

- Labour have embarked on a generously funded programme of 'restorative justice' and community crime reduction projects for disaffected youth, stressing reparation, mediation and mentoring for young offenders and those at risk of crime;

- Jack Straw took the brave decision to mount a public enquiry into the Stephen Lawrence case, in which the hugely bungled investigation by the Metropolitan Police of the murder of a black teenager by local white youths was defined as 'institutional racism' by the resulting Report;
- the UK, a long-term but reluctant signatory to the European Convention on Human Rights, has now incorporated its provisions into domestic law;
- the age of consent for homosexual relations should be reduced to 16, to match that for heterosexual relations.

The net result of all these measures remains, however, markedly punitive and penally expansionist, though some expert commentary (e.g. Morgan, 1998) sees Straw as acting '*sotto voce*' to 'manage' the prison population at roughly its current level. And the community measures are heavily dependent on marked improvements in the major public sector services of health, education and housing, which remain significantly underfunded by comparison with most European countries (Hills, 1997; Downes, 1998). Should crime rates recommence their annual rise, and the evaluation of community measures prove negative or equivocal, a further ratcheting up of prison populations seems inevitable.

The second common trajectory crucial to the politics of law and order is that

> the concern with crime and fear of victimization has grown out of all proportion to the actual increases in criminality; fear which typically is most focused on traditional 'street crimes' and crimes allegedly committed by powerless minority groups . . . Across Europe and in the US, increasing proportions of the prison population consist of 'minorities' and foreigners. (Marshall, 1996: 31)

In Europe, contradictory impulses are at work. On the one hand, the shared political aspiration is for a Europe *sans frontières*, with freedom of trade and movement, upheld by the European Court, the Convention on Human Rights, etc. On the other hand, the inflows of refugees, migrant workers and immigrants from both former communist and colonial societies provokes resentments that have, as Loïc Wacquant (1999) has stressed, fed into the politics of far Right ethnocentrism. One attempt at resolution is to legislate for equal opportunities but also to step up penalties for the offences in which the most discriminated against ethnic minorities are disproportionately involved (Tonry, 1995). The over-representation of Afro-Caribbean compared to white prisoners in Britain is much the same as in the USA. In The Netherlands, the proportion of non-Dutch prisoners rose from 12 percent in 1981 to 26 percent in 1992; and a growing proportion are from second-generation ethnic minorities (Van Swaaningen and De Jonge, 1995; Downes, 1998: 150). While much controversy surrounds the view that such minorities are disproportionately involved in crime, the perception has grown that they are unusually disaffected, resistant to welfare measures and recalcitrant. In this situation, even liberal elites are prone to disillusioned acceptance of exclusionary measures: in England, black children are permanently excluded from school at three times the rate of white children; and the scale of expulsions overall rose greatly during the 1990s to 12,668 in 1996/7 (10,400 in 1998/9) (Department for Education and Employment, 10 May 2000). These trends all hold potential for penal expansion.

Risk and security

More common ground between Europe and the USA can be found in the combination of a heightened awareness of victimization by crime and greater expectations of personal security and public safety. Expectations about safety and security have increased hugely in the post-war period. The Social Democratic ideal of cradle-to-grave work and welfare; immense improvements in medical care and surgery; the post-war settlement that, despite the nuclear threat, held out the prospect of peaceful international relations; and the makings of a system of world governance promised future stability. In the lives of most people in the democracies of the West, and with the single exception of the Vietnam war, victimization by crime was the principal source of risk that could not be personally controlled or ameliorated. Oral histories tend to confirm this sense of crime as an increasingly unwarranted scourge (Hood and Joyce, 1999). It has fuelled the growth of such movements as victim rights and victim support (Rock, 1987, 1990, 1998) and the vast and growing investment in situational crime prevention: mass electronic surveillance, target hardening, security checks and gated communities are now so pervasive that the crime rate might well be termed the displacement rate. Cars left unalarmed, property left unguarded and houses only minimally secured are now bad insurance risks, with the worst-hit communities becoming uninsurable. The more repressive the controls, the more regressive becomes the crime, with poorer areas – notoriously the deindustrialized wastelands – plagued by multiple victimization (Davies, 1998). The promise of situational control (Clarke, 1980) was that the contested terrain of 'root causes' could be ignored. But while such controls may have helped contain crime rates, they have hardly been reduced at all substantially. Insofar as crime rates persist at a high level or even increase despite such measures – which has immense implications for the exclusion and control of deviant groups and individuals – the potential for yet further resort to imprisonment is ever-present.

Among the more potent images of risk and insecurity are the mentally ill, decanted from dwindling institutions to insubstantial community care. What gets noticed in the community are the visibly distressed and deviant, whose often-unkempt appearance, verbal aggression and odd behaviour disturb harassed commuters and busy shoppers. Though it is no comfort to victims, their contribution to lethal violence is minute, but what there is has fuelled demands for 'something to be done' about the most dangerous, severely disordered personalities. The current British Home Office proposal (1999) is that indefinite detention should be the provision, even in the absence of offending behaviour. Given the difficulties of diagnosis, this is a recipe for expanding incarceration to a fresh target group of uncertain dimensions.

THE MACHO ECONOMY

The USA in the 1980s seemed to many observers (e.g. Paul Kennedy, 1993) to be losing its pre-eminence as *the* world power economically if not militarily. The 1990s saw its position not only restored but subject to a certain triumphalism. There remains, however, one contender against the US model of political economy: the social democratic 'welfare state', mixed economies, primarily of Europe, but also Canada, Australia and New Zealand. In this model, fundamentally capitalist societies intervene in the market for social, welfare and civic ends, especially in the fields of education, health, housing, income maintenance and personal social services. It has been a remarkable attempt, particularly in Scandinavia, to retain what Lionel Jospin termed 'a market economy but not a market society', and to protect the more vulnerable from pitiless economic forces on a more systematic basis than the vagaries of private charity.

International commentary often takes the USA to be some kind of ultracapitalist lost cause in terms of welfare spending. But this is a travesty. In 1993, even after a decade of Reaganomic tax cuts for the rich and welfare cuts for the poor, US spending on public welfare services still amounted to some 21 percent of GDP, compared to 26 percent in the UK and 29 percent in Germany (Hills, 1997). The UK and Germany are, on this measure, closer to the USA than to Scandinavian countries, where over 40 percent of GDP is devoted to public sector welfare. On health, the USA spent a slightly *higher* proportion of GDP on its public health sector than the British spent on the National Health Service, and over twice as much if private health spending is included. On education and social security they are roughly the same, though the US system favours the better off much more than in Britain; really big differences only obtain in housing. What this implies is the underlying strength of constituencies within the USA for a substantial mixed economy of welfare, rather than an absolute difference between the USA and Europe.

For the past two decades, however, the pressures towards privatization and a reduction of public spending have gathered pace. The impact of different interpretations of the 'Third Way' (Giddens, 1999) will be crucial in determining how far this tendency will be pushed. The debate is increasingly couched in terms of the greater success of deregulated market economies, most notably the USA, by comparison with the more 'corporatist' economies of Europe, with the UK occupying an intermediate position following the partial continuation of New Right privatizations by New Labour. At stake is the continuing commitment to far more substantial public sector investment in the lead countries of Scandinavia, The Netherlands, Belgium, France, Germany and Italy.

The sheer size of the US prison population has now become an important factor in this macroeconomic matrix as never before. As Beckett and Western (1997) have clearly spelt out, the US prison population now amounts to some 2 percent of the male labour force. As a result of prisoners being excluded from the labour force count, a convention which merits re-examination, this factor alone has reduced the official figure for male unemployment by some 30–40 percent since the early 1990s. And it is this unemployment figure that is endlessly cited, on both sides of the Atlantic, as a major sign of the superiority of the deregulated economy of the USA compared with the more corporatist economies of Western Europe. Few financial commentators seem aware of the significance of the penal factor – only Larry Elliott (*Guardian* 13 December 1999) has, to my knowledge, referred to it all, and then only in passing. Making some allowance for the huge job creation aspect of imprisonment for custodial and allied staff, especially in areas of high unemployment, would enhance its significance even further. It is a tragic irony that a major flaw in the political economy of the USA – its grotesquely high prison population – unduly inflates what is taken to signify a major success – its unusually low unemployment rate. Moreover, it is by now well established, thanks to the work of Michael Tonry (1995), Jerome Miller (1996) and Mark Mauer (1997), that these effects are most pronounced and devastating in the case of young black males, with one in three either in prison or under the penal disciplines of probation or parole. The penal factor has denuded some black inner-city neighbourhoods of young men: the female-headed household can now, but for children and the elderly, be writ large as communities virtually composed of women. And in the ghetto areas documented by William Julius Wilson, more or less devoid of economic activity, very high unemployment rates persist which would be even starker but for the high rate of imprisonment, fuelled by involvement in the drug trade. Yet informed commentators can still write: 'The economy is booming, and American blacks are today less likely to be out of work than Europeans. (Black unemployment is down to under 8 per cent.)' (Thernstrom, 1999). Taking those in prison into account, that figure would be at least 16 percent.

It may be, therefore, that mass imprisonment in the USA will make its impact on Europe less by the direct export of its components, such as privatization, and mandatory and tougher sentencing, and more by its masked impact on macroeconomic policy, encouraging a retreat from substantial welfare services, from the involvement of trade unions in economic regulation and from employment safeguards. 'If Europe continues to follow the lead of the US by continuing the gradual dismantlement of the welfare state, excluding growing segments of the population from full participation in society, Europe too may become a polarized society of winner versus losers' (Marshall, 1996: 32) with all that that implies by way of crime and its penal control.

In this retreat from welfarism, Britain leads the way: New Labour is

> on course to keep public spending at a lower level (as a proportion of the whole economy) than any government since Harold Macmillan's 35 years ago . . . Even if the extra money voted in the comprehensive spending review results in health, education and transport rising as a proportion of GDP in 1999–2000 and beyond, the changes are unlikely to make a radical difference to the average during the whole life of the present government. (Travers, 1999)[6]

The National Health Service has run for 20 years or more on at least 1 percent below average expenditure for the European OECD countries. That is currently £8 billion a year, which amounts over the 20-year period to a total of £160 billion of denied investment. Despite its efficiency, no system could flourish on such austere resourcing. As the health budget covers mental health, it is no surprise that 'care in the community' is at a low ebb. As, unlike mental hospitals, prisons are an ever-open door for whomever they are sent by the courts, transcarceration is more of a reality now than in the past, with prisoners suffering disturbingly high rates of some of the most serious mental illnesses.

There are at least four other respects in which the US penal phenomenon feeds into important debates in a distorting fashion. First, it is associated with both a successive stabilization and actual reductions in the US crime rate *and* with an unprecedentedly long period of economic growth. Both factors combine to lend mass incarceration an aura of hard-won success, of benefits outweighing costs, which may prove influential in other countries. It hallows the export of private prison systems by Wackenhut and Correctional Corporation of America. The fact that the economic growth is despite, not because of, the prison explosion may be swamped in the rush to buy into its apparent success.

Second, as Beckett and Western argue, imprisonment damages employment prospects after release and heightens risks of recidivism. The criminogenic effects of custody are met in circular fashion by yet more incarceration. This helps explain why the US prison population has risen so incessantly beyond all seeming limits, and suggests that the USA is now locked into a penal economy which is both self-replicating and subject to a multiplier effect due to progressively steepening mandatory sentences.

Third, and paradoxically, the tight labour market created in part by mass imprisonment *may* be one reason for the falls in crimes against property, as a consequence of rising prosperity and even low wage employment (W. Wilson, 1997). It is, however, the imprisonment and not the employment that gains popular credit.

Fourth, there is a *macho* quality to the long US boom that may be heightened by mass incarceration. High prison populations hold inflationary implications, due to the tight labour markets on which they exert a concealed effect, and due also to the huge, largely unproductive nature of the investment involved. These are currently masked by the low inflation achieved in the USA partly by productivity gains from information technology, but partly from high levels of foreign investment (Atkinson, 2000). A certain *machismo* inheres, however, in the steep disparity between Stock Market valuations and company profits; the size of the current account deficit; and high levels of consumer debt. When the downturn comes, it could be that mass incarceration will exert a Keynesian, stabilizing effect, to be sustained for economic reasons. But a recession will fall most damagingly on those ex-offenders and ex-prisoners who have been employed, if at all, in the most precarious and least protected jobs, and whose employability has been most eroded by custody. These pressures predictably heighten their risk of recidivism and reimprisonment (Beckett and Western, 1997). The interaction between these two trends could spell the even greater expansion of the prison population to well above the 2 million mark.

It is also the case that a *macho* economy produces a *macho* society. When economic strength and cut-throat profitability are the drivers of conduct; when job stability and decent wages are a folk memory; when skilled professionals can be told to clear their desks within the hour; when you are only as good as your last deal; and when secrecy in takeovers, asset stripping and head-hunting are conducted with sublime disregard for ethics, then the basis for some sort of Kantian respect for persons in social relationships can hardly be said to exist. The *machismo* of the street, in drug dealing, hustling and physical intimidation, with its lack of eye contact, demand for 'respect' (Bourgois, 1995) and contempt for weakness, is – as William Julius Wilson has said – a poor basis for primary labour market employment. It is, however, a good preparation for street crime and survival in prison. The *machismo* of the powerless is a symmetrical parody of that of the powerful in a winner/loser culture.

CONCLUSIONS

'Europe has to withstand the American 'example'! . . . It is improbable that it will become like the US in the future. The latter has given them too bad an example of what a failure can look like' (Kuhn, 1996: 39). One can only hope that this is indeed to be the case. But the burden of this analysis is that the components of a steep rise in imprisonment in Europe, especially in Britain, have been assembled. At the macroeconomic level, the case against more regulated economies is strengthened by fallacies about low unemployment fostered by mass incarceration itself. And Europe does not have to *match* the US rate of imprisonment for Europe to experience the makings of a social and political disaster: even to reach half the US level, or 330 per 100,000, would mean tripling current rates of imprisonment in Europe. The off-the-scale character of US imprisonment may even induce complacency elsewhere that their prison populations are so much lower that even steep rises in their terms would be comparatively negligible.

It is certainly the case that Europe and other societies should resist the US example on the penal front. But what are the prospects for resistance within the USA itself? Here there is much common ground with Europe. 'We think of the US as a nation dedicated to private enterprise. Yet [unlike in Britain] its water supply remains in public hands, as do some important rail lines; and there are no plans to privatise the federal mails' (Blackburn, 2000: 25). And, as noted above, education, health and social security remain major public services, despite the huge inroads of the grossly enlarged criminal justice and penal systems. In other words, there is a basis for interpretations of American exceptionalism to be reclaimed from the New Right by the constituencies which created the New Deal and the Great Society programmes. It may be that those constituencies have been fragmented by deindustrialization and suburbanization, but the potential for their reassembly surely lies in the need for security against the hazards of the 'risk society' that can only be collectively provided.

The crime form most unique to American society, lethal violence, presents awesome problems of regulation, but Zimring and Hawkins have documented the links with lack of gun control to provide a case which can be tirelessly put for far greater restrictions, even if they are dubious about its prospects. On racial discrimination and drug law enforcement, we should heed William Julius Wilson's prescription on joblessness and inequality: that although they affect young black men most adversely, they are trans-racial problems that are best dealt with as needing common solutions.

Taken together, these three strands provide a front on which to contest the case for mass incarceration. Otherwise, the country which invented the juvenile court but is now executing juveniles, and in which no presidential candidate opposes capital punishment, will carry on, and seek to carry others with it, as if it had no alternative.

Acknowledgements

My thanks to David Piachaud, Paul Rock and Andrew Wilson for timely help and stimulating criticism. It was David Piachaud who coined the term 'the *macho* economy' to parody those economists who dismiss what goes on at the micro-level as of no account. I am also grateful to Kate Malleson, Maurice Punch, Mick Ryan and Jo Sparkes for ready answers on what, for me, were difficult points.

Notes

1 Except Britain, where poverty levels came to surpass those in the USA.

2 One sign of active resistance to the American trend is the Canadian Solicitor General's web-site Home Page *Myths and realities: dispelling myths about Canada's criminal justice system* (4 February 2000), which explicitly challenges the morality and efficacy of US penal policy.

3 David Greenberg's Commentary (this issue) criticizes this approach by linking the long-term decline in violence in England since the 13th century with the rise of the spirit of capitalism. I prefer to see the two as mutually dependent on the establishment of the rule of law, a settled state with authorities strong enough to uphold it, and the long haul to democratic citizenship. Moreover, the immense decline in rates of homicide had

already been substantially accomplished by the advent of capitalism in the late 18th century.

4 Thus, for example, the 1995 Republican political agenda *Restoring the Dream* contained 'the toughest crime package approved by the House of Representatives in decades', stepping up already huge budgets for additional prison construction from 8 to 10.5 billion dollars, converting elements of Democrat social spending into law enforcement programmes, limiting the scope for death penalty appeals, allowing 'good faith' exemptions to exclusionary rules on evidence, making victim restitution mandatory for federal crimes and easing the deportation of criminal aliens (see Windlesham, 1998: 129–30; and throughout for an impressively documented analysis of the past two decades of law and order politics in the USA).

5 Against this view, Matthews (1999) argues, citing Lynch (1988) and the work of Farrington and Langan (1992) and Farrington et al. (1994), that the USA is not especially punitive once the more serious character of crime in America is taken into account: 'The differences between the USA and England and Wales are largely a product of different rates of crime rather than major differences in sentencing practice . . . However, the USA tends to impose longer prison sentences for those convicted' (Matthews, 1999: 99). This conclusion seriously understates substantial differences between the two societies, and between the USA and other Western European countries, in sentences for non-violent crimes and drug offences, the fastest growing component of US incarceration rates. Even Lynch (1995), who is also keen to challenge the image of the USA as relatively punitive, summarizes Farrington and Langan's (1992) data as follows:

> The probability of incarceration following conviction was not radically different across nations for violent crimes, but it was substantially different for property crimes . . . A person found guilty of burglary in the United States had a.74 probability of a custodial sentence but only a.40 chance in England and Wales . . . The large differences in time served between the United States and the other countries occurs for property crimes – burglary and larceny. (Lynch, 1995: 33–4)

For burglary, the same source gives the US average of time served as 10.6 months compared with 6.8 months in England and 5.3 in Canada. For larceny, the mean time served is 7 months in the USA compared with 4.65 in England and 2 months in Canada. For drug offences, the differences are even more substantial. And, as Currie notes, these figures are mostly based on mid-1980s data, so that 'after nearly a decade and a half of relentlessly stiffening sentences [in the US] . . . our comparative severity has increased substantially' (Currie, 1998: 19). Moreover, while within offence differences, such as carrying weaponry, may account for steeper sentences for robbery, this factor is far less likely to apply to burglary and larceny (see Zimring and Hawkins, 1997: 44–6). Matthews' argument is, however, a timely reminder that we lack up-to-date, close-grained analyses of comparative sentencing practice. The urge to normalize American punitiveness also encourages playing down, or ignoring, what is happening at the extremes of the sentencing spectrum, as distinct from its middle range. Thus 'it is curious that those who argue that the US is not especially punitive generally fail to mention that we are the only industrial democracy that still makes significant use of the death penalty for homicide (Currie, 1998: 17). And for the least serious offences, the USA has pioneered, or reactivated, an array of 'quality of life' crimes, for whose violation the risks of arrest, detention and subsequent imprisonment are now greatly increased (Parenti, 1999: Ch. 4).

6 The March 2000 Budget changes the picture for health spending, adopting annual increases far higher than those previously enacted, and aiming to raise government resourcing of the National Health Service to European average levels by 2007. With this exception, New Labour policies on welfare are tending towards a liberal-democratic rather than the social-democratic tradition of previous Labour and most Western European governments.

References

Ashworth, A. et al. (1998) 'Neighbouring on the oppressive: the government's "Anti-Social Behaviour Order" proposals', *Criminal Justice* 16(1): 7–14.

Atkinson, M. (2000) 'Dollar beware', *Guardian* 18 January.

Beckett, K. (1997) *Making crime pay: law and order in contemporary American politics.* New York: Oxford University Press.

Beckett, K. and Western, B. (1997) 'The penal system as labor market institution: jobs and jails, 1980–95', *Overcrowded Times* 8(6).

Blackburn, R. (2000) 'How to bring back collectivism', *New Statesman* 17 January 2000.

Bottoms, A. (1995) 'The philosophy and politics of punishment and sentencing', in C. Clarkson and R. Morgan (eds) *The politics of sentencing reform.* Oxford: Clarendon Press.

Bourgois, P. (1995) *In search of respect.* Cambridge: Cambridge University Press.

Bowling, B. (1999) 'The rise and fall of New York murder: zero tolerance or crack's decline?', *British Journal of Criminology* 39(4).

Bowling, B. (2000) 'New Labour, racism, crime and justice', paper presented to the British Society of Criminology, 19 January.

Chambliss, W. (1999) *Power, politics, and crime.* Boulder, CO: Westview.

Christie, N. (1993) *Crime control as industry: towards gulags, western style?* London: Routledge.

Clarke, R. (1980) 'Situational crime prevention', *British Journal of Criminology* 20(2): 136–47.

Cohen, S. (1985) *Visions of social control.* Cambridge: Polity.

Collini, S. (2000) 'The end of the world as we know it', *Guardian* 1 January.

Currie, E. (1998) *Crime and punishment in America.* New York: Holt.

Davies, N. (1998) *Dark heart.* London: Chatro & Windus.

Department for Education and Employment (2000) *Permanent exclusions from schools and exclusion appeals, England 1998/9 (provisional).* London: Government Statistical Service.

Downes, D. (1998) 'The buckling of the shields: Dutch penal policy 1985–95', in R. Weiss and N. South (eds) *Comparing prison systems.* Amsterdam: Gordon & Breach.

Downes, D. (1998) 'Toughing it out: from Labour opposition to Labour government', *Policy Studies* 19(3/4): 191–8.

Downes, D. and Morgan, R. (1997) 'Dumping the hostages to fortune: the politics of law and order', in M. Maguire, R. Morgan and R. Reiner (eds) *The Oxford handbook of criminology, 2nd edn.* Oxford: Clarendon Press.

Farrington, D. and Langan, P. (1992) 'Changes in crime and punishment in England and America in the 1980s', *Justice Quarterly* 9: 5–46.

Farrington, D., Langan, P. and Wikstrom, P. (1994) 'Changes in crime and punishment in England, America and Sweden in the 1980s and 1990s', *Studies in Crime and Crime Prevention*, 104–31.

Feeley, M. and Simon, J. (1992) 'The new penology: notes on the emerging strategy on corrections and its implications', *Criminology* 30(4): 449–74.

Garland, D. (1990) *Punishment and modern society.* Oxford: Clarendon Press.

Garland, D. (1996) 'The limits of the sovereign state: strategies of crime control in contemporary society', *British Journal of Criminology* 36(4): 445–71.

Garland, D. (forthcoming) *The culture of control: crime and social order in contemporary society.* Oxford: Clarendon Press.

Giddens, A. (1999) *The third way.* Cambridge: Polity.

Gray, J. (1998) *False dawn: the delusions of global capitalism.* Cambridge: Granta.

Greenberg, D. (1999) 'Punishment, division of labor, and social solidarity', in W. Laufer and F. Adler (eds) *The criminology of criminal law: advances in criminological theory, vol. 3.*

Hills, J. (1997) *The future of welfare: a guide to the debate.* York: Rowntree Foundation.

Home Office (1999) *Managing dangerous people with severe personality disorder: proposals for policy development.* London: Home Office, July.

Hood, R. and Joyce, K. (1999) 'Three generations: oral testimonies on crime and social change in London's East End', *British Journal of Criminology* 39(1).

James, O. (1993) *Juvenile violence in a winner/loser culture.* London: Free Association Books.

Junger-Tas, J. (1998) 'Dutch Penal Policies Changing Direction' *Overcrowded Times*, 9(5).

Kennedy, P. (1993) *Preparing for the twenty-first century.* New York: Random House.

King, R. (1999) 'The rise and rise of supermax: an American solution in search of a problem?', *Punishment & Society* 1(2): 163–86.

King, R. and Morgan, R. (1980) *The future of the prison system.* Farnborough: Gower.

Kuhn, A. (1996) 'Incarceration rates: Europe versus USA', *European Journal on Criminal Policy and Research (Developments in the Use of Prisons)* 4(3): 46–73.

Kuhn, A. (1999) 'Incarceration rates around the world', *Overcrowded Times* 10(2).

Lynch, J. (1988) 'A comparison of prison use in England, Canada, West Germany and the United States', *Journal of Criminal Law and Criminology* 79: 108–217.

Lynch, J. (1995) 'Crime in international perspective', in J. Wilson and J. Petersilia (eds) *Crime.* San Francisco, CA: ICS Press.

Madsen, D. (1998) *American exceptionalism.* Edinburgh University Press.

Marshall, I. (1996) 'How exceptional is the United States? crime trends in Europe and the US', *European Journal on Criminal Policy and Research (Europe Meets US in Crime and Policy)* 4(2): 7–35.

Mathiesen, T. (1990) *Prison on trial: a critical assessment.* London: Sage.

Matthews, R. (1999) *Doing time: an introduction to the sociology of imprisonment.* London: Macmillan.

Mauer, M. (1997) *Intended and unintended consequences: state racial disparities in imprisonment.* Washington, DC: The Sentencing Project.

Melossi, D. and Lettiere, M. (1998) 'Punishment in the American democracy: the paradoxes of good intentions', in R. Weiss and N. South (eds) *Comparing prison systems.* Amsterdam: Gordon & Breach.

Miller, J. (1996) *Search and destroy: African-American males in the criminal justice system.* Cambridge University Press.

Ministry of Justice (1985) *Society and crime: a policy plan for the future.* The Hague: Ministry of Justice.

Morgan, R. (1998) 'Imprisonment in England and Wales: flood tide, but on the turn?', *Overcrowded Times* 9(5).

Parenti, C. (1999) *Lockdown America: police and prisons in the age of crisis.* London: Verso.

Pease, K. (1998) 'Crime, Labour and the wisdom of Solomon', *Policy Studies* 19(3/4): 255–66.

Radzinowicz, L. (1991) 'Penal regressions', *Cambridge Law Journal* 50: 422–44.

Rock, P. (1986) *The view from the shadows.* Oxford: Clarendon Press.

Rock, P. (1990) *Helping victims of crime.* Oxford: Clarendon Press.

Rock, P. (1998) *After homicide: practical and political responses to bereavement.* Oxford: Clarendon Press.

Rothman, D. (1971) *The discovery of the asylum: social order and disorder in the new republic.* Boston, MA: Little, Brown.

Rothman, D. (1980) *Conscience and convenience: the asylum and its alternatives in progressive America.* Boston, MA: Little, Brown.

Rothman, D. (1995) 'Perfecting the prison: United States, 1789–1865', in N. Morris and D. Rothman (eds) *The Oxford history of the prison: the practice of punishment in western society.* New York: Oxford University Press.

Ruggiero, V., Ryan, M. and Sim, J., eds (1995) *Western European penal systems: a critical anatomy.* London: Sage.

Rutherford, A. (1996) *Transforming criminal policy.* Winchester: Waterside.

Rutherford, A. (1999) 'New Labour, new Democrats, new criminality', paper given at Mannheim Centre, London School of Economics, 21 January.

Ryan, M. (1999) 'Penal policy making towards the millennium: elites and populists; New Labour and the new criminology', *International Journal of the Sociology of Law* 27: 1–22.

Sennett, R. (1998) *The corrosion of character: the personal consequences of work in the new capitalism.* New York: Norton.

Simon, J. (1993) *Poor discipline: parole and the social control of the underclass.* Chicago University Press.

Sparks, R. (forthcoming) 'State punishment in advanced capitalist societies.' University of Keele: Dept. of Criminology.

Stern, V. (1998) *A sin against the future: imprisonment in the world.* London: Penguin.

Taylor, I. (1999) *Crime in context: a critical criminology of market societies.* Cambridge: Polity.

Thernstrom, A. (1999) 'The kids are all right: why fears that America has lost its moral compass are misplaced', *Times Literary Supplement* 30 July.

Tonry, M. (1995) *Malign neglect: race, crime and punishment.* New York: Oxford University Press.

Tonry, M. (1996) 'The effects of American drug policy on black Americans, 1980–1996', *European Journal of Criminal Policy and Research (Europe Meets US in Crime and Policy)* 4(2) 36–62.

Tonry, M. (1999) 'Why are US incarceration rates so high?', *Overcrowded Times* 10(3).

Travers, T. (1999) 'Squaring the circle', *Guardian* 22 September.

Van Swaaningen, R. and De Jonge, G. (1995) 'The Dutch prison system and penal policy in the 1990s: from humanitarian paternalism to penal business management', in V. Ruggiero, M. Ryan and J. Sim (eds) *Western European penal systems: a critical anatomy.* London: Sage.

Von Hirsch, A. (1976) *Doing justice.* New York: Hill & Wang.

Wacquant, L. (1999) '"Suitable enemies": foreigners and immigrants in the prisons of Europe', *Punishment and Society* 1(2): 215–22.

Walmsley, R. (1999) *World prison population list.* London: Home Office.

Wilson, J. (1975) *Thinking about crime.* New York: Basic Books.

Wilson, W. (1997) *When work disappears: the world of the new urban poor.* New York: Knopf.

Windlesham, Lord (1998) *Politics, punishment, and populism.* Oxford University Press.

Young, J. (1986) 'The failure of criminology: the need for a radical realism', in R. Matthews and J. Young (eds) *Confronting Crime* London: Sage.

Young, J. (1999) *The exclusive society: social exclusion, crime and difference in late modernity.* London: Sage.

Zimring, F. and Hawkins, G. (1997) *Crime is not the problem: lethal violence in America.* New York: Oxford University Press.

DAVID DOWNES is Professor of Social Administration and Director of the Mannheim Centre for Criminology and Criminal Justice at the London School of Economics. His books include *The delinquent solution* (1966), *Contrasts in tolerance* (1988) and, with Paul Rock, *Understanding deviance* (3rd edn 1998).

[14]
Toughing It Out: From Labour Opposition to Labour Government

Abstract *Labour's criminal justice policy has remained strikingly consistent in the move from Opposition to Government. That policy was fashioned in the break with key aspects of past Labour policy after Tony Blair's 'Tough on crime; tough on the causes of crime' statement of 1993. The tensions implicit in this approach flow from the relatively short-term demands of the first part of the phrase and the longer term requirements of the second part. In the context of punitive populism, being tough on crime came to mean being as tough as (if not tougher than) the Tories on crime. And the need to head off a repetition of the Conservative 'tax bombshell' in the 1992 defeat for Labour seems to have meant (despite the Comprehensive Spending Review) an excessive caution on public expenditure. These tensions now threaten to undermine the most positive aspects of Labour's programme, not only in criminal justice, but more broadly in relation to social exclusion and the labour market. They have generated perverse incentives to over-heat the penal economy, to blow the prospects for restorative justice off-course, and to repeat in different guise some of the mistakes of the 1970s. As a result, Jack Straw remains somewhat imprisoned by the agenda set by Michael Howard.*

'Law and order', as distinct from plain 'order', is a recent issue in party politics. In electoral terms, 1970 marked its entry, 1979 its high water-mark. It is now just part of the landscape. When Rod Morgan and I (Downes & Morgan, 1994, 1997) examined the course of its partisan history, we were struck by the central paradox that Labour's record on law and order was just as good as, if not decisively better than, that of the Conservatives, yet the Tories were always regarded as *the* party of law and order, with Labour correspondingly nervous about challenging their record – even when, as in 1992, they had presided over a 40% rise in the crime rate in three short years. Why?

We argued that certain 'hostages to fortune' made it difficult for Labour to handle the issue in a forthright way. These hostages were key constituencies or symbolic issues central to Labour's history, but which were freighted with a set of connotations that could be exploited politically to associate Labour either with support for law-violation or with being 'soft' on crime. First, the links with trade unionism and the Labour movement carried associations with strikes, occupations, Scargill and flying pickets, which were remorselessly milked for their full deviancy potential by the Tories. Secondly, the rough working-class – or emerging 'underclass' – engaged disproportionately in crime, delinquency and riotous behaviour, which defied explanation that could not be traduced as excuse in political exchanges. On this front, the nadir was Bernie Grant's 1985 remark after the Broadwater Farm riot, in which a police officer was hacked to death: "The police got a good hiding." Thirdly, the long and usually honourable history of civil disobedience, from Poplar to the Poll Tax, was fraught with Labour support for law violation, albeit by individual MPs rather than the Party as a whole.

David Downes, Professor of Social Administration, London School of Economics and Political Science, Houghton Street, London WC2A 2AE, UK. Tel: 0171 955 7344; Fax: 0171 955 7415.

And fourthly, civil libertarianism – again an honourable strand, embracing homosexual law reform, anti-censorship and the abolition of capital punishment – could be tarred as the making of the 'permissive society'.

Following the unexpected defeat of 1992, New Labour embarked on a course of decisively dumping these hostages, at least in the sense of distancing the Party from militant trade unionism; taking a very proactive stance towards the control of beggars, 'squeegee merchants' and rowdyism; and backing away from any hint of support for the decriminalisation of cannabis, let alone other illegal drugs. All this paid off handsomely in the context of Tory discomfiture over 'back to basics', Neil Hamilton, sleaze, and even Government Ministers ensnared in corrupt practice.

Although in office there has been no relaxation but even, in some respects, a toughening of this stance, the distinctive achievements of New Labour should be registered: the reinstatement of union rights at GCHQ; the minimum wage; signing up to the European Convention on Human Rights; the New Deal for the long-term unemployed in particular; the Stephen Lawrence Inquiry; and the Social Exclusion Unit. None of these would have been achieved under another Conservative government. It does not do to belittle them. That said, there are real grounds for doubt that the Labour Party has got it right on crime and criminal justice, partly because of the legacy of two decades of New Right government, but partly because of shortcomings in the strategy itself, both in relation to the criminal justice system and in the broader political project: the so-called 'Third Way'.

The first year of 'New Labour' government was significant for a remarkable consistency of purpose and strategy born of the remoulding of criminal justice policy after 1992. With a few exceptions, such as the prison privatisation programme, Labour's very own penal U-turn, the first year of government saw the development of plans to give legislative shape to the series of measures formulated in opposition. Labour are clearly determined to stick closely to the electorally successful formula that emerged from what Ian Dunbar and Anthony Langdon (1998) have termed the 'watershed': Tony Blair's statement 'tough on crime; tough on the causes of crime' proved a potent political winner. In one breath, it broke with the discourse on purely individual responsibility for crime of the Right, and with that on a barely qualified societal responsibility for crime of the Left. It symbolised a refusal to be defined as 'soft on crime' combined with an acknowledgement that crime is not committed in a vacuum, but in a social context that might be rendered less crime-prone by political choice in relation to social and economic policies.

In the process, however, a distinct set of 'perverse incentives' evolved. First, being 'tough on crime' became 'being as tough as (or even tougher than) the Tories on crime'. The stakes were raised to embrace such measures as the activation of the minimum mandatory sentences of the 1997 Crime (Sentencing) Act, the proposed Anti-Social Behaviour Order, and the declaration by the Prime Minister that those convicted of soccer hooliganism abroad should lose their jobs at home – the forging of a novel link between crime and unemployment. Yet there were already clear signs that a penal expansionism had taken hold which rendered minimum mandatory sentencing unnecessary. The judiciary had already stepped up custodial sentencing without benefit of any such mandate. The prison population had risen by 50% in just over four years. The penal economy was already over-heating, and the measures and proposals of the government can only, on balance, stoke it up even higher. The crime rate has fallen for the fourth year running, and for some that may constitute evidence for the 'prison works' philosophy. But crime rates have also fallen in many European countries, irrespective of trends in imprisonment, the most likely explanation being the immense increase in security and target hardening, on the one hand, and emergence from recession on the other. On the other hand, if drug-specific (as distinct from drug-related) offending – which is very largely hidden – was included, the crime rate would long since have gone through the roof, with the addition of hundreds of thousands of illegal transactions daily. The Office of National Statistics estimates that illegal drug sales amount to between £4.3 and £9.9 billion, between 1.3 and 2.5% of annual consumer spending (*Guardian*, 10 July 1998).

Secondly, and symmetrically, government policy is based on a 'tough on public spending; tough on the causes of public spending' logic, the results of which are already plain in severe spending constraints. Nor has the Comprehensive Spending Review changed the picture dramatically. The prospect is for modest rather than radical increases, except – very selectively – on health and education. This strategy will make an unduly adverse impact on the most positive aspects of the Crime and Disorder Act. The entire 'restorative justice' policy depends heavily on new resourcing for services that have been grossly depleted over the past two decades, both in criminal justice and in health, education, housing and personal social services. The proportion of Gross Domestic Product (GDP) spent in 1993 on welfare services was almost the lowest in Europe, and lower than the average for Organisation of Economic Cooperation and Development (OECD) countries as a whole (Hills, 1997). For example, public spending on education in the UK was 5.1% of GDP compared with an OECD average of 5.8% – despite the great increase in demands made on these services. The Spending Review would halve that gap – but the bulk of the new resourcing would go towards meeting new commitments, for nursery provision and cutting class sizes. Yet, having boxed itself in on spending levels and personal taxation over the whole Parliament, Labour can do little to change the basic pattern. Moreover, by being forced to rely on interest rate changes rather than taxation to control inflation, it is risking a recession which will damage the prospects for its main innovation, the New Deal and Welfare to Work. David Piachaud (1998) has estimated that at best the New Deal could reduce unemployment by 400,000, whilst a recession raising unemployment levels to the 1990–96 average of 2.4 million would add 800,000 to the jobless total.

In sum, the strategy which helped to win the election is likely to prove counter-productive in office.

Looking back, 1993 was indeed a watershed year. Blair's challenge to the Tories on crime pushed Labour ahead for the first time on law and order as a 'valence issue', and goaded first Kenneth Clarke and secondly Michael Howard into the U-turn on penal policy which fuelled the steep rise in imprisonment. As Shadow Home Secretary, Blair lambasted the Tory government's failure to stem the unprecedented rise in the crime rate between 1989 and 1992 as "giving up on law and order" (*Guardian*, 2 February 1993). Yet he did so less by connecting the 40% + rise in crime with their economic policies leading to a long and deep recession, than by linking it with the falling arrest and prosecution rate and the shortcomings of the 1991 Criminal Justice Act. This set the tone for the next five years in which, while Labour maintained a focus on the need to address the causes of crime in the wider society, the foreground and main emphasis became the need to be 'tough on crime'. A symbol of this priority was Jack Straw's up-staging of Michael Howard by his attack on a range of targets from squeegee merchants – echoing the zero tolerance policing of the New York Police Department – to the lack of progression in sentencing recidivist offenders, the outcome (or at least main aim) of the 1991 Act. It is now difficult for Jack Straw to talk the prison population down, having outdone Michael Howard on his own ground.

The story goes on. As the economy moved out of recession, following the forced devaluation of October 1992, crime rates predictably fell (or, as in the British Crime Survey, rose only negligibly). Yet Labour could hardly credit the Conservatives with economic responsibility for the *fall* in crime. And the Tories themselves could hardly abandon the rhetoric of two decades and claim it. Crime, after all, for them, was a purely personal responsibility, to be disconnected from social and economic trends, despite their own Home

Office and Cambridge economists' research that convincingly linked the two (see, e.g., Field, 1990; Wells, 1995). As a result, all that registered publicly and politically about falling crime rates was their equation with 'prison works' in both the UK and the US. Stable or falling crime rates elsewhere, in several European countries and in Canada, where imprisonment either fell or remained little changed, did not register as important counter-examples. Only the zero-tolerance policing and sentencing trends in the US attracted media and political attention, despite the lack of fit between them and falling crime rates (Currie, 1996, 1998; Young, 1997). As a result, tragically as it is turning out, tough policing, tough justice and tough custody are wrongly credited with stemming the rise in crime.

The equation of more prison equals less crime is most marked in the US, where the adult prison population now amounts to 2% of the male labour force (Western & Beckett, 1997), 4% if prison staff are included. The effects of this mass incarceration, which impacts most heavily on the black and Hispanic minority groups, are now being felt in macro-economic policy terms. One-third of the low US unemployment rate is attributable to imprisonment, yet this hidden factor is left out of account in cross-national comparisons of unemployment. As a result, influential commentators conclude that American anti-union and deregulated labour markets are superior to their more protected European counterparts. And, ironically, prison may be 'working' to reduce unemployment enough to assist in reducing crime rates in US cities (Downes, 1997). However, as prison damages the employability of ex-prisoners, a self-confirming vicious spiral is kept in motion. *More* imprisonment is needed to offset its own adverse effects in terms of higher crime among ex-prisoners, a locking-in of the US to a penal economy which is highly unstable. The costs of prison increasingly bite into education and welfare budgets, thus heightening the likelihood of more crime, and thus more imprisonment (Christie, 1993; Stern, 1998).

All of which makes the emphasis in the UK Crime and Disorder Act on restorative justice all the more important as an antidote to the custodial sway of the 'prison works' discourse. For it is arguably the case that restorative justice, with its built-in principle of opposition to social exclusion and its emphasis on reintegrative shaming, reparation and mediation, is one sure bulwark against punitive policies. Other philosophies of punishment – just deserts, rehabilitation, even abolitionism – harbour the risk of being hi-jacked by tough justice interpretations, on the one hand, or by populist backlash, on the other, against offenders seemingly acting with impunity. Restorative justice must, however, take account of these alternative philosophies in its turn. Otherwise, it risks inequity (von Hirsch, 1997; Blagg, 1997); an anti-therapeutic stance, even when it 'works' (McGuire, 1995), and a drift into net-widening and 'disintegrative shaming' (Cohen, 1979; Vagg, 1998). The recent Home Office circular to magistrates urging them to 'name and shame' young offenders smacks of 'disintegrative' rather than 'reintegrative' shaming.

Contemporary governments, even of a reformist or liberal bent, are increasingly subject to what David Garland (1996) has termed "the limits of the sovereign state":

> State sovereignty over crime has been simultaneously denied and symbolically reasserted. The limits of police and punishment are recognised in one policy only to be ignored in another ... The preventative strategies are premised upon consolidated research results and clear administrative rationalities, the 'punitive' strategy is driven by a political dynamic rather than a punitive one ... They operate on quite contradictory assumptions about the character of offending and the possibilities for criminal justice interventions. [Also] the rhetoric, perceptions and emotions evoked by the punitive strategy have the effect of undermining the preventative, responsibilising strategy, making it more difficult for those committed to the latter to carry their policies through. (Garland, 1996, pp. 462–3)

This analysis of what amounts to a penological 'double-bind' is well exemplified by the UK Crime and Disorder Act. Certain measures have already been much criticised for their punitive, costly and likely counter-productive character. Andrew Ashworth, Rod Morgan, Andrew von Hirsch and other law professors (Ashworth *et al.*, 1998) have attacked the Anti-Social Behaviour Orders as unnecessary, over-harsh, blurring civil and criminal canons of proof, and infringing the European Convention on Human Rights, signing up to which has been one of the Labour government's most significant achievements. Proposals to tag selected prisoners in the last 3 months of their sentences seems a costly way of enriching private security firms for monitoring 'safe bets' for early release. Both this and curfews for juveniles harbour a 'thin end of the wedge' potential for zero tolerance.

The Act is also over-interventionist in ways that recall the mistakes made in the 1970s, when 'up-tariffing' responses to early juvenile offending led to the over-use of both criminal and civil forms of institutional disposals. The system became harder and harder, whilst appearing to be softer and softer, which Cavadino and Dignan (1992) called 'system disaster' leading to more than the doubling of custody for juveniles by the end of the 1970s. The system of Final Warning and Parenting Orders holds the potential for just such a chain-reaction of up-tariffing to recur:

> Effectively, Labour is moving the current community supervision resources, used for young people as a last chance before custody, down tariff to become the first intervention. The resource implications of this early input are phenomenal as are the consequences for young people if they should be reconvicted. (Jones, 1996, p. 4)

One experienced youth justice worker estimated that of every 100 juvenile cases a year going through the courts, 80 could now end up with parenting assessments, yielding a large crop of parenting orders. Agencies (other than the police) could not cope with such demands, and the likely result would be a high rate of breaching, worsening intra-familial conflicts and, at worst, 12-year-olds being escorted to prison by youth justice workers. Moreover, unless other agencies are strengthened, the police are bound to emerge as the senior partner in youth justice matters:

> Some agencies are more powerful than others (the most powerful state agencies are the police and the housing departments) and there is a tendency for the preoccupations of these agencies to dominate inter-agency agendas, with a corresponding likelihood that other important interests become marginalised or ignored. (Pearson *et al.*, 1992, p. 70)

These punitive and net-widening aspects of the UK Crime and Disorder Act make it even more important that the restorative justice components are given the maximum feasible chance to succeed. Yet the most positive measures in the Act are subject to the second set of constraints, the 'tough on public spending' principle. The youth justice and drug testing and treatment provisions are in principle humane ways of putting restorative justice into effect. Several areas practice such measures already, with seeming success, such as the much-publicised mediation scheme for juvenile offenders in Buckinghamshire, though they await proper evaluation, particularly in relation to the more traditional cautioning and youth justice approaches. But what experience should already teach us is glossed over in the Act. First, inter-agency co-operation is actually costly, and unlikely to lead to rapid savings, not least because it draws heavily on the full-time professional staff of several agencies, some of whom are in desperately short supply; and it raises expectations for access to allied services. A young offender who is encouraged to take advantage of education, job training, youth work and special needs facilities for, say, dyslexia and/or school phobia, will initially need more services, not less, even if he or she desists from offending. The pay-off is in the long-term, when he or she holds down a decent job, but the costs are in the short-term. Some of the most recent proposals acknowledge this – such as Sure Start, a British equivalent of the American Headstart programme – but these are exceptions.

The justification is that it is more humane and, by the building of trusting relationships, works better, in the long term, not that it cuts costs in the short-term. Yet the resource assumptions in the Act are that the latter will be the case. Secondly the work-rate of existing staff cannot be increased indefinitely. For example, Pamela Taylor, a leading forensic psychiatrist, recently wrote on mental disorder and the risk of violence that:

> access to alcohol and other drugs of abuse is the side effect of community care for those with a serious mental disorder for which patients, their families and professional staff have been least prepared. Resources for accommodation, occupation and specific treatment are scarce, resources for understanding and managing drug abuse in this context have been almost non-existent ... Of most concern is that reliance on or belief in 'actuarially based assessment' could come to substitute for resources appropriate to management ... After any inquiry there is a clamour for better assessment and prediction ... There is little evidence of a rush to enhance specialist provision across all levels of service. A checklist, or a new piece of legislation, however, allows a tick in the box that something has been done. (1997, pp. 158–9)

Similarly, the Audit Commission Report on *Misspent Youth* (1996) found, in their review of the soaring rate of school exclusions and its role in delinquency, that "mental health professionals – who said that they had provided support to schools in the past – reported that health commissioners were no longer prepared to fund activity to help teachers deal with difficult pupils" (p. 69). A recent report on school exclusion in the *Observer* (28 June 1998) found that "the waiting list for child guidance is three years ... The whole system is waiting to explode" (p. 18). Since *anything* involving psychiatry and mental health adds weeks if not months on to the judicial process, owing to the huge backlog of work due to the shortage of key personnel, the prospects for speeding up the youth justice process, without damage to due process, are seriously dented.

Another front on which a poverty of resource thinking is evident is that of probation and local authority social services. Probation Service cuts have been mounting for several years as demands on it have grown. Over the past four years, probation staff have been cut by 3000 (15%) while their caseload has risen by nearly 40,000 (20%). Thanks to Michael Howard's closure of university training courses for probation staff, a major hiccup is occurring in the recruitment of those with professional social work training. The Spending Review should enable that shortfall to be made good, though the case for restoring university training is unlikely to be heard. Yet practically every aspect of the Act makes extra demands on probation and social service workers. They are crucial for the speeding-up of court procedures; the co-ordination of local crime strategies; the operation of youth justice services and youth offending teams in particular. The thinking behind the Act builds on the fact that very much good work with young offenders is very cheap – such as mentoring, and work with drug users by ex-addicts. What the costing of the Act neglects is that such work needs co-ordination by well-resourced full-time professionals. Otherwise, it is very uneven, lacking basic knowledge and short-term in its effectiveness. Nor can the New Deal be a good basis for reintegrative programmes *unless* it is accompanied by other forms of support, which cannot be supplied without better resourced basic services. One early study found an "alarming" shortfall of referrals to the training agency from New Deal:

> Even allowing for a margin of error, the result of the research in Lambeth so far has serious implications for New Deal. If offenders form such a small percentage of the New Deal cohort, then this could well apply to other 'socially excluded' groups. (Conalty, 1998, p. 10)

This poverty of resource thinking tends to run throughout the entire strategy. The new local authority co-ordinating role for community safety is crucial, but local authorities are so strapped for cash in the very areas where crime is rife that it is hard to see how they can function effectively in this role. Thanks to the Poll Tax, they cannot rely on the 1991 census at enumeration district level, as the Audit Commission recommended, since the under-count of young males aged 19–34 topped a million (Heady *et al.*, 1994). As Andrew Rutherford commented, if you don't count, you don't get counted. Moreover, local authorities have been progressively stripped of their co-ordinating role in so many fields, education in particular, that they will face a set of contradictory pressures, in formulating their strategy, which are largely beyond their control. School exclusions, which are driven by parental choice and league tables, can only be tackled by resources and powers, which the local authority no longer command. For example, Further Education is crucial to the success of the New Deal, but is now a commercialised morass no longer accountable to local authorities or to meeting the needs of local pupils and trainees. Such examples illustrate how the criminal justice system is all too often a surrogate for the failure of basic services.

Similarly, the poor resourcing of the Crown Prosecution Service has dogged its performance from the outset. Any serious attempt to speed up youth justice must involve the Crown Prosecution Service, but its poor resourcing is compounded by its resistance to joint co-ordination as incompatible with its judicial function. These contradictions need to be sorted out if the best proposals in the UK Crime and Disorder Act are to hold out any real prospect of success.

Finally, we must at least raise the question of how far the New Labour strategy involves "giving up on" what Garland (1996) called "the solidarity project": the search over the past two centuries for a truly inclusive society based on social democracy and social justice. So far, the 'Third Way' has laudably tackled social exclusion, but on terms that draw back from tackling its institutional sources. The veto on increases in personal taxation rules out any direct assault on inequality. The New Deal relies on employer subsidy rather than job creation (which was the hallmark of its US original under Roosevelt). Apart from the 'windfall' tax, the privatised utilities and services are not only to be left alone: they are to be augmented. The minimum wage creates a bottom line but otherwise the steep growth in labour market inequalities, with its weaponry of down-sizing, asset stripping and insecure job tenure, is left intact. Crime rates may be held in check for a time but only at the cost of massive social fortification: gated communities and electronically monitored lives. As Will Hutton argued about a speech by Jack Straw:

> There are weaknesses to the social philosophy of the third wayers, notably that most of the obligations that accompany rights in a New Labour order are shouldered by the bottom of society rather than those at the top, which is let off largely scot-free ... Until the third way incorporates a modernised version of a Left critique of markets into their model, they will talk well-intentioned hot air and stay locked in a blind alley. (*Observer*, 5 July 1998)

For these reasons, the Blairite formula, which proved so signal a success in electoral terms, will – unless imaginatively revised and properly resourced – prove unlikely to stave off a systems disaster in the years to come.

Acknowledgements

My thanks for constructive criticism and ideas to Dermot Brady, John Carrier, John Harding, Denis Jones, Jill Peay and Robert Reiner.

References

ASHWORTH, A., GARDNER, J., MORGAN, R., SMITH, A.T.H., VON HIRSCH, A. & WASIK, M. (1998) Neighbouring on the oppressive: the government's 'Anti-Social Behaviour Order' proposals *Criminal Justice* 16(1), 7–14.

AUDIT COMMISSION (1996) *Misspent Youth: Young People and Crime.* London: Audit Commission.

BLAGG, H. (1997) A just measure of shame *British Journal of Criminology* Autumn, 481–501; and the Reply by J. Braithwaite, 502–6.

CAVADINO, M. & DIGNAN P. (1992) *The Penal System.* London: Sage.

CHRISTIE, N. (1993) *Crime Control As Industry.* London: Routledge.

COHEN, S. (1979) The punitive city *Contemporary Crises* 3(8), 339–63.

CONALTY, J. (1998) *Working Together for the Best Deal,* report on the partnership between the Inner London Probation Service and the employment service in Lambeth during the New Deal (18–24s). Pathfinder period (5th January to 6th April 1998). London: ILPS/Lambeth Employment Service.

CURRIE, E. (1996) *Is America Really Winning the War on Crime and Should Britain Follow its Example?* NACRO.

CURRIE, E. (1998) *Crime and Punishment in America.* New York: Holt.

DOWNES, D. (1997) Prison does wonders for the jobless figures. *Guardian,* 25 November.

DOWNES, D. and MORGAN, R. (1997) Dumping the hostages to fortune: the politics of law and order, in M. MAGUIRE, R. MORGAN & R. REINER (eds) *The Oxford Handbook of Criminology,* 2nd edn. Oxford: Clarendon Press.

DUNBAR, I. and LANGDON, A. (1998) *Tough Justice: Sentencing and Penal Policies in the 1990s.* London: Blackstone Press.

FIELD, S. (1990) *Trends in Crime and their Interpretation.* London: Home Office.

GARLAND, D. (1996) The limits of the sovereign state: strategies of crime control in contemporary society *British Journal of Criminology* 36(4), 445–71.

HEADY, P., SMITH, S. & AVERY, V. (1994) *1991 Census Validation Survey Coverage Report,* Ch. 5. London: HMSO.

HILLS, J. (1997) *The Future of Welfare* (rvd edn). York: Rowntree Foundation.

JONES, D. (1996) Tough on crime and nasty to children *Prison Report* Autumn, 4–5.

MCGUIRE, J. (1995) *What works: Reducing Reoffending.* Chichester: John Wiley.

PEARSON, G., BLAGG, H., SMITH, D., SAMPSON, A. and STUBBS, P. (1992) Crime, community and conflict: the multi-agency approach, in D. DOWNES (ed.) *Unravelling Criminal Justice.* Basingstoke: Macmillan.

PIACHAUD, D. (1998) The prospects for poverty: poverty is set to increase, despite Government initiatives *New Economy* 5(1), 8–13.

STERN, V. (1998) *A Sin against the Future: Imprisonment in the World.* Harmondsworth: Penguin.

TAYLOR, P.J. (1997) Mental disorder and risk of violence *International Review of Psychiatry* 9(2/3), 156–61.

VAGG, J. (1998) Delinquency and shame: data from Hong Kong *British Journal of Criminology* Spring, 247–67.

VON HIRSCH, A. (1997) Restorative justice: some queries, in M. TONRY (ed.) *Oxford Crime and Justice Handbook.* New York: Oxford University Press.

WELLS, J. (1995) Crime and unemployment, in COATES, K. (ed.) *The Right to Work.* Nottingham.

WESTERN, B. and BECKETT, M. (1997) The penal system as labour market institution: jobs and jail, 1980–95 *Overcrowded Times* 8(6), 1, 9–13.

YOUNG, J. (1997) *The Criminology of Intolerance.* University of Middlesex: Centre for Criminology.

[15]
Visions of Penal Control in The Netherlands

ABSTRACT

Following three decades of prolonged decarceration from 1947 to 1974, Dutch penal policy underwent first a gradual, then a more radical, reversal in a period of sustained recarceration after 1975. David Garland's (2001) theory of the "culture of control" emergent in late modernity to combat rising crime and insecurity is a necessary but insufficient account of the transition. Additional elements in the invocation of pathology legitimizing the transition are periods of unusually steep rises in crime rates, resort to "heart of darkness" symbolism by the media and members of key elites, and a sense of relative underprotection by a critical mass of the public. This combination of influences also drove penal expansion in England and the United States. The past half century has seen the rise and fall of penal hope in the Netherlands. It is, for penal reformers at least, a story that is both inspiring and dispiriting: inspiring because it shows that, even in a modern industrial society and in the context of modest rises in crime rates, a substantial reduction in the prison population can be achieved over decades, not just a few years; but dispiriting because even a prolonged decarceration proved unsustainable. Developments in penal expansion over the past two decades represent a radical departure from those of the three preceding decades.

The first few decades after World War II were years of growing optimism and prosperity that gave penal reformers the opportunity to embrace what David Garland (1985) termed "penal-welfarism," a framework of generous welfare provision for all, within which prisoners came to be included. For some decades Dutch penal policy was the epitome of this era. A social democratic political economy linked sci-

David Downes is professor emeritus of social administration and a member of the Mannheim Centre for Criminology and Criminal Justice, London School of Economics.
An earlier version of this essay formed the basis for an address to the annual conference of the Dutch Society of Criminology, June 16, 2005.

entific modernism with liberal social and cultural values within a shared moral framework. Momentum was given to reductionist penal policies by the unique philosophy of the "Utrecht School" and by a crime rate that rose only slowly until the end of the 1960s. To use Norbert Elias's key concept, Dutch elites in effect embarked on a civilizing mission that embraced the Common Market, decolonization, international law-making, and support for the United Nations. A minimal resort to coercion and punishment combined with a maximum investment in welfare and rehabilitation was the dominant narrative in relation to crime. Even when the crime rate rose steeply in the 1970s and a key error in forecasting future prison capacity led to a shortfall in prison cells, Dutch liberal pragmatism evolved several devices for avoiding overcrowding: waiting for a prison place, juggling with home leave, and so on. By the 1980s, however, extra capacity could no longer be deferred without breaching the one-to-a-cell principle. By 1985, the *Society and Crime* report signaled a distinct change in the penal climate toward more extensive use of prosecution and available sentencing options, including custody. By 2006, Dutch imprisonment rates had sextupled.

This essay outlines and reflects on the evolution of Dutch penal policy since the early 1970s.[1] Throughout I compare Dutch developments with those in England and Wales and the United States, and contrast them to those of countries—such as Canada, Finland, or Scotland—that did not experience rapidly rising prison populations. Sections I and II discuss Dutch policies before and after the shift toward greater punitiveness became clear and won support from key officials. Sections III and IV discuss pathology in two senses, first in the characterization of crime as one among various social pathologies warranting firm responses and second as a symbol for excesses of punitiveness initiated in the name of control. Section V speculates on alternative futures.

I. The Era of Tolerance

On the cusp of change between 1981 and 1985, I embarked on a comparative study of postwar penal policy and practice in the Netherlands and England and Wales, taking as the starting point the striking difference between their daily average prison populations per 100,000,

[1] For a more detailed analysis of Dutch postwar penal policies, see Downes and van Swaaningen (2007).

which were then a ratio of one to four.[2] The conventional wisdom of the time in Britain was that if the crime rate rose, the prison population would inevitably rise with it. There was strikingly little awareness of the situation in other countries, and the National Association for the Care and Resettlement of Offenders was well ahead of the time in inviting Hans Tulkens, head of the prison department in The Hague, to give a lecture on the Dutch approach to penal policy (Tulkens 1979). That lecture made it clear that comparing the two countries' approaches to the use of imprisonment, far from being a waste of time, had a real point: there *was* an alternative to penal expansion, even in the context of a rising crime rate.

The first step was to establish the reality of the basis for comparing the two situations: how far like was being compared with like. The crime rates could mask substantial differences. But comparing sentencing trends over time (1950–81) in relation to three offenses regarded as serious in both societies—burglary, rape, and robbery—showed sharply divergent trends, with the clear tendency in England being to sentence a growing proportion of offenders to imprisonment for longer terms, whereas in the Netherlands the clear tendency was the reverse: to waive prosecution in growing proportions of cases and to reduce both the use of custody and the lengths of sentences (Downes 1988, pp. 37–41). In retrospect, a closer inspection of seriousness *within* offense categories might have blunted the force of the contrast. For example, the first bank robbery in the Netherlands occurred as late as 1965. By that point, armed bank robberies were an established if rare event in England. Even so, the trends remained markedly divergent after the growth of more serious robberies in the Netherlands.

A second "reality check" was to establish how far the custody figures masked other institutional measures that fell outside the frame for imprisonment. In the Netherlands, mental institutionalization was a substantial alternative to imprisonment in the 1950s and 1960s, though less so in later decades. At its apex proportionally, in 1955, offenders detained in mental hospitals under the TBR provisions[3] amounted to

[2] The imprisonment rate per 100,000 population is often criticized as too crude a measure of the resort to imprisonment in a society. However, as it is a product of the average length of time served and the annual number of admissions to prison, it remains the best single indicator of the scale of imprisonment.

[3] Until 1988, TBR was the abbreviation for the Dutch term for the semi-indeterminate detention of offenders in mental institutions (see Tak [2002, chap. 6] for changes since 1988).

fully one-third of the combined institutional population. Two decades later by the mid-1970s, that had fallen to one-tenth. Though using the combined figures made little difference to comparative trends, they do show vividly the extent to which the Dutch judiciary accepted for well over a decade the appeal of a psychiatric model for the treatment of offenders. Resistance set in during the 1960s, and in interviews, more than one judge joked that in the 1950s you could get TBR for bicycle theft.

A third reality check, a few years later in 1985, was to interview prisoners to establish to what extent, if at all, and in what ways, if any, the experience of imprisonment in the Netherlands differed from that in England. It was all too easy to assume that the former would be far less inhumane than the latter. In the event, the conventional wisdom was amply borne out. Interviews with fourteen Dutch prisoners in England and twelve British prisoners in the Netherlands, half of whom had also experienced custody in their own countries, provided a reasonable basis for comparisons, especially by those who had been through both systems (Downes 1988, chap. 6). If anything, my assumptions had been too guarded. The Dutch system proved far more humane than the English, even though I was allowed access to a variety of prisons in the Netherlands and officially steered well clear of the overcrowded local prisons in England. Twenty years later, the English system has improved somewhat in limited ways, thanks to the 1991 Woolf Report, and the Dutch system has become more disciplinary: my guess, however, is that the differences remain substantial.

Explaining the origins and character of postwar Dutch decarceration is more complex and difficult than documenting its extent. Almost my first contact with informed Dutch sources was, thanks to Eryl Hall Williams of the London School of Economics, with Professor Nico Keijzer, who answered my queries by reference to the influence of the so-called Utrecht School. This proved seminal in my eventual attempt to account for how the judiciary came to embrace so minimal a use of custody from the late 1940s (its decline till then had been largely due to the release of several thousand wartime detainees). Otherwise, the informed view was that Dutch imprisonment rates had traditionally been very low, and postwar policy was therefore more of the same. While that did not account for the falling rate of imprisonment at a period of rising crime rates in the 1960s and early 1970s, it was in line with a general theory of Dutch tolerance as the ultimate reason for the trend. However, the long-term data on Dutch and English prison population rates do not support this view. For most of the century before the Dutch prison levels dipped below that in England in 1955, the English prison population rate had been lower than the Dutch (Downes 1988, p. 7). Neither appealing to history nor invoking a traditional culture of tolerance could, therefore, explain what happened after 1945.

What, then, *did* account for the strength and duration of Dutch decarceration, which lasted from 1947 until 1975 and ebbed only gradually until the late 1980s and early 1990s? One theory to make evident good sense was that the Nazi occupation led to the imprisonment of a critical mass of the judicial and political elite who, as a result of their experience of imprisonment, after the war were determined to minimize its extent and transform its character. Having posed this question to the twenty-six judges and prosecutors I interviewed on the subject, I was surprised at how little credence they gave it. Indeed, though none put it in these terms, to be imprisoned under a fascist regime for refusing to commit crimes is hardly the same thing as being imprisoned in a democracy for committing them. Even so, it is difficult to deny it some role in predisposing Dutch elites to accept the broad reformist program set out in the Fick Report of 1947 (Franke 1995).

In reviewing theories of decarceration (Downes 1988, chap. 3), my approach was first to differentiate those that were compatible with the Dutch case from those that were not and, second, to assess the broadly acceptable theories against the criterion of how far they connected with the actual accomplishment of sentencing by the prosecutors and judges themselves. On the first count, Andrew Scull's explanation (1977) of the decarceration of the "mad" and the "bad" in the economic context of fiscal crisis accounted very well for the widespread closure of mental hospitals in the United States and Britain but not for the expansion to come of prisons. In the Dutch case, the coincidence of decarceration with economic prosperity and recarceration with economic exigency was the very converse of his thesis. Nevertheless, decarceration may be connected with recarceration in other respects dealt with below.

Similarly, Alfred Blumstein's theory of the "stability of punishment" (Blumstein and Cohen 1973) seemed simply incongruent with the trends of penal expansion and overcrowding in England and the shape of things to come in the United States by way of mass imprisonment. By contrast, Blumstein's emphasis on the limits of capacity did register with pragmatic devices evolved by the Dutch judiciary to restrain prison numbers in the context of rising crime rates (e.g., by creating queues of sentenced prisoners who were expected to wait until cells became available). But this was not some functional requisite of Dutch society; rather it was the outcome of a tiny cadre struggling to make ends meet.

A third theory that seemed starkly at odds with the Dutch case was Foucault's "power-knowledge" thesis of the prison as a disciplinary bastion in an oppressive society. However, as elaborated by Stanley Cohen (1979, 1985) in his "dispersal of discipline" approach, this theory gained resonance in the recarceration phase to come.

Theories that lent themselves more readily to explaining the Dutch case were those seeking the causes of decarceration in the peculiarly Dutch form of a "culture of tolerance"; in the uniquely Dutch "politics of accommodation"; in a generous welfare state; and in the culture of the judiciary.

The "culture of tolerance" was undeniably a reality in the Netherlands, a matter of historic record of religious and political freedoms, reaffirmed by the early abolition of capital and corporal punishment, and, by comparison with Belgium and France, for example, a strikingly nonpunitive approach to war criminals and collaborators (Buruma 2007). Yet invoking that culture did not fit the need to account for a history of imprisonment in the Netherlands, which exceeded that in England in its scale. Nor did it automatically translate into more lenient sentencing at a time of rising crime.

The "politics of accommodation" (dealt with much more fully in Downes and van Swaaningen [2007]) may have explained *how* but not *why* such a policy and set of sentencing practices came to be adopted. For example, the reversal in 1971 of the principle of legality, which had entailed the prosecution of every case unless the public interest was seen by the prosecutor as better served by its waiving, was a major statement of policy that would hardly have gone unchallenged in a political culture less attuned to interelite and expert-run negotiation.

Generous welfare may have eased the passage of decarceration but could not be said to require it. Welfare provision and mental health provision in western Europe *at that time* showed only a negligible correlation with prison population rates (Downes 1988, pp. 78–81), though the scale of resource commitment to welfare has since then increased as a negative correlate of, and thus arguably a growing constraint on, the growth of imprisonment (Downes and Hansen 2006). Also, the trend toward the closure of mental hospitals came later in the Netherlands than in Britain and the United States, postponing the drift toward the "transcarceration" (Lowman, Menzies, and Palys 1987) of a growing number and proportion of prisoners with severe mental illness who would formerly have been detained in mental institutions. By the mid-1990s, however, "10 percent of the prison population cope with grave mental problems, while in total 36 percent have personality disorders of some kind. The number of mentally disordered offenders is increasing due to the lack of places in non-judicial psychiatric clinics and the decrease in ambulatory health care in the community" (van Swaaningen and de Jonge 1995, p. 31).

All the above considerations seemed germane to accounting for the decarceration trend but as facilitating rather than direct influences in the causal matrix, which ultimately had to engage with the prime agencies involved in sentencing, the prosecutors, and the judges. Their culture came across very strongly in interviews, in such responses as "I have to tell you that a sentence of a year or more is, in our opinion, in our custom, already a long sentence" (prosecutor) or "In a certain way, we think that giving one a prison sentence of several years will not solve the problem of handling the criminality" (senior prosecutor) (quoted in Downes 1988, p. 84).

One memorable exchange took place with a judge who was the epitome of an utterly dedicated and intensely focused professional jurist. In the course of the interview, I asked her how she would have sentenced the three young offenders aged sixteen to seventeen in the notorious case of an elderly man mugged for a pittance in Handsworth, Birmingham, in 1974. The case and its aftermath formed the centerpiece for the major study linking crime and its control to issues of race, ethnicity, and political economy by the "Birmingham School" (Hall et al. 1978). Having heard my description of the crime, which involved the youths returning to inflict further injuries on the victim (the case hinged on whether they intended his death), she replied that she could not comment since she would need to know far more about the case. Suitably chastened, I apologized for having expected her to. "But tell me," she said, "what were the sentences?" "One of twenty years and two of ten years." There was a sharp intake of breath. "Oh, I had been thinking of between three months' and six months' imprisonment."

Such a marked contrast with the English sentence could be understood only in the context of a judicial culture animated by a strong aversion to imprisonment as a damaging and further criminalizing experience, and with confidence in a probation and welfare system that would reduce the likelihood of further offending after release. The pivotal and lasting impact of the work of the Utrecht School on this judicial generation at least was due to the philosophy of criminal law and the sentencing of offenders that the principal exponents articulated at different levels and in varied roles in legal training, juridical commentary, higher education, and the Ministry of Justice (Junger-tas and Junger 2007). The contributions of Willem Pompe, Pieter Baan, and Thomas Kempe held substantial weight with the judiciary, psychiatrists, and social workers. They fashioned an inclusionary ethic of penality that argued for the minimal use of custody, the humanization of prison regimes, and the re-engagement of the offender in the moral community. Their effect on the judiciary was best expressed in judges' frequent references to the book based on prisoners' own accounts of their experience of imprisonment by a leading member of the School: "One of the books that made a great impression on me was the 'green book' of Professor Rijksen [1958; so-called because its cover was green]. . . . For most people the only time that really counts are the first weeks, the first months in prison, and the first *time* they are in prison, and every other time doesn't make any difference. So why should we do it when it costs so much to put them in prison?" (judge, quoted in Downes [1988, pp. 84–85]). While the School as a whole did not share some of its members' enthusiasm for the psychiatric treatment of offenders, there was for at least a decade a remarkable efflorescence of what would now be called "multiagency" decision making in sentencing a number of more serious offenders, in which the heads of the relevant ministries and departments met at the Utrecht Classification Clinic to assess the most appropriate mode of disposition, at times in discussion with the offenders themselves. So intense a commitment to the principle of resocialization proved short-lived, but the overriding shared commitment to the reduction of imprisonment as far as possible became a central strand in judicial culture. But for the rising crime rate, it could plausibly have had a permanent rather than a declining impact on sentencing and penal policy after 1980.

II. The Era of Sustained Recarceration

Despite what at least one formidable critic (Franke 1990) saw as my starry-eyed view of Dutch tolerance, I was made fully aware at the outset of my research of a hardening of mood and policy. For example, field notes record the following, after meetings with leading Dutch criminologists at the Ministry of Justice and the Free University, Amsterdam: "But it looks as if any attempt to use the Dutch situation as a goad to the English law and order lobby are now sunk. The rise in the [crime] rate looks far steeper than our own, and they have started putting serious offenders away for longer" (January 15, 1981). However, somewhat stiffer sentencing seemed at that point a wholly understandable response to what had been a steepening crime rate over a period of several years, and that was to persist for four more, much of it drug-related if largely minor. It did not help that in the Central Bureau of Statistics (CBS) annual summary of trends in criminal justice, the layout made the crime rate look like a cliff face (CBS 1986, p. 5; see fig. 1). Nevertheless, my hope, and indeed expectation, was that the accompanying rise in imprisonment would level out when the crime rate stabilized. I would have expected the Dutch to behave like the Nordic countries, reining imprisonment in to Swedish or Danish levels. This is a telling example of just how difficult prediction can be. For far from stabilizing, the Dutch recarceration was sustained, quintupling the imprisonment rate in thirty years from roughly twenty to 100 per 100,000 of the general population between 1973 and 2003.[4]

Accounting for so sustained a recarceration is no less difficult than explaining the previous trend of decarceration. Hanns von Hofer has suggested that the convergence, after three decades, of the prison population rates in Finland, Sweden, and the Netherlands, via a falling, a stable, and an expansionist set of contrasting trends, indicates "that there might be some kind of an adaptation process at work (the mysterious 'regression to the mean'?) somehow pulling prison populations towards some kind of [European] 'standard'" (von Hofer 2003, p. 21). This intriguing possibility skates over the problem of explaining just how three different sets of politicians and judicial sentencers contrive such a perfect match. It is much more likely, as von Hofer himself argues, that trends in prison populations are, or have come to be, fundamentally political constructs of a dynamic and often volatile char-

[4] A rate of 123 per 100,000 is given for the Netherlands as of July 1, 2004 (Walmsley 2005).

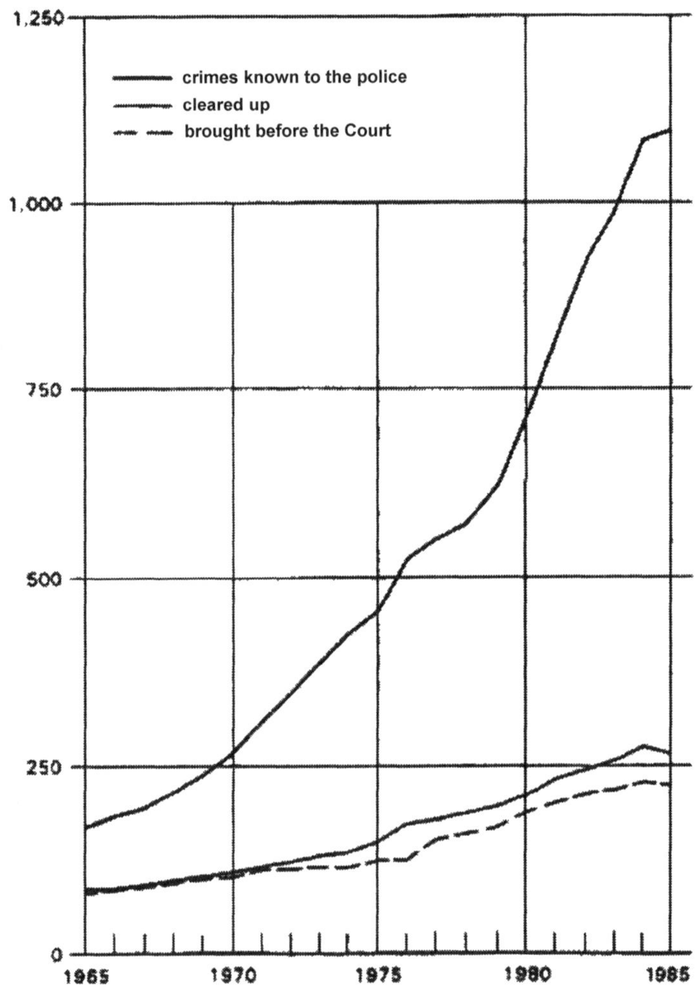

FIG. 1.—Crimes known to the police, crimes cleared up, and crimes brought before the court, Netherlands, 1965–85.

acter. On this basis, the direction of the trends and what drives their trajectories matter much more than the coincidental levels. By these criteria, the Netherlands is closer to the situation in England and Wales (though not Scotland) and even the United States, which has also experienced a quintupling of its prison population over the past twenty-five years, albeit from a much higher baseline.

In one very fundamental sense, it may be thought outrageous to bracket these three societies together in relation to penal futures. Imprisonment in Europe, especially western Europe, remains vastly lower than that in the United States: imprisonment rates in Europe are on average about one-seventh those in the United States. As Franklin Zimring put it, comparing increases in imprisonment rates of the last thirty years in Europe to those in the United States is like comparing a haircut to a beheading. The key question is, is the United States an outlier or a harbinger of things to come elsewhere? Is a haircut the prelude to a beheading? I do not think that we can dismiss these questions as dystopian (see Zedner 2002). England and Wales have already reached the level of 142 prisoners per 100,000 population (Walmsley 2005), not far short of the level of the United States in the early 1970s at which the great leap forward to mass imprisonment began. And one does not have to envisage a full-scale matching of the American case to be profoundly pessimistic about changes to the character of European society were levels of imprisonment to reach even halfway to the U.S. state of penal affairs. In England and Wales, the Conservative opposition at the 2005 election signaled its willingness to raise the prison population to 100,000, a rate of 200 per 100,000, double the western European average (Conservative Party 2005), beyond the foothills to the lower slopes of mass imprisonment. That this rather desperate proposal passed without comment is a sign of how far such rhetorical pledges have become normalized, part of the small change of party political maneuvering.

I do not wish to suggest that politics in the Netherlands has reached these depths, but common trends in criminal justice and penal policies within a number of other Western countries suggest that the Netherlands experience is not the norm. For in several western European countries, including Scotland, the penal population trend so far remains more stable, registering only slight increases over the past two decades. This is even more strikingly the case with Canada, the country one might have thought most vulnerable to emulating the American example. "[Selective focus] on *change* in imprisonment rates—largely in terms of increases—is not without limitations. Specifically, by their very nature and scope, they tend to exclude or erroneously subsume countries such as Canada that have experienced relative stability in levels of incarceration" (Webster and Doob, in this volume, p. 298). Canadian imprisonment rates have not shown any substantial increases for more than a quarter century. In practice, Canada adopts an explicitly non- or even anti-American position on penal policy. In some of these countries, current daily prison numbers are higher than in the Netherlands. But they have remained little changed for some two decades. It may well be, of course, that now that the Netherlands imprisonment rates have reached levels characteristic of many Western countries, around 120 per 100,000, the Dutch situation will also stabilize, though that did not happen in England and Wales.

Extrapolating trends is, of course, no valid guide to penal futures. The key questions are how to factor in the components of policy relevance that drive the trends in one direction or another. Recent theories that might account for the key variations include those of David Garland (2001), Jonathan Simon (2006), James Whitman (2003), Michael Tonry (2001), and Nils Christie (1993). The "culture of control" thesis of Garland seems to capture trends in the Netherlands as well as England and the United States extraordinarily well, though his theory does not fully account for the immense scale of mass imprisonment in America. That, in my view, has a lot to do with the unique American sense of mission, of being a "city on a hill," a "perfect society" in embryo,[5] and a model that, as the sole superpower, the United States can aspire to export to the rest of the world. It is worth remembering that the Pilgrim fathers left Leiden via Plymouth because they found Dutch Calvinism too permissive! Their potent sense of mission survives to this day as a legitimation for America to be "not only a model nation, but also the world's guardian, regulating the conduct of other nations, and representing the world's last and best chance of salvation" (Madsen 1998, p. 38).

Following the demise of rehabilitation and social reform as the means of crime control, that principle serves to legitimate mass incarceration as the chief strategy for its achievement. Interacting with the "war on drugs" and the infliction of harsh justice on black and Hispanic ethnic minority offenders (Tonry 1995; Wacquant 2001), a model of social salvation by penal incapacitation has been fashioned that exceeds the predictive potential of Garland's depiction of the "culture of control." However, it is arguably the case that Garland was not aiming to account for the full extent of mass imprisonment in the United States, but to analyze the commonalities in a more widespread cultural shift

[5] John Pratt (1992, 2006) has developed this concept in relation to the relatively high rate of incarceration in New Zealand. See also Downes (2001, pp. 53–55).

emerging across a range of societies in response to the political economy of late modernity.

At least six key steps from among twelve Garland analyzes as marking the shift from "penal-welfarism" to a "culture of control" apply to the Netherlands as well as to England and the United States. First is the decline of the rehabilitative ideal, with which there can be little dispute. In the Netherlands, the use of TBR declined from some one-third of all institutional dispositions in 1955 to about one-tenth by 1975 and 7.5 percent in 2004. Reports from the national Social and Cultural Planning Bureau show marked reductions in the proportion of Dutch people agreeing that treatment rather than punishment is the preferred response to criminal offending.

Second is the politicization of law and order and a new populism: experts are devalued, though policies are claimed to be "evidence-based." In the Netherlands, the politicization of law and order had reached the symbolic point in 1994 at which "no left-wing politician can afford to be seen as 'soft' on law and order" (quoted in Downes 1998, p. 153). Currently, "crime and safety have become important societal themes in the Netherlands to the extent that even in Amsterdam, once the preserve of highly ideological 'red' officials who were automatically antagonistic to the police, a left-wing politician can become a supporter of zero tolerance (albeit in a balanced form)" (Punch 2005, p. 58).

Third is the reinvention of the prison—"Prison Works," to quote the former British home secretary, Michael Howard: it is now a "pillar" of social order. In the Dutch case, prisons in effect have been recast from their role in a civilizing mission to being a bulwark against social collapse. As the key report *Law in Motion* (Ministerie van Justitie 1990) stated, "What is at stake is nothing less than the credibility of constitutional government and its democratic and social values. . . . Our highest policy priority is, of necessity, to combat crime by preventive and repressive means" (pp. 85–86).

Fourth is a "perpetual sense of crisis": the citizenry live in a full-on state of red alert, are bombarded with incessant crime news and dramas, and are exhorted to be "active citizens" in the "War on Crime," a state of affairs that is not relaxed even when the crime rate is going down. In the Dutch case, this is reflected by the consistent appearance of "fighting crime" as the top political priority in 1992–2000, overtaken in 2002 only by "maintaining order" (Roes 2004, p. 73). Insofar as the measures used to encourage a war on crime consciousness have worked to reduce the crime rate by, for example, a massive step change in private security measures, target hardening, and neighborhood watch, fear of crime is logically reinforced on a daily basis (Tonry 2004*a*). As long as the "causes of crime," especially those that flow from growing inequalities, remain unaddressed, the citizenry are all too aware that crime prevention entails constant watchfulness and anxiety.

Fifth is the transformation of criminological thought that followed the shift to "administrative criminology" (Young 1999), which is also apparent in Britain and the United States. A survey of developments in the 1980s found that "whereas the percentage of externally financed . . . policy-oriented studies has increased tremendously, financial sources for fundamental research . . . are getting more and more scarce," with content monitoring at times coming close to "financial censorship" (van Swaaningen, Blad, and van Loon 1992, p. 91). Topics are increasingly of a short-term, narrowly focused policy agenda, with "a boom of studies on migrant-groups and juveniles as 'problem-categories' in the field of crime" (p. 92). Moreover, "critical inquiries into sentencing and the effectivity of criminal law are disappearing."

Sixth, new management styles and working practices are incessantly promulgated. In both Britain and the Netherlands, the probation service has increasingly been detached from face-to-face work with clients, which in England has devolved onto untrained staff and is increasingly enmeshed in risk assessment and performance evaluation. At least two commentators in England (N. Cohen 2005; Dean 2005) have compared the endless reorganizations to a capitalist version of Maoist "cultural revolution." In the Netherlands in the late 1980s and early 1990s, consultancies brought in to report on practically every aspect of the Prosecution Service sprouted to such an extent that jokes were made about the "Samsonite circuit"—a reference to the briefcases then fashionable in business circles.

For Garland, incessantly rising crime rates since the mid-1950s, at least until the mid-1990s, are among the principal causes of what amounts to a paradigmatic revolution in the conventional wisdom about punishment, particularly as it impinged on the heartlands of support for penal reform: the liberal middle and upper-middle classes, which had previously been relatively untouched by criminal victimization. As a *New Yorker* cartoon is commonly said to have put it, "A conservative is a liberal who's been mugged." Other causes of the new "culture of control" include the upsurge of illicit drug use and drug-related crime, from trafficking to street dealing, and from money laundering to street crimes to finance the habit; the unpredictable shocks to civic peace by assorted terrorist activities; and the intense emotionality and sophistication that the media bring to bear in reporting and dramatizing crime, all of which promote a fear of crime far beyond that due to the actual experience of crime: as a result, fear of crime is little affected by falls in the crime rate.

The principal and seemingly permanent change resulting from these developments is what Jonathan Simon (2006) has memorably termed "governing through crime." It is worth remembering that even in the United States, the politics of law and order in relation to crime is of relatively recent vintage: dating from 1964, and the pitch on the need for far tougher crackdowns on crime by the losing candidate, Barry Goldwater. In Britain the change was first registered in the 1970 general election, when the Conservatives asserted—with what now seems a model of reticence—that "the Labour Government cannot entirely shrug off responsibility for . . . the serious rise in crime and violence" (Downes and Morgan 1997, p. 90).The first real watershed was the 1979 election, when Margaret Thatcher fused crime and industrial conflict as a pivotal issue. Striking workers were portrayed as no better than hooligans. In the Netherlands, it was only in the late 1980s that this change occurred.

But there is a crucial *caveat* to be entered here. Not all societies have undergone this transformation in the politics of law and order. Indeed, even in Britain the *real* watershed was 1992, when Labour abandoned what had been defined by the Conservatives as a "soft on crime" approach to embrace the Blairite slogan "tough on crime, tough on the causes of crime." The decarceration in England of the 1980s and early 1990s, when the prison population fell from 50,000 to 43,000 in the space of four years, 1988–92, would not have been possible under a Conservative government if the Labour opposition had at that stage accused *them* of being soft on crime. From 1993 onward, however, both major parties vied with each other for the "toughest on crime" image, with the result that the prison population almost doubled in the space of ten years. Much the same "governing through crime" ethos also came to obtain in the Netherlands. As yet, no society to embrace this discourse, by which being tough on crime becomes the precondition for governmental legitimacy, has managed to engineer an alternative strategy compatible with electoral success.

The trick, clearly, is not to go there in the first place, and this consideration lends particular importance to the question, alluded to above, of why and how several major societies have contrived to finesse the problems of managing rising crime without resorting to rising imprisonment. The major recent theories of punishment do not really address this difference. As James Whitman (2003) put it, Foucault does not do variation. Nor for that matter does David Garland (2001) or Jonathan Simon (2006). They are mainly concerned with what they see as the immanent trends and properties of punishment in late modernity, with an especial focus on the United States.

Whitman (2003) addresses the major and growing differences between America and Europe in his supremely scholarly *Harsh Justice*, which sees the crucial source of divergence as being between two forms of democracy. In the American case, punishment has always been harsh, as democratic forms have lent themselves to populist measures without an intervening paternalistic bureaucracy. In Europe, democracy has sought to level down from the baseline of aristocratic privilege, which in punishment terms has ultimately benefited even the worst off. The judiciary and the relevant bureaucracies have not been subject to populist demands from which they have secured a relative autonomy. It is an impressive thesis and works to some extent even in ways internal to the United States: the most "European" states, such as Minnesota and Maine, have relatively lenient sentencing policies, Maine even allowing prisoners to vote.

Two gaps in Whitman's thesis are that, first, he does not address the recency and sheer scale of mass imprisonment in the United States and, second, he does not "do" variation within Europe.

Nor does Nils Christie or Stan Cohen, who otherwise come closest in many respects to assembling a theoretical armory to account for what is going on. For example, the privatization of prisons for profit, one of Christie's main themes, is as yet only a marginal component of "the trend towards Gulags, Western-style." Stan Cohen's seminal work (1979, 1985)—to whose *Visions of Social Control* the title of this essay pays tribute—analyzed the potency of "net-widening," "mesh-thinning," and the penetration of the state into civil society as noncustodial processes more likely to generate penal expansion rather than contain it, but his work awaits a systematic application to assess how far these possibilities have been realized across different societies. The work of Maeve McMahon (1992) argued that no such outcomes occurred in Canada, but they do seem to have done so in the United States, England, and the Netherlands.

The far-ranging and detailed comparative study of penal systems by Michael Cavadino and James Dignan (2006) employs a typology of political economy as an analytical framework to account for variations in imprisonment. Four models are discerned: neoliberal (United States, South Africa, New Zealand, England and Wales, and Australia), conservative corporatist (Italy, Germany, the Netherlands, and France), social democratic (Sweden and Finland), and oriental corporatist (Japan). Basically, and compellingly, societies characterized by competitive individualism are seen as generating higher rates of incarceration than those typified by more welfare-based inclusiveness. Thus imprisonment rates broadly decline from the extreme neoliberal case of the United States to the oriental corporatism of Japan. The Netherlands is seen as a "beacon of tolerance dimmed," largely for reasons to do with weakening of traditions of consensus-based policy making in the context of late modernity and globalization, with marked problems of multicultural integration and, thanks to Dutch fluency in the English language, an uncommon openness to neoliberal and individualistic influences from the United Kingdom and the United States, respectively. Crime trends are not seen as a key variable in this matrix, though, like Garland, Cavadino and Dignan see the broad upward trend in crime rates as implicated in the general trend toward more incarceration cross-nationally.

It may be that, by looking almost entirely at the dynamics and power implications of the new forms of actuarial and punitive justice, sociologists (myself included) have come to see these developments as too disconnected from crime trends; and, with Garland, viewing crime trends as tending to drive "culture of control" trends along in a universal fashion. Yet countries such as Canada, Sweden, Denmark, Norway, Finland, Germany, France, and Scotland have hardly been unaffected by rising crime. Crime has risen in those countries more or less as much as in England and the Netherlands since the 1950s or 1960s. And it has stabilized and fallen in much the same way over the past decade. Most strikingly, Canada's homicide rate has risen and fallen in near symmetry with that of the United States over almost half a century, but without provoking engulfment by mass imprisonment (Webster and Doob, in this volume). Michael Tonry refers, in his *Thinking about Crime* (2004*b*), to "the falling crime rate in the 1990s in most Western countries, and within federal countries, in most states, irrespective of wide variations in crime policies, imprisonment rates, and punitive sensibilities" (p. 105). In other words, above a minimal level (and there should be more debate about what that level may be), crime trends are only negligibly affected by trends in control and punishment.

III. The Invocation of Pathology

However, by the same token we should not altogether rule out the possible influence of crime trend variables on punishment. What might distinguish societies that, over the past two to three decades, have maintained a "steady-state" or "stable" penal population from those that have markedly increased prison numbers are arguably three linked factors: first, a crime rate that rose over a period of years with *disproportionate* steepness; second, accompanying events that are taken to symbolize the imminent danger of moral or social collapse; and third, a perception that the criminal justice and penal systems have left society underprotected. In the United States, England and Wales (though not Scotland), and the Netherlands, such phenomena occurred and arguably provoked moral panics of a sufficiently alarming character to change the course of criminal justice and penal policies in fundamental and basically punitive respects. Once they were locked into such policies, subsequent falls in the crime rate were attributed to tougher measures. The "Prison Works" narrative could claim a happy ending as well as endless sequels. Yet countries that had not experienced such developments as traumatic could manage to maintain a stable penal policy, and when it came, the falling crime rate was not associated with tougher policies, *but with the effectiveness of alternatives to prison.*

It is important to stress in what follows that a Durkheimian vocabulary is being drawn on without an acceptance of functionalist logic. The *perception* of pathology lends itself rather to an interactionist stress on the primacy of meaning. Two examples illustrate the point. First, the contrast between the "stable" penal climate of Sweden, Norway, and Denmark and the more volatile climate of the Netherlands is not explained by long-term crime rate trends, which "support the general criminological conclusion that crime and incarceration rates are fairly independent of one another; each rises and falls according to its own laws and dynamics" (Lappi-Seppälä, in this volume, p. 239). In Sweden in particular, two of the three "conditions" outlined above were present in the steep rise in crime rates from the late 1970s until the late 1980s and the assassination of the prime minister in 1986; but these phenomena did not trigger penal escalation.

Second, even the singularly tragic cases of child-on-child homicides in England and Norway led to sharply differing responses. The children responsible for killing James Bulger in England in 1993 were subjected to imprisonment and attributions of evil; the children who killed Silje Redergård in Norway were protectively shielded and assisted by all means toward social reintegration. In his comparative study of the two cases, David Green (in this volume) concludes that the crucial sources of difference are to be found in the contrasting political cultures. In Britain, the term "moral panic" (S. Cohen 1972) captures all too well the demonization of the two ten-year-old boys responsible for the killing of two-year-old James Bulger. The case was fed into a tabloid-fueled and highly emotive politics of law and order. By contrast, in Norway, the media supported the government's backing for social workers and psychiatrists to counsel the families of both the five-year-old victim and the six-year-old perpetrators. In the view of the Norwegian media and experts involved, the age gap in the Bulger case would not have made any substantial difference to that response. In short, there is no neat positivist formula for predicting the invocation of pathology, but a combination of phenomena that heighten the probability that it will ensue.

I will examine each case in turn. In the United States, between 1964 and 1975, the murder rate doubled, that for rape rose by 150 percent, and robbery rates quadrupled (see Tonry 2004*b*, p. 114). In the same period, four major political assassinations occurred: of President John F. Kennedy, Robert Kennedy, Martin Luther King Jr., and Malcolm X. As if that were not enough, America underwent military defeat and a humiliating withdrawal from Vietnam; the war, the Watergate scandal, and racial conflict, with outbreaks of serious urban rioting, bitterly divided America; student unrest erupted on campuses; and illicit drug use proliferated. The mid-1970s not surprisingly in retrospect was the point at which the trend to mass imprisonment began, though its extent and scale were predicted by nobody, not even its intellectual apologists, such as James Q. Wilson. That period also witnessed not only the end of the rehabilitative ideal as a dominant force in sentencing and penal policy but also the long-drawn-out demise of the New Deal era. In closing down both rehabilitation and what David Garland called the "solidarity project," in its modified American form, preventive policies of a broad social welfare character were marginalized in favor of the punitive.

In England, the 1980s began with a Foucauldian sense of inevitability that criminal justice and penal policy would increasingly take a repressive and punitive turn. The New Right government of Margaret Thatcher took office in 1979 dripping with punitive rhetoric about the necessity for taking far tougher measures against crime and delinquency. Yet as the decade wore on, a liberal consensus about the need to reduce levels of custody grew steadily from successful, practitioner-led diversionary projects for young offenders to include the adult population also. The decarceration of the late 1980s and early 1990s saw the prison population drop from 50,000 to 43,000. The fateful twist was that this brief three-year period coincided almost exactly with the crime rate soaring by 50 percent (fig. 2), in part driven by a long and deep recession.

This period of rising crime concern was surmounted in 1993 by the murder of James Bulger. The ensuing moral panic gave Labour, which as the opposition had hitherto criticized the policies of decarceration as not going far enough, the opportunity to challenge the Conservative lead on the law and order issue, which the new shadow home secretary, Tony Blair, increasingly framed as a crisis in terms of undue leniency in sentencing. This was a real break with the position of Labour up to that point.

As a result, both major parties vied with each other to be tougher on crime, and the country became locked into penal expansion with no obvious end in sight, despite substantial falls in the crime rate. Over the next ten years the prison population almost doubled, from 43,000 to 75,000. Over that period England became the most intensively and extensively surveilled society on earth, by closed-circuit television and other forms of electronic monitoring. The issue of the introduction of identity cards, on what would amount to compulsory grounds, carrying an array of biometric data, which hold the potential for indefinite "function creep," is now to be mandatory for passport holders from 2010. Technology is increasingly exploited by the state as a means of controlling the citizenry rather than its role being seen as to protect

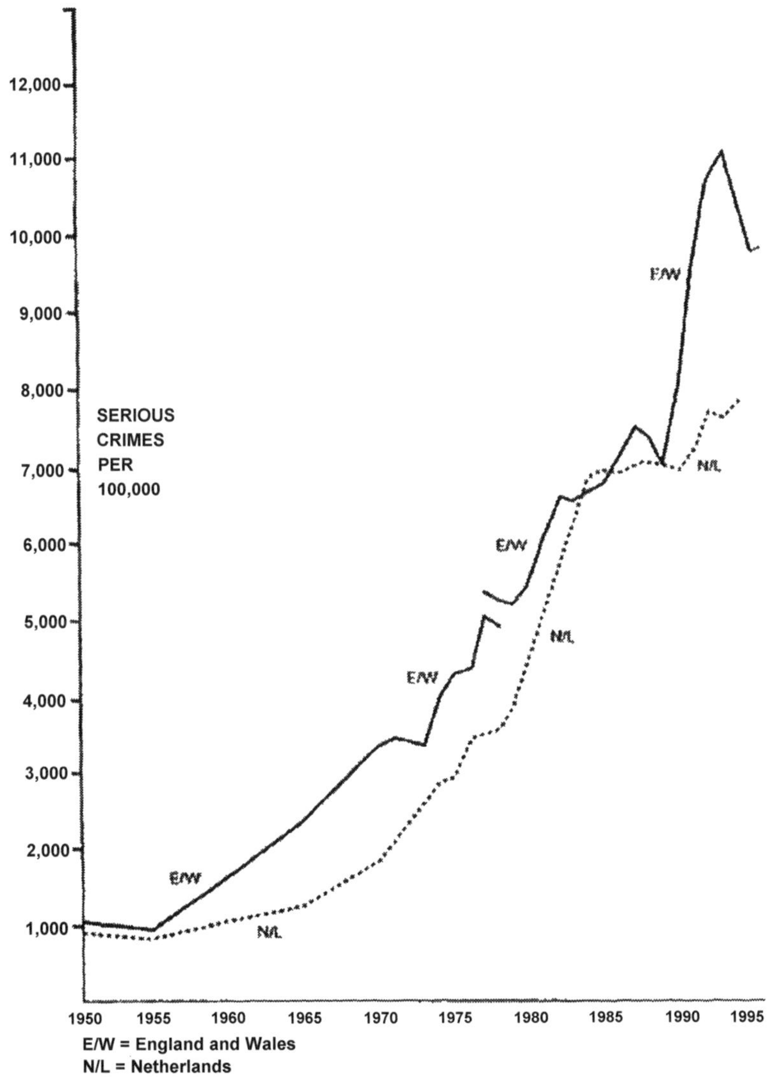

FIG. 2.—Crime rates in England and Wales and the Netherlands, 1950–95. Serious crimes per 100,000 population.

citizens from abuse by technological intrusions. This is far from being the full-blown Orwellian nightmare, but were "Big Brother" to seize power, he would have the machinery of near-total control already in place.

Similarly in the Netherlands, special factors, though of a different kind, operated to sustain recarceration into the late 1980s and beyond, even though the crime rate overall had stabilized. First, fears of the growth of organized crime fused with anxieties about drug-related crime. As Europe's entrepot nation, a far higher percentage of the gross domestic product of the Netherlands than is the case for other OECD countries comprises imports and exports, roughly 50 percent (van Dijk and de Waard 2000, p. 32). Organized crime in the form of transit crime has now been identified as the downside of that trading status (Kleemans 2007). But ten to fifteen years ago, more diffuse fears had arisen concerning a much more corrosive and pervasive mafiaization of Dutch economic and even political institutions. These have now been allayed, but then they were very real.

Second, it was in that period that the sheer scale and complexity of multicultural problems began to surface, generating alarm about the disproportionate involvement of ethnic minority youths in street crime, just as the character and scope of a decline in consensus-based policy making were also becoming evident (Engbersen, van der Leun, and de Boom 2007).

Third, there was increasing concern about the extent to which penal capacity was not keeping pace with the scale of custodial sentencing in the 1980s. A perception of an underprotected society gained ground, with the low prison population clearly a factor in elite as well as public alarm. Even a liberal critic of the more instrumental approach to criminal justice such as A. C. 't Hart stated that "in cases where the criminal law still retains a task, it must be carried out efficiently and consistently. It is, for example, absolutely inexcusable that prison sentences imposed by the courts should be allowed to lapse by prescription" (1986, p. 96).

It is, of course, impossible to say how far, if at all, the low prison population, "shielded" by a burgeoning "waiting list," contributed to the steep rise in crime, not least because crime rates also increased steeply in the United States and England when punishment and incarceration were set at much higher levels. But the perception is what counts.

Similarly, it is impossible to say how far the increased prison population in the Netherlands contributed to the stemming of the rise in the crime rate after 1985, a trend that also occurred in countries that resisted penal expansion, albeit from a higher baseline. Most likely is a "Durkheimian" effect—a broad, consciousness-raising determination to combat rising crime by an array of responses, in which custody was but one element—stiffening informal controls, reduced unemployment, greater investment in noncustodial measures, and greatly increased situational crime prevention.

These and other factors, not least the far more crime-conscious media, sustained recarceration throughout the 1990s, setting the scene for even tougher measures to be introduced in the aftermath of the assassinations of Pim Fortuyn and Theo van Gogh. These developments imply a continuing rise in the prison population in the wake of more severe crackdowns on ethnic minority youths, street crime, and so-called quality of life crimes. The introduction of identity cards and the threatened deportation of some 26,000 largely Moslem immigrants whose legal rights to residence are problematic can only aggravate rising tensions between the mainstream and already marginalized communities. Nevertheless, the tensions stoked by large-scale migration are very real (Cavadino and Dignan 2006, pp. 47–48), especially those that stem from globalization and its discontents rather than from long-established patterns of resettlement. Japan in particular has not had to contend with the scale and diversity of immigration of the Netherlands. On the other hand, Canada—a "stable" penal culture—has long been the destination of a wide variety of immigrants.

What all three societies, the Netherlands, England, and the United States, have in common, despite the immense differences in their scale and character, is the experience of defining the nature of the threats they face in terms of imminent social collapse. There is an apocalyptic tone to much of the political and media coverage of crime, and not only the more extreme crimes, redolent of Joseph Conrad's *Heart of Darkness*. This sense of impending and palpable horror is then the basis for severe measures to be taken that jettison liberal values.

A good example in England was the indefinite detention without trial of twelve Moslems allegedly linked to terrorism. Though released after three years following appeal to the Law Lords, they remain under indefinite house arrest, under a new law that can now be applied in such cases to all U.K. citizens.

But the onset of this extreme response to crime predated terrorism by several years in the Netherlands and the United States: England had experienced Irish Republican Army terrorism for rather longer. For example, even so senior a figure in Dutch criminal justice as Dato Steenhuis, who directed the training of public prosecutors in the 1980s, could register his view, to a Council of Europe seminar in 1986, that "the walls of the criminal justice system-building, once a stable rock in a society morally in decay, are tottering" (Rutherford 1996, p. 70).

So strong an invocation of pathology signifies the extent to which the Dutch judicial elite had been riven by changing crime trends, which at the same time weakened the credibility of the upholders of a more "tolerant" and rehabilitative approach to offending. Though much talk of this kind is rhetorical, it does pave the way for increasingly punitive and repressive measures to be taken against minor as well as major forms of crime and deviance, minor acts of vandalism as much as major acts of violence. The consequences for penal policy and prison regimes are therefore both expansionist and dehumanizing. Moreover, if the culture of the judiciary was arguably the prime mover in Dutch decarceration, we should look to changes in that culture that may be pivotal to the shift toward recarceration for explanation.

> Crime and safety have become important social and political themes in the Netherlands (SMVP 2004). Within the last decade there has been a major shift in thinking; its spokespeople want to rid society of the shortcomings they associate with tolerance, "*gedogen*," and the wheeling-dealing, consensus model, and want to tackle societal problems firmly. The new language reflects the "neo-liberal" thrust in NPM (New Public Management): NPM proponents speak of clear agreements (in "contracts" or "covenants"), setting targets, improved performance, low discretion, consistent enforcement and a fundamental determination to "solve" problems. This turnaround and its new approach had been promulgated in The Netherlands within the jargon of neo-liberalism and far less in a punitive and strongly ideological rhetoric than is the case in the US and UK. (Punch 2005, pp. 62–63)

Nevertheless, the outcomes are arguably similar and have come to permeate the approach of the judiciary also.

Thus changes since the mid-1980s to the prosecution service and the police were criticized as strengthening their powers to the detriment of due process and that of the judges (Peters 1986, p. 31; 't Hart 1986; Kelk 1995). As Fionda (1995, p. 113) commented in a comparative study of prosecutorial discretion,

> It seems appropriate to talk of recent Dutch prosecution policy in terms of a harsher philosophy: indeed, persons interviewed often used the words 'repression' and 'severity' to describe that new philosophy. This spirit of repression and severity, which is clearly the foundation of the two recent policy plans [*Law in Motion* 1990 and *The Functioning of the Public Prosecution Office within Law Enforcement* 1994 (the Donner Report)], has also been present in the day-to-day practice of prosecutors. . . . [Their] approach seems to have changed, and cases which would have been considered too trivial to warrant formal intervention are now being considered as serious.

In relation to robbery, that conclusion is borne out by research that compared street bag snatching on a case-by-case study in 1977 and 1989 (Freeling 1993). It was found that in 1989 every such case was categorized as robbery and duly prosecuted, whereas in 1977 in some instances a charge of theft would have eventuated and prosecution been waived. Also, prison sentences in 1977 were more lenient and often conditional, whereas in 1989 they were harsher and usually unconditional (see also de Haan nd, 1994).

IV. The Pathology of Overcontrol

In speculation about prisons of the future, two models have evolved: the incapacitative and the restorative. The second type, which in many respects was pioneered in the Netherlands, stresses the need to normalize the experience of the prison as far as possible in line with the standards of the outside world; to maximize contacts with family and community ties, by extensive visiting and even so-called conjugal visits; to maximize opportunities for work training, education, and recreation; to encourage insight into offending behavior; and to minimize the depth and weight of imprisonment, not least by keeping sentences and time served as short as possible. The incapacitative prison, seen at its most extreme form in the supermax prisons in America, such as Pelican Bay, reverses all these precepts. Prisoners are held in solitary confinement, with minimal human contact even with prison guards; are sentenced to life or extremely long sentences; and have no possibility of progression toward early release or enhanced regime conditions (Shalev 2005). As many as 20,000 prisoners[6] in the United States are

[6] If to this estimate are added the numbers of death row inmates in isolation awaiting execution and prisoners confined in punitive and protective custody, the numbers held in isolation may "well reach over 150,000" (Shalev 2005, p. 10, n. 8).

now held under such regimes, which amounts to double imprisonment: a prison within a prison, being buried alive. The Dutch have a supermax prison in miniature at Vught, which, though it holds only a small number of prisoners designated as dangerous, is the clearest manifestation of a shift toward the incapacitative principle (Downes 1998, pp. 166–69).

The great majority of prisons embody elements of both approaches, even in the United States, and until relatively recently, the trend moved from the incapacitative toward the restorative in most developed countries. However, the lesson of the past two decades is that things can change with extraordinary speed in the opposite direction: from the restorative to the incapacitative. And, given the lengths of sentences in the United States, it is virtually impossible to see how they could be shifted back again toward the restorative with anything like equal pace.

To adapt both John Donne and Aleksandr Solzhenitsyn, the prison system may be an archipelago, but it is not an island. The prison-industrial complex in America is now so huge that it has become a real factor in political economy. The prison guards union in California is a major constituency for the Republican Party. The staple economic base for employment and services of a growing number of communities in America is the local prison. Moreover, prisoners and ex-prisoners are denied the vote in many U.S. states, and the electoral repercussions, given the voting preferences of the ethnic minorities from which most prisoners are drawn, were a pivotal factor in the 2000 presidential election of George W. Bush. For the first time since the ending of transportation, therefore, penal policy has become a factor in global politics. Moreover, the United States is an aggressive exporter of its penal ideas and management systems, as it is of policies, especially concerning illicit drugs, that are a growing contribution to rising prison populations. In short, once a country is locked into penal expansionism, it can become self-replicating. Thus American correctional industries trawl the world for markets, finding ready buyers in England even for a twentieth-century version of the prison hulks.

The American influence aside, there are three reasons why in England and even in the Netherlands the drift is toward the incapacitative and away from the restorative model. Not least, the huge cost of imprisonment makes for endless budget cuts as prison numbers grow. A recent cut in England has ended the long tradition of supplying a free newspaper to prisoners, a highly symbolic signal of the loss of momentum toward penal reform.

In the Netherlands, several developments since the early 1990s have encouraged a similar trend. First, several incidents of hostage taking in 1991–92 shattered the confidence placed by prison staff in the assumption that treating prisoners decently is a guarantee of good institutional order. The result was to step up security measures and create total security facilities that, in one case at least, invited censure from the Council of Europe (1993, 1994). Second, the report on *Effective Detention* in 1994 rationed what had been the universal provision of educational and other provisions to only those prisoners deemed suitable. Third, specialized regimes have been created for drug users and short-term prisoners that are more austere even than the general norm. Fourth, the one-to-a-cell principle has been definitively ended, opening the possibility of greatly increased capacity without the need for new building programs: a crucial restraint against increasing expansion has been removed. Fifth, a Dutch version of "three strikes and you're out," the so-called ISD Act, has been established that has the potential, according to Arjan Blokland, Catrien Bijleveld, and Paul Nieuwbeerta (2003), to raise the prison population seven times, to the American level of 700 detainees per 100,000! Managerial and actuarial criteria, rather than humanist and rehabilitative considerations, are invoked to justify changes in the values underlying developments in criminal justice policy. The net result is, sadly, for the most likely vision of penal control to prevail in the Netherlands to take increasingly incapacitative rather than restorative shape.

V. Alternative Realities

So is the story simply one of doom and gloom? Is there no escape from the looming prospect of Max Weber's "iron cage" after so long a history, especially in the Netherlands, of a far more humane alternative? There *are* clear alternatives, but they are that much more difficult to retrieve in societies that are seemingly locked into penal expansion and still experiencing a "heart of darkness" sense of mortal, not just moral, panic.

The partial reason is that populist fears do have a basis in reality and politicians are by definition answerable to electorates in a way criminologists and the judiciary are not. As a consequence, penal conservatives have no problem in embracing incapacitation simply on an axiomatic basis. Liberal and radical penologists, whose claims to expertise become eroded by rapid surges in crime, have only two methods to argue their case: the empirical and the moral. But those methods, especially drawn from comparative study, still offer a balance of evidence and ethics against imprisonment as the solution to crime problems. They provide a set of alternatives that are already familiar but unwarrantedly devalued or abandoned because of our inability or unwillingness to adapt them to conditions transformed by rapid structural change.

They are a mixture of the macro matters of political economy and the micro, relatively small, doable changes even within the current sociopolitical matrix. A good example of the latter was furnished by the introduction of the minimum wage in Britain, which was significantly linked with crime reduction by area (Hansen and Machin 2002). As Richard Wilkinson (2000) put it in his defense of altruism compared with competitiveness in evolutionary terms, we do not have to embrace some notion of total egalitarianism to make changes that reduce crime by reducing inequality. Another example would be the innovation of deliberative polling (Green, in this volume), a more informed and lengthy process of coming to opinions about, inter alia, crime and punishment, as distinct from the tabloid-driven snapshot of opinion forced into set responses. Much evidence suggests that outcomes of deliberative polling are less punitive and more restorative than "instant opinion" polling allows; yet it is the latter that too often fuels media and thus political campaigns for ever tougher punishment.

Important links are also to be found between forms of political economy and the resort to imprisonment, as Cavadino and Dignan (2006) conclude after their wide-ranging comparative study. The main promise still resides in social democracy as the principal antidote to imprisonment—a genuine "Third Way" as against market capitalism and state socialism. Comparative evidence confirms that welfare capital is increasingly the alternative to penal capital, the extent of commitment to welfare being inversely related to the size of prison populations (Downes and Hansen 2006). But for the increases in welfare spending between 1988 and 1998, we estimate that the rise in the prison population in England and Wales would have been 20 percent higher. This implies that penal-welfarism is far from dead and can be extended. However, both these measures are arguably best read as aspects of inequality, which is now rampant in the turbo-capitalist era. What Jock Young terms the "chaos of reward" (1999, p. 152) remains a recipe for anomie, corrosive of social capital, social cohesion, and disrespect for "losers" in "winner/loser cultures" and therefore hugely exclusionary. Cultural criminology (Hayward 2004) discerns increasing links in a deindustrialized world between identity formation and the means of consumption rather than production. Street crime enables losers to afford the fashionable brand-name clothing and gear that are emblems of status in a consumer culture but are otherwise out of reach. It is mainly by tackling these long-standing issues that the social democratic "solidarity project" will be restored. It is by these means that ethnic minorities will be more successfully integrated into society, rather than by subjecting them to an increasingly repressive culture of control.

As it is, the Dutch tradition of pragmatic tolerance is in danger of being swamped by fears of ethnic minority crime and disorder. Yet it is still active, albeit within increasingly circumscribed parameters. Crimes without victims, except for hard-drug use, are still creatively addressed by this approach, in relation to prostitution, euthanasia, and soft-drug consumption (Pakes 2004; Buruma 2007). The Netherlands should be more aggressive in international debate in promulgating the successes of its policies in these respects. It is to be hoped that Dutch society can recover lost ground and become the first to break free from a culture of control that, once in place, has so far proved a permanent fixture.

REFERENCES

Blokland, Arjan, Catrien Bijleveld, and Paul Nieuwbeerta. 2003. "Kosten en baten van de invoering van three strikes and you're out in Nederland: Een scenariostudie." *Tijdschrift voor Criminologie* 45:178–92.

Blumstein, Alfred, and Jacqueline Cohen. 1973. "A Theory of the Stability of Punishment." *Journal of Criminal Law and Criminology* 64(2):198–206.

Buruma, Ybo. 2007. "Dutch Tolerance: On Drugs, Prostitution, and Euthanasia." In *Crime and Justice in the Netherlands*, edited by Michael Tonry and Catrien Bijleveld. Vol. 35 of *Crime and Justice: A Review of Research*, edited by Michael Tonry. Chicago: University of Chicago Press.

Cavadino, Michael, and James Dignan. 2006. *Penal Systems—a Comparative Approach*. London: Sage.

CBS (Central Bureau of Statistics). 1986. *Justice and Security XXIII*. Reprinted from the *Statistical Yearbook of The Netherlands*. The Hague: CBS.

Christie, Nils. 1993. *Crime Control as Industry—towards Gulags, Western-Style?* London: Routledge.

Cohen, Nick. 2005. "Justice without Appeal: Government Plans to Abolish the Probation Service Are Sure to End in Tragedy." *Observer* (December 11), p. 31.

Cohen, Stanley. 1972. *Folk Devils and Moral Panics: The Creation of the Mods and Rockers*. London: MacGibbon and Kee.

———. 1979. "The Punitive City: Notes on the Dispersal of Social Control." *Contemporary Crises* 3:339–63.

———. 1985. *Visions of Social Control*. Cambridge: Polity.

Conservative Party. 2005. *Are You Thinking What We're Thinking? It's Time for Action; Conservative Election Manifesto 2005*. London: Conservative Party.

Council of Europe. 1993. *Report to the Dutch Government of the Visit to the Netherlands Carried Out by the European Committee for the Prevention of Torture and Inhuman or Degrading Treatment or Punishment (CPT) from 30 August to 8 September 1992*. Strasburg: Council of Europe.

———. 1994. *Response of the Netherlands Government*. Strasburg: Council of Europe. [Report in Dutch, December 20, 1993; in English, September 1994.]

Dean, Malcolm. 2005. "Shame of Blair's Market Madness." *Society Guardian* (December 14), p. 4.

de Haan, Willem. nd. "A Moral Panic on the Brink: Moroccan Gangs in the City of Amsterdam." Working paper. Utrecht: Willem Pompe Institute.

———. 1994. "Counting Muggers in a Local Area: A New Statistical Model for Estimating the Actual Number of Perpetrators." Working paper. Utrecht: Willem Pompe Institute.

Downes, David. 1988. *Contrasts in Tolerance: Post-war Penal Policies in the Netherlands and England and Wales*. Oxford: Clarendon.

———. 1998. "The Buckling of the Shields: Dutch Penal Policy 1985–95." In *Comparing Prison Systems*, edited by R. Weiss and N. South. Amsterdam: Gordon and Breach.

———. 2001. "The *Macho* Penal Economy: Mass Incarceration in the United States—a European Perspective." In *Mass Imprisonment: Social Causes and Consequences*, edited by David Garland. London: Sage.

Downes, David, and Kirstine Hansen. 2006. "Welfare and Punishment in Comparative Perspective." In *Perspectives on Punishment: The Contours of Control*, edited by Sarah Armstrong and Leslie McAra. Oxford: Oxford University Press.

Downes, David, and Rod Morgan. 1997. "Dumping the 'Hostages to Fortune'? The Politics of Law and Order in Post-war Britain." In *The Oxford Handbook of Criminology*, 2nd ed., edited by Mike Maguire, Rod Morgan, and Robert Reiner. Oxford: Oxford University Press.

Downes, David, and René van Swaaningen. 2007. "The Road to Dystopia? Changes in the Penal Climate of the Netherlands." In *Crime and Justice in the Netherlands*, edited by Michael Tonry and Catrien Bijleveld. Vol. 35 of *Crime and Justice: A Review of Research*, edited by Michael Tonry. Chicago: University of Chicago Press.

Engbersen, Godfried, Joanne van der Leun, and Jan de Boom. 2007. "The Fragmentation of Migration and Crime in the Netherlands." In *Crime and Justice in the Netherlands*, edited by Michael Tonry and Catrien Bijleveld. Vol. 35 of *Crime and Justice: A Review of Research*, edited by Michael Tonry. Chicago: University of Chicago Press.

Fionda, Julia. 1995. *Public Prosecutors and Discretion: A Comparative Study*. Oxford: Clarendon.

Franke, Herman. 1990. "Dutch Tolerance: Facts and Fables." *British Journal of Criminology* 30:81–93.

———. 1995. *The Emancipation of Prisoners: A Socio-historical Analysis of the Dutch Prison Experience*. Edinburgh: Edinburgh University Press.

Freeling, W. 1993. "De stratoptasjeroof: Hoe het strafklimaa strenger werd." *Proces* 5:76–82.

Garland, David. 1985. *Punishment and Welfare: A History of Penal Strategies*. Aldershot, UK: Gower.

———. 2001. *The Culture of Control*. Oxford: Clarendon.

Green, David A. In this volume. "Comparing Penal Cultures: Child-on-Child Homicide in England and Norway."

Hall, Stuart, Chas Critcher, Tony Jefferson, John Clarke, and Brian Roberts. 1978. *Policing the Crisis: Mugging, the State, and Law and Order*. London: Macmillan.

Hansen, Kirstine, and Stephen Machin. 2002. "Spatial Crime Patterns and the Introduction of the UK Minimum Wage." *Oxford Bulletin of Economics and Statistics* 64(supplement):677–97.

Hayward, Keith. 2004. *City Limits*. London: Sage.

Junger-Tas, Josine, and Marianne Junger. 2007. "The Dutch Criminological Enterprise." In *Crime and Justice in the Netherlands*, edited by Michael Tonry and Catrien Bijleveld. Vol. 35 of *Crime and Justice: A Review of Research*, edited by Michael Tonry. Chicago: University of Chicago Press.

Kelk, Constantijn. 1995. "Criminal Justice in the Netherlands." In *Criminal Justice in Europe: A Comparative Study*, edited by P. Fennell et al. Oxford: Clarendon.

Kleemans, Edward R. 2007. "Organized Crime, Transit Crime, and Racketeering." In *Crime and Justice in the Netherlands*, edited by Michael Tonry and Catrien Bijleveld. Vol. 35 of *Crime and Justice: A Review of Research*, edited by Michael Tonry. Chicago: University of Chicago Press.

Lappi-Seppälä, Tapio. In this volume. "Penal Policy in Scandinavia."

Lowman, J., R. J. Menzies, and T. S. Palys, eds. 1987. *Transcarceration: Essays in the Sociology of Social Control*. Aldershot, UK: Gower.

Madsen, Deborah. 1998. *American Exceptionalism*. Edinburgh: Edinburgh University Press.

McMahon, Maeve. 1992. *The Persistent Prison? Decarceration and Penal Reform*. Toronto: University of Toronto Press.

Ministerie van Justitie. 1990. *Law in Motion: A Policy Plan for Justice in the Years Ahead.* The Hague: Ministry of Justice.

Pakes, F. 2004. "The Politics of Discontent: The Emergence of a New Criminal Justice Discourse in the Netherlands." *Howard Journal of Criminal Justice* 43:284–98.

Peters, Antonie A. G. 1986. "Main Currents in Criminal Law Theory." In *Criminal Law in Action*, edited by Jan van Dijk et al. Arnhem: Gouda Quint.

Pratt, John. 1992. *Punishment in a Perfect Society.* Wellington, NZ: Victoria University Press.

———. 2006. "The Dark Side of Paradise: Explaining New Zealand's History of High Imprisonment." *British Journal of Criminology* 46:541–60.

Punch, Maurice. 2005. *From "Anything Goes" to "Zero Tolerance": Policy Transfer and Policing in the Netherlands.* The Hague: Dutch Ministry of the Interior and Kingdom Relations.

Rijksen, R. 1958. *Meningen van Gedetineerden over de Strafrecht-splaging* [Prisoners speak out]. Assen: van Gorcum.

Roes, Theo. 2004. *The Social State of the Netherlands.* The Hague: Social and Cultural Planning Office.

Rutherford, Andrew. 1996. *Transforming Criminal Policy.* Winchester, UK: Waterside Press.

Scull, Andrew. 1977. *Decarceration: Community Treatment and the Deviant—a Radical View.* Englewood Cliffs, NJ: Prentice-Hall.

Shalev, Sharon. 2005. "Solitary Control and Punitive Isolation: 'New' Forms of Solitary Confinement in Supermax Prisons of the USA." PhD thesis, London School of Economics, Department of Sociology.

Simon, Jonathan. 2006. *Governing through Crime: The War on Crime and the Transformation of American Governance, 1960–2000.* New York: Oxford University Press.

SMVP (Stichting Maatschappij, Veiligheid en Politie [Dutch Society, Security and Police Foundation]). *Klem van Gedogen.* Dordrecht: SMVP.

Tak, Peter. 2002. *Essays on Dutch Criminal Policy.* Nijmegen: Wolf Legal Publishers.

't Hart, A. C. 1986. "Criminal Law Policy in the Netherlands." In *Criminal Law in Action*, edited by J. van Dijk et al. Arnhem: Gouda Quint.

Tonry, Michael. 1995. *Malign Neglect: Race, Crime and Punishment in America.* New York: Oxford University Press.

———. 2001. "Unthought Thoughts: The Influence of Changing Sensibilities on Penal Policies." In *Mass Imprisonment: Social Causes and Consequences*, edited by David Garland. London: Sage.

———. 2004*a*. *Punishment and Politics: Evidence and Emulation in the Making of English Crime Control Policy.* Cullompton, Devon, UK: Willan.

———. 2004*b*. *Thinking about Crime: Sense and Sensibility in American Penal Culture.* New York: Oxford University Press.

Tulkens, Hans. 1979. *Some Developments in Penal Policy and Practice in Holland.* Chichester, UK: Barry Rose.

van Dijk, Frans, and Jaap de Waard. 2000. *Legal Infrastructure of the Netherlands in International Perspective*. The Hague: Ministry of Justice.

van Dijk, Jan, Charles Haffmans, Fritz Ruter, Julian Schutte, and Simon Stolwijk, eds. 1986. *Criminal Law in Action: An Overview of Current Issues in Western Societies*. Arnhem: Gouda Quint.

van Swaaningen, René, John Blad, and Reinier van Loon, eds. 1992. *A Decade of Criminological Research and Penal Policy in the Netherlands—the 1980s: The Era of Business-Management Ideology*. Rotterdam: Erasmus University.

van Swaaningen, René, and Gerard de Jonge. 1995. "The Dutch Prison System and Penal Policy in the 1990s: From Humanitarian Paternalism to Penal Business Management." In *Western European Penal Systems: A Critical Anatomy*, edited by V. Ruggiero, M. Ryan, and J. Sim. London: Sage.

von Hofer, Hanns. 2003. "Prison Populations as Political Constructs: The Case of Finland, Holland and Sweden." *Journal of Scandinavian Studies in Criminology and Crime Prevention* 4(1):21–38.

Wacquant, Loic. 2001. "Deadly Symbiosis: When Ghetto and Prison Meet and Mesh." In *Mass Imprisonment: Social Causes and Consequence*, edited by David Garland. London: Sage.

Walmsley, Roy. 2005. *World Prison Population List*. 6th ed. London: Kings College, International Centre for Prison Studies.

Webster, Cheryl Marie, and Anthony N. Doob. In this volume. "Punitive Trends and Stable Imprisonment Rates in Canada."

Whitman, James. 2003. *Harsh Justice: Criminal Punishment and the Widening Divide between America and Europe*. New York: Oxford University Press.

Wilkinson, Richard. 2000. *Mind the Gap: Hierarchies, Health and Human Evolution*. London: Weidenfeld and Nicolson.

Young, Jock. 1999. *The Exclusive Society: Social Exclusion, Crime and Difference in Late Modernity*. London: Sage.

Zedner, Lucia. 2002. "Dangers and Dystopias in Penal Theories." *Oxford Journal of Legal Studies* 22(2):341–66.

Name Index